W9-BQI-873

DATE DUE

JY 1 4'01		
JA 2 5'02		
JA 2 9'02		
JY 2 4'02		
MY 27'05		
FE 2 3'06		

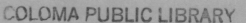

BASIC MARKETING
a managerial approach

About the author

E. Jerome McCarthy received his Ph.D. from the University of Minnesota in 1958. Since then he has taught at the Universities of Oregon, Notre Dame, and Michigan State. He has been deeply involved in teaching and developing new teaching materials. Besides writing various articles and monographs, he is the author of textbooks on data processing and "social issues in marketing."

Now 52 years old, Dr. McCarthy is active in making presentations to academic conferences and business meetings. He has worked with groups of teachers throughout the country and has addressed international conferences in South America, South Africa, and India.

Dr. McCarthy was voted one of the "top five" leaders in Marketing Thought in 1975 by marketing educators. He was also a Ford Foundation Fellow in 1963–64 doing independent research on the role of marketing in economic development. In 1959–60 he was a Ford Foundation Fellow at the Harvard Business School—working on mathematical methods in marketing.

Besides his academic interests, Dr. McCarthy is involved in consulting for and guiding the growth of several businesses. He has worked with executives from Lear-Siegler, Rockwell International, General Motors, Cordemex, Grupo Industrial Alfa, and many smaller companies. He has also been director of several for-profit and not-for-profit organizations. His primary interests, however, are in (1) "converting" students to marketing and marketing strategy planning and (2) preparing teaching materials to help others do the same. This is why he has continued to spend a large part of his time revising and improving *Basic Marketing*. This is a continuing process, and this seventh edition incorporates the latest thinking in the field.

*   *   *   *   *

Andrew A. Brogowicz graduated from Wayne State University with B.S. and M.B.A. degrees in Marketing and received his Ph.D. in Business Administration from Michigan State University in 1977. He was a Ford Motor Company Summer Marketing Fellow in 1968, doing marketing research, analysis, and planning in the Tractor Division Equipment Marketing Operations Office. Prior to receiving his Ph.D., he worked in food retailing and served as a management and economic planning consultant for the Lansing Model Cities Program.

Dr. Brogowicz has been involved in writing various parts of the *Basic Marketing* teaching package since 1970. He is co-editor of *Readings in Basic Marketing* and assisted Dr. McCarthy in writing *Essentials of Marketing*.

Currently on the Marketing Faculty of Western Michigan University, Dr. Brogowicz has also taught at Wayne State University, Michigan State University, and the University of Illinois at Chicago Circle, where he served as faculty advisor for the Circle Marketing Club. In addition to teaching introductory marketing, his primary teaching and research interests include strategic planning, marketing channels, and sales management.

BASIC MARKETING

a managerial approach

SEVENTH EDITION

E. Jerome McCarthy, Ph.D.
Michigan State University

with the assistance of
Andrew A. Brogowicz, Ph.D.
Western Michigan University

1981

RICHARD D. IRWIN, INC.
Homewood, Illinois 60430

© RICHARD D. IRWIN, INC., 1960, 1964, 1968, 1971, 1975, 1978, and 1981

ISBN 0-256-02533-9

Library of Congress Catalog Card No. 80–85240

Printed in the United States of America

3 4 5 6 7 8 9 0 K 8 7 6 5 4 3 2

Preface

This text is designed for use in an introductory course in marketing—either in schools with one or two marketing courses or in the larger business schools with a full complement of marketing courses.

All business students should be introduced to the basic problems and practices in marketing management. At the same time, it is wishful thinking to assume that a student can be taught all there is to know about marketing in one or two courses. And it is also clear that—even in larger schools with a range of marketing courses—less than one third of all business students become marketing majors.

This text, then, aims to meet the needs of the majority of beginning marketing students who are taking their first and perhaps only course in marketing. It tries to give the student an understanding and a feel for the marketing manager's job—and the world in which the job must be performed.

This text does not offer a complete and detailed description of all possible problems or solutions in marketing. But it does offer a broad and necessary understanding of marketing problems—giving the student a foundation for investigating more comprehensive references. A student must see the whole picture before the details can be appreciated.

As a basic introductory text, *Basic Marketing* differs considerably from other books. First, it is designed to facilitate learning. In other words, it is intended to be a learning aid—helping the student and instructor to accomplish specific objectives (which begin each chapter and are discussed in the *Teacher's Manual*). Second, it has a logical flow from chapter to chapter—taking an integrated, analytical approach to both macro- and micro-marketing problems. Third, it has a distinct and consistent focus throughout the text. While the text material, of course, is similar to that found in many other texts—the focus definitely is not. We will be primarily concerned with micro-marketing. That is, we will see marketing through the marketing manager's eyes—because that manager can affect the performance of both the individual firm and the macro-marketing system.

Marketing strategy planning—including designing a marketing mix (but not day-to-day implementation)—is stressed to give the student the big-picture view of micro-marketing. This planning takes place within a dynamic social and political environment which affects the macro-marketing system. Therefore, the effect of the environment on the macro-marketing system (and vice versa) is given extensive treatment.

The first chapter stresses that there is much more to marketing than selling and advertising. Our macro-marketing system works because of the decisions of many producers and consumers. The importance of understanding the macro-marketing system is stressed—while the point that changes in our macro system are likely to come from the actions of individual consumer/citizens and business people is emphasized. This sets the stage for focusing on the actions and potential contributions of business people and, in particular, marketing managers.

Following the introductory chapter, micro-marketing and the vital role of marketing management are stressed. Developing marketing strategies to satisfy target markets is emphasized especially. Finding attractive opportunities—within an uncontrollable environment—is discussed in the next few chapters. The chapter on marketing research is concerned not only with finding possible target markets but with finding attractive strategies and correcting problems—using a "scientific approach." Then, the next several chapters describe the characteristics and buying habits of potential target markets—both final consumers and intermediate customers such as businesses, farmers, and governments. This leads into how to segment markets and forecast market potential and likely sales.

Next, based on the behavior of target markets and the company's own objectives, a marketing mix is developed using the four Ps: Product, Place (that is, channels and institutions), Promotion, and Price. These sections are the bulk of the text—and are concerned with developing the "right" Product and making it available at the "right" Place with the "right" Promotion and the "right" Price—to satisfy target customers and still meet the objectives of the business.

These materials are presented in an integrated, analytical way so that there is a logical, cumulative development of the student's thinking. After some final chapters on integrating the four Ps into marketing plans and programs, their application to international marketing is shown. While there is a multinational emphasis throughout the text, this separate chapter is provided for those wishing special emphasis on international marketing.

The final chapter returns to the question, "Does marketing cost too much?" Here we consider the many criticisms of marketing and evaluate the effectiveness of both micro- and macro-marketing—considering whether any changes are needed. This final analysis is important because marketing people must be concerned about their impact on the economy—and how they can help our system work more effectively.

Some textbooks treat currently "hot" topics such as "social responsibility" and "consumerism" as a basis for separate chapters. That is not done in this text. Instead, they are treated in their appropriate places within the integrated whole. That is, these materials are not only treated in the beginning and end of the text, but also are woven into the text—to emphasize that marketing managers must continually be aware of and work within their environment. Isolating such materials in a separate chapter would lead to an unfortunate "compartmentalization" of ideas.

It is hoped that—in this framework—marketing will be looked upon by more students as a useful, fascinating, and very necessary function in our American economy.

This material can be studied in a number of ways. *One,* the text material can be supplemented by lectures and class discussion of the text material and perhaps additional readings. A separate *Readings in Basic Marketing* provides additional complementary materials. *Two,* understanding of the text material can be enhanced by discussion of conventional questions and problems at the end of each chapter. Further, a separate *Learning Aid* offers additional opportunities to obtain a deeper understanding of the material. This *Learning Aid* includes an introduction to each chapter, a list of the important new terms, self-testing true-false and multiple-choice questions (with answers) as well as cases and exercises. *Three,* thought-provoking questions included at the end of the chapters can be used to encourage the student to investigate the marketing process and organize an individual way of thinking about it. Some of the questions and exercises in the *Learning Aid* also can be used to implement this third approach.

The text is organized so that any of the approaches or any combination of them can be used—depending upon the time available and the objectives of the instructor. All are compatible. However, at least experimentation with the third approach is highly recommended. It is not only educationally sound, but can be exciting too—for both the student and the instructor. The thinking behind this third approach is elaborated upon in the following paragraphs.

I reevaluated my approach to teaching beginning marketing when some educators made some interesting observations. Dr. J. S. Bruner, at Harvard, found that a child learned more geography when given a map and asked to predict where the biggest cities *should be*—rather than by straight memorization of where they actually are. Other educators had success using similar methods, such as asking children to "invent" multiplication as a short cut to addition.

Trying to apply these ideas using conventional marketing texts was difficult, however, since most of the "answers" were given early—sometimes in the first chapter or two. Thus, it was not possible to have the student read the text and still develop his own ideas as the text moved along.

This text works differently. It assumes that the student comes to the beginning marketing course with some experience—if nothing else, as a consumer—and ability to project what "should be" or "probably will be" on the basis of this prior knowledge. Certainly the student's vocabulary—in the sense of conventional marketing terms and definitions—will be lacking. But the nature of these terms—and especially the functions which should be provided by business firms—can be anticipated.

It is for this reason—that the student should be encouraged to "think ahead"—that this text deliberately avoids introducing some concepts and definitions before they are needed. Precise definitions of wholesaling and retailing, for example, are delayed until midway in the book—when "where and how goods should be made available" is considered.

When all the details are not presented early, then creative thought can be encouraged by the questions following each chapter. These questions encourage the student to think ahead and develop what "ought to be." Then subsequent chapters present commonly accepted definitions and methods of operation. For example, following the introductory chapters, customers—both intermediate customers and final customers—are analyzed. The questions here encourage the student to think about the kind of products these customers might like, their likely shopping behavior, where the goods should be made available, and how they should be priced and promoted.

In the Product area—after the student has had a chance to roughly categorize the products which will be available—the conventional terms are introduced and past experience is organized.

The questions at the end of the Product chapters ask how these products should be made available. After a try at this, the conventional definitions and institutional material on wholesaling and retailing are introduced in the Place area; and so on.

This approach follows in sequence four basic steps in psychological learning theory:

1. Motivation.
2. Investigation.
3. Organization.
4. Utilization.

The first few chapters attempt to motivate the student by encouraging interest in the subject and indicating how important marketing and marketing management are to the operation of a company and the whole economy. The questions at the end of the early chapters encourage independent investigation. Then subsequent chapters provide the commonly accepted organization.

In the middle chapters, the approach is to alternate between steps 2 and 3—from investigation to organization and then to further investigation, building upon the material previously organized. The cases at the end of the text or the many caselets in the *Learning Aid* can be used to encourage the student to utilize the thinking done in the investigation and organization stages. Ideally, some cases or caselets should be tried during and at the end of the course—to "set" the material and give the student a chance to use the fruits of independent thinking. This completes the learning cycle. By the end of the course, the student should be better prepared to move on to a subsequent case analysis course in marketing or other management areas.

As indicated earlier, this third approach need not be used—the first two can be used quite satisfactorily. But I have thoroughly enjoyed teaching the course since experimenting with its use. Most students feel they know quite a bit about marketing when they come into this course. When the entire course is "high spotted" in the first few chapters, it becomes difficult to maintain interest in "old stuff." If, instead, the instructor and text encourage organization and use of experience and common sense to almost "write" the book, the student becomes involved. Many even enjoy the course. And this is one of my major objectives for these teaching materials.

To facilitate student understanding, important new concepts are given special treatment. Important new terms are shown in red in the body of the text—and defined right there—and may also appear in the headings for emphasis. They are also listed separately in the *Learning Aid*—with page numbers. We feel this will help the student note important concepts and aid review before examinations.

Finally, feedback—from both students and instructors—is encouraged. It is our intention to prepare the best teaching materials we can. Learning should not only be fun—but should accomplish specific objectives. Any suggestions for improving the learning process in the marketing area will be greatly appreciated.

E. Jerome McCarthy

Acknowledgments

This book is a result of the blending of my experiences at Northwestern University, Michigan State University, and the Universities of Minnesota, Oregon, and Notre Dame—as well as my business experiences. Many people—too numerous to mention—have had an influence on this text. My colleagues at the University of Notre Dame had a profound effect on my thinking during the years we were developing a beginning course emphasizing marketing management. The original edition of this text grew out of that effort. To all of them, and especially to the many students who suggested case materials—and have criticized and made comments about all of the editions—I am most grateful.

Helpful criticisms and comments were made by the following: David Rink of Northern Illinois University, Homer M. Dalbey of San Francisco State University, Stanley J. Shapiro of McGill University, Thomas J. Killoran of CUNY (Baruch College), Gary M. Armstrong of the University of North Carolina, J. H. Faricy of the University of Florida, David Lambert of the University of Wisconsin at Milwaukee, Walter Gross of the University of Georgia, Guy R. Banville of St. Louis University, and John F. Grashof of Temple University.

I was helped by the participants in a "focus group discussion" at a Southern Marketing Association meeting. The following persons were willing to interact with others on the pros and cons of various aspects and proposed changes in this edition of *Basic Marketing:* Barbara Bart of Georgia Southern College, Robert C. Stephens III of Kennesaw College, Harry Summers of Memphis State University, and Gerald Waddell of Clemson University.

I am also deeply indebted to Yusaku Furuhashi of the University of Notre Dame for reading several versions of the various editions, making numerous suggestions, and giving on-going counsel on the multinational emphasis. His insightful comments have been invaluable.

Andrew A. Brogowicz of the Western Michigan University continues to expand his impact with each edition. Besides collaborating on the *Learning Aid, Teacher's Manual,* and *Readings in Basic Marketing,* Dr. Brogowicz made many suggestions and drafted changes for many chapters.

Joanne McCarthy provided invaluable editorial assistance and many fresh ideas. Mary McCarthy suggested where pictures and other illustrations might help communicate more effectively—and took or selected appropriate pictures. Also of great help was Carol McCarthy who did library research and helped reorient Appendix C, "Career Planning in Marketing"—reflecting her needs and experiences as a college student looking for a career in advertising. And Ellen Vander Lugt was a great help handling transcription and typing of sometimes illegible manuscript. Finally, I must thank my wife, Joanne, for much patience and advice throughout the process—and then for assistance during the final proofreading which occurs under typically chaotic conditions.

To all of these persons—and to the many publishers who graciously granted permission to use their material—I am deeply grateful. Responsibility for any errors or omissions is certainly mine, but the book would not have been possible without the assistance of many others. My sincere appreciation goes to everyone who helped in their own special way.

E. J. McC.

Contents

Contents

xiv

Contents

xvi

Contents

xviii

PART ONE

Introduction to marketing and its environment

The first three chapters (and Appendix A, which follows Chapter 2) are intended to give you a "big picture" of what marketing is all about. First, we will look at where marketing fits into our whole economic system—and then discuss where marketing fits within a business firm or a nonprofit organization. Here we will learn what marketing strategy planning is all about—and get an overview of what the rest of this book is about.

Chapter 3 and Appendix A are concerned with the uncontrollable environments which the marketing manager must understand and work with when planning marketing strategies. These uncontrollable variables are becoming more and more important as the role of government expands—and fluctuations in the economic environment have a greater impact on an individual firm.

It is quite clear that a marketing manager must know how to plan strategies—but this must be done with a full understanding of the uncontrollable environments. It is almost "suicide" to try to plan in a vacuum. This points up the importance of a marketer having a broad view of the world—being an "educated person" in the broadest and best sense of the word. In fact, marketing can be thought of as an integrating discipline. An effective marketer must be able to tie together the various parts of a business—and help it adjust to the uncontrollable environments in which it must operate.

1

When you finish this chapter, you should:

1. **Know what marketing is and why you should learn about it.**
2. **Know why and how macro-marketing systems develop.**
3. **Know why marketing specialists—including middlemen and facilitators—develop.**
4. **Know the marketing functions and who performs them.**
5. **Recognize the important new terms (shown in red).**

1

Marketing's role in society

"Marketing affects almost every aspect of your daily life."

Some students study marketing because they've heard that there are many good job opportunities available to marketing graduates. Some study marketing because they want to work in sales or advertising—and they know this has *something* to do with marketing. Some study marketing just to be able to list some business courses on their resumés. And, finally, many students take a beginning course in marketing simply because it's a required subject.

Regardless of why they study marketing, most beginning marketing students have one thing in common: they have little idea of what marketing is all about—or how it affects their daily lives.

If you are one of these students, don't worry—you're not alone! Few people really understand what marketing is all about. In fact, more than a few marketing graduates—and even some business people—would be hard pressed to give a precise definition of marketing.

Nevertheless, marketing is a very important subject which has and will continue to affect every aspect of your daily life. Therefore, before trying to define marketing in formal terms, we would first like to give you a general idea of what marketing is all about—and how you can benefit from studying marketing.

MARKETING—WHAT'S IT ALL ABOUT?

Marketing is more than selling or advertising

If forced to define marketing, most people would probably say that marketing means "selling" or "advertising"—words that leave negative thoughts in some people's minds. By the time you finish this book, it is hoped that you will see

3

that selling and advertising are legitimate professions—that not all salespeople and advertisers are "flim-flam artists." For now, however, it is crucial to recognize that—while selling and advertising are very important parts of marketing—*marketing is much more than just selling and advertising.*

How did all those tennis rackets get here?

Mary McCarthy

To illustrate, consider all those tennis rackets being swung with varying degrees of accuracy by millions of tennis players all around the world. Most of us were not born with a tennis racket in our hand. Nor do most of us make our own tennis rackets. Instead, the tennis rackets we use were manufactured by firms such as Wilson, Spaulding, Slazenger, Davis, Head, and Bancroft.

Most tennis rackets look pretty much alike. All are intended to do the same thing—hit the ball over the net. Nevertheless, a tennis player can choose from among a wide assortment of rackets. Not only do tennis rackets come with different shapes, weights, and handle sizes, but one can also choose from rackets made of different materials—such as wood, steel, aluminum, fiberglass, or graphite. In addition, a racket can be strung with either nylon or gut. These different materials involve various tradeoffs, not the least of which is price. One can purchase a prestrung racket for less than $10. Or one can spend more than $100 for just a frame!

This variety—of sizes and materials—complicates the production and sale of tennis rackets. To illustrate just how complex the whole process can become, let us consider some of the many things a firm should do *before* and *after* it decides to manufacture tennis rackets. In addition to simply manufacturing rackets, the firm should:

1. Estimate how many people will be playing tennis over the next several years and how many tennis rackets they will buy.
2. Predict exactly when people will want to buy tennis rackets.
3. Determine which handle sizes, shapes, and weights people will want and in what proportion.
4. Decide what materials these tennis rackets should be made of—as well as where and how these materials can be obtained.
5. Estimate what price the different tennis players will be willing to pay for their rackets.
6. Determine where these tennis players will be located and what method of distribution should be used to get the firm's rackets to them—including what wholesalers and retailers to use.
7. Decide which methods of promotion should be used to inform potential customers about the firm's tennis rackets.
8. Estimate how many other firms will be manufacturing tennis rackets, how many rackets they will produce, what kind, at what prices, and so forth.

The above activities are *not* part of what is called manufacturing—actually *producing* goods and services. Rather, they are part of a larger process. If it is carried out effectively, it can provide needed direction for manufacturing—and ensure that the right products find their way into the hands of the final consumer. This process is called "marketing." As our tennis racket example shows, it involves far more than selling or advertising. As a matter of fact, marketing involves many more activities too detailed to mention in our example. You will learn much more about these activities before you finish this book. For now, it is enough to see that marketing plays an essential role in providing consumers with need-satisfying goods and services.

HOW MARKETING RELATES TO MANUFACTURING

Manufacturing is a very important economic activity. Whether for lack of skill, resources, or just plain time, most people do not make most of the products they consume. Picture yourself, for example, building a ten-speed bicycle, a component stereo system, or a digital watch—starting from scratch! Clearly, the high standard of living that most Americans enjoy would not be possible without modern manufacturing.

Tennis rackets, like mousetraps, don't sell themselves

Although manufacturing is an essential economic activity, some people overrate its importance in relation to marketing. Their attitude is reflected in Emerson's old saying: "If a man . . . makes a better mousetrap . . . the world will beat a path to his door!" (A good product—in other words—is all you need to succeed in business. Make that better product and the customers will find you!)

The mousetrap theory probably was not true in Emerson's time. And it certainly isn't true today. In modern economies, the grass grows high on the path to the Better Mousetrap Factory—if the new mousetrap is *not* properly marketed. We have already seen, for example, that there is a lot more to selling tennis rackets than simply manufacturing them. The same holds true for most other products.

The point is that manufacturing and marketing are both important parts of a total business system—whose purpose is providing consumers with need-satisfying goods and services. Together, manufacturing and marketing combine to provide the four basic economic utilities—form, time, place, and possession utility—from which (economists tell us) consumer satisfaction comes. Here, **utility** means the power to satisfy human needs.

Tennis rackets do not automatically provide utility

Form utility is provided when a manufacturer makes something—for instance, a tennis racket—out of other materials. But contrary to those who believe in the mousetrap theory, just manufacturing tennis rackets does not result in consumer satisfaction. Time, place, and possession utility must also be provided.

Time utility means having the product available *when* the customer wants it. And **place utility** means having the product available *where* the customer wants it. For example, how much satisfaction would a tennis player in California get from a tennis racket in a manufacturer's warehouse in Pennsylvania? Obviously, that tennis racket wouldn't win many games unless it were available *when* (time utility) and *where* (place utility) the tennis player wanted it. Further, to have the legal right to use the racket, the tennis player would have to pay for it before enjoying possession utility. **Possession utility** means completing a transaction and gaining possession so that one has the right to use a product.

Stated simply, the job of manufacturing is to create form utility, while marketing's job is to provide time, place, and possession utility. And to the extent that marketing information helps decide what products to produce, it can also be

6

This player needs a new racket immediately (time utility) at the court (place utility) or the game has to stop.

Mike Kelly

argued that marketing helps create form utility. In any case, those who question the value of marketing should ask themselves how much satisfaction a pound of coffee in Brazil would give a consumer in Boston—or what is the value to consumers of tire chains in a factory during a snowstorm—or air conditioners in a warehouse during a heat wave?

It should be clear that successful manufacturing depends on successful marketing—getting the right goods to the right place at the right time at a price that will allow the buyer to take possession. How marketing creates time, place, and possession utility will be explored later in this chapter. First, we want to tell you why you should study marketing—and then we'll define marketing in more detail.

MARKETING AND YOU

Why you should study marketing

One reason for studying marketing is that *a large share of your buying dollar goes for marketing.* Prof. Reavis Cox estimated that 41.7 percent goes for marketing activities. Other analysts—using other methods—have calculated it is up to 58.9 percent. So a reasonable estimate is that the cost of marketing is about 50 percent of the consumer's dollar.[1]

Another important reason for learning about marketing is that *marketing is all around you. It affects almost every aspect of your daily life.* The products you buy, the stores where you shop, the salespeople that approach you, all that advertising you see and hear—they are all part of marketing. Further, the newspapers and magazines you read, the radio programs you listen to, and the television shows you watch, are largely paid for by advertisers—again, part of marketing. Even your job resumé is part of a marketing campaign to sell yourself to some employer.

Another reason for studying marketing is that *there are many exciting and rewarding career opportunities in marketing.* Marketing is often the route to the top executive's position. At several places in this book you will find descriptions of career opportunities in marketing—in sales, advertising, product management, marketing research, physical distribution, and so forth.

For those of you who are seeking nonmarketing jobs in business, *you will probably have to work with marketing people.* Knowing something about marketing will help you relate better to those people. In the final analysis, a company that cannot successfully market its products will have no need for accountants, computer programmers, financial managers, personnel managers, production managers, traffic managers, credit managers, and so on. As is often said: "Nothing happens unless the cash register rings."

Even if you are not planning a business career, *marketing concepts and techniques have broad application for nonprofit organizations too.* The same basic approaches used to sell soap can also be used to "sell" ideas, politicians, mass transportation, health care services, energy conservation, and museums. Some hospitals even have "marketing directors."

A final and even more basic reason for studying marketing is that *marketing is vital for economic growth and development.* Marketing stimulates research and innovation—resulting in new products—which—if found attractive by customers—can lead to fuller employment, higher incomes, and a higher standard of living. An effective marketing system is vital, therefore, to the future of our nation—as well as all other nations.

HOW SHOULD WE DEFINE MARKETING?

As we said earlier, most people would probably define marketing as selling or advertising. On the other hand, one marketing scholar defined marketing as "the creation and delivery of a standard of living."[2]

There is a big difference between these two definitions—besides the fact that one is very narrow while the other is very broad. The first definition focuses on activities performed by an individual business firm. The second focuses on the economic welfare of a whole society. In other words, the first is a *micro*-level definition while the second is a *macro*-level definition.

This is a very important difference. Traditionally, marketing has been seen at the micro level—as a set of business activities performed by individual firms. Recently, we have seen that many of these activities are also performed by nonprofit organizations which try to serve their clients' needs.[3] But this wider view still focuses on activities performed by individual organizations.

Some students of marketing feel that this micro-level view of marketing is too narrow. They prefer to view marketing from a macro level—as a "fundamental societal process which necessarily and inherently evolves within a society to facilitate the effective and efficient resolution of the society's needs for exchange of consumption values."[4]

Micro- or macro-marketing?

Which view is correct? Is marketing a set of activities done by individual firms or organizations? Or is it a social process?

To answer this question, let's go back to our tennis racket example. We saw that to be successful, a manufacturer of tennis rackets would have to perform several customer-related activities in addition to simply producing rackets. The same would be true for an art museum or a family service agency. This would seem to support the idea of viewing marketing as a set of activities done by individual organizations.

On the other hand, people cannot live on tennis rackets and art museums alone! In an advanced economy—like that of the United States—it takes thousands of goods and services to satisfy the many needs of society. A large supermarket may handle as many as 15,000 products. And a typical Kmart stocks 15,000 different items.[5] Clearly, a society needs some sort of marketing system to organize the efforts of all the producers that are needed to satisfy the needs of all citizens. Thus, it would appear that marketing is a vital social process.

The answer to our question is that *marketing is both a set of activities performed by organizations **and** a social process.* In other words, marketing exists at both the micro and macro levels. Therefore, it must be defined at both levels. We will present two definitions of marketing—one for *micro*-marketing and another for *macro*-marketing. The first focuses on customers and the organizations that serve them. The second one takes a broad view of our whole production-distribution system.

MICRO-MARKETING DEFINED

> **Micro-marketing** is the performance of activities which seek to accomplish an organization's objectives by anticipating customer or client needs and directing a flow of need-satisfying goods and services from producer to customer or client.

Let's examine this definition.

Applies to profit and nonprofit organizations

To begin with, this definition applies to both profit and nonprofit organizations. Their customers or clients may be individual consumers, business firms, nonprofit organizations, government agencies, or even foreign nations. While most custom-

Society needs many different goods to satisfy varied customers.

Mary McCarthy

ers and clients will probably have to pay for the goods and services they receive, others may receive them free of charge or at a reduced cost—through private or government subsidies.

It is more than selling and advertising

Is micro-marketing only personal selling and advertising? Unfortunately, many executives think this is true. They feel that the job of marketing is to "get rid of" the product that has been produced and priced by the production, accounting, and finance executives.

This narrow view of marketing should be rejected. As noted management consultant Peter Drucker has stated:

> There will always, one can assume, be need for some selling. But the aim of marketing is to make selling superfluous. The aim of marketing is to know and understand the customer so well that the product or service sells itself.
>
> Ideally, marketing should result in a customer who is *ready* to buy. All that should be needed then is to make the product or service available. . . .[6]

Thus, when we define micro-marketing as those activities which anticipate customer or client needs and direct a flow of need-satisfying goods and services, we mean just that.

Begins with customer needs

Marketing should begin with potential customer needs—not with the production process. Marketing should try to anticipate needs. And then, marketing rather than production should determine what products are to be made—including decisions about product development, product design, and packaging; what prices or fees are to be charged; credit and collection policies; transporting and sorting policies; when and how the products are to be advertised and sold; and after-sale warranty, service, and perhaps even disposal policies.

Provides a sense of direction

This does *not* mean that marketing should take over production, accounting, and financial activities. Rather, it means that marketing—by interpreting consumers' needs—should provide direction for these activities and seek to coordinate them. After all, the purpose of a business or nonprofit organization is to satisfy customer or client needs. It is *not* to supply goods or services which are *convenient* to produce and which *might* sell or be accepted free.

THE FOCUS OF THIS TEXT—BUSINESS-ORIENTED MICRO-MARKETING

Assuming that most of you are preparing for a business career, the main focus of this text will be on micro-marketing—as seen from the viewpoint of the marketing manager. Much of the material will also be relevant for individuals who plan to work for nonprofit organizations.

It is very important, however, that marketing managers never forget that their organizations are just small interacting components of an enormously complex macro-marketing system. Changes in the system can affect any marketing manager. Therefore, the rest of this chapter will examine the macro—or "big picture"—view of marketing. Let's begin by defining macro-marketing and then review some basic concepts.

MACRO-MARKETING DEFINED

> **Macro-marketing** is a social process which directs an economy's flow of goods and services from producers to consumers in a way which effectively matches supply and demand and accomplishes the objectives of society.

Emphasis is on whole system

Like micro-marketing, macro-marketing is concerned with the flow of need-satisfying goods and services from producer to consumer. However, the emphasis is not on the activities that *individual* organizations perform. Rather, the emphasis is on *how the whole system works*—and how it affects society and vice versa.

Every society needs a macro-marketing system—but not all systems are equally "good." They can vary both in how *effectively* the society uses its scarce resources and how *fairly* it allocates its output of goods and services.

Supply and demand must be matched

Achieving effectiveness and fairness is not easy. Not all producers share the same goals, resources, and skills. Likewise, not all consumers share the same goals, resources, and needs. In other words, within any society there are both heterogeneous supply capabilities and heterogeneous demands for goods and services. The role of a macro-marketing system is to effectively match this heterogeneous supply and demand—*and* at the same time accomplish society's objectives.

Is it effective and fair?

Given that not all nations share the same objectives, the effectiveness and fairness of a particular macro-marketing system must be evaluated in terms of that society's objectives. If the people of a society really want a higher standard of living—but a military dictator uses most of the resources for internal security—this might be "ineffective" in the minds of the people. And if most of the "non—defense" income went to the "ruling elite"—this might be "unfair"—again in the minds of the people. Clearly, what is fair and effective depends on the objectives of a society—and whose objectives are called *the objectives*.

Let's look more closely into macro-marketing. And to make this more meaningful to you, consider (1) what kind of a macro-marketing system we have and (2) how effective and fair it is.

EVERY SOCIETY NEEDS AN ECONOMIC SYSTEM

All societies must provide for the needs of their members. Therefore, every society needs some sort of **economic system**—the way an economy is organized (with or without the use of money) to use *scarce* productive resources (which could have alternative uses) to produce goods and services and distribute them for consumption—now and in the future—among various people and groups in the society.[7]

How an economic system operates will depend upon a society's goals and the nature of its political institutions.[8] But, regardless of what form these take, all economic systems must develop some method—along with appropriate economic institutions—to decide *what* and *how much* is to be produced and distributed *by whom, when,* and *to whom. How* these decisions are made may vary from nation to nation—but the macro-level objectives are basically similar: to create goods and services and make them available when and where they are needed—to maintain or improve each nation's standard of living.

We are producers and consumers

It is very useful (although greatly oversimplified) to think of an economic system as consisting of *producers* and *consumers.* In a pure subsistence economy, individual family units produce all the goods that they themselves consume. In more advanced economies, most people are also both producers and consumers—but the goods and services that they produce are not necessarily those that they consume.

As *producers,* we are mainly concerned with our income. This represents our claim against the output of the economy. As *consumers,* on the other hand, we are concerned with what our income will buy. While these two roles are inherent in any economy, they can lead to conflicts and difficulties. This is called the **micro-macro dilemma**—*what is "good" for some producers and consumers may not be "good" for society as a whole.*[9] This problem complicates economic decision making considerably. It means that there may not always be obvious right answers that everyone will agree upon. Many compromises may have to be reached.

HOW ECONOMIC DECISIONS ARE MADE

There are two basic kinds of economic systems: planned systems and market-directed systems. Actually, no economy is *entirely* planned or market-directed. Most fall somewhere between the two extremes.

Government planners may make the decisions

In **planned economic systems,** government planners decide what and how much is to be produced and distributed by whom, when, and to whom. Producers generally have very little choice about product design. Their main task is to meet their assigned production quotas. Prices are set by the planners and tend to be very rigid—not fluctuating according to supply and demand. Consumers usually have *some* freedom of choice—because it is impossible to control every single detail. But the assortment of goods and services offered to them is often quite limited. Activities such as market research, branding, and advertising typically receive little emphasis. Sometimes they are not done at all.[10]

Government planning may work fairly well as long as an economy is simple and the variety of goods and services is small. It may even be necessary under certain conditions—during wartime, for example. However, as economies become more complex, government planning becomes more difficult. It may even break down. Planners may find themselves overwhelmed by many complex decisions. And consumers may lose patience if the planning bureaucracy does not respond satisfactorily to their needs. In an effort to reduce consumer dissatisfaction, planners in the Soviet Union and other socialist countries have placed more emphasis on marketing (branding, advertising, and market research) in recent years.

A market-directed economy runs itself

In **market-directed economic systems,** the individual decisions of the many producers and consumers make the macro-level decisions for the whole economy.

Consumers decide—with their dollar votes—what is to be produced.

Don Smetzer

The individual decisions may be small, but together they determine the macro-level decisions for the whole economy. For the most part, such an economy is free from the bureaucratic controls that go along with government planning.

In a pure market-directed economy, consumers determine a society's production decisions when they make their choices in the marketplace. In a sense, they decide what is to be produced and by whom—through their dollar votes. At the same time, whenever a new consumer need arises, an opportunity is created for some profit-minded business. All consumer needs that can be served profitably—not just the needs of the majority—will generate producers to meet those needs. Thus, ideally, the control of the economy is completely democratic—with power spread throughout the economy.

Consumers in a market-directed economy enjoy maximum freedom of choice. They are not forced to buy any goods or services, except those that must be provided for the good of society—things such as national defense, schools, police and fire protection, mass transportation, and public health services. These are provided by the community—and citizens are taxed to pay for them.

Similarly, producers are free to do whatever they wish—provided that they stay within the rules of the game established by government *and* that they receive sufficient dollar votes from consumers. If they do their job well—if, through sound decision making, they satisfy enough consumers—they will earn a profit and stay in business. But profit, survival, and growth are not guaranteed.

Price is a measure of value

Since the bulk of the U.S. economy (and most Western economies) is market-directed, it is important that you understand how such an economy works—in particular, the role of market price. The prices of consumer goods and services serve roughly as a measure of their social importance. If consumers are willing to pay the market prices, apparently they feel they are getting at least their money's worth. Similarly, the cost of resources is a rough measure of the value of the resources used in the production of these goods and services. In a market-directed economy, the prices in both the production sector (for resources) and the consumption sector (for goods and services) fluctuate to allocate resources and distribute income in the light of consumers' preferences. The result is a balance of demand and supply, and the coordination of the economic activity of many people and institutions.

Consumers and producers must continually interact

The interaction among various people and institutions in a market-directed economy is shown in a very simplified manner in Figure 1–1. Here we see that consumers offer their resources in the resource market (human resources as well as land and capital) for use in producing goods and/or services by business firms. (A firm is defined broadly to include any producing entity which acts as a unit—from a farm family to a large industrial corporation.)

Figure 1–1
Model of a market-directed economy

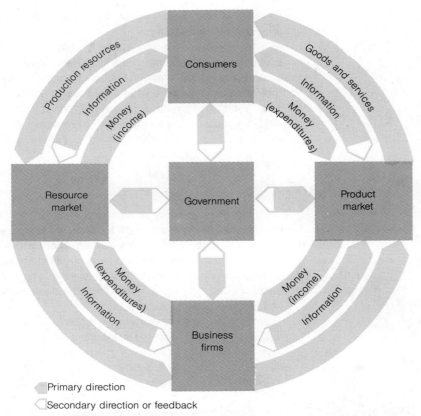

Primary direction

Secondary direction or feedback

Source: Adapted from Y. H. Furuhashi and E. J. McCarthy, *Social Issues of Marketing in the American Economy* (Columbus, Ohio: Grid, Inc., 1971), p. 5.

These firms, in turn, make payments to people for use of these resources. These people—in their role as consumers—can take the payments into the product market to buy finished goods and services. Their money is exchanged for goods and services, and then flows to the business firms—which can continue hiring and buying factors for further production.

Such a system requires continual flows within the system—to keep it going. Ideally, the participants have enough information to make wise decisions about where they offer their resources for sale and what they buy.

The role of government

Government is included in Figure 1–1 to show that a market-directed society may assign the supervision of the system to the government. Since proper functioning of a market-directed system depends on continual, smooth flows throughout the system, the government is expected to ensure that the market system continues to work properly. To protect the rights and freedoms of all, the government usually sets rules to ensure that property is protected, contracts are enforced, individuals are not exploited, no group monopolizes the resource market or the product market, the various resources are compensated at competitive levels, and that producers do, in fact, deliver the kinds and quality of goods they claim to be offering.

The American economy is mainly—but not entirely—market-directed. For example, in addition to the previously mentioned tasks, the federal government controls interest rates and the supply of money. Further, it sets import and export restrictions, regulates radio and TV broadcasting, alternately restricts and stimulates agricultural production, controls prices and wages on occasion, and so on. Some observers see increasing government interference as a growing threat to the survival of our market-directed system and the economic and political freedom that goes with it.[11]

ALL ECONOMIES NEED MACRO-MARKETING SYSTEMS

At this point you may be saying to yourself: "All this sounds like economics—where does *marketing* fit in?" Studying a *macro-marketing system* is a lot like studying an economic system—except more detailed attention is given to the "marketing" components of the system—including consumers and other customers, middlemen, and marketing specialists. The focus is on the activities they perform—and how the interaction of the components affects the effectiveness and fairness of a particular system.

In general, we can say that no economic system—whether planned or market-directed—is likely to achieve its macro-level objectives without an effective macro-marketing system. In explaining why this is so, we will first look at the role of marketing in primitive economies. Then, we will see how macro-marketing tends to become increasingly complex in advanced economic systems.

Marketing involves exchange

Our earlier statement that all economies need macro-marketing systems was not entirely true. One big exception would be a *pure subsistence economy*—

where each family unit produces all the goods that it consumes. In such a primitive economy, there would be no need for producers and consumers to exchange goods and services. Each producer-consumer unit would be totally self-sufficient. Therefore, no marketing would take place. *Marketing does not occur unless there are two or more parties who each have something of value they want to exchange for something else.*

This is not to suggest that marketing begins and ends with the exchange process. As our tennis racket example showed, there is more to marketing than simply producing and selling something in exchange for cash. However, the need for exchange—which is found in almost all societies—is at the core of marketing.

What is a market?

The term "marketing" comes from the word **market**—which means a group of buyers and sellers (usually producers and consumers) bargaining over the terms of exchange for goods and/or services. This can be done face-to-face at some physical location (for example, a farmers' market). Or it can be done indirectly—through a complex network of middlemen who link buyers and sellers who are separated geographically (for example, the stock market).

In primitive economies, markets tend to be located in central places. **Central markets** are convenient places where buyers and sellers can meet face-to-face to exchange goods and services. You will better understand macro-marketing by analyzing how and why central markets develop.

Central markets facilitate exchange

Imagine a small village consisting of five families—each with some special skill for producing some need-satisfying product. After meeting basic subsistence needs, each family might decide to specialize. This decision would be very practical. It is easier for one family to make two pots and another to make two baskets

Producers come face-to-face with consumers in many markets.

Peter Le Grand

Figure 1–2
**Ten exchanges required when a
central market is not used**

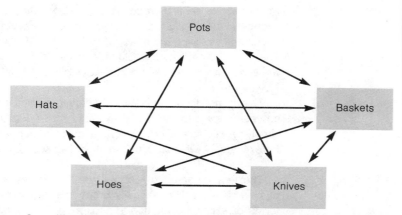

Source: Wroe Alderson, "Factors Governing the Development of Marketing Channels," in *Marketing
Channels for Manufactured Products,* ed. Richard M. Clewett (Homewood, Ill.: Richard D. Irwin, 1954), p.
7. © 1954 by Richard D. Irwin, Inc.

than it is for either to make one pot and one basket. Specialization makes labor
more efficient and more productive. It may also increase the total amount of
form utility created.

If these five families specialize in one product each, they will have to trade
with each other. As Figure 1–2 shows, it would take the five families ten separate
exchanges to obtain some of each of the products. If the families live near each
other, the exchange process would be relatively simple. But if they are far apart,
travel back and forth will be time-consuming. And who would do the traveling
and when? Obviously, this type of marketing system would not be very effective
for creating time, place, and possession utility.[12]

Faced with this problem, the families could agree to come to a central market
and trade on a certain day. Then, each family would need to make only one
trip to the market to trade with all the others—reducing the total number of
trips. This would facilitate exchange, leave more time for production and consumption, and also provide for social gatherings. In total, much more time, place,
possession, and even form utility would be enjoyed by each of the five facilities.

*Money system speeds
trading*

While a central meeting place would simplify exchange, the individual bartering
transactions would still take much time. Bartering takes another party who wants
what you have and vice versa. Each trader must find others who have products
of approximately equal value. After trading with one group, a family might find
itself with a collection of hats, knives, and pots. Then it would have to find others
willing to trade for these products.

A money system would change all of this. A seller would merely have to
find a buyer who wants his product, negotiate the price, and be free to spend
his money to buy whatever he wants.

*Middlemen facilitate
exchange even more*

Even though the development of a central market and a money system would
simplify the exchange process among the five families in our imaginary village,

a total of ten separate transactions would still be required. Thus, it would still take much time and effort to carry out exchange among the five families. Each family head might have to open (and pay for) a stall at the market, while other family members shop at other parts of the market.

This clumsy exchange process could be made much simpler by the appearance of a **middleman**—someone who specializes in trade rather than production—who is willing to buy each family's goods and then sell each family whatever it needs. He would charge for this service, of course. But this charge might be more than offset by savings in time and effort.

In our simple example, using the services of a middleman at a central market would reduce the necessary number of transactions for all families from ten to five. See Figure 1–3. Each family would have more time for production, consumption, and visits to other families. Moreover, each family could specialize in production, thereby creating greater form utility. Meanwhile, by specializing in trade, the middleman could provide additional time, place, and possession utility. In total, all the villagers might enjoy greater economic utility—and thus greater consumer satisfaction—as a result of using a middleman in the central market.[13]

Note that the reduction in transactions that results from using a middleman in a central market becomes more significant as the number of families increases. For example, if the population of our imaginery village were to increase from five to ten families, 45 transactions would be required without a middleman. Using a middleman would reduce the necessary number of transactions to ten—one for each family.

Such middlemen—offering permanent trading facilities—are known today as *wholesalers* and *retailers*. The advantages of working with middlemen increase rapidly as the number of producers and consumers, their distance from each other, and the number and variety of competing products increase. That is why there are so many wholesalers and retailers in more complex economic systems.

Figure 1–3
Only five exchanges are required when a middleman in a central market is used

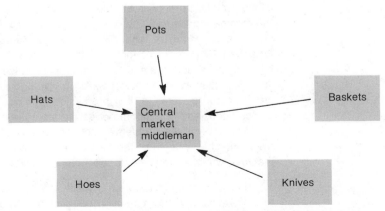

Source: Adapted from Wroe Alderson, ''Factors Governing the Development of Marketing Channels,'' in *Marketing Channels for Manufactured Products,* ed. Richard M. Clewett (Homewood, Ill.: Richard D. Irwin, 1954), p. 7. © 1954 by Richard D. Irwin, Inc.

18

THE ROLE OF MARKETING IN ECONOMIC DEVELOPMENT

Modern economies have advanced well beyond the five-family village—but the same principles still apply. The main purpose of markets and middlemen is to facilitate exchange and allow greater time for production, consumption, and other activities—including recreation.

Effective marketing system is necessary

Although it is tempting to conclude that more effective macro-marketing systems are the result of greater economic development, just the opposite is true. *An effective macro-marketing system is a necessary ingredient for economic development.* In fact, management expert Peter Drucker has suggested that marketing may even be the key to growth in less-developed nations. In his words:

> Marketing occupies a critical role in respect to the development of such "growth areas." Indeed, marketing is the most important "multiplier" of such developments. It is in itself in every one of these areas, the least developed, the most backward part of the economic system. Its development, above all others, makes possible economic integration and the fullest utilization of whatever assets and productive capacity an economy already possesses. It mobilizes latent economic energy. It contributes to the greatest needs: that for the rapid development of entrepreneurs and managers, and at the same time it may be the easiest area of managerial work to get going.[14]

Breaking the vicious circle of poverty

Without an effective macro-marketing system, the less-developed nations may be doomed to a "vicious circle of poverty"—that is, people will not leave their subsistence way of life to produce for the market, because there are no buyers for any goods they might produce. And there are no buyers because everyone else is producing for their own needs.[15]

How can this vicious circle of poverty be broken? There is much evidence to suggest that what may be most needed is a major overhaul of the antiquated micro- and macro-marketing systems that are typical in the less-developed nations.

The inefficiency of these marketing systems results in very high food prices in the rapidly growing urban areas of these nations.[16] The lower two thirds of the income groups in these urban areas often spend two thirds or more of their disposable income on food. (By way of comparison, most U.S. families spend less than 30 percent of their income for food, beverages, and tobacco.) The high prices reduce demand for food crops and leave the urban consumers with little discretionary income to spend on nonfood products. As a result, farmers are reluctant to increase their production. The manufacture of nonfood items is discouraged. And real income does not increase.

The answer to this problem—according to Prof. W. W. Rostow—is reorganizing the marketing systems of the less-developed nations. In particular, he suggests that four major jobs must be done together as part of a conscious national strategy:

1. A buildup of agricultural productivity.
2. A revolution in the marketing of agricultural products in the cities.
3. A shift of industry to the production of simple agricultural equipment and consumer goods for the mass market.

4. A revolution in marketing methods for such cheap manufactured goods—especially in rural areas.[17]

Studies conducted in Latin American countries indicate that this "marketing revolution" should center around the development of marketing middlemen who are willing to adopt innovative methods, assume greater risks, increase their operating efficiency, and create multiproduct retail outlets with high turnover–low margin operations.[18]

CAN MASS PRODUCTION SATISFY A SOCIETY'S CONSUMPTION NEEDS?

Urbanization brings together large masses of people who must rely on others to produce the bulk of the goods and services that are necessary to satisfy their basic needs. Further, in advanced economies consumers often enjoy considerable discretionary income. This allows them to seek goods and services that satisfy higher-level needs as well. Such economies face a stiff challenge to create sufficient economic utility to satisfy these consumption needs.

Fortunately, advanced economies can take advantage of mass production with its **economies of scale.** This means that as a company produces larger numbers of a particular product, the cost for each of these products goes down. Further, aided by specialization and the division of labor, modern economies can apply modern manufacturing methods to convert raw materials into a massive output of goods and services with need-satisfying potential.

Is mass production the solution to the problem of satisfying a society's consumption needs? Some would answer *yes* to this question. But the truth is that mass production is a necessary *but not the only* condition for satisfying consumers' needs. Effective marketing is also needed.

Barriers to effective marketing

Effective marketing involves getting all the goods and services that consumers need and want to them at the right time, in the right place, and at the terms that will allow them to take possession. This is a very complicated task, given the heterogeneous nature of supply in an advanced economy's production sector and the heterogeneous nature of demand in its consumption sector.

Achieving effective marketing in an advanced economy is complicated further by the fact that producers are separated from consumers in several ways.[19] As Figure 1–4 illustrates, exchange between producers and consumers is generally hampered by spatial separation, separation in time, separation in information, separation in values, and separation of ownership. Exchange is complicated further by "discrepancies of quantity" and "discrepancies of assortment" between producers and consumers. That is, individual producers specialize in producing and selling large quantities of a narrow assortment of goods and services, while individual consumers need small quantities of a wide assortment of goods and services.

Universal marketing functions must be performed

The role of a macro-marketing system is to provide the marketing capability that is necessary to overcome these separations and discrepancies—and thereby provide for an effective matching of heterogeneous supply and demand between

Figure 1–4
Marketing facilitates production and consumption

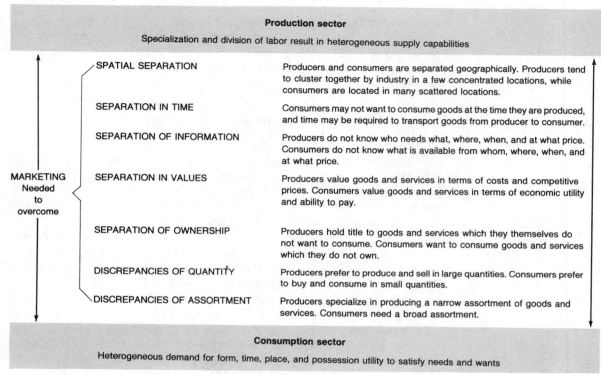

Production sector
Specialization and division of labor result in heterogeneous supply capabilities

MARKETING Needed to overcome	SPATIAL SEPARATION	Producers and consumers are separated geographically. Producers tend to cluster together by industry in a few concentrated locations, while consumers are located in many scattered locations.
	SEPARATION IN TIME	Consumers may not want to consume goods at the time they are produced, and time may be required to transport goods from producer to consumer.
	SEPARATION OF INFORMATION	Producers do not know who needs what, where, when, and at what price. Consumers do not know what is available from whom, where, when, and at what price.
	SEPARATION IN VALUES	Producers value goods and services in terms of costs and competitive prices. Consumers value goods and services in terms of economic utility and ability to pay.
	SEPARATION OF OWNERSHIP	Producers hold title to goods and services which they themselves do not want to consume. Consumers want to consume goods and services which they do not own.
	DISCREPANCIES OF QUANTITY	Producers prefer to produce and sell in large quantities. Consumers prefer to buy and consume in small quantities.
	DISCREPANCIES OF ASSORTMENT	Producers specialize in producing a narrow assortment of goods and services. Consumers need a broad assortment.

Consumption sector
Heterogeneous demand for form, time, place, and possession utility to satisfy needs and wants

Source: Adapted from William McInnes, "A Conceptual Approach to Marketing," in *Theory in Marketing*, 2d ser. ed. Reavis Cox, Wroe Alderson, and Stanley J. Shapiro (Homewood, Ill.: Richard D. Irwin, 1964), pp. 51–67. © 1964 by Richard D. Irwin, Inc.

producers and consumers. This is achieved through the performance of the **universal functions of marketing:** buying, selling, transporting, storing, standardization and grading, financing, risk-taking, and market information.

These marketing functions are *universal* in the sense that they must be performed in *all* macro-marketing systems—regardless of whether an economy is planned or market-directed. It is largely through these marketing functions that economic utility is created. *How* these functions are performed and *by whom* may differ among nations and systems, but their performance is essential in the marketing of all goods and services.

Because these functions are the foundation for any macro-marketing system, some explanation is necessary to help you understand what they involve.

The exchange functions

Buying and selling lead to exchange. The **buying function** involves looking for and evaluating goods and services. For middlemen, this means a search for products that will appeal to their customers. The **selling function** involves promoting the product. It includes the use of personal selling and advertising and other mass selling methods. This is the best-known—and some people feel the only—function of marketing.

The physical distribution functions

The **transporting function** means the movement of goods from one place to another. The **storing function** involves holding goods. These are the major activities of many marketing institutions—especially warehouses, transportation agencies, wholesalers, and some retailers.

The facilitating functions

Standardization and grading, financing, risk taking, and market information are the facilitating functions that aid the performance of the exchange and physical distribution functions. **Standardization** and **grading** involve sorting products according to size and quality. This simplifies the exchange process by reducing the need for inspection and sampling. **Financing** provides the necessary cash and credit to manufacture, transport, store, sell, and buy products. **Risk taking** involves bearing the uncertainties that are a part of the marketing process. A firm can never be certain that customers will want to buy its products, and the products could also become damaged, stolen, or obsolete. The **market information function** involves the collection, analysis, and distribution of information needed to plan, carry out, and control marketing activities.

WHO PERFORMS MARKETING FUNCTIONS?

Producers, consumers, and marketing specialists

From a macro-level viewpoint, these marketing functions are all part of the marketing process and must be performed by someone. *None* of them can be eliminated. In a planned economy, some of the functions might be performed by government agencies, while others might be left to individual producers and consumers. In a market-directed economy, marketing functions are performed by producers, consumers, and a variety of marketing institutions which serve as producers of time, place, and possession utilities. See Figure 1–5.

It would be possible for individual producers and consumers to perform all the marketing functions themselves. In a very simple economy, this might actually happen. However, while producers and consumers must perform *some* marketing functions themselves, it generally would not be very efficient if they were to try to perform *all* the functions.

Earlier in this chapter, we saw that the addition of a middleman in a simple five-family village of producers and consumers would both simplify exchange and increase the total amount of economic utility. This effect is multiplied many times over in a large, complex economy. This helps explain why the bulk of the products sold in the United States are distributed through wholesalers and retailers—rather than directly from producers to consumers.

Just as producers and consumers benefit when marketing specialists take over the exchange functions of buying and selling, they also benefit when marketing specialists perform the remaining marketing functions. Thus, we find marketing functions being performed not only by marketing middlemen—but also by a variety

Figure 1–5
Model of U.S. macro-marketing system*

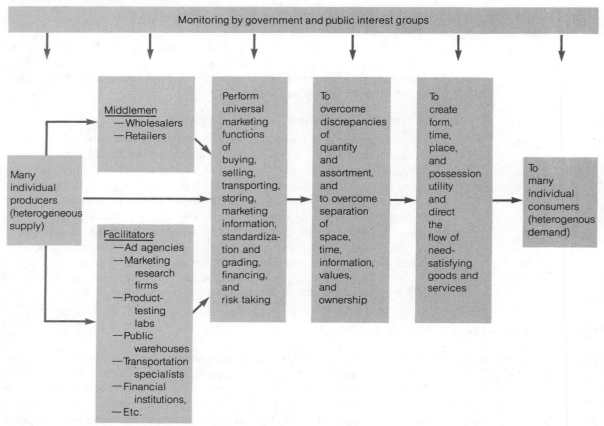

*Our nation's macro-marketing system must interact with the macro-marketing systems of many other nations.
Source: This model was suggested by Prof. A. A. Brogowicz of Western Michigan University.

of other *facilitators.* These include advertising agencies, marketing research firms, independent product-testing laboratories, public warehouses, transportation firms, and financial institutions. Through specialization and economies of scale, marketing middlemen and facilitators are often able to perform the marketing functions more effectively and at a lower cost than producers or consumers could. At the same time, they allow producers and consumers to spend more of their time on production and consumption.

Functions can be shifted and shared

From a macro viewpoint, all of the marketing functions must be performed by someone. But, *from a micro viewpoint not every firm must perform all of the functions.* While some marketing specialists perform all the functions, others specialize in only one or two. For example, marketing research firms specialize in the market information function.

Determining the most efficient path to the consumer's door is one of the most important jobs of marketing management. Because of the benefits of specialization, distributing goods through a series of marketing specialists is often more efficient than distributing directly from producer to consumer. When several specialists are used, some of the marketing functions may be performed several times. But the key point to remember is this: *Responsibility for performing the marketing functions can be shifted and shared in a variety of ways, but no function can be completely eliminated!*

HOW WELL DOES OUR MACRO-MARKETING SYSTEM WORK?

It connects remote producers and consumers

A macro-marketing system does more than unite an economy's production and consumption sectors. It also provides an organizational, transportation, and communications network which links small, geographically isolated markets to larger, inter-regional markets which have enough demand to make mass production possible. This also helps distribute goods from surplus areas to deficit areas under changing supply and demand conditions.[20]

It encourages growth and new ideas

In addition to making possible the mass production of goods, our market-directed macro-marketing system encourages innovation. Research effort and investment capital are attracted when customers are willing to pay for a new good or service. And competitive pressures and changing consumer needs force firms to develop further innovations and improvements. In recent years, industries that have followed this pattern include business machines and electronics.

It has its critics

In trying to explain marketing's role in society, we have tended to describe our macro-marketing system in a very positive light. In general, we feel this approach is fully justified. After all, our macro-marketing system has provided us—at least in material terms—with one of the highest standards of living in the world. It seems to be both "effective" and "fair."

We would not be honest, however, if we failed to point out that marketing—as we know it in the United States—has its critics. Marketing activity is especially open to criticism because it is the part of business most visible to the public. There is nothing like a pocketbook issue for getting consumers aroused!

Typical complaints about marketing include:

Advertising is annoying, deceptive, and wasteful.

Product quality is terrible—they just don't build things like they used to!

Marketing makes people too materialistic—it motivates them toward the "almighty dollar" instead of social needs.

Easy consumer credit makes people buy things they don't need and cannot really afford.

Planned product obsolescence wastes our precious resources.

Packaging and labeling are often confusing and deceptive.

Middlemen add to the cost of distribution and raise prices without providing anything in return.

Consumer dissatisfaction shouldn't be taken lightly.

Mike Kelly

Marketers are destroying our environment.

Advertising is corrupting the minds of children and putting too much sex and violence on TV.

Greedy business people create monopolies which restrict output and raise prices.

Distribution costs are too high.

Retailers are cheating the public.

There are too many unsafe products on the market.

Marketing serves the rich and exploits the poor.

Such complaints cannot and should not be taken lightly. They show that many Americans are less than enchanted with some parts of our marketing system. Certainly, the strong public support that consumer advocates like Ralph Nader have received is clear indication that not all consumers feel they are being treated like kings and queens. If these complaints are ignored, there could be strong pressure for the government to restructure our macro-marketing system. Already, some of our nation's leaders are calling for national economic planning instead of reliance on a market-directed system.[21]

CONCLUSION

In this chapter we have defined two levels of marketing: micro-marketing and macro-marketing. A close review of the complaints against marketing suggests that there are basically two levels of criticism. One level is concerned with marketing's overall role in society. The other is concerned with the activities of individual firms. In other words, some criticisms are directed at our macro-marketing system, while others apply mostly to micro-marketing. This reinforces our earlier stand that marketing must be defined and evaluated at both the micro and macro levels.

The major thrust of this book is on *micro*-marketing. We believe that most criticisms of marketing are the result of inefficient and socially irresponsible micro-level decision making. Therefore, the best way to answer such criticism is to educate future business people—such as yourself—to be more efficient and socially responsible decision makers. This will not only improve the performance of individual firms and organizations, but it should also make our macro-marketing system perform more effectively.

In the chapters that follow, we will see how organizations can better satisfy their customers' and clients' needs. We will not spend much time on how present organizations operate. Instead, we will focus on *why* they do what they do, and *how* they might do it better. Ultimately, you should be able to understand the *why* of present marketing efforts, *how* they might be improved, and *how* you can contribute to the marketing process in the future.

The impact of micro-level marketing decisions on society will be discussed throughout the text. Then—in Chapter 24—after you have had time to develop a deeper understanding of how and why producers and consumers think and behave the way they do—we will reexamine macro-marketing. There we will evaluate how well both micro-marketing and macro-marketing perform in our market-directed economic system.

QUESTIONS AND PROBLEMS

1. It is fairly easy to see why people do not beat a path to the mousetrap manufacturer's door, but would they be similarly indifferent if some food processor developed a revolutionary new food product which would provide all necessary nutrients in small pills for about $100 per year per person?

2. Distinguish between macro- and micro-marketing. Then explain how they are interrelated, if they are.

3. Explain in your own words what the macro-micro dilemma is, using an example.

4. Identify the two roles that most individuals play in our economic system. Are these roles incompatible? Why?

5. Distinguish between how economic decisions are made in a centrally planned economy and in a market-directed economy.

6. Explain *(a)* how a central market facilitates exchange and *(b)* how the addition of a middleman facilitates exchange even more.

7. Identify a "central market" in your city and explain how it facilitates exchange.

8. Discuss the nature of marketing in a socialist economy. Would the functions which must be provided and the development of wholesaling and retailing systems be any different?

9. Describe a recent purchase you have made and indicate why that particular product was available at a store, and, in particular, at that store.

10. Define the functions of marketing in your own words. Explain how they can be shifted and shared—using an example.

11. Explain, in your own words, why the emphasis in this text is on micro-marketing.

12. Why is satisfying customers or clients apparently considered of equal importance as satisfying an organization's objectives—in the text's definition of micro-marketing?

SUGGESTED CASES

NOTES

1. Reavis Cox, *Distribution in a High-Level Economy* (Englewood Cliffs, N.J.: Prentice-Hall, Inc., 1965), p. 149; and Paul W. Stewart and J. Frederick Dewhurst, *Does Distribution Cost Too Much?* (New York: Twentieth Century Fund, 1963), pp. 117–18.

2. Malcolm P. McNair, "Marketing and the Social Challenge of Our Times," in *A New Measure of Responsibility for Marketing*, Keith Cox and Ben M. Enis, eds. (Chicago: American Marketing Association, 1968.)

3. Philip Kotler and Sidney J. Levy, "Broadening the Concept of Marketing," *Journal of Marketing*, January 1969, pp. 10–15; Philip Kotler, "Strategies for Introducing Marketing into Nonprofit Organizations," *Journal of Marketing*, January 1979, pp. 37–44; and Shelby D. Hunt, "The Nature and Scope of Marketing," *Journal of Marketing*, July 1976, pp. 17–28.

4. Daniel J. Sweeney, "Marketing: Management Technology or Social Process," *Journal of Marketing*, October 1972, p. 7.

5. "The Hot Discounter," *Newsweek*, April 25, 1977, p. 70.

6. Peter F. Drucker, *Management: Tasks, Responsibilities, Practices* (New York: Harper & Row, Publishers, 1973), pp. 64–65.

7. Paul A. Samuelson, *Economics: An Introductory Analysis*, 7th ed. (New York: McGraw-Hill Book Company, 1967), p. 5.

8. Much of the material on this topic has been adapted from Y. H. Furuhashi and E. J. McCarthy, *Social Issues of Marketing in the American Economy* (Columbus, Ohio: Grid, Inc., 1971), pp. 4–5; see also J. F. Grashof and A. Kelman, *Introduction to Macro-Marketing* (Columbus, Ohio: Grid, Inc., 1973).

9. Furuhashi and McCarthy, *Social Issues of Marketing*, p. 6.

10. For more on this topic, see Reed Moyer, "Marketing in the Iron Curtain Countries," *Journal of Marketing*, October 1966, pp. 3–9; and G. Peter Lauter, "The Changing Role of Marketing in the Eastern European Socialist Economies," *Journal of Marketing*, October 1971, pp. 16–20.

11. See, for example, Milton Friedman, *Capitalism and Freedom* (Chicago: University of Chicago Press, 1962); and Murray L. Weidenbaum, *Business, Government, and the Public* (Englewood Cliffs, N.J.: Prentice-Hall, Inc., 1977). For a contrasting point of view, see John Kenneth Galbraith, *Economics and the Public Purpose* (Boston: Houghton-Mifflin Company, 1973).

12. Wroe Alderson, "Factors Governing the Development of Marketing Channels," in *Marketing Channels for Manufactured Products*, ed. Richard M. Clewett (Homewood, Ill. Richard D. Irwin, Inc., 1954).

13. Ibid.

14. Peter F. Drucker, "Marketing and Economic Development," *Journal of Marketing* (January 1958), p. 253. Reprinted from the *Journal of Marketing*.

15. Ragnar Nurkse, *Problems of Capital Formation in Underdeveloped Countries* (Oxford: Basil Blackwell, 1953), p. 4.

16. The bulk of this discussion is based on Charles C. Slater, "Marketing Processes in Developing Latin American Societies," *Journal of Marketing*, July 1968, pp. 50–55.

17. W. W. Rostow, *View from the Seventh Floor* (New York: Harper & Row, Publishers, 1964), p. 136.

18. Slater, "Marketing Processes in Developing Latin American Societies."

19. This discussion is based largely on William McInnes, "A Conceptual Approach to Marketing," in *Theory in Marketing*, second series, ed. Reavis Cox, Wroe Alderson, and Stanley J. Shapiro (Homewood, Ill.: Richard D. Irwin, Inc., 1964), pp. 51–67; see also Grashof and Kelman, *Introduction to Macro-Marketing*, pp. 69–78.

20. Reed Moyer, *Macro Marketing: A Social Perspective* (New York: John Wiley & Sons, Inc., 1972), pp. 3–5.

21. *Forging America's Future: Strategies for National Growth and Development*, Report of the Advisory Committee on National Growth Policy Processes, reprinted in *Challenge*, January/February 1977.

H. Armstrong Roberts

When you finish this chapter, you should:

1. **Know what the marketing concept is and how it should affect a firm's strategy planning.**

2. **Understand what a marketing manager does.**

3. **Know what marketing strategy planning is and why it will be the focus of this book.**

4. **Be familiar with the four Ps in a marketing mix.**

5. **Know the difference between a strategy, a strategic plan, and a marketing program.**

6. **Recognize the important new terms (shown in red).**

2

Marketing's role within the firm

"A master plan to hit the target" is not a James Bond story line—but the goal of a good marketing manager.

Marketing and marketing management are important in our society—and in business firms. As you saw in Chapter 1, marketing is concerned with anticipating needs and directing the flow of goods and services from producers to consumers. This is done to satisfy the needs of consumers and carry out both the economy's (the macro view) and the firm's (the micro view) objectives.

To get a better understanding of both macro- and micro-marketing, we are going to emphasize micro-marketing. That is, we are going to look at things from the point of view of the marketing manager—the one who makes a company's important marketing decisions.

MARKETING'S ROLE HAS CHANGED A LOT OVER THE YEARS

In a modern economy, marketing management plays a very important role. But it hasn't always been so important—or so complex. Relatively little marketing was done in ancient Egypt, for example, or in feudal Europe.

Early economies counted on middlemen

Early humans simply scratched out an existence—and there are still many parts of the world that have not advanced much beyond this subsistence living. Some people still raise and consume almost everything they produce—living without money, and sharing most of the work and output of their communities.

In other economies, specialization in production took place at an early stage. About 2100 B.C., the Code of Hammurabi was set down to help regulate the highly developed society that had grown up on the fertile valleys of the Tigris and Euphrates Rivers—in what is now Iraq. Trade flourished—and these communities rose above the subsistence level because of (1) specialization in production and distribution and (2) an assurance that the specialization would work. That is, some people were willing to leave self-sufficient farms when they were fairly sure of being fed by the food production of others.

Trade tended to grow whenever there was political stability—especially during the long period when the Romans ruled the Mediterranean area—and controlled its commerce. During the following centuries, production and trade continued growing—with some ups and downs due to wars, famines, and plagues. But the main emphasis was on producing more and expecting middlemen to distribute whatever was produced.

Evolution from the production era to the marketing era

It is only in recent years that an increasing number of producers, wholesalers, and retailers have recognized the importance of marketing. These companies have grown from the days when the basic emphasis was producing or stocking products. Now, they focus their attention on customers—and try to integrate the company's total effort toward satisfying them.

Identifying the following four eras should help clarify this evolution: (1) production or product era, (2) sales era, (3) marketing department era, and (4) marketing company era.

The story of this change was told very well by R. J. Keith—a top manager of Pillsbury, Inc.—a manufacturer of flour, cake mixes, and animal feeds.[1]

From the production to the sales era

Marketing was a long time coming to Pillsbury. The company was formed in 1869 and continued until about 1930 in what Keith called the production era. The **production era** is a time when a company focuses on production—perhaps because few products are available in the market. Beginning in 1930, the company went into the sales era. The **sales era** is a time when a company emphasizes

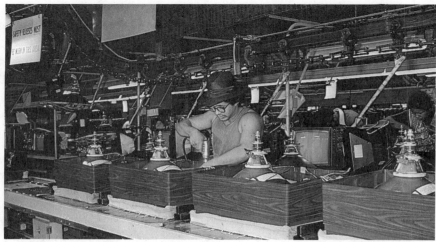

Specialization helps an economy become more productive.

Milt & Joan Mann

selling—because of increased competition. Selling became more important at Pillsbury as the firm became aware that it needed to attract both its middlemen and the middlemen's customers.

To the marketing department era

The sales era continued until about 1950. By then, Pillsbury had developed many new products. Sales were growing rapidly. Someone was needed to tie together the efforts of production, research, purchasing, and sales. As Pillsbury faced up to this job, the sales era was replaced by the marketing department era. The **marketing department era** is a time when all marketing activities are brought under the control of one department—to improve short-run policy planning—and to try to integrate the firm's activities. Finding people trained in short-run marketing policy making was difficult. For three or four years, the company worked at learning how to turn ideas into products and then products into profits.

To the marketing company era

In a relatively few years, Pillsbury had developed a staff with a marketing management approach. Then, in 1958, the company went all the way—into the marketing company era. The **marketing company era** is a time when—in addition to short-run marketing planning—marketing people look and plan three to ten years ahead and the whole company effort is guided by the *marketing concept*.

WHAT DOES THE MARKETING CONCEPT MEAN IN BUSINESS?

The **marketing concept** means that a firm aims all its efforts at satisfying its customers—at a profit. This is really a fairly new idea in business. It replaces the production-oriented way of thinking. **Production orientation** means making products which are easy to produce—and *then* trying to sell them. **Marketing orientation** means trying to carry out the marketing concept.

The marketing concept calls for changing the firm's ways of doing things. Instead of trying to get customers to buy what the firm has produced, a marketing-oriented firm would try to produce what customers need.

Those who believe in the marketing concept feel that customer needs should be the firm's main focus. They feel that the firm's resources should be organized to satisfy those needs.

Three basic ideas are included in the definition of the marketing concept.

1. A customer orientation.
2. A total company effort.
3. Profit—not just sales—as a goal of the firm.

Carrying out the marketing concept, therefore, might require three related changes:

1. A change in management attitudes.
2. A change in the firm's organization structure.
3. A change in its management methods and procedures.

Changes in all three areas would probably be needed if the firm really wanted to adopt the marketing concept.

The typical production orientation is a road block

Give the customers what they need—this may seem so obvious and logical that it may be hard for you to understand why the marketing concept is such a new idea. However, people haven't always done the logical and obvious. In a typical company, production managers thought mainly about getting out the product. Accountants were interested only in balancing the books. Financial people looked after the company's cash position. And sales people were mainly concerned with getting orders. Each person saw the rest of the business working around him. No one was concerned with the whole system. As long as the company made a profit, each department went merrily on—"doing its own thing." Unfortunately, this is still true in most companies today.

"Production orientation" refers to the typical lack of a central focus in a business firm. To be fair to the production people, however, it also is seen in sales-oriented sales representatives, advertising-oriented agency people, finance-oriented finance people, and so on. We will use "production orientation" to cover all such narrow thinking.

It should be a "sharing" situation

Ideally, all managers should work together—because the output from one department may be the input to another. But managers in production-oriented firms tend to build "fences" around their own departments—as seen in Figure 2–1(A). Each department runs its own affairs for its own benefit. There may be meetings to try to get them to work together—but usually each department head comes to such meetings with the idea of protecting his own department's interests.

It's easy to slip into a production orientation

It is very easy to slip into a production-oriented way of thinking. Production managers, for example, might prefer to have long production runs of easy-to-produce, standardized products. And retailers might prefer only day-time weekday hours—avoiding nights, Saturdays, and Sundays—when many customers would prefer to shop. Differences in outlook between production-oriented and marketing-oriented managers are shown in Figure 2–2.

Figure 2–1
A. A business as a box (most departments have high fences)

B. Total system view of a business (implementing marketing concept; still have departments but all guided by what customer wants)

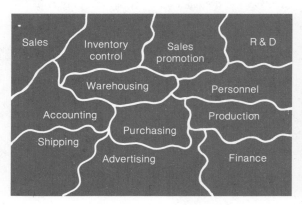

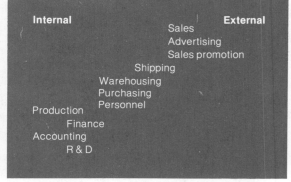

Figure 2–2
Some differences in outlook between adopters of the marketing concept and the typical production-oriented managers

Marketing orientation	Attitudes and procedures	Production orientation
Customer needs determine company plans	Attitudes toward customers	They should be glad we exist, trying to cut costs and bring out better products
Company makes what it can sell	Product offering	Company sells what it can make
To determine customer needs and how well company is satisfying them	Role of marketing research	To determine customer reaction, if used at all
Focus on locating new opportunities	Interest in innovation	Focus is on technology and cost cutting
A critical objective	Importance of profit	A residual, what's left after all costs are covered
Seen as a customer service	Role of customer credit	Seen as a necessary evil
Designed for customer convenience and as a selling tool	Role of packaging	Seen merely as protection for the product
Set with customer requirements and costs in mind	Inventory levels	Set with production requirements in mind
Seen as a customer service	Transportation arrangements	Seen as an extension of production and storage activities, with emphasis on cost minimization
Need-satisfying benefits of products and services	Focus of advertising	Product features and quality, maybe how products are made
Help the customer to buy if the product fits his needs, while coordinating with rest of firm—including production, inventory control, advertising, etc.	Role of sales force	Sell the customer, don't worry about coordination with other promotion efforts or rest of firm

Source: Adapted from R. F. Vizza, T. E. Chambers, and E. J. Cook, *Adoption of the Marketing Concept—Fact or Fiction* (New York: Sales Executives Club, Inc., 1967), pp. 13–15.

Work together . . . do a
better job

In a firm that has accepted the marketing concept, however, the fences come down. There are still departments, of course, because there are efficiencies in specialization. But the total system's effort is guided by what customers want—instead of what each department would like to do.

In such a firm, it is more realistic to view the business as a box with both an internal and an external section. See Figure 2–1(B). Here, there are some internal departments concerned mainly with affairs inside the firm—production, accounting, and research and development (R&D). And there are external departments concerned with outsiders—sales, advertising, and sales promotion. Finally, there are departments that must be concerned with both the internal and the external sections—warehousing, shipping, purchasing, finance, and personnel. The efforts of *all* of these departments are aimed at satisfying some market needs—at a profit—because they have accepted the marketing concept.

*Marketing concept
forces change*

The marketing concept is really very powerful—if taken seriously. It forces the company (1) to think through what it is doing, and why, and then (2) to develop a plan for accomplishing its objectives. Where the marketing concept has been wholeheartedly accepted and carried out, it has led to major changes in the way the firm operates—and often to higher profits.

ORGANIZING TO IMPLEMENT THE MARKETING CONCEPT

*Pointing the company
toward its goal*

The first and most important step in applying the marketing concept is a serious commitment to a customer orientation. Without acceptance of this idea—at least by top management—any change in the organization structure won't really matter.

Some organization helps

After top management has accepted the marketing concept, some formal reorganization is usually desirable. The product planning function is often under the production or R&D (research and development) department. Pricing is under the finance or accounting department. And sales and advertising are often separate departments.

All these activities involve the customer, so they should be under the direction of the marketing manager. The marketing manager should report directly to top management—along with the heads of production, R&D, finance, and accounting.

Figure 2–3
A company's organization chart before and after acceptance of the marketing concept

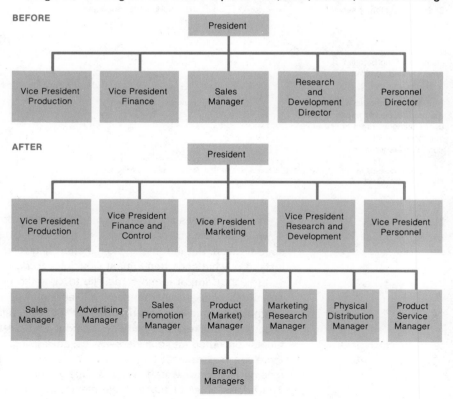

The arrangement of a particular marketing department depends on the strategies of that company and the personalities involved. Organization charts in one company before and after adoption of the marketing concept are shown in Figure 2–3.

Who should organize and run the total system?

Top management is responsible for developing and running a *total system* designed to meet the needs of target customers. Ideally, the whole company becomes customer-oriented. All departments pull together to reach the objectives. (Note: We will still have departments—because there are advantages in job specialization.) Instead of battles between various departments, a marketing-oriented system would do some marketing research, perhaps run some market tests, and figure potential costs and *company* (not departmental) profits for possible strategies. Then, it would decide what is best for the *firm*—not just what is best for any one department.

In such a system, the marketing manager would help develop this "total system" attitude within the firm. He must work regularly with customers and is in an ideal position to tie things together.

Who is suited to lead a marketing-oriented company?

Many marketing managers probably will come out of sales management because they are more likely to be familiar with the firm's customers. But this isn't always true. The marketing manager and a marketing-oriented president could come from any specialty. In one cosmetic company—as might be expected in this type of business—the advertising and sales promotion manager gradually assumed major planning and coordinating responsibilities. In another firm, however—which produced highly technical custom-built products—the production manager was the leader in applying the marketing concept.

The most important point is that the prospective marketing manager and top manager accept the marketing concept.

ADOPTION OF THE MARKETING CONCEPT HAS NOT BEEN EASY OR UNIVERSAL

The marketing concept seems so logical that you would think that it would have been readily accepted by most firms. In fact, it was not. Further, there are still many firms which are production-oriented. In fact, the majority are either production-oriented—or regularly slip back that way—and must consciously bring the customers' interests to bear in their planning.

The marketing concept was first accepted by consumer goods companies—such as General Electric and Procter & Gamble. Competition was intense in some of their markets—and trying to satisfy customers' needs more fully was a way to win in this competition. Further, organizing the company around the marketing concept helped to integrate all of the company's activities. General Electric was the pacesetter in accepting the marketing concept. As GE saw it, a logical implementation of the marketing concept would provide a systematic approach to managing the marketing process in any business—large or small.[2]

General Electric's success with the marketing concept—and widespread publicity about what it was doing and why—helped spread the "message" to other consumer goods and industrial goods companies.

Producers of industrial commodities—steel, coal, paper, glass, chemicals—have accepted the marketing concept more slowly—if at all. Similarly, many retailers have been slow to accept the marketing concept—in part because they are so close to the final consumer that they "feel" that they really know their customers.

In the last ten years or so, "service" industries—including banks, airlines, lawyers, physicians, accountants, and insurance companies—have begun to consider the marketing concept. Acceptance varies widely in these industries. The government has even encouraged more emphasis on marketing by encouraging advertising and price competition among lawyers, accountants, and other professional groups. This has led many in these professions to pay more attention to their customers' needs. And some have been forced into it by aggressive competitors who are advertising and using price to attract new customers—which is contrary to long-accepted professional practice.

THE MARKETING CONCEPT IS USEFUL FOR NONPROFIT ORGANIZATIONS, TOO

Most of this book will focus on how to use the marketing concept in a specific business firm—be it a manufacturer, farmer, miner, wholesaler, or retailer—selling goods *or* services. Our primary focus will be on business firms which typically have some kind of a profit orientation.

But the same general principles can be applied directly to nonprofit organizations. All that must be changed are the objectives against which possible plans are measured. The Red Cross, art museums, and government agencies, for example, are all seeking to satisfy some consumer groups—and most of the ideas and principles are directly applicable.[3]

Like businesses, nonprofit organizations must focus on *some* particular customers—because their resources are usually limited. A visiting nurses organization, for example, defined its goal as providing "better" nursing services for "everyone." But this led to troubles—because most of its clients had "infinite" needs for more service—and it was difficult to know where to spend its limited funds. By more carefully defining whom they were serving, they saw that some customers simply needed "house-keeping care and comfort," while others needed "temporary nursing care," and others, "terminal nursing care." This clearer view of the needs of their clients enabled the nurses to rethink their efforts and focus on the ones they decided needed their service the most—the latter two groups.

HOW FAR SHOULD THE MARKETING CONCEPT GO?

The marketing concept is so logical, it's hard to see why anyone would argue with it. However, in recent years a new attitude is gaining importance. Some people have pointed out—correctly—that when a firm focuses its efforts on satisfying *some* consumers—to gain its objectives—the effect of this on society may be completely ignored. Further, the long-run welfare of the target consumers

Non-profit organizations must be sensitive to their target markets to be successful.

A Public Service of this newspaper & The Advertising Council

Today is the first day of the rest of your life.
Give blood,
so it can be the first day of somebody else's, too.

Red Cross is counting on you.

Courtesy The American Red Cross

may be neglected in favor of satisfying their short-term needs. For example, some critics argue that businesses should not offer cigarettes, high-heeled shoes, alcoholic beverages, soft drinks, and many processed foods—because they are either "empty calories" or may be detrimental to health in the long run. These critics raise the basic question: "Is the marketing concept really desirable?"[4]

Should all consumer needs be satisfied?

Remember the micro-macro dilemma we discussed in Chapter 1. What is "good" for some individual consumers in the short run may not be good for society as a whole. Further, what is "good" for some individual consumers in the short run may not be good for them in the long run. Consumers may *enjoy* diet soft drinks and cigarettes. In this sense, these are "good" products. But these same products may contain ingredients which—in the long run—may be harmful to the consumer. Should manufacturers continue to produce them?

Some marketing managers and socially conscious marketing companies are beginning to face this problem. Their definition of customer satisfaction is changing to include long-range effects—as well as immediate customer satisfaction. They are trying to bring social cost/benefit analysis into their decision making—with a view to balancing consumer, company, and social interests.

What if it cuts into profits?

It is interesting to note that being more "socially conscious" often seems to lead to positive customer response when built into strategies. For example, some supermarkets have had success offering nutritional labeling. And some food manufacturers are now trying to increase the nutritional value of their products—or bringing out new products which offer greater nutrition value. But these are the easy changes. What about changes that actually cut into profits? For example,

Figure 2–4
The management job (given the company's objectives and present resources)

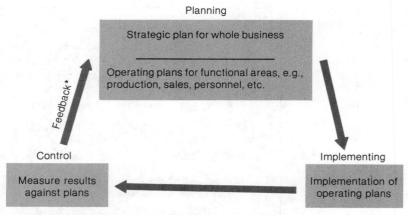

Planning

Strategic plan for whole business

Operating plans for functional areas, e.g., production, sales, personnel, etc.

Feedback*

Control

Measure results against plans

Implementing

Implementation of operating plans

* In the form of information concerning results of management planning.

given the hazards of tobacco and alcoholic beverages, should the companies offering these products go out of business? Motorcycles, bicycles, small cars, skis, and many other products are extremely hazardous to users. Should these be offered to consumers just because they want them? Who should decide? Is this a micro-marketing issue or a macro-marketing issue?

Being "socially conscious" and trying to carry out the marketing concept can be difficult. It may mean reducing short-term profitability. But socially responsible business managers have to face this issue. We will talk about it again in Chapter 24—after you have a better understanding of marketing.

THE MANAGEMENT JOB IN MARKETING

Hitting some target customers

The marketing manager wants to anticipate and then meet the needs of a group of customers (the target group) with a particular good or service. Out of the almost infinite number of products offered to consumers, the marketing manager wants to be sure that *his product* will succeed. How can he do it?

First, the marketing manager is a *manager*. It is helpful, therefore, to look closely at the role of any manager.

Nature of management job

Management generally has three basic tasks:

1. To set a general plan for the business.
2. To direct the implementation of this plan.
3. To control the plan in actual operation.

For simplicity, this can be thought of as: planning, implementing, and control. The three-cornered diagram in Figure 2–4 shows the interrelation of these basic tasks. The relationship of the control and planning jobs is very important—information feedback often leads to changes in the general plan or even to a totally new plan. Thus the management job is *continuous*.

The marketing management job is continuous

The **marketing manager's job** consists of the basic management tasks: planning, implementing, and control. But—as shown in Figure 2–5—the planning job consists of two parts: (1) finding attractive opportunities and (2) developing marketing strategies. The marketing manager cannot be satisfied with planning present strategies. In a dynamic marketplace, he must always look for new opportunities and make new plans. Competitors continually search for ways of improving their offerings—and consumers are always willing to try something newer and better.

Besides looking for opportunities, the marketing manager must also develop marketing strategies—aimed at particular groups of customers. Planning marketing strategy is the basic topic in this text. Without a well-defined "master plan," there are no guidelines for implementing or control.

Marketing strategies must be turned into strategic plans—one for each strategy—which spell out the time-related details. Going further, all of a firm's plans must be merged together into one program—which is then implemented and controlled.

Planning strategies to guide the whole company is called **strategic planning**—the managerial process of developing and maintaining a match between the resources of an organization and its market opportunities. This is even bigger than developing a marketing program—because it includes planning for production, research and development, and other functional areas in more detail than is necessary when planning marketing strategies.

We will not get into such detail in this text—but it is important to see that the marketing department's plan is not the whole corporate plan. On the other hand, it is clear that a good corporate plan should be market-oriented. And to the extent that the corporate plan is simply the sum of the various department plans, the marketing department's strategic plans may set the tone and direction for the whole company. In other words, if the marketing department applies the marketing concept, then this could lead the whole company to do so.

After the basic strategies are planned, management can concern itself with

Figure 2–5
The marketing management process

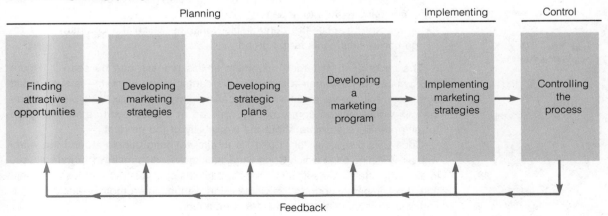

Planning				Implementing	Control
Finding attractive opportunities	Developing marketing strategies	Developing strategic plans	Developing a marketing program	Implementing marketing strategies	Controlling the process

Feedback

the implementation of these strategies—that is, with personnel selection, salary administration, middleman selection, commission rates, and so on. Implementation may, in fact, take up a greater part of the manager's time—but it is not the major concern here. Detailed study of implementation decisions must be left for advanced work—after you have learned about planning marketing strategy.

We will discuss control, too, since it provides the feedback that leads to modifying marketing strategies. The tools most frequently used by the marketing manager—to maintain his control—are electronic data processing, marketing research, and accounting.

All marketing jobs require planning and control

At first, it might appear that planning and control are of concern only to the top management of large companies. This is *not* true. Even the smallest farmer, retailer, or wholesaler should plan and control strategies.

Similarly, all salespeople—however limited their territory or department—also must have a plan of attack. They may not have complete freedom—because of the master strategy already outlined—but they usually have some choice. They should develop their own strategies—in the light of their abilities and the problems of their particular areas.

This means that marketing strategy planning may be very important to you—soon—maybe even in your present job or college activities.

WHAT IS MARKETING STRATEGY PLANNING?

Marketing planning means finding attractive opportunities and developing profitable marketing strategies. But what is a "marketing strategy"? We have used these words rather casually so far. Now let's see what they really mean.

What is a marketing strategy?

A **marketing strategy** is a target market and a related marketing mix. It is a "big picture" of what a firm will do in some market. Two interrelated parts are needed:

1. A **target market**—a fairly homogeneous (similar) group of customers to whom a company wishes to appeal.
2. A **marketing mix**—the controllable variables which the company puts together to satisfy this target group.

Figure 2–6
A marketing strategy

THE MARKETING MIX

C

The importance of target customers in this process can be seen in Figure 2–6, where the customer—the "C" in the center of the diagram—is surrounded by the controllable variables which we call the "marketing mix." A typical marketing mix would include some product, offered at a price, with some promotion to tell potential customers about the availability of the product.

Coca-Cola's strategy for "Coke" is to aim at young people around the world with a refreshing drink which Coca-Cola packages or dispenses in various ways—in as many retail outlets as it can reach. While its pricing is more or less competitive, the company supports the whole effort with much promotion—including advertising, personal selling, and sales promotion.

A marketing manager has to identify a target market to whom he wishes to appeal.

Peter Le Grand

SELECTING A MARKET-ORIENTED STRATEGY IS TARGET MARKETING

Target marketing is not mass marketing

It is important to see that a marketing strategy focuses on *some* particular target customers. We will call this market-oriented approach "target marketing"—to distinguish it from "mass marketing." **Target marketing** focuses on some specific target customers. **Mass marketing**—the typical production-oriented approach—aims at "everyone." Production-oriented managers just assume that everyone is the same—and will want whatever their firms offer. They don't try to find out what *some* customers might want. Instead, everyone is considered a potential customer. See Figure 2–7.

"Mass marketers" may do target marketing

Commonly used terms can be confusing here. The words "mass marketing" and "mass marketers" do not mean the same thing. Far from it! "Mass *marketing*" means selling to "everyone," as explained above—while "mass *marketers*" like General Electric, Procter & Gamble, and Sears, Roebuck are *not* aiming at "everyone." They do aim at clearly defined target markets. The confusion with "mass marketing" occurs because their target markets usually are large and spread out.

Target marketing— maybe big markets and profits

It is important to see that target marketing is not limited to small market segments—only to fairly homogeneous ones. A very large market—even what is sometimes called the "mass market"—may be fairly homogeneous in some cases and the target marketer will deliberately aim at it.

The basic reason for this focus on some specific target customers is to gain a competitive advantage by developing a more satisfying marketing mix—which should also be more profitable for the firm.

Figure 2–7
Production-oriented and marketing-oriented managers have different views of the market

Production-oriented manager sees everyone as basically similar and practices "mass marketing"

Marketing-oriented manager sees everyone as different and practices "target marketing"

DEVELOPING MARKETING MIXES FOR TARGET MARKETS

There are many marketing mix variables

There are many possible ways to satisfy the needs of target customers. A product can have many different features, colors, and appearances. The package can be of various sizes, colors, or materials. The brand names and trademarks can be changed. Services can be adjusted. Various advertising media (newspapers, magazines, radio, television, billboards) may be used. A company's own sales force or other sales specialists can be used. Different prices can be charged, and so on. With so many variables available, the question is: Is there any way of simplifying the selection of marketing mixes? And the answer is *yes*.

The four "Ps" make up a marketing mix

It is useful to reduce the number of variables in the marketing mix to four basic ones:

Product.
Place.
Promotion.
Price.

Figure 2–8
A marketing strategy—showing the 4 Ps of a marketing mix

It helps to think of the four major parts of a marketing mix as the "four Ps." Figure 2–8 emphasizes their relationship and their focus on the customer—"C."

Customer is not part of the marketing mix

The customer is shown surrounded by the four Ps in Figure 2–8. This has led some students to think that the customer is part of the marketing mix. This is not true. The customer should be the target of all marketing efforts. The customer is placed in the center of the diagram to show this—the C stands for the specific customers, the target market.

Table 2–1 shows some of the variables in the four Ps—which will be discussed in later chapters. For now, let's just describe each P briefly.

Product—the right one for the target

The Product area is concerned with developing the right "product" for the target market. This product may involve a physical good and/or service. The important thing to remember in the Product area is that your good—and/or service—should satisfy *some* customers' needs.

Under Product we will discuss developing and managing new products and product lines. We will also talk about the characteristics of various kinds of products—so that you will be able to make generalizations about product classes. This will help you develop whole marketing mixes more quickly.

Although this text may seem to emphasize physical goods, the principles also apply to services. This is important—because the service side of our economy is large and growing. We will use Product to mean a "bundle" of goods and/or services. Most products are a combination of both goods and services.

Place—reaching the target

Place is concerned with getting the right product to the target market. A product isn't much good to a customer if it isn't available when and where it's wanted. In the Place area, we will see where, when, and by whom the goods and services can be offered for sale.

Goods and services move to consumers through channels of distribution. A **channel of distribution** is any series of firms (or individuals) from producer to final user or consumer. A channel can include several kinds of middlemen and specialists. Marketing managers work with these channels. So our study of Place is very important to marketing strategy planning.

Sometimes a channel system is quite short. It may run directly from a producer to a final user or consumer. Usually, it is more complex—involving many different kinds of middlemen and specialists. And if a marketing manager has several different target markets, several channels of distribution might be needed. See Figure 2–9.

Promotion—telling and selling the customer

The third P—Promotion—is concerned with telling the target market about the "right" product. Promotion includes personal selling, mass selling, and sales promotion. It is the marketing manager's job to blend these methods.

Personal selling involves direct face-to-face communication between sellers and potential customers. Personal selling lets the salesperson adapt the firm's marketing mix to each potential customer. But this individual attention comes at a price. Personal selling can be very expensive. Often this personal effort has to be blended with mass selling and sales promotion.

**Table 2–1
Strategic decision areas**

Product	Place	Promotion	Price
Features	Channels	Promotion blend	Flexibility
Accessories	Market exposure	Kind of sales people	Level
Installation	Kinds of middlemen	Selection	Introductory pricing
Instructions	Who handles storing	Training	Discounts
Service	and transporting	Motivation	Allowances
Warranty	Service levels	Kind of advertising	Geographic terms
Product lines		Media type	
Package		Copy thrust	
Brand name		Publicity	
		Sales promotion	

Figure 2–9
Four possible (basic) channels of distribution for consumer goods

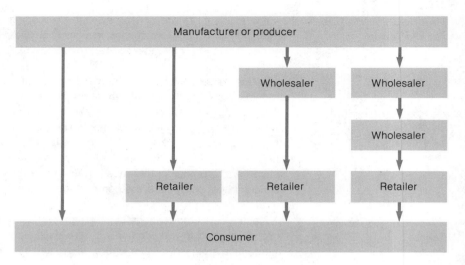

Mass selling is communicating with large numbers of customers at the same time. **Advertising** is any paid form of nonpersonal presentation of ideas, goods, or services by an identified sponsor. It is the main form of mass selling.

Sales promotion refers to those promotion activities which complement personal selling and mass selling. This can involve designing and arranging for the distribution of novelties, point-of-purchase materials, store signs, catalogs, and circulars. Sales promotion people try to help the personal selling and mass selling specialists.

Price—making it right

In addition to developing the right Product, Place, and Promotion, marketing managers must also decide the right Price. In setting a price, they must consider the kind of competition in the target market. They must also try to estimate customer reaction to possible prices. Besides this, they also must know current practices as to markups, discounts, and other terms of sale. Further, they must be aware of legal restrictions on pricing.

If customers won't accept the Price, all of the planning effort will be wasted. So you can see that Price is an important area for the marketing manager.

Relative importance of the four Ps

All four Ps are needed in a marketing mix. In fact, they should all be tied together. But is any one more important than the others? Generally speaking, the answer is *no*—all contribute to one whole. When a marketing mix is being developed, all (final) decisions about the Ps should be made at the same time. That's why the four Ps are arranged around the customer (C) in a circle—to show that they all are equally important.

Strategy guides implementing

Let's sum up our discussion of marketing mix planning this far. We develop a *Product* that we feel will satisfy the target customers. We find a way *(Place)* to reach our target customers. *Promotion* tells the target customers about the availability of the product that has been designed for them. Then, the *Price* is set after estimating expected customer reaction to the total offering and the costs of getting it to them.

Both jobs must be done together

It is important to stress—*it cannot be overemphasized*—that selecting a target market and developing a marketing mix are interrelated. A marketing manager cannot do one step and then another. Both steps must be done together. It is *strategies* which must be evaluated against the company's objectives—not alternative target markets or alternative marketing mixes.

Strategy sets details of implementation

The needs and attitudes of a target market determine the nature of an appropriate marketing mix. So marketers have to analyze their potential target markets with great care—*segmenting* them into sub-markets and identifying the dimensions which really make a difference in these alternative market segments. Throughout the rest of the book, we will explore ways of identifying attractive market opportunities and developing appropriate strategies. Ideally, we will try to understand not only the needs and attitudes of potential target markets, but also enough of their other dimensions so that logical marketing mixes will follow quickly. Such target market descriptions may require imaginative combining of several dimensions to completely describe potential target markets. It will help estimating the size of potential markets if we can tie each to demographic characteristics—such as age, sex, income, geographic area, and so on.

These ideas can be seen more clearly with an example in the home decorating market.

A British paint manufacturer looks at the home decorating market

The experience of a paint manufacturer in England illustrates the strategic planning process and how strategic decisions help decide how the plan is carried out.

First, this paint manufacturer's marketing manager interviewed many potential customers and studied the various needs for the products he could offer. By combining several kinds of customer needs and some available demographic data, he came up with the view of the market shown in Figure 2–10. In the following description of these markets, note that useful marketing mixes come to mind immediately.

Figure 2–10
The home decorating market (paint area) in England

There turned out to be a large (but hard to describe) market for "general-purpose paint"—about 60 percent of the potential for all kinds of paint products. The manufacturer did not consider this market—because he did not want to compete "head-on" with the many companies already in this market. The other four markets—which were placed in the four corners of a market diagram simply to show that they were different markets—he called Helpless Homemaker, Handy Helper, Crafty Craftsman, and Cost-Conscious Couple.

The Helpless Homemaker—the manufacturer found out—really didn't know much about home painting or specific products. This customer needed a helpful paint retailer who could supply not only paint and other supplies—but also much advice. And the retailer who sold the paint would want it to be of fairly good quality so that the homemaker would be satisfied with the results.

The Handy Helper was a jack-of-all-trades who knew a great deal about paint and painting. He wanted a good-quality product and was satisifed to buy from an old-fashioned hardware store or lumber yard—which usually sells mainly to men. Similarly, the Crafty Craftsman was willing to buy from a retailer who would not attract female customers. In fact, these older men didn't want to buy paint at all. They wanted pigments, oils, and other things to mix their own paint.

Finally, the Cost-Conscious Couple was young, had low income, and lived in an apartment. In England, an apartment dweller must paint the apartment during the course of the lease. This is an important factor for some tenants as they choose their paint. If you were a young apartment dweller with limited income, what sort of paint would you want? Some couples in England—the manufacturer discovered—did not want very good paint! In fact, something not much better than whitewash would do fine.

The paint manufacturer decided to cater to "Cost-Conscious Couples" with a marketing mix flowing from the description of that market. That is, knowing what he did about them, he offered a low-quality paint (Product), made it available in lower-income apartment neighborhoods (Place), aimed his price-oriented ads at these areas (Promotion), and, of course, offered an attractive low price (Price). The manufacturer has been extremely successful with this strategy—giving his customers what they really want—even though the product is of low quality.

DIFFERENTIATING BETWEEN STRATEGY AND TACTICS

Our main emphasis in this text is on strategy planning—but a lot more than strategy planning is involved in successful marketing. Strategies work out as planned only when they are effectively carried out. Many decisions have to be made during these implementing efforts. These decisions are concerned with tactics—short-run plans to help implement strategic plans.

Tactical decisions can enhance the basic strategy

Tactical decisions should be made within the guidelines set down during strategy planning. Product policies, place policies, and so on, are developed as part of strategy planning. Then, tactical decisions within these policies probably will be necessary—while carrying out the basic strategy. It is important to realize, however, that as long as these tactical decisions stay within the guidelines, no change is being made in the basic strategy. If tactical decisions do not produce

Table 2–2
Relation of strategic policies to tactical decisions for paint manufacturer

Strategic policies	Likely tactical decisions
Product—Carry as limited a line of colors and sizes as will satisfy the target market.	Add, change, or drop colors and/or can sizes as customer tastes and preferences dictate.
Place—Try to obtain distribution in every conceivable retail outlet which will handle this type of paint in the areas where the target customers live or buy.	If a new retailer opens for business in these market areas, immediately solicit his order.
Promotion—Promote the "low price" and "satisfactory quality" to meet the needs of the market.	Regularly change the point-of-purchase and advertising copy to produce a "fresh" image. Media changes may be necessary also. Sales people have to be trained, motivated, etc.
Price—Maintain a low "one-price" policy without "specials" or other promotional deals.	If paint companies in other markets cut prices, do not follow.

Figure 2–11
Elements of a firm's marketing program

Target market
+
Marketing mix
} = Marketing strategy + Time related details and control procedures = Strategic plan + Other strategic plans } A firm's marketing program

the desired results, however, it may be necessary to reevaluate the whole strategy—rather than just "redoubling the effort" in a tactical decision area.

It's easier to see the difference between strategic policies and tactics if we illustrate these ideas using our paint manufacturer example. Possible four-P or basic strategic policies are shown in the left-hand column in Table 2–2—and likely tactical decisions are shown in the right-hand column.

It should be clear that some tactical decisions are made regularly—even daily—and such decisions should not be confused with strategic ones. Certainly, a great deal of effort can be involved in these tactical decisions. They might take up a good part of the time of a sales manager, advertising manager, and others. But they are not the strategic decisions which will be our primary concern. In later chapters, we will discuss the policies which provide guidelines for such tactical changes—but details of implementation are the subject of advanced texts and courses in marketing.

STRATEGIC PLANS AND PROGRAMS MUST BE DEVELOPED—EVENTUALLY

Our focus has been—and will continue to be—on developing marketing strategies. But it is also important to see that eventually marketing managers must develop strategic *plans* and a marketing *program*. See Figure 2–11. We discuss them briefly here and more fully in Chapter 21.

What is a strategic plan?

A strategy is a "big picture" of what a firm will do in some market. A strategic plan goes farther. A **strategic plan** includes a strategy and the time-related details for carrying out the strategy. It should spell out the following in detail: (1) what marketing mix is to be offered to whom (that is, the target market), and for how long; (2) what company resources (shown as costs) will be needed—at what rate (month by month, perhaps); and (3) what results are expected (sales and profits, perhaps month by month). It should also include some control procedures—so that whoever is to carry out the plan will know when things are going wrong. This might be something as simple as comparing actual sales against expected sales—with a "warning flag" to be raised whenever total sales fall below a certain level.

Several plans make a program

Most companies implement more than one strategic plan at the same time. Typically, they aim at several target markets and prepare different marketing mixes for each one. A **marketing program** blends all of a firm's strategic plans into one "big" plan. This program, then, is the responsibility of the whole company.

THE IMPORTANCE OF MARKETING STRATEGY PLANNING

Most of our emphasis in this book will be on the planning phase of the marketing manager's job—for a good reason. The "one-time" strategy decisions—the decisions that decide what business the company is in and the strategies it will follow—may be more important than has been realized. In fact, an extremely good plan might be carried out badly and still be profitable, while a poor but well-implemented plan can lose money. The case histories that follow show the importance of planning—and why we are going to emphasize strategy planning throughout this text.

Sears, Roebuck found its own market—for many years

Sears, Roebuck has had great success since World War II because of a good new plan. Before this time, department stores had always been located in the downtown area. Sears tried a new strategy. The company built its new stores in the rapidly growing suburban areas—away from downtown competition. Sears provided ample parking space—and stores so large and well stocked that customers could do all their shopping under one roof. Conventional retailers said Sears would fail, because the "right" place for big department stores was downtown. But Sears had correctly predicted that people were shifting to the suburbs. Their new strategy was a big success—for many years.

Sears has not been doing as well in recent years, however, as new kinds of retailers have moved to the outlying areas. These newer competitors included various kinds of specialized discounters who offered knowledgeable salespeople—as well as large self-service operations which emphasized lower prices, like Kmart and Woolco. In other words, the newcomers emphasized lower prices—some with service and some self-service—as they moved right near Sears' previously well-chosen locations.

In the face of this new competition, Sears held the firm to its original strategy and saw some of its business picked off by the new competitors. The Christmas toy business, for example, was cut into drastically by the "discounters." Sears

Sears predicted correctly that people were moving away from the city—and found their market there.

Kenneth Yee

Henry Ford saw a market for millions of cars.

tried various strategy changes—including raising price and quality as it felt its customers were becoming more affluent. When they found that they had gone too far, they tried to return to the original strategy of appealing to the large middle-income group. This has confused some consumers about what Sears is actually doing—and perhaps made them more willing to try the newer competitors.

Also contributing to Sears' problems is trying to staff a "full-service" store with competent salespeople for the extra hours they are now open to compete with the self-service stores. It is one thing to have a core of trained salespeople for a 9-to-5, six-days-a-week operation and quite another thing to be open from 9 to 9, six days a week and 10 to 6 on Sunday.

So you can see, that while Sears had a successful strategy for a while, newcomers have come along with different—and perhaps more effective—strategies which "chip away" at Sears. These competitors are attracting customers who might otherwise have been reasonably or even well satisfied by Sears' marketing mix—until they were exposed to different marketing mixes.

Henry Ford's strategy worked—until General Motors caught up

Henry Ford is remembered for developing the mass production techniques that produced a car for the masses. His own view of his approach, however, was that mass production developed *because* of his basic decision to build a car for the masses. In those days, cars were almost custom-built for the wealthy, the sports drivers, and other specialty buyers. Ford decided on a different strategy. He wanted to produce a car that could appeal to most potential buyers.

Certainly, new production ideas were needed to carry out Ford's strategy. But the really important decision was the initial *market-oriented* decision that there was a market for millions of cars in the $500 price range. Much of what followed was just carrying out this decision. Ford's strategy to offer a low-priced car was an outstanding success and millions of Model Ts were sold in the 1910s and 1920s. But there was a defect in his strategy. To keep the price down, a very basic car was offered with "any color you want as long as it's black."

In the 1920s, General Motors' management felt that there was room for a new strategy. Their basic decision was to add colors and styling—even if this meant raising prices. They also hit upon the idea of looking at the market as having several segments (based on price and quality)—and then offering a full line of cars with entries at the top of each of these price ranges. They planned to appeal to quality-conscious consumers—always offering good values. The General Motors strategy was not an immediate success. But they stuck with their plan through the 1920s and slowly caught up with Ford. Finally, in May 1927, Ford closed down his assembly line for 18 months, switched his strategy, and introduced the more market-oriented Model A. But General Motors was already well on its way to the commanding market position it now holds.[5]

General Motors and the replacement parts market

It is important to note that while General Motors was successfully capturing a giant share of the automobile market, it was neglecting another very important market—the automobile replacement parts market. Of course, parts were supplied—they had to be. But in those early days, they were more concerned with making and selling cars than with keeping them running. Supplying parts was seen more as a "necessary evil" than an important business in itself. As a result, the market was left to many smaller suppliers—who were willing to move into this profitable market.

Even today, General Motors does not have the commanding position in the replacement parts and service market that it has in the car market. In other words, the successful strategy of General Motors was concerned with making and selling automobiles—not with the broader concept of personal transportation and keeping the cars moving.

The watch industry sees new strategies

The conventional watchmakers—both domestic and foreign—had always aimed at customers who thought of watches as high-priced, high-quality symbols to mark special events—like graduations, retirement, and so on. These manufacturers produced expensive watches—and stressed their symbolic appeal in advertising. Their promotion was heavily concentrated in the gift-buying seasons of Christmas and graduation time. Jewelry stores were the main retail outlets—charging large markups.

This commonly accepted strategy of the major watch companies ignored those who just wanted to tell the time—and were interested in low-priced watches that kept time reasonably well. So the U.S. Time Company developed a successful strategy around its "Timex" watches—and became the world's largest watch company.[6]

U.S. Time completely upset the watch industry—both foreign and domestic—by not only offering a good product (with a one-year repair or replace guarantee) at a lower price, but also by using new, lower-cost channels of distribution. Its watches are widely available in drug stores, discount houses, and nearly any other retail outlet which will carry them.

Now, Timex itself faces serious competition—electronics firms have entered the market with an entirely new way of keeping time—digital watches. They have also been cutting prices drastically—while following Timex's lead into widespread distribution. Some of the traditional watchmakers are closing their factories. Even Timex is threatened because it is not deeply involved in the new technology and production methods. Here, technological improvements—combined with modern marketing strategy planning—may completely change this whole industry in only a few years.[7]

Creative strategy planning needed for survival

Such dramatic shifts in strategy may surprise conventional, production-oriented managers. But such changes are becoming much more common—especially in industries where some of the firms have accepted the marketing concept.

What all this means is that a marketing manager and his firm will have to spend less time finding ways to use a company's present resources—a typical production-oriented approach—and pay more attention to locating new market opportunities. By looking for breakthrough opportunities, a company may find many profit possiblities which might otherwise be missed. This is discussed in Chapter 4.

Creative strategy planning is becoming even more important—because profits no longer can be won just by spending more money on plant and equipment. Moreover, domestic and foreign competition threatens those who can't create more satisfying goods and services. New markets, new customers, and new ways of doing things must be found if companies are to operate profitably in the future—and contribute to our macro-marketing system.

Strategy planning helps nonmarketing people, too

Clearly, good strategy planning can help ensure a firm's success. At the same time, it can satisfy consumers and, therefore, contribute to more effective operation of our macro-marketing system.

While strategy planning is helpful to marketers, it is also important to recognize that it is needed by accountants, production and personnel people, and all other specialists. A strategic plan lets everybody in the firm know what "ball park" they are playing in and what they are trying to accomplish. In other words, it gives direction to the whole business effort. It helps them to proceed with their various jobs. An accountant cannot set budgets if there is no plan, except perhaps mechanically projecting last year's budget. Similarly, a financial manager cannot project cash needs without some notion of expected sales to some customers—and the costs associated with satisfying them. Also, the personnel department needs to know what kinds of tasks the firm must accomplish—before it can hire and train people. And, obviously, the purchasing and production departments need to know how much of what is to be produced before they can make their plans.

We will use the term "marketing manager" for editorial convenience, but really, when we are talking about marketing strategy planning, we are talking about the planning which a market-oriented manager should do when developing a firm's strategic plans. This kind of thinking should be done, or at least understood, by everyone in an organization who is responsible for planning—and this means even the lowest-level salesperson, production supervisor, retail buyer, or personnel counselor.

Figure 2–12
Marketing manager's
framework

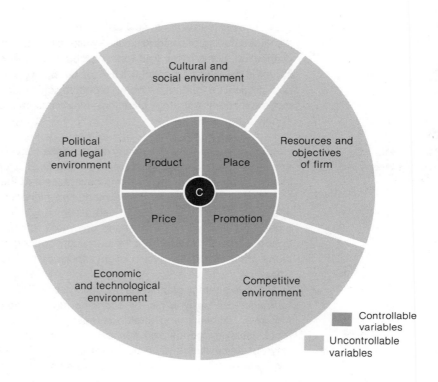

STRATEGY PLANNING DOESN'T TAKE PLACE IN A VACUUM

Strategy planning takes place within a framework

A marketing manager's strategy planning does not take place in a vacuum. Instead, the manager works with controllable variables within a framework involving many uncontrollable variables—which must be considered even though the manager cannot control them. Figure 2–12 illustrates this framework and shows that the typical marketing manager must be concerned about the cultural and social environment, the political and legal environment, the economic and technological environment, the competitive environment, and the resources and objectives of the firm. These uncontrollable variables are considered in more detail in the next two chapters. But clearly, the framework within which the marketing manager operates has a bearing on his strategy planning.

CONCLUSION

Marketing's role within a marketing-oriented firm is to tie the company together. The marketing concept provides direction. It stresses that the firm's efforts should be focused on satisfying some target markets—at a profit. Production-oriented firms tend to forget this. Often, the various departments within such a firm let their natural conflicts of interest lead them to building "fences" around their areas. Then, even coordinating committees may not be able to redirect the firm's efforts.

Complete acceptance of the marketing concept would probably lead to new organization arrangements. But the really important matter is acceptance by top management of the marketing concept. Without this, new arrangements probably won't make much difference.

The job of marketing management is one of continuous planning, implementing, and control. The marketing manager must constantly study the environment—seeking attractive opportunities. And new strategies must be planned continually. Potential target markets must be matched with marketing mixes that the firm can offer. Then, attractive strategies—really, strategic plans—are chosen for implementation. Controls are needed to be sure that the plans are carried out successfully. If anything goes wrong along the way, this continual feedback should cause the process to be started over again—with the marketing manager planning more attractive marketing strategies.

A marketing mix has four variables—the four Ps—Product, Place, Promotion, and Price. Most of this text is concerned with developing profitable marketing mixes for clearly defined target markets. So, after several chapters on selecting target markets, we will discuss each of the four Ps in greater detail.

QUESTIONS AND PROBLEMS

1. Define the marketing concept in your own words, and then explain why the notion of profit is usually included in this definition.

2. Define the marketing concept in your own words, and then suggest how acceptance of this concept might affect the organization and operation of your college.

3. Distinguish between "production orientation" and "marketing orientation," illustrating with local examples.

4. Explain why a firm should view its internal activities as part of a "total system." Illustrate your answer for (a) a large grocery products manufacturer, (b) a plumbing wholesaler, and (c) a department store chain.

5. Does the acceptance of the marketing concept almost require that a firm view itself as a "total system"?

6. Distinguish clearly between a marketing strategy and a marketing mix. Use an example.

7. Distinguish clearly between mass marketing and target marketing. Use an example.

8. Why is the customer placed in the center of the four Ps in the text diagram of a marketing strategy? Explain, using a specific example from your own experience.

9. Explain, in your own words, what each of the four Ps involves.

10. Evaluate the text's contention that "a marketing strategy sets the details of implementation."

11. Distinguish between strategy and tactics, illustrating for a local retailer.

12. Distinguish between a strategy, a strategic plan, and a marketing program—illustrating for a local retailer.

13. Outline a marketing strategy for each of the following new products:
    a. A radically new design for a haircomb.
    b. A new fishing reel.
    c. A new "wonder drug."
    d. A new industrial stapling machine.

14. Provide a specific illustration of why marketing strategy planning is important for all business people, not just for those in the marketing department.

SUGGESTED CASES

NOTES

1. Robert J. Keith, "The Marketing Revolution," *Journal of Marketing,* January 1960, pp. 35–38.

2. Edward S. McKay, "How to Plan and Set Up Your Marketing Program," *A Blueprint for an Effective Marketing Program, Marketing Series* No. 91 (New York: American Management Association, Inc., 1954), p. 15.

3. Philip Kotler, "Strategies for Introducing Marketing into Nonprofit Organizations," *Journal of Marketing,* vol. 43, January 1979, pp. 37–44.

4. Leslie M. Dawson, "Marketing for Human Needs in a Humane Future," *Business Horizons,* June 1980, pp. 72–82; Hiram C. Barksdale and William D. Perreault, Jr., "Can Consumers Be Satisfied?" *MSU Business Topics,* Spring 1980, pp. 20–30; Peter C. Riesz, "Revenge of the Marketing Concept," *Business Horizons,* June 1980, pp. 49–53; and Alan M. Kantrow, "The Strategy-Technology Connection," *Harvard Business Review,* July–August 1980, pp. 6–21.

5. Alfred P. Sloan, Jr., *My Years with General Motors* (New York: MacFadden Books, 1965), Introduction, chaps. 4 and 9.

6. Daniel Yankelovich, "Psychological Market Segmentation," in *Some Bold New Theories of Advertising in Marketing,* ed. Jack Z. Sissors (Evanston, Ill.: Northwestern University, 1963), pp. 23–25.

7. "Japanese Heat on the Watch Industry," *Business Week,* May 5, 1980, pp. 92–106; "A Reclusive Tycoon Takes Over at Timex," *Business Week,* April 14, 1980, p. 32; "Texas Instruments Wrestles with the Consumer Market," *Fortune,* December 3, 1979, pp. 50–57; "The Great Digital Watch Shake-Out," *Business Week,* May 2, 1977, pp. 70–80; "The Digital Watch Becomes the World's Cheapest Timepiece," *The Wall Street Journal,* April 18, 1977, p. 11; "Gruen Industries Asks Chapter 11 Status," *The Wall Street Journal,* April 15, 1977, p. 9; "Why Gillette Stopped Its Digital Watches," *Business Week,* January 31, 1977, pp. 37–38; and "Digital Wristwatch Business is Glowing, but Rivalry Winds Down Prices, Profits," *The Wall Street Journal,* August 24, 1976, p. 6.

Appendix A

Economics fundamentals

When you finish this appendix, you should:

1. Understand the "law of diminishing demand."
2. Know what a market is.
3. Understand demand and supply curves—and how they set the size of a market and its price level.
4. Know about elasticity of demand and supply.
5. Recognize the important new terms (shown in red).

A good marketing manager should be an expert on markets and the nature of competition in markets. The economist's traditional demand and supply analysis are useful tools for analyzing the nature of demand. In particular, you should master the concepts of a demand curve and demand elasticity. A firm's demand curve shows how the target customers view the firm's product. And the interaction of demand and supply curves helps set the size of the market and the market price. These ideas are discussed more fully in the following sections.

PRODUCTS AND MARKETS AS SEEN BY CUSTOMERS AND POTENTIAL CUSTOMERS

Economists provide useful insights

How *potential customers* (not the firm) see a firm's product has an important bearing on how much they are willing to pay for it, where it should be made available, and how eager they are to obtain it—if at all. In other words, it has a very direct bearing on marketing strategy planning.

Economists have been concerned with these basic problems for years—and their analytical tools can be quite helpful in summarizing how customers view products and how markets behave.

Economists see individual customers choosing among alternatives

Economics is sometimes called the "dismal" science because it shows that customers simply cannot buy everything they want. Since most customers have a limited income over any period of time, they must balance their needs and the costs of various products.

Economists usually assume that customers have a fairly definite set of preferences. It is assumed that they evaluate alternatives in terms of whether they will make them feel better (or worse)—or in some way improve (or change) their situation.

But what exactly is the nature of the customer's desire for a particular product? Usually the argument is given in terms of the extra utility the customer can obtain by buying more of a particular product—or how much utility would be lost were he or she to have less of the product. (Students who wish further discussion of this approach should refer to indifference curve analysis in any standard economics text.)

Utility is a conceptual framework. It may be easier to grasp this idea if we look at what happens when the price of one of the customer's usual purchases changes.

The law of diminishing demand

Suppose that a consumer were buying potatoes in ten-pound bags at the same time he bought other foods—such as meat and vegetables. If the consumer is mainly interested in purchasing a certain amount of foodstuffs—and the price of the potatoes drops—it seems reasonable to expect that he will switch some of his food money to potatoes—and away from some other foods. But if the price of potatoes rose, you would expect our consumer to buy fewer potatoes—and more of other foods.

The general interaction of price and quantity illustrated by this example has been called the **law of diminishing demand**—which says that if the price of a product is raised, a smaller quantity will be demanded—and if the price of a product is lowered, a greater quantity will be demanded.

A group of customers makes a market

When our hypothetical consumers are considered as a group, we have a "market." It seems reasonable that many consumers in a market will behave in a similar way—that is, if price declines, the total quantity demanded will increase—and if the price rises, the quantity demanded will decrease. Experience supports this reasoning—especially for broad product categories, or commodities such as potatoes.

The relationship between price and quantity demanded in a market is illustrated in Table A–1. It is an example of what economists call a "demand schedule." Note that as the price decreases, the quantity demanded increases. In the third column, total dollar sales or *total revenue* of the potato market is shown. Notice, however, that as prices go lower, the total unit volume increases, yet the total revenue decreases. It is suggested that you fill in the missing blanks and observe the behavior of total revenue—an important figure for the marketing manager. We will explain what you should have noticed—and why—a little later.

Table A–1
Demand schedule for potatoes

Point	(1) Price of potatoes per bag (P)	(2) Quantity demanded (bags per month) (Q)	(3) Total revenue per month ($P \times Q = TR$)
A	$0.80	8,000,000	$6,400,000
B	0.65	9,000,000	
C	0.50	11,000,000	5,500,000
D	0.35	14,000,000	
E	0.20	19,000,000	

**Figure A–1
Demand curve for potatoes
(ten-pound bags)**

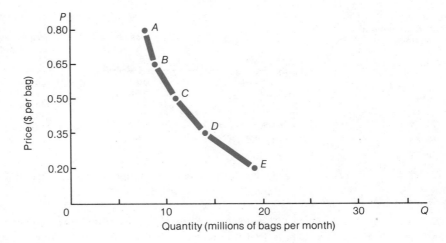

**The demand curve—
usually down-sloping**

If your only interest is seeing at which price customers would be willing to pay the greatest total revenue, the demand schedule may be adequate. But a demand curve may be more helpful. A **demand curve** is a "picture" of the relationship between price and quantity in a market—assuming that all other things stay the same. It is a graph of the demand schedule. Figure A–1 shows the demand curve for potatoes—really just a plotting of the demand schedule. It shows how many potatoes would be demanded by potential customers at various possible prices. This is known as a "down-sloping demand curve."

Most demand curves are down-sloping. It just means that if prices were decreased, the quantity that customers would demand would increase.

Note that the demand curve only shows how customers would react to various prices. In a market, we see only one price at a time—not all of these prices. The curve, however, shows what quantities will be demanded—depending upon what price is set. It would seem that most business people would like to see the price set at the point where the resulting revenue was large.

Before discussing this, however, we should consider the demand schedule and curve for another product—to get a more complete picture of what is involved in demand-curve analysis.

**A refrigerator demand
curve looks different**

A different demand schedule is the one for refrigerators shown in Table A–2. Column (3) shows the total revenue that would be obtained at various possible prices and quantities. Again, as the price of refrigerators goes down, the quantity demanded goes up. But here, unlike the potato example, total revenue increases—at least until the price drops to $150.

**Every market has a
demand curve—for
some time period**

These general demand relationships are characteristic of all products—but each product has its own demand schedule and curve *in each potential market*—no matter how small the market. In other words, a particular demand curve has meaning only with reference to a particular market. We can think of demand curves for individuals, regions, and even countries. And the time period covered

Point	(1) Price per refrigerator (P)	(2) Quantity de- manded per year (Q)	(3) Total revenue per year ($P \times Q = TR$)
A	$300	20,000	$ 6,000,000
B	250	70,000	17,500,000
C	200	130,000	26,000,000
D	150	210,000	31,500,000
E	100	310,000	31,000,000

really should be specified—although this is often neglected, as we usually think of monthly or yearly periods.

The difference between elastic and inelastic

The demand curve for refrigerators (see Figure A–2) is down-sloping—but note that it is flatter than the curve for potatoes. It is quite important that we understand what this flatness means.

We will consider the flatness in terms of total revenue—since this is what interests business managers.*

When you filled in the total revenue column for potatoes, you should have noticed that total revenue would decrease continually if the price were reduced. This looks undesirable from a manager's point of view—and illustrates inelastic demand. Inelastic demand means that although the quantity demanded would increase if the price were decreased, the quantity demanded would not "stretch" enough—that is, it is not elastic enough—to avoid a decrease in total revenue.

In contrast, elastic demand means that if prices were dropped, the quantity demanded would stretch enough to increase total revenue. The upper part of the refrigerator demand curve is an example of elastic demand.

But note that if the refrigerator price were dropped from $150 to $100, total revenue would decrease. We can say, therefore, that between $150 and $100, demand is inelastic—that is, total revenue would decrease if price were lowered to $100.

Thus, elasticity can be defined in terms of changes in total revenue. *If total revenue would increase if price were lowered, then demand is elastic. If total revenue would decrease if price were lowered, then demand is inelastic.*

Total revenue may decrease if price is raised

A point that is often missed in discussions of demand is what happens when prices are raised instead of lowered. With elastic demand, total revenue will *decrease* if the price is *raised.* If total revenue remains the same when prices change, then we have a special case known as "unitary elasticity of demand."

The possibility of raising price and increasing revenue at the same time is of special interest to managers. This only occurs if the demand curve is inelastic. If this is the case, it is obviously an attractive situation. Total revenue would

---

* Strictly speaking, two curves should not be compared for flatness if the graph scales are different, but for our purposes now we will do so to illustrate the idea of "elasticity of demand." Actually, it would be more correct to compare two curves for one product—on the same graph. Then, both the shape of the demand curve and its position on the graph would be important.

increase if price were raised, but costs probably would not increase—and might actually go down.

The ways total revenue changes as prices are raised are illustrated in Figure A–3. Here, total revenue is the rectangular area formed by a price and its related quantity.

P_1 is the original price here—and the total potential revenue with this original price is shown by the area with the diagonal lines slanted down from the left. The total revenue area with the new price, P_2, is shaded with lines running diagonally upward from the left. In both cases, there is some overlap—so the important areas are those with only a single shading. Note that in the left-hand figure—where demand is elastic—the revenue added when the price is increased is less than the revenue lost (compare only the single-shaded areas). When demand is inelastic, however, only a small single-shaded revenue area is given up for a much larger one when price is raised.

An entire curve is not elastic or inelastic

It is important to see that it is *wrong to refer to a whole demand curve as elastic or inelastic*. Rather, elasticity for a particular curve refers to the change in total revenue between two points on a curve—and not along the whole curve. The change from elasticity to inelasticity can be seen in the refrigerator example. Generally, however, nearby points are either elastic or inelastic—so it is common to refer to a whole curve by the degree of elasticity of the curve in the price range that normally is of interest—the *relevant range*.

Demand elasticities affected by availability of substitutes and urgency of need

At first, it may be difficult to see why one product has an elastic demand and another an inelastic demand. Many factors affect elasticity—such as the availability of substitutes, the importance of the item in the customer's budget, and the urgency of the customer's need and its relation to other needs. By looking at one of these factors—the availability of substitutes—we should better understand why demand elasticities vary.

Substitutes are goods or services that offer a choice to the buyer. The greater the number of "good" substitutes available, the greater will be the elasticity of demand—"good" here referring to the degree of similarity—or homogeneity—

Figure A–2
Demand curve for refrigerators

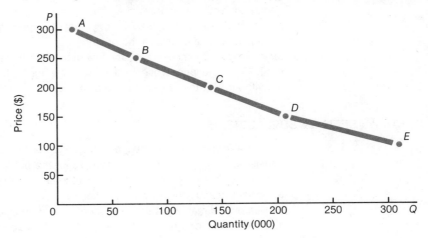

Figure A–3
Changes in total revenue as prices increase

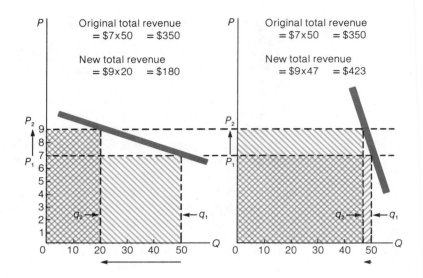

that customers see. If they see the product as extremely different—or heterogeneous—then a particular need cannot easily be satisfied by substitution—and the demand for the most satisfactory product may be quite inelastic.

As an example, if the price of hamburger is lowered (and other prices stay constant), the quantity demanded will increase a lot—as will total revenue. The reason is that not only will regular hamburger users buy more hamburger, but those consumers who formerly bought hot dogs, steaks, or bacon probably will buy hamburger too. But if the price of hamburger rose, the quantity demanded would decrease—perhaps sharply. Consumers would still purchase some hamburger—depending on how much the price had risen, their individual tastes, and what their guests expect (see Figure A–4).

In contrast to a product which has many "substitutes"—such as hamburger—consider a product with few or no substitutes. Its demand curve will tend to be inelastic. Salt is a good example. Salt is needed to flavor food. Yet no one person or family uses great quantities of salt. And even with price changes *within a reasonable range,* it is not likely that the quantity of salt purchased would change much. Of course, if the price dropped to an extremely low level, manufacturers might buy more—say, for low-cost filler, instead of clay or sand (Figure A–5). Or, if the price rose to a staggering figure, many people would have to do without. But these extremes are outside the relevant range.

MARKETS AS SEEN BY SUPPLIERS

Demand curves are introduced here because the degree of elasticity of demand shows how potential customers feel about the product—and especially whether there are substitutes for the product. But to get a better understanding of markets, we must continue this economic analysis.

Customers may want some product—but if suppliers are not willing to supply it, then there is no market. So we will study the economist's analysis of supply—

and then bring supply and demand together for a more complete understanding of markets.

Economists often use the kind of analysis we are discussing here to explain pricing in the marketplace. This is *not* our intention. Here we are interested in markets—and the interaction of customers and potential suppliers. The discussion in this appendix does *not* explain how individual firms set prices or should set prices. That will come in Chapters 19–20.

Supply curves reflect supplier thinking

Generally speaking, suppliers' costs have a bearing on the quantity of products they are willing to offer in the market during any period. In other words, their costs affect their supply schedules and supply curves. While a demand curve shows the quantity of goods customers would be willing to buy at various prices, a **supply curve** shows the quantity of goods that will be supplied at various possible prices. Eventually, only one quantity of goods will be offered and pur-

Figure A–4
Demand curve for hamburger (a product with many substitutes)

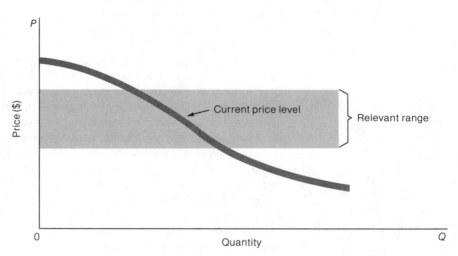

Figure A–5
Demand curve for salt (a product with few substitutes)

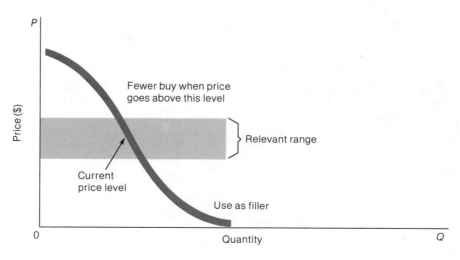

chased—so a supply curve is really a hypothetical description of what would be offered at various prices. It is, however, a very important curve. Together with a demand curve, it summarizes the attitudes and probable behavior of buyers and sellers about a particular product in a particular market.

Some supply curves are vertical

We usually assume that supply curves tend to slope upward—that is, suppliers will be willing to offer greater quantities at higher prices. If a product's market price is very high, it seems only reasonable that producers will be anxious to produce more of the product—and even put workers on overtime or perhaps hire additional workers to increase the quantity they can offer. To go further, it seems likely that producers of other products will switch their resources (farms, factories, labor, or retail facilities) to the product that is in great demand.

On the other hand, if a very low price is being offered for a particular product, it's reasonable to expect that producers will switch to other products—reducing supply. A supply schedule (Table A–3) and a supply curve (Figure A–6) for potatoes illustrate these ideas. This supply curve shows how many potatoes would be produced and offered for sale at each possible market price in a given month.

In the very short run (say, over a few hours, a day, or a week), a supplier may not be able to increase the supply at all. In this situation, we would see a vertical supply curve. This situation is often relevant in the market for fresh produce. Fresh strawberries, for example, continue to ripen, and a supplier wants to sell them quickly—preferably at a higher price—but in any case, he wants to sell them. For less perishable products, he may set a minimum price and, if necessary, store them until market conditions are better.

If the product is a service, it may not be easy to expand the supply in the short run—and there is no way to store it either. Additional barbers or medical doctors are not quickly trained and licensed—and they only have so much time to give each day. When the day is done, the unused "supply" is lost. Further, the prospect of much higher prices in the near future cannot easily expand the supply of many services. For example, a good play, or an "in" restaurant or nightclub is limited in the amount of "product" it can offer at a particular time.

Elasticity of supply

The term *elasticity* also is used to describe supply curves. An extremely steep or almost vertical supply curve—often found in the short run—is called inelastic

Table A–3
Supply schedule for potatoes

Point	Possible market price per 10-lb. bag	Number of bags sellers will supply per month at each possible market price
A	$0.80	17,000,000
B	0.65	14,000,000
C	0.50	11,000,000
D	0.35	8,000,000
E	0.20	3,000,000

Note: This supply curve is for a month to emphasize that farmers might have some control over when they deliver their potatoes. There would be a different curve for each month.

Figure A–6
Supply curve for potatoes
(10-pound bags)

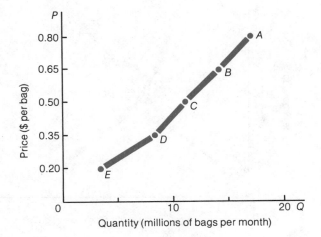

supply because the quantity supplied does not stretch much (if at all) if the price is raised. A flatter curve is called **elastic supply** because the quantity supplied does stretch more if the price is raised. A slightly up-sloping supply curve is typical in longer-run market situations. Given more time, suppliers have a chance to adjust their offerings—and competitors may enter or leave the market.

DEMAND AND SUPPLY INTERACT TO DETERMINE THE SIZE OF THE MARKET AND PRICE LEVEL

We have treated market demand and supply forces separately. Now we must bring them together to show their interaction. The *intersection* of these two forces determines the size of the market and the market price—at which point the market is said to be in *equilibrium.*

The intersection of demand and supply is shown for the potato data discussed above. The demand curve for potatoes is now graphed against the supply curve in Figure A–6—see Figure A–7.

In this potato market, the demand is inelastic—the total revenue of all the potato producers would be greater at higher prices. But the market price is at the **equilibrium point**—where the quantity and the price sellers are willing to offer are equal to the quantity and price that buyers are willing to accept. The $0.50 equilibrium price for potatoes yields a smaller *total revenue* to potato producers than a higher price would. This lower equilibrium price comes about because the many producers are willing to supply enough potatotes at the lower price. *Demand is not the only determiner of price level. Cost also must be considered—via the supply curve.*

Some consumers get a surplus

It is important to note that not everyone gets only his money's worth in a sales transaction. Presumably, a sale takes place *only* if both buyer and seller feel they will be better off after the sale. But sometimes the price is better than "right."

Figure A–7
**Equilibrium of supply and
demand for potatoes**

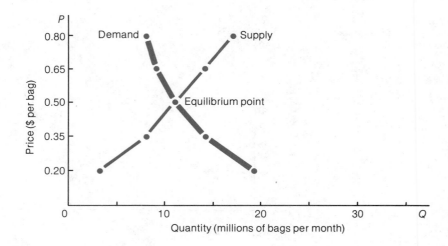

The price we are talking about is the equilibrium price related to demand and supply forces. Typically, demand curves are down-sloping and some of the demand curve is above the equilibrium price. This is simply a graphic way of showing that some customers would be willing to pay more than the equilibrium price if they had to. In effect, some of them are getting a "bargain" by being able to buy at the equilibrium price. Economists have traditionally called these bargains the **consumer surplus**—that is, the difference to consumers between the value of a purchase and the price they pay.

It is important to see that there is such a surplus—because some business critics assume that consumers do badly in any business transaction. In fact, a sale takes place only if the consumer feels he is at least "getting his money's worth." As we can see here, some would be willing to pay much more than the market price.

DEMAND AND SUPPLY HELP UNDERSTAND THE NATURE OF COMPETITION

The elasticity of demand and supply curves—and their interaction—help predict the nature of competition a marketing manager is likely to experience. For example, extremely inelastic demand curves together with the usual up-sloping supply curves mean that the firm will have much latitude in its strategy planning. Apparently customers like the product and see few substitutes—they are willing to pay higher prices before cutting back much on their consumption.

Clearly, the elasticity of a firm's demand curves has great relevance for strategy planning—but there are other factors which affect the nature of competition. Among these are the number and size of competitors—and the uniqueness of each firm's marketing mix. These ideas are discussed more fully in Chapter 3 in the section on "competitive environment." That discussion presumes a real understanding of the contents of this appendix—so now you should be ready to handle that—and later material involving demand and supply analysis (especially Chapters 19 and 20).

CONCLUSION

The economist's traditional demand and supply analysis provides useful tools for analyzing the nature of demand and competition. It is especially important that you master the concepts of a demand curve and demand elasticity. How demand and supply interact helps determine the size of a market—and its price level. It also helps explain the nature of competition in different market situations. These ideas are discussed in Chapter 3—and then built upon throughout the text. So careful study of this appendix will build a good foundation for later work.

QUESTIONS AND PROBLEMS

1. Explain in your own words how economists look at markets and arrive at the "law of diminishing demand."

2. Explain what a demand curve is and why it is usually downsloping.

3. What is the length of life of the typical demand curve? Illustrate your answer.

4. If the general market demand for men's shoes is fairly elastic, how does the demand for men's dress shoes compare to it? How does the demand curve for women's shoes compare to the demand curve for men's shoes?

5. If the demand for fountain pens were inelastic above and below the present price, should the price be raised? Why or why not?

6. If the demand for steak is highly elastic below the present price, should the price be lowered?

7. Discuss what factors lead to inelastic demand and supply curves. Are they likely to be found together in the same situation?

When you finish this chapter, you should:

1. **Know the uncontrollable variables the marketing manager must work with.**

2. **Know how—and how quickly—the cultural and social environment can change.**

3. **Know why you could go to prison by ignoring the political and legal environment.**

4. **Know the effect of the different kinds of market situations on strategy planning.**

5. **Understand how the economic environment can affect strategy planning.**

6. **Recognize the important new terms (shown in red).**

3

Uncontrollable environments affecting marketing management

Marketing managers do not plan strategies in a vacuum. They have to work with several uncontrollable variables when choosing target markets and developing the four Ps.

As we saw in Chapter 2 (and as is shown again in Figure 3–1) these variables fall in the following areas:

1. Cultural and social environment.
2. Economic and technological environment.
3. Competitive environment.
4. Political and legal environment.
5. Resources and objectives of the firm.

In the long run, marketing managers may affect some or all of these variables. In the short run, however, they must be taken as "given." Now we will see how the first four uncontrollable variables add to the complexity and challenge of marketing management. And in Chapter 4, we will see how the resources and objectives of the firm can limit its opportunities—as well as the strategies it eventually chooses.

CULTURAL AND SOCIAL ENVIRONMENT

The cultural and social environment affects how and why people live and behave as they do. This variable is very important—because it has a direct effect on customer buying behavior.

Markets consist of real people—with money to spend. But the number and location of these people is pretty much set. And, many of their attitudes and

Figure 3–1
Marketing manager's
framework

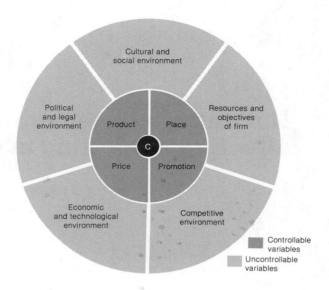

behavior patterns are fixed—or changing only slowly. In other words, we already know a great deal about our cultural and social environment.

Since the demographic and behavioral dimensions of buyer behavior are given extensive treatment in Chapters 6–8, we will present only a few examples here—to emphasize the possible impact of this variable on marketing strategy planning.

The American "melting pot" is not homogenized

Americans are often stereotyped as friendly people—but actually this varies by regions. People on the West Coast, for example, tend to be more open and—at least superficially—more friendly. This is, in part, because many have moved west to find a new life—and have left behind the more tradition-bound social structures of the smaller towns of the Midwest and East. People on the West Coast also seem more willing to travel great distances. Some Californians, for example, thought nothing of driving several hundred miles on a weekend (before the energy crisis). This had an effect on the location of retail facilities—and loyalty to particular stores.

Even eating habits vary in different regions and within urban areas. Biscuits and grits are much more popular in the South, for example. And Mexican food has long been favored in the Southwest. Within the large cities, we still find ethnic and religious groups which are separate markets for some goods and services. Large urban areas often have neighborhoods of Irish, Italians, Poles, Jews, Puerto Ricans, Hispanics, and Blacks. Some have newspapers, radio stations, restaurants, grocery stores, and record shops which aim at these culturally defined markets.

Women are being liberated

The last decade has seen much discussion about women's roles in our culture. Some of this has generated more heat than understanding—but it is clear that a shift in thinking is taking place. Women are now freer to seek any kind of job they want—and many are. Greater financial freedom is making many women less dependent on marriage as a career. So, more women are not marrying at all or marrying later—and planning to have fewer children. This is affecting manufacturers of housing, baby foods, convenience foods, clothing, and cosmetics—among many others.

It is no longer socially acceptable or sensible to think of women as docile "chattel" of men. Increasingly, they are playing equal roles in society. And it is likely that this change in thinking will continue to affect not only the younger women—who were the leaders in the women's liberation movement—but all women.

This is a major shift in American thinking which must be considered in marketing strategy planning and implementation. It will affect not only what is offered to consumers—but also how and by whom. We will see many more women in managerial positions—as well as in responsible selling and advertising jobs. Ineffective and untrained males are in for some real shocks as more women get business training and go out to compete as equals—taking jobs which once might have gone to less able males. This is happening already.

Work and growth are important to some

Marketers also must adjust for cultural attitudes toward life and work—which are a reflection of religious, ethical, and moral values. It is clear that national attitudes have an effect on a country's rate of growth—and the direction of its development.[1]

The American culture tends to encourage the belief that hard work leads to achievement and material rewards—while other societies seem less concerned about what they feel are materialistic values. Most Americans are willing to work—but they also expect rewards and material comforts. This has led us to focus on growth—and producing and distributing goods and services. Much of our analysis of the U.S. market will be within this cultural framework.

In some other societies, on the other hand, far more stress is placed on

The U.S. is not a homogenous whole—so markets must be analyzed carefully by marketing managers.

Mike Jaeggi

leisure and the enjoyment of life. More holidays are built into the working year. The output of such economies may not be quite as high as it could be—but the people may not feel that they are suffering because of it.

What quality of life do we want?

It seems that the attitudes of some people—especially younger people—may be changing—placing greater emphasis on leisure and personal comfort. They have been nicknamed the "me generation." Each person seems primarily concerned with taking care of him- or herself—*now*—rather than building enduring relationships—and planning and working to build for the future. For some, this has a direct impact on their work habits—whether they come in regularly and are willing to do a good job, and/or take on greater responsibilities.

The current movement of industrial activity from the North and Midwest to the "Sun Belt" is in part due to the southern worker's greater enthusiasm about work—and a greater willingness to put in a full day's work for the pay. According to one business analyst: "Southern workers seek out work, they work 60 minutes of every hour. In the North, they try to find ways to get out of work and get more money doing it. They coast 10 to 15 minutes of every hour."[2]

If work attitudes in the "Snow Belt" are shifting, it may be caused by a growing interest in the "quality of life." But a desire for less materialistic solutions may also reduce our productivity and income. In time, we may learn to live a slower paced, less materialistic life.

Bribes or tips?

What some Americans call a "bribe" may be commonplace—and accepted as a necessary business expense—in other countries. Some cultures even have a special word for financial "favors" and treat them much like Americans treat tips. It's "just the way things are done." Recently, however, the difference between American attitudes toward "bribes" and the practices in other countries has gotten

Americans are changing their lifestyles—toward more relaxed, less materialistic living.

Peter Le Grand

some American firms into legal difficulties. The U.S. investigations initially focused on international sales of aircraft—but then shifted to domestic deals—and in particular the traditional arrangements in the beer industry, including under-the-table payments, free dispensing equipment, and free stools and glasses.

What is "right" in such cases may depend on the attitudes and laws in the particular social and cultural environment. This is an area which must be watched carefully by business managers—because attitudes seem to be changing. As one accountant said, "The morals of business aren't changing, the ground rules are. There's a demand for lily-white hands."[3]

Changes come slowly

Regarding the possibility of changing the cultural and social environment, it's important to see that changes in basic attitudes come slowly. An individual firm could not hope to encourage big changes in the short run. Instead, it should identify these attitudes and work within these constraints in the short run—while making long-run plans.

Sometimes, however, strong outside forces—such as energy shortages, riots, or boycotts—may force more rapid changes in the cultural and social environment, or cause clashes with the political and economic environments.

ECONOMIC ENVIRONMENT

The **economic and technological environment** affects the way firms—and the whole economy—use resources. We will treat the economic and technological environments separately—to emphasize that the technological environment provides a base for the economic environment. Technical skills and equipment affect the way resources of an economy are converted into output. The economic environment, on the other hand, is affected by the way all of the parts of our macroeconomic system interact. This, then, affects such things as national income, economic growth, and inflation.

National economic fluctuations make a difference

Even a well-planned marketing strategy may fail if the country goes through a depression or rapid business decline. As customers stop buying, people and businesses have to shift their spending patterns—perhaps completely eliminating some types of purchases. The oil-related layoffs during the recession of 1973–75 weakened many producers and retailers—even of lower-priced goods which sometimes sell well in recessions. Finally, the largest retail bankruptcy in U.S. history was announced by the W. T. Grant chain in 1976. And the Robert Hall chain selling lower-priced clothing went bankrupt in 1977. The 1980 recession was even deeper. Many firms had to retrench, cut product lines, and change strategies to avoid similar fates. Clearly, such strong forces are beyond a firm's control. Still, strategy must be changed to adjust to powerful economic conditions.

Resource scarcities may depress economic conditions

The growing shortage of some natural resources—in particular, energy resources—may cause severe upsets. In the petrochemical industry, for example, some plastic manufacturers find their costs rising so high that they are priced out of the market. Rising gasoline prices are causing consumers to be less interested in the larger, more profitable (to the auto industry) cars. Further, important shifts in auto-buying patterns will have a ripple effect throughout the economy—because the automobile industry is a major buyer of metals, plastics, fabrics, and tires.[4]

These problems may be even greater in resource-poor countries—such as Japan—which are almost wholly dependent on others for raw materials, including energy sources.[5]

Higher fuel prices may cut economic growth

The continued economic growth which we have come to accept may be slowed or stopped by higher fuel costs. Put simply, higher fuel prices for the large amounts of imported oil have shifted income out of the United States—and reduced our real incomes. Further, lower real incomes are possible in the future—because of technological factors. Much of our existing plant and equipment is energy-intensive. Some industrial processes that were profitable with low energy prices are now less profitable—or may actually be obsolete. It is likely that the average job in the future will use less machinery and be less productive. In effect, rising energy costs will increase real incomes in the few countries with large energy reserves—but the balance of the world may see lower real incomes. The United States will definitely feel the impact—because we are such big energy users *and* oil importers.

Continued inflation changes government policies and business strategies

Inflation is a major factor in many economies. When people assume that prices will keep going up, they buy and sell accordingly. This behavior adds fuel to the inflationary fires. Some Latin American countries have had from 25 to 100 percent inflation per year for many years. In contrast, the 6- to 20-percent levels reached in recent years in the United States were "low." Nevertheless, these U.S. rates caused—properly—great concern about whether our inflation was out of control. This led to restrictive monetary and fiscal policies which *did* reduce income and employment *and* consumer spending.

The government-encouraged recession of 1980 was the most severe one since the great depression of the 1930s. But it was generally agreed that some pulling back was necessary—to stop the inflationary thinking. Figure 3–2 shows

Figure 3–2
Rising cost of living in the United States 1950–1980 (Using Consumer Price Index, 1967–100)

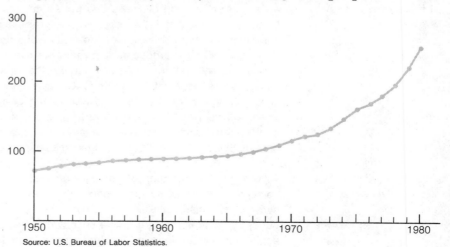

Source: U.S. Bureau of Labor Statistics.

how rapidly the cost of living was rising in the 1970s—and why the government chose such drastic action in 1980. But even though there was good reason, the economic hardship was widespread—especially among the producers and retailers of major durable goods.

You can see that the marketing manager must watch the economic environment carefully. In contrast to the cultural and social environment, economic conditions change continuously. And they move rapidly—up or down—requiring tactical and even strategic responses.

TECHNOLOGICAL ENVIRONMENT

The technological base affects opportunities

Underlying any economic environment is the **technological base**—the technical skills and equipment which affect the way the resources of an economy are converted to output. In tradition-bound societies, relatively little technology may be used—and the output may be small. Modern economies, on the other hand, make greater use of the technological base, so labor can be more productive.

Spectacular advances in technology were made in the last 30 years. This was due in part to our new-found interest in and support of research and development. Almost all of the technological developments since the beginning of man have occurred in that time period. It is estimated that about 90 percent of the scientists that ever lived are alive and working today. This has caused an explosion of scientific literature—which makes it difficult, and in some fields, impossible—to keep up. New engineers who are not working on the frontiers of their field become obsolete in about ten years!

More technological developments probably can be expected—although not as many from the United States. Support in the United States for R&D has been cut back in recent years as fighting recessions, inflation, and energy shortages have taken center stage. Some foreign producers—especially Japan—have pioneered recent breakthroughs, for example, in applying basic research findings to electronic products.

Some of these developments certainly will affect marketing—just as previous ones have had their impact. The modern automobile, for example, has enabled farmers to come to town—and urban people to go wherever they want—thereby destroying the local "monopolies" of some retailers and wholesalers. Modern trucks and airplanes have opened up many new markets and permitted production for national or international markets—with resulting competition and benefits for consumers. Electronic developments have permitted mass promotion via radio, TV, and telephone—reducing the relative importance of other media. And, in time, we may be able to shop in the home with a combination TV-computer system—eliminating the need for some retailers and wholesalers.

Computers have also permitted more sophisticated planning and control of businesses. Electronic equipment may allow us to return to custom production methods—but this time in automated factories which will let customers decide more exactly what they want and then get almost immediate delivery. This will cause drastic changes in internal company affairs—including sales forecasting, production scheduling, warehousing, and so on.

In recent years there has been more emphasis on research and development around the world.

Peter Le Grand

As we move through the text, you should see that some of the major advances in business have come from creative and early recognition of new ways to do things. Additional breakthrough opportunities probably will arise as our technological base changes.

Marketing managers should help their firms see such opportunities by trying to understand the "why" of present methods—and what is keeping their firms from doing things more effectively. Then, as new developments come along, they will be sensitive to possible applications—and be able to see how opportunities can be turned into profitable realities.

Further, they can make a contribution by developing a sense of what technical developments would be acceptable to society. With the growing concern about environmental pollution, the quality of life, working conditions, and so on, it is possible that some potentially attractive techological developments should be rejected—because of their long-run impact. Perhaps what might be good for the firm and the economy's *economic* growth might not fit with the cultural and social environment—and thus the political and legal environment. The marketing manager's closeness to the market could give him a better feel for what people are thinking—and allow him to help the firm avoid blunders.[6]

THE COMPETITIVE ENVIRONMENT

(Note: The following materials assume some familiarity with economic analysis—and especially the nature of demand curves and demand elasticity. For those wishing a review of these materials, see Appendix A, which follows Chapter 2.)

The **competitive environment** refers to the number and types of competitors the marketing manager must face—and how they might behave. Although these factors can't be controlled by the marketing manager, he can choose strategies which will avoid head-on competition.

Manager may be able to avoid head-on competition

By correctly understanding the nature of the competitive environment, the manager's chances may be improved. He should expect many competitors—and probably price competition—in an industry composed of many small producers and retailers. This is the case, for example, in the boating industry—where hundreds of boat builders and thousands of engine and accessory manufacturers try to sell their products through more than 17,000 marine retailers and 3,500 marinas.[7] Competitive strategies in this industry are very different from those in the aluminum or computer industries—where there are relatively few competitors.

You can get a greater depth of understanding of the nature of competition by identifying four kinds of market situations. We will emphasize three kinds: pure competition, oligopoly, and monopolistic competition. A fourth type—monopoly—is so rare that it will not be treated separately. Usually, monopolies are controlled by local, state, or federal authorities. When they are not, they can be treated as monopolistic competition—since monopolies are simply an extreme case of monopolistic competition.

Understanding these market situations is quite important—because the freedom of a marketing manager is greatly reduced in some situations. The important dimensions in these situations are summarized in Figure 3–3.

When competition is pure

Many competitors offer about the same thing

Pure competition is a market situation which develops when a market has:

1. Homogeneous (similar) products.
2. Many buyers and sellers, who have full knowledge of the market.
3. Ease of entry for buyers and sellers, that is, new firms have little difficulty starting in business—and new customers can easily come into the market.

More or less pure competition is found in many agricultural markets. In the potato industry, for example, there are tens of thousands of producers—and they are in pure competition. Let's look more closely at these small producers.

Figure 3–3
Some important dimensions regarding market competitors

Important dimensions \ Types of situations	Pure competition	Oligopoly	Monopolistic competition	Monopoly
Uniqueness of each firm's product	None	None	Some	Unique
Number of competitors	Many	Few	Few to many	None
Size of competitors (compared to size of market)	Small	Large	Large to small	None
Elasticity of demand facing firm	Completely elastic	Kinked demand curve (elastic and inelastic)	Either	Either
Elasticity of industry demand	Either	Inelastic	Either	Either
Control of price by firm	None	Some (with care)	Some	Complete

Figure 3–4
Interaction of demand and
supply in the potato industry
and the resulting demand curve
facing individual potato
producers

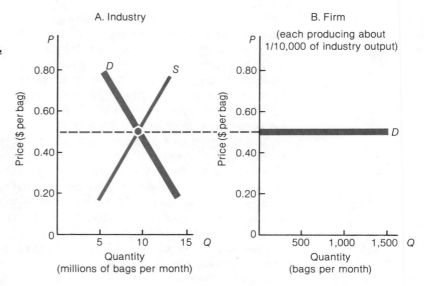

In pure competition, these many small producers see almost a perfectly flat demand curve facing each one of them. The relation between the industry demand curve and the demand curve facing the individual farmer in pure competition is shown in Figure 3–4. Although the potato industry as a whole has a down-sloping demand curve, each individual potato producer has a demand curve that is perfectly flat at the **equilibrium price**—the going market price.

To explain this more clearly, let's look at the demand curve for the individual potato producer. Assume that the equilibrium price for the industry is 50 cents. This means the producer can sell as many potatoes as he chooses at 50 cents. The quantity that all producers choose to sell makes up the supply curve. But acting alone, a small producer can do almost anything he wants to do.

If this individual farmer raises 1/10,000th of the quantity offered in the market, for example, you can see that there will be little effect on the market if he goes out of business—or doubles his production.

The reason an individual's demand curve is flat in this example is that the farmer probably could not sell any potatoes above the market price. And there is no point in selling below 50 cents.

Not many markets are *purely* competitive. But many are close enough to allow us to talk about "almost" pure competition situations—ones in which the marketing manager has to accept the going price.

Squeeze on the orange growers

Florida orange growers, for example, have basically homogeneous products. They have no control over price. When there is a very large supply, prices drop rapidly and are beyond the producers' control. When supplies are short, the reverse happens. During one year, the crop was 50 percent larger than the previous crop—and most growers sold their oranges below their costs. Oranges "on the tree" which cost 75 cents a box to grow were selling for 35 cents a box.

Supply turned around the next year, however, and oranges were selling for $2.40 to $2.60 a box.[8]

Similar situations are found with many agricultural commodities. Farmers often seek government help to "save" them from pure competition. Agricultural parity programs are designed in part for this purpose—usually working to increase price by reducing supply.

Profit squeeze is on in many markets

Such highly competitive situations are not limited to agriculture. In any field where many competitors sell homogeneous products—such as chemicals, plastics, lumber, coal, printing, and laundry services—the demand curve seen by *each producer* tends to be flat. Assuming no collusion among the firms, there is a tendency for each firm to expand production—and the action of all producers forces down the market price.

Industries tend to become more competitive—that is, move toward pure competition (except in oligopolies—see below). More competitors enter the market, the supply is increased, and the current equilibrium price is pushed downward. This tends to force profits down—until some competitors are eliminated. Economists describe the final equilibrium position as that point at which there is only enough return to keep the survivors in the business.

On the way to this final equilibrium position, competition becomes so tough that companies actually lose money—as the price goes below the long-run equilibrium level—and some firms are driven out of the market. It also may take some time before the industry price moves up to the equilibrium level—so that the remaining companies can survive. At the economist's final equilibrium point, however, none of the firms makes a profit! Each just covers all its costs.

When competition is oligopolistic

Few competitors offering similar things

Not all industries or markets move toward pure competition. Some become oligopolies.

Oligopoly situations are special market situations which develop when a market has:

1. Essentially homogeneous products—such as basic industrial chemicals or gasoline.
2. Relatively few sellers—or a few large firms and many smaller ones who follow the lead of the larger ones.
3. Fairly inelastic industry demand curves.

The demand curve facing each firm is unusual in an oligopoly situation. Although the industry demand curve can be inelastic throughout the relevant range, the demand curve facing each competitor looks "kinked." See Figure 3–5. The current market price is at the kink.

There is a "market price" because the competing firms watch each other carefully—and know it is wise to be at the kink. Each marketing manager must expect that raising his own price above the market for such a homogeneous product would cause a big loss of sales. Few, if any, competitors would follow his price increase. So, his demand curve would be relatively flat above the market

**Figure 3–5
Oligopoly—kinked demand
curve—situation**

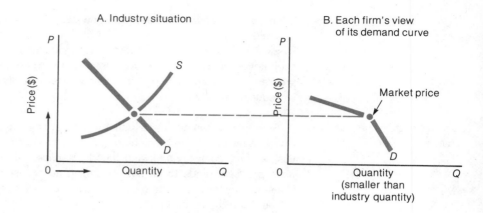

A. Industry situation

B. Each firm's view
of its demand curve

price. But if he lowers his price, he must expect competitors to follow. Therefore, given inelastic industry demand, his own demand curve would be inelastic at lower prices. Since lowering prices along such a curve would drop total revenue, he probably should not do it. That is, he should leave his price at the kink—the market price.

Actually, however, there are price fluctuations in oligopolistic markets. Sometimes this is due to firms that don't understand the market situation—and cut their prices to get business. In other cases, big increases in demand or supply change the basic nature of the situation—and lead to price cutting. Sometimes the price cuts are drastic—such as Du Pont's Dacron price cut of 25 percent. This happened when Du Pont decided that industry production capacity already exceeded demand and more was due to start into production.[9]

Price wars are sometimes started

A common example of price fluctuations can be seen in retail gasoline marketing—at a major intersection where there are several obvious competitors. Apparently enough final consumers think of gasoline as homogeneous to create oligopoly conditions. And oligopoly-type "price wars" are common. These usually start when some gasoline discounter successfully attracts "too much" business— perhaps by cutting his prices one cent a gallon below his usual price. The war proceeds for a time—with everyone losing money—until one of the retailers calls a meeting and suggests that they all "get a little sense." Sometimes these price wars will end immediately after such a meeting—with prices returning to a "reasonable and proper" level.

As in pure competition, oligopolists face a long-run trend toward an equilibrium level—where profits are driven toward zero. Along the way, a marketing manager might try to avoid price competition—relying more on other elements in the marketing mix. This is extremely difficult, however. If all of the potential customers view the products as essentially similar, how can a firm obtain some differential advantage?

*When competition is
monopolistic*

A price must be set

You can see why firms would want to avoid pure competition or oligopolistic situations. They would prefer a market in which they have more control. Aggressive marketing managers do seek to develop a differentiated or heterogeneous product (in the eyes of some consumers, not just the firm)—in order to gain more control. But if they still have to face some fairly direct competitors, we have a market situation called monopolistic competition.

Monopolistic competition is a market situation which develops when:

1. A market has different (heterogeneous) products—in the eyes of some customers.
2. Sellers feel they do have some competition in this market.

The word *monopolistic* means that each firm is trying to get its own little monopoly. But the word *competition* means that there are still substitutes. The vigorous competition of the purely competitive market is reduced. Each firm has its own down-sloping demand curve. But the shape of the curve depends on the similarity of competitors' products and marketing mixes. Each monopolistic competitor has freedom—but not complete freedom—in its own little "industry."

Judging elasticity will help set the price

Since a firm in monopolistic competition has its own down-sloping demand curve, it must make a price decision as part of its strategy planning. Here, estimating the elasticity of the firm's own demand curve is helpful. If it is highly inelastic, the firm may decide to raise prices to increase total revenue. But if demand is highly elastic, this may mean many competitors with acceptable substitutes. Then the price may have to be set near "competition." And the marketing manager probaby should try to develop a better marketing mix.

Why some products are offered in pure competition

Why would anyone compete in profitless pure competition? The usual explanation is that the firm was either already in the industry—or enters without knowing what is happening or is going to happen—and must stick it out until its resources are gone.

In oligopolistic markets, prices are usually at the "kinked" price.

Mary McCarthy

Production-oriented people seem more likely to make such a mistake than market-oriented managers. Avoiding pure competition seems advisable—and certainly fits with our emphasis on target marketing.

Pure competition cannot always be avoided

Despite their desire to avoid pure competition, some firms find that (at least for part of their operation) they can't. In some cases, production processes make this inevitable. For instance, in the chemical industry, caustic soda is produced as a by-product in the production of more profitable chlorine. At one time, the supply of caustic soda was so great that it was being dumped as waste into the Gulf of Mexico. Obviously, this large supply had a depressing influence on the price (to say nothing about the water)!

Some industries appear to be almost purely competitive, yet new firms keep entering—replacing the casualties—possibly because they don't have more attractive alternatives and can at least earn a living in the industry. Examples include small retailing and wholesaling, especially in less-developed economies. Also, farmers continually try to shift their production to more profitable crops, but since there are many thousands of other farmers making similar choices, almost pure competition is typical.

POLITICAL ENVIRONMENT

The attitudes and reactions of people, social critics, and governments are becoming increasingly important to marketing managers—because they all affect the political environment. In our discussion, we will separate political and legal questions—although in practice this separation is hard to maintain. A change in the political environment often leads to changes in the legal environment— or the administration of existing laws.

Consumerism is here— and basic

Perhaps the consumerism movement should have been treated under the cultural and social environment—because it reflects the values of many people in our society. But it is discussed here because these values may be changing rapidly. As a well-known business consultant, Peter Drucker, wrote: "We have been a very patient people, by and large. Now people are fed up, and I do not blame them."[10]

Consumerism is a social movement seeking to increase the rights and powers of consumers and buyers. Its continued growth may flow out of a change in thinking which began in the 1950s—with books like Rachel Carson's *The Silent Spring*—and was reinforced by President John F. Kennedy's "Consumer Bill of Rights." He stated these in 1962. Although they did not become law, they have affected people's thinking—including some in government regulatory agencies and courts.

President Kennedy's "Consumer Bill of Rights" includes the following:

The right to safety.
The right to be informed.
The right to choose.
The right to be heard.

Consumerists are slowly having an effect on businesses through their demands for "consumer rights."

Peter Menzel—Stock, Boston

Kennedy did not include "the right to a clean and safe environment"—probably because the environment had not yet become a public concern. But most people are now concerned with such a right. Increasingly, government pressure is being applied on everyone—including businesses and government units—to improve our waste handling and to clean our chimneys and motor exhaust systems. This is probably the outstanding recent example of a rapid change in cultural values which has been converted into action by the political authorities.

This change was preceded by the rapid and visible deterioration of the physical environment—and was facilitated by our democratic political process which capitalizes on "dramatic" problems. And we may see more such changes—if the notions of "safety" and "quality of life" are applied to personal and property safety (from criminals) and moral safety (from pornographers, and movie and mass media producers).

Kennedy's "rights" are not as likely to cause dramatic changes as the anti-pollution moves. Instead, individual firms and government agencies must change their behavior on a day-to-day basis. This is not as easy to legislate. Basic changes in attitudes about what is "right" and "wrong" are needed—and this doesn't happen quickly. So there may be an ongoing need for consumerists to help assure that the "little guy" is not ignored or "wronged" by business or government authorities. This need is being filled by institutions at the federal, state, and local levels. So the consumerism movement is not likely to die overnight.

It is important to see that consumerists are concerned about protecting consumers not only against business—but also against government regulations and administrative groups. Some federal agencies—such as the Federal Trade Commission and the Consumer Product Safety Commission—may want to "do good," but it appears that some consumer protection actions have been wasteful. There is growing interest both inside and outside the government in assuring that a proper balance among all parties is achieved.[11]

*Public interest groups
are growing*

Public interest groups—sometimes called "consumerists"—have multiplied in recent years. Probably the best known—and perhaps the most successful—of these groups is Ralph Nader's *Public Citizen* organization. Its most successful effort focused on auto safety—and eventually led to the National Traffic and Motor Vehicle Safety Act of 1966.

Hundreds of public interest groups have developed or expanded in the last 20 years. Some seek to protect the environment (the Sierra Club, the Save the Whales Foundation, and so on); others seek to protect or expand the rights of women (NOW), blacks (NAACP), senior citizens (AARP and the Grey Panthers), and so on.

Clearly, the various public interest groups limit the freedom of marketing managers. Some have responded by fighting such groups—feeling that it limited "free enterprise"—while others have simply accepted the consumer groups as another variable which must be considered in strategy planning. But it does mean that a marketer must spend more time with the legal and public relations departments when planning strategies. Focusing only on the company's target markets—without considering the interests of other "publics"—is no longer a practical approach.

*And not meeting
consumer expectations
could be drastic*

A recent poll showed the business community "out of step" with the American public on consumerism issues. Generally, the public seems to like what the consumerists are trying to do.[12] Marketers shouldn't forget that the role of businesses is to satisfy consumers. No firm has a God-given right to operate any way it wants to.

This means that the marketing manager—as well as top management—should pay more attention to consumers' attitudes in marketing planning. Ignoring the consumer movement could be fatal. The rules governing business could change. Specific businesses might be told they could not operate. Or they might face such heavy fines that they would be forced out of business. And, in an "antibusiness" environment, fines could be quite large. A Utah family was awarded $450,000 when a court ruled that the Ford Bronco was a dangerous vehicle—and was, in part, the cause of a fatal accident.[13] Such an award against a small company could wipe it out. For a large company, it opens the door to additional lawsuits which could be costly—and damage its reputation.

Clearly, more attention must be paid to product design and safety in our social and political environment. The old, production-oriented ways of doing things are no longer acceptable.

*Nationalism can be
limiting in international
markets*

Strong sentiments of nationalism—an emphasis on the country's interests before everything else—may also affect the work of some marketing managers. These feelings can reduce sales or even block marketing activity in some international markets. Oil and copper mining firms have felt such pressures in recent years—for example, in Latin America, Africa, and the Middle East.

To whom the firms could sell, and how much, have been dictated by national interests. The Arab boycott of firms doing business with Israel is probably the outstanding example in recent years. But the "Buy American" policy in many government contracts reflects similar attitudes in the United States. And there seems to be growing support for protecting U.S. producers from foreign competi-

Peter Le Grand

tion—especially of color TVs, footwear, textiles, and cars. Similarly, Philippines business people have tried to drive "excessively aggressive" Chinese merchants out of the Philippines. And Africans have driven Indian merchants out of their countries.

Countries may choose to issue guidelines to foreign firms—as Canada did recently to encourage "good corporate behavior." These guidelines sometimes are supplemented with new laws or the threat of legislation. Laws were passed in Canada, for example, to restrict the flow of U.S. advertising and culture—via television—into the Canadian market. British Columbia banned cigarette and liquor ads in all media—including the U.S. press.[14]

Such guidelines can be extremely important in both domestic and international business—because often businesses must get permission to operate. In some political environments, this is only a routine formality. In others, a lot of red tape is involved—and personal influence and/or "bribes" are sometimes necessary.

Multinational firms may be affected

Corporations that routinely operate in several countries have grown in size and importance in the last few decades. But growing nationalistic sentiments must be even more seriously considered by such firms in the future. Many countries require multinational firms to employ nationals, use locally produced parts, and so on. Multinational corporations are discussed in Chapter 23—but here it should be noted that their occasional disregard for feelings in individual countries has now given way to serious efforts to understand the people and the politicians within each particular country.

Political environment may offer new opportunities

The political environment is not always a negative variable. Governments may decide that encouraging business and opening markets are good for their people. Japan recently opened its market more to foreign investors and competitors. The United States and Western European countries may give industrial development a boost in Latin America, Africa, and Asia—by allowing manufactured goods from those areas to be imported at lower duty rates.

Within the United States, special programs and financial incentives encourage urban redevelopment and minority-owned businesses—as well as employment and training of the hard-core unemployed. State and local governments also try to attract and hold businesses—sometimes with tax incentives.

Some business managers have become very successful by studying the political environment—and developing strategies which use these political opportunities.

LEGAL ENVIRONMENT

Trying to encourage competition

American economic and legislative thinking has been based on the assumption that competition among many small firms will guide the economy with an "invisible hand." This idea became popular after the publication of Adam Smith's *Wealth of Nations* in 1776. Great Britain accepted this idea during the 1800s—in principle at least—and it was included in common law there and in the United States. According to this concept, attempts to restrain or limit trade are against the public interest and unenforceable. Practices tending to fix prices, limit markets, or in any other way control trade were considered undesirable.

This laissez-faire approach did not last long in Great Britain. But Americans have been reluctant to give up Adam Smith's free enterprise ideal. After the Civil War, however, some companies grew large—and some were combined into trusts, cartels, and monopolies by wealthy tycoons—often called "robber barons." This led to restraint of competition and hardships for smaller producers and consumers. As a result, there was a movement—especially among Mid-western farmers—to limit monopolists.

Beginning in 1890, a series of laws were passed that were basically *antimonopoly* or *procompetition*. The names and dates of these laws are shown in Table 3–1.

Antimonopoly law and marketing mix planning

Specific application of antimonopoly law to the four Ps will be presented in later chapters. To round out our discussion here, you should know what kind of proof the government must have to obtain a conviction under each of the major laws. You should also know which of the four Ps have been most affected by each law. Figure 3–6 provides such a summary—with a phrase following each law to show what must be proved to obtain a conviction. Note how the wording of the laws is moving to the side of protecting consumers.

Prosecution is serious— one can go to jail

Businesses and *business managers* are subject to both criminal and civil laws. Many business activities are regulated by civil laws—and penalties are limited to blocking or forcing certain actions, together with fines. Where criminal law applies, jail sentences can be imposed. For example, the Sherman Act now provides for fines up to $1 million for corporations, as well as fines of up to $100,000 and/or up to three years in prison for individuals.

This is an important point to understand. Some business managers have gone to jail—or received suspended jail sentences—in recent years because they violated the criminal law provisions of antitrust legislation.

Jail sentences are a recent development. Usually only fines were imposed upon the company. Given the potential profitability of activities such as price fixing, fines were not much more than "slaps on the wrist." But the government and courts are cracking down. Jail sentences have been imposed in cases where the firms and managers plead "no contest"—that is, they do not plead guilty.

Table 3–1
Outline of federal legislation now affecting competition in marketing

Year	Antimonopoly (procompetition)	Anticompetition	Antispecific practices
1890	Sherman Act		
1914	Clayton Act Federal Trade Commission Act		Clayton Act
1936	Robinson-Patman Act	Robinson-Patman Act	Robinson-Patman Act
1938			Wheeler-Lea Amendment
1950	Antimerger Act		Antimerger Act
1975	Magnuson-Moss Act		Magnuson-Moss Act

Figure 3–6
Focus (mostly prohibitions) of federal antimonopoly laws on the four Ps

Law	Product	Place	Promotion	Price
Sherman Act (1890) Monopoly or conspiracy in restraint of trade	Monopoly or conspiracy to control a product	Monopoly or conspiracy to control distribution channels		Monopoly or conspiracy to fix or control prices
Clayton Act (1914) Substantially lessen competition	Forcing sale of some products with others— tying contracts	Exclusive dealing contracts (limiting buyers' sources of supply)		Price discrimination by manufacturers
Federal Trade Commission Act (1914) Unfair methods of competition		Unfair policies	Deceptive ads or selling practices	Deceptive pricing
Robinson-Patman Act (1936) Tends to injure competition		Prohibits paying allowances to "direct" buyers in lieu of middlemen costs (brokerage charges)	Prohibits "fake" advertising allowances or discrimination in help offered	Prohibits price discrimination on goods of "like grade and quality" without cost justification, and quantity discounts limited
Wheeler-Lea Amendment (1938) Unfair or deceptive practices	Deceptive packaging or branding		Deceptive ads or selling claims	Deceptive pricing
Antimerger Act (1950) Lessen competition	Buying competitors	Buying producers or distributors		
Magnuson-Moss Act (1975) Unreasonable practices	Product warranties			

Recently, for example, several packaging executives were given prison terms and fines up to $35,000 each in a "no contest" case.[15] As further evidence of the government's seriousness about prosecuting price fixers, a Justice Department office opened a "hotline" to enable consumers to complain about possible antitrust violations. This way it can learn about regional price-fixing schemes that it would not otherwise discover. The many small businesses that have tended to ignore these laws—because they felt they were "too small for the government to worry about"—may be in for a shock.[16] The government's new seriousness should cause marketing managers to pay more attention to the political and legal environment in the future.

Consumer protection laws are not new

There is more to the legal environment than just the antimonopoly laws. Some consumer protections were built into the English and U.S. common law system. A seller had to tell the truth (if asked a direct question), fulfill contracts, and stand behind the firm's product (to some reasonable extent). But beyond this, it was expected that vigorous competition in the marketplace would protect consumers—so long as they were careful. Within this framework, the procompetition thrust of the antitrust laws is understandable.

Focusing only on competition did not protect consumers very well in some areas, however. Some dishonest or production-oriented businesses and their "letter of the law" advisors found ways of cutting corners—or staying just barely within the law. So the government has found it necessary to pass other laws—usually involving specific types of products.

Foods and drugs are controlled

Consumer protection laws go back at least to 1906. The Pure Food and Drug Act was passed then. Colorful exposés of unsanitary meat-packing practices in the Chicago stockyards caused consumer interest in this act. After much debate, it was decided to pass a general law to control the quality and labeling of food and drugs in interstate commerce. This was a major victory for consumer protection. Before this, it was assumed that common law and the old warning "let the buyer beware" would take care of consumers.

Some loopholes in the law were corrected in following acts. The law now bans the shipment of unsanitary and poisonous products—and requires much testing of drugs. The Food and Drug Administration (FDA) attempts to control manufacturers of these products. It has the power to seize products that violate its rules. It also has regulations on branding—and requires that food shipped in interstate commerce contain labels which correctly describe the contents. In general, it has done a good job. But the outcry over a recent proposal to ban the use of saccharin may force the government to decide how much protection consumers really want. In this case, there were many users who felt that the government should first ban the use of many other products whose bad effects

Government agencies have made many sanitary and safety improvements, but some consumers feel they go too far in some cases.

Milt & Joan Mann

had already been more thoroughly proved—for example, alcohol and cigarettes. Clearly, more thinking is needed in this area.

Product safety is controlled

The Consumer Product Safety Act (of 1972) is another important consumer protection law. It set up the Consumer Product Safety Commission to control product safety. This group has broad power to set safety standards and penalties for failure to meet these standards. Again, there is some question as to how much safety consumers want. The Commission found the bicycle the most hazardous product under its control!

But given that the Commission has the power to force a product off the market, it is obvious that safety must be considered in product design. This is an uncontrollable variable which must be treated seriously by marketing managers.[17]

State and local laws affect strategy planning, too

In addition to federal legislation which affects interstate commerce, marketers must be aware of state and local laws which affect intrastate commerce. Here, legal advice and/or extensive knowledge of community or state politics are even more important. Some laws may be obsolete or impose such harsh penalties that local prosecutors are reluctant to enforce them. For practical purposes, these particular laws do not exist.

There are state and city laws regulating minimum prices and the setting of prices; regulations for starting up a business (licenses, examinations, and even tax payments); and in some communities, regulations prohibiting certain activities—such as door-to-door selling or selling on Sundays or during evenings.

Some states have regulations about movement or importation of agricultural commodities—supposedly to protect product quality or to prevent the spread of animal or crop diseases. Some of these, of course, are justifiable. Others are simply devices to let local producers get higher prices. This has been especially true for milk, some citrus products, and wine. This is also true of the buy-local and buy-American provisions of some government contracts.

Consumerists and the law say "let the seller beware"

Traditional thinking about buyer-seller relations has been *"let the buyer beware"*—but now it seems to be shifting to *"let the seller beware."* The number of consumer protection laws has been increasing. These laws and court interpretations suggest that the emphasis now is on protecting consumers *directly*—rather than *indirectly* by protecting competition. Production-oriented businesses may find this frustrating—but they will just have to adapt to this new political and legal environment.

Much of the impact of this consumer protection legislation tends to fall on the manufacturers—because they are the producers of the product and, under common law, are supposed to stand behind what they make. Generally these guarantees have been fairly weak—what was "reasonable" or what the courts would consider "reasonable." But increasingly, the courts are putting greater responsibility on the manufacturers—even holding them liable for any injury that their product causes—even injury caused by users' carelessness. Recently, for example, a manufacturer was held liable for damages because one of its vacuum cleaners blew up when it was plugged into a 220-volt circuit. The label clearly

Figure 3–7
Some important federal
regulatory agencies

Agencies	Responsibilities
Federal Trade Commission (FTC)	Enforces laws and develops guidelines regarding unfair business practices
Food and Drug Administration (FDA)	Enforces laws and develops regulations to prevent distribution and sale of adulterated or misbranded foods, drugs, cosmetics, and hazardous consumer products
Consumer Product Safety Commission (CPSC)	Enforces the Consumer Product Safety Act—which covers any consumer product not assigned to other regulatory agencies
Interstate Commerce Commission (ICC)	Regulates interstate rail, bus, truck, and water carriers
Federal Communications Commission (FCC)	Regulates interstate wire, radio, and television
Environmental Protection Agency (EPA)	Develops and enforces environmental protection standards
Office of Consumer Affairs (OCA)	Handles consumers' complaints

stated that the product was to be used in 115-volt outlets—but the court concluded that the manufacturer failed to warn the customer that the results of plugging the unit into anything stronger would be disastrous.[18] In such an environment, it is clear that businesses must "lean over backwards." Times have changed—let the seller beware.

Know the laws—follow
the courts and federal
agencies

Because legislation must be interpreted by federal agencies and the courts, students should carefully study both legislative developments and the thinking of the courts and agencies. Often laws are vaguely phrased by legislators—to convey intent—but not specific detail. It is then up to the courts and administrative bodies to spell out the details. And good legal assistance is needed to keep up with these details. See Figure 3–7 for a description of some important federal regulatory agencies which should be considered in strategy planning.

If marketing managers had a better understanding of the intent of the makers and interpreters of the laws, there would be less conflict between business and government—and fewer embarrassing mistakes. With such an understanding, managers might come to accept the political and legal environment as simply another framework within which business must function and develop its marketing strategies. After all, it is the consumers—through their government representatives—who determine the kind of economic system they want.

CONCLUSION

This chapter was concerned with the forces which—while beyond the marketing manager's control—profoundly affect strategy planning. Some uncontrollable variables can change faster than others. But all can change—requiring adjustments in plans. Ideally, likely changes would be considered in the planning.

As we have seen, a marketer must develop marketing mixes appropriate to the customs of the people in his target markets. He must be aware, for example, that promotion which is suitable in Gary, Indiana, may be offensive to citizens of New Orleans, Louisiana, or Yokohama, Japan.

The marketing manager also must be aware of legal restrictions—and sensitive to changing political climates. The growing interest in consumerism may force many changes.

The economic environment—the chances of business recessions or spiraling inflation—also will affect the choice of strategies. And the marketer must try to anticipate, understand, and deal with such changes—as well as changes in the technological base underlying the economic environment.

A manager must also examine the competitive environment. How well established are competitors? What action might they take? What is the nature of competition?

Developing good strategies is obviously a very complicated job. The marketing manager must be well informed. He can benefit by increased knowledge of the social and natural sciences. Most important, he must know his own field thoroughly—for he will have to use the information from all these sources when developing his own strategies. Marketing management—as you can see—is an integrating and challenging discipline.

QUESTIONS AND PROBLEMS

1. For a new design of haircomb, or one of the items mentioned in Question 13 of Chapter 2, discuss the uncontrollable factors that the marketing manager will have to consider.

2. Discuss the relative importance of the uncontrollable variables, given the speed with which these variables move. If some must be neglected because of a shortage of executive time, which would you recommend for neglect?

3. Discuss the probable impact on your hometown of a major technological breakthrough in air transportation which would permit foreign producers to ship into any U.S. market for about the same transportation cost that domestic producers must incur.

4. If a manufacturer's well-known product is sold at the same price by many retailers in the same community, is this an example of pure competition? When a community has many small grocery stores, are they in pure competition? What characteristics are really needed in order to have a purely competitive market?

5. List three products that are sold in purely competitive markets and three sold in monopolistically competitive markets. Do any of these products have anything in common? Can any generalizations be made about competitive situations and marketing mix planning?

6. Cite a local example of an oligopoly, explaining why it is an oligopoly.

7. Which way does the U.S. political and legal environment seem to be moving (with respect to business-related affairs)?

8. Why is it necessary to have so many laws regulating business? Why has Congress not just passed one set of laws to take care of business problems?

9. What and whom is the government attempting to protect in its effort to preserve and regulate competition?

10. For each of the *major* laws discussed in the text, indicate whether in the long run this law will promote or restrict competition (see Figure 3–6). As a consumer, without any financial interest in business, what is your reaction to each of these laws?

11. Are consumer protection laws really new? Discuss the evolution of consumer protection. Is more such legislation likely?

SUGGESTED CASES

1   Quenton, Incorporated
5   Midwest Steel Company

NOTES

1. David C. McClelland, "Business Drive and National Achieve-
    ment," *Harvard Business Review*, July–August 1962, pp. 91–112.

2. "Sunbelt Secret: 'Workers Work.' " *The Lansing State Journal*,
    June 15, 1977, p. A–9.

3. "Conflict of Interest: Moral Climate Changes," *Business Week*,
    April 14, 1973, pp. 56–62. See also "Del Monte Corp. Finds a
    Foreign 'Consultant' Can Help a Great Deal," *The Wall Street
    Journal*, July 14, 1975, p. 1; "Beer Firms Are Target as Agencies
    Extend Bribery Probes to U.S.," *The Wall Street Journal*, July
    10, 1976, p. 1 f; "Schlitz Expects U.S. Investigators to Urge
    Legal Action in Improper Marketing Case," *The Wall Street Jour-
    nal*, March 28, 1977, p. 9; "Canada's Flexible Bribery Standards,"
    Business Week, June 13, 1977, pp. 35–36; and "Misinterpreting
    the antibribery law," *Business Week*, September 3, 1979, pp.
    150–51.

4. "The petro-crash of the 80's," *Business Week*, November 19,
    1979, pp. 176–90; "The Shrinking Standard of Living," *Business
    Week*, January 28, 1980, pp. 72–78; "Howard Johnson Says
    Inflation Fuel Woes Could Hurt Business," *The Wall Street Jour-
    nal*, April 3, 1980, p. 29; "Tire Industry Drops into a Deep Reces-
    sion; Gasoline Shortage, Rising Costs Take Toll," *The Wall
    Street Journal*, October 17, 1979, p. 40; "For Some U.S. Con-
    cerns, Energy Crisis Fuels Greater Profits and Employment,"
    The Wall Street Journal, December 7, 1979, p. 18; "How OPEC's
    High Prices Strangle World Growth," *Business Week*, December
    20, 1976, pp. 44–50; "Will Energy Conservation Throttle Eco-
    nomic Growth?" *Business Week*, April 25, 1977, pp. 66–80; and
    "Economic Shock Wave from Oil Price Rises in '73 Still Hurts
    West," *The Wall Street Journal*, March 10, 1977, pp. 1 f.

5. N. Hanna, A. H. Kizilbash, and A. Smart, "Marketing Strategy
    under Conditions of Economic Scarcity," *Journal of Marketing*,
    January 1975, pp. 63–67.

6. George C. Sawyer, "Social Issues and Social Change: Impact
    on Strategic Decisions," *MSU Business Topics*, Summer 1973,
    pp. 15–20.

7. "From Back Yard Boats to Yachts," *Business Week*, August
    28, 1965, pp. 28–29.

8. "Oranges Start Coming Up Roses," *Business Week*, May 4,
    1968, pp. 127–30.

9. *Business Week*, June 24, 1967, p. 85.

10. "The U.S.'s Toughest Customer," *Time*, December 12, 1969,
    pp. 89–98.

11. "The FTC Reviews Its Own Consumer Rules," *Business Week*,
    March 28, 1977, p. 92; Norman Kangun, "The Failings of Regula-
    tion," *MSU Business Topics*, Spring 1976, pp. 5–14; "Govern-
    ment Intervention," *Business Week*, April 4, 1977, pp. 42–95;
    "Federal Commissions Draw Increasing Fire, Called Inept and
    Costly," *The Wall Street Journal*, October 9, 1974, pp. 1 f; "The
    Hidden Cost of Drug Safety," *Business Week*, February 21, 1977,
    pp. 80–84; and "A Subtle Easing of the Price-Fixing Rules,"
    Business Week, December 24, 1979, pp. 90–92.

12. "Business Out of Sync with Public, Pollster Says," *Advertising
    Age*, May 23, 1977, p. 4 f.

13. "Crash Suit Costs Ford $450,000," *Detroit Free Press*, Decem-
    ber 14, 1972.

14. "Trudeau's New Rules for Foreign Investors," *Business Week*,
    August 24, 1974, pp. 58–59; *The Wall Street Journal*, May 1,
    1972, p. 22; and "Ottawa Restricts U.S. Ads," *Business Week*,
    September 4, 1965, p. 36.

15. "Packaging Firm Is Found Guilty of Price Conspiracy," *The Wall
    Street Journal*, January 21, 1977, p. 3. See also T. McAdams
    and R. C. Milgus, "Growing Criminal Liability of Executives,"
    Harvard Business Review, March–April 1977, pp. 36–40; and
    "Antitrust Ruling on Certain Bags Is Left Standing," *The Wall
    Street Journal*, January 15, 1980, p. 5.

16. "Antitrust: A Hotline to Nab Price Fixers," *Business Week*, May
    30, 1977, p. 34; "New Antitrust Chief to Seek Jail Terms in
    Price-Fix Cases," *The Wall Street Journal*, January 24, 1980,
    p. 2; and J. G. Van Cise, "For Whom the Antitrust Bell Tolls,"
    Harvard Business Review, January–February 1978, pp. 125–30.

17. Paul Busch, "A Review and Critical Evaluation of the Consumer
    Product Safety Commission: Marketing Management Implica-
    tions," *Journal of Marketing*, October 1976, pp. 41–49.

18. "Business Responds to Consumerism," *Business Week*, Sep-
    tember 6, 1969, p. 95.

PART TWO

Selecting target markets

In this part, we will talk about finding potentially attractive target markets and how to evaluate their potential. First (in Chapter 4) we will discuss what marketing opportunities are and how to find—and evaluate—them. Then (in Chapter 5) we will discuss how to gather information to aid in marketing strategy planning. This "marketing research" chapter is really concerned with much more than just analyzing target markets—so it could be studied here or near the end of the book, when you have some questions you might want answered about marketing mix planning.

The next three chapters (Chapters 6–8) are concerned with possible dimensions of target markets. In Chapters 6 and 7 we will look at the dimensions of the consumer market—both demographic and behavioral. And in Chapter 8 the possible dimensions of the many different kinds of intermediate customers will be considered.

Finally, in Chapter 9 we will wind up this section with a discussion of segmenting markets and estimating their potential. This is a very important chapter, because it is necessary to correctly define markets and their relevant dimensions—in order to plan effective marketing mixes. Without knowing the dimensions of the target market, a marketing manager has to fall back on production-oriented "mass marketing"—which is almost a guarantee of failure in our increasingly competitive markets.

This part leads logically into the next section—on developing marketing mixes. In fact, it is not possible to select target markets without tying them to marketing mixes. We implement whole strategies, not target markets, and so you should see this part as the first step in learning how to develop more effective marketing mixes—and eventually develop effective strategic plans.

Milt & Joan Mann

1. Understand how to find marketing opportunities.
2. Understand how to define relevant markets, generic markets, and product-markets.
3. Know about the different kinds of marketing opportunities.
4. Understand how to screen and evaluate opportunities.
5. Understand how the resources and objectives of the firm can help in the search for opportunities.
6. Understand why the firm would want to match its opportunities to its resources and objectives.
7. Recognize the important new terms (shown in red).

4

Marketing opportunity analysis

Finding attractive opportunities is part of marketing strategy planning.

The primary focus of this text is on marketing strategy planning—an important part of which is finding attractive opportunities. Let's define what we mean by "attractive opportunities"—and then see how the company's objectives and resources can affect the search for these opportunities. Remember, strategic planning is concerned with matching a firm's resources to its market opportunities.

We will also discuss the kinds of opportunities available—and how to evaluate them. This chapter is important—because attractive opportunities make the rest of marketing strategy planning easier.

WHAT ARE ATTRACTIVE OPPORTUNITIES?

Optimists see opportunities everywhere. Should a marketing manager pursue all of the possibilities he finds? Is every one really an attractive marketing opportunity for his firm? The answer, in general, is *no!* Attractive opportunities for a particular firm are those the firm has some chance of doing something about—given its resources and objectives. Strategic planning tries to match opportunities to the firm's resources—what it can do—and its objectives—what it wants to do.

Usually, attractive opportunities are fairly close to markets the firm already knows. It makes sense to build on a firm's strengths—and avoid its weaknesses. This may allow it to capitalize on changes in its present markets—or more basic changes in the uncontrollable environment.

How many opportunities a firm "sees" depends on the thinking of top management—and the objectives of the firm. Some want to be innovators—and eagerly search out new opportunities. Others are willing to be creative imitators of the leaders. And others are willing to be risk-avoiding "me-too" marketers.

Figure 4–1 shows the process we will be discussing throughout the chapter—finding possible opportunities and then screening them to choose the ones which will be turned into strategies and strategic plans. As Figure 4–1 shows, we will first look for possible opportunities—and then evaluate them against screening criteria. These criteria develop out of analysis of the company's resources, the long-run trends facing the company, and the objectives of top management.

Breakthrough opportunities are needed

Throughout this book we will emphasize finding **breakthrough opportunities**—opportunities which enable the innovators to develop hard-to-copy marketing mixes which will be very profitable for a long time. Really, what we would like to find is attractive enough opportunities so we can achieve a "competitive differential advantage" which will give the firm a "competitive edge" over competitors—and at least a temporary monopoly in "its own little market." Such a breakthrough opportunity will help the firm capture a large market share—which may delay "imitators." This will prolong its monopoly—and the attractive profits which come with real breakthrough opportunities.

Our emphasis on finding breakthrough opportunities is important—because such opportunities are needed just for survival in our increasingly competitive markets. The "me too" products which production-oriented people like to turn out are not very profitable anymore. They must face head-on competition with similar products from all over the world—and much of this competition emphasizes lower prices.

Should seek a competitive differential advantage

It is important to emphasize that a firm should seek to obtain a "competitive differential advantage"—just to ensure its survival. The marketing concept helps encourage this point of view—but aggressive application of this concept *is* needed.

Figure 4–1
Finding and evaluating opportunities

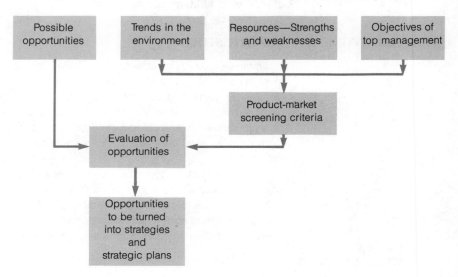

Too many firms—even those who supposedly have adopted the marketing concept—are worried about holding on to their share of their *current* market—rather than trying to expand that market or to find totally new ones. They are competitive—rather than innovative. They try to get by with yesterday's strategies—rather than creating more effective new ones. This accounts in part for the declining profit rates we see in some industries and firms.[1]

New markets, new customers, and new ways of doing things must be found if companies are to operate profitably in the future—and contribute to our macro-marketing system. By looking for breakthrough opportunities, a company may expand its horizon—and find profit possibilities which might otherwise be missed.

SEARCH FOR OPPORTUNITIES CAN BEGIN WITH DEFINING THE FIRM'S MARKETS

Accurately identifying the firm's current markets may suggest attractive opportunities which production-oriented competitors won't see. When marketing managers really understand their target markets, they can develop marketing mixes which are far better than those of competitors. Such understanding can provide breakthrough opportunities. Such mixes may not mean very big changes—perhaps only in advertising or pricing—but can lead to large sales and profit growth *quickly*. Or, a clear understanding of the target market may require greater changes in the marketing mix—but produce a much better strategy.

An example will show you how a real understanding of a target market can suggest new opportunities—and lead to a much better marketing mix. Eastman Kodak—well known for cameras and photographic supplies—also produces an industrial good, X-ray film. Until a few years, ago, Kodak felt this market wanted faster X-ray pictures at cheaper prices. Their marketing mix was aimed to satisfy those needs. But closer study of this market showed that the real need in hospitals and health-care units was saving the radiologist's time. Time was precious—and just giving the radiologist a faster picture wasn't enough. Something more was needed to help him do the whole job faster. Kodak came to see that its business was not just supplying X-ray pictures, but really helping to improve the health care supplied to patients. As a result, Kodak came up with two new time-savers for the radiologist: a handy cassette film pack and a special identification camera that records all vital patient data directly on the X-ray at the time that the X-ray is made. Previously, this tagging had to be done in the darkroom during developing—which took more time and created the possibility of error. This was a different marketing mix aimed at satisfying a different need.[2] And it worked very well.

What is a firm's market?

What is a firm's market is a very important—but sticky—question. A "**market**" is a group of potential customers with similar needs—and sellers offering various products—that is, ways of satisfying those needs. Obviously, the description for a market should focus on customers and the needs they want satisfied by some product(s). But how specific should we get? We have a need for food—but should a flour producer define his market as the hunger market? The food market? The flour market? The flour producer will have to compete with other flour produc-

Mary McCarthy

ers—but all of them must also compete with the producers of other kinds of food in a "bigger" market. You can see this more clearly if you think of a market as including sellers who offer substitute ways of satisfying needs. So wheat flour has to compete with other kinds of flour as well as rice, potatoes, and beans—and perhaps even less direct substitutes like meat, vegetables, and dairy products.

Companies sometimes avoid the difficulties of defining markets by describing them in terms of the products the firm sells. This production-oriented approach is easy—but it may also cause the firm to miss good opportunities. Producers and retailers of Christmas cards, for example, may define their market very narrowly as the "Christmas card" market. Or, if they think a little broader, they might define their market as the "greeting card" market—including birthday cards, Easter cards, "all occasion" cards, and "humorous" cards. But by taking a broader, more customer-oriented view, the firm might define its market as the "personal expression" market. And this might lead the firm to offer all kinds of products which could be sent as gifts—to express one person's feelings towards another. The possibilities beyond greeting cards include jewelry, plaques, candles, puzzles, and so on. Companies like Hallmark have this bigger view of a market—and they have expanded far beyond selling just standard greeting cards for the major "greeting card" occasions—birthdays and Christmas.

From generic market to product-markets

It is useful to think of two basic types of market—a generic market and a product-market. A **generic market** is a market in which sellers offer substitute products which are quite different physically or conceptually. In contrast, a **product-market** is a market in which sellers offer substitute products which are similar—either physically or conceptually.

A generic market description looks at markets broadly and from the customers' viewpoint. People seeking "status," for example, have several very different ways to satisfy their "status" needs. A status-seeking consumer might buy an expensive car, take a luxury cruise to Hawaii, or buy designer clothes at an exclusive shop.

See Figure 4–2. Any one of these very different products might satisfy the "status" need. Sellers in this generic "status" market will have to focus on the needs the *customer* wants satisfied, *not* on how one seller's car (or vacation, or designer label) is better than that of another producer. By really understanding people's needs and attitudes, it may be possible for producers of "status symbols" to encourage shifts to their particular product.

The fact that quite different products may compete with each other in the same generic market may make it harder to define the market. But if customers see all these products as substitutes—as competitors in the same generic market—then marketers will have to live with this complication.

Suppose, however, that our status-seeking consumer decides to satisfy his status need with a new, expensive car. Then—in this *product*-market—Mercedes, Cadillac, or Ferrari may compete with each other for the status-seeker's dollar.

To summarize—in the broad, *generic* market for status—cars, designer clothes, or expensive vacations may all be competing with each other. In a narrower *product*-market concerned with status—consumers compare similar products to satisfy their status needs (i.e., a Ferrari with a Mercedes or a Cadillac).

Most companies quickly narrow their focus to product-markets—because of the firm's past experience, resource commitments, or management preferences. And we will usually be thinking of product-markets when we refer to markets. But this should be done carefully when one is searching for opportunities—because it is so easy to miss opportunities—as the Christmas card example showed.

DEFINING THE RELEVANT MARKET

A marketing manager may find it useful to work with several market definitions—all the way from a very broad generic market definition to a very narrow product-market definition. Broader definitions are more useful for finding opportu-

Figure 4–2
The position of some products in a "status symbol" market

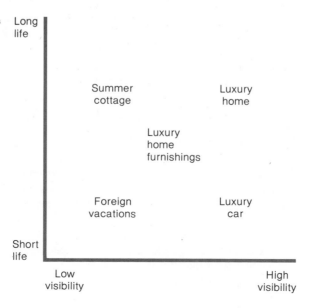

nities—and avoiding competitive surprises from competitors which a too-narrow view would ignore. Narrow market definitions, on the other hand, can be useful for handling short-run tactical problems. For example, the New York City market for a particular product line may be of great relevance for handling a price war among a few New York discounters.

Broaden market definitions for finding opportunities

Broader market definitions—including broader product-market definitions and generic market definitions—are useful for finding opportunities. But deciding how broad to go—that is, deciding on the relevant market area—is a creative process. Too narrow a definition will limit a firm's opportunities—but too broad a definition will make the company's efforts and resources look insignificant.

Fortunately, our strategic planning process provides some guidelines for defining a firm's **relevant market,** the market which is suitable for the firm's purpose. Here, we are trying to match opportunities to the firm's resources and objectives—so the *relevant market for finding opportunities* should be bigger than the firm's present product-market—however it is defined—but not so big that the firm couldn't expand and be an important competitor in this "relevant" market. A small manufacturer of screw drivers, for example, shouldn't define its market as broad as "the world-wide tool market" or as narrow as "our present screw driver customers." But it might have the production and/or marketing capabilities to consider "the U.S. hand tool market." It might be able to offer hammers, pliers, and wrenches to present customers. Or, this broader market definition might suggest other sub-markets into which the firm could expand with screw drivers. These might be other parts of the country—using the same type of channel of distribution—or other kinds of customers—using different kinds of channels.

Naming a market

A product-market description should include some customer-related terms— *not* just product-related terms. Product-related terms are *not*—by themselves— an adequate description of a market. Further, a generic market description would *not* include *any* product-related terms. The emphasis, instead, would be on the needs or benefits sought—for example personal expression, or status, or personal transportation.

It is better to name markets with customer-related terms as much as possible— only adding product-related terms for clarity—or to narrow the size of the relevant market. It is important to recognize, however, that focusing only on customer-related terms may lead to dealing with markets which are too broad. So, depending on the company's resources and objectives, it often will be desirable to narrow the firm's relevant market down to one or more product-markets. If an auto manufacturer does not already have a well-recognized brand which can compete in the "status symbol" market—but does have a brand which can compete successfully in the "personal transportation" market—then it might want to define its relevant market accordingly—so that it only analyzes market areas where it has some chance of matching opportunities to its own resources. Similarly, a U.S. manufacturer of bicycles with special skills in this area might define its relevant market as the world-wide market for personal transportation bicycles *and* status symbol bicycles.

Are these cars in the same product-market?

Don Smetzer

Identifying geographic boundaries may help

When trying to name present or potential markets, it usually is desirable to start with the customers' views of the geographic boundary of the market—and then move on to the needs that the company's present offering might satisfy. Just identifying the geographic boundaries of the present market can suggest new opportunities. A supermarket in Los Angeles is not catering to all consumers in the Los Angeles area—and so there may be opportunities for expansion to unsatisfied customers in that market. In general, it is good practice to identify the geographic boundaries of all markets.

Identifying customers' needs can help, too

Potential customers' needs and attitudes toward the products in the general area being considered can help name the relevant product-market or generic market. If the firm were interested in the automobile market, for example, it should think about the basic reasons why people buy automobiles. At a very general level, they probably buy them for transportation and/or status. If we were to focus on the world-wide transportation market and look at how this general need is being satisfied, we would see that the various competitors are offering mass and personal solutions to this need. In particular, and in varying degrees, the following products are substitutes—airplanes, pickup trucks, cars, motorcycles, mopeds, bicycles, skateboards, and shoes. And by thinking about why some of these substitutes are better than others, we can convert these product-related solutions to more particular needs or benefits sought. For example, some of these substitutes are better than others with respect to speed, convenience (in all weather), personal versus group transportation, size of load, and cost.

Creative analysis of the needs and attitudes of present and potential target markets—in relation to the benefits being offered by the firm and competitors—will help you see new opportunities. In the next several chapters we will be studying the many potential dimensions of markets—and suggesting ways of segmenting these markets. But, for now, you should see that markets can be defined in various ways—and defining them only in terms of current *products* is *not* the best way for finding new opportunities and planning marketing strategies. Instead, you should try to define *generic markets* and *product-markets*—with emphasis on the customer-related characteristics, including geographic dimensions and needs and attitudes.

TYPES OF OPPORTUNITIES TO PURSUE

Most people have unsatisfied needs—and alert marketers can find opportunities all around them. Starting with the firm's present product-markets is useful. This may require marketing research, research and development (R&D), analysis of profitable companies' activities, and analysis of the environmental trends we discussed in the last chapter. In fact, a creative marketer should be continually scanning the environment for opportunities which may match with the firm's resources.

It is also possible to go beyond the firm's present activities. It helps to visualize the kinds of opportunities which may be found. Figure 4–3 shows that there are four possibilities: market penetration, market development, product development, and diversification.

Market penetration

Market penetration: a firm trying to increase sales of its present products in its present markets—probably through a more aggressive marketing mix. The firm might try to increase the customers' rate of use—or attract either the competitors' customers or current nonusers. New promotion appeals might be effective. McDonald's may have "Ronald McDonald" invite the kids in for a special offer. More stores may be added in present areas—for greater convenience. Short-term price cuts might be a help. Obviously, effective planning would be greatly aided by a real understanding of why some people are buying now—and what might motivate them to buy more—or motivate others to shift brands or begin or resume buying.

Market development

Market development: a firm trying to increase sales by selling present products in new markets. This might involve, for example, McDonald's adding new stores in new areas—perhaps in downtown locations, in schools or hospital lobbies, or even in foreign countries. Or it might only involve advertising in different media to reach new target customers.

Product development

Product development: a firm offering new or improved products for present markets. Here, presumably, the firm knows the market's needs and might see the possibility of adding or modifying product features, or creating several quality

Figure 4–3
Four basic types of opportunities

	Present products	New products
Present markets	Market penetration	Product development
New markets	Market development	Diversification

levels, or adding more types or sizes—to better satisfy the present market. For example, McDonald's now offers breakfasts for adults—and cookies for kids.

Diversification

Diversification: a firm moving into totally different lines of business—which might include entirely unfamiliar products, markets, or even levels in the production-marketing system. For example, manufacturers might go into wholesaling or retailing—or buy their suppliers.[3]

Which opportunities come first?

Most firms tend to be production-oriented and think first of greater market penetration. If they already have as big a share as they can get in their present markets, they may think of market development—finding new markets for their present products—including expanding regionally, nationally, or even internationally.

Marketers who have a good understanding of their present markets may see opportunities in product development—especially because they already have a way of reaching their present customers.

The most challenging opportunities involve diversification. Here, both new products and new markets are included. The further the opportunity is from what the firm is already doing, the more attractive it may look to the optimists—and the harder it will be to evaluate. The firm may have a good understanding of all the problems close to its current operations—that is why it is considering other opportunities! But opportunities which are far from a firm's current operations may involve much higher risks. This is why it is very important to have ways of avoiding wasteful searches for opportunities—as well as for efficiently evaluating those which are finally considered. How this can be done is discussed in the following pages.

Many firms go for diversification

The last 20 years has seen much diversification in the United States. As the stock market was rising in the 1960s, it was "easy" for firms with rising stock prices to purchase other companies by trading stock for stock. As a result, many firms have divisions producing and selling completely unrelated products. Gulf & Western is in real estate, financial services, entertainment, electronics, and many other fields. And Beatrice Foods Company has moved from its early focus on dairy products into many other areas. See Figure 4–4.

Obviously, such "conglomerates" have diversified far beyond businesses which have a common thread. Each of these separate divisions seemed to offer an attractive opportunity—and each now requires strategic plans, and a program (probably) for each division.

COMPANY RESOURCES LIMIT THE SEARCH FOR OPPORTUNITIES

Every firm has some resources—hopefully some unique resources—which distinguish it from other firms. Attractive opportunities should make use of these strong points—while avoiding direct competition with firms having similar strengths.

To find its strengths, the firm must evaluate functional areas (production, research and engineering, marketing, general management, and finance) as well

Product-markets	Brands
Dairy and soft drink	Meadow Gold, Dannon Yogurt, Johnston's, Viva, Swiss Miss, and bottlers of Royal Crown, 7-Up, Schweppes, and others
Grocery	La Choy, Burny Brothers Bakeries, Krispy Kreme, Mario's, Beatrice, Shedd's, Gebhard, and Rosarita
Food distribution & warehousing	Sexton, MIS, Cal-Compac Foods, and various public warehouse operations
Confectionery & snack	Fisher, Doumak, M. J. Holloway, Clark, Switzer, and Brenner
Specialty meats	Eckrich, Lowrey's, Kneip, R. F., and Pepi's
Agri-products	Vigortone, Pfister & Vogel, and various by-product and feed producers
Institutional & industrial	Excel, Taylor Freezer, Wells, Vogel Peterson, Day-Timers, Cryogenic Associates, Design West, World Dryer, and others
Travel & recreational	Samsonite, Buxton, Bonanza, Velva Sheen, Monticello, Airstream, Morgan Yacht, and others
Housing & home environment	Harman International, Liken, Aristo Kraft, Stiffel, Holiday Homes, Melnor, Samsonite, Chicago Specialty, A. H. Schwab Co., Fort Smith Folding Tables and Chairs, and others
Chemical & allied products	Stahl Finish, Polyvinyl, Chemical Industries, Imperial Oil and Grease Co., Farboil, Triton Ink Co., Standard Drywall, Envelope Adhesive Corp., and others
International	Brands in all of the above categories in 28 countries

Source: Beatrice Foods Company.

as present products and markets. By analyzing outstanding successes and failures—in relation to the firm's capabilities, talents, and skills—it should be possible to find patterns which explain why it was successful—or why it failed—in the past.

Resources which should be considered—as part of an evaluation of strengths and weaknesses—are discussed in the following sections.

Financial strength

Some industries—such as steel and public utilities—require large amounts of capital to achieve economies of scale. For them, the cost of production per unit decreases as the quantities produced increase. Therefore, smaller producers would be at a great disadvantage if they tried to compete in these lines. Some industries, however, do not have economies of scale—and smaller, more flexible firms may be quite effective. In fact, large companies often have difficulties when they enter low-investment businesses. For example, a large chemical processor tried to make and sell decorated shower curtains—because it was producing the basic plastic sheets. It lost heavily on the experiment, however. The smaller shower curtain manufacturers and middlemen were much more flexible—changing their styles and price policies more rapidly. Here, financial strength was a strength in the basic plastic sheet business—but it was a weakness where style and flexibility in adapting to customer needs was important.

Raw material reserves

Firms that own or have assured sources for basic raw materials have a head start in businesses that need these resources. But companies—large or small—that are not in this position may find—especially in times of short supply—that they have difficulty even staying in business. Chemical and paper manufacturers, for example, usually try to control timber resources. Metals and petroleum companies have controlled their own resources. Now that we see a growing scarcity of raw materials, it probably will be desirable for a firm to control or have assurances of supply before building a marketing strategy which depends upon raw materials.

Physical plant

Some lines of business—railroads, utilities, oil refineries, ice-skating rinks—require large special-purpose physical plants. If these are well-located, they are a strength. On the other hand, badly located or obsolete plants—or wholesale or retail facilities—can be real weaknesses. The existing physical plant can have a big impact on marketing strategy planning—because one of the firm's objectives probably will be to use the existing plant as fully as possible. Any logical strategy will, therefore, try to use the existing facilities—or provide for their disposal so that the capital can be used more effectively elsewhere.

Patents

Patents are of primary concern to manufacturers. A patent owner has a 17-year "monopoly" to develop and use its new product, process, or material as it sees fit. If a firm has a patent on a basic process, potential competitors will be forced to use second-rate processes—and their efforts may be doomed to failure. If a firm has such a patent, it is a resource—while if its competitors have it, it may be a weakness which cannot be overcome with other aspects of a marketing mix.

Brands

If a firm has developed a loyal following of customers which prefer or insist upon its product, others may have difficulty invading this market. A strong brand is a valuable resource that a marketing manager can use in developing marketing strategies.

Skilled people

Some firms deliberatley pay high wages to attract and retain skilled workers—so they can offer high-quality products. A skilled sales force is also a strength—lack of good salespeople can limit strategy planning. Even if skilled employees can produce a new product, the sales force may not have the contacts or know-how to sell it. This is especially true when a firm moves from consumer products to industrial products—or vice versa.

Management attitudes

The attitude of top management toward growth is important in strategy planning—especially as it affects the development and introduction of new products.

The president of a New England manufacturing company was enthusiastic about the prospects for a new product. But after evaluating the attitudes of his company's personnel—and especially his management people—he dropped his plans for the product. Why? He found that his employees had no ambition or interest in growth.[4]

Even if the capital is available, some people aren't interested in expansion because they're happy in their own niche.

Karen A. Yops

OBJECTIVES MAY LIMIT THE SEARCH FOR OPPORTUNITIES

A company's objectives should shape the direction and operation of the whole business. If it has already been decided that the firm is to stay small—so the owner has plenty of time for golf—then this objective will obviously limit the firm's opportunities. (Actually, of course, it probably would not even be looking for opportunities!) On the other hand, if a large, aggressive firm seeks sales growth—then the range of opportunities expands quickly. If this firm has almost unlimited capital, then the strategy planners have even more freedom to search for good opportunities.

You can see that objectives are important regarding marketing strategy planning. So we will treat this matter in some depth—referring to its effect both on finding attractive opportunities and developing marketing strategies.

OBJECTIVES SHOULD SET FIRM'S COURSE

A company should know where it is going—or it is likely to fall into the trap expressed so well by the quotation: "Having lost sight of our objective, we redoubled our efforts."[5] In spite of their importance, objectives are seldom stated explicitly. In small businesses, they appear to be stated *after the fact!* And in some large businesses, there may be *several* implicit—but conflicting—objectives held by different managers. The relative importance of these objectives may depend upon the point of view of the person being interviewed.[6]

It would be convenient if a company could set one objective—such as making a profit—and let that serve as the guide. Actually, however, setting objectives is much more complicated—which explains why it is done so poorly, if it's done at all.

Setting objectives that really guide the present and future development of the company is a soul-searching process. It forces top management to look at the whole business, relate its present objectives and resources to the external environment, and then plot what it wants to do in the future.

Three basic objectives provide guidelines

Taken together, the following three objectives provide a useful starting point for objective setting for a particular firm. These three objectives could be phrased and made more specific in many ways. But they should be sought together because—in the long run—a failure in even one of the three areas could lead to total failure of the business.

1. Engage in some specific business activity that will perform a socially and economically useful function.
2. Develop an organization to carry on the business and implement its strategies.
3. Earn enough profit to survive.[7]

Should be socially useful

The first objective suggests that the company should do something society considers useful. This isn't just a "do good" objective. Businesses exist on the approval of consumers. If the activities of a business appear to be against the consumer "good," that firm can be wiped out almost overnight by political or legal action—or the customer's own negative response.

The first objective also implies that the firm should see its purpose as satisfying customer needs—rather than focusing only on internal concerns such as using the company's resources, exploiting a patent, and so on. The firm should define its efforts broadly—setting need-satisfying objectives rather than product-oriented objectives.

The importance of a broad market-oriented view should be obvious—if the objectives are supposed to help a company plan for the future. Too narrow a view may lead the company into a product-market area in which the product itself—because of changing customer needs—will soon be obsolete.[8]

Should organize to innovate

In a macro-marketing sense, consumers have granted businesses the right to operate—and to make a profit if they can. They also expect businesses to be dynamic—agents of change—adjusting their offerings to customers' needs. Competition is supposed to encourage innovation and efficiency. Assuming that our society will continue this approach, a business firm should develop an organization that will ensure that these consumer-assigned tasks are effectively carried out—and that the firm itself continues to prosper.

Should earn some profit

It is sometimes assumed that profit is the only objective of business—and it certainly is true that in the long run a firm must make profits to survive. But simply saying that a firm should try to make a profit isn't enough. The time period involved must also be specified—since long-run profit maximization may require losing money during the first few years of a plan.

Further, trying to maximize profit won't necessarily lead to large profits. Competition may be so fierce that failure may be almost guaranteed in a particular industry. It might be better to set some target rate of profit return that would lead the firm into areas having some possibility of such a return. In fact, some firms probably should seek even higher rates of return than they are now earning—and more than is available in their *present* activities.

Setting objectives is complicated further by the need of specifying the degree of risk that management is willing to assume for larger returns. Very large profits might be possible in the oil prospecting business, for example, but the probability of success in that field might be quite low. If the business is to take a long-run view—if it intends to survive and be a useful member of the business community—it probably should include the costs of risk and potential losses in its calculation of long-run returns.

Both hands must work toward the same objectives

Whatever objectives are chosen by top management, they should be compatible with each other—or frustrations and even failure may result. The three broad objectives suggested above would help a firm avoid this mistake. But as these three guidelines are made more specific, care is necessary. For example, top management might set a 10-percent return on investment each year as one objective, while at the same time specifying that the current plant and equipment be used as fully as possible. Competition might make it impossible to use the resources fully and achieve this return—but the managers might try to follow the resource-use objective through the course of the year and only discover at the end of the year that the two objectives are impossible to achieve together!

Top management myopia may straitjacket marketing

We are assuming that it is the marketing manager's job to work within the framework of objectives provided by top management. But some of these objectives may limit marketing strategies—perhaps damaging the whole business. This is why it is desirable for the marketing manager to help shape the company's objectives.

A few examples will help show how the marketing manager might be forced to choose undesirable strategies.

A quick return on investment is sometimes sought by top management. This might lead the marketing manager to select marketing strategies that would yield quick returns in the short run—but kill brand loyalty in the long run.

Top management might decide on diversification. This might force the marketing manager to choose strategies that are badly matched to the company's resources.

Some top managements want a large sales volume or a large market share—because they feel this assures greater profitability. Recent studies seem to support the idea that larger market share leads to greater profitability. But how you define markets affects these results—and the suggested relation may be only a coincidence. A better explanation may be found in the quality of the marketing strategies—rather than the quantity of sales or market share. Recently there have been many bankruptcies of large firms with big market shares—some railroads, for example which seemed to dominate their markets. A&P has been a leader in some food store markets, and yet profits have been very disappointing. Increasingly, companies are shifting their objectives toward *profitable* sales growth rather than just larger market share—as they realize that the two do not necessarily go together.[9]

Objectives should guide the whole management process

Ideally, the marketing manager should be involved in setting objectives, but regardless, these objectives should guide the search for and evaluation of opportunities—as well as later planning of marketing strategies. Particular marketing objectives should be set within the framework of these overall objectives. As shown in Figure 4–5, there should be a hierarchy of objectives—moving from company objectives, to marketing department objectives. For each marketing strategy, there should also be objectives for each of the four Ps—as well as sub-objectives. For example, in the Promotion area we might need advertising objectives, sales promotion objectives, and personal selling objectives.

The company objectives would also be used as input to the development of the product-market screening criteria—for screening opportunities—as explained below.

HOW TO EVALUATE OPPORTUNITIES

Once some opportunities have been identified, then it is necessary to screen and evaluate them. Usually, it is not possible for a firm to pursue all of its opportunities. Instead, it should try to match its opportunities to its resources and objectives. So, the first step is to quickly screen out the obvious mismatches. Then, it can analyze the remaining ones more carefully. Let's look at some approaches for screening and evaluating opportunities.

Developing and applying screening criteria

We have already evaluated the firm's resources (for strengths and weaknesses), the environmental trends facing the firm, and the objectives of top management. Now these should be merged into a set of product-market screening

Figure 4–5
A hierarchy of objectives

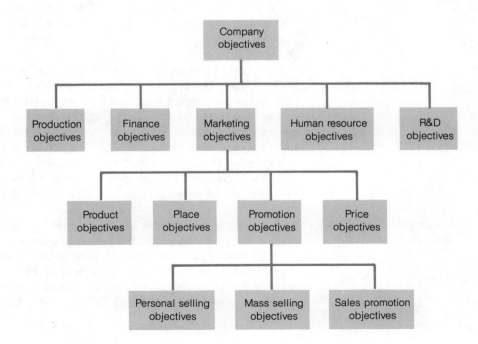

Figure 4-6
An example of product-market
screening criteria for a small
retailer ($300,000 annual sales)

1. Quantitative criteria
   a. Increase sales by $100,000 per year for the next five years.
   b. Earn ROI of *at least* 25 percent before taxes on new ventures.
   c. Break even within one year on new ventures.
   d. Opportunity must be large enough to justify interest (to help meet objectives) but small enough so company can handle with the resources available.
   e. Several opportunities should be needed to reach the objectives—to spread the risks.
2. Qualitative criteria
   a. Nature of business preferred.
      1. Goods and services sold to present customers.
      2. "Quality" products which can be sold at "high prices" with full margins.
      3. Competition should be weak and opportunity should be hard to copy for several years.
      4. Should build on our strong sales skills.
      5. There should be strongly felt (even unsatisfied) needs—to reduce promotion costs and permit "high" prices.
   b. Constraints
      1. Nature of businesses to exclude.
         (a) Manufacturing.
         (b) Any requiring large fixed capital investments.
         (c) Any requiring many people who must be "good" all the time and would require supervision (e.g., "quality" restaurant).
      2. Geographic
         (a) United States and Canada only.
      3. General
         (a) Make use of current strengths.
         (b) Attractiveness of market should be reinforced by *more than one* of the following basic trends: technological, demographic, social, economic, political.
         (c) Market should not be bucking *any* of above trends.

criteria. These criteria should include both quantitative and qualitative components. The quantitative components summarize the objectives of the firm—sales, profit, and return on investment (ROI) targets for each strategy.* The qualitative components summarize what kind of business the firm wants to be in, what business it wants to exclude, what weaknesses it should avoid, and what strengths and trends it should build on.[10]

Developing screening criteria is a difficult process—because they summarize in one place what the firm wants to accomplish—in quantitative terms—and roughly how and where it wants to accomplish it. The criteria should be realistic—that is, they should be achievable. Opportunities that pass the screen ought to be ones that could be turned into strategies which the firm could implement with its current resources.

Figure 4–6 illustrates the product-market screening criteria for a small retailer. This whole set would help the firm's managers eliminate unsuitable opportunities—and find attractive ones to turn into strategies and plans.

Whole plans should be
evaluated

Forecasts of the probable results of implementing whole strategic *plans* are needed to apply the quantitative part of the screening criteria—because it is "implemented plans" which generate sales, profits, and return on investment (ROI). For a rough screening, we only need an estimate of the likely results of implementing alternative opportunities over logical planning periods. If a product's life (before withdrawal from the market) is likely to be three years, for example,

* See Appendix B (following Chapter 19) for definitions of these terms.

then a good strategy may not produce profitable results during the first six months to a year. But evaluate the plan over the projected three-year life, and it might look like a winner. When evaluating the potential of alternative opportunities—strategic plans—it is important to evaluate similar things—that is, *whole* strategic plans.

Opportunities that pass the screen—or any opportunities, if screening criteria are not used—may be evaluated more thoroughly before being turned into strategic plans for implementation. Usually, there are more opportunities than resources and the marketing manager must choose among them—to match the firm's opportunities to its resources and objectives. The following approaches can be useful in selecting among alternative strategic plans.

Total profit approach can help evaluate alternative plans

The total profit approach to evaluating plans requires forecasts of potential sales and costs during the life of the plan.

The prospects for each plan might be evaluated over a five-year planning period—with monthly and/or annual estimates of sales and costs. This is illustrated graphically in Figure 4–7.

Note that—as shown in Figure 4–7—quite different strategic plans can be evaluated at the same time. In this case, a substantially improved product and product concept (Product A) is being compared with a "me too" product for the same target market. In the short run, the "me too" product would break even sooner and might look like the better choice—if only one year's results were considered. The new product, on the other hand, will take a good deal of pioneering but—over its five-year life—will be much more profitable.

Return-on-investment (ROI) approach can help evaluate alternative plans, too

Besides evaluating the profit potential of alternative plans, it may also be necessary to calculate the return on investment of resources needed to implement a plan. One plan might require a heavy instrument in advertising and channel development, for example, while another relies primarily on lower price. (Note: ROI analysis is discussed briefly in Appendix B), which follows Chapter 19.

ROI analyses can be useful for selecting among alternative plans—because equally profitable plans may require vastly different resources—and offer different rates of return on investment. Some firms are very much concerned with ROI—because they must borrow money for working capital and there is little point in

Figure 4–7
Expected sales and cost curves of two strategies over five-year planning periods

borrowing to implement strategies that won't even return enough to meet the cost of borrowing.[11]

Expected-value approach can handle uncertainty

The total profit approach and the ROI approach require estimates of sales and profits. If fairly definite estimates can be made for alternative strategies, these can be compared and the "best" one selected.

Where there is uncertainty about the likely outcome of individual plans, however, one might wonder which profit figures to use. If one can estimate the probability of the possibilities happening, however, then it is possible to use the *expected-value approach*—that is, to compute the expected profit (or sales) and compare these expected profits for alternative plans.

See Table 4–1 for an illustration of how expected profit could be calculated for four alternatives. Assuming that the marketing manager is willing to accept expected profit as the criterion, then the strategy that is likely to produce the highest expected profit can be chosen. For example, in Table 4–1, Strategy 3 would be chosen. A more conservative decision maker, however, might select Strategy 2 because of the certainty of *some* profit. In other words, even though profit is one of the objectives of management, the risk associated with alternative plans might lead different managers to select different plans.

Decision trees may show alternatives more clearly

When many alternative plans must be evaluated, a visual aid—called a *decision tree*—may be helpful. The tree diagram in Figure 4–8 shows several alternatives clearly. At the end of each branch, a measure of effectiveness—such as total profit and/or return on investment—can be shown for comparison. And, if the success of any of the plans is uncertain, the expected values can be calculated and compared—as illustrated in Table 4–1. As a further aid, it might be useful to show the resources required for each alternative—beside the total profit and return on investment. Most firms try to make a profit—while using their resources effectively—but sometimes these are conflicting objectives. So, it helps to have all the relevant information conveniently displayed when management attempts to apply its judgment in choosing the best opportunities.

PLANNING GRIDS HELP EVALUATE DIFFERENT KINDS OF OPPORTUNITIES

When a firm has many possibilities to evaluate, it usually has to compare quite different ones. This can present a real problem—but the problem has been

Table 4–1
Evaluation of various alternatives with expected-value approach

Alternative strategies	Payoff (in dollars of profit)	Probability of occurrence	Expected profit
1	$ 100,000 or 0	.50 .50	$ 50,000
2	25,000 or 10,000	.90 .10	23,500
3	1,000,000 or −10,000	.20 .80	192,000
4	500,000 or −100,000	.30 .70	80,000

Figure 4–8
Decision tree for evaluation of alternative one-year plans, given that the target market and product have already been selected and one-year plans are realistic

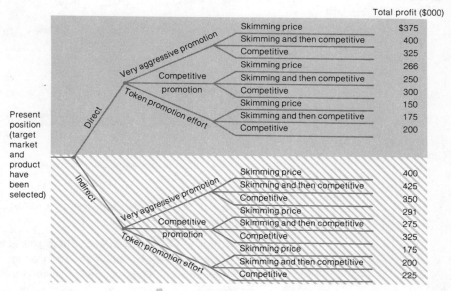

			Measure of effectiveness
			Total profit ($000)
		Skimming price	$375
	Very aggressive promotion	Skimming and then competitive	400
		Competitive	325
	Competitive promotion	Skimming price	266
Direct		Skimming and then competitive	250
		Competitive	300
	Token promotion effort	Skimming price	150
		Skimming and then competitive	175
Present position (target market and product have been selected)		Competitive	200
		Skimming price	400
	Very aggressive promotion	Skimming and then competitive	425
		Competitive	350
Indirect	Competitive promotion	Skimming price	291
		Skimming and then competitive	275
		Competitive	325
	Token promotion effort	Skimming price	175
		Skimming and then competitive	200
		Competitive	225

reduced by the development of some graphical approaches—usually relying on four- or nine-box grids. The easiest to understand and apply is the Boston Consulting Group growth-share matrix approach—which is discussed first. A more subjective approach developed by General Electric is discussed second.

Boston Consulting Group approach

The Boston Consulting Group (BCG) is a well-known consulting firm which has popularized a four-box matrix approach which evaluates opportunities (as well as the company's present product lines) in terms of "stars," "cash cows," "dogs," and "question marks."[12]

The BCG approach requires measures of market growth and relative market share for the various alternatives. With just these two pieces of information, the various opportunities can be plotted on the BCG growth-share matrix. See Figure 4–9. The vertical axis refers to the *annual growth rate* of the market for each alternative. In this figure, the market growth rate axis goes from a low of 0 percent (below zero is considered *very bad*) to a high of 20 percent. Higher-level growth rates could be used, of course, but these opportunities are not too common. Then, the market growth axis is divided into high and low growth ranges—using a 10 percent growth rate as an arbitrary cut-off point.

The horizontal axis shows *relative market share*—the alternative's share relative to the share of the industry's leading competitor. A relative market share of 0.1 means the alternative has 10 percent of the industry leader's share. A relative market share of 10—at the other extreme—means that the alternative has a share that is 10 times larger than that of the next largest competitor in the market. As above, the horizontal axis is divided into high and low share—using 1.0 as the middle—so that a four-box matrix results.

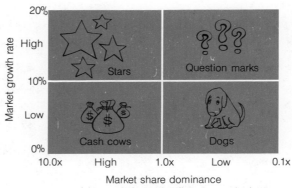

Given a four-box grid, this growth-share matrix approach helps identify four kinds of alternatives:

Stars—Stars are high-growth, high-share products. It is usually assumed that these are, or will be, profitable products, although cash is needed to finance their rapid growth. Generally, it is assumed that financing stars is desirable because eventually their growth will slow down and they will turn into cash cows—which will become major cash suppliers for other products.

Cash cows—Cash cows are low-growth, high-share products. These are profitable products which generate a lot of cash that the company can use to support other products.

Question marks—Question marks are high-growth, low-share products. Because of their low-share, it is assumed that they require a lot of cash to maintain or increase their share—which is very important in the BCG approach. These products are called question marks—or "problem children" or "wildcats"—because it is not as clear what to do about them. Management has to think about whether it wants to spend more money to build them into market leaders—or to phase them down or out.

Dogs—Dogs are low-growth, low-share products. They are also called "cash traps." They may produce enough cash to break even—but they do not appear to be a potential source of cash or profits.

When a company's present products—as well as its opportunities—are placed within the BCG matrix, it helps everyone see the relative attractiveness of the alternatives. And given the resources and objectives of the company, it helps decide what to do with each of the alternatives. Ideally, the firm would probably want a blend of different kinds of strategic plans. So it might choose to invest cash in some of them—perhaps some of the more attractive question marks, continue the present strategies for some others—perhaps the strong cash cows, seek short-run profits with some—perhaps weaker cash cows which should be "milked" in the short run—regardless of the long-run effect, and sell or eliminate some—perhaps some of the weaker question marks as well as the dogs.

Evaluating alternatives using this approach would be an ongoing process, of course. Some alternatives might be moved from question marks to stars and later become cash cows. But by seeking a blend of stars and cash cows, a company might be able to achieve profitable growth—while offsetting the "negative" impact of some question marks and dogs.

General Electric uses strategic planning grid

General Electric feels it has gone beyond the BCG approach with a nine-box grid. (See Figure 4–10). People who use the nine-box grid feel that focusing only on market growth and market share may not capture all the variables which should be considered. The nine-box grid forces company managers to make three-part judgments (high, medium, and low) about the business strengths and industry attractiveness of all proposed or existing products or businesses.

GE looks for green positions

GE feels that opportunities that fall into the green boxes in the upper left-hand corner of the grid are its growth opportunities—the ones that will lead the company to invest and grow with these businesses. The red boxes in the lower right-hand corner of the grid, on the other hand, suggest a no-growth policy. Existing red businesses might continue to generate earnings—but GE figures they no longer deserve much investment. The yellow businesses are the borderline cases—which could go either way. An existing yellow business might be continued and supported—but a proposal for a new yellow business would have a greater chance of being rejected by top management.

GE's "stop light" evaluation method is a very subjective, multiple-factor approach—because GE has concluded that there are too many traps and possible errors if it tries to use over-simplified, single-number criteria—like ROI and market share—for judging "attractiveness" or "strength." Instead, top managers review written summaries of about a dozen factors (see Figure 4–10) which help them make summary judgments. Then they make a collective judgment based on the importance they attach to each of the factors. GE reports that the approach generally leads to agreement and, further, a good understanding about why some businesses or new opportunities are supported—while others are not. Further, it appears that high-high green businesses are uniformly good on almost any

**Figure 4–10
General Electric's strategic planning grid**

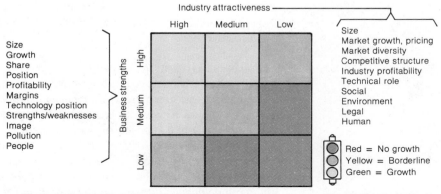

Source: Adapted from M. G. Allen, "Strategic Problems Facing Today's Corporate Planner" (speech given at the Academy of Management, 36th Annual Meeting, Kansas City, Missouri, 1976).

quantitative or qualitative measure used. This interaction among the relevant variables makes it practical to boil them all down into a "stop light" framework.[13]

Factors reflect GE's objectives

The various factors which General Electric considers in its subjective evaluation would, of course, reflect the corporation's objectives. The various "business strength" factors are related to the size of business it would like to be in—and the business's growth potential and profitability. The "industry attractiveness" variables also reflect GE's objectives in that ideally it would want to be involved in industries where the firm has a good chance of growth and profitability—while still contributing to the economy. In summary, the use of many factors simply helps ensure that all the concerns of the corporation are properly considered when it is evaluating alternative opportunities.

The General Electric approach can be useful for deciding which opportunities to develop, that is, which markets the firm should stay with or go into. Then, the marketing planner must go on to the second part of the marketing planning job—developing strategies.

MULTIPRODUCT FIRMS HAVE A DIFFICULT STRATEGY PLANNING JOB

Multiproduct firms—like General Electric and Beatrice Foods—obviously have a more difficult strategic planning job than a firm with only a few products or product lines aimed at the same or similar target markets. They have to develop strategic plans for very different businesses. And the corporate level must try to balance the plans and needed resources for the various businesses in such a way that the whole corporation reaches its objectives—perhaps continued sales and profit growth. This requires analyses of the various alternatives—using approaches similar to the BCG approach or the General Electric strategic planning grid—and approving strategic plans which make sense for the whole corporation—even if it means harvesting some divisions and eliminating others.

Details on how to manage such a complicated firm are beyond our scope. But it is important to recognize (1) that there are such firms and (2) that the principles we will discuss in this text are applicable—they just may have to be extended. For example, some firms have developed strategic business units (SBUs) and others are applying a portfolio management approach. These topics are discussed next.

Strategic business units may help

Some multiproduct firms have tried to improve their operations by forming strategic business units. A **strategic business unit (SBU)** is an organizational unit within a larger company which focuses its efforts on some product-markets and is treated as a separate profit center. Forming SBUs formally recognizes that a company is composed of quite different activities—some of which may be growing rapidly and require a great deal of attention and resources—while others may be only in the middle in terms of profitability, and should be "harvested"—that is, they should be allowed to generate cash for the businesses with more potential. There also may be product lines with poor market position, low profits, and poor growth prospects—and these should be dropped or sold.

Companies which set up strategic business units usually do change their attitudes and methods of operation. Managers are rated in terms of achieving their strategic plans—rather than short-term profits. Without SBUs, it is all too easy to emphasize only profits—especially short-run profits. It is a temptation for an eager manager to go for the short-term results—while sacrificing long-term gains. With SBUs, the emphasis is on developing plans which, when accepted, are to be implemented aggressively. Under this concept, some managers would be equally successful phasing out some product lines, while other managers are moving ahead aggressively—expanding sales in other markets.

The point here is that each manager would be carrying out a market-oriented strategic plan approved by top management. The manager's job would be to help develop effective plans and then implement them to ensure that the company's resources are used effectively—and that the firm accomplishes its corporate objectives.[14]

Some firms use portfolio management

Some top managements handle strategic planning for a multiproduct firm with an approach called **portfolio management**—which treats alternative products, divisions, or strategic business units (SBUs) as though they were stock investments—to be bought and sold using financial criteria. These managers see themselves making trade-offs among very different opportunities. They simply treat the various alternatives as investments—which should be supported, "milked," or sold off—depending upon profitability and return on investment (ROI). In effect, each alternative is evaluated as a stock market trader evaluates a stock.[15]

This approach makes some sense if the alternatives are really quite different. It is unlikely that top managers can become very familiar with the prospects for all of their alternatives. So they fall back on the easy-to-compare quantitative criteria. And because the short run is much clearer than the long run, heavy emphasis is usually placed on *current* profitability and return on investment. This puts great pressure on the operating managers to "deliver" *in the short run*—perhaps even neglecting the long run. (There have even been cases of managers manipulating their accounting records—to make the short-run results look better!)

Portfolio management would be greatly improved by encouraging the development of market-oriented strategic plans—which would make it possible to more accurately evaluate the short-run and long-run prospects of the many alternatives. If market-oriented strategies were spelled out in complete detail, it would be easier for experienced managers to evaluate the "quality" of the plans. They would not only have a better basis for deciding how to allocate resources among the various plans, but they also would be able to make specific suggestions about modifying plans. In other words, they would actually become involved—again—in the management process—instead of relying on a few financial criteria which may fail to capture the long-run value of their alternatives.

This approach focuses—excessively—on the short run—just as most stock market traders are concerned with the short-run fluctuations of the market. Mechanical application of the portfolio management approach may cause firms to "sell" their future for the short run. This would be most unfortunate—and it is important to see that a market-oriented approach to strategic planning can provide the input for a more in-depth evaluation of alternative opportunities.

CONCLUSION

Innovative strategy planning is needed for survival in our increasingly competitive marketplaces. This requires not only developing marketing strategies but finding attractive opportunities—which was the focus of this chapter.

We discussed ways of finding attractive opportunities—and breakthrough opportunities. And we saw that the firm's own resources and objectives may help limit the search for opportunities.

Eventually, some procedures are needed for screening and evaluating opportunities. We explained an approach for developing screening criteria—from the output of an analysis of the strengths and weaknesses of the company's resources, the environmental trends it faces, and top management's objectives. We also considered some quantitative techniques for evaluating opportunities. And we discussed procedures for evaluating quite different opportunities—BCG and GE strategic planning grid. We also recognized that a multiproduct firm may use a portfolio management approach to developing its whole program.

Now that we have discussed how to find and evaluate attractive opportunities, we must go on to discuss how we turn these opportunities into profitable marketing strategies. This will require us to get into marketing research (Chapter 5), analyzing demographic trends and customer buying behavior (Chapters 6–8), and segmenting markets (Chapter 9). After these chapters, we will go on to developing marketing mixes and strategies (Chapters 10–20).

QUESTIONS AND PROBLEMS

1. Distinguish between an attractive opportunity and a breakthrough opportunity.

2. Explain how new opportunities may be seen by defining a firm's markets more precisely. Illustrate for a situation where you feel there is an opportunity—i.e., an unsatisfied market segment—even if it is not very large.

3. Distinguish between a generic market and a product-market. Illustrate your answer.

4. Explain the major differences among the four basic types of opportunities discussed in the text, and cite examples for two of these types of opportunities.

5. Explain why a firm might want to pursue a market penetration opportunity before pursuing one involving product development or diversification.

6. Explain how a firm's resources might limit its search for opportunities. Cite a specific example for a specific resource.

7. Discuss how a company's financial strength might have a bearing on the kinds of products it might produce. Will it have an impact on the other three Ps as well? If so, how? Use an example in your answer.

8. Explain how a firm's objectives might affect its search for opportunities.

9. Specifically, how would various company objectives affect the development of a marketing mix for a new type of baby shoe? If this company were just being formed by a former shoemaker with limited financial resources, list the objectives he might have and then discuss how they will affect the development of his marketing strategy.

10. Explain the components of product-market screening criteria—which are used to evaluate opportunities.

11. Explain the differences among the following approaches to evaluating alternative plans: total profit approach, return-on-investment approach, and expected value approach.

12. Compare and contrast the following approaches to evaluating opportunities: Boston Consulting Group approach and General Electric's strategic planning grid approach.

13. Distinguish between the operation of a strategic business unit and a firm which has only paid "lip service" to adopting the marketing concept.

SUGGESTED CASES

4 Redi, Incorporated
12 Ski Haus Sports Shop

29 Rundle Manufacturing Company

NOTES

1. Robert H. Hayes and William J. Abernathy, "Managing Our Way to Economic Decline," *Harvard Business Review,* July–August 1980, pp. 67–77, and Peter C. Riesz, "Revenge of the Marketing Concept," *Business Horizons,* June 1980, pp. 49–53.

2. "How Kodak Will Exploit Its New Instamatic," *Business Week,* March 18, 1972, pp. 46–48.

3. Igor Ansoff, *Corporate Strategy* (New York: McGraw Hill Book Co., 1965).

4. Based on Charles H. Kline, "The Strategy of Product Policy," *Harvard Business Review,* July–August 1955, pp. 91–100.

5. Charles H. Granger, "The Hierarchy of Objectives," *Harvard Business Review,* May–June 1964, p. 63.

6. Charles P. Edmonds III and John H. Hand, "What Are the Real Long-Run Objectives of Business?" *Business Horizons,* December 1976, pp. 75–81; Douglas S. Sherwin, "Management of Objectives," *Harvard Business Review,* May–June 1976, pp. 149–60; and M. J. Etzel and J. M. Ivancevich, "Management by Objectives in Marketing: Philosophy, Process, and Problems." *Journal of Marketing,* October 1974, pp. 47–55; "Informatics' New Push on Profits," *Business Week,* May 26, 1980, pp. 118–26; and "Sears' Strategic About-Face," *Business Week,* January 8, 1979, pp. 80–83.

7. Adapted from Peter F. Drucker, "Business Objectives and Survival Needs: Notes on a Discipline of Business Enterprise," *Journal of Business,* April 1958, pp. 181–90.

8. This point of view is discussed at much greater length in T. Levitt, "Marketing Myopia," *Harvard Business Review,* July–August 1960, pp. 45 f.

9. "A Turnaround 'Master' Takes on Kroehler," *Business Week,* June 16, 1980, pp. 86–89; "A Painful Attempt to Aid Ampex," *Business Week,* February 12, 1972, p. 17; "Ford Motor Company Adopts New Tactics to Boost Its 'Big Three' Standing," *The Wall Street Journal,* May 15, 1973, pp. 1 f; "RCA's New Vista: The Bottom Line," *Business Week,* July 4, 1977, pp. 38–44; "The Luster Dims at Westinghouse," *Business Week,* July 20, 1974, pp. 53–63; and "Market-Share-ROI Corporate Strategy Approach Can Be an 'Oversimplistic Snare,' " *Marketing News,* December 15, 1978, pp. 1 f.

10. Frank R. Bacon, Jr., and Thomas W. Butler, Jr., *Planned Innovation,* revised edition, Institute of Science and Technology, The University of Michigan, Ann Arbor, 1980.

11. J. Fred Weston, "ROI Planning and Control," *Business Horizons,* August 1972, pp. 35–42; Richard T. Hise and Robert H. Strawser. "Application of Capital Budgeting Techniques to Marketing Operations," *MSU Business Topics,* Summer 1970, pp. 69–76; and Louis V. Gerstner, "Can Strategic Planning Pay Off?" *Business Horizons,* December 1972, pp. 5–16; "Esmark Is Growing Impatient with Swift as Meat Packer Remains a Drag on Profits," *The Wall Street Journal,* April 29, 1980, p. 40; "Esmark Facing Financial 'Realities' with Its Decision to Lop Off Two Units," *The Wall Street Journal,* July 1, 1980, p. 10; "Borden, Inc. Plans to Lop Off Units with 20% of Sales," *The Wall Street Journal,* July 11, 1980, p. 5; "P&G's New New-Product Onslaught," *Business Week,* October 1, 1979, pp. 76–82; and Edward D. Roberts, "New Ventures for Corporate Growth," *Harvard Business Review,* July–August 1980, pp. 134–42.

12. George S. Day, "Diagnosing the Product Portfolio, *Journal of Marketing,* April 1977, pp. 29–38.

13. M. G. Allen, "Strategic Problems Facing Today's Corporate Planner," a speech given to the Academy of Management, 36th annual meeting, Kansas City, Missouri, 1976; and "General Electric's 'Stoplight Strategy' for Planning." *Business Week,* April 28, 1974, p. 49. For other approaches, see Frank R. Bacon, Jr. and T. W. Butler, Jr., *Planned Innovation,* rev. ed. (Ann Arbor: Institute of Science and Technology. The University of Michigan, 1980); and Y. Wind and H. J. Claycamp, "Planning Product Line Strategy: A Matrix Approach," *Journal of Marketing,* January 1976, pp. 2–9.

14. "GE's New Strategy for Faster Growth," *Business Week,* July 8, 1972, pp. 52–58; "Italy: A Big Overseas Turn-Around for GE," *Business Week,* September 23, 1972, p. 45; and "General Electric's 'Stoplight Strategy' for Planning," *Business Week,* April 28, 1974, p. 48.

15. George S. Day, "Diagnosing the Product Portfolio," *Journal of Marketing,* April 1977, pp. 29–38.

When you finish this chapter, you should:

1. Understand a scientific approach to marketing research.
2. Know how to go about defining and solving marketing problems.
3. Know about getting secondary and primary data.
4. Know about the validity and reliability of research data.
5. Understand the three research approaches—and their advantages and disadvantages.
6. Know about marketing information systems.
7. Recognize the important new terms (shown in red).

Gathering information for marketing planning

"Hello. I'm conducting a survey . . ." Marketing research? Yes, but there's a lot more to the job than that.

Successful planning of marketing strategies requires information—information about potential target markets and their likely responses to various marketing mixes, and about competition and other uncontrollable factors.

It is the job of marketing research to help the marketing manager gather the information needed to make wise decisions. This isn't easy, because people and competitors are so unpredictable. It has to be done, however. Without good marketing information, managers have to "fly by the seat of their pants"—and in our dynamic and highly competitive economy, this almost guarantees failure.

WHAT IS MARKETING RESEARCH?

Marketing research gathers and analyzes data to help marketing managers make decisions. One of the important jobs of a marketing researcher is to get the "facts" and interpret them. This can be done with special projects or on a continuing basis—depending on the purpose. Marketing research is much more than a bunch of techniques—or a group of specialists in survey design or statistical methods. Good marketing researchers must be both marketing *and* management-oriented—to be sure that their research focuses on real problems on which action can be taken.

Research provides a bridge to consumers

Today, many marketing managers are isolated in company offices—far from their potential customers. For this reason, they *must* rely on research to know what is going on. This point cannot be overemphasized—it is very easy for management to lose touch with its markets. All the potential markets in the United States *and* abroad are not like those in which the typical middle-class suburban managers live.

Managers must know what researchers do

Marketing research details may be handled by staff or outside specialists—but marketing managers must know how to plan and evaluate research projects. That is, they should be able to communicate with specialists in *their* language. They may only be "consumers" of research—but they should be informed consumers, to be able to specify exactly what they want to buy.

For this reason, our discussion of marketing research will not focus on mechanics—but rather on how to plan and evaluate research. The marketing researcher must excel in these areas also. So, in the following discussion we will take the marketing researcher's view—realizing that both researcher and manager should participate in the research process—if the results are going to lead to action.

Researchers are improving and inspiring more faith

Marketing research, as we know it today, began around 1900—and grew as more companies became interested in regional and, then, national markets. The development of sampling techniques in the 1930s, the use of the psychological interview, and other attitude and opinion measurement techniques have expanded the field.

These and other refinements have increased the dependability of the findings. And this—together with more decision-oriented researchers—has encouraged firms to put more money and faith in research. In some consumer goods companies, no major decisions are made without the support—and sometimes even the official approval—of the marketing research department. As a result, some marketing research directors rise to high levels in the organization. For example, this activity is headed by the Vice President of Growth and Technology at Pillsbury.

OUR STRATEGIC PLANNING FRAMEWORK CAN GUIDE RESEARCH

Marketing researchers often become involved with strategic as well as tactical planning. They also can be helpful in evaluating how strategies are working out—providing "feedback"—which may lead to new plans. Thus, research is a continuing process. Some marketing researchers see themselves at the center of an information system which works to integrate all activities of the company.

With such a wide range of potential responsibilities, it is important that marketing researchers see clearly what kinds of problems they are being asked to work on—and what information is really needed to solve the problems.

Finding the right problem level almost solves the problem

The strategic planning framework introduced in Chapter 2 can be especially useful here—helping the researcher to see where the real problem lies. Do we really know enough about target markets?—enough to work out all of the four Ps? And so on down through tactical problems—such as how to motivate an older salesperson or handle a price war in New York City or Tokyo.

The importance of understanding the nature of the problem—and then trying to solve *that* problem—can be seen more clearly in the following example of a

manufacturer of a new easy-to-use baking mix. Top management had chosen apartment dwellers, younger couples, and the too-busy-to-cook crowd as target markets—a logical market at first glance. Some modest research on the *size* of this market—*not* their interest in this product concept—indicated that if these consumers responded as expected, there were enough of them to create a profitable baking mix market. The company decided to aim at this market—and developed a logical marketing mix.

Why didn't this baking mix sell?

During the first few months, sales were disappointing. The manufacturer "guessed" that the product itself might be unacceptable—since the promotion seemed to be adequate. At this point, a consumer survey was run—with surprising results. The product was apparently satisfactory—but the target consumers were just not interested. Easier preparation of this kind of product didn't particularly grab them. Instead, the best market turned out to be families who did their own cooking. They appreciated the convenience of the mix—especially when they needed something in a hurry.

In this case, the original strategy planning was done sloppily. The original choice of target markets was based on executive guesswork. This led to an unsuitable strategy—and wasted promotion money. Some research with consumers—about their needs and attitudes—might have avoided this costly error. Both marketing research and management fumbled the ball—by not studying the attitudes of the target market. Then, when sales were poor, the company compounded the error by assuming that the product was at fault—overlooking consumers' real attitudes about the product. Fortunately, research finally uncovered the real problem—and the strategy was changed quickly.

The moral of this story is that our strategic planning framework can be useful for guiding marketing research efforts. If the marketing managers have the facts on the potential target markets, then they can focus their research on marketing mix ingredients, their sensitivity to change, and the effectiveness of various tactics. Without such a framework, marketing researchers can get sidetracked into working on the wrong problems.

Quick answers are often needed

In our dynamic marketplace, marketing research often must try to provide answers to urgent questions—both strategic and tactical. Sometimes answers are needed so soon that quick-and-rough research work must be done. A little information may be better than total ignorance. Even though the most scientific approach is not possible when time is short, researchers should use the best procedures possible. For this reason, we will begin by showing that the scientific method is a logical approach to marketing problems. This scientific approach—combined with a strategic planning framework—can provide direction in the typically chaotic atmosphere of the business world.

THE SCIENTIFIC METHOD AND MARKETING RESEARCH

In relating the scientific method to marketing research, we are not trying to cloak marketing research with scientific "respectability." Managers want to make

Sometimes information is needed too fast to allow for in-depth research.

Peter Le Grand

the best decisions possible—and this can't be done consistently without a logical approach.

The scientific method is such an approach. In marketing, this logical method forces the researcher to follow procedures that reduce the possibilities of sloppy work—or of relying on intuition.

The scientific method is a research approach which consists of four stages:

1. Observation.
2. Developing hypotheses.
3. Predicting the future.
4. Testing the hypotheses.

With this method, researchers use their intuition and observations to develop hypotheses —educated guesses about the relationships between things or what will happen in the future—such as "There is no significant difference between brands A and B in the minds of consumers." Then they test each hypothesis.

Application of the scientific method helps the marketing manager develop and test the best hypotheses. It takes a commonsense but rigorous approach—developing hypotheses, testing, perhaps modifying, and testing again. The feedback principle is applied throughout the process.

The scientific approach to pain

To illustrate these stages in a simple nonmarketing case, consider a college student who develops a painful, swollen ankle after a skiing accident. The ankle could be bruised, sprained, or broken. What should he do? If he goes to a doctor, he will probably find the doctor following the scientific method:

1. Observation: Pain seems to increase if foot is twisted, but pain is not unbearable.
2. Developing an hypothesis: Since a sprain would be more painful than this, the ankle is broken.
3. Predicting the future: Pain and swelling will reduce, but bone may heal improperly if not set.

4. Testing the hypothesis: X-ray the ankle; don't wait to see if hypothesis is correct in this case.

Let us now use the same framework to show how a marketing manager might use this method.

The scientific approach to offering shirt wrappers

A manufacturer of men's shirts wanted to find new opportunities. The approach they took is shown here:

1. Observation: Notice some competitors' sales increasing and many competitors shifting to a new plastic wrapping.
2. Developing hypotheses: Assume *(a)* that plastic wrapping is the cause of competitors' sales increases and *(b)* that the firm's products are similar.
3. Predicting the future: Firm's sales ought to increase if it shifts to the new wrapping.
4. Testing the hypotheses: Produce some shirts in the new package and test them in the market.

The market test revealed that the prediction was correct—sales did increase. But what if they had not? In the answer to this question lies one important benefit of the scientific approach. Through careful control (making certain that the test was correctly designed and run) and evaluation of results, we should be able to isolate the reason *why* a given test failed—and determine where the hypotheses were in error.

In this case, either one of the hypotheses could have been wrong. Either increased sales by competitors were *not* caused by the new wrapping—or this manufacturer's products were *not* similar.

Assuming that the first hypothesis was wrong, further research might show that competitors' sales were up simply because their promotion had been more effective. Or, if the second hypothesis was wrong, it might show how the product differed—and the product could be changed.

FOUR-STEP APPROACH TO SOLVING MARKETING PROBLEMS

In marketing research, there is a four-step application of the scientific method:

1. Definition of the problem.
2. Situation analysis.
3. Informal investigation.
4. Formal research project.

See Figure 5–1.

Observation—the first stage in the scientific method—can be used during all four marketing research steps. Once the problem is defined, *developing hypotheses* takes place—perhaps during the situation analysis or the informal investigation. *Predicting the future* occurs any time before a formal research project is begun. And *testing the hypotheses* is completed in the formal research project—unless, as frequently happens, informal investigation solves the problem. Table

Figure 5-1
Four-step approach to solving
marketing problems

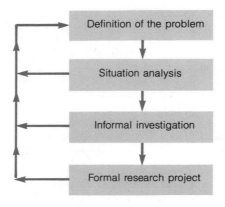

Table 5-1
Relation of scientific method to
marketing research

Scientific method stages	Used during the following marketing research steps
Observation	Definition of problem Situation analysis Informal investigation Formal research
Developing hypotheses	Situation analysis Informal investigation Formal research (planning)
Predicting the future .... (action implications)	Situation analysis Informal investigation Formal research (planning)
Testing hypotheses	Formal research (unless management is satisfied with an earlier but more intuitive solution)

5-1 helps see the relationships. The meaning of these terms is explained in the following pages.

Note—again—that this orderly procedure helps clarify just what you are doing. Mastery of this approach will greatly improve your ability to plan marketing research projects—and solve the right problems.

DEFINITION OF THE PROBLEM—STEP ONE

Defining the problem is the most important—and often the most difficult—job of the marketing researcher. It is slow work—requiring careful observation—and sometimes taking over half the time spent on a research project. But it is time well spent if the problem is correctly defined. The best research job on the wrong problem is wasted effort. It may even lead to costly mistakes—such as introducing a poor product—or ineffective advertising.

The typical problem arises when a firm is not able to reach one of its objectives. This may be a top management objective of increasing sales for the company as a whole—or in a particular geographic territory—or for a particular product.

Or, it might be as low level as finding a way to motivate one salesperson to make more frequent sales calls on some less attractive customers.

Don't confuse problems with symptoms

Problem definition sounds simple—and that's the danger. Objectives are seldom stated clearly—if at all. So it's easy to fall into the trap of mistaking identification of symptoms for the definition of the problem. For example, suppose that the company's sales are dropping in certain territories—while sales expenses remain constant—with a resulting decline in profits. Will it help to define the problem by asking: How can we stop the sales decline? Probably not. This would be like asking how to lower a patient's temperature—instead of first trying to find the cause of the fever.

We must discover *why* sales are declining (rather than increasing—which is the objective). Is the cause competitive activity, product deficiencies, inadequate support by company salespeople, noncompetitive prices, inefficient advertising, or some other reason? If one or more of these factors can be isolated as the cause, then the marketer is on the way to a solution. The general problem would be how to reach the objective of increasing sales. But the specific problem might focus on how to accomplish the objectives assigned to one or more of the four Ps. Perhaps advertising had been assigned the job of increasing awareness of the company's offerings to pave the way for the company's salespeople. If the advertising is ineffective, then the company's whole marketing plan may fail. The specific problem to be worked on in this case, then, might be how to improve the advertising—or overall promotion effort.

The real problem may be hard to isolate. The marketing manager should think of several likely problems to investigate. He can start with the strategic planning framework, for example, and evaluate what is known about the target market—and the compatability of the marketing mix ingredients. If there are doubts about one or more of these factors, these possible problem areas may be explored. But without more investigation and evidence, the marketing manager should not assume too quickly that the real problem has been defined. Instead, he should take his list of possible problems and go on to the next step—trying to discover which is the basic cause of the trouble.

SITUATION ANALYSIS—STEP TWO

When the marketing manager feels the problem has begun to surface, a situation analysis can be useful. A **situation analysis** is an analysis of information inside the firm and in already published sources. A complete commitment to a particular problem isn't necessary yet. Through this and the following steps, the problem may be revised or restated—in the light of new facts. *This reevaluation should be continuous.* Even after a hypothesis has been developed and tested by formal research, new factors can come up—so that a new statement of the problem and a new hypothesis test is necessary.

No talks with outsiders

In the situation analysis, the researchers first try to size up the situation—but without talking to outsiders. They talk to informed executives within the com-

When analyzing the situation, a researcher has to know what he's looking for before he can try to find it.

Mary McCarthy

pany, and study internal company records—which are generated as part of the control function. They also search libraries for available published material.

This research is important—since researchers should know the environment in which they work. They analyze information about their own company, its products, the industry, specific markets in which it is operating, middlemen, its own promotion, and its competitors' activities. Libraries contain vast amounts of information—but once the researchers have begun to zero in on the problem, they can look there for specific kinds of information.

Unless they know what they are looking for, researchers may be overwhelmed by the information available within their own company or in libraries. Let's take a closer look at the type of information we're talking about.

Secondary data is available now

A situation analysis evaluates **secondary data**—information which is already published or collected. **Primary data** is information which is gathered specifically to solve a current problem. See Figure 5–2.

Gathering primary data is discussed later. But it must be emphasized here that too often researchers rush out to gather primary data when there is already a plentiful supply of secondary information. And this data may be available immediately—at little or no cost!

One of the first places a researcher should look for secondary data—after looking within the firm—is in a good library. Frequently, your local library has the answer you need. Well-trained librarians can be a big help. Ask! They will be glad to help you.

Government sources

The federal and state governments publish data on almost every conceivable subject. The federal government publishes a monthly guide to its current publications. But it is more practical to refer to summary publications—to get leads to more detailed documents.

The most useful summary—the *Statistical Abstract of the United States*—is

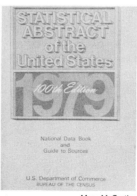

STATISTICAL ABSTRACT of the United States 1979

National Data Book and Guide to Sources

U.S. Department of Commerce
BUREAU OF THE CENSUS

Mary McCarthy

like an almanac. It is issued each year—and lists more than 1,000 summary tables from published sources. References to world markets are included. Detailed footnotes can guide you to more specific detail on a topic.

Every marketing student should be familiar with the *Abstract*—because it is probably the best starting point for locating statistical data. Marketers must be experts on sources of information—and the time to start developing this skill is *now*.

The U.S. Department of Commerce distributes statistics compiled by all other federal departments. Commerce Department branch and field offices—located in major cities throughout the United States—are good sources of data. Staff members provide assistance and suggestions for locating specific data.

Some city and state governments have similar agencies that provide leads for local data. University bureaus of business research may also prove useful.

Private sources

Many private research organizations—as well as advertising agencies, newspapers, and magazines regularly compile and publish data. A good business library is valuable here for sources such as *Sales and Marketing Management, Industrial Marketing, Advertising Age*—and the publications of the National Industrial Conference Board. Some information is available inexpensively as a customer service to clients of advertising agencies—or buyers of advertising space or time. For example, J. Walter Thompson Co.—an advertising agency—and the *Chicago Tribune* maintain continuing panels of consumers for research purposes.

Trade associations can also be a good source of information about a particular industry. They not only compile data from and for their members, but also publish magazines that focus on the problems and important topics in the industry. Some of these magazines will be found in business libraries.

Research by subscription

Some private research firms specialize in supplying—by subscription—research data that will aid the marketing manager in situation analysis. Some firms measure the sales and market shares of foods and drugs at retail by auditing retail stores. Others try to estimate the same information by measuring wholesale shipments. And others measure movement at the consumer level using consumer panels.

Two of the better-known organizations specializing in continuing research are the Market Research Corp. of America (MRCA) and A. C. Nielsen Co. The MRCA maintains a consumer panel of about 7,500 families located throughout the United

Figure 5–2
Sources of data

Primary data sources	Secondary data sources

Surveys—Mail
   telephone
   personal interviews
Market tests
Panels
Observation—Personal
   mechanical
	Company files
	Libraries
	Governments
	Private research organizations
	Trade associations
	University business research bureaus

States. These families are expected to record, in diaries, all of the food and drug items, plus selected other items purchased each week. They list not only the item itself, but the price paid and the store from which it was purchased. This panel is used by many large food and drug manufacturers to obtain a measure of the rate of consumption of their products at the consumer level.

Similar reports are provided by A. C. Nielsen—well known for the radio and television "Nielsen ratings"—which audits about 1,600 retail food and drug stores to measure movement at the retail level. The two services ought to provide roughly the same measure of movement of products at the consumer level. The Nielsen study, however, provides additional information about retail displays, tie-in sales, and other activities. For this reason, some large companies subscribe to both services. They find out more about the activity and sales of their smaller competitors than some of these competitors know about themselves.

Problem solving during the situation analysis

If the problem is clear-cut, it can sometimes be solved at this point—without additional expense. Perhaps someone else already has done a study that answers almost exactly the same question.

The fact that further research *may* be reduced or eliminated is important. Too often, researchers rush out a questionnaire to 100 or even several thousand persons or firms. This gives the impression that the researcher is "really doing something." An effective situation analysis, unfortunately, usually is less impressive. If a supervisor asks the researcher what he is doing, about all he can say is, "I'm sizing up the situation" or "I'm studying the problem."

Actually, the situation analyst is really trying to determine the exact nature of the situation—and the problem. The person who rushes out all the questionnaires may be doing this too—although this fact may surprise him! The point is that when the results of the questionnaire come in, he may finally see the problem—but he still won't have the answer. He will still have to go to the next step in analysis—just like the more "scientific" researcher.

INFORMAL INVESTIGATION—STEP THREE

During the informal investigation, the researcher is still trying to define the problem and develop hypotheses. But now the idea is to get outside the company and the library—and to talk to informed people. By informed people, we mean intelligent and efficient retailers, wholesalers, customers, and other knowledgeable people in the industry. No formal questionnaire is used—because the researcher is not yet *testing* hypotheses—except intuitively.

When developing new machine tool products, for example, it would make sense to talk to a few machine operators, plant superintendents in more efficient factories, design engineers at independent research organizations or universities, and perhaps a few good wholesalers who have close contact with potential customers.

Fast, informative, inexpensive

While these talks would be informal, they should help the researcher narrow down the problem and hypotheses. This is important—because asking informed

Informed people can help a researcher identify and clarify problems.

Mike Jaeggi

people to discuss *general* problems won't be productive. Only specific questions will obtain specific answers.

The virtues of the informal investigation are that it takes little time and can be very informative. Moreover, it is inexpensive compared with a large-scale survey.

On the basis of the information gathered in a situation analysis and informal investigation, the researcher should now be developing some specific hypotheses. Or he may be able to refine the hypotheses at this point—solving the problem without further research. This is especially likely in industrial goods markets—where the number of customers is limited and buying behavior is fairly predictable. Here, the views of a few well-informed people may be representative of the industry.

If management has to make a decision quickly—if it can't wait for a formal test—then well-considered hypotheses may lead to a practical solution. Sometimes, speed is more important than precision. In such cases, care in the early steps may bear fruit far beyond the extra time and effort spent there.

PLANNING THE FORMAL RESEARCH PROJECT—STEP FOUR

Gathering primary data

If the researcher has failed to solve the problem by this time, the next step is to plan a formal research project to gather primary data. Three basic methods can be used: (1) the observation method, (2) the survey method, or (3) the experimental method.

Each method has its uses. But unless the problem is complex, only one method would be used in a project. It is the researcher's job to choose which method is best—depending on the problem—as well as the time, funds, facilities, and people available.

The **observation method** involves observing potential customers' behavior.

This method avoids face-to-face interviews—because asking direct questions may not get very good results. Sometimes, however, asking questions can't be avoided. Then, the survey method—which asks people questions—may be helpful. Telephone, mail, or personal interviews can be used for surveys. The experimental method uses experiments to test hypotheses. Either the observation method or the survey method—or both—could be used. But usually control groups are needed.

Observation method

In pinpointing the problem, we have been using observation—asking ourselves what is happening inside and outside the firm. When planning a research project, it is logical to continue using observation. This differs from the earlier type of observation, however, in that it focuses on a well-defined problem rather than on broad activity.

Here the researcher avoids talking to the subjects. If a retailer or a bread manufacturer were interested in bread-buying behavior in supermarkets, for example, he could station someone at the bread counter to observe what takes place. The observer could gather information about the length of deliberation, the choice of a brand, the amount of label reading that takes place, or the extent of multiple purchases.

In some situations, movies are taken of consumers under varying situations. Then their behavior can be analyzed carefully by running the films at very slow speeds—or actually analyzing each frame. This might be useful, for example, in studying product selection in a supermarket or department store.

Mary McCarthy

Or if a supermarket operator were interested in the distance customers traveled to his store, he could take down license numbers in the parking lot. The addresses of all license holders could be obtained at the state license bureau and plotted on a map—the density of the dots would show where the traffic was coming from. Further, if a shopping center were being considered for a particular corner, the traffic flowing by this location could be counted to measure potential.

A device, the "Audimeter," permits adaptation of the observation method to radio and television audience research. This machine is attached to the radio and/or the TV set in the homes of selected families, and records when the set is on and what station is turned on. This method is used by the A. C. Nielsen Co., and the results are widely used for popularity ratings. It is claimed that once families get used to the meter, their behavior is no longer influenced by its presence. This method does not "observe" whether anyone is listening or viewing, however. Also the sample sizes normally used may not be adequate to yield the precise ratings users would like. This is basically a matter of economics, however. If users want more accurate ratings, more families will have to be audited—and this may make the information too costly.

The distinguishing characteristics of the observation method are that (1) no one is directly questioned, as in the survey method, and (2) no formal plan is developed to give consumers alternatives or obstacles which might require them to change their normal behavior—as in the experimental method.

Survey method

Surveys are used when the researchers feel that they must talk directly to someone to solve their problems. Sometimes surveys are used for testing hypotheses—but they may also be just exploratory efforts, to evaluate the situation before doing more research. Such an exploratory survey might provide the background data which in another case would already have been located during the situation analysis.

There are basically three types of surveys: telephone, mail, and personal interview. Each has its advantages and disadvantages.

Telephone surveys

Telephone interviews are effective for getting quick answers to short, simple questions—especially when it isn't important to identify the respondent or to know any of the characteristics of the person or family. If consumer characteristics—such as age, income, condition of personal belongings, household furnishings, or family composition—have a bearing on the analysis, then another survey method may be more appropriate.

Telephone interviewing is relatively low in cost and is satisfactory where the researcher is primarily interested in people who are likely to own telephones. In some areas, however, 10 to 20 percent of the families do not have telephones—and excluding them may lead to bias in the results.

Mail surveys

The mail questionnaire is useful when extensive questioning is necessary. This is especially true if potential respondents are widely scattered. With the mail questionnaire, the person can take all the time he wishes to complete the questions—and may be more willing to fill in personal or family characteristics. Unfortunately, the response rate on mail questionnaires is not very high—unless there is extensive follow-up or the questionnaire is especially interesting. Only 1 to 10 percent may respond—and the respondents may not be at all representative. Those who respond may be entirely different kinds of people than those who do not—and the results could be very misleading.

Mail questionnaires are inexpensive—per interview—if a large number of people respond. Conversely, they may be quite expensive if the response rate is poor—as it typically is—or if extensive follow-up is required. With mail questionnaires, moreover, it is difficult to probe for additional answers—or to encourage respondents to expand on particular points.

Personal interview surveys

The personal interview is often used because many people would rather talk than write. A personal interview survey may be more expensive per interview than a mail or telephone survey—but it offers the interviewers a chance to probe deeply on certain questions.

It also allows the interviewer to follow new lines of thought which might not have been anticipated earlier. New hypotheses or even new problems might be uncovered in the personal interviews. There is a chance to judge socio-economic characteristics from observation—and to follow up people who are not at home the first time or those who would not ordinarily answer mail questionnaires. In this sense, the researcher has greater control over his sample—and the results of a personal interview survey may be much more "representative."

*Personal interview surveys are more
expensive but they can get more
information because of interviewer
flexibility and people's willingness to
talk.*

Peter Le Grand

An extension of personal interviews is the **focus group interview**—which involves interviewing a group of people rather than one at a time. The purpose is to get group interaction—to stimulate thinking and get immediate reaction—perhaps expanding an idea or rejecting it in favor of another, and so on. This approach can be useful early in a research effort—to check hypotheses or just to find out how consumers think about a product or a market—what dimensions they talk about, or what's bothering them. These are informal sessions—but trained interviewers can get a lot of valuable information out of this approach. It helps to have specific questions and hypotheses in mind to guide the discussion. But an open mind helps pick up new ideas and potential hypotheses.

*Validity and reliability
of surveys*

When considering whether to use a survey—and in particular which type of survey—it is necessary to consider both the validity and reliability of the proposed survey. Really, these matters should be considered when doing any research—including observation and experimental research.

Validity

Validity is concerned with whether the research actually measures what it intends to. One sure way to get invalid findings is to ask consumers something they don't know. Although they don't know—and may not even know that they don't know—most respondents are obliging and will give answers.

Consumers think only in terms of what they are acquainted with. If in the 1880s you had asked a consumer what improvements should be made in lighting, he might have suggested a longer wick or a lamp that did not smoke. He was acquainted with the kerosene lamp and could not have been expected to say he wanted an electric light—because he had never heard of it.[1]

Sometimes it is even a question whether a survey measures anything at all. In one survey, the researcher wanted to get some direction for his company's activities. After a great deal of effort, an eight-page questionnaire was sent to the company's *present list of customers*. They were, in effect, asked what other lines of business the company ought to go into. Many of them tried to answer— but the answers were not too helpful—as they were not familiar with the company's resources or alternate target markets. Finally—after several months of work— the research project was dropped.

In evaluating the validity of surveys—really, all research—the research user should continually question: (1) whether the data was obtained from an informed source, and (2) whether the problem has been answered with this data.

Reliability

Reliability is concerned with the representativeness of the data. For most commercial research, it is economically and physically impossible to survey the total population. If the total population includes all retail stores, then only some of them may be used. If the population were all college students, then only some of them would be chosen. These are *samples*. The representativeness of the sample affects the reliability of the research results.

When only a small fraction of the relevant population is interviewed or observed, the results *may be* biased—because some members of the population may not be represented in the data. *May be* is emphasized because a small but carefully designed sample may provide a very close representation of the total population.

If a sample is chosen in a random manner from a population, this sample will *tend to* have the same characteristics and be representative of the population. *Tend to* is important because it is *only* a tendency. The possible deviation of sample results can be predicted by sampling theory, *if* some random sampling technique has been used.

Sampling technique, then, is of great importance. While the theory of sample design is beyond the scope of this text, in practice the marketing manager ought to know enough about sampling theory to recognize if a sample has been drawn in some specified random manner—and therefore whether it is possible to determine the reliability of the sample results.

"Random" does not mean that the sampling procedure is free from "rigging" or "fixing." Rather, a **random sample** is one in which some very specific statistical techniques have been used to ensure that all members of the population have a chance of being included in the sample.

One researcher might, for example, estimate the behavior of all people in a city by basing his conclusions on the responses of those who went through the railroad station—or those who were shopping downtown on a particular day. But it is clear that not everyone had a chance of being included in this sample. Many persons would be working or at home taking care of children. This is obvious, but many samples are still designed in this manner. During the 1930s and early 1940s, this was accepted practice.

If a random sampling technique has been used in designing the sample, then methods are available for stating the degree of reliability of the data obtained. These statements are in terms of **confidence intervals**—the range on either side of an estimate which is likely to contain the "true value" with some percent of certainty (which depends on the size of the sample). For example, if a sample of 100 were taken (using a strictly random sample), and it were found that 10 percent of the population preferred a new cake mix, the following statement could be made (with 95 percent certainty): The true percent preferring the new mix is between 4 and 16 percent of the population.

If this range of accuracy is not good enough for management action, then a larger sample should be used to narrow the confidence interval. If a sample size of 1,000 were used, and the same 10 percent preference were obtained, then the confidence interval would be approximately 8 to 10 percent—instead of 4 to 16 percent.[2]

Reliability affects management's confidence

Statistical reliability and confidence intervals should be part of the planning of the formal research project. This can ensure that the final results will be stated with enough confidence to encourage action by the marketing manager. Usually, on the basis of the preliminary analysis, the researcher will understand the accuracy needed for action. He should use this knowledge in setting the sample size—rather than waiting until the results come in and then finding that no meaningful conclusions are possible.

When a nonrandom sampling method is used, it is impossible to measure the amount of sampling bias which may have been introduced. Technically, confidence intervals cannot be computed. It cannot be said that a large (or small) amount of bias has entered—or that the results may be statistically unreliable (or reliable). Nothing at all, in fact, can be said about the reliability of such a sample.

Even so, some researchers using nonrandom samples are inclined to imply a great deal. Much commercial research does use nonrandom sampling—because of the higher cost of selecting more reliable samples—and are subject to criticism on these grounds. But some researchers claim that such samples may give good results. This may be true in certain cases—especially in the industrial area where the total number of customers may be relatively small—but such research must be used with care.

A brief example will illustrate the importance of using a carefully designed sample. Suppose a researcher wants to find out how many readers Magazine X and Magazine Y have. He knows something about the distribution of income of the population (from Census data), and makes the assumption that income has something to do with the purchase of X and Y. Assume further that there are only 40 people in the whole population and that he takes a sample of 20 to ask how many read each of the magazines. The answer he gets may depend on how the 20 are chosen.

If an interviewer sets out to talk to *any* 20 persons he chooses out of the 40, it seems likely that he would talk to the extroverts because they would be more easily approachable. Given the extrovert distribution in Table 5–2, 14 of the 20 would read Y and 6 would read neither X nor Y.

We would conclude that 70 percent of the population read magazine Y and 0 percent read magazine X. This result—it might be claimed—was based on a "representative" sample.

In the table, however, it can be seen that 14 of the 40—all the extroverts—

Table 5–2
Readership distribution in total population of 40

Income per week	Introverts	Extroverts
$1000	XXXXX	YYYYY
700	XXXXO	OYYYY
300	XXXOO	OOYYY
100	XXOOO	OOOYY

X indicates reader of X magazine.
Y indicates reader of Y magazine.
O indicates reader of neither magazine.

Source: Adapted from Robert Ferber, *Statistical Techniques in Marketing Research* (New York: McGraw-Hill Book Co., Inc., 1949), pp. 221–22.

read magazine Y, while 14—all the introverts—read magazine X, and 12 persons read neither of the magazines. Thus the sample results are completely in error. In real research, of course, it is not possible to check as we have done here, and the errors of this kind of sampling procedure may be hidden.[3]

It is important that both factors—validity and reliability—be considered in evaluating research. One study may be extremely valid—but of questionable reliability—whereas another study—using precise statistical techniques—may have only pseudo accuracy because of lack of validity. Either might lead to expensive mistakes.

Selecting the general approach to a survey

When developing a survey, there are two extremes which can be used—the quantitative or the qualitative approach.

Quantitative approach

Here the researcher asks how many persons do certain things, how many products are purchased in certain quantities, and so on. Simple "yes or no" or multiple-choice questions often are used. This approach is characterized by rather large—and perhaps statistically reliable—samples varying from several hundred to several thousand respondents. If the solution of a problem requires quantitative data, this approach can provide it. It also is used for "keeping tabs" on the market, as discussed below.

Much care should be used in writing questionnaires—to simplify tabulating the replies. Questions should also simplify the interviewing—since it usually is done by part-time interviewers with varying degrees of training. These questionnaires usually emphasize yes-no or true-false questions—or simple estimates of quantities used. Neither is likely to be confusing to either the respondent or the interviewer.

For some purposes, this approach may be useful. By keeping up-to-date on what the consumer is doing and thinking, management may be able to spot a trend or develop some hypotheses which can be tested by a specific research project. Some large companies maintain their own panels to keep "tabs" on consumers—while others take periodic surveys. Both help tell what, when, and where consumers are buying products.[4]

Keeping up with current activity is especially important for consumer goods—because of the time lag between purchases by consumers at the retail level

Researchers should write questionnaires to make them easier to complete and analyze.

Peter Le Grand

and the restocking of the product by the retailer through the wholesaler and then restocking by the wholesaler from the manufacturer. The time lag may be three to six months. If consumer demand falls off drastically, the manufacturer may be embarrassed with a large stock of goods which he has produced in anticipation of continued consumer purchases.

An outstanding example of what can happen was the introduction of whole canned chickens by the George A. Hormel Co. The product was introduced experimentally and was welcomed by wholesalers, retailers, and consumers alike. Everyone was buying, and employment at the factory increased markedly. In fact, many people left other jobs to go to work in Hormel's factory.

Then consumer buying slowed down. Consumers tried the product once or twice and found it satisfactory for emergency purposes, such as when unexpected company dropped in. They purchased one more can as insurance against such an occurrence—and then virtually stopped buying.

The retailers and wholesalers, however, were not immediately aware of this. Retailers continued buying until they were overstocked; wholesalers, in turn, continued buying from Hormel until they were overstocked. Finally Hormel found itself with the production line running full blast and practically no orders. Then the whole bubble burst—and many employees were laid off amid cries of "unfair treatment."[5]

Qualitative approach

The strictly quantitative approach is concerned with historical "facts"—with the what, where, and when—rather than the why. But when a researcher is interested in *what* customers are going to do *in the future* or *why* they did something in the past, then some kind of qualitative questions may be necessary.

Qualitative questions may be dangerous—and reduce research validity, however. Good judgment and careful design are vital in qualitative research—as the following case illustrates.

A researcher—trying to predict newsstand sales of pocket-size books six months before they were marketed—asked a group of people what titles they preferred. He got the usual answers—the Bible, Shakespeare, and so on. Then—at the end of the interview—he handed respondents a list of book titles. He said that he wanted to send them a free book for their cooperation. All they had to do was pick the title they wanted by number. Included in the list were pocket-sized editions of the Bible, Shakespeare, and other classics—as well as many of the titles which the company was considering. The favorite of respondents was *Murder of a Burlesque Queen!*[6]

The research moral is that when you ask someone a question, he may react to you or try to give you the answer he thinks you want. Given the list by this interviewer, however, he acted in his own self-interest and exposed his true preferences.

There has been enough evidence of this kind of consumer reaction in applied research to convince researchers that special techniques are necessary when trying to determine consumers' real attitudes—and needs and preferences.

Motivation research—a qualitative tool

Motivation research applies the clinical-type methods of the psychologist and sociologist to qualitative questions. Rather than using large samples, the motivation researcher works with relatively small samples—perhaps only 25 to 50 persons. And instead of one, two, or five-minute interviews, depth interviews taking one or two hours may be used.

In this situation, the interviewer attempts to get into the respondent's subconscious mind. The purpose is to find the basic needs and drives of this person—and how they affect the particular problem involved. Specially trained interviewers are required. It appears that the results obtained are, in part, related to the experience, training, and judgment of the person analyzing the data—as well as the answers of the individual respondents.

There is little or no possibility of quantifying the answers—or developing an objective measure of the results of this approach. This is an important criticism, because the results seem to depend so heavily on the training of the research worker and his own point of view. This adds complications—since one study identified 39 different psychological schools of thought on human behavior.[7] Yet only one group—Freudians—have been prominent in motivation research.

To illustrate these complications, two of the top motivation research agencies in the country were hired independently by two different groups interested in why consumers bought so few prunes.

One agency interviewed a sample cross-section of Americans and presented a 52-page report explaining why people dislike prunes—they were "dried-out, worn-out symbols of old age; the prune fails to give security; it is a plebeian food without prestige; and the prune is a witch." Based on these findings it was suggested that the California Prune Advisory Board "rename them black diamonds; surround prunes with an aura of preciousness and desirability; and take prunes out of the fruit family and put them in the same context as nuts."

At the same time, the other research agency presented a 61-page report which concluded that Americans have no emotional block about the prune's "laxative connotation." On the basis of this finding, the researcher suggested that they "exploit the core of the prune market by advertising the laxative features—and don't pussyfoot about this angle, either."

If only one of these studies had been made, then the prune producers would have had little difficulty in following the advice. But when two studies come up with such conflicting advice, there would seem to be reason to question the procedures.[8] Perhaps the results could be used in aiming at different target markets, but with the small samples used in this type of research it would be difficult to determine which specific markets had which views.

Interest in motivation research—especially the Freudian variety—is declining. As one researcher commented: "After all, Freud dealt with the abnormal personality, but the person we want to understand is the average consumer."[9]

Modified qualitative approach

Not all qualitative research is motivation research, however. Some motivation researchers have—in the interest of promoting their own techniques or agencies—tried to imply this. But any research which seeks "why" replies can be considered qualitative.

Some researchers have borrowed some of the more promising methods of the psychologist and sociologist—including some of the motivation research techniques—and "remodeled" them for use with traditional quantitative questionnaires. In this modified approach, respondents are given a better chance to express their attitudes.

Instead of giving respondents the choice of "Yes" of "no" on whether they plan to buy a product, for example, the researcher might allow five alternatives: "Definitely yes," "I am pretty sure," "I think so," "I do not think so," and "Definitely no." Or "open-end" questions seeking short, "free" answers may be used. Then the answers are classified for tabulation.

To encourage responses on such questions, cartoons with unfilled word-balloons may be used. The cartoon may show a situation such as a woman buying coffee in a supermarket. The respondent may be asked to fill in the balloon—explaining what the woman is saying to her friend. Or the balloon might be removed and the respondent might be asked to comment on her feelings about a woman, say, buying instant coffee. Then these responses would be classified and tabulated.

Surfacing approach

Some researchers make effective use of qualitative techniques—such as focus group interviews—as preparation for more quantitative studies. The qualitative research may suggest hypotheses which then can be tested.

The name, "surfacing approach" has been given to this method of using several different techniques—each one less and less subjective—until the final effort is fairly objective. As its name implies, it means beginning at the subconscious level (pure motivation research) and working closer and closer toward the surface of consciousness.[10]

Qualitative techniques, for example, might suggest that consumers would prefer real fruit flavor to artificial flavoring in a fruit dessert being designed to compete with Jello gelatin dessert. Then a quantitative approach might put the identical product in each of two packages—marked to show that one product was made with pure fruit flavor while the other was made with artificial flavoring. If consumers showed a strong preference for one or the other product—after using it—there would be a quantitative measure of the importance of this claim—and the company could consider this in the development of the product and its promotion.

The appeal of the surfacing approach is that the strictly qualitative techniques provide ideas—while the quantitative techniques provide "harder" measurements which give marketing managers more confidence in taking action.

Most marketers feel that both qualitative and quantitative research have their place.

Experimental method

The observation method avoids approaching the customer—while the survey method relies upon direct interview. The experimental method uses either or both of these methods.

The major difference—as the name implies—is that experiments are set up. Statistical controls may be used in a market test—so that random variations can be factored out by statistical analysis. Or mathematical models—perhaps using computers—can simulate customer behavior or total marketing system behavior.

While we don't have room here for a detailed discussion of these techniques, you should be aware that they are becoming increasingly important in marketing research. This emphasizes again the growing sophistication of marketing management and the challenge this career offers.[11]

The experimental method is often used in traditional sales and use tests. In a sales test, for example, a new product might be tried in one store, city, state, or region—while the marketing mix was held constant elsewhere. If a sales change takes place in all territories, only the net change in the trial territory will be attributed to the new factor. This method has been used by retailers to test packaging, displays, pricing, promotion plans, new products, and store equipment.

By this method, a bread manufacturer or retailer could check the importance of positions in different stores. Some bread deliverymen on commission have done this on their own. They have found that a front position increases sales so much that they have been known to pay a store clerk—out of their own pocket—to come to the bread display occasionally and move their company's bread to the front.

In other situations, use tests may be developed. Potential customers are given the same or different products in different packages. Then their response is analyzed using various statistical techniques.

Another method is to have a representative group of consumers play experimental "games" in which various products, prices, or other alternatives are offered in turn. This is not fully realistic, but some interesting and encouraging results have been obtained.[12]

The experimental method is not used much at the present time for three reasons. First, it takes time, when most marketing decisions must be made quickly. Second, it may be more costly. And third, many marketing researchers have

For the best and fastest results, the marketing manager and research manager should work together.

H. Armstrong Roberts

not had the statistical and mathematical training needed to conduct such tests effectively. This latter factor is being overcome rapidly—and this type research may become more common as more skilled researchers are trained and enter the field.

Managers should share in research design

The mechanics of designing research projects are beyond the scope of this text—but they are extremely important to the final results. Therefore, marketing managers should be involved in the process. At least, they should be familiar with some of the design details—so they can evaluate the validity and reliability of the research and be confident that the results will have action implications.

Some researchers imply a great deal about the reliability of their research methods. But they may be using samples which are not representative, yet try to pass off the results as reliable. A marketer should not be deceived by such sloppy work. He should understand that technical matters—such as research design and the size and representativeness of samples—do have relevance for the validity and reliability of the results.

EXECUTION AND INTERPRETATION OF THE RESEARCH PROJECT

How to conduct and interpret a formal research project involves training a field staff, tabulating, interpreting, and presenting results—as well as following through to make sure results are used effectively. We cannot treat this in detail here. Such matters are explained in most *marketing research* texts.[13]

Marketing manager and researcher should work together

Conducting and interpreting a research project involves some technical details. But it should be obvious that the marketing researcher and the marketing manager should have a close working relationship—to be sure that they really do solve the problems facing the firm.[14] If the whole research process has been a joint effort, then the interpretation step can move quickly into decision making.

When the researcher and the manager have not cooperated, the interpretation step becomes more important. While managers may not be research specialists, they have to evaluate research results. And the interpretation and presentation of the final results can be a clue to the quality of the research—and its planning. If a report does not have action applications, for example, it may have little value to management—and suggests poor planning by the researcher.

Further, if the research method and the reliability of the data are not clearly explained, the marketing manager must use even greater judgment in evaluating the data. In fact, if the researcher does not explain his methods—and then suggest specific action—he should not be surprised if the marketing manager ignores the work. Unfortunately, this happens far too often—and emphasizes the importance of the two working together to solve problems.

REAL PROBLEM SOLVING MAY REQUIRE ALL FOUR STEPS

Logical flow of steps may help

Marketing research usually must combine several steps to do an effective job. This is shown by an example of a company interested in expanding its market for interior decorating products.

The company wanted to increase its sales—but did not know how many interior decorators were in their market or how much money consumers spent on the company's product type *(definition of the problem)*. A review of U.S. *Census of Business* data showed that there were approximately 1,300 interior decorators. According to their own sales records *(situation analysis)* this would not leave much room for expansion with their present line. Management decided, tentatively, to branch out into other lines *(hypothesis*—that business would improve in another market).

Before going in this direction, the company decided to do more research in its present market. They interviewed the company's sales reps, checked the circulation data of an interior decorators' magazine (more *situation analysis*), talked with informed credit people *(informal investigation),* and made a limited mail survey to check on the size of the market (a *formal research project* to test an hypothesis that there were more potential customers).

This research revealed that there were actually 9,700 interior decorators who spent some $75 million on the company's type of product alone. For some reason—probably their small size—the decorators had not all been included in the published census data. it was clear at this point that the company's biggest and best market was the one which they were already selling.

In this case, no research at all—or a sketchy situation analysis—would have led to incorrect results. But further analysis—along with an informal investigation and a limited survey—got results that proved very satisfactory.[15] This type of research is within the reach of even small firms. You should now be able to understand and help in such an effort.

COST AND ORGANIZATION OF MARKETING RESEARCH

Relatively little—perhaps too little—is spent on the typical marketing research department. Often the research department's budget is about 0.2 percent of sales—or $100,000 for a company with a $50 million annual sales volume.[16] This is in contrast to research and development budgets that often run to 5 or 10 percent of sales. Unfortunately, this situation sometimes leads to developing products with little or no market potential.

Shortcuts cut cost, add risk

Even on modest budgets, however, good research can be done.[17] When a problem is carefully defined, formal research projects may *not* be necessary. This is especially true in industrial marketing research—because of the relatively small number of industrial customers. But taking shortcuts increases the risk.

Dependable research can become expensive. A large-scale survey could easily cost from $10,000 to $100,000—and the continuing research available from companies such as A. C. Nielsen can cost a company from $25,000 to $100,000 or more a year. And a market test for 6–12 months may cost $100,000 to $300,000 per test market. But companies willing and able to pay the cost of *marketing* research may learn more about their competitors and their market than the competitors know themselves.

Who does the work?

Most larger companies have a separate marketing research department to plan and conduct research projects. These departments often use outside specialists—such as interviewing or tabulating services—to handle particular assignments. This points up, again, the importance of good research planning—because when part of the research job is sent out, it must be accurately described. Further, specialized marketing consultants and marketing research organizations may be called in on more difficult problems—or in "frontier" research areas.

Few companies with sales of less than $2.5 million have separate marketing research departments—relying instead on salespeople or top managers for what research they do.[18]

HOW MUCH RESEARCH SHOULD BE DONE?

No firm can afford to do without marketing research

Most companies do some marketing research—even if it is not called by that name. Most marketers would agree with the manager of marketing research for Dow Chemical Co., who states:

> I feel that it is impossible to run a company today without market research, whether it is done by the president, the sales manager, or a separate group set up specifically to perform the function. Few companies are small enough to afford the luxury of having their market research done by the president. No company can afford not to do market research at all.[19]

What is the value of information?

The high cost of good research must be balanced against its probable value to management. You never get all the information you would like to have. Very sophisticated surveys or experiments may be "too good" or "too expensive" or "too late"—if all that is needed is a rough sampling of retailer attitudes toward a new pricing plan *by tomorrow.* Further, no matter how good the research was, the findings are always out of date—because "past" behavior was studied. It's the decision maker's job to evaluate—beforehand—whether research findings will still be relevant.

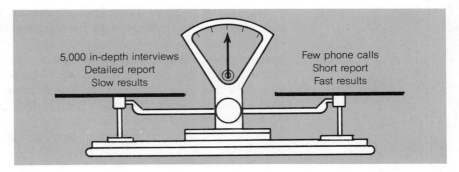

Researchers must try to balance the cost and value of more information.

5,000 in-depth interviews
Detailed report
Slow results

Few phone calls
Short report
Fast results

Marketing managers must take risks because of incomplete information. That is part of their job—and always will be. They might like more data—but they must weigh the cost of getting it against its likely value. If the risk is not too great, the cost of getting more information may be greater than the potential loss from a poor decision. A decision to expand into a new territory with the present marketing mix, for example, might be made with greater confidence after a $5,000 survey. But simply sending a sales rep into the territory for a few weeks to try to sell the potential customers would cost less than $5,000—and if successful, the answer is in *and* so are some sales.

Faced with a continuous flow of risky decisions, the marketing manager should only seek help from research for problems where he feels the risk can be greatly reduced at a reasonable cost.[20]

SOME FIRMS ARE BUILDING MARKETING INFORMATION SYSTEMS

In some companies, marketing researchers enjoy high status—and are deeply involved in major marketing decisions. In other companies, they tend to be only data collectors. They may analyze the company's sales, and sales call reports—or they may conduct special surveys to answer pressing problems. But they have not sold the idea that ongoing *information* (not just data) will improve decision making. Some may not even understand the difference between "one-shot" surveys to answer specific questions and developing a *continual flow of information* to help marketing managers make better decisions. Because of this, in some companies, marketing managers make decisions based almost totally on their own judgment—with very little hard information—even though much data is or could be made readily available.

Separate department may be needed

Some companies are setting up marketing information systems to improve the quality and quantity of information available to their managers. A **marketing information system (MIS)** is an organized way of continually gathering and analyzing data to get information that will help marketing managers make decisions. Sometimes this means expanding the job of the marketing research department. In other companies, this information function is separated into a new department. Management wants to make sure that this function does not get "lost" in the present activities of the marketing research department.

The need for a marketing information system (MIS) grows out of the recognition that most firms can generate more market-related data than they can possibly digest and turn into useful information. Computers can now print much faster than anyone can read. Some way must be found to convert raw data into information. Fortunately, one can build up to a MIS in stages. The sales and cost analysis techniques discussed in Chapter 22 are illustrations of relatively easy kinds of analysis that can be done. Going further, careful analysis of this data—perhaps using simulations and experiments—can help the managers develop greater insights into the relation of marketing inputs to outputs. This will improve their planning.

Information may make managers greedy

Once marketing managers see how a functioning MIS can help their decision making, they are eager for more information. They see that they can improve all aspects of their planning—blending individual Ps, combining four Ps into mixes, and developing and selecting plans. Further, they can monitor the implementing of ongoing plans—comparing results against plans and making necessary changes more quickly. Figure 5–3 shows all the interacting parts in an MIS—showing that it really is an information *system* intended to help managers make better decisions—not just to collect and massage data.

We probably will see more marketing information systems—as researchers become more experienced and computer costs continue to decline. The major obstacle may be the reluctance of marketing managers to ask for more useful information—and to use it in their decision making. Unfortunately, modern decision-making techniques haven't been used very much in most companies. There is still lots of room in marketing for able students willing to apply advanced techniques to solving real marketing problems.[21]

CONCLUSION

In this chapter, we have seen that marketing research is not a mysterious cult practiced by statisticians. In the best sense, it is a management tool that helps the marketing manager make better decisions—based not on feel and intuition, but on useful information. The manager should understand research procedures—and the researcher should understand management's problems of planning, implementing, and controlling marketing strategies. Without such close cooperation, the output of a marketing research department may be useless—and the department may become just a collector of data.

Marketing researchers should apply the scientific method to the solution of marketing problems. Some organized approach is needed—because very often a researcher does not have the time or money to complete a whole research project. If the early stages of the research effort have been effectively done, he may be able to "jump" to a solution early in the process. A scientific approach to solving marketing problems involves four steps: definition of the problem, a situation analysis, an informal investigation, and, if necessary, a formal research project.

Definition of the problem is obviously the most crucial step—because even good research on the wrong problem would be of no use. Then, a good situation

Figure 5–3
A diagram of a marketing information system showing various inputs to a computer and outputs to managers

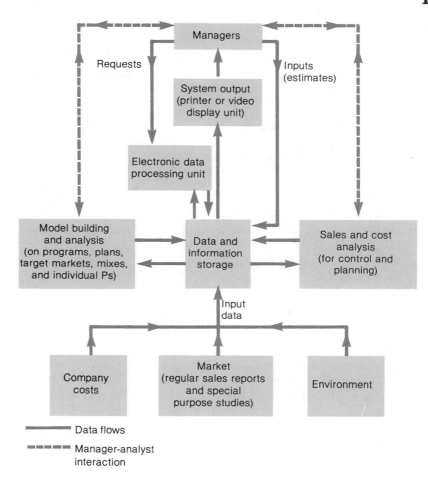

analysis—using secondary data—may help the researcher to solve the problem without going on to further steps in the analysis.

An informal investigation—like a situation analysis—may let a researcher solve the problem. This step requires informal interviewing of informed people. This moving up on the problem should be stressed—because there is more to marketing research than surveys. Yet surveys often are seen as the *only* activity of marketing research by outsiders. Surveys can provide helpful information, but there are many times when other methods provide better information—at the same or lower cost.

As part of a formal research design, surveys might be needed—or the observation or experimental methods may be used. Great care must be taken in research design and execution—because these are technical subjects. It is very easy to make errors which will reduce the validity and/or reliability of the results.

Our strategic planning framework can be a great help in finding the real problem. By focusing on the real problem, the researcher may be able to move quickly to a useful solution—without the cost and risks of a formal research project. If the firm has more time and an adequate budget, it may be able to enjoy the luxury of more detailed and more sophisticated analysis. Some firms have even developed marketing information systems—which help them make better decisions.

QUESTIONS AND PROBLEMS

1. Marketing research entails expense—sometimes a considerable expense. Why does the text recommend the use of marketing research even though a highly experienced marketing executive is available?

2. Explain the steps in the general scientific method and then show how the steps in marketing research are similar.

3. How is the situation analysis any different from the informal investigation? Could both these steps be done at the same time to obtain answers sooner? Is this wise?

4. Explain how you might use each of the research methods (observation, survey, and experiment) to forecast market reaction to a new kind of margarine which is to receive no promotion other than what the retailer will give it. Further, it should be assumed that the new margarine's name will not be associated with other known products. The product will be offered at competitive prices.

5. Distinguish between primary data and secondary data, illustrating your answer.

6. If a firm were interested in determining the distribution of income in the state of Ohio, how could it proceed? Be specific.

7. If a firm were interested in sand and clay production in Georgia, how could it proceed? Be specific.

8. Go to the library and find (in some government publication) three marketing-oriented "facts" which you did not know existed or were available. Record on one page and show sources.

9. Distinguish between reliability and validity (of research)—illustrating your answer.

10. Distinguish betweeen qualitative and quantitative approaches to surveys.

11. Discuss the concept that some information may be too expensive to obtain in relation to its value. Illustrate.

12. Discuss the concept of a marketing information system and how its output would differ from the output of the typical marketing research department.

13. Discuss what will be needed before marketing information systems become common. Also, discuss the problem facing the marketer in a small firm which is not likely to be able to afford the development of a marketing information system.

SUGGESTED CASES

4 Redi, Incorporated

6 The Capri

7 Sleep-Inn Motel

NOTES

1. "Finding Out What Consumers Will Buy," *Steel,* July 14, 1958, p. 106.

2. Detailed treatment of confidence intervals is beyond the scope of this text and can be found in any introductory statistics book. Just to refresh memories for those who have had statistics, however, the formula used here for a 95 percent certainty confidence interval is: $P \pm 2 \sqrt{\frac{p \times q}{n}}$. p is the percent result; q is $100 - p$; and n is the sample size. For the 10 percent preference this yields: $10 \pm 2 \times \sqrt{(10 \times 90) \div n}$. Obviously increasing n will decrease the confidence interval, as stated.

3. Robert Ferber, *Statistical Techniques in Marketing Research* (New York: McGraw-Hill Book Co., Inc., 1949), pp. 221–22.

4. "Good listener: At Procter & Gamble Success Is Largely Due to Heeding Consumer," *The Wall Street Journal,* April 29, 1980, pp. 1–2.

5. *The Hormel Annual Wage* (Austin, Minn.: Geo. A. Hormel & Co., undated), pp. 1–2.

6. "Don't Believe All That You Hear," *The Courier-Journal,* Louisville, Ky., May 26, 1957.

7. Wroe Alderson, *Marketing Behavior and Executive Action* (Homewood, Ill.: Richard D. Irwin, Inc., 1957), p. 189.

8. A good review of the arguments on both sides and the techniques involved can be found in Robert Ferber and Hugh Wales, eds., *Motivation and Market Behavior* (Homewood, Ill.: Richard D. Irwin, Inc., 1958).

9. "New Way to Size Up How Consumers Behave," *Business Week,* July 22, 1961, p. 74.

10. C. Joseph Clawson, "The Coming Breakthroughs in Motivation Research," *Cost and Profit Outlook* (Philadelphia: Alderson Associates, Inc., May–June 1958), p. 3.

11. *A Basic Bibliography on Marketing Research, No. 2,* and *Market Segmentation: A Selected and Annotated Bibliography, No. 28* (Chicago: American Marketing Association).

12. Alan G. Sawyer; Parker M. Worthing, and Paul E. Fendak, "The Role of Laboratory Experiments to Test Marketing Strategies," *Journal of Marketing,* Summer 1979, pp. 60–67.

13. Harper W. Boyd, Jr., Ralph Westfall, and Stanley F. Stasch, *Marketing Research: Texts and Cases,* 4th ed. (Homewood, Ill.: Richard D. Irwin, Inc., 1977).

14. J. G. Keane, "Some Observations on Marketing Research in Top Management Decision Making," *Journal of Marketing,* October 1969, pp. 10–15; B. A. Greenberg, Jac L. Goldstucker, and D. N. Bellenger, "What Techniques Are Used by Marketing Researchers in Business?" *Journal of Marketing,* April 1977, pp. 62–68; and R. J. Small and L. J. Rosenberg, "The Marketing Researcher as a Decision Maker: Myth or Reality?" *Journal of Marketing,* January 1975, pp. 2–7; and Danny N. Bellenger; "The Marketing Manager's View of Marketing Research," *Business Horizons,* June 1979, pp. 59–65.

15. Arthur P. Felton, "Conditions of Marketing Leadership," *Harvard Business Review,* March–April 1956, pp. 117–27.

16. "Scouting the Trail for Marketers," *Business Week,* April 18, 1964, pp. 90–116.

17. Donald F. Mulvihill, "Marketing Research for the Small Company," *Journal of Marketing,* October 1951, pp. 179–82.

18. *The Role and Organization of Marketing Research,* Experiences in Marketing Management, No. 20 (New York: National Industrial Conference Board, 1969), 65 pp.

19. William A. Marsteller, "Can You Afford a Market Research Department?" *Industrial Marketing,* March 1951, pp. 36–37; see also "Top Executives Keep Tabs on the Consumer—or Contend They Do." *The Wall Street Journal,* July 1, 1976, p. 1 f.

20. For more discussion, see P. E. Green and D. S. Tull, *Research for Marketing Decisions,* 2d ed. (Englewood Cliffs, N.J.: Prentice-Hall, Inc., 1970), chap. 1.

21. Richard H. Brien and James E. Stafford, "Marketing Information Systems: A New Dimension for Marketing Research," *Journal of Marketing,* July 1968, p. 21; David B. Montgomery and Charles B. Weinberg, "Toward Strategic Intelligence Systems," *Journal of Marketing,* Fall 1979, pp. 41–52; and "Market Research by Scanner," *Business Week,* May 5, 1980, pp. 113–116.

When you finish this chapter, you should:

1. Know about population and income trends.
2. Understand how population is growing—but at different rates for different age groups.
3. Know about the distribution of income.
4. Know how final consumer spending is related to population, income, family life cycle, and other variables.
5. Know how to estimate likely consumer purchases for broad classes of products.
6. Recognize the important new terms (shown in red).

6

Demographic Dimensions of the U.S. Consumer Market

Markets are people with money to spend to satisfy needs.

Target marketers believe that the *Customer* should be the focus of all business and marketing activity. These marketers hope to develop unique marketing strategies—by finding unsatisfied customers and offering them more attractive marketing mixes. They want to work in less competitive markets with more inelastic demand curves. Finding these attractive opportunities takes really knowing what makes potential customers tick. This means finding those market dimensions that make a difference—in terms of population, income, needs, attitudes, and buying behavior.

Three important questions should be answered about any potential market:

1. What are its relevant dimensions?
2. How big is it?
3. Where is it?

The first question—about relevant dimensions—is basic. Management judgment—perhaps aided by analysis of existing data and new findings from marketing research—is needed to pick the right dimensions.

To help build your judgment regarding buying behavior, this and the following two chapters will discuss what we know about various kinds of customers and their buying behavior. Keep in mind that we are not trying to make generalizations about "average customers" or how the "mass market" behaves—but rather how *some* people in *some* markets behave. You should expect to find differences.

We will begin with final consumer demographics because markets consist of *people* with *money* to spend to satisfy needs.

Figure 6–1

A. A New Yorker's eye view of the
United States

B. A Texan's eye view of the
United States

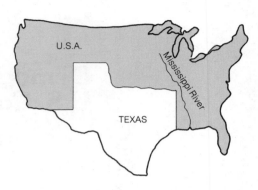

Forget the Texas or New York stereotypes

The marketing manager should not fall into the trap of accepting common stereotypes about the size or potential of various markets—such as those illustrated in one artist's version of a New Yorker's and a Texan's view of the United States (Figure 6–1). These may be humorous—but are of no real value to a marketer.

When valid data is available, there is no excuse for decisions based on such misconceptions—or regional propaganda. Try to see the data in the next few chapters in terms of selecting relevant dimensions—and estimating the potential in different market segments. Also, check your own assumptions against this data. Marketing decisions often must be made in a hurry—under pressure. Then, if you feel you really do know the relevant market dimensions, you may decide without even looking at the available data. Now is a good time to get the "facts" straight.

POPULATION—PEOPLE WITH MONEY MAKE MARKETS

Which states are bigger?

Table 6–1 shows the population by states for 1980. California as Number 1 should sober the New Yorker and the Texan—and explain why some marketers are going after the West Coast market. On the other hand, the heavy concentration of population in New York and nearby states—more than twice as populous as the whole West Coast—does lend some support to the New Yorker's view of the U.S. market. The population of Texas is large—but its supporters' views are based on area, not population—and now that Alaska is a state, Texas is no longer even the biggest state.

The map in Figure 6–2 emphasizes the concentration of population in different geographic regions. It shows the area of each state in proportion to its population. Notice the importance of the midwestern states and the southern states. These regions are often viewed as unique target markets by marketers anxious to avoid the extremely competitive East and West Coast markets. Note, too, the few people in the Plains and Mountain states—which explains why some "national" marketers pay less attention to these areas. Yet these states can provide an opportunity for an alert marketer looking for less competitive markets.

Where are the people today and tomorrow?

Population figures for a single year don't show the dynamic aspects of markets. The U.S. population has been growing continuously since the founding of the country—more than doubling in the 70 years from 1910 to 1980. But—and this is important to marketers—the population did *not* double everywhere. Some states have seen very rapid growth. Others have grown only a little—and at a slower rate.

California and the southwestern states, as well as Florida, have seen very rapid growth—while the Middle Atlantic and Plains states have grown more slowly. See the percent change column in Table 6–1.

Table 6–1.
Population by states, 1960 and 1980

State or other area	Population (000) 1960	Population (000) 1980	Percent change	State or other area	Population (000) 1960	Population (000) 1980	Percent change
United States	179,323	221,582	23.57	West North Central	15,394	17,247	12.04
New England	10,509	12,350	17.52	Minnesota	3,414	4,072	19.27
Maine	969	1,106	14.14	Iowa	2,758	2,924	6.02
New Hampshire	607	898	47.94	Missouri	4,320	4,899	13.40
Vermont	390	497	27.44	North Dakota	632	668	5.70
Massachusetts	5,149	5,788	12.41	South Dakota	681	702	3.08
Rhode Island	859	933	8.61	Nebraska	1,411	1,590	12.69
Connecticut	2,535	3,128	23.39	Kansas	2,179	2,391	9.73
Middle Atlantic	34,168	36,887	7.96	East South Central	12,050	14,229	18.08
New York	16,782	17,776	5.92	Kentucky	3,038	3,554	16.98
New Jersey	6,067	7,342	21.02	Tennessee	3,567	4,425	24.05
Pennsylvania	11,319	11,769	3.98	Alabama	3,267	3,815	16.77
South Atlantic	25,972	35,339	36.07	Mississippi	2,178	2,434	11.75
Delaware	446	587	31.61	West South Central	16,951	22,683	33.02
Maryland	3,101	4,183	34.89	Arkansas	1,786	2,222	24.41
D.C.	764	662	−13.35	Louisiana	3,257	4,028	23.67
Virginia	3,967	5,261	32.62	Oklahoma	2,328	2,971	27.62
West Virginia	1,860	1,885	1.34	Texas	9,580	13,462	40.52
North Carolina	4,556	5,670	24.45	Mountain	6,855	10,773	57.16
South Carolina	2,383	2,968	24.55	Montana	675	801	18.67
Georgia	3,943	5,166	31.02	Idaho	667	915	37.18
Florida	4,952	8,957	80.88	Wyoming	330	458	38.79
East North Central	36,225	41,419	14.34	Colorado	1,754	2,784	58.72
Ohio	9,706	10,812	11.40	New Mexico	951	1,248	31.23
Indiana	4,662	5,386	15.53	Arizona	1,302	2,496	91.71
Illinois	10,081	11,259	11.69	Utah	891	1,363	13.02
Michigan	7,823	9,223	17.90	Nevada	285	708	48.42
Wisconsin	3,952	4,739	19.91	Pacific	21,198	30,656	44.62
				Washington	2,853	3,911	37.08
				Oregon	1,769	2,535	43.30
				California	15,717	22,871	45.52
				Alaska	226	422	86.73
				Hawaii	633	918	45.02

Source: *Statistical Abstract of the United States, 1976.* for 1960 data. 1980 data estimates from "1980 Survey of Buying Power," *Sales & Marketing Management,* July 28, 1980.

Figure 6–2
Map showing each state's area in proportion to its 1980 population

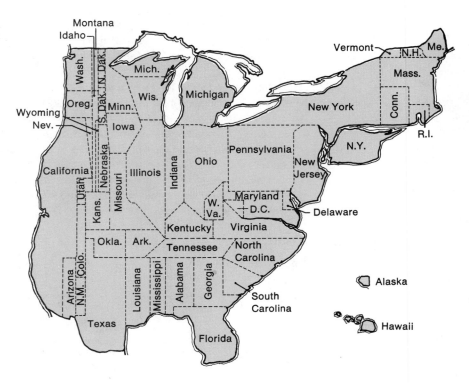

These different rates of growth are especially important to marketing. For example, sudden growth in one area may create a demand for many new shopping centers—while existing centers may be more than adequate in other areas. In fact, the introduction of new marketing facilities in slow-growing areas can create severe competitive problems for existing retailers. In other areas, however, demand may be growing so rapidly that even poorly planned facilities can be profitable.

Population will keep growing, but . . .

It seems certain that U.S. population will continue to grow—at least for another 50 years or more. The big questions are: "How much and how fast?"

Fertility rate has declined

The "baby boom" of the 1950s and 1960s turned into the "baby bust" of the 1970s. The fertility rate—number of children per woman—fell from a postwar high of 3.8 children per woman in 1957 to 1.8 in 1976—and then rose only to 2.0 in 1980. At the same time, however, people are living longer. So we can expect the total population to continue to grow. But there will be less need for baby food, toys, teachers, and child-oriented recreation.[1]

Average age will rise

Although population will continue to grow, a major transformation in our society may occur because the average age is going to continue to rise for many years.

The major reason is that the post–World War II baby boom—lasting roughly from 1947 to 1957—produced about 43 million children—or about one fifth of our present population. This large group crowded into the schools in the 1950s and 1960s—and then into the job market in the 1970s. By the 1980s and 1990s they will be swelling the middle-aged group. And early in the 21st century, they will reach retirement—still a dominant group in the total population. According to one population expert, "It's like a goat passing through a boa constrictor."

The twin impact of declining birthrates and the postwar babies moving through their life cycle can be seen in Figure 6–3. The median age will continue to rise with fewer young people and more older people. The figure shows that the traditional population triangle with many more young people at the bottom will turn into a rectangle—with all groups about the same size. This means smaller household units, with less need for big "family" homes and large "family size" packages of food—and more demand for small apartments, out-of-home entertainment, travel, and smaller packages of food.

Older people will want larger share of the resources

Eventually, America's "youth culture" will give way to a new kind of society.

Figure 6–3
An aging population

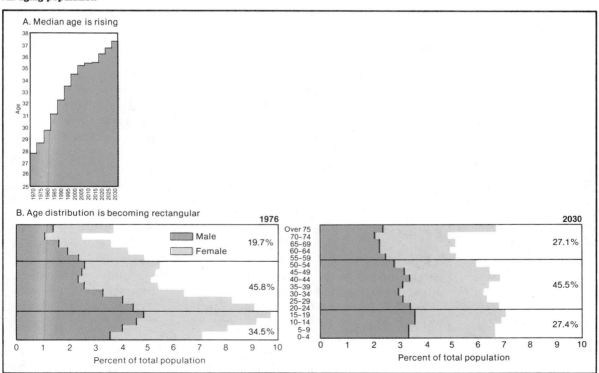

Source: Based on the U.S. Census and *Newsweek*, February 28, 1977, p. 52.

In fact, the aging of the population is seriously concerning some future thinkers—because it is possible that the younger people will not be able or willing to support all of the older people in the style they expect. Certainly the costs will continue to rise as there are relatively more retired people being supported by fewer young people. Already, the Social Security system is in trouble.

Fertility rate should be watched

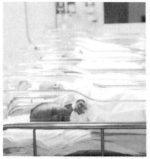

Mary McCarthy

Some of these population projections may be changed by new attitudes toward marriage, family size, and family planning—but others are fixed because the people are already born. These numbers can't be ignored by marketing managers—because the baby bust may continue. One reliable indicator of fertility trends—the number of children that potential mothers say they plan to have—fell from an average of 3.1 in 1967 to 2.4 in 1977, but the fertility rate did rise from 1977 to 1980. And there are so many potential mothers around that only a small increase in the fertility rate would lead to a large number of new babies. This could happen. Many women say they want to have a family—and have only postponed the decision.[2] So these figures should be watched carefully by marketers—because they obviously have an impact on future market sizes. For the present, however, it is clear that population will continue to grow—although not as fast as in the past—and most of this population expansion will be in already crowded metropolitan areas.

Household composition is changing

We often think of the "typical" American household as a married couple with two children and living in the suburbs. This never was true, and it is even less true now. Although almost all Americans marry, they are marrying later—delaying child bearing—and having fewer children. Couples with no children under 18 now account for almost half of all families. And couples do not stay together as long—or as much—as they used to. The United States has the highest divorce rate in the world—about 38 percent ending in divorce. Almost 80 percent of divorced people remarry—so we see a growing number of "his and hers" families. Still—even with all this shifting around—more than two thirds of all males and females are married.[3]

Nonfamily households are increasing

Once we get rid of the "couple with two children" stereotype of family life, we should also recognize that there are many households which are not families in the usual sense. *Single-adult households* account for about 20 percent of all households—this is more than 15 million people! These include young adults who leave home when they finish school—as well as divorced and widowed people who live alone. These people need smaller apartments, smaller cars, smaller food packages—and in some cases, less expensive household furnishings because they do not have very much money. Other "singles" have ample discretionary income—and may be attractive markets for "top of the line" stereos, "status" cars, travel, and nice restaurants and bars.

We should also note that there are several million unmarried people living together—either in couples or in groups. Some of these arrangements are temporary—as in college towns or in large cities when recent graduates go to the "big city" for their first "real" job. They have to set up households—but they may not have as much money to begin with—and may be interested in renting or buying inexpensive furnishings. But many also have more money than they ever thought they would have—and are good markets for clothing, cars, and eating and drinking places.

Marketers should probably pay special attention to these nonfamily households—because they are growing more rapidly than the traditional family households. And they have different needs and attitudes than the stereotype picture of an American family which you regularly see on television.

The shift to urban and suburban areas

Migration from rural to urban areas has been continuous in the United States since 1800. In 1920, about half the population lived in rural areas. By 1950 the number living on farms had dropped to 15 percent—and in 1980 it was below 4 percent. We have become an industrialized society—and it seems that farming will eventually be dominated by corporate agricultural enterprises.

From city to suburbs to city again

Since World War II, there has been a continual race to the suburbs. By 1970, more people were living in the suburbs than in the central cities. As people moved to the suburbs, retailers followed. And as middle-income people have moved out of the cities, lower-income consumers—often with different ethnic backgrounds—have moved in—thereby changing the nature of markets in the center of the city.

A partial reversal of this trend seems possible, however. Some families have become disenchanted with the suburban dream. They found it to be a nightmare of commuting, yard and house work, rising local taxes, and gossiping neighbors.

The movement back to the city is most evident among older and sometimes wealthier families. Their children have left or are ready to leave home. They feel hemmed in by the expansion of suburbia—and especially by the large number of lower-income families moving in. These older families are showing interest in condominiums and high-rise apartments close to downtown or outer belt line shopping, recreation, and office facilities.

Developing a new concept of the urban area

These continuing shifts—to and from urban and suburban areas—mean that the usual practice of recording population by city and county boundaries may lead to misleading descriptions of markets. Marketers are more interested in

The growing number of single nonfamily households should be watched by marketers.

Mary McCarthy

the size of homogeneous *marketing* areas—than in the number of people within political boundaries. To meet this need, the U.S. Census Bureau has developed a separate population classification—the Standard Metropolitan Statistical Area—and much data is collected on the characteristics of people in these areas.

The **Standard Metropolitan Statistical Area (SMSA)** is an integrated economic and social unit having a fairly large population nucleus. Specifically, an SMSA must contain one city or urbanized area of 50,000 or more inhabitants—and contiguous "urban" areas which give a combined population of at least 100,000. The SMSA includes the county of such a central area—and adjacent counties that are metropolitan in character and economically and socially integrated with the central area.

SMSAs are defined differently in New England—because many cities in that compact, densely populated region are closer together, and counties must be split. Other SMSAs—especially those in the western part of the country—are exceptionally large geographically because of huge county boundaries. Generally, however, SMSAs are urbanized—with a central city and surrounding suburbs.

Figure 6–4 shows the location of the nation's biggest urban areas. 288 SMSAs account for over two thirds of the country's population. This map further emphasizes the concentration of population in specific places—here, in SMSAs.

Big targets are easier

Some "national" marketers sell only in these metropolitan areas because of the large, concentrated population. Table 6–2 shows the size of the top 15 SMSAs in 1980.

These larger markets also offer greater sales potential than population alone would indicate—because of (1) generally higher wages in metropolitan areas and (2) the concentration of higher-paying occupations.

The SMSAs should be considered as potential dimensions when analyzing markets. The farther customers are from large market centers, the more the suburb seems likely to continue. A growing population must go somewhere—and the suburbs can combine pleasant neighborhoods with easy transportation to higher-paying jobs in the city or, increasingly, in the suburbs. The continuing

Table 6–2
Rank and population of top 15 Standard Metropolitan Statistical Areas in 1980

Rank		Population
1	New York, NY–NJ	9,266,300
2	Los Angeles–Long Beach, CA	7,161,300
3	Chicago, IL	6,998,400
4	Philadelphia, PA–NJ	4,771,500
5	Detroit, MI	4,371,900
6	Boston–Lowell–Brockton–Lawrence–Haverhill, MA–NH	3,901,600
7	San Francisco–Oakland, CA	3,222,700
8	Washington, DC–MD–VA	3,054,600
9	Dallas-Fort Worth, TX	2,798,000
10	Houston, TX	2,779,400
11	Nassau-Suffolk, NY	2,699,900
12	St. Louis, MO–IL	2,390,300
13	Pittsburgh, PA	2,249,700
14	Baltimore, MD	2,158,200
15	Minneapolis–St. Paul, MN	2,074,600

Source: Metro market estimates from "1980 Survey of Buying Power," *Sales and Marketing Management*, July 28, 1980, p. B-9.

Figure 6-4
Standard metropolitan statistical areas

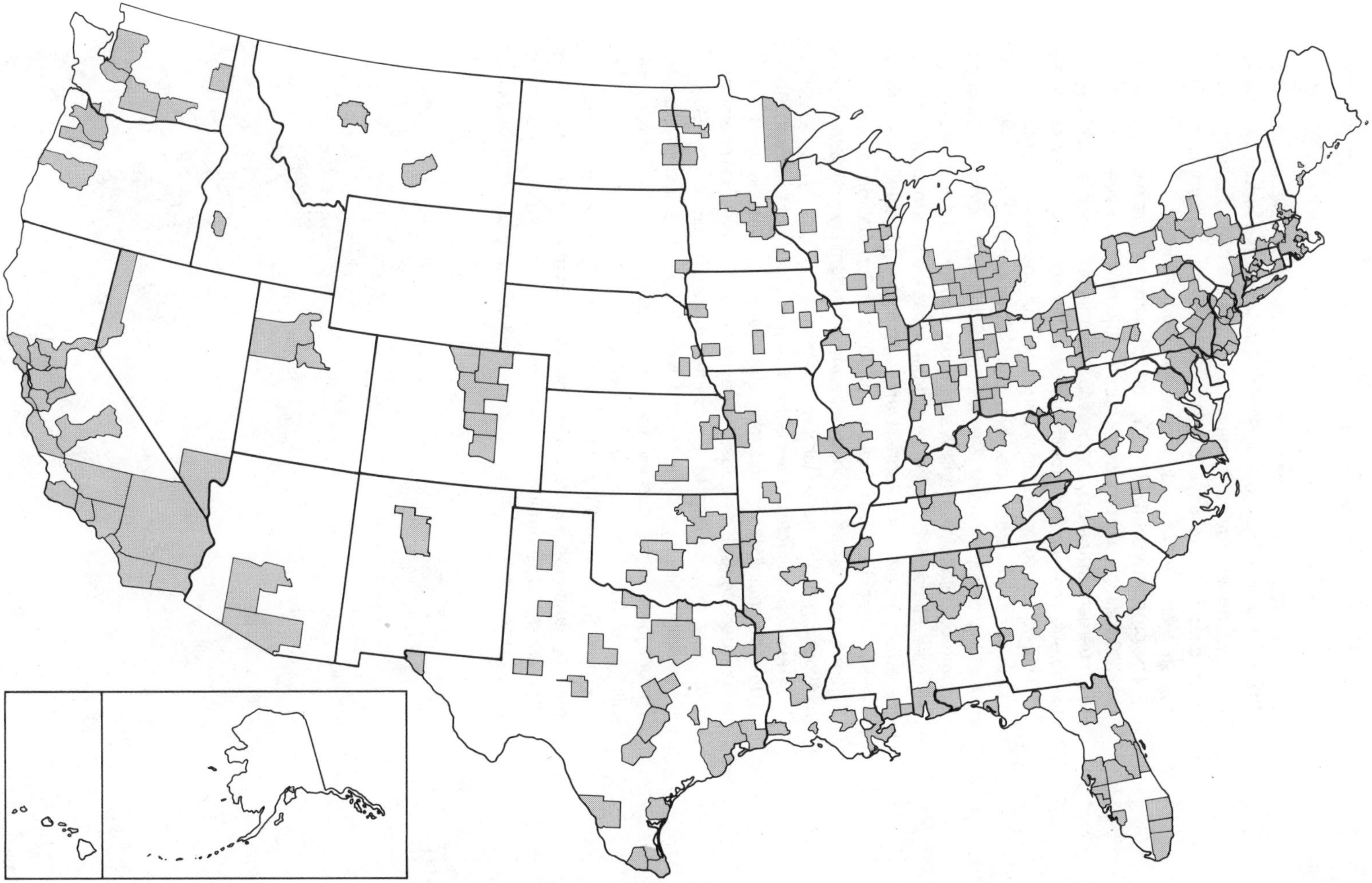

Source: *Census of Wholesale Trade*, U.S. Department of Commerce, June 1980, pp 52–2 and 52–3.

decentralization of industry may move jobs closer to the suburbs than to the central city. Not only people—but also industries—have been fleeing the old cities. Higher energy costs may change this—but probably not very fast, because such changes take time. Besides we may be developing an urban economic system which is not as dependent on central cities.

The proportion of the U.S. population living in large metropolitan areas—those over 2.5 million—will probably double in the next 50 years—from about 20 percent to 40 percent of the population. Much of this shift will probably be people moving to the suburbs—and to growing cities in the southern and western "Sun Belts."[4]

This continued growth in urban-suburban population is creating interurbias— a strip of several urban-suburban areas. Some people see a 600-mile-long "city" stretching along the East Coast and joining the people of Boston, New York, Baltimore, Philadelphia, and Washington, and their suburbs into one giant community (see Figure 6–5). Other interurbia areas occur around the Great Lakes and the adjoining areas in Pennsylvania, Ohio, and Missouri; in southern Florida; in the San Francisco Bay region; and in southern California. The darker parts in Figure 6–5 are areas which are already quite densely populated—and can expect continued growth and suburban "sprawl."

The economic role of the center of large cities is not too clear. Modern transportation, communication, and long single-story production lines make working in a crowded central area less necessary—and even uneconomical. In the long run, there may be less and less interest in the central city. By the year 2000, for example, it is estaimated that New York City will have lost about half its current jobs. Some jobs will have gone south and west, of course—but others will just shift to less crowded areas.[5]

The U.S. city of the last 80 years has been described as a series of concentric rings or bands ranging from low-income slums at the city center outward through progressively higher-income areas to the wealthy suburban areas at the outer fringe. The metro areas of tomorrow will probably be more heterogeneous with

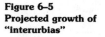
Figure 6–5
Projected growth of
"interurbias"

Many moves are caused by job promotion—creating more affluent target markets.

Mary McCarthy

many small neighborhoods—some wealthy, some middle income, and some poor—intermingled from the central city to the suburbs. This pattern of urban redevelopment already can be seen in Los Angeles, Chicago, and Philadelphia. This will make target marketing even more important.

The mobile ones are an attractive market

It is important to remember that none of these population shifts is necessarily permanent. People move, stay awhile, and then move on again. In fact, nearly 20 percent of Americans move each year. The mobile people are an important market—because their moves are often caused by promotions and job transfers—and they have money to spend. Moreover, they must make many market-oriented decisions fairly quickly after their move. They must locate new sources of food, clothing, medical and dental care, and household goods. Alert marketers should try to locate these people—and inform them of their marketing mix.[6]

Not only are Americans mobile with respect to their home base, but they also travel about and try new things. Better highways have encouraged more distant vacationing—and ownership of second homes, vacation cabins, travel trailers, and boats. This, in turn, has led to more retail stores, marinas, and recreation areas. Even the growth of suburban areas was encouraged by a willingness to travel farther to work. And growing suburban areas encouraged the growth of outlying shopping centers. With rising energy costs, we may see less growth of this kind—or even a reversal. This could offer new opportunities for alert marketers closer to population centers.

INCOME—PEOPLE WITH MONEY MAKE MARKETS

So far we have been concerned mainly with geographic characteristics. It is obvious, however, that unless people have income, they are not potential customers. The amount of money they can spend also will affect the type of goods they are likely to buy. For this reason, most marketers study income data, too.

Growth may continue

Income comes from producing and selling goods or services in the marketplace. A widely available measure of the output of the economy is the **gross** national product (GNP)—the total market value of goods and services produced in a year. The GNP has increased at the rate of approximately 3 percent a year since 1880. This means that GNP doubled—on the average—every 20 years. Total GNP of the United States reached over $2 trillion dollars—or just under $10,000 per capita in 1980.

It is not clear that total GNP will continue to grow as in the past. GNP is related to the output of employees. If the population growth rate slows, there will be fewer young workers and more retired people. This may become a serious political problem—as everyone expects the economy to deliver more, while fewer young people are available to support the older ones.

Although many forecasters continue to expect growth in GNP—in part because it is government policy to seek "full employment"—the reduction in population growth, the rising cost of energy,[7] and new thinking about the desirability of growth could lead to "no growth." This might cause severe unemployment and hardships. Politically, this would be very difficult to manage, so it seems more likely that the government will stimulate continued growth in GNP—although different kinds of goods and services may be produced.

The income pyramid capsized

Total GNP figures are more meaningful when converted to family or household income—and its distribution. Family incomes in the United States have been increasing continuously. But even more important to marketers is that the distribution of income has been changing drastically.

Figure 6–6 shows that as recently as 1930, most U.S. families were bunched together in the lower income levels—and the distribution looked something like a pyramid. By the 1970s, real incomes (buying power) had risen so much that the pyramid had turned over! This is important to marketers because it means that now more families are important customers. Before this upward shift in real income, the U.S. market had a large number of people at the bottom of the income distribution—and a relative handful forming an "elite" market at the top. This is a significant revolution which has broadened markets and drastically

**Figure 6–6
Redistribution of income—a revolution**

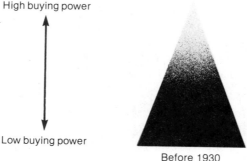

Proportion of families with various levels of buying power

High buying power

Low buying power

Before 1930
most U.S. families
had lower
buying power

After 1960
many more families
had higher
buying power

Source: Based on study in *Business Week*, October 16, 1965; and other data showing real incomes continuing to rise.

Figure 6–7
Total household income distribution by income levels in 1978

Household Income Level	Number of Households (millions)	Percent of Total Household	Percent of Total Income
$25,000 and over	17.6	22.8	48.1
$15,000-24,999	21.3	27.5	30.3
$10,000-14,999	12.9	16.7	11.5
$ 5,000-9,999	14.2	18.3	7.7
Under $5,000	11.4	14.7	2.4
Total	77.3	100.0	100.0

Mean household income equal to $17,730.
Source: *Current Population Reports,* U.S. Department of the Census, P–60, No. 120.

changed our marketing system. This situation is found only in the United States, Canada, many Western European countries, Australia, New Zealand, and Japan.

Real incomes may stop growing

It is hoped that real family incomes will continue upward—but this may not happen. In 1975, the real purchasing power of the average U.S. household dropped 3 percent and continued to drop until 1980. Maybe the peak of real family income in the United States has already been reached.

Middle-income families may get squeezed

Further, the distribution may be changing again, with the middle groups getting squeezed. Their real incomes have stayed steady for the last decade—unless the wife went to work outside the home. This could have a serious impact on marketers aiming at this big group.[8]

The higher-income groups receive a large share of the income

Although the pyramid has capsized, higher-income groups do receive a large share of total income. They are attractive markets—especially for "luxury" items. Figure 6–7 shows that although the average income of U.S. households in 1978 was $17,730, about 17.6 million households—22.8 percent of the 77.3 million households—had incomes over $25,000 and accounted for 48 percent of the total income of the nation. Another 30.3 percent of the total income went to 27.5% of households with incomes of $15,000–$25,000. In other words, more than three fourths of the income went to a little more than one half of the households—those with incomes over $15,000.

At the lower end of the scale, 11.4 million households had incomes under $5,000—and received only 2.4 percent of the total income. Although their incomes might seem high to peasants in less-developed countries, these are our "poor." However, they are attractive markets for some basic commodities—especially food and clothing.

Even though many people have low incomes they are still a market for some products.

John Penzari

How much income is "enough"

The importance of income distribution cannot be stressed too much. Bad marketing strategy errors have been made by overestimating the amount of income in various target markets. It is all too easy for marketers to fall into such errors because of our natural tendency to associate with others in similar circumstances—and then to assume that almost everyone lives the same way.

The $17,730 average household income for 1978 is a useful reference point—because a college graduate might start near this level (and a young working couple together can easily go way over this figure). This will seem like a lot of money in the initial flush of making money—but it is surprising how soon needs and expenses rise and adjust to available income. Before long, it's difficult to see how anyone can live on less—and U.S. Labor Department estimates help explain why. They felt that at least $11,546 a year was necessary in 1978 for an urban American family of four to maintain an "austere" living standard. So, the fact that there *is* an income distribution—and that many households must make do on much less than $10,000 or $17,730—should not be forgotten in marketing strategy planning.

CONSUMER SPENDING PATTERNS ARE RELATED TO POPULATION AND INCOME

We have been using the term *family income* because consumer budget studies show that most consumers spend their incomes as part of family or household units. If the women or children work, they usually pool their incomes with the men when planning expenditures. Thus, most of our discussion will be on how households or families spend their income.

Disposable income is spendable income

It should be remembered, however, that families do not get to spend all of their income. Disposable income is what is left of income after taxes. Out of its disposable income—together with gifts, pensions, cash savings, or other assets—the family makes its expenditures. Some families do not spend all their disposable income—saving part of it. Therefore, we should distinguish between disposable income and actual expenditures when trying to estimate potential expenditures in target markets.

Discretionary income is elusive

Not all of peoples' income is uncommitted. Most households spend a good portion of their income on "necessities"—food, rent or house payments, car and house furnishings payments, insurance, and so on—which are defined in various ways by different researchers and consumers. A family's purchase of "luxuries" comes from **discretionary income**—what is left of disposable income after paying for necessities.

Discretionary income is an elusive concept—because the definition of "necessities" varies from family to family—and over time. A color television set might be purchased out of discretionary income by a lower-income family—while being considered a necessity by a higher-income family. But if many people in a lower-income neighborhood start buying color television sets, then this might become a necessity for the others—and severely reduce the discretionary income available for other purchases.

Measuring discretionary income in a specific situation would require marketing research—but it is clear that the majority of U.S. families *do not* have enough discretionary income to afford the leisure-class lifestyles seen on TV and in other mass media. On the other hand, some young adults and older people without family responsibilities may have a large share of the discretionary income in a market. They may be especially attractive for sellers of stereos, cameras, new cars, foreign travel, and various kinds of recreation—tennis, skiing, plays, concerts, and fine restaurants.

Engel's laws show basic spending relationships

Engel's laws are generalizations about consumer spending patterns. These generalizations grew out of the work of a German statistician who published the first study of consumer spending patterns in 1857. Followers have rephrased these laws, until now they are stated in three parts:

1. As a family's income increases, the percentage spent on food will decrease.
2. As a family's income increases, the percentage spent on housing and household operations will be roughly constant (with the exception of fuel, light, and refrigeration, which will decrease).
3. As a family's income increases, the percentage spent on all other categories and the amount saved will increase (with the exception of medical care and personal care items, which are fairly constant).

Engel studied working-class families who spent *all* their income. This fits in with our emphasis on analyzing consumer *expenditures*. Note that as a family's income increases, *more money will be spent in total in all categories*. The decreases or increases are as a percentage of the total.

Engel's laws are useful only for predicting the behavior of an individual family—or groups of families moving from one income category to another. They should be used with care when predicting what happens in the whole economy when GNP changes. Engel's laws were not based on such movements—but rather on a comparison of the budgets of individual families. They can still be useful to marketers, however. A retailer, for example, might use Engel's laws to forecast how the expenditure patterns of his present customers would change if a new industrial plant coming into the community was likely to increase their incomes.

Expenditure data provides harder numbers

Generalizations such as Engel's laws are valuable when precise data is not available—but we do not have some detailed information on consumer expenditure patterns. The Bureau of Labor Statistics (BLS) and the U.S. Census Bureau have gathered detailed family spending data for 1972–73 to help the BLS with the consumer price index—but it also can be extremely useful for marketers. It is currently the most comprehensive and detailed data which is easily available. Some updating of income distribution data from a source such as *Sales and Marketing Management's* "Survey of Buying Power" probably would be desirable if this data were to be used in a real business situation. But for our purposes, we will discuss and illustrate the use of this basic information.

Estimating how potential customers spend their money

Table 6–3 shows the average annual spending by families for major categories of expenditures. These measures can serve as reference points—and should keep you from making wild estimates based only on your own experience. The amount spent on major categories such as food, housing, clothing, transport, and so on does vary by income level. And the relationships are logical when you realize that many of the purchases in these categories are "necessities."

Data such as in Table 6–3 can help a marketing manager understand how potential target customers spend their money. For example, if he is seriously considering consumers in the $15,000–$19,999 income bracket, he can analyze how families in this category spend their money. Then he can consider how they would have to rearrange spending to purchase his product. A swimming pool manufacturer could see that such families spend about $896 on recreation of all kinds. If a particular pool costs $600 a year, including depreciation and maintenance, it follows that the average family in this income category would have to make a big shift in lifestyle if it bought the pool.

This data will not tell the pool maker whether these potential customers will buy the pool. But it does supply useful input to help make a sound decision. If a manager feels that more information is needed, perhaps about the strength of their attitudes toward recreation products, then some marketing research may be needed. For example, a manager may want to make a budget study on consumers who already have swimming pools to see how they adjusted their spending patterns—and how they felt before and after the purchase.

EXPENDITURE PATTERNS VARY WITH OTHER MEASURABLE FACTORS

Income has a direct bearing upon spending patterns—but there are other factors that should not be ignored in any careful analysis of potential markets.

Spending affected by location of household

The 1973 Consumer Expenditure Study data show that the location of a consumer's household does affect the household's spending habits. We will not present detailed tables here—but will summarize a few important differences. The detailed BLS data should be analyzed to answer specific questions.

Table 6-3
Family spending by family income level—1972–1973

	All families	Under $3,000	$3,000 to $3,999	$4,000 to $4,999	$5,000 to $5,999	$6,000 to $6,999	$7,000 to $7,999	$8,000 to $9,999	$10,000 to $11,999	$12,000 to $14,999	$15,000 to $19,999	$20,000 to $24,999	$25,000 and over
Food	$1,554	$739	$943	$1,071	$1,126	$1,157	$1,288	$1,392	$1,563	$1,750	$2,010	$2,293	$2,651
Housing	2,435	1,310	1,539	1,614	1,709	1,818	1,964	2,128	2,342	2,591	3,027	3,495	4,682
Clothing	653	218	311	310	394	427	493	517	617	692	867	1,082	1,564
Transport	1,629	508	631	783	892	1,096	1,257	1,422	1,697	1,956	2,257	2,712	3,202
Health care	486	227	309	381	387	410	423	456	482	508	578	697	887
Personal care	101	36	53	59	69	77	77	81	96	105	130	159	226
Education	98	14	17	25	18	27	33	35	53	74	132	253	425
Reading	49	17	23	24	31	32	38	36	47	54	67	82	108
Recreation	657	174	238	241	334	288	371	470	586	683	896	1,297	1,834
Alcohol	78	25	39	45	50	52	65	63	84	79	106	117	177
Tobacco	129	72	77	90	96	108	119	135	142	155	172	172	148
Personal insurance	257	55	84	84	103	109	135	175	236	277	370	459	771
Retirement, pensions	595	239	279	261	291	334	354	392	557	626	820	1,071	1,480
Gifts, contributions	432	128	157	175	210	280	268	311	314	403	492	669	1,604

Source: *Consumer Expenditure Survey Series: Interview Survey, 1972 and 1973*, Report 455-3, pp. 19–23.

Where a family lives affects how they spend their income.

Kenneth Yee

Expenditures on transportation, housing, and food do seem to vary by geographic location. Consumers in central cities spend less on transportation and more on housing than those in rural areas outside SMSAs—probably because of higher land and construction costs, and greater population density. A rural family spends a larger share on food—perhaps because there is less competition in rural areas for a grocery dollar. But incomes tend to be lower in rural areas, so Engel's laws may explain some of this.

Also, by geographic boundaries

Geographic boundaries also are related to expenditures. Total expenditures in the South are lower than in other regions—because incomes there are lower. But the important differences are in the relative shares going for food and housing. Consumers in the northeastern part of the United States tend to spend more on these categories (especially for food, utilities, and shelter costs).

Stage of family life cycle affects spending

Two other demographic dimensions—age and number of children—affect spending patterns. Put together, these dimensions are concerned with the life cycle of a family. See Figure 6–8 for a summary of life cycle and buying behavior.

Young people and families accept new ideas

Younger people seem to be more receptive to new products and brands—but they are not foolish or innocent shoppers. One study of 14–25-year-olds showed that 74 percent of the respondents compared prices and brands before buying. Although the median income of these younger people is lower than that of older groups, they spend a greater proportion of their income on "discretionary" items—because they don't have major financial responsibilities for housing, education, and family rearing.[9] Although many are waiting longer to marry—or not marrying—some young people are getting married. These younger families—especially those with no children—are still accumulating durable goods such as automobiles and house furnishings. They need less food. It is only as children begin to arrive and grow that the family spending shifts to soft goods and services—such as education, medical, and personal care. This usually happens when the household head reaches the 35–44 age group.

Reallocation for teenagers

Once the children become teenagers, further shifts in expenditures occur. Teenagers eat more, begin to wear expensive clothes, and develop recreation and education needs that are hard on the family budget. The parents may be forced to reallocate their expenditures to cover these expenses—spending less on durable goods such as appliances, automobiles, household goods, and houses.

Many teenagers do earn much or all of their own spending money—and this has made an attractive market. Marketers who have catered to teenagers are beginning to feel the decline in birthrates—and probably will face harder times in the future. Motorcycle manufacturers, for example, have already been hurt— as teenagers are their heaviest buyers.[10]

Selling to the "empty nesters"

An important group in the 50–64 age category is called the "empty nesters." Their children are grown—and they are able to spend their money in other ways. It is an elusive group, however, because some people marry later and are still

Figure 6–8
Stages in the family cycle

Stage	Characteristics and buying behavior
1. Singles: Unmarried people living away from parents	Feel "affluent" and "free." Buy basic household goods. More interested in recreation, cars, vacations, clothes, cosmetics, and personal care items.
2. Divorced or separated	May be financially squeezed to pay for alimony or maintaining two households. Buying may be limited to "necessities"— especially for women who had no "job skills."
3. Newly married couples: No children	Both may work and so they feel financially well-off. Buy durables: cars, refrigerators, stoves, basic furniture—and recreation equipment and vacations.
4. Full nest I: Youngest child under six	Feel squeezed financially because they are buying homes and household durables—furniture, washers, dryers, and TV. Also buying child-related products—food, medicines, clothes and toys. Really interested in new products.
5. Full nest II: Youngest child over five	Financially are better off as husband earns more and/or wife goes to work as last child goes to school. More spent on food, clothing, education, and recreation for growing children.
6. Full nest III: Older couples with dependent children	Financially even better off as husband earns more and more wives work. May replace durables and furniture, and buy cars, boats, dental services, and more expensive recreation and travel. May buy bigger houses.
7. Empty nest: Older couples, no children living with them, head still working	Feel financially "well-off." Home ownership at peak and house may be paid for. May make home improvements or move into apartments. And may travel, entertain, go to school, and make gifts and contributions. Not interested in new products.
8. Sole survivor, still working	Income still good. Likely to sell home and continue with previous life style.
9. Senior citizen I: Older married couple, no children living with them, head retired	Big drop in income. May keep home but cut back on most buying as purchases of medical care, drugs, and other health related items go up.
10. Senior citizen II: Sole survivor, not working	Same as senior citizen I, except likely to sell home, and has special need for attention, affection, and security.

Source: Adapted from William D. Wells and George Gubar, "Life Cycle Concept in Marketing Research," *Journal of Marketing Research*, August 1968, p. 267.

raising a family as they move into this age group. It is the "empty nesters" who move back into the smaller, more luxurious apartments in the city. They may also be more interested in travel, small sports cars, and other things that weren't realistic possibilities before. Much depends on their income, of course, but this is a high-income period for many workers—especially white-collar workers.

Senior citizens are a big new market

Finally, the senior citizens—people over 65—should not be neglected. The number of people over 65 is increasing rapidly—because of modern medicine, improved sanitary conditions, and better nutrition. This group is now over 10 percent of the population—and growing.

Although older people generally have reduced incomes, many have adequate incomes and very different needs. Many firms, in fact, are already catering to the senior citizen market—and more will be coming. Gerber, for example, faced with a declining baby market, started producing some products for older people.[11] Some firms have gone into special diet supplements and drug products. Others have designed housing developments to appeal to older people.

Do ethnic groups buy differently?

America may be called the "melting pot," but ethnic groups require special attention when analyzing markets. This is obvious for some products, but there are other differences that may be ignored by the superficial observer.

This is an area where stereotype thinking is the most common—and where marketing research may be especially desirable. All blacks, for example, do not have big cars—in fact, black consumers spend less on automobile transportation than do whites with comparable incomes.[12] And those of Irish extraction do not eat just corned beef and cabbage or potatoes—just as those of Italian extraction buy food products other than pasta.

Ethnic dimensions must be studied and watched carefully—because they may be subtle and fast changing. Hair straighteners, for example, are no longer selling well to blacks.[13] But different kinds of cosmetics and hair preparation products do seem to be wanted. At the same time, a young, middle-income, black working

Ethnic groups read different media.

Kenneth Yee

couples' market may be developing. This may be an "almost ignored" $25-billion-a-year market. These working couples have accepted the values of middle America—but they have their own needs and ways of thinking—and importantly, they live in different areas and read different media. It might be wise to have separate dimensions for them—but the evidence is not clear on this[14]

The median age of U.S. blacks and Spanish-speaking people is much lower than that of whites. This means that many more are in earlier stages of the life cycle and, therefore, are a better market for certain goods—especially durable goods.

Some minority groups seem to be striving for what they believe to be white middle-income standards in material goods—and current products may be quite acceptable. Others have abandoned this goal in favor of their own sets of values. Clearly, separate strategies may be needed for these ethnically or racially defined markets. Perhaps some of these strategies would require only changes in Place and Promotion—but they would be separate strategies.

When the wife earns, the family spends

Another factor that deserves attention is the growing number of married women with paying jobs. In 1950, only 24 percent of wives worked outside the home, but this rose to about 50 percent by 1980.[15]

In families where the wife works, about 30 percent of all the family spending power comes from her income.[16] This is why the median family income is as high as it is. But many families feel they need this income to make ends meet.

A study by the U.S. Department of Agriculture showed that while a wife's job outside the home seems to have little effect on the nutritive value of her family's food, working wives do *spend more* for food—and do choose more expensive types of food.

Families with working wives also spend more on clothing, alcohol and tobacco, house furnishings and equipment, and automobiles.

In short, when a wife works, it affects the spending habits of the family. This fact must be considered when analyzing markets.

CONCLUSION

We studied population data—getting rid of various misconceptions about how our more than 200 million people are spread over the United States. It is clear that the potential of a given market cannot be determined by population figures alone. Income, stage in life cycle, geographic location of people, and other factors are important, too.

We also noted the growth of interurbias—such as along the Atlantic Seaboard. These urban-suburban systems suggest the shape of future growth in this country. It is also apparent that one of the outstanding characteristics of Americans is their mobility. For this reason, even relatively new data is not foolproof. Available data can only aid judgment—not replace it.

Engel's "laws" are useful generalizations about consumption patterns. They help predict individual and family buying behavior. But American consumers are different from Engel's workers in a very important way—they are among the most affluent in the world. And this affluence affects purchasing behavior. Beyond buying the essentials of life, they have "discretionary income"—and are able to buy a wide variety of "luxuries." And even when buying essentials—like food and clothing—they have many choices, and they use them.

The kind of data discussed in this chapter can be very useful for estimating the market potential within possible target markets. But, unfortunately, it is not very helpful in explaining specific customer behavior—why people buy *specific* products and *specific* brands. And such detailed forecasts are obviously important to marketing managers. Fortunately, better estimates can come from a fuller understanding of consumer behavior—which is the goal of the next chapter.

QUESTIONS AND PROBLEMS

1. Discuss how slower population growth, and especially a decline in the number of babies, will affect the businesses in your local community.

2. Discuss the impact of our "aging culture" on marketing strategy planning.

3. Some demographic characteristics are likely to be more important than others in determining market potential. For each of the following characteristics, identify two products for which this characteristic is *most* important: *(a)* size of geographic area, *(b)* population, *(c)* income, *(d)* stage of life cycle.

4. If a large, new atomic research installation were being built in a formerly small and sleepy town, how could the local retailers use Engel's laws in planning for the influx of newcomers, first of construction crews and then of scientists?

5. Name three specific examples (specific products or brands—not just product categories) illustrating how demand will differ by geographic location *and* market location, that is, with respect to size and location inside or outside a metropolitan market.

6. Explain how the continuing mobility of consumers as well as the development of "interurbia" areas should affect marketing strategy planning in the future. Be sure to consider the impact on the four Ps.

7. Explain how the redistribution of income has affected marketing planning thus far and its likely impact in the future.

8. Explain why the concept of the Standard Metropolitan Statistical Area was developed. Would it be the most useful breakdown for retailers?

9. With the growing homogeneity of the consumer market, does this mean there will be fewer opportunities to segment markets? Do you feel that all consumers of about equal income will probably spend their incomes similarly and demand similar products?

SUGGESTED CASES

6 The Capri

8 Arctic Palace

NOTES

1. "The Graying of America," *Newsweek*, February 28, 1977, pp. 50–55; and "The Family: Internal 'Violent Changes,' " *The (Lansing, Michigan) State Journal*, January 6, 1980, p. D–1.

2. Based on U.S. Census, and *Newsweek*, February 28, 1977, p. 52, and "The Baby Boom Muddies the Picture," *The Wall Street Journal*, March 27, 1980, p. 22.

3. "Advertisers Take Aim At a Neglected Market: The Working Women," *The Wall Street Journal*, July 5, 1977, p. 1; "A Living-Alone Affects Housing, Cars, and Other Industries," *The Wall*

Street Journal, November 15, 1977, p. 1; and "New Benefits for New Lifestyles," *Business Week*, February 11, 1980, p. 111.

4. "Cities May Flourish in South and West, Decline in Northeast," *The Wall Street Journal*, April 6, 1976, p. 1f; and "Smaller Cities with No End to Suburbanization," *Business Week*, September 3, 1979, p. 204–206.

5. Ibid.; and "The Prospect of a Nation with No Important Cities," *Business Week*, February 2, 1976, pp. 66–69.

6. James E. Bell, Jr., "Mobiles—A Possible Segment for Retailer

Cultivation," *Journal of Retailing,* Fall 1970, pp. 3–15; "Mobile Americans: A Moving Target with Sales Potential," *Sales and Marketing Management,* April 7, 1980, p. 40.

7. "Will Energy Conservation Throttle Economic Growth?" *Business Week,* April 25, 1977, pp. 66–80; and "The Future: How U.S. Business Will Change in the Next 50 Years," *Business Week,* September 3, 1979, pp. 169–212.

8. "The New Two-Tier Market for Consumer Goods," *Business Week,* April 11, 1977, pp. 80–83.

9. "Young Market Becoming More Conventional," *Advertising Age,* May 16, 1977, p. 84; "On a Fast Track to the Good Life," *Fortune,* April 7, 1980, pp. 74–84; "Demography's Good News for the 80's," *Fortune,* November 5, 1979, pp. 92–106; and "The Upbeat Outlook for Family Incomes," *Fortune,* February 25, 1980, pp. 122–130.

10. "Motorcycles: The Dip Continues," *Business Week,* May 3, 1976, pp. 80–81.

11. "Why Gerber Makes an Inviting Target," *Business Week,* June 27, 1977, pp. 26–27.

12. Marcus Alexis, "Some Negro-White Differences in Consumption," *American Journal of Economics and Sociology,* January 1962, pp. 11–28.

13. "When Black Is Beautiful," *Business Week,* September 8, 1973, p. 51.

14. *Marketing News,* American Marketing Association, September 15, 1973, p. 5; and Andrew A. Brogowicz, "Race as a Basis for Market Segmentation: An Exploratory Analysis," Ph.D. thesis, Michigan State University, 1977; and "The Upbeat Outlook for Family Incomes," *Fortune,* February 25, 1980, p. 130.

15. *The Nielsen Researcher,* no. 1, 1977, p. 7; and *Sales & Marketing Management,* July 28, 1980, p. A–8.

16. T. F. Bradshaw and J. F. Stinson, "Trends in Weekly Earnings: An Analysis," *Monthly Labor Review,* August 1975, pp. 25–26; and W. Lazer and J. E. Smallwood, "The Changing Demographics of Women," *Journal of Marketing,* July 1977, pp. 14–30; Mary Lou Roberts and Lawrence H. Wortzel; "New Life-Style Determinants of Women's Food Shopping Behavior," *Journal of Marketing,* Summer 1979, pp. 29–39.

Mary McCarthy

When you finish this chapter, you should:	1. Know about the various "black box" models of buyer behavior.
	2. Understand how the intra-personal variables affect an individual's buying behavior.
	3. Understand how the inter-personal variables affect an individual's and household buying behavior.
	4. Know how consumers use problem-solving processes.
	5. Have some "feel" for how all the behavioral variables and incoming stimuli are handled by a consumer.
	6. Recognize the important new terms (shown in red).

7

Behavioral dimensions of the consumer market

Which car will the customer buy—the Ford Mustang or the Audi Fox?

How can marketing managers predict which specific products consumers will buy? In what quantities? Why does a consumer choose a particular product?

Basic data on population, income, and consumer spending patterns in U.S. markets were presented in the last chapter. With this information, it is possible to predict basic *trends* in consumer spending patterns.

Unfortunately, when many firms sell similar products, this demographic analysis isn't of much value in predicting which *products* and *brands* will be purchased. Yet whether its products and brands will be chosen—and to what extent—is extremely important to a firm.

THE BEHAVIORAL SCIENCES HELP UNDERSTAND BEHAVIOR

To find better answers, we need to understand more about people. For this reason, many marketers have turned to the behavioral sciences for help. In this chapter we will explore some of the approaches and thinking in psychology, sociology, and the other behavioral disciplines.

Buying in a black box

A simplified way of summarizing the way various behavioral scientists understand consumer purchasing behavior is shown in Figure 7–1. Potential customers are exposed to various stimuli—including the marketing mixes of various competitors. Somehow, an individual person internalizes some or all of these stimuli. This person is usually shown in a mysterious black box that we can't see into—implying that we can observe his behavior, but not his decision-making processes.

**Figure 7–1
Simplified buyer behavior
model**

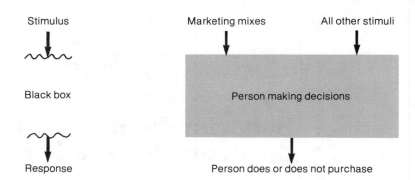

Then, for some reasons, he responds to the stimuli—and may buy a marketer's product.

This is the classical model of buyer behavior. This **stimulus-response model** says that people respond in some predictable way to a stimulus. The model does not explain *why* they behave the way they do—only that there is a predictable response to a stimulus. This is the model we were using in the last chapter. There, we hoped to find some relationship between demographic characteristics (of customers in the black box), products (stimulus), and the customer's buying behavior (response). We did find some relationships—but now we want to go even deeper. This will require a better understanding of how the consumer decision-making process works.

There are many black box theories

Depending on a person's behavioral science training—and which theories he accepts—we find many descriptions of how the black box works. These varying theories lead to different predictions about how consumers will react. So it helps to have some feel for the differences.

How the economist views the black box

The economist typically assumes that consumers are **economic men**—people who logically compare choices in terms of cost and value received—to maximize their satisfaction from spending their time, energy, and money. Therefore, the economist collects and analyzes demographic data when predicting consumer behavior. It was a logical extension of the economic-man theory which led us to look at demographic characteristics in the last chapter. Certainly, there is validity to this model—since consumers must at least have income to be in the market. But other behavioral scientists suggest that the black box works in a more complicated way than the economic-man model.

How we will view the black box

Consumers are multi-dimensional—so we will try to combine their various dimensions into a more complete model of how consumers make decisions.

Figure 7–2 presents a simple view of the black box. Here, we see the individual consumer—shown by a dot in the center of the diagram—surrounded by many influencing factors. Presumably the individual has needs. But these, in turn, are influenced by family, social class, other reference groups—and the culture in which he lives—no person is an island. Yet, ultimately, the individual makes decisions for or against our offerings—so we need to understand how an individual solves problems.

A more detailed view of the black box is shown in Figure 7–3. Here, we see both intra-personal and inter-personal variables affecting the person making decisions. Both sets of variables affect how a person sees and processes incoming stimuli. These topics are discussed in the next few pages, and then, we will look at the consumer's problem-solving process.

INTRA-PERSONAL VARIABLES FOCUS ON THE INDIVIDUAL

The intra-personal variables come from the field of psychology. In this section we will discuss some variables of special interest to marketers, that is, motivation, perception, learning, attitudes, and personality.

Motivation determines what is wanted

Everybody is motivated by needs and wants. **Needs** are the basic forces which motivate an individual to do something. Some needs are physiological—concerned with a person's physical body. Examples are the needs for food, drink, sex, warmth, and cooling. Other needs are psychological—concerned with the individual's view of himself and his relationship with others. Wants are less basic. **Wants** are "needs" which are learned during an individual's life. For example, everyone needs food, but some people also have a learned want for a "Big Mac."

When a need or want is not satisfied, it leads to a drive. The food need, for example, leads to a hunger drive. A **drive** is a strong stimulus which causes a tension that the individual tries to reduce by finding ways of satisfying this drive. Drives are internal—they are the reasons behind certain behavior patterns.

We all are a bundle of needs and wants. Some marketers work with long lists of needs. But lists can be most frustrating—because they can't include all relevant dimensions—especially product-related benefits. So it is easy to ignore a need (or benefit sought) which may turn out to be key to understanding some consumer's behavior. Nevertheless, lists of needs can stimulate thinking. Figure 7–4 presents such a list. It should *not* be thought of as complete—but only as

Figure 7–2
The individual decision maker (shown as a dot) nestled in an environment

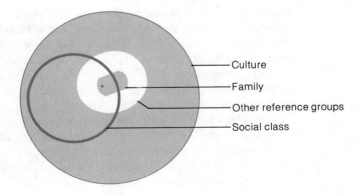

Culture

Family

Other reference groups

Social class

**Figure 7–3
More complete buyer behavior
model**

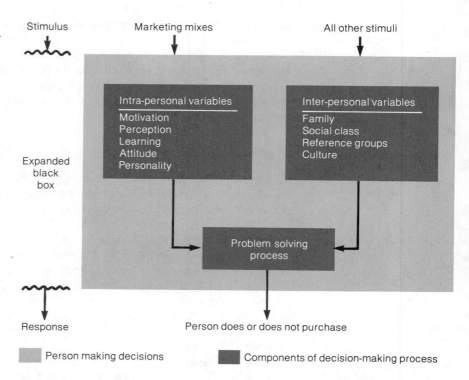

Stimulus

Marketing mixes

All other stimuli

Expanded
black
box

Intra-personal variables

Motivation
Perception
Learning
Attitude
Personality

Inter-personal variables

Family
Social class
Reference groups
Culture

Problem solving
process

Response

Person does or does not purchase

Person making decisions

Components of decision-making process

suggestive. The needs listed in this figure are people-related needs. They can also be thought of as *benefits sought* in a general sense. When a marketer has narrowed his target down to a fairly specific product-market, then the general benefits sought may become quite specific—for example, the food need might become as specific as wanting the benefits offered by a pizza. So, you can see that in developing a marketing strategy, the benefits sought could be matched against benefits offered by the company's marketing mix—to try to develop a match between what is wanted and what the firm should offer.

Are there hierarchies of needs?

Some psychologists feel that a person may have several reasons for buying—at the same time. They see people trying to develop a balance among the forces driving them. Some psychologists even see a hierarchy of needs. Maslow is well known for his five-level hierarchy. But we will discuss a similar four-level hierarchy which is easier to apply—and is supported by more recent research on human motivation.[1] The four levels are illustrated in Figure 7–5. The lowest-level needs are physiological. Then come safety, social, and personal needs. As a study aid, think of the "PSSP needs."

The **physiological needs** are concerned with food, drink, rest, sex, and other biological needs. The **safety needs** are concerned with protection and physical well-being (perhaps involving health, food, drugs, and exercise). The **social needs** are concerned with love, friendship, status, and esteem—all things that involve a person's interaction with others. The **personal needs,** on the other hand, are concerned with the need of an individual to achieve personal satisfaction—

Figure 7–4
Possible needs motivating a
person to some action

Physiological needs

Food	Warmth	Activity
Drink	Coolness	Rest
Sex—tension release	Body elimination	Self-preservation
Sleep		

Psychological needs

Abasement	Deference	Order
Acquisition	Distinctive	Personal fulfillment
Affiliation	Discriminating	Playing—competitive
Aggression	Discriminatory	Playing—relaxing
Beauty	Dominance	Power
Belonging	Emulation	Pride
Being constructive	Exhibition	Security
Being part of a group	Family preservation	Self-expression
Being responsible	Imitation	Self-identification
Being well thought of	Independence	Symmetry
Companionship	Individualism	Tenderness
Conserving	Love	Striving
Curiosity	Nurturing	Understanding (knowledge)
Discovery		

Desire for:

Acceptance	Prestige
Achievement	Recognition
Affection	Respect
Affiliation	Retaliation
Appreciation	Satisfaction with self
Comfort	Security
Contrariness	Self-confidence
Dependence	Sensuous experiences
Distance—"space"	Sexual satisfaction
Distinctiveness	Sociability
Fame	Status
Happiness	Sympathy
Identification	

Freedom from:

Anxiety	Imitation
Depression	Loss of prestige
Discomfort	Pain
Fear	Pressure
Harm—Psychological	Ridicule
Harm—Physical	Sadness

Source: Adapted from C. Glenn Walters, *Consumer Behavior*, 3d ed. (Homewood, Ill.: Richard D. Irwin, 1979); R. M. Liebert and M. D. Spiegler, *Personality*, 3d ed., (Homewood, Ill.: Dorsey Press, 1978); and others. © 1979 by Richard D. Irwin, Inc., and © 1978 by The Dorsey Press.

unrelated to what others think or do. Examples here include self-esteem, accomplishment, fun, freedom, and relaxation.

Motivation theory suggests that we never reach a state of complete satisfaction. As soon as lower-level needs are reasonably satisfied, those at higher levels become more dominant. It is important to see, however, that a particular good or service might satisfy more than one need at the same time. A hamburger in a friendly environment, for example, might satisfy not only the physiological need to satisfy hunger—but also some social need. In fact, it seems necessary to think of individuals as need-satisfying mechanisms who try to fill a *set* of needs— rather than just one need or another in sequence. You should also be aware that: (1) a higher-level need may develop before lower needs are satisfied, and (2) the order in which needs are satisfied can vary from one group to another.

Higher-level needs may be important for "commodities"

While the four basic needs can help us understand some buying behavior, other market situations may involve such basic "commodities" that neither producers nor consumers give much thought to what needs are being satisfied—resulting in undifferentiated marketing mixes. But a creative marketer may see that *several* basic needs are involved—and be able to segment the market. Or if this isn't possible, he may be able to appeal to the higher-level needs to differentiate his marketing mix. Gasoline illustrates this idea. Gasoline might help one consumer obtain food to satisfy a hunger (physiological) need—by driving safely to a store and therefore avoiding a walk through a dangerous neighborhood (safety need). But gasoline could be used to pick up a friend and satisfy social needs—or simply for a drive to satisfy a personal need for "freedom." Here, given that motorists must buy gas to get around, there is no point in selling the "gas is a good commodity" story. But a particular brand might offer more safety and dependability because of quality control. Or racing or beach scenes might try to associate the brand with fun, speed, and excitement.

Figure 7–5
The PSSP hierarchy of needs

While these "commodity-type" markets are often identified with product-related names—like the gasoline market—relying on such product-related "needs" is risky—because it's easy to miss seeing what is really motivating (or could motivate) some consumers. Just a simple knife, for example, might be treated as a commodity for satisfying the "knife" or "food cutting" need. But the same knife might help a cook satisfy several levels of need. A market-oriented firm might see that some cooks are interested in high-quality cutlery for their own personal satisfaction—or name brands to impress their guests. In these cases, different markets are involved and the appropriate marketing mixes should be different. An imaginative marketer might be able to develop a unique strategy—while competitors wouldn't even understand what's going on.

Economic needs affect how we satisfy basic needs

The four basic needs can help explain *what* we buy—but the economic needs help explain *how* we buy and *why* we want specific product features.

Economic needs are concerned with making the best use of a customer's limited resources—as the customer sees it. Some people look for the best price. Others want the best quality—almost regardless of price. And others settle for the best value. It's helpful to think of eight economic needs:

1. Convenience.
2. Efficiency in operation or use.
3. Dependability in use.
4. Reliability of service.
5. Durability.
6. Improvement of earnings.
7. Improvement of productivity of property.
8. Economy of purchase or use.

With economic needs, measurable factors can be emphasized. These might include specific dollar savings, differences in weight, or in length of product life.

Consumers are more aware of some needs than others

Trying to determine the relevant needs—either informally or through market research—is complicated by the fact that consumers may not be willing to discuss—or may not even know—what drives them. There are three degrees of awareness of needs: conscious, preconscious, and unconscious.[2]

At the **conscious level**. consumers are aware of their needs and are willing to talk to others about them. At the **preconscious level** they may be aware of their needs, but would rather not discuss them with others. They are not fully conscious of why they behave the way they do. A desire for status might be quite strong, for example, but they can't explain why. If pushed to explain, they might rationalize their purchases in terms of usefulness. Finally, at the **unconscious level,** people are not even aware of what forces are driving them. A direct promotion appeal aimed at such needs would not be effective.

Perception determines what is seen and felt

Stimuli may be bombarding consumers—yet they may not hear or see anything. This is because we apply the following selective processes:

1. **Selective exposure**—our eyes and mind seek out and notice only information that interests us.
2. **Selective perception**—we screen out or modify ideas, messages, and information that conflict with previously learned attitudes and beliefs.
3. **Selective retention**—we remember only what we want to remember.

These selective processes help explain why some people are not at all affected by some advertising—even offensive advertising. They just don't see or remember it!

A person's attitudes affect these selective processes. Further, decisions that the consumer is currently making and typically concerned about will affect which attitudes are relevant. If a consumer is thinking about buying an automobile, for example, then he may become quite interested in available cars, people's attitudes toward them, and car advertising. At the same time, if a house purchase isn't being considered at all, housing-related stimuli may be completely screened out.

A consumer may have a strong desire for status but can not explain why.

Mary McCarthy

When planning strategies, it would be useful to know how potential customers see their problems, what kind of information they are looking for, and what choice criteria they are using. This would help an advertiser to catch the attention of relevant problem solvers—as they are scanning the incoming stimuli.

Perception skills are learned. This has led some marketers to pay special attention to the learning process.

Learning determines what is remembered

Learning theorists describe a number of steps in the learning process. They define a "drive" as a strong stimulus that motivates an individual. Depending on the **cues**—products, signs, ads, and other stimuli in the environment—an individual chooses some specific response. A **response** is an effort to satisfy a drive. The specific response chosen depends on the cues and the person's past experience.

Reinforcement—of the learning process—occurs when the response is followed by satisfaction—that is, reducing the drive tension. Reinforcement strengthens the relationship between the cue and the response. And it may lead to a similar response the next time the drive occurs. Repeated reinforcement leads to the development of a habit—making the decision process routine for the individual. The relationships of the important variables in the learning process are shown in Figure 7–6.

Figure 7–6
The learning process

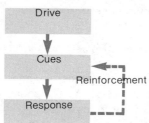

The learning process can be illustrated by a hungry person. The hunger *drive* could be satisfied in a variety of ways. But if the person happened to be driving around and saw a McDonald's sign—a *cue*—along the highway, then he might satisfy the drive by buying a McDonald's hamburger—the *response*. If the experience is satisfactory, *reinforcement* would occur—and our friend might be quicker to satisfy this drive in the same way in the future. This emphasizes the importance of developing good products which live up to the promises of the firm's advertising. People could learn to like or dislike McDonald's hamburgers—that is, learning works both ways.

Good experiences can lead to positive attitudes about a firm's product. Bad experiences can lead to negative attitudes—which even good promotion won't be able to change. In fact, the subject of attitudes is extremely important to marketers—and is discussed more fully in a following section.

Are needs learned?

Trying to separate learned from unlearned needs isn't very useful—and we won't try to here. But brief consideration of the idea is necessary—because some critics feel that marketing creates and warps many needs.

It can be argued that people are born with all the *basic* needs. A small child develops strong desires for "things"—certainly before advertisers have had a chance to influence him.

Even the need for status—which some marketing critics feel is related to the influence of advertising—is found among animals and in human societies where there is no such influence. Studies of birds show that there is a definite pecking order in flocks. In a study of jackdaws, for instance, it was found that the female, upon mating, acquires the status of her mate. In the human realm,

Whether or not needs are innate or learned—they are real.

Mary McCarthy

African villagers raise domesticated cattle and goats purely as signs of wealth and social status. For food, they hunt wild animals.[3]

Wanting a hamburger is learned behavior

Some needs may be culturally (or socially) determined, however. When human babies are born, their needs are simple. But as they grow, they learn complex behavior patterns to satisfy the drives stemming from these needs. As their needs become more sophisticated and specific, the needs can be described as wants. The need for food, for instance, may lead to many specific food wants—depending on the experience of the person. The resulting hunger drive may be satisfied only by the specific food desired. The people of Western nations like beef—and their children learn to like it. In India, however, Hindus regard the cow as sacred and will not eat beef. Hindu children learn to eat and like other foods. Many foods, in other words, can satisfy the hunger drive—but in a particular culture, an individual might *want* a hamburger. And the hunger drive might not be fully satisfied until he has eaten one.

Attitudes limit what decisions are made

Attitudes are an important topic for marketers—because attitudes affect the selective processes, learning, and eventually the buying decisions which people make. "Attitude" is commonly given several meanings—and it is important that we properly understand what we mean by the word. Coming from social psychology, it means: "An emotionalized predisposition to respond, positively or negatively, to an object or class of objects." "Emotionalized" separates attitudes from opinions and beliefs. "Predisposition" refers to the whole set of attitudes, opinions, and beliefs which are assumed to affect how a person learns and behaves.

For our purposes, **attitudes** are reasonably permanent points of view about an object or class of objects. Attitudes are things people believe strongly enough to be willing to take some action. Opinions and beliefs are not so action-oriented. It would be possible to have a belief—say that the world is round—without having an attitude about the world. And if you weren't sure it was round, you still might have an opinion about its shape.

Some marketers have stretched the meaning of attitude to include "preference" or, in the extreme, "intention to buy"—to make it easier to get from attitude to behavior. This logical extension occurred as it became clear that an attitude toward a specific object is not the same as an attitude toward a specific behavior regarding that object. In other words, a person might have a positive attitude toward a Cadillac—without having any intention to buy one. So, finding a positive attitude toward the car itself might be of little help in forecasting future behavior. But it is this narrow meaning of attitude—intention to buy—which is of most interest to managers who must forecast how much of their specific brand consumers will buy. So it would be desirable to try to link attitudes to intentions to buy.

Attitudes are important in marketing—because consumers are constantly faced with purchasing situations which require them to take some action. If they have a positive attitude toward a particular product or store, they may be more likely to buy that product, or shop in that store. Measuring these general attitudes might help to estimate a product's or a store's prospects. As we have said, these attitudes may not be directly related to buying behavior, but they *can* help a marketing manager get a better picture of present and potential markets. Some competitors may already have developed very positive attitudes toward their offerings. Or consumers may not have very strong attitudes toward a proposed product. They may be perfectly satisfied with their present ways of doing things—or simply "don't care."

Consumers' attitudes—both positive and negative—are learned from previous experiences with a product, exposure to the attitudes of others, or promotion which affects their own attitudes. If a marketer can discover the attitudes of the firm's potential target markets, then he can know whether there are positive attitudes to appeal to—or whether he must change existing attitudes—or perhaps even create new attitudes. Each of these jobs would require a different approach, of course.

Marketers generally try to understand the attitudes of their potential customers and work with them—perhaps directing positive attitudes toward the firm's own brand. This is much easier and more economical than trying to change attitudes. Changing present attitudes—especially negative ones—toward a specific brand—is probably the most difficult job that marketers face. If really negative attitudes are held by the target market, it may be more practical to try another strategy.[4]

Personality affects how people see things

Much research has been done on how personality affects people's behavior—and the results have been disappointing to marketers. Certainly, personality traits such as dominance, aggressiveness, dependence, sociability, responsibility, and friendliness would seem relevant to how people behave. And although traits like neatness have been associated with users of types of products—like cleaning materials—they haven't been much help in predicting which specific products or brands are chosen. Further, many personality variables would be hard to measure in an actual situation. Moodiness, for example, might be found among buyers of a product class—but of what use would this information be? Copywriters probably would not want to make a direct appeal to this variable. And salespeople would not want to ask customers to take a personality test before talking to them about their needs and what they might like to buy.

In summary, people's individual personalities probably do affect their buying behavior. But we do not now have general principles about personalities which can help us much in strategy planning.

Psychographic and life-style analysis may help

Some researchers have tried to find meaning in sets of personality traits—or in sets of customer-related dimensions that include personality traits. When only personality traits are used, the approach is sometimes calls "psychographics." More commonly, however, **psychographics** or **life-style analysis** refers to the analysis of many dimensions—including consumers' demographics, *A*ctivities, *I*nterests, and *O*pinions. The latter three sets are referred to as the "AIO variables." Typical life-style dimensions are shown in Table 7-1.

Life-style analysis assumes that the more you know and understand about your potential customers, the more effectively you can plan strategies to reach them.

Life-style analysis usually involves many items—perhaps on questionnaires as long as 25 pages—because several statements must be answered for each of the AIO variables. For example, if a marketer wanted to learn whether his target market included "sports spectators," he could list statements such as:

"I like to watch or listen to baseball or football games."
"I usually read the sports pages in the daily paper."
"I thoroughly enjoy conversations about sports."
"I would rather go to a sporting event than a dance."[5]

Potential customers would be asked how strongly they agreed with the statements—from "definitely agree" to "definitely disagree." Hundreds of such statements are used—and then a computer tries to find patterns among all of the answers. Many of the statements turn out to be irrelevant—but if meaningful market segments do emerge, then the answers provide insights about their life styles—as well as their demographics.

Life-style research can provide interesting insights about markets—but so far the results have been special purpose, rather than yielding general principles.

Table 7-1
Life-style dimensions

Activities	Interests	Opinions	Demographics
Work	Family	Themselves	Age
Hobbies	Home	Social issues	Education
Social events	Job	Politics	Income
Vacation	Community	Business	Occupation
Entertainment	Recreation	Economics	Family size
Club membership	Fashion	Education	Dwelling
Community	Food	Products	Geography
Shopping	Media	Future	City size
Sports	Achievements	Culture	Stage in life cycle

Source: Joseph T. Plummer, "The Concept and Application of Life-Style Segmentation," *Journal of Marketing*, January 1974, pp. 33–37.

A specific analysis, for example, might isolate clearly defined segments such as swingers, conservatives, etc.

The answers to the AIO questions provide a marketer with an in-depth view of how people think, and buy specific products. Sometimes it will show that changing products and/or target markets are needed. White Stag, for example, modified its missy-size sportswear lines when a life-style study showed that what the firm thought was the "missy-market" was really five different kinds of women with varied life-styles. This led to new lines for the various sub-markets—and new promotion to consumers and retailers.[6]

INTER-PERSONAL VARIABLES AFFECT THE INDIVIDUAL'S BUYING BEHAVIOR

So far we have been discussing findings from psychology. Yet consumer behavior may be determined not only by a person's needs and attitudes, but also by his relations to others.

Social psychologists and sociologists see market behavior as a response to the attitudes and behavior of others. We will look at their thinking about the interaction of the individual with family, social class, and reference groups.

Family consideration may overwhelm personal ones

Most decisions are made within a framework developed by experience within the family. An individual may go through much thinking about his own preferences for various products and services. But this analysis may be only one of the influences in the final decision. Social processes—such as power, domination, and affection—may be involved, too. This decision-making behavior is often the result of much social learning.

A boat for father or a TV for mother

The interaction of various social forces can be illustrated by a choice between two products—a television set and a boat with outboard motor.

The husband in a family might be particularly interested in the boat and motor for his camping and fishing trips. Weekend pleasure outings with the family would be only incidental. But in his arguments, he can present his preference in the desirable terms of *family wants and uses*. At the same time, his wife might prefer a new television set. It would improve the beauty of her home and, secondarily, would be used as an entertainment medium for herself, her husband, and the children. She, too, could argue that this purchase is *for the family*.

The actual outcome in such a situation is unpredictable. It depends on the strength of the husband's and the wife's preferences; their individual degree of dominance in the family; who contributes the most money to the family's income; the need for affection; and the response of other family members.

Knowing how all these forces interact would be helpful to the marketing manager. Unfortunately, each family behaves differently—and a marketing strategy usually has to deal with groups. But an individual retail salesperson in direct contact with the family might sense how the family operates and be able to adjust the marketing mix—especially the sales presentation to fit the situation.

The dynamics of family buying differs from family to family.

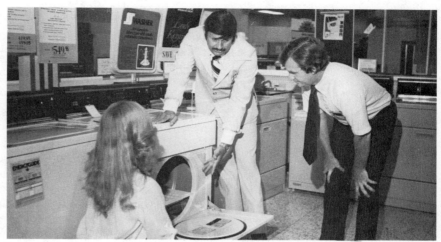

Peter Le Grand

Who is the real decision maker?

Although one person in the family often makes the purchase, in planning strategy it is important to find out who is the real decision maker.

Traditionally, the wife has been considered the family purchasing agent. She has been the one who had the time to shop and run the errands. As a result, most promotion has been aimed at women. But the situation may be changing. As more women work—and as night and Sunday shopping become more popular—the wife may be playing a less dominant role as family buyer and decision maker. Men now have more time for—and interest in—shopping. And they may make decisions involving large purchases—or buy products of special interest to them. Apparently buying varies greatly, depending on the product and the family—so research probably would be desirable for an important decision. But some generalizations can be helpful.

The nature of the product makes a difference

The husband is usually concerned with buying decisions that involve functional items. He tends to be more concerned with matters external to the family. The woman is more likely to make those buying decisions that have expressive value—and she is more concerned with internal matters. These distinctions may apply even if the user of a purchased product is the other person. For example, the wife may buy the husband's clothing accessories—while the husband might buy household appliances.

The husband and wife may work together where internal-functional or external-expressive matters are involved—and because the husband-wife roles may overlap. Husbands and wives may share in home improvements, for example, because they involve both functional and internal matters.[7] The relationships may be changing as women's roles change—presenting new opportunities for marketers.

Some buy for themselves or others

The question of spending by the family is not limited to parents. As the life-cycle stages of the family change—see Chapter 6—the children begin to handle and spend more money.

In many cases, moreover, the person actually doing the shopping is only acting as an agent for persons who may have specified which products should be bought. Small children may want specific kinds of cereals. The father may want a certain brand of cigarettes or golf balls.

Social class affects buying of specifics

Up to now, we have been concerned with the individual and his relation to his family. Now let's consider how society looks at an individual and perhaps the family—in terms of social class.

The mere mention of class distinctions in the United States provokes a defensive reaction. We like to think of America as a land of equality. We have been brought up to revere the statement in the Declaration of Independence, "All men are created equal."

Our class system is far less pronounced than those in European and Asiatic nations—where the system is tried to religion, blood kinship, or landed wealth. Nevertheless, sociological research shows that a class structure *does* exist in this country.

In discussing class structure, we will use the traditional technical terms—"upper," "middle," and "lower." But a word of warning is needed. The choice of these terms—even though in general use—is unfortunate, because they imply "superior" and "inferior." In sociological and marketing usage, however, no value judgment is intended. In fact, it is not possible to state that a particular class is "better" or "happier" than any other.

Some people strive to enter a "higher" class—because they find the values of that class more admirable. Others are comfortable with the standards of their own group—and prefer to remain where they are. And even what they think about people in the other social classes depends on where they are in the class system. See Figure 7–7.

The marketer's goal should be to learn the characteristics and typical behavior patterns of each class—so that he will be better able to develop unique marketing strategies based on class differences.

Characteristics of the U.S. class system

The U.S. class system is an individual and a family system. While a child is a member of a family—his social status will depend on the status of his family. But grown children often "join" a different class than their parents. This is especially true when they reach higher education levels—or take up different occupations from those of their parents.

The U.S. class system is usually measured by *occupation, education,* and *type and location of housing.* The *source* of income is related to these variables, but *there is not a direct relation between amount of income and social class.* In fact, some white-collar workers earn much less than some blue-collar workers—who are typically placed in a "lower" class.

Figure 7–7
Each class sees the other classes differently

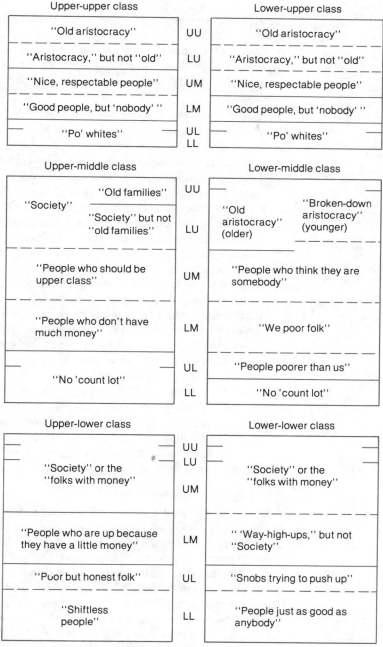

Upper-upper class

"Old aristocracy"	UU
"Aristocracy," but not "old"	LU
"Nice, respectable people"	UM
"Good people, but 'nobody' "	LM
"Po' whites"	UL / LL

Lower-upper class

"Old aristocracy"
"Aristocracy," but not "old"
"Nice, respectable people"
"Good people, but 'nobody' "
"Po' whites"

Upper-middle class

"Society" — "Old families" / "Society" but not "old families"	UU / LU
"People who should be upper class"	UM
"People who don't have much money"	LM
"No 'count lot"	UL / LL

Lower-middle class

"Old aristocracy" (older) / "Broken-down aristocracy" (younger)	
"People who think they are somebody"	
"We poor folk"	
"People poorer than us"	
"No 'count lot"	

Upper-lower class

"Society" or the "folks with money"	UU / LU / UM
"People who are up because they have a little money"	LM
"Poor but honest folk"	UL
"Shiftless people"	LL

Lower-lower class

"Society" or the "folks with money"
" 'Way-high-ups," but not "Society"
"Snobs trying to push up"
"People just as good as anybody"

Source. A. Davis, B. B. Gardner, and M. K. Gardner, *Deep South* (Chicago: University of Chicago Press, 1941).

The early work on social class in the United States was done for cities in the 10,000–25,000 population range. Later, the *Chicago Tribune* developed a population breakdown for metropolitan Chicago—which is probably typical of a big industrial city. Many of the findings are interesting to marketing managers. Let us look at the *Chicago Tribune* breakdown first and then consider some of the findings.

1. **Upper class** (0.9 percent of population): This was defined as wealthy old families (**upper-upper class**) and the socially prominent new rich (**lower-upper class**). This group has been the traditional leader in the American community. Most large manufacturers, bankers, and top marketing executives belong to it. It represents, however, less than 1 percent of the population. Being so small, the two upper classes are often merged into one.

2. **Upper-middle class** (7.2 percent of population): These are the successful business people, professionals, and top salespeople. The advertising professional usually is part of this class—reflecting the tastes and codes of the first two groups. Yet, combined, groups 1 and 2 still represent only 8.1 percent of the population.

3. **Lower-middle class** (28.4 percent of population): These are the white-collar workers—small business people, office workers, teachers, technicians, and most salespeople. The American moral code and the emphasis on hard work have come from this class. This has been the most conforming, church-going, morally serious segment of society. We speak of America as a middle-class society, but the middle-class value system stops here. Two thirds of our society is *not* middle class.

4. **Upper-lower class** (44.0 percent of population): These are the factory production line workers, the skilled workers, the service workers—the "blue collar" workers—and the local politicians and union leaders who would lose their power if they moved out of this class.

5. **Lower-lower class** (19.5 percent of population): This group includes unskilled laborers and people in nonrespectable occupations.[8]

What do these classes mean?

The *Chicago Tribune* class studies suggest that an old saying, "A rich man is simply a poor man with more money," may not hold true. While Engel's laws may still apply in general, it appears that a person belonging to the lower class—given the same income as a middle-class person—handles himself and his money very differently. The various classes buy at different stores, would prefer different treatment from salespeople, buy different brands of products (even though their prices are approximately the same), and have different spending-saving attitudes. Some of these differences are summarized in Figure 7–8.[9]

The marketing implications of this and other studies are most interesting. Selection of advertising media should be related to social class, for example. Customers in the lower classes would have little interest in *Fortune, New Yorker, Vogue,* or *Ladies' Home Journal*—while the middle and upper classes probably would have little desire to read *True Story, Modern Romances,* or *True Confessions.*

Class differences also have a bearing on product design and the kinds of

Figure 7–8
A comparison of attitudes and characteristics of middle and lower social classes

Middle class	Lower class
1. Pointed to the future.	1. Pointed to the present and past.
2. Viewpoint embraces a long expanse of time.	2. Lives and thinks in a short expanse of time.
3. More urban identification	3. More rural identification.
4. Stresses rationality.	4. Nonrational essentially.
5. Has a well-structured sense of the universe.	5. Vague and unclear structuring.
6. Horizons vastly extended or not limited.	6. Horizons sharply defined and limited.
7. Greater sense of choice making.	7. Limited sense of choice making.
8. Self-confident, willing to take risks.	8. Very much concerned with security and insecurity.
9. Immaterial and abstract in thinking (idea-minded).	9. Concrete and perceptive in thinking (thing-minded).
10. Sees himself tied to national happenings.	10. World revolves around family.

Source: P. Martineau, "The Pattern of Social Classes," in *Marketing's Role in Scientific Management*, ed. R. L. Clewett (Chicago: American Marketing Association, 1957), pp. 246–47.

products carried by retailers. The *Chicago Tribune* studies found that the customers in the lower class tend to prefer overstuffed or ornate house furnishings, while those in the middle and upper classes were more receptive to severely plain, functional styles. Further, those in the lower classes seemed to be confused by variety—and apparently had difficulty making choices. As a result, such buyers looked on furniture salespeople as friends and advisors. The middle-class buyers, on the other hand, were more self-confident. They knew what they wanted—and preferred the salesclerk to be an impersonal guide.

Clearly, social class has an impact on buying processes and cannot be ignored when developing marketing strategies. Fortunately, too, some fairly objective and readily available data can be used for determining social class. In particular, U.S. Census Bureau data on occupation, education, and expenditures on housing can be used.

Reference groups have relevance, too

A **reference group** is the people to whom the individual looks when forming attitudes about a particular topic. A person normally has several reference groups—for different topics. Some he meets face-to-face. Others he may just wish to imitate. In either case, he may take his values from these reference groups—and make buying decisions based on what he feels they would accept. *Playboy* magazine editors, for instance—and the "in" people who presumably read it—might be a reference group for *some Playboy* readers.

The importance of reference groups depends somewhat on the nature of the product—and on whether anyone else will be able to "see" which product and which brand is being used. Figure 7–9 suggests the interrelations. For example, an individual may smoke cigarettes because his reference group smokes—and the group's preference may even determine the brand he chooses. At the other extreme, most people in our society use laundry soap—and which brand is not easily known. In this case, reference group influence may be less relevant.

Inner- versus other-directed people

The reference-group concept has grown in importance in recent years as more people live and work together in today's larger organizations. The "organiza-

Figure 7–9
Reference-group influence

Brand type \ Product class	Weak	Strong
Weak	Canned peaches Laundry soap Refrigerator (brand) Radios	Air conditioners* Instant coffee* TV (black and white)
Strong	Clothing Furniture Magazines Refrigerator (type) Toilet soap	Cars* Cigarettes* Beer (premium versus regular)* Drugs*

* Classification by the extent to which reference groups influence their purchase based on actual experimental evidence. Other products listed are classified speculatively on the basis of generalizations derived from the sum of research in this area and confirmed by the judgment of seminar participants.
Source: Adapted from work of Bureau of Applied Social Research, Columbia University, New York, N.Y.

tion man" seems to be especially responsive to group pressures—and puts "getting along" with the group above other values.

This group consciousness has been described by Riesman as a sign of the transition from the "inner-directed" to the "other-directed" person. Inner-directed people have their own value systems and direct their own activities. Other-directed people are the ones whose characters are formed mainly by those around them. Other-directed people—a large proportion of our society according to Riesman—are led by each other. Consequently, there is a strong tendency to conform.[10]

Reaching the opinion leaders who are buyers

A trend toward other-directedness could have a major effect on the way individuals and groups change their values and desires. Advertising—and promotion in general—might have to be more concerned with affecting opinion leaders.[11]

Opinion leaders are people who influence others. Opinion leaders are not necessarily wealthier or better educated. And opinion leaders on one subject are not necessarily opinion leaders on another subject. Homemakers with large families may be consulted for advice on cooking. Young girls may be leaders in new clothing styles and cosmetics. This may occur within the various social classes—with different opinion leaders in the various classes.[12]

Culture surrounds the whole decision-making process

Culture is the whole set of beliefs, attitudes, and ways of doing things of a reasonably homogeneous set of people. We can think of the American culture, the western Canadian culture, the French culture, or the Latin American culture. People within these cultural groupings would be more similar in outlook and behavior than those in other groups. And sometimes it is useful to think of subcultures within such groupings. For example, within the American culture there are various religious and ethnic subcultures.

From a target marketing point of view, a marketing manager would probably want to aim at people within one culture. So, if a firm were developing strategies for two cultures—two different strategic plans would be needed.[13]

The attitudes and beliefs that we usually associate with culture tend to change slowly. So once you develop a good understanding of the culture for which you are planning, it probably will be practical to ignore this variable in favor of the more dynamic variables discussed above.

CONSUMERS USE PROBLEM-SOLVING PROCESSES

Behavioral scientists generally agree that people are problem solvers—that is, individuals are motivated by needs and drives which they try to satisfy. An unsatisfied need leads to tension and the desire to solve that problem. How the individual solves a particular problem depends on his own intra- and interpersonal variables. We saw this in Figure 7–4.

A common problem-solving process seems to be used by most consumers. The basic problem-solving process consists of five steps:

1. Becoming aware of—or interested in—the problem.
2. Gathering information about possible solutions.
3. Evaluating alternative solutions—perhaps trying some out.
4. Deciding on the appropriate solution.
5. Evaluating the decision.[14]

An expanded version of this basic process is presented in Figure 7–10. Here, the evaluation of information about alternatives would include not only a product type in relation to other types of products, but also brands within a product type *and* the stores where they might be available. This is a complicated evaluation procedure and—depending on their choice criteria, consumers may make seemingly "irrational" decisions.[15] If convenient service is crucial, for example, a person might pay list price for an "unexciting" car from a *very convenient* dealer.

People use different opinion leaders for different products.

Mary McCarthy

**Figure 7–10
Consumer's problem-solving
process**

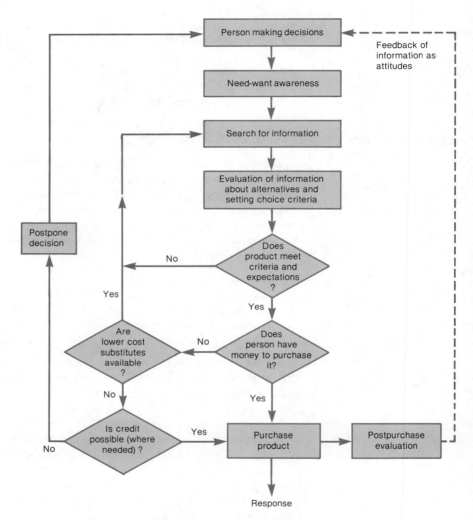

*Three levels of problem
solving are useful*

The basic problem-solving process shows the steps a consumer might go through while trying to find a way to satisfy his needs—but it does not show how long this will take—or how much thought will be given to each step. Some individuals have had much experience solving certain problems—and can move quickly through some of the steps or almost directly to a decision.

It is helpful, therefore, to recognize three levels of problem solving: extensive problem solving, limited problem solving, and routinized response behavior.[16] These problem-solving approaches might be used for any kind of good or service.

Extensive problem solving is involved when a need is completely new to a person—and much effort is taken to understand the need and how to satisfy it. A new college student, for example, may have feelings of loneliness, a need for companionship, a need for achievement, and so on. It may take him some time to figure out how and what he wants to do.

Limited problem solving involves *some* effort to understand a person's need and how best to satisfy it. Our college student, for example, might have tried various ways of satisfying his needs and come up with several fairly good choices. So, limited problem solving would mean deciding which choice would be best at a particular time.

Routinized response behavior involves mechanically selecting a particular way of satisfying a need whenever it occurs. When our college student feels the need for companionship, for example, it might be quickly solved by meeting with friends in familiar surroundings. A daily trip to the local "hang out" might become the answer to this problem.

Problem solving is a learning process

The reason problem solving becomes simpler with time is that people learn from experience—both positive and negative things. As a person approaches the problem-solving process, he brings with him attitudes formed by previous experiences and social training. Each new problem-solving process may then contribute to or modify this attitude set.

New concepts require an adoption process

Really new concepts present a problem solver with a harder job—handling the adoption process. The **adoption process** means the steps which individuals go through on the way to accepting or rejecting a new idea. It is similar to the problem-solving process, but the adoption process makes clearer the role of learning and the potential contribution of promotion in a marketing mix.

The adoption process for individuals moves through some fairly definite steps, as follows:

1. Awareness—the potential customer comes to know about the product but lacks details. He may not even know how it works or what it will do.
2. Interest—*If* he becomes interested, he gathers general information and facts about the product.
3. Evaluation—He begins to make a mental trial, applying the product to his personal situation.
4. Trial—The customer may buy the product so that he can experiment with it in use. A product that is either too expensive to try or isn't available for trial may never be adopted.
5. Decision—He decides on either adoption or rejection. A satisfactory evaluation and trial may lead to adoption of the product and regular use. According to psychological learning theory, reinforcement will lead to adoption.
6. Confirmation—The adopter continues to rethink his decision and searches for support for his decision—that is, further reinforcement.[17]

Dissonance may set in after the decision

After a decision has been made, a buyer may have second thoughts. He may have had to choose from among several attractive alternatives—weighing the pros and cons and finally making a decision. Later doubts, however, may lead to **dissonance**—a form of tension growing out of uncertainty about the rightness of a decision. Dissonance may lead a buyer to search for additional information—to confirm the wisdom of the decision and, so, reduce tension. This points up the importance of providing the information the consumer might want

Dissonance may set in after a purchase.

Mary McCarthy

at this step. Without this confirmation, the adopter might buy something else next time—also, he might *not* give very positive comments to others.[18]

Several processes are related and relevant to strategy planning

The interrelation of the problem-solving process, the adoption process, and learning can be seen in Figure 7–11. It is important to see this interrelation—and to note that they can be modified or accelerated by promotion. Also, note that the problem-solving behavior of potential buyers would affect the design of distribution systems. If they aren't willing to travel far to shop, then more outlets may be needed if you want their business. Similarly, their attitudes may help determine what price to charge. You can see that knowing how a target market handles these processes would aid marketing strategy planning.

INTEGRATING THE BEHAVIORAL SCIENCE APPROACHES

We have been examining the impact of many variables on a consumer's problem-solving behavior. Hopefully, the decision processes within a consumer's "black box" are somewhat clearer. But to tie this all together, we will present the various processes in one integrated diagram—and suggest how it might help you plan better marketing strategies—and understand new research findings.

Problem-solving model can aid strategy planning

The integrated model in Figure 7–12 can be useful for estimating what type of problem-solving behavior the target customers are likely to use in a specific product-market.

Extensive problem solving may be necessary if the information at some of the decision-making steps is inadequate. Then the consumer must get the needed information and apply it. Routine buying behavior, on the other hand, could occur if the consumer is quite familiar with the incoming stimuli—perceives them accurately (at least in his own mind)—and has already learned that a particular product would be very satisfactory.

Running through this decision-making model could help a marketing manager focus on what he knows—and does not know—about his target customers' decision-making processes. If he doesn't know how they search for information, for example, this might require some marketing research to be sure he understands how they behave. He might also discover their attitudes toward the firm's product.

If the target customers are perceiving the product incorrectly, a promotion effort might try to clarify the information entering the buyer's "black box." Or if there is confusion about how to evaluate all the information, advertising or personal selling efforts might be designed to help potential customers choose among the various offerings.

Model can incorporate research findings

Finally, this model gives marketing managers a way to handle new research findings in a meaningful way. Instead of just saying, "Well, that's very interesting—and wondering how it all fits—they can organize their thoughts within the model, modifying or changing their understanding of whichever variables are involved in the research findings.

Intuition and judgment are still needed

The present state of our knowledge about consumer behavior is such that we still must rely on intuition and judgment to develop useful descriptions of the "why" of consumer behavior in specific market segments. Demographic characteristics help some—and behavioral theories provide additional insights. But, finally, the marketing manager still has to mix in a dash of personal intuition and judgment to find homogeneous groups of customers.

By applying our model, however, "guesses" should be limited to areas where knowledge is lacking or vague. There is no excuse for "guessing" about the impact of variables which have already been well researched.

Some people feel that understanding consumers is just "common sense," but actually they are applying some model—perhaps a very simple one. As we have seen, economists tend to apply the "economic man" model—and some

Figure 7–11
Relation of problem-solving process, adoption process, and learning (given a problem and drive tensions)

Problem-solving steps	Adoption process steps	Learning steps
1. Becoming aware of or interested in the problem	Awareness and interest	Drive
2. Gathering information about possible solutions	Interest and evaluation	Cues
3. Evaluating alternative solutions, perhaps trying some out	Evaluation, maybe trial	
4. Deciding on the appropriate solution	Decision	Response
5. Evaluating the decision	Confirmation	

Reinforcement

Figure 7–12
Integrated buyer behavior model

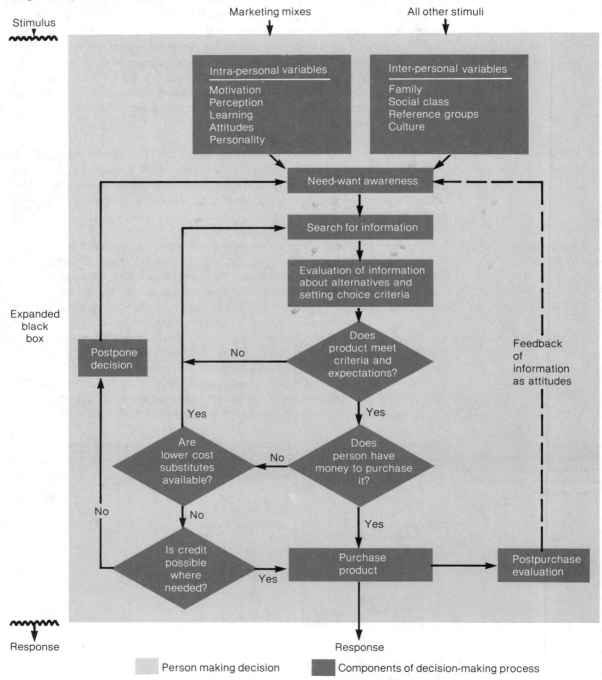

very price-oriented retailers seem to rely on this model. But typically, consumer behavior is much more complicated—and better strategies will result from making use of all the information available about how the intra-personal and inter-personal variables affect the target customers' problem solving in a particular market.

CONCLUSION

In this chapter, we have analyzed the individual consumer as a problem solver who is influenced by intra- and inter-personal variables. Our "black box" model of buyer behavior helps integrate a large number of variables into one process. A good grasp of this material is needed in marketing strategy planning—because an assumption that everyone behaves the way you do—or even like your family or friends do—can lead to expensive marketing errors.

Consumer buying behavior results from the consumer's efforts to satisfy needs and wants. We discussed some reasons why consumers buy—and saw that consumer behavior can't be explained by only a list of needs.

We also saw that our society is divided into social classes—which does help explain some consumer behavior. The impact of reference groups and opinion leaders was discussed, too.

A buyer behavior model was presented to help you interpret and integrate the present findings—and any new data you might obtain from marketing research. As of now, the behavioral sciences can only offer insights and theories which the marketing manager must blend with intuition and judgment in developing marketing strategies.

Marketing research may have to be used to answer specific questions. But if neither the money nor the time is available for research, then management will have to rely on the available description of present behavior and "guesstimates" about future behavior. You should study the popular magazines and the leading newspapers carefully—they often reflect the public's shifting attitudes. You also should be familiar with the many studies concerning the changing consumer that are published regularly in the business and trade press. This material—added and related to the information in these last two chapters—will help your decision making.

Remember that consumers—with all their needs and attitudes—may be elusive—but not invisible. We have more data and understanding of consumer behavior than is generally used by business managers. Applying this information may help you find your breakthrough opportunity.

QUESTIONS AND PROBLEMS

1. What is the behavioral science concept which underlies the "black box" model of consumer behavior? Does this concept have operational relevance to marketing managers, i.e., if it is a valid concept, can they make use of it?

2. Explain what is meant by a hierarchy of needs and pro-

vide examples of one or more products which enable *you* to satisfy each of the four levels of need.

3. Cut out two recent advertisements: one full-page color ad from a magazine and one large display from a newspaper. Indicate which needs are being appealed to in each case.

4. Explain how an understanding of consumers' learning processes might affect marketing strategy planning.

5. Explain psychographics and lifestyle analysis. Explain how it might be useful for planning marketing strategies to reach college students as compared to the "average" consumer.

6. How do society's values have an impact on purchasing behavior? Give two specific examples.

7. How should the social class structure affect the planning of a new restaurant in a large city? How might the four Ps be adjusted?

8. What social class would you associate with each of the following phrases or items?
   a. Sport cars.
   b. *True Story, True Romances,* etc.
   c. *New Yorker.*
   d. *Playboy.*
   e. People watching "soap operas."
   f. TV bowling shows.
   g. Families that serve martinis, especially before dinner.
   h. Families who dress formally for dinner regularly.
   i. Families which are distructful of banks (keep money in socks or mattress).
   j. Owners of French poodles.
   In each case, choose one class, if you can. If you are not able to choose one class, but rather feel that several classes are equally likely, then so indicate. In those cases where you feel that all classes would be equally interested or characterized by a particular item, choose all five classes.

9. Illustrate how the reference group concept may apply in practice, by explaining how you personally are influenced by some reference group for some product. What are the implications of such behavior for marketing managers?

10. What new status symbols are replacing the piano and automobile? Do these products have any characteristics in common? If they do, what are some possible status symbols of the future?

11. Illustrate the three levels of problem solving with an example from your own personal experience.

12. On the basis of the data and analysis presented in Chapters 6 and 7, what kind of buying behavior would you expect to find for the following products: *(a)* canned peas, *(b)* toothpaste, *(c)* ballpoint pens, *(d)* baseball gloves, *(e)* sport coats, *(f)* dishwashers, *(g)* encyclopedias, *(h)* automobiles, and *(i)* motorboats? Set up a chart for your answer with products along the left-hand margin as the row headings and the following factors as headings for the columns: *(a)* how consumers would shop for these products, *(b)* how far they would go, *(c)* whether they would buy by brand, *(d)* whether they would wish to compare with other products, and *(e)* any other factors they should consider. Insert short answers—words or phrases are satisfactory—in the various grid boxes. Be prepared to discuss how the answers you put in the chart would affect each product's marketing mix.

SUGGESTED CASES

7 **Sleep-Inn Motel**

9 **Annie's Floral**

NOTES

1. K. H. Chung, *Motivational Theories and Practices* (Columbus, Ohio: Grid, Inc., 1977), pp. 40–43; and A. H. Maslow, *Motivation and Personality* (New York: Harper & Brothers, 1954).
2. G. H. Smith, *Motivation Research and Advertising in Marketing* (New York: McGraw-Hill Book Co., 1954). pp. 19–21.
3. Robert Ardrey, *African Genesis* (New York: Atheneum Publishers, 1961), chap. 4.
4. Donald G. Morrison; "Purchase Intentions and Purchase Behav-ior," *Journal of Marketing,* Spring 1979, pp. 65–74; Paul W. Miniard and Joel B. Cohen, "Isolating Attitudinal and Normative Influences in Behavioral Intentions Models," *Journal of Marketing Research,* February 1979, pp. 102–10; Russell I. Haley and Peter B. Case, "Testing Thirteen Attitude Scales for Agreement and Brand Discrimination," *Journal of Marketing,* Fall 1979, pp. 20–32; Paul R. Warshaw; "Predicting Purchase and Other Behaviors from General and Conceptually Specific Intentions," *Journal of Marketing Research,* February 1980, pp. 26–33; Paul R. War-

shaw, "A New Model for Predicting Behavioral Intentions: An Alternative to Fishbein," *Journal of Marketing Research,* May 1980, pp. 153–72; Michael J. Ryan and E. H. Bonfield, "Fishbein's Intentions Model: A Test of External and Pragmatic Validity," *Journal of Marketing Research,* Spring 1980, pp. 82–95. This discussion is based on J. Pavasars and W. D. Wells, "Measures of Brand Attitudes Can Be Used to Predict Buying Behavior," *Marketing News,* April 11, 1975, p. 6; and F. E. Webster, Jr., *Social Aspects of Marketing* (Englewood Cliffs, N.J.: Prentice-Hall, Inc., 1974), pp. 44–46.

5. William D. Wells and Douglas J. Tigert, "Activities, Interests, and Opinions," in *Market Segmentation,* ed. James F. Engel et al. (New York: Holt, Rinehart & Winston, Inc., 1972), p. 258.

6. Alvin C. Burns and Mary C. Harrison, "A Test of the Reliability of Psychographics," *Journal of Marketing Research,* February 1979, pp. 32–38; "Information on Values and Lifestyles Needed to Identify Buying Patterns," *Marketing News,* October 5, 1979, p. 1 f; and *Marketing News,* December 31, 1976, p. 8. See also "Life Style Research Inappropriate for Some Categories of Products," *Marketing News,* June 17, 1977, p. 9; M. E. Goldberg, "Identifying Relevant Psychographic Segments: How Specifying Product Functions Can Help," *Consumer Research,* December 1976, pp. 163–69; and W. D. Wells, "Psychographics: A Critical Review," *Journal of Marketing Research,* May 1975, pp. 196–213.

7. W. H. Reynolds and James H. Meyers, "Marketing and the American Family," *Business Topics,* Spring 1966, pp. 58–59. See also G. M. Munsinger, J. E. Weber, and R. W. Hansen, "Joint Home Purchasing Decisions by Husbands and Wives," *Consumer Research,* March 1975, pp. 60–66; E. P. Cox III, "Family Purchase Decision Making and the Process of Adjustment," *Journal of Marketing Research,* May 1975, pp. 189–95; R. T. Green and I. C. M. Cunningham, "Feminine Role Perception and Family Purchasing Decisions," *Journal of Marketing Research,* August 1975, pp. 325–32; I. C. M. Cunningham and R. R. Green, "Purchasing Roles in the U.S. Family, 1955 & 1973," *Journal of Marketing,* October 1974, pp. 61–64; and Harry L. Davis, "Decision Making within the Household," *Journal of Consumer Research,* March 1976, pp. 241–60; Patrick E. Murphy and William A. Staples; "A Modernized Family Life Cycle," *Consumer Research,* June 1979, pp. 12–22; David J. Curry and Michael B. Menasco, "Some Effects of Differing Information Processing Strategies on Husband-Wife Joint Decisions," *Consumer Research,* September 1979, pp. 192–203; George J. Szybillo et al., "Family Member Influence in Household Decision Making," *Consumer Research,* December 1979, pp. 312–16; and Harry L. Davis, "Decision Making within the Household," *Consumer Research,* March 1976, pp. 241–60.

8. Adapted from P. Martineau, *Motivation in Advertising* (New York: McGraw-Hill Book Co., 1957), p. 164.

9. P. Martineau. "The Pattern of Social Classes," in *Marketing's Role in Scientific Management,* ed. R. L. Clewett (Chicago: American Marketing Association, 1957), pp. 246–47. See also James A. Carman, *The Application of Social Class in Market Segmentation* (Berkeley: Institute of Business and Economic Research, University of California, 1965); William H. Peters, "Relative Occupational Class Income: A Significant Variable in the Marketing of Automobiles," *Journal of Marketing,* April 1970, pp. 74–78; and Arun K. Jain; "A Method for Investigating and Representing

an Implicit Theory of Social Class," *Consumer Research,* June 1975, pp. 53–59.

10. David Riesman, N. Glaser, and R. Denney, *The Lonely Crowd* (Garden City, N.Y.: Doubleday & Co., Inc., 1950). For additional discussion on reference groups, see James H. Donnelly, Jr., "Social Character and Acceptance of New Products," *Journal of Marketing Research,* February 1970, pp. 111–16; and Yoram Wind, "Preference of Relevant Others and Individual Choice Models," *Consumer Research,* June 1976, pp. 50–57; Jeffrey D. Ford and Elwood A. Ellis; "A Reexamination of Group Influence on Member Brand Preference," *Journal of Marketing Research,* February 1980, pp. 125–32.

11. Harold H. Kassarjian, "Social Character and Differential Preference for Mass Communication," *Journal of Marketing Research,* May 1965, pp. 146–53; and James H. Myers and Thomas S. Robertson, "Dimensions of Opinion Leadership," *Journal of Marketing Research,* February 1972, pp. 41–46.

12. James A. Carman, *The Application of Social Class in Market Segmentation* (Berkeley: Institute of Business and Economic Research, University of California, 1965) pp. 21 and 61; and Elihu Katz and Paul E. Lazarsfeld, *Personal Influences* (Glencoe, Ill.: Free Press, 1955). See also John O. Summers, "The Identity of Women's Clothing Fashion Opinion Leaders," *Journal of Marketing Research,* May 1970, pp. 178–86; and Charles W. King and John O. Summers, "Overlap of Opinion Leadership across Consumer Product Categories," *Journal of Marketing Research,* February 1970, pp. 43–50.

13. Walter A. Henry, "Cultural Values Do Correlate with Consumer Behavior," *Journal of Marketing Research,* May 1976, pp. 121–27.

14. Adapted from James H. Myers and William H. Reynolds, *Consumer Behavior and Marketing Management* (Boston: Houghton Mifflin Co., 1967), p. 49.

15. Richard W. Olshavsky and Donald H. Granbois, "Consumer Decision Making—Fact or Fiction?" *Consumer Research,* September 1979, pp. 93–100; David A. Sheluga; James Jaccard; and Jacob Jacoby, "Preference, Search, and Choice: An Integrative Approach," *Consumer Research,* September 1979, pp. 166–176; Jack J. Kasulis, Robert F. Lusch, and Edward F. Stafford, Jr., "Consumer Acquisition Patterns for Durable Goods," *Consumer Research,* June 1979, pp. 47–57; and Lawrence X. Tarpey, Sr., and J. Paul Peter, "A Comparative Analysis of Three Consumer Decision Strategies," *Consumer Research,* June 1975, pp. 29–37.

16. John A. Howard and Jagdish N. Sheth, *The Theory of Buyer Behavior* (New York: John Wiley & Sons, Inc., 1969), pp. 46–48. See also C. Whan Park, "Students and Housewives: Differences in Susceptibility to Reference Group Influence," *Consumer Research,* September 1977, pp. 102–10.

17. Adapted from E. M. Rogers, *The Diffusion of Innovations* (New York: Free Press of Glencoe, 1962); and E. M. Rogers with F. Schoemaker, *Communication of Innovation: A Cross Cultural Approach* (New York: Free Press of Glencoe, 1968).

18. For further discussion on this topic, see James H. Myers and William H. Reynolds, *Consumer Behavior and Marketing Management (Boston: Houghton-Mifflin Co., 1967);* and J. F. Engel, D. T. Kollat, and R. D. Blackwell, *Consumer Behavior* (New York: Holt Reinhart & Winston, Inc., 1968).

When you finish this chapter, you should:	1.	Know who the intermediate customers are.
	2.	Know about the number and distribution of manufacturers.
	3.	Understand the problem-solving behavior of manufacturers' purchasing agents.
	4.	Know the basic methods used in industrial buying.
	5.	Know how buying by retailers, wholesalers, farmers, and governments is similar to—and different from—industrial buying.
	6.	Recognize the important new terms (shown in red).

8

Intermediate customers and their buying behavior

Intermediate customers buy more than final consumers!

Most of us would probably define the term *customer* as the individual final consumer (or family). Actually, most purchases are made by intermediate customers. This chapter will discuss these intermediate customers: Who they are. Where they are. What their buying habits are.

There are great marketing opportunities in serving intermediate customers—and a student heading toward a business career has a good chance of working in this area. While we will limit the discussion to the United States to keep it specific—most of the ideas apply to international markets.

INTERMEDIATE CUSTOMERS ARE DIFFERENT

Intermediate customers are any buyers between producers of basic raw materials and final consumers. The various types and their number are shown in Table 8–1. There are only about 15 million intermediate customers in the United States—compared to more than 220 million final consumers. These customers do many different jobs—and many different market dimensions are needed to describe all these different markets.

The main focus in this chapter will be on the buying behavior of manufacturers—because we know the most about them. Other intermediate customers appear to behave similarly—especially in the way they buy plant and equipment.

Even trivial differences are important

Understanding how and why intermediate customers buy is important because competition is often rugged in intermediate markets. Even "trivial" differences may affect the success of a marketing mix.

201

**Table 8–1
Kind and number of
intermediate customers in
1976–77**

Services.	3,833,000
Agriculture, forestry, and fisheries.	3,653,000
Retailers.	2,440,000
Construction	1,221,000
Wholesalers	591,000
Manufacturers	468,000
Governmental units	80,000
Others.	2,225,000

Source: *Statistical Abstract of the United States, 1979.*

Since sellers usually approach each intermediate customer directly—through a sales rep—there is more chance to adjust the marketing mix for each individual customer. It is even possible that there will be a special marketing strategy for each individual customer. This is carrying target marketing to its extreme. But when the customer's size and sales volume make this possible, it may be not only desirable but necessary in order to compete.

In such situations, the individual sales rep will have to carry more responsibility for strategic planning. This is relevant to career planning—since these jobs are very challenging and pay well.

Let's see how these intermediate customers behave.

MANUFACTURERS ARE IMPORTANT CUSTOMERS

*There are not many big
ones*

One of the most striking facts about manufacturers is how few there are compared to final consumers. In the industrial market, there were about 313,000 factories in 1972—and the majority of these are quite small. See Table 8–2. The owners are often the buyers in small plants. And they buy less formally than buyers in the relatively few large manufacturing plants—which employ most of the workers and produce a large share of the value added by manufacturing. In 1972, plants with 250 or more employees numbered only 13,622—4.3 percent of the total, yet they employed 57 percent of the production employees and produced 63 percent of value added by manufacture. These large plants are important—and it may be desirable to segment potential customers on the basis of size.

*Customers cluster in
geographic areas*

In addition to concentration by size, industrial markets are concentrated in particular geographic areas—both regions and cities. The Middle West, Middle Atlantic states, and California are important industrial markets—as are the big metropolitan areas.

The buyers for some of these larger manufacturers are even further concentrated in home offices—often in large metropolitan areas. One of the large building material manufacturers, for example, does most of its buying for more than 50 plants from its Chicago office. In such a case, a sales rep may be able to sell all over the country without leaving his home city. This makes selling easier for competitors too—and the market may be extremely competitive. The importance of these big buyers has led some companies to set up "national account" sales forces—specially trained to cater to their needs. A geographically bound salesperson can be at a real disadvantage against such competitors.

Concentration by industry

Not only do we see concentration by size of firm and geographic location, but also by industry. Manufacturers of advanced electronics systems are concentrated in the Boston and New York areas—and on the West Coast. The steel industry is heavily concentrated in the Pittsburgh, Birmingham (Alabama), and Chicago areas. Other industries have similar concentrations—based on the availability of natural or human resources.

Much data is available on industrial markets by SIC code

In industrial markets, marketing managers can focus their attention on a relatively few clearly defined markets and reach the majority of the business. Their efforts can be aided by the availability of very detailed information. The federal government regularly collects data on the number of establishments, sales volumes, and number of employees of a large number of industry groups—broken down by county and SMSA. The data is reported for Standard Industrial Classification code industries *(SIC Codes)*. These codes are a real help to market research for those who can relate their own sales to their *customers'* type of activity. SIC code breakdowns start with such broad industry categories as food and related products (code 20), tobacco products (code 21), textile mill products (code 22), apparel (code 23), and so on.

Within each two-digit industry breakdown, much more detailed data may be available for three-digit and four-digit industries (that is, sub-industries of the two- or three-digit industries). Within the apparel (23) industry, for example, the three-digit industry 232—men's, youths', and boys' furnishings, work clothing, and similar garments—contains the following four-digit industries: shirts, collars, and night wear (2321), underwear (2322), neckwear (2323), separate trousers (2327), work clothing (2328), and NEC (not elsewhere classified) (2329).

Four-digit detail isn't available for all industries in every geographic area—because industries tend to concentrate and the Census will not reveal data when only one or two plants are located in an area. But, the point is that a lot of good information is available. If companies aiming at industrial target markets can specify who they are aiming at, readily available data organized by SIC codes may be valuable. Besides the federal government, most trade associations and private organizations which gather data in the industrial area do so by SIC code.[1]

Mary McCarthy

Table 8–2
Size distribution and manufacturing establishments, 1972*

Size in terms of number of employees	Number of establishments	Value added by manufacturing ($ million)	Total number of employees (000)	Percent of firms	Percent of value added	Percent of employees
1–4	112,289	3,752.9	196.8	35.9	1.06	1.09
5–9	46,696	5,248.5	312.0	14.9	1.48	1.7
10–19	43,735	10,126.1	605.4	13.9	2.86	3.35
20–49	49,892	25,625.8	1,568.5	15.9	7.2	8.69
50–99	25,628	29,244.4	1,787.1	8.19	8.26	9.9
100–249	20,800	56,466.7	3,232.0	6.65	15.95	17.9
250–499	8,032	51,426.0	2,785.2	2.56	14.5	15.4
500–999	3,481	48,496.9	2,370.0	1.1	13.7	13.1
1,000–2,499	1,527	50,488.2	2,248.6	0.48	14.26	12.46
2,500 and over	582	73,097.7	2,926.8	0.18	20.65	16.2

* Due to census compilation problems, this was the latest data available.

Source: 1972 Census of Manufactures.

INDUSTRIAL BUYERS ARE PROBLEM SOLVERS

Some people think of industrial buying as entirely different from consumer buying—but a closer look at buying processes suggests that there may be many similarities. In fact, it appears that the problem-solving framework introduced in Chapter 7 can be applied here.

Three kinds of buying processes are useful

In Chapter 7 we discussed three kinds of buying by consumers: extended, limited, and routine buying. In industrial markets, it is useful to adapt these concepts slightly—and work with three similar buying processes: a *new-task buying* process, a *modified rebuy* process, or a *straight rebuy*.[2]

New-task buying occurs when a firm has a new need and the buyer wants a great deal of information. New-task buying can involve setting product specifications, sources of supply, and an order routine which can be followed in the future if satisfactory results are obtained.

The **modified rebuy** is the in-between process where some review of the buying situation is done—though not as much as in new-task buying. Since buyers may want more information, an alert marketer would provide it.

A **straight rebuy** is a routine repurchase which may have been made many times before. Buyers probably would not bother looking for new information—or new sources of supply. Most of a company's purchases might be this type—but they would take a small part of an organized buyer's time.

A particular product might be considered in any of the three ways. Careful market analysis is needed to determine how the firm's products are accepted—and by whom. A new-task buy will take much longer than a straight rebuy—and provide much more chance for a promotion impact by the seller. This can be seen in Figure 8–1—which shows the time and many influences involved in the purchase of a special drill.

Industrial buyers are becoming specialists

The large size of some manufacturers has created a need for buying specialists. **Purchasing agents** are buying specialists for manufacturers. Some of these have banded together—forming the National Association of Purchasing Agents—in an effort to improve the effectiveness and status of professional buyers. This

Straight rebuys use the same sources routinely.

Mary McCarthy

Figure 8–1
Decision network diagram of the buying situations: Special drill

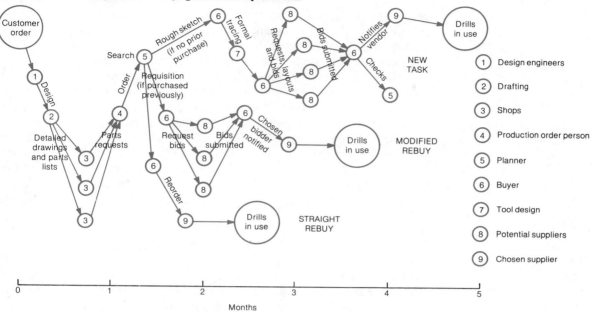

Source: Patrick J. Robinson and Charles W. Faris, *Industrial Buying and Creative Marketing* (Boston: Allyn & Bacon, Inc., 1967), p. 33. Reprinted by permission of the publisher.

is the well-informed, modern-day buyer who will face *you* if you want to sell to the industrial market.

The industrial buyer—or purchasing agent—usually must be seen first—before any other employee is contacted. The buyers hold important positions and take a dim view of sales reps who try to go around them. In large companies, purchasing agents specialize by product area—and are real experts.

Rather than being "sold," these buyers expect accurate information that will help them buy wisely. They like information on new goods and services—and tips on potential price changes, strikes, and other changes in business conditions. Most industrial buyers are serious and well educated—and sales representatives should treat them accordingly.

Basic purchasing needs are economic

Industrial buyers are usually less emotional in their buying habits than final consumers. Buyers look for certain product characteristics—including economy, both in original cost and in use; productivity; uniformity; purity; and ability to make the buyer's final product better.

In addition to product characteristics, buyers consider the reliability of the seller, general cooperativeness, ability to provide speedy maintenance and repair, past and present relationships (including previous favors), continuous supply under all conditions, and reliable and fast delivery.

Emotional needs are relevant, too

Industrial purchasing does have some emotional overtones, however. Modern buyers are human—and want friendly relationships with suppliers. Some buyers seem eager to imitate progressive competitors—or even to be the first to try new products. Such "innovators" might deserve special attention—when new products are being introduced.

Buyers are also human with respect to protecting their own interests—and their own position in the company. Most buyers—like people everywhere—want to survive and improve their chances for promotion—without taking too many risks. "Looking good" is a serious matter for some purchasing agents—because they have to buy a wide variety of things from many sources and make decisions involving many factors beyond their control. A new source may deliver low-quality materials, for example, and the buyer may be blamed. Or, poor service or late delivery may reflect on his ability. Therefore, anyone or anything that helps the buyer look good to higher-ups has a definite appeal. In fact, this one factor might make the difference between a successful and an unsuccessful marketing mix.

Supply sources must be dependable

This matter of dependability deserves further emphasis. There is nothing worse to a purchasing agent and a production manager than shutting down a production line because sellers have not delivered the goods. Product quality is important, too. The cost of a small item may have little to do with its importance. If it causes the breakdown of a larger unit into which it goes, it may result in a large loss completely out of proportion to its own cost. To try to assure dependable quality, some buyers inspect all incoming lots with statistical quality control procedures. Such buyers give preference to producers whose products are slightly better than required specifications—thereby giving greater assurance of reliability and quality. This is *the* important selling point for some firms. In effect, this "makes" their marketing mix—because it gives the buyer an extra margin of safety.

A seller's marketing mix should satisfy both the needs of the buyer's company as well as the buyer's individual needs. Therefore, it helps to find an overlapping area where both can be satisfied. See Figure 8–2 for a graphic model of this concept.

Multiple influences on buying

Much of the work of the typical purchasing agent consists of straight rebuys—routine placing of orders to fill requisitions flowing from various production, warehouse, and office departments. For such requisitions, the order can be placed without consultation with anyone.

In other cases—especially new-task buying—a multiple buying influence may be important. **Multiple buying influence** means the buyer shares the purchasing

Figure 8–2
A model of individual industrial buyer behavior—showing overlapping needs (shaded area)

Individual buyer needs

Company needs

A salesperson may have to work with multiple buying influences.

Luis Medina

decision with several people—perhaps even top management. Possible buying influences include:

1. *Users*—perhaps production line workers or their supervisors.
2. *Influencers*—perhaps engineering or R&D people who help write specifications or supply information for evaluating alternatives.
3. *Buyers*—the purchasing agents who have the responsibility for selecting suppliers and arranging the terms of the sale.
4. *Deciders*—the persons in the organization who have the power to select or approve the supplier—usually the purchasing agent for small items, but perhaps top management for larger purchases.
5. *Gatekeepers*—people who control the flow of information within the organization—perhaps purchasing agents who shield users or other deciders. Gatekeepers could also include receptionists, secretaries, research assistants, and others who can influence the flow of information about potential purchases.[3]

Each of these buying influences may be interested in different aspects of the buying situation—and the sales rep should study each case carefully. The salesperson might have to talk to every one of the possible influences—choosing different topics and stressing different factors for each. This not only complicates the promotion job—but also lengthens it. Approval of a routine order may take anywhere from a week to several months. On very important purchases—say, the purchase of a new computer system, a new plant, or major equipment—the selling period may stretch out to a year or more.

BASIC METHODS AND PRACTICES IN INDUSTRIAL BUYING

Not only the nature of the buyer—but also the nature of the buying situation—may be the basis for segmenting markets. Some buyers use different methods of evaluating products and sellers. And because of their methods of buying, there may be times when the market potential dries up completely—or there is no way for a new supplier to break into a market.

Should you inspect, sample, describe, or negotiate?

Industrial buyers (really, buyers of all types, including final consumers) can use four basic approaches to evaluating and buying products: (1) *inspection,* (2) *sampling,* (3) *description,* and (4) *negotiated contracts.*

In modern economies, most products are purchased by description or negotiated contracts. By contrast, most buying in less-developed economies is done by inspection or sampling—regardless of the products. The reason is skepticism and uncertainty about quality—or lack of faith in the seller. Some U.S. buyers of chicken feathers for fishing tackle, for example, must go personally to Calcutta to select their feathers—because the producers and middlemen cannot be trusted to send the right kinds—even though it is obvious that they know what is wanted. And understanding of the differences in these buying methods is important in strategy planning.

Inspection looks at everything

Inspection buying means looking at every item. It is used for products that are not standardized—and require examination. Here, each product is different—as in the case of some fruits and vegetables, and livestock. One-of-a-kind products, such as used buildings and cars, must also be inspected. These products are often sold in open markets—or at auction if there are several potential buyers. These buyers inspect the goods and either "haggle" with the seller—or bid against competitors.

Sampling looks at some

Sampling buying means looking at only part of a potential purchase. As products become more standardized—perhaps because of more careful grading and better quality control—buying by sample becomes feasible. The general price level may be set by demand and supply factors—but the actual price level may be adjusted from this level, depending on the quality of the specific sample. This kind of buying is used in grain markets, for example—where the actual price is based on a sample which has been withdrawn from a carload of grain and analyzed.

Description just describes accurately

Description buying means buying from a written (or verbal) description of the product. The product is not inspected. Most manufactured items and many agricultural commodities are bought this way—because quality control or grading procedures can be used. When quality can almost be guaranteed, buying by description—grade, brand, or specification—may be satisfactory—especially when there is mutual trust between buyers and sellers. Many wholesale and retail buyers have come to accept government grading standards for fruits and vegetables. Now, many of these goods are packed in the fields—and sold without any further inspection or sampling. This, of course, reduces the cost of buying and is used by buyers whenever practicable.

Negotiated contracts explain how to handle relationships

Negotiated contract buying means agreeing to a contract that allows for changing the purchase arrangements.

Sometimes, the buyer knows roughly what is needed—but can't describe it exactly. Perhaps the specifications or total requirements may change as the job progresses—or maybe some of the details cannot be anticipated. This is found, for example, in research and development work—and in the building of special-purpose machinery and large buildings. In such cases, the general project is described and a basic price may be agreed upon—with provision for adjustments both upward and downward. Or a supplier may be willing to work under a contract that provides some type of incentive—such as full coverage of costs plus a fixed fee, or full costs plus some percentage profit based on costs. The whole contract may even be subject to renegotiation as the work proceeds.

Buyers may favor loyal, helpful suppliers

To be sure of dependable quality, a buyer may develop loyalty to certain suppliers. This is especially important when buying nonstandarized products. When a friendly relationship is developed over the years, the supplier practically becomes a part of the buyer's organization.

Most buyers have a sense of fair play. When a seller proposes a new idea that saves the buyer's company money, the seller is usually rewarded with orders. This encourages future suggestions. In contrast, buyers who use a bid system exclusively—either by choice or necessity, as in some government and institutional purchasing—may not be offered much beyond the basic goods or services. They are interested primarily in price. Marketing managers who have developed better products may not seek such business—at least with their better mix.

But buyers must spread their risk—seeking several sources

Even if a firm has developed the most ideal marketing mix possible, it probably will not get all the business of its industrial customers. Purchasing agents usually look for several dependable sources of supply—to protect themselves from unpredictable events, such as strikes, fires, or floods in one of their suppliers' plants. Still, a good marketing mix is likely to win a larger share of the total business.

Most buyers try to routinize buying

Most firms use a buying procedure that tries to routinize the process. When some person or unit wants to buy something, a requisition is filled out. After approval by some operating supervisor, the requisition is forwarded to the buyer for placement with the "best" seller. These requisitions have already been approved—and now the buyer is responsible for placing a purchase order and getting delivery by the date requested.

Buyers use several sources to guard against unpredictable events.

Mike Voss

Ordering may be routine after requisitioning

The requisitions are converted to purchase orders as quickly as possible. Straight rebuys are usually made the day the requisition is received—while new-task and modified rebuys take longer. If time is important, the buyer may place the order by telephone—and then a confirming purchase order is typed and sent out. Routine straight rebuys would consist of the buyer (1) deciding which of several sellers would get this order, (2) filling in the seller's name and other details on the requisition, and (3) forwarding it to the clerical pool for typing into a purchase order and mailing.

It pays to know the buyer

Notice the importance of being one of the regular sources of supply. The buyers don't even call potential sources for straight rebuys. Sellers' sales reps regularly call on these buyers—*not* to sell a particular item but to maintain relations—or to become a source—and/or to point out new developments which might cause the buyer to reevaluate the present "straight rebuy" procedure and give some business to the sales rep's company.

The fact that a lot of buying is of the "straight rebuy" type points up the importance of being on the buyer's list of potential sellers. The seller can't always be there exactly when the requisitions come in—and the buyer may not call all potential sources before placing orders.

Obviously, having a favorable image is an advantage for a seller. Unless a definite share of the business must be allocated to each of several sources, it is likely that a favored source might get a slightly larger share. Moving from a 20-percent to a 30-percent share may not seem like much from a buyer's point of view, but for the seller it would be a 50-percent increase in sales!

Some buy by computer

Some buyers delegate a large part of their routine order-placing to computers. They develop decision rules that tell the computer how to order—and leave the details of following through to the computer. They then watch the general movement of economic conditions. When conditions require, the buyers modify instructions to the computer. When nothing unusual happens, however, the computer system continues to routinely rebuy as needs develop—printing out new purchase orders to the regular suppliers.

It is important, then, for a supplier to be in the computer's memory. In this situation, the seller just aims to be one of the major suppliers. Obviously, this a big "sale." It also is obvious that such a buyer would be more impressed by an attractive marketing mix for a whole *line* of products than just a lower price for a particular order. It might be too expensive and too much trouble to change the whole buying system just because somebody is offering a low price on a particular day.

Paying taxes affects spending decisions

How the cost of a particular purchase is handled on a firm's profit and loss statement has a big effect on the buyer. If—in computing profits—the cost of a large machine could be charged to the current year's expenses, the company might be more willing to buy it. Even though the cost of the equipment reduced current profits, it also would reduce taxes and increase the company's assets. Typically, however, such purchases *cannot* be charged off in one year, due to government regulations.

...are two general methods of charging costs: as capital and as expense
...th are determined primarily by U.S. Internal Revenue Service regulations.

...items are depreciated

...al items are durable goods—such as large machinery or factories—
...re charged off over many years, that is, depreciated. Internal Revenue
...ns and accepted accounting procedure require that only a part of the
original cost be charged off each year—for a period of 2 to 50 years, depending
on the item.

The federal government has relaxed depreciation rules to stimulate the economy and then tightened them—to cool inflationary booms. These efforts have
been effective—and you can see why managers do look at capital investments
differently from expense items. Capital items are likely to lead to "new-task"
purchasing—because of their importance to a company.

Business managers generally are slow to buy capital items. The purchase
of a capital item is, in effect, a long-term claim against future revenues. Yet
management can't predict exactly what the future holds. Since an error in judgment can have an influence for many years, managers understandably don't
want to make quick decisions. There seems to be little agreement on the best
approach to capital expenditure decisions,[4] however, and emotional considerations may become important.

Expense items are expensed

In contrast to capital items, **expense items** are short-lived goods and services
which are charged off as they are used—usually in the year of purchase. The
potential value is more easily forecast—and can be compared with the cost.
Since the company is not mortgaging its future when it buys expense items, it
tends to be less concerned about these costs—especially if business is good.
The multiple-buying influence is less here—and straight rebuys become more
common. If a firm's sales decline, however, some expense purchases may be
cut back sharply—or eliminated temporarily. There may also be a return to the

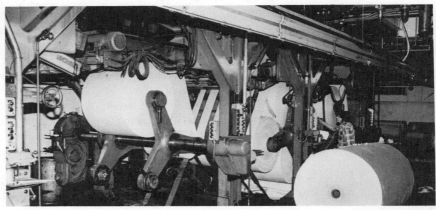

A newspaper printing press is a capital item while the paper is an expense
item.

Mary McCarthy

modified rebuy process—as buyers reevaluate their sources of supply and the prices being offered to them.

Inventory policy may determine purchases

Industrial firms generally try to maintain an adequate inventory—at least enough to keep production lines moving. There is no greater disaster in a factory than to have a production line close down.

Adequate inventory is often expressed in terms of number of days' supply—for example, 60- or 90-days' supply. But what is a 60- or 90-days' supply depends upon the level of demand for the company's products. If the demand rises sharply—say by 10 percent—then total purchases will expand by more than 10 percent to maintain customary inventory levels *and* meet the new needs. On the other hand, if sales decrease by 10 percent, actual needs and inventory requirements decrease—and total purchases may decrease drastically while the inventory is being "worked off." During such a cutback, a seller probably couldn't stimulate sales—even by reducing price—or offering more favorable credit terms. The buyer is just not in the market at that time.

Anticipating the future may lead to buying fluctuations

Demand at the manufacturer level may fluctuate much more than at the final consumer level—because manufacturers earlier in the channel try to predict the behavior of middlemen and other producers. If manufacturers believe prices are going to drop further, they may postpone all purchases. If they feel that prices are at their lowest point, they may buy in large quantities—anticipating future needs.

Buyers' needs may be hard to forecast when other intermediate customers try to anticipate growing demand. Home air-conditioners, for example, are sold to final consumers mostly in hot weather. Orders for air-conditioner compressors, however, may be heavy *before* the summer selling season, as retailers and wholesalers are building their stocks. Compressor producers may have to accelerate production—perhaps even going on overtime. If really hot weather never comes, however, then everyone may be overstocked—and the orders for compressors may stop completely. Yet, a prolonged heat wave may run down retailers' stocks—and start a chain reaction backward to the component manufacturers—and all their suppliers.

Reciprocity helps sales, but . . .

Reciprocity means trading sales for sales—that is, "if you buy from me, I'll buy from you." If a company's customers also can supply products which the firm buys, then the sales departments of both buyer and seller may try to "trade" sales for sales. Purchasing agents generally resist reciprocity—but often it is forced on them by their sales departments.

Reciprocal buying and selling is common in some industries—particularly in paints, chemicals, and petroleum. Usually both prices and product qualities are competitive—and it becomes difficult to ignore the pressure of the sales departments involved. One chemical company brought purchasing under marketing to handle this problem.

When prices and quality are competitive, an outside supplier seldom can break such a reciprocal relationship. He can only hope to become an alternate source of supply—and wait for the competitors to let their quality slip or prices rise. The U.S. Justice Department frowns upon reciprocity. It has tried to block reciprocal buying on the grounds that it is an attempt to monopolize—restricting the normal operation of the free market. This may force those firms that rely heavily on reciprocity dealing to reevaluate their marketing strategies.[5]

Buying practices vary by product

These general buying methods and practices apply in the purchase of many industrial products. Specific habits and practices, however, vary according to the type of product—a subject covered in Chapter 10.

RETAILERS AND WHOLESALERS ARE PROBLEM SOLVERS, TOO

They must buy for their customers

Most retail and wholesale buyers see themselves as purchasing agents for their target customers—remembering the old saying: "Goods well bought are half sold." Typically, they do *not* see themselves as sales agents for manufacturers. They buy what they think they can sell. And wholesalers buy what they think their retailers can sell. They don't try to make value judgments about the desirability or "worth" of what they are selling. Rather, they focus on the needs and attitudes of *their* target customers. Recognizing the close relationship of buying and selling, the buyers in some smaller firms are also responsible for sales and the sales force. This permits immediate feedback from the salespeople to affect buying.

They must buy too many items

Most retailers carry a large number of items—drugstores up to 12,000 items, hardware stores from 3,000 to 25,000, and grocery stores up to 10,000 items— and they just don't have the time to pay close attention to individual items. Often retail buyers are annoyed by the number of wholesalers' and manufacturers' representatives who call on them. These retailers feel that their sales of each item are so small that they can't afford to spend much time over each product. Wholesalers, too, handle so many items that they can't give continuous atten-

Most retailers carry too many items to spend much time on any one item.

Mary McCarthy

tion to each one of them. A grocery wholesaler may stock up to 20,000 items—a drug wholesaler up to 125,000—and a dry-goods wholesaler up to 250,000 items.

Understandably, most retailers and wholesalers buy most of their products on a routine, automatic reorder basis—straight rebuys—once the initial decision to stock products has been made. Sellers to these markets must understand the size of the buyer's job—and have something useful to say and do when they call. For example, besides just maintaining relationships, they might take inventory, set up displays, or arrange shelves—while trying to get a chance to talk about specific products.

In larger firms, on the other hand, we see buyers spending more time on individual items. Buyers may specialize in certain lines. Some large chains buy such large lots that they assign buyers to find additional and lower cost sources of supply.[6]

They must watch inventories and computer output

The large number of items bought and stocked by wholesalers and retailers means that inventories must be watched carefully. Most modern retailers and wholesalers try to carry adequate but *not* excessive inventories. Instead, they want to maintain a selling stock and some reserve stock—and then depend on a continual flow through the channel. Smaller firms use hand inventory control methods—but even small firms are moving more to automatic inventory control procedures. Large firms use quite sophisticated computer-controlled inventory control systems. Large retail discounters have even moved to unit control systems—to quickly pinpoint sales of every product on their shelves. As one discounter put it, "we are not satisfied to know what we are selling in a thousand-foot area—we want to know quickly what we are selling on each table."[7] Similarly, drug wholesalers maintain perpetual inventory on their important items. One drug wholesaler maintains a perpetual inventory record on 800 items that are important to its operation. A plumbing-heating wholesaler maintains an automated perpetual inventory on 13,000 items. The system so speeds pricing and other activities—thus cutting other costs—that this inventory control system operates "for free."[8] For this reason, more and more wholesalers and retailers are adopting such systems. This is especially relevant to marketing managers selling to them—because buyers with this kind of information know their needs and become more demanding about dependability of delivery. They also know more about how goods move—and where promotion assistance might be desirable.

Some are not always "open to buy"

Just as manufacturers may sometimes be trying to reduce their inventory and are "not in the market," retailers and wholesalers may stop buying for similar reasons. No amount of special promotion or price cutting will cause them to buy in these situations.

In retailing, another dimension may become important—buyers may be controlled by a fairly strict budget. This is a miniature profit and loss statement for each department or merchandise line. In an effort to make a profit, the buyer tries to forecast sales, merchandise costs, and expenses. The figure for "cost of merchandise" is the amount the buyer has to spend over the budget period. If the money has not yet been spent, the buyer is "open to buy"—that is, the buyer has budgeted funds which he can spend during the current time period.

Owners or professional buyers may buy

The buyers in small stores and for many wholesalers are the owners or managers—since there is a very close relationship between buying and selling. In larger operations, buyers may specialize in certain lines—but they still may supervise the salespeople who sell what they buy. These buyers are in close contact with their customers—*and* with their salespeople, who are sensitive to the effectiveness of the buyer's efforts—especially when they are on commission. A buyer may even buy some items to satisfy the preferences of salespeople. Therefore they should not be neglected in the promotion effort. The multiple buying influence may be important.

As sales volumes rise, a buyer may specialize in buying only—and have no responsibility for sales. Sears is an extreme case, but it has a buying department of more than 3,000—supported by a staff department exceeding 1,400. These are professional buyers—who may know more about prices and quality and trends in the market than their suppliers. Obviously, they are big potential customers—and should be approached differently than the typical small retailer.[9]

Resident buyers may help a firm's buyers

Resident buyers are independent buying agents who work in central markets for several retailer or wholesaler customers in outlying markets. They work in cities like New York, Chicago, Los Angeles, and San Francisco. They buy new styles and fashions—and fill-in items—as their customers run out of stock during the year. Some resident buying organizations buy everything except furniture, shoes, and food for their stores. Some resident buyers have hundreds of employees—and buy more than $1 billion worth of goods a year.

Resident buying organizations fill a need to reach the many small manufacturers who can't afford to maintain large sales departments. Resident buyers usually are paid an annual fee—based on their purchases.

Committee buying happens, too

In some large companies—especially in those selling foods and drugs—the major decisions—to add or drop lines or change buying policies—may be delegated to a *buying committee*. The seller still will call on the buyer—but the buyer does not have final responsibility. In some companies, the buyer prepares forms summarizing proposals for new products. The seller completes these forms—but may not get to present his story in person to the buying committee.

This rational, almost cold-blooded, approach reduces the impact of the persuasive salesperson. It has become necessary because of the flood of new products. Consider the problem facing grocery chains. In an average week, 150 to 250 new items are offered to the buying offices of the larger food chains. If all were accepted, 10,000 new items would be added during a single year—maybe more than their present stock! Obviously, buyers must be hard-headed and impersonal. About 90 percent of the new items presented to food stores are rejected.

Wholesalers' and manufacturers' marketing managers must develop good marketing mixes when buying becomes so sophisticated and competitive. This approach is likely to become more common—as computers improve sales analysis and inventory control. How possible target markets buy should affect marketing strategy planning.

Committee buying reduces the impact of the persuasive salesperson.

H. Armstrong Roberts

THE FARM MARKET

Agriculture underlies almost all economies. In some countries, agriculture uses almost all the work force—but in the United States the percentage of the population working in agriculture has declined to less than 4 percent.

Farmers are the most numerous intermediate customers. But just as the percentage of the population working in agriculture has declined, so has the number of farms. In the 40 years from 1940 to 1980, more than 3 million farm units disappeared. The total dropped from more than 6 million to less than 3 million farms. The remaining farms have absorbed some of this acreage. From 1940 to 1980, the average farm increased in size from less than 200 acres to just over 400 acres.

As in manufacturing, there are still many small farms—though the large ones produce most of the output. About half the farmers produce almost 90 percent of the total farm output. Many of the small farmers are not much more than subsistence farmers—and are not an especially attractive market. Quite simply, many farmers do not have the money to buy much.

The owners of large farms are another matter. They tend to run their farms as a business—rather than a way of life. They can be influenced by sales presentations stressing savings—and increases in productivity. Further, they are better informed and receptive to change—and, they may have the assets to act on their decisions.

Some studies of farmer purchasing behavior, however, show that—for some products—buying motivations are not much different from those for consumer goods.

Many farmers are unwilling to shop around for the lowest price—preferring the convenience of the nearest farm implement or feed dealer. Some emulation is found—especially in the purchase of farm machinery. This is understandable when you consider that a farmer's home and place of business are the same. Some manufacturers take pride in office facilities and factories—and the same sort of need may affect farmer purchasing behavior. Among owners of smaller farms, a new tractor may offer must as much status as a new car would to an urban resident. Moreover, the farmer's roles in business and as a final consumer sometimes overlap. For example, a station wagon might be used for carrying feed and the family's groceries. So the needs that drive both final consumers and business people may become mixed.

Tailoring products to customers' specialization

Farmers are tending to specialize in one or a few products—such as wheat alone, or wheat plus oats or corn, or fruit and nuts, or poultry. These farmers are interested in only specific kinds of products.

A cotton farmer, for example, may have little interest in hen houses or antibiotics. Or a wheat farmer in the northern plains—where hard wheat is grown—would have different needs from those of a farmer further south—where the crop is soft wheat. Fortunately, much data is available on such differences from the U.S. Department of Agriculture.

Marketing mixes may have to be tailored for each individual farmer—and this is happening. Fertilizer producers now go far beyond selling an all-purpose bag of fertilizer. Now they blend the exact type needed to each farm—and load it directly onto fertilizer spreaders which do the job more economically than manual methods. Some producers are working directly with farmers, providing a complete service—including fertilizing, weeding, and debugging—all tailored to each individual farmer's needs.[10]

Agriculture is becoming agribusiness

Some farmers are going into contract farming. **Contract farming** means the farmer gets supplies and perhaps working capital from local middlemen or manufacturers who agree to buy the farmer's output—sometimes at guaranteed prices. This limits his buying freedom—since the farmer becomes, in effect, an employee. Such arrangements are becoming more common, especially in raising chickens and turkeys—and in growing fresh vegetables for commercial canning. These arrangements give stability to the agricultural structure—but also limit the markets for sellers. It is all part of the move toward **agribusiness**—the move toward bigger and more businesslike farms.

Milt & Joan Mann

Where such contractual arrangements (or actual ownership) are common, marketing managers will have to adjust their marketing mixes. They may have to sell directly to the large manufacturers or middlemen who are handling the arrangements—rather than to the farmer.

In summary, the modern farmer is becoming more educated and more businesslike—and seems willing to accept help and new ideas—but only when it is certain they will help improve production.

THE GOVERNMENT MARKET

Size and diversity

Government is the largest customer group in the United States—and many other countries. About 21 percent of the U.S. gross national product is spent by various government units—and the figure is much higher in more planned economies. Governments buy almost every kind of product. They run not only schools, police departments, and military organizations—but also supermarkets, public utilities, research laboratories, offices, hospitals, and liquor stores. Government expenditures cannot be ignored by an aggressive marketing manager.

Bid buying is common

Many government customers buy by description—using a mandatory bidding procedure which is open to public review. Often the government buyer is required to accept the lowest bid. His biggest job—after deciding generally what is wanted—is to correctly describe the need—so that the description is precise and complete. Otherwise, the buyer may find sellers bidding on a product he doesn't even want. By law, the buyer might have to accept the low bid for an unwanted product.

Writing specifications is not easy—and buyers usually appreciate the help of well-informed salespeople. Legally, the buyer cannot write the specifications so that only one supplier will be able to meet them (although this has been done!). But if all relevant specifications are included, bidding must be on the items desired. The customer can then obtain the product wanted. And the more experienced salesperson may get the business—even with a bid that is not the lowest—because the lower bids don't meet minimum specifications.

Not all items that governments buy cause specification difficulties. Many branded items—or items for which there are widely accepted standards—are routinely purchased through the conventional bidding procedures. School supplies, construction materials, and gasoline, for example, are bought this way.

Negotiated contracts are common, too

Contracts may be negotiated directly for items that are not branded or easily described—or for products requiring research and development—or in cases in which there would be no effective competion. Depending on the government involved, the contract may be subject to audit and renegotiation—especially if the contractor makes a larger profit than was expected.

Negotiation is often necessary when there are many qualitative and intangible factors. Unfortunately, this is exactly where favoritism and "influence" can slip in. Such influence is not unknown—especially in city and state government. Nevertheless, negotiation is an important buying method in government sales—and here a marketing mix should emphasize more than just low price.

Learning what government wants

Since most government contracts are advertised, potential suppliers focus on the government agency they want to cater to—and learn the bidding methods of that particular agency. The marketer can make a big contribution here—because there are so many different bidding procedures.

A marketer can learn a lot about potential government target markets from government directories. The U.S. government offers a purchasing directory that explains its procedures—and various state and local governments also offer guidance. And there are trade magazines and trade associations providing information on how to reach schools, hospitals, highway departments, park departments, and so on. These are unique target markets—and must be treated as such when developing marketing strategies.

CONCLUSION

In this chapter we have considered the number, size, location, and buying habits of various intermediate customers—to try to identify logical dimensions for segmenting markets. We saw that the nature of the buyer and the buying situation are relevant—and that the problem-solving models of buyer behavior introduced in Chapter 7 apply here—with modifications.

The chapter focused mainly on buying in the industrial market—because more is known about manufacturers' buying behavior, and buying in other markets is likely to be similar. Some differences in buying by retailers and wholesalers were discussed. Characteristics of the farm market and government market were also considered. The trend toward fewer, larger, more productive farms with better-informed and more progressive farmers was emphasized. The government market was described as an extremely large, complex set of markets requiring much market analysis.

A clear understanding of intermediate customer buying habits, needs, and attitudes can aid marketing strategy planning. And since there are fewer intermediate customers than final consumers, it may even be possible for some marketing managers (and their salespeople) to develop a unique strategy for each potential customer.

This chapter suggested some general principles which would be useful in strategy planning—but the nature of the products being offered may require some adjustments in the plans. The nature of specific industrial products is discussed in Chapter 10. These variations by product may provide additional segmenting dimensions—to help the marketing manager fine-tune his marketing strategies.

QUESTIONS AND PROBLEMS

1. Discuss the importance of thinking "target marketing" when analyzing intermediate customer markets. How easy is it to isolate homogeneous market segments in these markets?

2. Explain how SIC codes might be helpful in evaluating and understanding industrial markets.

3. Compare and contrast the problem-solving approaches used by final consumers and by industrial buyers.

4. Describe the situations which would lead to the use of the three different buying processes for a particular product, such as computer tapes.

5. Compare and contrast the buying processes of final consumers and industrial buyers.

6. Distinguish among the four methods of evaluating and buying (inspection, sampling, etc.) and indicate which would probably be most suitable for furniture, baseball gloves, coal, and pencils, assuming that some intermediate customer is the buyer.

7. Discuss the advantages and disadvantages of reciprocity from the industrial buyer's point of view. Are the advantages and disadvantages merely reversed from the seller's point of view?

8. Is it always advisable to buy the highest quality product?

9. Discuss how much latitude an industrial buyer has in selecting the specific brand and the specific source of supply for that product, once a product has been requisitioned by some production department. Consider this question with specific reference to pencils, paint for the offices, plastic materials for the production line, a new factory, and a large printing press. How should the buyer's attitudes affect the seller's marketing mix?

10. How does the kind of industrial good affect manufacturers' buying habits and practices? Consider lumber for furniture, a lathe, nails for a box factory, and a sweeping compound.

11. Considering the nature of retail buying, outline the basic ingredients of promotion to retail buyers. Does it make any difference what kinds of products are involved? Are any other factors relevant?

12. Discuss the impact of the decline in the number of commercial farmers on the marketing mixes of manufacturers and middlemen supplying this market. Also consider the impact on rural trading communities which have been meeting the needs of farmers.

13. The government market is obviously an extremely large one, yet it is often slighted or even ignored by many firms. "Red tape" is certainly one reason, but there are others. Discuss the situation and be sure to include the possibility of segmenting in your analysis.

14. Based on your understanding of buying by *(a)* manufacturers, *(b)* farmers, and *(c)* governments, outline the basic ingredients of promotion to each type of customer. Use two products as examples for each type. Is the promotion job the same for each pair?

SUGGESTED CASES

3 **Kemek Manufacturing Company**

5 **Midwest Steel Company**

NOTES

1. For more detail, see *Facts for Marketers,* U.S. Department of Commerce.

2. Patrick J. Robinson and Charles W. Faris, *Industrial Buying and Creative Marketing* (Boston: Allyn & Bacon, Inc., 1967), chap. 2. See also Frederick E. Webster, Jr., and Yoram Wind, "A General Model for Understanding Organizational Buying Behavior," *Journal of Marketing,* April 1972, pp. 12–19; Urban B. Ozanne and Gilbert A. Churchill, Jr., "Five Dimensions of the Industrial Adoption Process," *Journal of Marketing Research,* August 1971, pp. 322–28; and Donald R. Lehmann and John O'Shaughnessy, "Difference in Attribute Importance for Different Industrial Products," *Journal of Marketing,* April 1974, pp. 36–42; Lowell E. Crow; Richard W. Olshavsky; and John O. Summers, "Industrial Buyers' Choice Strategies: A Protocol Analysis," *Journal of Marketing Research,* February 1980, pp. 34–44; and Robert E. Spekman and Louis W. Stern; "Environmental Uncertainties and Buying Group Structure: An Empirical Investigation," *Journal of Marketing,* Spring 1979, pp. 54–64.

3. Frederick E. Webster, Jr., and Yoram Wind, *Organizational Buying Behavior* (Englewood Cliffs, N.J.: Prentice-Hall, 1972), p. 6; and Frederick E. Webster, Jr., "Management Science in Industrial Marketing," *Journal of Marketing,* January 1978, pp. 21–27.

4. Donald F. Istvan, *Capital-Expenditure Decisions: How They Are Made in Large Corporations,* Indiana Business Report No. 33 (Bloomington: Indiana University, 1961), p. 97; and James D. Edwards, "Investment Decision Making in a Competitive Society," *MSU Business Topics,* Autumn 1970, pp. 53–60.

5. "Federal Suit Charges GE with Reciprocity on Purchasing; Vigorous Defense Is Vowed," *The Wall Street Journal,* May 19, 1972, p. 2; see also Robert E. Weigand, "The Problems of Managing Reciprocity," *California Management Review,* Fall 1973, pp. 40–48; and Reed Moyer, "Reciprocity: Retrospect and Prospect," *Journal of Marketing,* October 1970, pp. 37–54.

6. For a detailed discussion of supermarket chain buying, see J. F. Grashof, *Information Management for Supermarket Chain Product Mix Decisions* (PhD thesis, Michigan State University, 1968.)

7. "What's the Sales Potential of Those Products Taking Up Space on a Store's Valuable Shelves," *Systems Management,* January 1962, p. 35 ff.

8. "Aaron Company's Total Inventory Control of 13,000 Items," *Supply House Times,* February 1959, pp. 48–70.

9. "Why Sears Stays the No. 1 Retailer," *Business Week,* January 20, 1968, pp. 65–73.

10. "Monsanto Moves into Farmers' Back Yard," *Business Week,* February 6, 1965, pp. 60–62; see also "Agricorporations Run into Growing Criticism as Their Role Expands," *The Wall Street Journal,* May 2, 1972, p. 1 f; "How the Family Farm Can Harvest Millions," *Business Week,* July 4, 1977, pp. 68–70; and "The Billion-Dollar Farm Coops Nobody Knows," *Business Week,* February 7, 1977, pp. 54–64.

Mary McCarthy

1. Know what market segmentation is.

2. Understand the three approaches to target marketing.

3. Know the dimensions which have been useful for segmenting markets.

4. Understand how to segment markets into sub-markets.

5. Know a seven-step approach to segmenting which you can do yourself.

6. Understand several forecasting approaches which extend past behavior.

7. Understand several forecasting approaches which do not rely on extending past behavior.

8. Recognize the important new terms (shown in red).

9

Segmenting markets and forecasting their potential

You have to aim at somebody—not just everybody—to make a profit.

Aiming at specific "somebodies" is the big difference between production-oriented managers and target marketers. Production-oriented managers think of their markets in terms of *products* and aim at everybody. They think of the "women's clothing" market or the "car" market. Target marketers think of product-markets—that is, they think first of markets in terms of *customers' needs*—and then of products to satisfy these needs. And they segment such markets into sub-markets as they look for attractive opportunities.

The great importance of segmenting markets as part of marketing strategy planning helps explain why we have been talking about possible market dimensions for several chapters.

In this chapter, we'll talk about segmenting markets—and forecasting sales in these markets. Segmenting markets is not just a classroom exercise—if a product isn't aimed at a specific target market, all the effort may be wasted.

TARGET MARKETING REQUIRES EFFECTIVE MARKET SEGMENTATION

What is market segmentation?

We have been casually referring to how target marketers segment markets, but now we must become more formal about what segmenting involves. **Market segmentation** is the process of identifying more homogeneous sub-markets or segments within a market—for the purpose of selecting target markets and developing appropriate marketing mixes. You can see that market segmentation or "segmenting" is not planning marketing strategies. It is only concerned with identifying markets or sub-markets which might become parts of marketing strategies.[1]

The basic idea underlying market segmentation is that any market is likely to consist of sub-markets which might need separate marketing mixes. (In the extreme, we are all unique individuals, so each of us might be considered a separate target market within many product-markets.) So target marketers segment markets into smaller, more homogeneous markets which they may be able to satisfy more exactly than if they treat everybody alike.

MARKET SEGMENTATION LEADS TO THREE APPROACHES TO TARGET MARKETING

Target marketers aim at specific targets

There are three basic ways of developing market-oriented strategies—that is, doing target marketing—for a product-market:

1. The **single target market approach**-segmenting the market and selecting one of the homogeneous sub-markets as the target market.
2. The **multiple target market approach**—segmenting the market and selecting two or more homogeneous sub-markets, each of which will be treated as a separate target market requiring a different marketing mix (as Procter & Gamble does with Crest, Gleem, and so on).
3. The **combined target market approach**—combining two or more homogeneous sub-markets into one larger target market as a basis for one strategy.

Note, all three approaches involve target marketing—they are all aiming at specific and clearly defined target markets. See Figure 9–1. For convenience, we will call people who follow the first two approaches the "segmenters," and the people who use the third approach "combiners."

**Figure 9–1
Target marketers have specific aims**

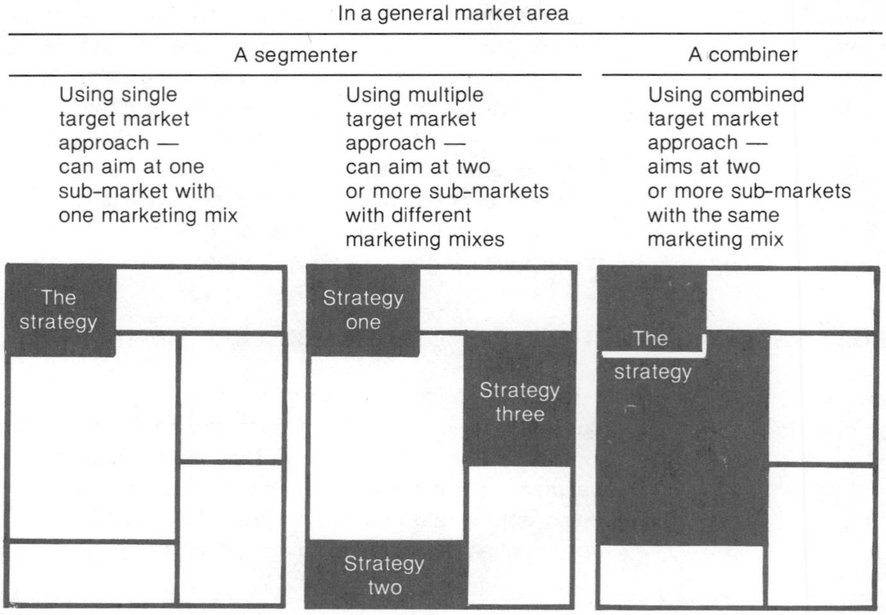

Figure 9–2
There may be different demand curves in different market segments*

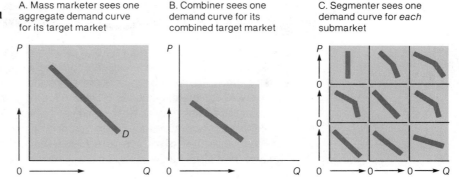

A. Mass marketer sees one aggregate demand curve for its target market

B. Combiner sees one demand curve for its combined target market

C. Segmenter sees one demand curve for *each* submarket

* Note: A familiarity with economic analysis and especially demand curves and demand elasticity is assumed in this text. Those desiring a review of these materials should see Appendix A at the end of Chapter 2.

Combiners try to satisfy "pretty well"

Combiners try to increase the size of their target markets by combining two or more sub-markets—perhaps to gain some economies of scale, to minimize their risk, or simply because they do not have enough resources to develop more than one marketing mix. Combiners look at various sub-markets for similarities—rather than differences. Then they try to extend or modify their basic offering to appeal to these "combined" customers—with just one marketing mix. See Figure 9–2. For example, combiners may try a new package, a new brand, new features, or new flavors. But even if physical changes are made, their aim is *not* at smaller sub-markets. Instead, combiners try to improve the general appeal of their marketing mix to appeal to a bigger "combined" target market.

Combiners tend to rely heavily on promotion—to convince the different sub-markets that a single product or marketing mix satisfies each segment's needs. Relying more on promotion is also necessary because there are probably fewer product differences from competition. And the differences may be quite small. But these little differences—in color, texture, or ease of use—may be *very* important to some customers. Also, the many different customers combined into one target market may be interested in different features of the same product. In the cosmetics market, the same product may have different meanings—and fill different needs—for different customers. For example, some women may be concerned with cleanliness, others with beauty, and others with glamour. One cosmetic advertisement for one product might appeal to all of them—but for different reasons. A combiner might see that the firm might be able to serve *all* these needs at the same time. If they aren't too different, this may not only be possible—but will make economic sense for the firm.

Segmenters try to satisfy "very well"

Segmenters, on the other hand, aim at one or more homogeneous sub-markets and try to develop a different marketing mix for each sub-market—one that will satisfy each sub-market very well.

Segmenters may make more basic changes in marketing mixes—perhaps in the physical product itself—because they are aiming at smaller, more homogeneous target markets. Each sub-market would be seen as needing a separate marketing mix. A segmenter would worry that trying to appeal to *several* sub-markets at the same time—with the same mix—might confuse the customers about the nature of the product. For example, some of the early entries in the "instant breakfast" market failed with combination appeals to dieters (as a low-calories meal), harried commuters (as a breakfast substitute), working mothers (for a quick, complete, nutritious breakfast for kids), and housewives (as a nutritious snack between meals). Now, some segmenters have aimed at the "nutritious snack" market and succeeded with "crunchy granola" bars. It is interesting to note that while their direct appeal is to the snack market, they are also getting some of the "quick lunch" and "fast breakfast" customers.

Segmenters see each sub-market's demand curve

Segmenters see different demand curves in different parts of a market area. Instead of assuming that the whole market consists of a fairly homogeneous set of customers—as the mass marketer does—or merging various sub-markets together—as the combiner does—the segmenter sees sub-markets with their own demand curves—as illustrated in Figure 9–2. Segmenters believe that focusing on one or some of these smaller markets will provide greater satisfaction to the target customers—and greater profit potential and security for the segmenter.

Although a combiner might attempt to satisfy a lot of people "pretty well," a segmenter would attempt to satisfy a smaller number of people "very well." Ideally, total sales would be greater with the same effort—because the segmenter's market penetration in its chosen target market would probably be much higher.

Segmenting may produce bigger sales

It is very important to understand that a segmenter is not settling for a smaller sales potential. Instead, by focusing the firm's efforts on only a part of a larger market, the segmenter expects to get a much larger share of his target market(s). In the process, total sales may be larger. The segmenter may even get almost a monopoly in "his" market(s).

A segmenter may be able to separate himself from extremely competitive market conditions. For example, the Wolverine World Wide Company came out with "Hush Puppies"—a casual, split-pigskin shoe that moved the firm into the very competitive U.S. shoe market with spectacular success—while conventional small shoe manufacturers were offering just "shoes" and facing tough competition.

Should you segment or combine?

Which approach should be used? This depends on many things, including the firm's resources, the nature of competition, and—most importantly—the degree of similarity that exists with regard to customer needs, attitudes, and buying behavior.

It is tempting to aim at larger combined markets instead of smaller segmented markets. If successful, such a strategy could result in significant economies of scale. Also, offering one marketing mix to two or more segments usually requires less investment—and may appear to involve less risk—than offering different marketing mixes to different market segments.

However, combiners face the continual risk of segmenters "chipping away" at the various sub-markets of their combined target markets—especially if the combined markets are quite heterogeneous. In the extreme, a combiner may create a fairly attractive marketing mix but then watch segmenters capture one after another of its sub-markets with more targeted marketing mixes—until finally the combiner is left with no market at all!

The single or multiple target market approaches may be better

In general, it's safer to be a segmenter—that is, to try to satisfy customers *very* well instead of only *fairly* well. That's why many firms use the single or multiple target market approach—instead of the combined target market approach. Procter & Gamble, for example, markets many products which—on the surface—may appear to be directly competitive with each other (e.g., Tide versus Cheer or Crest versus Gleem). However, P&G follows a strategy of offering "tailor-made" marketing mixes (including products) to each sub-market that is large enough and profitable enough to merit a separate marketing mix. This approach can be extremely effective, but it may not be possible for a smaller firm with more limited resources. It may have to use the single target market approach—aiming at the one sub-market which looks "best" for it.

TARGET MARKETERS CAN BE INNOVATIVE OR IMITATIVE

Both segmenters and combiners can be *innovators* or *imitators*. An **innovative segmenter** would look for sub-markets with relatively "unsatisfied" needs and try to develop a uniquely satisfying marketing mix for one (or more) of them. An **imitative segmenter,** on the other hand, would try to offer a better marketing mix to a market segment that has already been identified by an innovator—and perhaps even by other imitators. Obviously, this is likely to lead to "me too" products and marketing mixes. Note, however, that an aggressive imitator can respond quickly to newly identified customer needs with a well-conceived marketing mix and achieve great success—out-performing an innovative segmenter who is using only a "so-so" marketing mix.

Similarly, an **innovative combiner** would seek to find a new combination of sub-markets for which he could offer a differentiated marketing mix. And the **imitative combiner** would try to offer a better marketing mix for the innovator's target market. As with the imitative segmenters, this is likely to lead to "me too" products and mixes. In fact, it is probably more likely to lead to such offerings here, because the innovative combiner probably would be offering a less-targeted mix to begin with—to appeal to more people—so copies of a bland offering would be more likely to be a more exact copy. These important ideas are expanded upon below.

Innovators may have to become imitators

Innovative segmenters often find that one or more competitors will quickly follow them. Then they can either try to segment the market further or attempt to differentiate their marketing mix more effectively than the imitators. Or, an imitator may discover a more satisfying marketing mix and the innovator may have to become an imitator. This could happen as the market's needs shift through time.

J. C. Penney has segmented clothing markets.

Courtesy J. C. Penney

The producers of Top-siders and Deckers (shoes) now face many copiers at similar and lower prices. Similarly, although auto manufacturers have developed many different kinds of cars to appeal to different target markets, the various companies and divisions within companies quickly copy each other. Sometimes, car builders frankly admit that one car is designed to compete directly with another. Then, the competitive focus shifts to minor differences in features, trim, and accessories—together with different psychological perceptions of the products, styles, and brand names.

A brutally competitive market can develop when imitative combiners copy each other. Vague or seemingly meaningless claims may be made for trivial or even nonexistent differences. Promotion costs may rise—and price dealing and eventually price cutting may reduce profitability in such markets.

Even marketing managers who would prefer to be innovative segmenters may be forced to compete more or less directly with imitative segmenters—unless they have some unique insights about their target markets and/or unique patents, resources, brand names, or other strengths which the "me too" competitors are not able to duplicate.

Both segmenters and combiners must expect competition—but an innovative segmenter who does a good job of satisfying his target market is generally less vulnerable to competitors. So an aggressive marketing manager should attempt to segment effectively to begin with, and then continually check the effectiveness of the firm's efforts—to improve future strategy planning. This will help ensure that it satisfies its current target markets—and spots new opportunities while they are developing. This is important because it is clear that innovative target marketing is necessary to survive in our competitive marketplaces.

WHAT DIMENSIONS ARE USED TO SEGMENT MARKETS?

Segmenting forces the marketing manager to decide which dimensions might be useful for planning marketing mixes. Ideally, of course, the dimensions should help guide marketing mix planning. Table 9–1 shows some of the kinds of dimensions we have been talking about in the last several chapters—and their probable effect on the four *P*s. Ideally, we would like to describe any potential market in terms of all three types of dimensions—because these dimensions will help us develop better marketing mixes.

Consumers have many dimensions—and several may be useful for segmenting a market. Table 9–2 shows some geographic and demographic segmenting dimensions—and their typical breakdowns.

Figure 9–3 shows the major segmenting dimensions that have been used for final consumer markets. As the figure shows, there are customer-related dimensions and situation-related factors—which are more important in some markets. When all competitors in a market are imitating each other, for example, then some product feature may be *the most important demension*. Or the degree of brand loyalty or even whether the brand is in a store when it is wanted (that

Table 9–1
Relation of potential target market dimensions to marketing mix decision areas

Potential target market dimensions	Effects on decision areas
1. Geographic location and other demographic characteristics of potential customers	Affects size of *Target Markets* (economic potential) and *Place* (where products should be made available) and *Promotion* (where and to whom to advertise)
2. Behavioral needs, attitudes, and how present and potential goods or services fit into customers' consumption patterns	Affects *Product* (design, packaging, length or width of product line) and *Promotion* (what potential customers need and want to know about the product offering, and what appeals should be used)
3. Urgency to get need satisfied and desire and willingness to compare and shop	Affects *Place* (how directly products are distributed from producer to consumer, how extensively they are made available, and the level of service needed) and *Price* (how much potential customers are willing to pay)

Table 9–2
Some segmenting dimensions and typical breakdowns

Dimensions	Typical breakdowns
Geographic	
Region	Pacific, Mountain, West North Central, West South Central, East North Central, East South Central, South Atlantic, Middle Atlantic, New England
City, county, or SMSA size	Under 5,000; 5,000–19,999; 20,000–49,999; 50,000–99,999; 100,000–249,999; 250,000–499,999; 500,000–999,999; 1,000,000–3,999,999; 4,000,000 or over
Demographic	
Age	Infant, under 6; 6–11; 12–17; 18–24; 25–34; 35–49; 50–64; 65 and over
Sex	Male, female
Family size	1–2, 3–4, 5+
Family life cycle	Young, single; young, married, no children; young, married, youngest child under 6; young, married, youngest child 6 or over; older, married, with children; older, married, no children under 18; older, single; other
Income	Under $5,000; $5,000–$7,999; $8,000–$9,999; $10,-000–$14,999; $15,000–$24,999; $25,000 or over
Occupation	Professional and technical; managers, officials, and proprietors; clerical, sales; craftsmen, foremen; operatives; farmers; retired; students; housewives; unemployed
Education	Grade school or less, some high school, graduated high school, some college, college graduate
Religion	Catholic, Protestant, Jewish, other
Race	White, Negro, Oriental, other
Nationality	American, British, French, German, etc.
Social class	Lower-lower, upper-lower, lower-middle, upper-middle, lower-upper, upper-upper

is, the buying situation) may decide which product is purchased. Let's look at these potential dimensions now—to see which ones will be the most useful.

Geographic dimensions can be useful

Geographic dimensions are a sensible basis for segmenting because consumers in different areas do have different lifestyles and needs. Further, customers in different areas may have to be served by different middlemen—and reached with different media. In fact, this is such a basic segmenting dimension, that it may be more practical to use it in the title of a product-market—rather than as a segmenting dimension, for example, the "West Coast market for. . . ."

Using geographic dimensions usually leads to a quick split of a market—but it does not give the detail needed for planning a marketing strategy. So, more segmenting of each geographic market is usually necessary.

Other demographic dimensions are useful, too

Demographic variables (such as age, sex, family size, income) have been popular segmenting dimensions—because they are easy to measure and data is easy to get. These reasons, however, are not good reasons for using demographics. Often, product choice—and especially brand choice—are only slightly related to demographics. Higher-income consumers may be able to afford more expensive items—but that doesn't mean they'll buy them. Luxury cars aren't bought only by the wealthy. So, mechanically segmenting with demographics only should be avoided.

**Figure 9–3
Types of segmenting
dimensions**

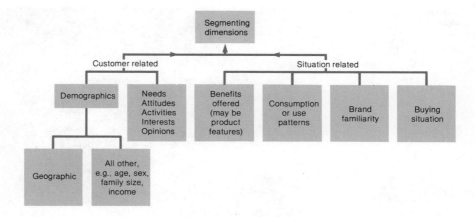

*Attitudes and life-style
affect buying*

Because demographics don't give very good answers by themselves, behavioral dimensions have been getting increasing attention. Sometimes two or three attitude dimensions can help segment a market. But generally, life-style specialists work with many variables at the same time (maybe 25 to 100). And different sets of variables are found useful in different markets. See Chapter 7.

Need-satisfying benefits

Customers buy products to satisfy needs. We discussed various kinds of needs and wants in Chapter 7. Recall the PSSP needs, the economic needs, and a long list of needs to stimulate one's thinking.

It is important to understand that customers buy need-satisfying benefits— not products. So it is sometimes useful to segment a market based on needs and/or the benefits sought or being offered. Benefit dimensions usually are specific to a product-market—the benefits from buying skis are quite different from buying snack foods. Segmenting based on benefits can be tricky. Not everyone may be interested in the same benefits. Nevertheless, benefits sought—sometimes described in terms of product features—can provide understanding about how customers see a market. For example, "high-performance" athletic equipment—like some snow skis—may give status to those who can really use them, but make fools of beginners who buy them to impress others.[2]

*Consumption or use
patterns—related to how
much is bought*

Segmenting by whether people are current product users and at what rate— heavy, medium, light—has helped some target marketers. Research often shows, for example, that a small group of "heavy users" accounts for a large part of sales. "Heavy" beer drinkers, for example—those who consume one or more bottles or cans per day—account for more than three fourths of some brewers' sales. The firm may want to aim at these heavy users to make sure they keep on buying. Or, the present non-users or light users might be attractive target markets.[3]

*Brand familiarity affects
brand choice*

Some firms segment their markets by how familiar present customers are with the various brands. This approach can be interesting—especially if some brand has reached the stage where customers demand it. This may suggest

Consumption patterns can help segment markets.

Kenneth Yee

that competitors should change their focus—to people less attached to a particular brand.

This approach must be used with care. It is possible to measure whether customers recognize, prefer, or even insist upon particular brands—but measuring brand loyalty is a more difficult matter. Much research has been done on this topic—but it is still not clear what brand loyalty means. Some people may keep buying a particular product out of habit—or because of its low price—not because they "insist" on this one brand. If better substitutes were available, they might be quite willing to shift. Others may insist, but buy so infrequently that they are treated as non-users. Rather than trying to gauge brand loyalty by frequency and/or regularity of purchase, it may be more fruitful to determine people's degree of familiarity with various brands.

Buying situation—is the product in the store?

Some people have segmented markets based on how consumers behave in different buying situations. In a small convenience food store like a 7–11, for example, consumers may do less brand and price comparison than when on their weekly shopping trip to a supermarket. They may be willing to pay higher prices for convenience. This obviously affects marketing strategy planning.

Possible buying-situation dimensions include the kind of store, its depth of assortment, whether it is leisurely or rushed buying, or whether it is a "serious" or "browsing" shopping trip. Obviously, using these dimensions requires real knowledge of the market.

MARKET SEGMENTATION IS EASIER SAID THAN DONE

Segmenting does not mean "break down"

Segmentation efforts often prove unsuccessful because of a common tendency to start with the whole "mass market" and then try to "break it down" into sub-markets—often using one or two demographic characteristics. This approach usually fails because customer behavior is too complex to be explained in terms of just one or two demographic characteristics. For example, not all old men or all young women buy the same products or brands. Other customer dimensions must be considered—starting with customer needs.

Sometimes, many different dimensions are needed to describe the different sub-markets. This was the case in the home decorating market example we studied in Chapter 2. Recall that the British paint manufacturer finally settled on the "cost-conscious couple" as its target market. In that case, four possible target markets with very different dimensions were placed in the four corners of a market diagram. This is the kind of segmenting we want to do.

Segmenting is an aggregating process

Marketing-oriented marketers think of **segmenting** as an aggregating process. They start with the idea that each person is "one of a kind"—and can be described by a special set of dimensions. However, while it might be ideal to treat each person as a unique target market, this usually isn't practical in terms of manufacturing and distribution costs—the marketing mix might cost more than the customer would be willing and able to pay.

Therefore, segmenters look for similarities—customers who are quite similar in terms of their special set of dimensions—and then aggregate these customers into relatively homogeneous sub-markets that can be served effectively—and profitably. This is shown in Figure 9–4—where the many dots show each person's position in a product-market with respect to two possible segmenting dimensions—need for status and need for dependability. While each person's position is unique, it can also be seen that many of the people are similar in terms of how much status and dependability they need. Thus, the segmenter can aggregate these people into three (an arbitrary number) relatively homogeneous sub-markets—A, B, and C. Group A might be called "Status Oriented" and group C "Dependability Oriented." Members of group B want both—and might be called the "Demanders."

One of the difficult things about segmenting is that some potential customers just don't "fit" neatly into market segments. For example, not everyone in Figure 9–4 was put into one of the three groups. Forcing them into one of the three groups would have made these sub-markets more heterogeneous and harder to please. Further, forming additional segments to place them in probably would not be profitable—because they are too few in number and not very similar in terms of the two dimensions. These people are simply too "unique" to be catered

Figure 9–4
Every individual has his or her own unique position in the market—those with similar positions can be aggregated into potential target markets

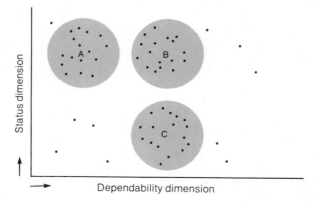

Status dimension

Dependability dimension

to and may have to be ignored—unless they are willing to pay a high price for special treatment.

How far should the
aggregating go?

Segmenters have basically three choices: They can treat everybody alike; they can treat everybody differently; or they can try to aggregate people into some workable number of relatively homogeneous sub-markets—and treat each sub-market differently. The first choice is seldom (if ever) effective—it is "mass marketing." The second choice is seldom practical for the economic reasons we have discussed. Thus, the only real choice is to look for homogeneous sub-markets that can be served profitably. The major problems with this choice are deciding: (1) *how many* sub-markets should be formed and (2) what the *boundaries* of these sub-markets should be.

Looking back at Figure 9–4, we assumed that there were three sub-markets. This was an arbitrary number, however. As Figure 9–5 shows, it may be that there are really *six* sub-markets. What do you think—does this product-market consist of three segments or six segments?

It's a matter of judgment

Actually, the number of sub-markets that can be formed is a decision that is based more on judgment than on some scientific rule. This decision is influenced basically by two things: how heterogeneous the market is with respect to the segmenting dimensions and how well the firm wants to—and can afford to—satisfy the needs of each potential customer.

There would be no point in trying to segment a market if customer needs were all basically the same. Typically, however, there are some important differences—and segmenting is desirable. In fact, in very competitive markets, even seemingly minor differences may make a big difference in how well a firm does against tough competitors. But it is necessary to have decision rules about how far to go.

Basically, profit-oriented firms would probably want to continue aggregating potential customers into a larger market as long as its marketing mix would be reasonably satisfying to all those within the segment—*and* the firm would be able to offer this marketing mix at a profit. The interaction of customer needs

Figure 9–5
How many segments are there?

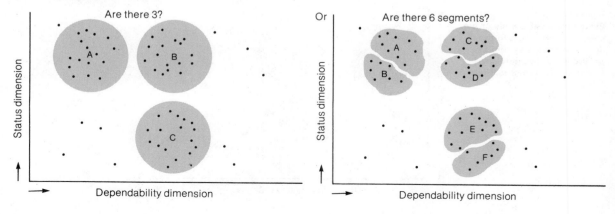

with what the firm can offer profitably should be noted. And present or potential competition must be figured in here when calculating profitability.

Criteria for selecting market segments

Ideally, "good" market segments would meet the following criteria:

1. *Homogeneous within*—the people within a market segment should be as homogeneous as possible with respect to the segmenting dimensions *and* their likely responses to marketing mix variables.
2. *Heterogeneous between*—the people in different market segments should be as heterogeneous as possible with respect to the segmenting dimensions *and* their likely responses to marketing mix variables.
3. *Substantial*—the segments should be big enough to be profitable.
4. *Operational*—the segmenting dimensions should be useful for identifying customers and deciding on marketing mix variables. There is no point in having a dimension that isn't useable.

Criterion 4 is especially critical—because it is possible to find dimensions which are useless. A personality trait such as moodiness, for example, might be found among the traits of particularly heavy buyers of a product—but what could one do with this knowledge? Personal sales people would have to take a personality inventory of each prospective buyer—clearly an impossible task. Similarly, advertising media buyers or copywriters could not make much use of this information. So, although moodiness might be related in some way to previous purchases, it would not be a useful dimension for marketing purposes.

Criterion 4 may lead to including readily available dimensions—such as demographics—to aid marketing mix planning. Dimensions such as age, income, location, and family size may be very useful—at least for Place and Promotion planning. In fact, it would be difficult to make some Place and Promotion decisions without information about such dimensions.

Profit is the balancing point

Target marketers do not segment markets without thinking of what could be done for them. Even how the market is segmented should be affected by these practical business matters. Target marketers develop whole strategies—they don't just segment markets. As a practical matter, this means that *more aggregating probably would be encouraged by cost considerations—to achieve economies of scale—while demand considerations would suggest less aggregating to satisfy needs more exactly.*

Profit would be the balancing point—determining how unique a marketing mix the firm can afford to offer to a particular group.

Too much aggregation leaves you vulnerable

Segmenters must be careful about not trying to aggregate too far in search of profit. As sub-markets are made larger, they become less homogeneous—and individual differences within each sub-market may even begin to outweigh the similarities. This makes it harder to develop marketing mixes which can do an effective job of satisfying potential customers within each of the sub-markets. And this in turn leaves the firm more vulnerable to competitive efforts—especially from innovative segmenters who are willing to offer more attractive marketing mixes to more homogeneous sub-markets.

THERE MAY BE BOTH QUALIFYING AND DETERMINING DIMENSIONS

We have already stressed that consumers are multi-dimensional. Some dimensions may be more important than others, however, and it is useful to distinguish between qualifying dimensions—the dimensions which are relevant to a product-market—and determining dimensions—the dimensions which actually affect the purchase of a specific product type or specific brand in a product-market. A consumer would have to have enough money to be in the market, for example, but this might only qualify him as a prospect. It does not tell us which kind of product he is likely to purchase or which brand. Several such qualifying dimensions may have to be present—and still we will not have determined what he will do. A prospective car owner, for example, would have to have enough income or credit to purchase a car—and also would have to be of driving age—and have or be able to obtain a driver's license. This still does not determine that he will buy a car. He may simply rent one—or continue borrowing his parents' or friends' car—or hitchhike. He may not get around to actually buying a car until not having one is annoying—until, for example, his status with his buddies is falling because he doesn't have "wheels." This need may lead him to buy *some* car—but it is not determining with respect to a specific brand or a specific model within a particular brand.

Determining dimensions may have to be very specialized

How specific the determining dimensions have to get depends on whether one is concerned with a general product type or a specific brand. This is shown in Figure 9–6. The more specific we want to be, the more particular the determining dimensions may have to be. In a particular case, the determining dimensions may seem minor—but they are important because they *are* the determining dimensions. In the car—status symbol market, for example, paint colors or the brand name may determine which cars people buy.

**Figure 9–6
Finding the relevant dimensions**

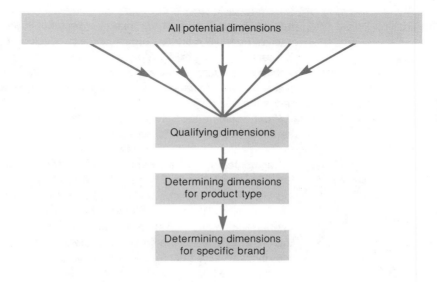

Qualifying dimensions are important, too

The qualifying dimensions are necessary to narrow down to the determining dimensions. But, once the determining dimensions have been identified, we can go back to the qualifying dimensions—for insights which can aid marketing mix planning and implementation. In other words, qualifying and determining dimensions work together to affect marketing strategy.

Different dimensions may be needed for different segments in a market

It is important to see that each different product-market *within the same broad market* may be motivated by a different set of dimensions. In the "snack food" market, for example, health food enthusiasts might be interested in nutrition, while dieters might care only about calories—and economical shoppers with lots of kids might be interested in volume to "fill them up." The related product-markets might be called: "health-conscious-snack food market," "dieters-snack food market," and "kids-snack food market."

A SEVEN-STEP APPROACH TO SEGMENTING CONSUMER MARKETS

Now that we have discussed the philosophy behind segmenting, let's go on to a logical, seven-step procedure which can be used without expensive marketing research or computer analyses. More sophisticated approaches discussed later are just extensions of this approach—but this approach is workable and has led to successful strategies. It is especially useful for finding the determining dimensions for *product types.* When you want to move down to specific brands—especially where there are several competing brands—then more sophisticated techniques may be necessary.

So that you can clearly grasp this approach, we will list each step separately, explain its significance, and provide a common example to illustrate how each step works. The example we will use is rental housing—in particular, the apartment market in a big urban area.

1. Select the product-market area to be considered.

After the firm has defined its objectives, it must determine what business it wants to be in. If it is already in some market, this might be a good starting point. If it is just starting out, then many more opportunities are open, although the available resources—including human and financial—should help limit the possibilities to a manageable number. Generally, it is better to build on strengths—while trying to avoid one's own weaknesses and competitors' strengths. Naming the product-market area should focus on *market* needs—not only present or possible products or product features.

Example: The firm might presently be in a part of the rental housing market—building small utility apartments for low-income families—basically just satisfying the physiological needs—for water, shelter, and so on. A narrow view of the product-market—that is, considering only products now being produced—might lead the firm to thinking *only* in terms of more low-income housing for other low-income families. A bigger view—considering more market needs—might see these compact apartments as only a small part of the total apartment or total rental housing market—or even the total housing market—in the firm's area. Taking an even bigger view, the firm could consider expanding to additional

"Brainstorming" aids creative segmenting.

Mary McCarthy

geographic areas—or diversifying out of housing into other "construction" markets.

Ultimately, some balance has to be struck between defining the product-market too narrowly (same old product, same old market) and defining it too broadly (the whole world and all its needs is our market). Here, the focus is on the whole rental housing-apartment market in one metropolitan area—because this is where the firm had had some experience and wanted to work.

2. List all needs that all potential customers may have in this product-market area.

This is just a "brainstorming" step. We want to write down as many needs as we can—as quickly as possible. The list does not have to be complete. The idea here is to have enough input to stimulate creativity in the next several steps. Some need dimension which is just "thrown in" now may be *the* determining dimension for a market segment. If that need were not included at this stage, it is possible that the existence of that market segment would be neglected.

Possible need dimensions can be identified by starting with the PSSP hierarchy of basic needs (see Chapter 7) to be sure that all potential dimensions have a chance of entering the process. Expanding these four basic needs into more specific needs can be done by thinking about why some people buy the present offerings in this product-market—perhaps using a long list like we presented in Chapter 7, to stimulate your thinking. The economic needs may be relevant in some cases, too. If the products are selling, presumably they are satisfying somebody's needs for something. They may not be doing it very well, but at least they are doing it better than competitors' offerings. Figuring out why will suggest more needs.

Example: In the rental housing-apartment market, it is fairly easy to list the following needs—which start with but move beyond the four basic needs: basic shelter, parking, play space, safety and security, distinctiveness, economy, privacy, convenience (to something), enough living area, attractive interiors, and good supervision and maintenance to assure trouble-free and comfortable living.

3. Form possible market segments.

Assuming that some market segments will have different needs than others,

Some people do not fit easily into "typical" market segments.

Ken Firestone

select out of the above list the most relevant ones for yourself, then for a friend, then for several acquaintances from widely different demographic groups. Form one segment around yourself or an obvious user—and then go on aggregating others into other segments until three or more market segments emerge. Be sure to identify the distinguishing demographic and customer-related characteristics of the segments—so it will be possible to name them later. For example, if the people in one segment tend to be college students looking for a "party-environment," then this will help understand what they want and why—and will help nickname the segment (perhaps as the "partyers").

This is obviously an intuitive process, but you should have some thoughts about how you behave. Given that you are unique, you must begin to recognize that others have different needs and attitudes. Once this is accepted, it is really remarkable how good your judgment becomes about how others behave. We all may have different preferences, but knowledgeable observers do tend to agree—at least roughly—on how and why people behave. Market-related experience and judgment are needed to screen all the possible dimensions. But at the least, the geographic, demographic, and behavioral topics discussed in earlier chapters should be considered when forming these market segments.

Example: A college student living off campus would probably want an apartment to provide basic shelter, parking, economy, convenience to school and work, and enough room either in the apartment or in common facilities to have parties. An older married couple, on the other hand, might have quite different needs—perhaps for basic shelter and parking, but *also* privacy and perhaps good supervision—so they would not have to put up with the rowdy party environment which might be attractive to the student. An older acquaintance with a family would also be interested in shelter and parking, but might be faced with a financial squeeze and, therefore, be interested in economy—while getting enough room for the children to live and play.

4. Look for determining dimensions.

Review the list of dimensions in each market segment and remove any that are common—as they apparently are not determining dimensions. They may be important qualifying dimensions—reflecting "core needs" which must be satisfied—but they are not the determining dimensions which we are seeking now.

A potential dimension such as low price or good value may be relevant for *all* potential customers and, therefore, not useful as a determining variable. It may be an extremely important qualifying dimension—which will have to be satisfied in any marketing mix. But for segmenting purposes, it may be only *qualifying*—not determining—and therefore should be removed *at this stage*.

Example: With our "apartment hunters," the need for basic shelter, parking, and safety and security appear to be *common* needs. Therefore—in this step—we will remove them from our list of dimensions.

5. Name the possible product-market segments.

Review the remaining dimensions—segment by segment—and tentatively name each segment—based on the relative importance of the determining dimensions—and distinguishing customer-related characteristics (as explained in Step 3). To visualize what this market looks like, draw a picture of the market and place these segments in it.

Here is where creativity and judgment are needed to weight the relative importance of the remaining dimensions. (Even sophisticated techniques require judgment at this stage!) What is required here is a feel for the relative importance of the remaining dimensions. This will lead to tagging each market segment with meaningful people-related words—or "nicknames." And to see the whole market, drawing a picture of the market will be helpful. Dimensions along the axes might be useful in some cases—but are by no means required. In fact, in complex markets, dimensions on the axes probably will be inappropriate and misleading.

Example: We can logically identify the following "apartment" segments at this time: swingers, sophisticates, family, job-centered, home-centered, and urban-centered. See Figure 9–7. Each segment has a different set of benefits sought—product features—which follow directly from the people types and the needs they have (see the legend at the bottom of Figure 9–7).

6. Seek better understanding of possible market segments.

After tentatively naming the segments as we did in Step 5, further study of what is already known about each segment—including demographics and other customer-related dimensions—is necessary—to deepen your understanding of how and why these market segments behave the way they do. This may help explain why some competitive offerings are more successful than others. It also can lead to splitting and renaming some segments.

Example: Newly married couples might have been treated as "swingers" in Step 5—because the "married" dimension was not considered determining. But, on further thought, we see that while some newly married couples are still swingers at heart, others have begun to shift their focus to buying a home. For these "newly married," the apartment is only a transitional place. Further, they are not like the sophisticates—as shown at the bottom of Figure 9–7—and probably should be treated as a separate segment. Note, however, that if the newly marrieds happen to have enough income, they might end up in a sophisticates apartment development—while waiting to move into a home of their own. The same apartment development might be able to cater to the sophisticates and to some of the newly married at the same time—but the advertising and personal selling appeals might be quite different. The point here is that these market differences might only be discovered in Step 6—and it would be at this stage that the "newly married" segment would be named.

7. Tie each segment to demographic and other customer-related characteristics, if possible, and then draw a new picture of the whole market to show the relative sizes of the segments.

Eventually, we are looking for profitable opportunities. So now we must try to tie our market segments to hard data—so it will be easier to estimate the sizes of the segments. We are *not* trying to estimate market potential here. Now we only want to provide the basis for later forecasting and marketing mix planning. The more we know about alternative target markets, the easier the following tasks will be.

Fortunately, much demographic data is available—and bringing in demographics adds a note of economic reality to the whole process. It is theoretically possible that some market segments will have almost no market potential. Without some

**Figure 9–7
Market for apartment dwellers in a metropolitan area**

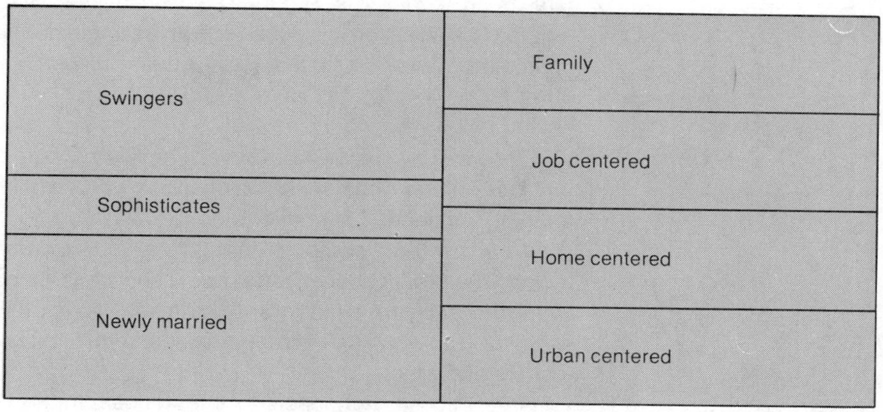

Swingers	Family
	Job centered
Sophisticates	Home centered
Newly married	
	Urban centered

Name of market segment	People types and needs characteristics	Determining benefits sought (Product features)
Swingers	Young, unmarried, active, fun-loving, party-going	Economy Common facilities Close-in location
Sophisticates	Young, but older than swingers, more mature than swingers, more income and education than swingers, more desire for comfort and individuality	Distinctive design Privacy Interior variety Strong management
Newly married	No longer swingers, want a home but do not yet have enough money, wife works so economy not necessary	Privacy Strong management
Job centered	Single adults, widows, or divorcees, not much discretionary income and want to be near job	Economy Close-in location Strong management
Family	Young families with children and not enough income to afford own home	Economy Common facilities Room size
Home centered	Former homeowners who still want some aspects of suburban life	Privacy Room size Interior variety
Urban centered	Former homeowners in the suburbs, who now want to be close to attractions of city	Distinctive design Close-in location Strong management

Source: Adapted from *House and Home*, April 1965, pp. 94–99.

hard data, the risks of attempting to pursue such a market increase rapidly.

To help understand the market—and explain it to others—it will be useful to draw a picture of the market with boxes that give some idea of the size of the various market segments. This will help the planners see the larger and perhaps more attractive opportunities.

Example: It is possible to tie the swingers to demographic data. Most of them are young, in their 20s, and the U.S. Census Bureau has very detailed information related to age. Given this data—and an estimate of what proportion are swingers—it would be easy to estimate the actual number of swingers in a metropolitan area.

Market dimensions suggest a good mix

Once we have followed all seven steps, we should be able to see the outlines—at least—of the kinds of marketing mixes which would be attractive to the various market segments. Let's take a look.

We know that "swingers" are active, young, unmarried, fun-loving and party-going. The product benefits (features) shown at the bottom of Figure 9–7 indicate what the swingers want in an apartment. (As an aside, it is interesting to note what they *do not want*—strong management. Most college students will probably understand why!)

A very successful appeal to the swingers in the Dallas, Texas, area includes a complex of apartments with a swimming pool, a putting green, a night club that offers jazz and other entertainment, poolside parties, receptions for new tenants, and so on. And to maintain their image, management insists that tenants who get married move out shortly—so that new swingers can move in.

As a result, apartment occupancy rates were extremely high in such buildings. At the same time, other builders were having difficulties filling their apartments—mostly because the units offered were hardly more than "little boxes" with few uniquely appealing characteristics.

SEVEN-STEP APPROACH APPLIES IN INDUSTRIAL MARKET, TOO

A similar seven-step approach can be used for intermediate markets, too. The major change would be in the first step—selecting the product-market area. To illustrate this idea—and to increase your understanding about segmenting markets, we will show how the first step would be different for industrial markets.

As with consumer markets, the first step is naming the general market area—

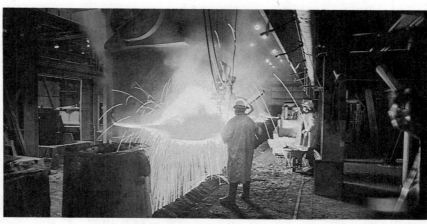

Understanding desired function helps segment industrial markets.

Milt & Joan Mann

which means specifying geographic dimensions, along with the basic functions desired. It is the basic functions which are different.

Industrial buyers are interested in accomplishing basic functions. Their demands are derived from final consumer demands—so the industrial market is concerned with finding or producing raw materials and converting them into finished goods and services. The basic functions which industrial buyers are concerned about include, but are not limited to: forming, bending, grading, boring, digging, cutting, fastening, heating, cooling, conducting, transmitting, controlling, switching, containing, filling, dumping, cleaning, preserving, dispensing, recording, analyzing, sorting, communicating, training, motivating, insuring, feeding employees, and so on.

Defining the market—using both geographic dimensions and the basic functions—will usually ensure that the focus is broad enough—that is, not exclusively on the product now being supplied to present customers. But it also keeps the focus from expanding to "all the industrial needs in the world."

It is better to focus on a basic function than specific product characteristics. Alternative ways of satisfying the basic function may be found—and completely surprise and upset the producers—if the market is too narrowly defined. For example, aluminum wire now competes in what some copper wire producers thought was the "copper wire market." And plastic products are taking more of this business. Perhaps this market should be called the "transmitting"or "conducting" market. Certainly, the "copper" view was too narrow. Market-oriented stragegic planners attempt to avoid surprises which result from such tunnel vision.

Finally, it is important to see that if a firm has been—or is thinking about being—in two or more quite different markets, these areas should be named separately—rather than trying to jam all of them into one. Serving several markets is becoming more common—as more firms expand their activities. Even simple product line extensions may cause the firm to move into new markets. So this first step is extremely important.

After the first step—in the seven-step approach—the other steps would be similar to segmenting consumer markets—only many of the dimensions discussed in Chapter 8 would be used here. For example, the size of the buyer's company, the nature of the buying situation, and the importance of multiple buying influence should be considered in identifying the qualifying and determining dimensions. Further, when it comes to estimating the size of the markets, SIC-coded information can be quite helpful. In fact, given all of the data which is available—and the relative ease of tying it to market segments—there is little excuse for ignorance about the size of industrial markets.

MORE SOPHISTICATED CLUSTERING TECHNIQUES MAY HELP IN SEGMENTING

The seven-step approach is logical and practical—and it works. But a marketing manager no longer is limited to such an intuitive, judgmental approach. Some quantitative techniques can help. Roughly called "clustering" techniques, they seek to do—mechanically—some of what previously was done with much intuition and judgment.

Figure 9–8
Toothpaste market segment description

Segment name:	The sensory segment	The sociables	The worriers	The independent segment
Principal benefit sought	Flavor, product appearance	Brightness of teeth	Decay prevention	Price
Demographic strengths	Children	Teens, young people	Large families	Men
Special behavioral characteristics	Users of spearmint flavored toothpaste	Smokers	Heavy users	Heavy users
Brands disproportionately favored:	Colgate, Stripe	Macleans, Plus White, Ultra Brite	Crest	Brands on sale
Personality characteristics	High self-involvement	High sociability	High hypochondriasis	High autonomy
Life style characteristics	Hedonistic	Active	Conservative	Value-oriented

Source: Russell I. Haley, "Benefit Segmentation: A Decision-Oriented Research Tool," *Journal of Marketing,* July 1968, p. 33.

Clustering usually requires a computer

Clustering techniques (which usually require marketing research to gather primary data and computer analysis) try to find similar patterns within sets of data. This data could include anything which might possibly turn out to be relevant—including demographic characteristics, attitudes toward the product or life in general, and previous purchasing behavior. The computer searches among all the data for homogeneous groups of people. When such groups have been found, then the dimensions of the people in the groups must be analyzed—by humans—for insights as to why the computer clustered them together. If the results make some sense—if they have face validity—they may suggest new, or at least better, marketing strategies.

A cluster analysis of the toothpaste market, for example, might show that some people buy toothpaste for its sensory satisfaction (the sensory segment), while others are concerned with the effect of clean teeth on their social image (the sociables). Others are worried about decay (the worriers), and some are strictly interested in the best value for their money (the economic men). See Figure 9–8. Each of these market segments calls for a different marketing mix—although some of the four Ps may be similar. Finally, a marketing manager would have to decide which one (or more) of these segments would be the firm's target market(s).

Much experimental work is being done with these techniques—and the results are encouraging. As more work of this kind is done, we may see similar kinds of clusters reoccurring in different product classes—for example (besides those mentioned above): the *status seeker,* the *swinger,* and the *conservative.*

It should be clear, however, that these techniques only aid the manager. Judgment is still required to develop an original list of possible dimensions—and then to name the resulting clusters, if they make market sense.[4]

Clustering works for services, too

These clustering techniques are generally useful for both goods and services—and consumer goods and industrial goods.

In a study of the commercial banking market for example, six different groups were isolated—each having relevance for marketing strategy planning. These groups were called the nonborrowers, value seekers, nonsaving convenience seekers, loan seekers, one-stop bankers, and a representative group (which was not strong on any dimensions). Subsequently, changes were made in the bank's strategy—focusing on each of the markets and treating them as the basis for separate strategies. Instead of the previous "we are friendly people" advertising campaign, the bank decided to focus on its products in an attempt to appeal to the different markets. The nonborrowers segment was appealed to with messages about the bank's checking account, bank charge card, insurance, and investment counseling. For the convenience seekers, on the other hand, stress was placed on faster teller service, express drive-in windows, overnight drop boxes, and deposit-by-mail accounts. In an effort to reach the loan seekers, promotion stressed auto-loan checking accounts, mail-loan request forms, and loan programs through automobile dealers.[5]

SEGMENTING SHOULD NOT BE CARRIED TO EXTREMES

Once a marketer gets a feel for segmenting markets, it is tempting to get carried away—and create a separate sub-market for every potential customer. Going to such extremes is not very practical, however. Seldom do we have data to evaluate such fine subdivisions. Further, most firms want to try to meet the needs of some target market which is large enough to support its efforts—and yield a profit.

FORECASTING TARGET MARKET POTENTIAL AND SALES

Target markets do not have potential all by themselves. Their attractiveness depends on the likely response of potential customers to a marketing mix—which is the subject of the rest of the book. So as you are learning to plan marketing mixes, you should keep in mind that eventually you will have to evaluate alternative strategies—not just target markets—and then pick those strategic plans which will be carried out by the company.

Estimates of target market potential and likely sales volumes are necessary for effective strategy planning. But a manager can't forecast *sales* without some possible plans. Sales are *not* just "out there for the taking." Market opportunities may be there—but whether a firm can change these opportunities into sales depends on the strategy it selects. Much of our discussion will be concerned with estimating **market potential**—what a whole market segment might buy—rather than a sales forecast. A **sales forecast** is an estimate of how much an industry or firm hopes to sell to a market segment. We must first try to judge the market potential before we can estimate what share a particular firm might be able to win—because of its marketing strategy and how well it implements it.

Our primary focus will be on forecasting for a reasonable planning period—such as a year—rather than on making long-run estimates, or weekly or monthly forecasts to guide current operations. Such forecasts require different techniques and are beyond our scope.

Figure 9–9
Straight-line trend projection—extends past sales into the future

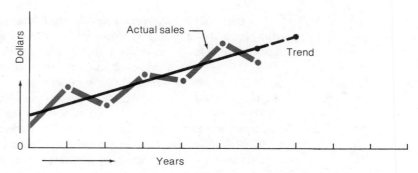

Trend extension is the basic method

Trend extension is the basic method

When we forecast for existing products, we usually have some past data to go on. The basic method—called **trend extension**—extends past sales experience into the future. See Figure 9–9.

Ideally—when extending past sales behavior—the marketer should decide why sales have varied in the past. This is a difficult and time-consuming part of sales forecasting. Usually we can gather a lot of data about the product or market—or about the economic environment. But unless the *reason* for past sales variations is known, it's hard to predict in what direction—and by how much—sales will move. Graphic analysis and statistical techniques—including correlation and regression analysis—can be useful here. These techniques are discussed in standard statistics texts.

Once we know why sales vary, it usually is easy to develop a specific forecast. Sales may be moving directly up as population grows, for example. So we can just get an estimate of how population is expected to grow—and then project the impact on sales.

Trend extension can miss turning points

The big limitation of trend-extension is that it assumes past conditions will continue unchanged into the future. In fact, the future is not always like the past. Trend-extension will be wrong whenever there are important variations. For this reason—although they may extend past behavior for one estimate—most managers look for another way to help forecast sharp economic changes.

THREE LEVELS OF FORECAST ARE USEFUL

We are interested in forecasting the potential in specific market segments. To do this, it helps to make several kinds of forecasts.

Some economic conditions affect the entire economy. Others may influence only one industry. And some may affect only one company or one product's sales potential. For this reason, a common approach to sales forecasting is to:

1. Develop a *national income forecast* and use this to:
2. Develop an *industry sales forecast,* which then is used to:
3. Develop *specific company* and *product forecasts.*

Generally, a marketing manager doesn't have to make forecasts for the national economy. This kind of forecasting—basically, trend projecting—is a specialty in itself. These forecasts are available in business and government publications, so managers can simply use one source's forecast or combine several together.

Developing industry sales forecasts

Once the future of the whole economy has been estimated, the next step is to make a forecast for industry sales, that is, sales in the firm's general product-market area. Since the two are often closely related, simply extending this past relationship may be effective. Automobile sales, for example, reflect the level of national income—since auto sales normally go up as national income rises. But it would be most unusual for such a relationship to be direct; that is, a 1 percent increase in some national figure seldom leads to a 1 percent increase in industry sales. Therefore, some statistical analysis is needed—to determine the relationship between the two (or more) variables. This relationship can then be used to adjust the forecast of national income to estimate expected industry sales.

Someone else may do the forecasting

Just as marketing managers do not have to develop their own national economy estimates, they may not have to do industry estimates either. Some industry estimates are published regularly by government agencies, banks, trade associations, and business publications—for such broad categories as steel, cement, plywood, and housing.

Unfortunately, most readily available industry forecasts are for general commodity groups—and reflect what appears to be production-oriented thinking. Such estimates may show market potential for broad *product* classes, but too narrow a view of a market can miss many opportunities. Recall that the copper wire producers lost some of their share to aluminum wire producers. The "industry" should be defined carefully—before the available data is assembled to make an industry forecast.

The more imaginative the previous segmenting effort has been, the less likely that available industry data will fit the firm's chosen product-markets. In fact, aggressive segmenters may create their own little "industries"—and thus have to move directly to estimating potential for their own company and specific products.

Developing company and product forecasts

Next, the marketing manager must try to forecast the size of product-market segments of interest only to his firm and direct competitors. This is the subject of the rest of this chapter.

Forecasting sales for new products is a tougher assignment than forecasting for established products—and calls for slightly different techniques. Therefore, we will discuss these two forecasting jobs separately.

FORECASTING COMPANY AND PRODUCT SALES BY EXTENDING PAST BEHAVIOR

Past sales can be extended

At the very least, a marketing manager ought to know what the firm's present markets look like—and what it has sold to them in the past. A detailed sales analysis—for products and geographic areas—gives such facts for projecting future results.

Just extending past sales into the future may not seem like much of a forecasting method. But it is better than just assuming that next year's *total* sales will be the same as this year's.

Simple extension of past sales gives one forecast. But it usually is desirable to tie future sales to something more than the passage of time. The factor method tries to do this.

The **factor method** tries to forecast sales by finding a relation between the company's sales and some other factor (or factors). The basic formula is: something (past sales, industry sales, etc.) *times* some factor *equals* sales forecast. A **factor** is a variable which shows the relation of some variable to the item being forecasted.

An example: Bread

The following example for a bread manufacturer shows how forecasts can be made for many geographic market segments—using the factor method and available data. This general approach can be useful for any firm—manufacturer, wholesaler, or retailer.

Analysis of past sales relationships showed that a particular bread manufacturer regularly sold one half of 1 percent (0.005) of the total retail food sales in its various target markets. This is a single factor. By using this single factor, estimates of the manufacturer's sales for the coming period could be obtained by multiplying a forecast of expected retail food sales by 0.005.

Retail food sales estimates are made each year by *Sales & Marketing Management* magazine. Figure 9–10 shows the kind of geographically detailed data available each year in its "Survey of Buying Power" issues.

Let's carry this bread illustration further, using the data in Figure 9–10 for Evanston, Illinois. Evanston's food sales were $64,732,000 for the previous year. By simply accepting last year's food sales as an estimate of next year's sales and multiplying the food sales estimate for Evanston by the 0.005 factor (the firm's usual share in such markets) the manager would have an estimate of his next year's bread sales in Evanston. That is, last year's food sales estimate $64,732,000) times 0.005 equals this year's bread sales estimate of $323,660.

Or going further, if the marketing manager expected that an especially aggressive promotion campaign would increase the firm's share by 10 percent, the single factor could be increased from 0.005 to 0.0055—and then multiplied by the food sales estimate for Evanston—to obtain an estimate for his Evanston bread sales.

The factor method is not limited to using just one factor. Several factors can be used together. For example, *Sales and Marketing Management* regularly gives a "buying power index" (BPI) as a measure of the potential in different geographic areas. See Figure 9–10. This index takes into consideration (1) the population in a market, (2) the market's income, and (3) retail sales in that market. The BPI for Evanston, Illinois, for example, is 0.0442—meaning that Evanston ac-

Figure 9–10
Sample of pages from *Sales & Marketing Management's* "Survey of Buying Power"

ILL. S*M*M ESTIMATES		POPULATION—12/31/79							RETAIL SALES BY STORE GROUP 1979						
METRO AREA County City	Total Population (Thousands)	% Of U.S.	Median Age of Pop.	% of Population by Age Group				Households (Thousands)	Total Retail Sales ($000)	Food ($000)	Eating & Drinking Places ($000)	General Mdse. ($000)	Furniture/ Furnish./ Appliance ($000)	Automotive ($000)	Drug ($000)
				18–24 Years	25–34 Years	35–49 Years	50 & Over								
CHAMPAIGN - URBANA - RANTOUL .	**167.3**	**.0755**	**24.2**	**28.8**	**18.1**	**12.8**	**15.6**	**56.1**	**750,659**	**141,217**	**84,645**	**104,559**	**32,169**	**124,322**	**21,335**
Champaign	167.3	.0755	24.2	28.8	18.1	12.8	15.6	56.1	750,659	141,217	84,645	104,559	32,169	124,322	21,335
• Champaign	59.1	.0267	24.1	33.1	16.5	12.2	17.1	20.5	372,676	51,957	42,145	59,268	22,841	71,285	13,034
• Rantoul	26.4	.0119	22.5	32.3	20.1	12.0	6.2	6.9	83,420	13,189	10,447	7,629	2,538	28,743	1,653
• Urbana	36.0	.0162	23.9	38.0	17.5	10.5	16.2	11.7	88,370	14,795	15,245	9,931	5,379	10,714	1,756
SUBURBAN TOTAL	45.8	.0207	27.1	13.4	19.5	16.0	18.7	17.0	206,193	61,276	16,808	27,731	1,411	13,580	4,892
CHICAGO	**6,998.4**	**3.1585**	**30.1**	**12.5**	**16.9**	**17.0**	**24.6**	**2,442.5**	**30,308,650**	**5,812,065**	**2,963,628**	**3,918,761**	**1,364,554**	**5,612,488**	**1,109,378**
Cook	5,200.6	2.3470	30.7	12.5	16.7	16.7	26.1	1,896.6	21,758,843	4,272,784	2,257,371	2,926,717	988,026	3,662,492	835,474
Arlington Heights	70.0	.0316	28.1	9.4	17.5	21.9	16.1	21.9	303,917	37,233	28,866	25,695	18,972	107,625	10,766
Berwyn	45.2	.0204	41.8	10.7	13.3	15.4	41.6	19.4	193,387	23,701	22,159	25,765	8,299	58,088	9,969
• Chicago	2,880.4	1.2999	31.2	13.1	16.4	15.8	27.9	1,143.7	9,558,408	1,909,397	1,086,762	1,159,167	446,674	1,244,572	417,578
Chicago Heights	39.1	.0176	28.1	12.5	17.0	16.4	21.9	12.7	216,723	34,203	24,875	21,698	7,976	80,712	5,720
Cicero	58.9	.0266	35.2	12.8	16.0	15.8	34.5	24.3	160,033	49,595	22,326	5,890	2,677	33,579	3,468
Des Plaines	55.7	.0251	29.8	10.7	17.8	19.4	21.4	18.5	315,331	54,393	36,688	34,346	2,288	88,503	11,272
Evanston	72.3	.0326	32.2	16.9	17.0	14.4	30.9	27.7	365,768	64,732	28,084	19,235	16,581	103,206	14,115

ILL. S*M*M ESTIMATES		EFFECTIVE BUYING INCOME 1979						S*M*M ESTIMATES		EFFECTIVE BUYING INCOME 1979					
METRO AREA County City	Total EBI ($000)	Median Hsld. EBI	% of Hslds. by EBI Group: (A) $8,000–$9,999 (B) $10,000–$14,999 (C) $15,000–$24,999 (D) $25,000 & Over				Buying Power Index	**METRO AREA** County City	Total EBI ($000)	Median Hsld. EBI	% of Hslds. by EBI Group: (A) $8,000–$9,999 (B) $10,000–$14,999 (C) $15,000–$24,999 (D) $25,000 & Over				Buying Power Index
			A	B	C	D					A	B	C	D	
CHAMPAIGN - URBANA - RANTOUL .	**1,255,818**	**18,171**	**5.7**	**15.6**	**29.6**	**30.4**	**.0792**	**CHICAGO** (Contd)							
Champaign	1,255,818	18,171	5.7	15.6	29.6	30.4	.0792	Arlington Heights	765,566	32,623	1.2	4.0	16.4	73.9	.0402
• Champaign	465,518	18,383	5.5	13.0	27.2	31.5	.0323	Berwyn	440,983	21,505	3.8	11.4	30.0	38.9	.0242
• Rantoul	153,282	15,315	7.5	27.6	32.3	19.2	.0099	• Chicago	22,980,979	17,646	5.2	15.2	29.7	28.7	1.2930
• Urbana	261,045	16,464	6.7	15.3	25.8	29.0	.0143	Chicago Heights	290,857	21,289	3.6	12.3	31.6	37.9	.0198
SUBURBAN TOTAL	375,973	20,195	4.7	14.2	33.5	34.6	.0227	Cicero	517,761	20,438	3.7	12.4	34.0	33.7	.0267
CHICAGO	**61,441,498**	**22,597**	**3.7**	**11.0**	**27.8**	**42.9**	**3.5542**	Des Plaines	571,729	28,991	1.7	5.9	22.4	64.2	.0334
Cook	45,761,030	21,611	4.0	11.8	28.0	40.2	2.6185	Evanston	818,151	24,442	3.9	11.4	23.8	48.6	.0442

Source: *Sales & Marketing Management*, July 28, 1980, C–68f.

counts for 0.0442 percent of the total U.S. buying power. This means that Evanston is a fairly attractive market—because its BPI is much higher than would be expected based on population alone. That is, although Evanston accounts for 0.0326 percent of U.S. population, it has a much larger share of the buying power—because its income and retail sales are above average.

Using several factors rather than only one factor enables us to work with more information. And in the case of the BPI, it gives a measure of a market's potential—which may be quite important if, for example, a company's sales are not limited to one type of retail store. Then, rather than falling back to using population only, or income only, or trying to develop one's own special index, the BPI can be used in the same way that we used the 0.005 factor in the bread example.

When several factors are used, they may be put together—as with the BPI—or used separately. But the basic factor method is the same. This is shown for a retailer who might be interested in estimating the potential for sets of novelty beer mugs in the New York City area. If about 10 percent of its target market could be expected to buy a $5 set within a one-year period, and this target market consisted of young, low-income families without children, the appropriate numbers could be multiplied to get a forecast as shown below. The example shows that 7,344 buying families will spend $5 each—for a total sales potential of $36,720.

Families in New York City	2,000,000
× Percent earning under $10,000	43.2
	864,000
× Percent under 25 years	20.0
	172,800
× Percent without children	42.5
Number of families	73,440
× Expected share of market (percent)	10.0
	7,344
× Price of product (in dollars)	5
Total sales potential	$ 36,720

Manufacturers of industrial goods can use several factors, too

Table 9–3 shows how one manufacturer estimated the market for fiber boxes for a particular county. This approach could be used county by county—to estimate the potential in many geographic target markets.

In this case, SIC code data is used. This is common in the industrial area—because SIC code data is readily available and often very relevant. In this case, the value of box shipments by SIC code were collected by a trade association—but the rest of the data was available from government sources.

Basically, the approach is to calculate the typical consumption per employee—for each SIC industry group in the particular county—to get a market potential estimate for each group. Then, the sum of these estimates becomes the total market potential in that county. A firm thinking of going into that market would need to estimate the share it could get with its own marketing mix.

Note that this approach can also aid management's control job. If the firm were already in this industry, it could compare its actual sales (by SIC code) with the potential and see how it is doing. If its typical market share is 10 percent of the market—and it is obtaining only 2–5 percent of the market in various SIC sub-markets—then some marketing mix changes may be in order.

Time series and leading series may help estimate a fluctuating future

Not all past economic or sales behavior can be neatly extended with a straight line or some manipulation. Much economic activity is characterized by ups and downs. To cope with such variation, statisticians have developed *time-series* analysis techniques. **Time-series** are historical records of the fluctuations in economic variables. We cannot go into a detailed discussion of these techniques here—but note that there are techniques to handle daily, weekly, monthly, seasonal, and annual variations.[6]

The dream of all forecasters is to find an accurate **leading series**—a time series which changes in the same direction *but ahead of* the series to be forecasted. For example, if an index of electrical power consumption always went up three months before a company's own sales of products which have some logical relation to electric power consumption (it is important that there be some logical relation!) then the managers might watch this "leading" series very carefully when forecasting monthly sales of those products.

Table 9–3
Estimated market for corrugated and solid fiber boxes by industry groups, Phoenix, Arizona, Standard Metropolitan Statistical Area

SIC major group code industry	(1) Value of box shipments by end use ($000)*	(2) Employment by industry groups†	(3) Consumption per employee by industry groups (1 ÷ 2) (dollars)	Maricopa County (4) Employment by industry groups†	(5) Estimated share of the market (3 × 4) ($000)
20 Food and kindred products	586,164	1,578,305	371	4,973	1,845
21 Tobacco	17,432	74,557	233	—	—
22 Textile mill products	91,520	874,677	104	—	—
23 Apparel	34,865	1,252,443	27	1,974	53
24 Lumber and products (except furniture)	19,611	526,622	37	690	26
25 Furniture and fixtures	89,341	364,166	245	616	151
26 Paper and allied products	211,368	587,882	359	190	68
27 Printing; publishing, and allied industries	32,686	904,208	36	2,876	104
28 Chemicals and allied products	128,564	772,169	166	488	81
29 Petroleum refining and related industries	28,328	161,367	175	—	—
30 Rubber and miscellaneous plastic products	67,551	387,997	174	190	33
31 Leather and leather products	8,716	352,919	24	—	—
32 Stone, clay, and glass products	226,621	548,058	413	1,612	666
33 Primary metal industries	19,611	1,168,110	16	2,889	46
34 Fabricated metal products	130,743	1,062,096	123	2,422	298
35 Machinery; except electrical	58,834	1,445,558	40	5,568	223
36 Electrical machinery, equipment, and supplies	119,848	1,405,382	391	6,502	553
37 Transportation equipment	82,804	1,541,618	53	5,005	265
38 Professional, scientific instruments, etc.....................	13,074	341,796	38	—	—
39 Miscellaneous manufacturing industries	200,473	369,071	543	376	204
90 Government	10,895	—	—	—	—
Total	2,179,049	—	—	—	4,616

* Based on data reported in *Fibre Box Industry Statistics,* Fibre Box Association.
† U.S. Bureau of the Census, *County Business Patterns.*

No single series has yet been found that leads GNP—or other important quantities. Lacking such a series, forecasters develop indices—statistical compilations of several series—in an effort to find some time series that will lead the series they are attempting to forecast. Some indices of this type are published by the U.S. Department of Commerce. And business magazines—such as *Business Week*—publish their own time series—updating them weekly.

APPROACHES THAT DO NOT EXTEND PAST BEHAVIOR CALL FOR MORE JUDGMENT AND SOME OPINIONS

The methods discussed above make use of "hard" data—projecting past experience into the future on the assumption that the future will be like the past. But this is a dangerous assumption in dymanic markets. Usually, it is desirable to add judgment to hard data to get better—or at least other—forecasts to be compared on the way to making the final forecast.

The following methods—which tend to be more subjective or qualitative—may be especially useful when: (1) conditions are changing in the marketplace, (2) the company's marketing mix has changed substantially, (3) the company is in unstable, fluctuating markets (such as fashion goods or seasonal businesses) and (4) the company is introducing new products which have no past history.

Jury of executive opinion adds judgment

One of the oldest and simplest methods of forecasting—the **jury of executive opinion**—combines the opinions of experienced executives—perhaps from marketing, production, finance, purchasing, and top management. Basically, each executive is asked to estimate market potential and sales for the *coming years*. Then, they try to work out a consensus. The idea is to use as much seasoned judgment as possible—in combination with past data.

The main advantage of the jury approach is that it can be done quickly—and easily. On the other hand, the results may not be spectacular. There may be excessive reliance on extending the past—because some of the executives may have little contact with outside market forces. At the worst, it could be an averaging of naïve extensions of the past. At the best, however, it could alert the forecasters to major shifts in customer demand or competition.

Estimates from salespeople can help, too

Using salespeople's estimates to forecast is like the jury approach. But salespeople are more likely than home office managers to be familiar with customer reactions—and what competitors are doing. Their estimates are especially useful in industrial markets—where a limited number of customers may be well known to the salespeople. But this approach is useful in any type of market. Good retail clerks have a "feel" for the market—their opinions should not be ignored.

Two limitations concerning the use of salespeople's estimates should be kept in mind. First, salespeople usually don't know about possible changes in the national economic climate—or even about changes in the company's marketing mix.

Salespeople know their market and can be helpful in sales forecasting.

Mary McCarthy

Second, salespeople may have little to offer if they change jobs often.

Surveys, panels, and market tests

Instead of relying heavily on salespeople to estimate customers' intentions, it may be desirable to do some marketing research. Special surveys of final buyers, retailers, and wholesalers can show what is happening in different market segments. Some firms use panels of stores—or final consumers—to keep track of buying behavior—and to determine when simply extending past behavior has become inadequate.

Surveys are sometimes combined with market tests—when the company wants to estimate the reaction of customers to possible changes in the marketing mix. A market test might show that a product increased its share of the market by 10 percent when its price was dropped one cent below competition. Yet this extra business might be quickly lost if the price were increased one cent above competition. Such market experiments help the marketing manager make realistic estimates of future sales when one or more of the four Ps are changed.

Sometimes the only way to estimate the market potential of a new product is to actually try it in the market. Several test markets can be used—and assuming they are fairly representative (a big assumption!)—the results can be projected to a larger area.

Forecasting from market test results can be misleading, however—since the very novelty of the product seems to attract some customers. This means that sales may shoot up just after a new product is introduced, then decline quickly, level off, and then *perhaps* rise as a market of repeat customers develops.

Another problem with market test results is that competitors may run special pricing offers or extra promotion—to meet or beat the introductory effort. And there's also the danger of wanting to rush the market test—which probably should take from 6–12 months—because of an initial sales boom *and* an eagerness to market the product ahead of competition. This is a serious matter, because extensive market testing may be a luxury in our highly competitive markets—especially if more aggressive competitors are monitoring the tests to try to beat the innovator to national distribution. This has happened often enough to discourage some firms from testing new products.[7]

Substitute method—nothing is completely new

The **substitute method** involves careful analysis of the sales of products which a new one may displace. Since few products are entirely new, this method can provide an upper limit on potential sales. With imagination and research, a company can list most possible uses and determine the potential in the present markets. Once the upper limits of the markets have been estimated, these figures can be scaled down by market realities—including likely customer preferences at various price levels, and the availability of good or better substitutes. Research and judgment are obviously needed with this approach—and several of the methods discussed above would be helpful. In the industrial goods area, SIC data would be especially useful—in estimating the potential in quite different kinds of markets.

Application of the substitute method can be illustrated by the forecasting done by Du Pont for a plastic resin product.[8]

The chemical company began by estimating the size of the various end-use markets—shown as the left series of boxes in Figure 9–11. These were markets where the resin product was technically suitable for use—including automotive, electrical, electronic, construction, personal, and toy products. The sum of the potential in all these boxes indicated the upper limit on demand. Then a harder look at the suitability of the product in comparison with those currently being used indicated that one of the planned automotive and construction applications should be dropped.

The markets where the new product was technically preferable for use are shown in Figure 9–11 in the second bar from the left. These first two market possibility bars, however, ignore potential selling prices—which are realities in any market. So the potential demand at various selling prices was considered. The five right-hand bars in Figure 9–11 show the various quantities of the product that, technically, should be used at various price levels. The extreme right-hand bar indicates that if prices were low enough, all of the potential users would use the product.

Many potentials but one forecast

The data in Figure 9–11 are shown in a different way and with more detail in Figure 9–12.

Here the impact of demand curves in different markets on marketing strategy planning becomes clearer. At a high selling price, interest would be shown by one of the potential automotive markets and by electrical and electronic users (markets a, b, and c). If the price were dropped slightly, additional automotive users (d and e) and a construction industry user (f) would add to the potential market. In other words, potential target markets are being specified as part of the sales forecasting procedure.

Figure 9–11
Estimating the size of the market possibilities

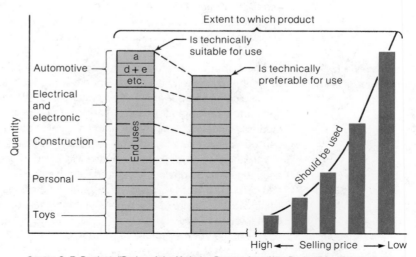

Source: G. T. Borchert, "Design of the Marketing Program for a New Product," in *Marketing's Role in Scientific Management*, ed. Robert L. Clewett (Chicago: American Marketing Association, 1957), p. 64.

Figure 9–12
Another way of seeing
Figure 9–11

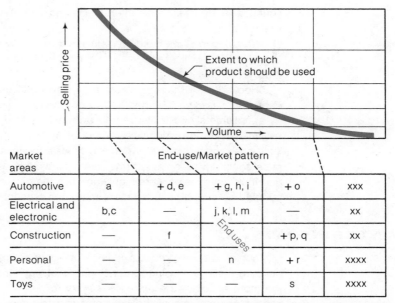

Market areas	End-use/Market pattern				
Automotive	a	+ d, e	+ g, h, i	+ o	xxx
Electrical and electronic	b,c	—	j, k, l, m	—	xx
Construction	—	f		+ p, q	xx
Personal	—	—	n	+ r	xxxx
Toys	—	—	—	s	xxxx

Source: G. T. Borchert, "Design of the Marketing Program for a New Product," in *Marketing's Role in Scientific Management*, ed. Robert L. Clewett (Chicago: American Marketing Association, 1957), p. 66.

Need analysis in possible market segments

If a product is so new that no present market can be used as a guide, then the marketing manager may have to use *need analysis*. This usually involves running a survey to determine who might be interested in the product and why. And the seven-step approach to segmenting markets could be applied.

This kind of forecasting may seem crude in comparison with the techniques described earlier—but it is still important. Careful analysis of this type may produce clear alternatives. It may show that either the highest potential sales volume for a product is too small to justify further research and development—or the outlook may prove to be so attractive that, despite the crude estimate, enthusiasm seems justified.

Calculations killed this slide rule

The following simple example illustrates this approach.

A firm developed a five-inch plastic slide rule that would help a shopper determine the "best buy" among several products and packages at a supermarket. After discussion with a few friends, the company's managers were sure that some shoppers would be interested. But how many? And which ones? Men probably should have been considered, too, because they do some shopping—but the managers limited their initial survey to women.

A small-scale survey was discouraging. Only 5 percent showed any interest. The survey was not large enough to enable the managers to understand all the relevant dimensions, but it appeared that only the more highly educated, younger women might be interested—and only if the retail price of the slide rule were under 70 cents.

The company then talked to retailers to see how they reacted to the product. Some retailers indicated a lack of enthusiam—though some were willing to give it a try.

It looked as if the achievable potential would be quite low. Specific figures confirmed this. The 5 percent of the women who *might* be interested—multiplied by approximately 60 million American families—suggested an upper limit of 2.5 million units. When potential retail availability was considered, this potential upper limit was reduced to 100,000 units *or less.* In view of the fact that a premium price could not be obtained (the rule itself would cost about 25 cents to make), and that repeat sales were highly unlikely, the project was dropped. Not enough people had strongly felt needs to make the product worthwhile to the firm.

ACCURACY OF FORECASTS

The accuracy of forecasts varies a lot—depending upon the number of components in the figure being forecast. The more general the figure being forecast, the more accurate the forecast is likely to be. This is because small errors in various components of the estimate tend to offset each other—and make the whole estimate more accurate.

Annual forecasts of national totals—such as GNP—may be accurate within 5 percent. Industry sales forecasts—which tend to be more specific—are usually accurate within 10 percent—depending upon the variability of the industry.

When estimates are made for individual products, there is even less chance of offsetting errors—except where errors from one salesperson or territory offset those in another. Where style and innovation are important factors in an industry, forecast errors of 10 to 20 percent for *established products* are not uncommon. The accuracy of specific *new-product* forecasts is even lower. Many new products fail completely—while others are extremely successful.

One forecaster of new consumer and industrial products claimed he had an excellent overall forecasting average for a particular year. He was off by only 2 percent on the average. His inaccuracy on specific product forecasts, however, was frightening. Many products did not sell at all—he missed by 100 percent—and others exceeded his expectations by 200 to 300 percent.[9]

CONCLUSION

This chapter discussed market segmentation—the process of segmenting markets—to find potentially attractive target markets. Some people try to segment markets by breaking them down into smaller sub-markets. But this can lead to poor results. Instead, segmenting should be seen as an aggregating process. The more similar the customers are, the larger the market segments can be. Four criteria for evaluating market segments were presented.

Ways of developing better strategies—segmenting (aiming at one or more sub-markets) and combining—were discussed. Segmenting aims the firm's efforts at smaller, more homogeneous target markets. Combining, on the other hand, builds up the size of a firm's target market by combining smaller homogeneous sub-markets into one larger target market.

Even "rough and ready" segmenting can add perspective about the nature of alternative markets—and may lead to breakthrough opportunities. Seemingly trivial determining dimensions may make a "winner" out of what appears to be a "me too" strategy. In fact, target marketers probably should continue to try to be segmenters to the very end.

We also talked about several approaches to forecasting market potential and sales. The most common approach is to extend past behavior into the future. This gives reasonably good results if market conditions are fairly stable. Methods here include extension of past sales data and the factor method. We saw that projecting the past into the future is risky when big market changes are likely. To make up for this possible weakness, marketers must use their own experience and judgment. They also may be able to bring in the judgment of others—using the jury of executive opinion method and salespeople's estimates. They may also use surveys, panels, market tests, the substitute method, and need analysis.

We saw that the accuracy of forecasts depends on how general a forecast is being made, with the most error when specific forecasts for products—and especially new products—are made.

Even though forecasts are subject to error, they are still necessary to help the firm choose among alternative strategic plans. Sloppy forecasting could lead to poor strategies. No forecasting at all is stupid!

Sales forecasting is not a mechanical task. Experience and judgment are needed to estimate the attractiveness of alternative marketing mixes. This is a learned skill—but you ought to be thinking about forecasting sales as we study how to develop attractive marketing mixes. Planning marketing mixes and forecasting their results go hand in hand. They are both part of effective market strategy planning.

In summary, a good marketer should be an expert on markets and likely relevant dimensions. By creatively segmenting markets, he may spot opportunities—even breakthrough opportunities—and enable his firm to succeed against aggressive competitors offering similar products. Segmenting is basic to target marketing. And the more you practice segmenting, the more meaningful market segments you will see.

QUESTIONS AND PROBLEMS

1. Explain what market segmentation is.

2. Explain the three approaches to developing market-oriented strategies for product-markets.

3. Distinguish between segmenters and combiners. Further, explain which approach is being followed if cold cream is offered in a new, more distinctively shaped jar. Which approach is being followed if only the label is changed to gold foil for distinctiveness?

4. List three products that seem to be offered by segment-

ers and three that seem to be offered by combiners. Do any of these products have anything in common?

5. List the types of potential segmenting dimensions and explain which you would try to apply first, second, and third in a particular situation. If the nature of the situation would affect your answer, explain how.

6. Explain why "first-tine" segmentation efforts may be very disappointing.

7. Illustrate the concept that segmenting is an aggregating

process by referring to the apparent admissions policies of your own college and a nearby college or university.

8. *(a)* Evaluate how "good" the seven markets identified in the market for apartments (Figure 9–7) are with respect to the four criteria for selecting good market segments. *(b)* Same as *(a)* but evaluate the four corner markets in the British home decorating market (Figure 2–10).

9. Review the types of segmenting dimensions listed in Figure 9–3 and Table 9–2 and select the ones which you feel should be combined to fully explain the market segment you, personally, would be in if you were planning to buy a new automobile today. Do not hesitate to list several dimensions, but when you have done so, then attempt to develop a short-hand name, like "swinger," to describe your own personal market segment. Then try to estimate what proportion of the total automobile market would be accounted for by your market segment. Next, explain if there are any offerings which come close to meeting the needs of your market. If not, what sort of a marketing mix is needed? Do you feel it would be economically attractive for anyone to try to satisfy your market segment? Why or why not?

10. Identify the determining dimension or dimensions which explain why you bought the specific brand you did in your most recent purchase of a: *(a)* soft drink, *(b)* pen, *(c)* shirt or blouse, and *(d)* larger, more expensive item, such as a bicycle, camera, boat and so on. Try to express the determining dimension(s) in terms of your own personal characteristics rather than the product's characteristics. Estimate what share of the market would probably be motivated by the same determining dimension(s).

11. Apply the seven-step approach to segmenting consumer markets to the college-age market for off-campus recreation, which can include eating and drinking. Then, evaluate how well the needs in these market segments are being met in your geographic area. Is there an obvious breakthrough opportunity waiting for someone?

12. Explain how the first step in the seven-step approach to segmenting markets would have to be changed to apply it in industrial markets. Illustrate your answer.

13. Explain the difference between a forecast of market opportunities and a sales forecast.

14. Suggest a plausible explanation for sales fluctuations for *(a)* bicycles, *(b)* baby food, *(c)* motor boats, *(d)* baseball gloves, *(e)* wheat, *(f)* woodworking tools, and *(g)* latex for rubber-based paint.

15. Discuss the relative accuracy of the various forecasting techniques. Explain why some are more accurate than others.

16. Explain the factor method. Illustrate your answer.

17. Given the following annual sales data for a company which is not planning any spectacular marketing strategy changes, forecast sales for the coming year (7) and explain your method and reasoning.

(a)		*(b)*	
Year	Sales ($000)	Year	Sales ($000)
1	$200	1	$160
2	230	2	155
3	210	3	165
4	220	4	160
5	200	5	170
6	220	6	165

18. Discuss the relative market potential of Cicero and Evanston, Illinois, for: *(a)* prepared cereals, *(b)* automobiles, and *(c)* furniture.

19. Discuss how a General Motors market analyst might use the substitute method if the company were considering the potential for an electric car which might be suitable for salespeople, commuters, homemakers, farmers, and perhaps other groups. The analyst is trying to consider the potential in terms of possible price levels—$2,000, $4,000, $6,000, $8,000, and $10,000—and driving ranges—10 miles, 20 miles, 50 miles, 100 miles, and 200 miles—which would typically be desired or needed before recharging. He is assuming that gasoline-powered vehicles would become illegal for use within the major urban cities. Further, it is expected that while personal gasoline-driven cars still would be used in rural and suburban areas, they would not be permitted within some suburban areas, especially around the major metropolitan areas.

SUGGESTED CASES

4 **Redi, Incorporated**

6 **The Capri**

8 **Arctic Palace**

NOTES

1. Nelson N. Foote, "Market Segmentation as a Competitive Strategy," in E. J. McCarthy et al., *Readings in Basic Marketing*, 3d ed, (Homewood, Ill.: Richard D. Irwin, Inc., 1981); and Alan J. Resnik; Peter B. B. Turney, and J. Barry Mason, "Marketers Turn to 'Countersegmentation,'" *Harvard Business Review*, September–October 1979, pp. 100–106.

2. For a classic article on the subject, see Russell I. Haley, "Benefit Segmentation: A Decision-Oriented Research Tool," *Journal of Marketing*, July 1968, pp. 30–35. See also Richard M. Johnson, "Market Segmentation: A Strategic Management Tool," *Journal of Marketing Research*, February 1971, pp, 13–18; James H. Myers, "Benefit Structure Analysis: A New Tool for Product Planning," *Journal of Marketing*, October 1976, pp. 23–32; and Roger J. Calantone and Alan G. Sawyer, "The Stability of Benefit Segments," *Journal of Marketing Research*, August 1978, pp. 395–404.

3. Dik W. Twedt, "How Important to Marketing Strategy Is the 'Heavy User'?" *Journal of Marketing*, January 1964, pp. 71–72.

4. Frederick W. Winter, "A Cost-Benefit Approach to Market Segmentation," *Journal of Marketing*, Fall 1979, pp. 103–11; Phillip E. Downs, "Multidimensional Scaling versus the Hand-Drawn Technique," *Journal of Business Research*, December 1979, pp. 349–58; John R. Houser and Rank S. Koppelman, "Alternative Perceptual Mapping Techniques: Relative Accuracy and Usefulness," *Journal of Marketing Research*, November 1979, pp. 495–506; Stephen John Arnold, "A Test for Clusters," *Journal of Marketing Research*, November 1979, pp. 545–51; and Henry Assael, "Segmenting Markets by Response Elasticity," *Journal of Advertising Research*, April 1976, pp. 27–35.

5. S. Arbeit and A. G. Sawyer, "Benefit Segmentation in a Retail Banking Environment," presented at the American Marketing Association Fall Conference, Washington, D.C., August 1973.

6. See most basic statistics textbooks under time-series analysis; and U.S. Bureau of the Census, *Estimating Trading Day Variation in Monthly Economic Time Series*, Technical Paper No. 12 (Washington, D.C.: U.S. Government Printing Office, 1965).

7. "New Dog Food Skips Tryouts (Carnation), *Advertising Age*, June 9, 1980, p. 1f.

8. G. T. Borchert, "Design of the Marketing Program for a New Product," in *Marketing's Role in Scientific Management*, ed. Robert L. Clewett (Chicago: American Marketing Association, 1957), pp. 64–66.

9. Checking the accuracy of forecasts is a difficult subject. See R. Ferber, W. J. Hawkes, Jr., and M. D. Plotkin, "How Reliable Are National Retail Sales Estimates?" *Journal of Marketing*, October 1976, pp. 13–22; D. J. Dalrymple, "Sales Forecasting Methods and Accuracy," *Business Horizons*, December 1975, pp. 69–73; P. R. Wotruba and M. L. Thurlow, "Sales Force Participation in Quota Setting and Sales Forecasting," *Journal of Marketing*, April 1976, pp. 11–16; R. Shoemaker and R. Staelin, "The Effects of Sampling Variation on Sales Forecasts for New Consumer Products," *Journal of Marketing Research*, May 1976, pp. 138–43; and R. Staelin and R. E. Turner, "Error in Judgmental Sales Forecasts: Theory and Results," *Journal of Marketing Research*, February 1973, pp. 10–16.

PART THREE

Developing the marketing mix

This part (Chapters 10–20) is concerned with developing effective marketing mixes for the potential target markets we discussed in Part Two. Here, we discuss the "four Ps"—the ingredients of a marketing mix. The four Ps are interrelated and must be blended into one integrated whole—to satisfy some target market's needs and preferences

First, we will discuss Product—in Chapters 10 and 11. We will explore what a "product" is, and introduce some goods classes to speed the development of your marketing sense—because they suggest the outlines of a marketing mix. Combined with a knowledge of the target market, you could begin to "rough out" a marketing mix fairly quickly. Chapter 10 is also concerned with the strategic packaging and branding decisions which are necessary in most marketing mixes. Then, Chapter 11 discusses new-product planning, a new-product development process, and the management of products over their life cycles.

Place is covered in Chapters 12–15. This is an important variable in marketing—because it deals with how products move from producers to consumers. Chapter 12 is concerned with the development and management of channel systems. Chapters 13–15 introduce some of the components of channel systems. Chapter 13 is concerned with retailing—and the many kinds of retailers. Wholesaling is discussed in Chapter 14—along with the many kinds of wholesalers and the

261

(continued)

functions they *may* perform for those above and below them in a channel of distribution. Chapter 15 is concerned with physical distribution—basically the transporting and storing functions which must be provided as products move from producers to final consumers.

The Place chapters are very important—study them carefully. This is where most of the "action" in marketing takes place. Much more than half of the cost of marketing is concerned with developing, managing, and operating channel systems. Physical distribution takes about half of the cost of marketing. A large part of the rest of the cost is for personal selling—which takes place in the channels of distribution.

Promotion is discussed in three chapters (Chapters 16–18). Chapter 16 explains the various promotion methods—personal selling, advertising, and sales promotion—and shows that a blend of these methods is usually needed. Effective blending requires a good understanding of some theoretical principles. These include the communication process—as well as how individuals and groups adopt products. Then, Chapter 17 applies some of these ideas to personal selling—emphasizing the importance of carefully defining what the personal selling job is. Selecting, training, and motivating the "right" people to do the personal selling job are also discussed. Chapter 18 focuses on the mass selling job—basically, advertising. Here, the importance of specific advertising objectives is stressed. These objectives then determine the kinds of advertising that should be used—as well as suggesting the kind of media and the copy thrust.

The final two chapters in this part (as well as Appendix B on Marketing Arithmetic) are concerned with Price. Chapter 19 discusses pricing objectives—and how they affect the strategic decisions which must be made in the pricing area. The many dimensions of Price are discussed in this chapter. Then, in Chapter 20 we talk about price setting in the real world. This involves mark-up pricing, average-cost pricing, break-even analysis, and the economist's traditional marginal analysis—which helps find the most profitable price and quantity.

In summary, by the time you have studied this part, you should have a good understanding of how to develop the "right" Product (including packaging and branding) which will be made available in the "right" Place, supported with the "right" Promotion at the "right" Price to satisfy some target market. Hopefully, you will be able to develop *profitable* strategies—target markets and marketing mixes. So the next job—in Part Four—will be to evaluate these potentially attractive strategies to decide which one or ones you will select for implementation.

Peter Le Grand

When you finish this chapter, you should:

1. Understand what "Product" really means.
2. Know the differences among the various consumer and industrial goods classes.
3. Understand how the goods classes can help a marketing manager plan marketing strategies.
4. Understand the strategic importance of packaging.
5. Understand what branding is and how it can be used in strategy planning.
6. Recognize the important new terms (shown in red).

10

Elements of product planning

The product must satisfy customers—what they want is what they'll get.

Developing the "right" product isn't easy—because customer needs and attitudes keep changing. Further, *most customers want some combination of goods and services in their product.* We'll talk about this first.

Then, to help you understand marketing strategy planning better, we will talk about some goods classes. The consumer goods and industrial goods classes introduced in this chapter should be studied carefully. They can speed your development as a marketing strategy planner.

We will also talk about packaging and branding. Most products need some packaging. And both physical goods and services should be branded. A successful marketer wants to be sure that satisfied customers will know what to ask for the next time.

In summary, we will talk about the strategic decisions of manufacturers or middlemen who must make these product, packaging, and branding decisions. These strategic decisions are shown in Figure 10–1.

WHAT IS A PRODUCT?

Customers buy satisfaction, not parts

First, we have to decide what we mean by a "product."

If we sell an automobile, are we selling a certain number of nuts and bolts, some sheet metal, an engine, and four wheels?

If we sell a detergent to be used in a washing machine, are we selling just a box of chemicals?

**Figure 10–1
Strategy planning for Product**

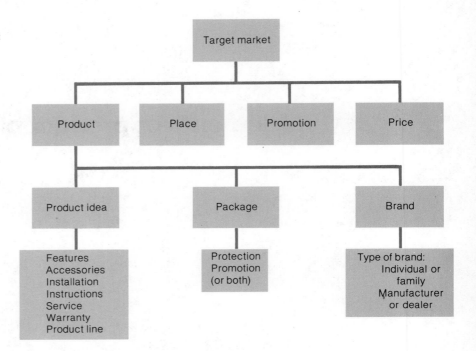

If we sell a delivery service, are we selling so much wear and tear on a delivery truck and so much operator fatigue?

The answer to all these questions is *no*. Instead, what we are really selling is the satisfaction, use, or profit the customer wants.

All the customers ask is that their cars look good, ride well, and keep running efficiently. They don't care how they were made. Further, they want to clean their clothes with the detergent—not analyze it. And when they order something to be delivered, they don't really care how much out of the way the driver has to go or where he has been. They just want their package.

Similarly, when producers and middlemen buy products, they are interested in the profit they will make from their purchase—through its use and resale—not how the products were made.

Product means the needs-satisfying offering of a firm.

The idea of Product as potential customer satisfactions or benefits is very important. Many business managers—trained in the production side of business—get wrapped up in the number of nuts and bolts, the tightness of the nuts, the fertilizer application per acre, and other technical problems. Middlemen, too, are often concerned with technical details. But while these are important to them, they have little effect on the way most customers view the product. What matters to customers is how *they* see what is being offered—not how the sellers see it. And these two views may be far apart.

Product is more than just a physical thing

A "Product" is more than just a physical good with its related features. It includes accessories, installation, instruction on use, the package, perhaps a

Figure 10–2
Possible blends of goods and services in a product

100% Good	50/50	100% Service
Common nails Dried beans	Auto rustproofing Restaurant meal	Medical exam Radio program

brand name which fills some psychological needs, a warranty, and confidence that service will be available after the purchase if it is needed.

Product may only be a service

"Product" may not include a physical good at all! The product of a barber or hair stylist is the trimming or styling of your hair. A medical doctor may just look at you—neither taking anything away nor giving you anything physical. Nevertheless, each satisfies needs—and provides a product in the sense we will use "product" in this book. Figure 10–2 emphasizes this point by showing that a "product" could range from 100 percent physical good—such as commodities like common nails or dried beans—to 100 percent service. Most products fit someplace in between—that is, they are a blend of physical goods *and* services.[1] This shows why it is so important to fully understand the needs and attitudes of target customers—and then develop a *complete* product to satisfy their needs.

Need satisfaction comes from a product

This bigger view of a product must be understood completely—it's too easy to slip into a *physical product* point of view. We want to think of a product in terms of the *needs it satisfies.* Customer needs are satisfied not only by physical goods but also by services. If the objective of the firm is to satisfy customer needs, it must see that service is part of or may be *the* product—and has to be provided as part of the marketing mix. An automobile without any repair service, for example, is not a very useful product.

Product assortment and product lines must be developed, too

We will usually talk about one product at a time—to simplify the discussion. But many businesses sell many products—each of which may involve a separate strategy. So it is useful to define **product assortment**—the set of all product

A Product is more than just a physical good.

Mike Jaeggi

lines and items that a firm sells, and **product line**—a set of products that are closely related. They may be seen as related by the seller because they are produced and/or operate in a similar way, or are sold to the same target market, or are sold through the same types of outlets, or are priced at about the same level. Procter & Gamble, for example, has many product lines within its product assortment—including soaps, detergents, toothpastes, shampoo, toilet tissue, disposable diapers, and so on. **Product item**—a particular product within a product line—usually is distinguished by brand, size, price, or some other characteristic—and identified with its own stockkeeping number. For example, each size of a brand of soap would be a separate item—and would require separate decisions!

Most manufacturers and wholesalers have to offer product assortments to satisfy their customers. Retailers also have to offer assortments. This makes the job of product planning harder. But if this is what customers want, then product lines and a whole product assortment have to be offered.

Goods and/or services are our Product

To further simplify our discussion, we will not make a distinction between goods and services—but will call them all *Products*. Within this broader concept of a Product, we can also consider the assortment of goods and services offered by a wholesaler or retailer as a Product. This will let us generalize about marketing strategy planning for any kind of firm.

GOODS CLASSES HELP PLAN MARKETING STRATEGIES

To avoid trying to treat *every* product as unique when planning strategies, it would help to have some product classes which would help plan marketing mixes. Luckily, products can be classified this way. These classes are a useful starting point for developing marketing mixes.

Note: we will call these classes "goods classes"—because this is traditional in marketing. But remember, goods classes refer to *products*—which can be goods and/or services.

Goods class depends on who will use the product

Whether a product should be treated as a consumer or industrial good depends on who will use it. **Consumer goods** are those products meant for the final consumer. **Industrial goods** are products meant for use in producing other products. All goods fit into one of these two groups.

Goods class depends on how customers see the product

There is no automatic classification for a particular product. Since different people may see the same product differently, several goods classes may be needed to correctly describe how all potential customers in a general market area view the product. This means there is no need to memorize a long list of products according to goods classes. It also helps explain why the same product must be marketed in several different ways.

Focusing on goods classes is a practical approach—and will provide a thread through the rest of this book. Research supports this approach—having found that these goods classes are relevant to marketing mix planning.[2]

Figure 10–3
Consumer goods classes and
marketing mix planning

1. *Convenience goods.*
   a. Staples—need maximum exposure—need widespread distribution at low cost.
   b. Impulse goods—need maximum exposure—need widespread distribution but with assurance of preferred display or counter position.
   c. Emergency goods—need widespread distribution near probable point of use.
2. *Shopping goods.*
   a. Homogeneous—need enough exposure to facilitate price comparison.
   b. Heterogeneous—need adequate representation, in major shopping districts or large shopping centers near other, similar shopping goods.
3. *Specialty goods*—can have limited availability, but in general should be treated as a convenience or shopping good (in whichever category product would normally be included), to reach persons not yet sold on its specialty-goods status.
4. *Unsought goods*—need attention directed to product and aggressive promotion in outlets, or must be available in places where similar products would be sought.

CONSUMER GOODS CLASSES

Based on customer buying behavior

Consumer goods classes are based on the way people think about and buy products. Since the aim of marketing is to satisfy consumers' needs, basing goods classes on consumer buying behavior makes sense. It also follows from our discussion—in Chapter 7—of the consumer as a problem solver. Consumer goods can be divided into four groups: (1) convenience goods, (2) shopping goods, (3) specialty goods, and (4) unsought goods. See Figure 10–3 for a summary of how these goods classes are related to a marketing mix.

CONVENIENCE GOODS—USUALLY PURCHASED QUICKLY

Convenience goods are products the customer needs but isn't willing to spend much time or effort shopping for. Examples are: cigarettes, soap, aspirin, newspapers, magazines, chewing gum, candy, and most grocery products. These products are bought often, require little service or selling, don't cost much, and may even be bought by habit.

Convenience goods are of three types—staples, impulse goods, and emergency goods—again based on *how customers think about products—not* the features of the products themselves.

Staples—purchased and used regularly

Staples are goods which are bought often and routinely—without much thought. Examples include food and drug items used regularly in every household. Here, branding can become important to help customers cut shopping effort.

Staples are sold in convenient places like food stores, drug stores, discount and hardware stores, and vending machines. Some customers want convenience so much that they have milk, bread, and newspapers delivered directly to their homes.

Shopping for staples may not even be planned. Many shoppers plan meals in the store—and modern supermarkets are laid out to make this easier. "Go-

Convenience goods should be easily available.

Mary McCarthy

togethers" like strawberries and sponge cake or ice cream and chocolate sauce are placed next to each other to encourage unplanned buying.

Such buying is not necessarily "impulse buying." One study showed that the purchase of about 50 percent of all grocery items might be classed as unplanned—but nearly 86 percent of these purchases were products and brands that had been bought before.[3] Experienced shoppers may be shifting their routine meal planning from home to store. This may be very sensible. The shoppers can see what is available this week—and what are the "best buys." They may even buy brands which are part of their consumption system—recall our discussion of routinized buying behavior in Chapter 7.

Impulse goods—bought immediately on sight

Impulse goods are goods which are bought quickly—as unplanned purchases—because of a strongly felt need. True impulse goods are items that the customer had not planned to buy, decides to buy on sight, may have bought the same way many times before, and wants "right now."

If a shopper passes a street corner vendor, for example, and gets a sudden urge for ice cream, that ice cream bar is an impulse good. But if the same shopper bought a box of ice cream bars in the supermarket as a family dessert, the bars would be staples—because the shopper was looking for a dessert.

There is an important difference between buying something to satisfy a current need and buying for later use. If the customer doesn't buy an impulse good immediately, the need may disappear and no purchase will be made. But if the customer needs a dessert, a purchase probably will be made eventually.

This difference is important because it affects Place and the whole marketing mix. Place is very important for impulse goods. If the buyer doesn't see them at the "right" time, the sale may be lost. As a result, special methods are developed for selling impulse goods. They are put where they'll be seen and bought—near front doors, near the checkout counters, or on display shelves in front of the store.

Emergency goods—purchased only when urgently needed

Emergency goods are goods which are purchased only when the need is great. Little shopping may be done. The customer needs the product immediately. Price isn't important. Examples are ambulance services, umbrellas or raincoats during a rainstorm, and tire chains during a snowstorm.

Some retailers carry emergency goods to meet such needs. They know that many potential customers will face certain kinds of emergencies. And they set up their operations to serve them. Small gasoline stations in rural areas and service stations on toll-roads carry tires to meet emergency needs. The buyer probably could get a tire at a lower price back home—but with a blowout, any price is right.

Some small, neighborhood grocery stores meet the "fill-in" needs of customers who need a few items between weekly supermarket trips. Usually these stores charge higher prices. But customers will pay it—because they think of these goods as "emergencies." One study found that almost 80 percent of households use such a "fill-in" store.[4] In the last 20 years, chains of such convenience food stores have been spreading. They provide "emergency" service—staying open "7 till 11" and stocking items that are needed in a hurry.

Place is an important part of the marketing mix for emergency goods. Clearly, the marketing mix for emergency goods will be different from the one for staples—at least regarding where products are placed.

SHOPPING GOODS

Shopping goods are those products that a customer feels are worth the time and effort to compare with competing products.

Shopping goods can be divided into two types—depending on what customers are comparing: (1) homogeneous and (2) heterogeneous shopping goods.

Homogeneous shopping goods—the price must be right

Homogeneous shopping goods are shopping goods that the customer sees as basically the same—and wants at the lowest price.

When consumers see the various brands of a product class as basically the same, each competitor has an almost perfectly elastic demand curve. Since a slight price cut on such products could greatly increase sales volume, we might expect vigorous price competiton.

This, in fact, is the condition in many markets. Some consumers feel that certain sizes and types of refrigerators, television sets, washing machines, and even automobiles are basically similar. They are mainly concerned about shopping for the best price.

Manufacturers try to emphasize their product differences—and retailers try to promote their "better service." But if the customers don't believe these differences are real, your Ford dealer who "wants to make you happy . . . keep you happy . . ." may not get the chance unless the price is right. This is particularly true in large urban areas where there are many firms selling the same physical good and similar service.

In one study of automobile purchasing behavior, about half of the people wanted the "best price" or "best deal" and did shop at more than one dealership.[5]

Three out of four supermarket shoppers shop for advertised specials every week.[6]

This buyer emphasis on price helps explain the rise of certain types of discount houses—and why some retailers emphasize "low prices" and "price cuts."

Low-price items are seen this way, too

Even some smaller items like butter, coffee, and other food items may be thought of as homogeneous shopping goods. Some customers carefully read food store advertising for the lowest prices—and then they go from store to store getting the items. They wouldn't do this for staples.

Heterogeneous shopping goods—the product must be right

Heterogeneous shopping goods are shopping goods that the customer sees as different—and wants to inspect for quality and suitability. Examples are furniture, dishes, some cameras, and clothing. Quality and style are important—price is less important.

Even if an item costs only $5 or $10, consumers may look in three or four stores to be sure they have done a good job of shopping.

Price is not totally ignored in this kind of buying. But for nonstandardized products, it's harder to compare prices. Once the customer has found the right product, price may not be significant—provided it is reasonable. That is, the demand for the product may be quite inelastic. The more close substitutes there are, the more elastic becomes the demand. But it does not approach the extreme elasticity found with homogeneous shopping goods.

Branding may be less important for heterogeneous goods. The more consumers want to make their own comparisons of price and quality, the less they rely on brand names and labels.

The buyer of heterogeneous shopping goods not only wants—but expects—some kind of help in buying. And, if the product is expensive, the buyer may want extra service—such as alteration of clothing or installation of appliances.

SPECIALTY GOODS

Specialty goods are consumer goods that the customer really wants—and is willing to make a special effort to buy. Shopping for a specialty good doesn't mean comparing—the buyer wants that special product and is willing to search for it. It is not the extent of searching, but the customer's *willingness* to search—if necessary—that makes it a specialty good.

Specialty goods usually are specific branded products—not broad product categories. But a unique new product—even though not branded—also might be a specialty good. This could be true of a new drug or fertilizer—available only by generic name. Generally, however, a specific brand is involved.

Don't want substitutes!

Contrary to a common view, specialty goods need not be expensive, durable items that are purchased infrequently. Any item that develops "brand insistence" is a specialty good. Consumers have been observed asking for a drug product by its brand name and, when offered a substitute (even though chemically identical), actually leaving the store in anger.

As might be expected, the demand for specialty goods is relatively inelastic—

Customers are willing to search for specialty goods.

Mary McCarthy

at least within reasonable price ranges—since target customers are willing to insist upon the product.

UNSOUGHT GOODS

Unsought goods are goods that potential customers do not yet want or know they can buy. Therefore, they don't search for them at all. In fact, consumers probably wouldn't buy these goods if they saw them—unless Promotion could show their value.

There are two types of unsought goods: new unsought and regularly unsought.

New unsought goods are products offering really new ideas that potential customers don't know about yet. Informative promotion can help convince customers to accept or even seek out the product—ending their unsought status.

James R. Holland— Stock, Boston

Regularly unsought goods are products—like gravestones, life insurance, and encyclopedias—that may stay unsought but not unbought forever. These products may become some of the biggest purchases a family ever makes— but few people would even drive around the block to find them. There may be a need—but the potential customers are not motivated to satisfy it. And there probably is little hope that they will move out of the unsought class for most consumers. For this kind of product, Promotion is very important.

ONE PRODUCT MAY BE SEEN AS SEVERAL CONSUMER GOODS

We have been looking at one product at a time. But the same product might be seen in different ways by different target markets *at the same time.*

The marketing manager might find that the market consists of several groups of people—each of which has similar attitudes toward the product. This is shown in Figure 10–4. This diagram groups people in terms of their willingness to shop as well as brand familiarity. It is a simple way of summarizing our discussion of consumer goods. Each of these groups might need a different marketing mix.

Figure 10–4
**How potential customers might
view some product***

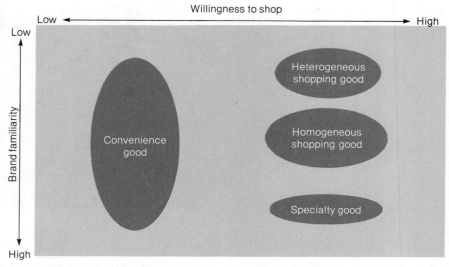

* The number of people holding each view is indicated roughly by the size of the cluster. Suggested by Prof. Yusaku Furuhashi, University of Notre Dame.

A tale of four motels

Motels are a good example of a service that can be seen as *four different* kinds of goods. Some tired motorists are satisfied with the first motel they come to—a convenience good. Other travelers shop for the kind of place they want at a fair price—a heterogeneous shopping good. Others shop for just basic facilities at the lowest price—a homogeneous shopping good. And others study tourist guides, talk with traveling friends, and phone ahead to reserve a place in a recommended motel—a specialty good.

Perhaps one motel could satisfy all potential customers. But it would be hard to produce a marketing mix attractive to everyone—easy access for convenience, good facilities at the right price for shopping goods buyers, and qualities special enough to attract the specialty goods travelers. As a result, we see very different kinds of motels—seemingly (but not really) competing with each other.

*Need for consumer
research—to classify
products*

Although the marketing manager can use market judgment to classify a product, a more reliable job could probably be done with marketing research. A formal research effort can uncover consumer attitudes, needs, and shopping behavior related to the product type and the company's particular product. Such analysis might show not only the relevant dimensions for deciding on the right goods class or classes—but also other segmenting dimensions.

*Goods classes can help
describe target markets*

With complete information about the relevant dimensions in potential target markets, it is "relatively easy" to develop "good" marketing mixes. Realistically, however, it should be increasingly obvious that this information is not always available—that we do not always know as much as we would like about our potential customers. This is where consumer goods classes can help.

A marketing manager may be able to make reasonably good judgments about how eager consumers are to satisfy their needs—and how willing they are to shop and compare. These judgments can help classify products. And these classes, in turn, will help us get started on marketing mix planning.

INDUSTRIAL GOODS ARE DIFFERENT

Industrial goods classes are useful for developing marketing mixes, too—since industrial firms use a logical system of buying related to these goods classes.

Before looking at industrial good *differences,* however, we will note some important *similarities* that have a direct impact on strategy planning.

GENERAL CHARACTERISTICS OF INDUSTRIAL GOODS[7]

One demand derived from another

The outstanding characteristic of the industrial goods market is **derived demand**—the demand for industrial goods is derived from the demand for final consumer goods.

Derived demand is clearly illustrated in the steel industry. Almost all steel is sold to manufacturers for the production of other products. About one fifth of all steel products go to the automotive industry—which is highly dependent on final consumer demand. If a car manufacturer expects to sell 50,000 cars of a particular model each month, it will need enough steel to produce them. No amount of price cutting or adjustments in the steel maker's marketing mixes will increase the total amount of steel needed.

As long as business is good and markets are growing, the derived nature of industrial demand does not seem very important—and is often neglected. But it becomes very important when final consumer demands are shifting rapidly—or in times of recession when even the most efficient and aggressive industrial goods companies lose sales because their customers cannot get business. At such times, some industrial goods producers advertise directly to final consumers—to try to stimulate demand. Cement and earth-moving equipment manufacturers, for example, have promoted road building to final consumers—to build demand for *their* products.

Price increases might not reduce quantity purchased

The fact that demand for most industrial goods is derived means that *industry demand for such goods will be fairly inelastic.* To satisfy final consumer needs, producers need a certain quantity of each of the components of their products—almost regardless of price. Since each of the components costs only a fraction of the total cost of their product, the price of any one item may have relatively little to do with the quantity of that item purchased. The cost of the spice in a box of cake mix, for example, might be only one half of 1 percent of the cake manufacturer's total cost. Even if the price of this spice were doubled and passed directly along to consumers, it would have relatively little impact on the cake producer's price or the quantity demanded by final consumers. Therefore, the price increase might not reduce the quantity of spice purchased.

Suppliers may face almost pure competition

Although the industry demand for industrial goods may be inelastic, the demand facing individual sellers may be extremely elastic. This will be true if competitive

Industrial buyers usually seek several sources of supply.

Mary McCarthy

products are basically homogeneous and there are many sellers—that is, if the market approaches pure competition.

In the case of the spice ingredients, if the spices available from all suppliers are basically similar and one spice supplier increases its price while competitors do not, buyers probably will shift their purchases to the competition. Thus *there may be nearly pure competition among the suppliers of a product even though there is inelastic industry demand.*

Buyers will help make the market as competitive as they can. Most industrial buyers seek several sources of supply to ensure production in their own plants. Their job is to buy as economically as possible—and they will be quick to spread the word that competitors are offering lower prices.

INDUSTRIAL GOODS CLASSES

Industrial goods buyers do little shopping—especially compared to consumer goods buyers. Usually the seller comes to the buyer. This means that goods classes based on shopping behavior are not useful.

Industrial goods classes are based on how buyers see products—and how the products are to be used. Expensive and/or long-lasting products are treated differently than inexpensive items. Products that become a part of a firm's own product are seen differently from those which only aid production. Finally, the relative size of a particular purchase can make a difference. An air compressor may not be very important to a buyer for General Motors, but it might be very important for a small garage owner.

The industrial goods classes are related to the way industrial purchasing departments and accounting control systems operate day to day. Buyers, for example, often specialize by product categories. And categories similar to our industrial goods classes are used for buying, maintenance, costing of orders, and control purposes.

The classes of industrial goods are: (1) installations, (2) accessory equipment, (3) raw materials, (4) component parts and materials, (5) supplies, and (6) services.

See Figure 10–5 for a summary of how these goods classes are related to what is needed in a marketing mix.

INSTALLATIONS—MAJOR CAPITAL ITEMS

Installations are important long-lived capital items—durable goods which are depreciated over many years. They include buildings and land rights, custom-made equipment, and standard equipment. Buildings and custom-made equipment generally require special negotiations for each individual product—because they are "one-of-a-kind." Standard major equipment is more homogeneous—and is treated more routinely. All installations, however, are important enough to require high-level and even top-management consideration. New-task buying or modified rebuying will be involved here.

Size of market small at any time

Installations are long-lasting goods—so they are not bought very often. The number of potential buyers *at any particular time* usually is small. For custom-made machines, there may be only a half-dozen potential customers—compared to a thousand or more potential buyers for similar standard machines.

Potential customers are generally in the same industry. Their plants are likely to be near to each other—which makes Promotion easier. The automobile industry, for example, is heavily concentrated in and around Michigan. The tire industry

Figure 10–5
Industrial goods and marketing mix planning

1. *Installations.*
   a. Buildings (used) and land rights—need widespread and/or knowledgeable contacts, depending upon specialized nature of product.
   b. Buildings (new)—*need technical and experienced personal contact, probably at top management level (multiple buying influence).*
   c. Major equipment.
      i. *Custom-made*—need technical (design) contacts by person able to visualize and design applications, and present to high-level and technical management.
      ii. Standard—need experienced (not necessarily highly technical) contacts by person able to visualize applications and present to high-level and technical management.
2. *Accessory equipment*—need fairly widespread and numerous contacts by experienced and sometimes technically trained personnel.
3. *Raw materials.*
   a. Farm products—need contacts with many small farmer producers and fairly widespread contact with users.
   b. Natural products—need fairly widespread contacts with users.
4. *Component parts and materials*—need technical contacts to determine specifications required—widespread contacts usually not necessary.
5. *Supplies.*
   a. Maintenance—need very widespread distribution for prompt delivery.
   b. Repairs—need widespread distribution for some, and prompt service from factory for others (depends on customers' preferences).
   c. Operating supplies—need fair to widespread distribution for prompt delivery.
6. *Services*—most need very widespread availability.

is in Ohio. Copper mining is in the western states. And the aircraft industry—from a world view—is in the United States.

Buying needs basically economic

Buying needs are basically economic—and concerned with the performance of the installation over its expected life. After comparing expected performance to present costs and figuring interest, the expected return on capital can be determined. Yet emotional needs—such as a desire for industry leadership and status—also may be involved.

Multiple buying influence important

The importance of installations leads to much multiple buying influence. Negotiations can stretch over months or even years—and often involve the top managers of the company, especially for buildings or custom-made products. This may complicate promotion, since these managers may be concerned with quite different problems than purchasing agents—and may not use the same evaluation criteria. The top managers may be less concerned, for example, with the product's suitability for current needs than with its flexibility and possible usefulness in a new venture being considered. The seller may need different sales approaches to cope with each of the possible influences.

Industry demand may be very inelastic, but sellers see elastic curves

The demand for a particular installation may be completely inelastic up to a certain price—especially if the firm badly needs expanded capacity. The potential return on the new investment may be so attractive that any reasonable price may be acceptable.

While the buyers' demand can be very inelastic, however, the situation for sellers may be different. There may be many suppliers—such as building contractors. So buyers of installations may be able to request bids and buy in a very competitive market.

Installation industry, a "boom-or-bust" business

The installation industry has been described as a "boom-or-bust" business. During the upswing of a business cycle, businesses want to expand capacity rapidly—and are willing to pay almost any reasonable price to do it. Competition is less vigorous—and profits are higher for the installation sellers. But during a downswing, buyers will have little or no need for new installations—and sales can fall off sharply.

Installations may have to be leased or rented

Since installations are relatively expensive, the producer will often lease or rent the product rather than sell it outright. Examples are buildings and land rights—and some specialized equipment, including electronic data processing machines.

Such lease or rental arrangements are attractive to some target markets—because they shift the expenditure from a capital item to an expense item—a short-lived good and/or service which—for accounting and tax purposes—is written off as it is used, usually in the year of purchase.

Specialized services are needed as part of the product

Since the expected return on an installation is based on efficient operation, the supplier may have to provide service to assure this efficiency. The sales contract may specify regular service visits. Service people may even be perma-

Service is important for some accessories.

Mary McCarthy

nently assigned to the company. Computer manufacturers sometimes station service people with the machines. The cost is included in the price or rent.

The more homogeneous the installation, the more likely it is that the seller will try to differentiate the product by offering specialized services—such as aid in installing the machine in the buyer's plant, training employees in its use, supplying repair service, and taking trade-ins.

ACCESSORY EQUIPMENT—IMPORTANT BUT SHORT-LIVED CAPITAL ITEMS

Accessory equipment includes short-lived capital items. They are the tools and equipment used in production or office activities. Examples include portable drills, sanding machines, electric lift trucks, typewriters, filing cases, accounting machines, wheelbarrows, hand trucks, and small lathes.

Since these products cost less and last a shorter time than installations, multiple buying influence is less important. Operating people and purchasing agents—rather than top managers—may do the buying.

More target markets requiring different marketing mixes

Accessories are more standardized than installations. And they are usually needed by more customers! A large, special-purpose belt sanding machine, for example, might be produced as a custom-made installation for wood-working firms. But small portable sanding machines would be considered accessory equipment. Since there are many more possible customers and less geographic concentration, different marketing mixes would be needed for accessory equipment than for installations.

Might prefer to lease or rent

Leasing or renting accessories is attractive to some target markets—because the costs can be expensed. A manufacturer of electric lift trucks, for instance, was able to expand its sales by selling the basic truck outright—but charging for the expensive battery system by the amount of time it was used. This increased sales because, as one of the managers said: "Nobody worries about costs which are buried as an operating expense."[8]

Buyers may have many substitutes

As accessory items become less expensive and more standardized, it is more likely that there will be substitutes. Then, although individual buyers may have inelastic demands, they still are able to buy in fairly competitive markets.

Special services may be attractive

Ordinarily, engineering services or special advice is less important for accessory equipment—because of its simpler operation. Yet, some companies have managed to add attractive services to their accessories. Office equipment firms, for example, offer advice on office layout and office systems.

RAW MATERIALS—FARM PRODUCTS AND NATURAL PRODUCTS ARE EXPENSE ITEMS

Become part of a physical good

Raw materials are unprocessed goods—such as logs, iron ore, sand, and freshly caught fish—that are handled as little as is needed to move them to the next step in the production process. Unlike installations and accessories, raw materials become part of a physical good—and are expense items.

We can break raw materials into two categories: (1) farm products and (2) natural products. **Farm products** are grown by farmers—examples are cotton, wheat, strawberries, sugar cane, cattle, hogs, poultry, eggs, and milk. **Natural products** are products which occur in nature—such as fish and game, lumber and maple syrup, and copper, zinc, iron ore, oil, and coal.

FARM PRODUCTS VARY IN QUALITY AND QUANTITY

Involve grading, storage, and/or transportation

The need for grading is one of the important differences between farm products and other industrial goods. Nature produces what it will—and someone must sort and grade farm products to satisfy various market segments. Some of the top grades of fruits and vegetables find their way into the consumer goods market. The lower grades are treated as industrial goods—and used in juices, sauces, and frozen pies.

Most farm products are produced seasonally—yet the demand for them is fairly constant all year. As a result, storage and transportation are important in their marketing process.

As noted, buyers of industrial goods usually don't seek suppliers. This complicates the marketing of farm products. The many small farms usually are widely scattered—sometimes far from potential buyers. Selling direct to final users would be difficult. So Place and Promotion are important in marketing mixes for these products.

Large buyers may encourage contract farming

Most buyers of farm products have specific uses in mind—and generally prefer that these products be sorted and graded. But since large buyers may have difficulty getting the quantities of the grades and types they want, they may encourage contract farming. This has two effects. It makes the supplier a part of the buyer's operation—and removes one more producer from the competitive market. This may be desirable from the suppliers' point of view—because it isolates them from a purely competitive market.

Each seller's demand curve is elastic

Most farm products have an inelastic *market* (industry) demand—even though the many small producers are in nearly pure competition. The market demand becomes more elastic when there are many substitutes (such as beef for pork or corn for wheat). But within the usual price ranges, the demand for agricultural products is generally inelastic. So these producers often try to control output and prices—usually with U.S. Department of Agriculture help.

Most attempts to control farm product prices are frustrated by slow adjustment of supply—and the difficulty of organizing the many producers. Once a crop is planted, the potential supply is more or less fixed (subject to weather, pests, and so on)—and it is too late to change crop size that year.

At the end of a growing season, the quantity is fixed. If this supply is large, the market price can be extremely low—if it is small, the price may be high. This can be seen in Figure 10–6—where vertical lines are used to show that in the short run, farmers would supply the same quantity regardless of the price.

NATURAL PRODUCTS—QUANTITIES ARE ADJUSTABLE

In contrast to the farm products market with its many producers, natural products are produced by fewer and larger companies. There are some exceptions—such as the coal and lumber industries—but oligopoly conditions are common.

Typically, the total supply of natural products is limited—and can't be expanded easily. But the supply harvested or mined in any one year *is* adjustable.

Most of the products are bulky and have transportation problems. But storage is less important—since few are perishable. And some can be produced year-round. Major exceptions are fish and game—which have "runs" or seasons—and are more like farm products than natural products in their marketing patterns.

As with farm products, buyers of natural products usually need specific grades and dependable supply sources—to be sure of continued production in their own plants. Large buyers, therefore, often try to buy—or at least control—their sources of supply. This is easier than with farm products—because fewer and larger production facilities are involved.

Figure 10–6
Effect of changes in supply on price in agricultural markets

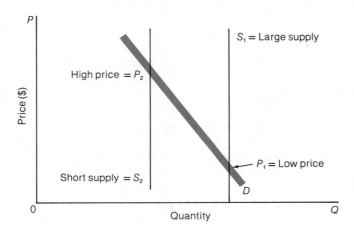

Production of natural products can be varied over time.

Milt & Joan Mann

One way to control supply sources is **vertical integration**—here meaning ownership of the natural product source by the user. Examples are paper manufacturers who control timber resources, oil refiners who control crude oil sources, and tire manufacturers who control rubber plantations.

Natural products sellers who do not integrate usually find that their customers want to be sure of dependable sources of supply. This is often done through contracts—perhaps negotiated by top-level managers—using standard grades or specifications.

Sellers' demand curves may be inelastic or elastic

The industry demand for natural products is derived and basically inelastic. The large producers understand and are quite responsive to market demands. They are inclined to limit supply to maintain stable prices. In the coal and lumber industries, however—where there are many producers—there is close to pure competition.

COMPONENT PARTS AND MATERIALS—IMPORTANT EXPENSE ITEMS

The whole is no better than . . .

Component parts and materials are expense items which have had more processing than raw materials. They require different marketing mixes than raw materials—even though they both become part of a finished product.

Component *parts* include those items that are (1) finished and ready for assembly or (2) nearly finished—requiring only minor processing (such as grinding or polishing) before being assembled into the final product. Examples are automobile batteries, small motors, and tires—all of which go directly into a finished product.

Component *materials* are items such as wire, paper, textiles, or cement. They have already been processed—but must be processed further before becoming part of the final product.

Multiple buying influences

Some component parts are custom-made. Much negotiation may be necessary between the engineering staffs of both buyer and seller to arrive at the right specifications. If the price of the item is high—or if it is extremely important in the final product—top managers may be involved. New-task buying is found here—to help set the specifications and sources.

Other component parts and materials are produced to commonly accepted standards or specifications—and produced in quantity. Production people in the buying firm may specify quality—but the purchasing agent will do the buying. And he will want several dependable sources of supply. Modified rebuys and straight rebuys are seen here.

Buying needs are economic

The needs involved in buying components are basically economic—price, availability, quality, and suitability. Assurances of availability and prompt delivery are most important. A purchasing agent must do everything possible to avoid a plant shutdown caused by lack of materials. Moreover, an assured source of supply will enable the buyer to reduce inventory—thus reducing both inventory investment and the risk of damage to, and obsolescence of, goods in stock.

Since components are incorporated into the firm's own product, quality is extremely important. The buyer's own name and whole marketing mix are at stake. Quality may be less important for some component parts, however, if they are well branded—such as a tire or spark plug—and the blame for a defective product can fall upon the component supplier. Generally, however, a progressive buyer will try to buy from component sources that help assure a satisfactory product.

Market may be very competitive

Although the industry and individual buyers' demands may be fairly inelastic for components, there usually are many willing suppliers—so buyers operate in a fairly competitive market. In fact, the market for many component parts and materials is extremely competitive. There are several reasons for this competition.

1. Most component buyers want to have several sources of supply—and encourage new suppliers.
2. There usually are many small producers—small fabricators, machine shops, and foundaries—with general-purpose machinery that can produce a great variety of component parts.
3. There usually are many component materials suppliers willing to produce to widely accepted specifications or standards.

Replacement markets may develop

Since component parts are incorporated into a finished product, a replacement market often develops. This market can be both large and very profitable—as in the case of automobile tires and batteries.

This replacement market *(after market)* may involve new target markets. The part originally may have been considered a component part when it was sold in the *OEM (original equipment market)*—but as a replacement, the same product might become a consumer good. The target markets are different—and probably different marketing mixes will be necessary.

Some component parts suppliers are eager to have their parts used in the OEM market—because the "after market" is so attractive.

The Mallory Battery Co. worked hard to get its small batteries installed as original components in cameras, watches, hearing aids, and dictating equipment—because marketing research told them that half of all final consumer battery buyers don't know what kind of battery powers their equipment. They simply walk into a store and say, "Gimme one just like this."

Mallory coordinated its efforts in both markets—the components and final consumer markets—and achieved a 50-percent increase in profits.[9]

SUPPLIES—EVERYBODY WANTS THESE EXPENSE ITEMS, BUT HOW MUCH?

Supplies are expense items that do not become a part of the final product. They may be treated less seriously by buyers. Although they are necessary, most supplies are not as vital to continued operations as the products in the first four classes. When a firm economizes, orders for supplies may be the first to go.

They are called MRO items

Supplies can be divided into three categories: (1) maintenance, (2) repair, and (3) operating supplies—giving them their common name: "MRO items."

Maintenance items include such things as paint, nails, light bulbs, sweeping compounds, brooms, and window-cleaning equipment. *Repair items* are nuts and bolts or parts needed to repair existing equipment. *Operating supplies* include lubricating oils and greases, grinding compounds, coal, typing paper, ink, pencils, and paper clips.

Important operating supplies

Some operating supplies needed regularly and in large amounts receive special treatment from buyers. Some companies buy coal and fuel oil in carload or tank-car quantities. Usually there are several sources for such homogeneous products—and large volumes may be purchased in highly competitive markets. Or contracts may be negotiated—perhaps by high-level executives. Such contracts have several advantages. Subsequent purchase requisitions may be drawn routinely against them—as straight rebuys. They sometimes assure lower prices. And they eliminate the buyer's concern about a dependable source for these important operating supplies.

When several dependable sources are available and orders are large, reciprocity may become important. If quality and price are roughly the same, it becomes more difficult to refuse the sales department's request for reciprocity relationships. Purchasing departments usually resist such efforts—but this is one place where the sales department's arguments are strong.

Maintenance and small operating supplies

These items are similar to consumer's convenience goods—and are so numerous that a purchasing agent cannot possibly be an expert in buying all of them. There usually is little multiple buying influence. They may not even justify modified rebuying.

Each requisition for maintenance and small operating supplies may be for a relatively few items. The purchase requisitions can amount to only $1 or $2. Although the cost of handling a purchase order may be from $5 to $10, the item will be ordered—because it is needed—but not much time will be spent on it.

Branding may become important for such products. It makes product identification and buying easier for such "nuisance" items.

Mary McCarthy

Industry demand for supplies is fairly inelastic—and sellers may see pretty inelastic demand curves, too. Since only small amounts of money are involved—and shopping around for bargains would hardly be worth the time—a purchasing agent might find several dependable sources of supply and buy from them for the bulk of such items.

A new company offering only one supply item might have trouble entering such a market. The job of buying these small items is difficult enough—and buyers usually don't have time to review the small advantages of some new product or supplier.

The purchasing agent wouldn't be as interested in price for such items—the breadth of assortment and dependability of the source are more important in buying supply items. But price is not unimportant—and a skilled purchasing agent continually shops for good value. The threat of losing a substantial amount of business from one buyer tends to keep the various suppliers' prices in line for their whole assortment.

Repair items

The original supplier of installations or accessory equipment may be the only source of supply for repairs and parts. The cost of repairs relative to the cost of disrupted production may be so small that buyers are willing to pay the price charged—whatever it is.

Demand for repair items is quite inelastic. But if the demand for such items is large and steady—say, for truck mufflers or power transmission belts—there may be many suppliers. The market then may become quite competitive—even though each buyer's demand is relatively inelastic.

SERVICES—YOU EXPENSE THEM

Services are expense items which support the operations of a firm. Engineering or management consulting services can improve the plant layout or the operation of the company. Design services can supply designs for the physical plant, products, and graphic materials. Maintenance services can handle window-cleaning, painting, or general housekeeping. Other companies can supply in-plant lunches—and piped-in music—to improve employee morale and production.

The cost of buying services outside the firm is compared with the cost of having company people do them. For special skills needed only occasionally, an outsider can be the best source. And service specialists are growing in number in our complex economy.

The demand for special services is often inelastic—if the supplier has a unique product. And the supply may be fairly inelastic, too. The suppliers may consider themselves professionals and charge accordingly. For example, engineers, architects, and medical doctors have commonly accepted fee schedules. The competition among them is not based on price—but on quality of service.[10]

INDUSTRIAL GOODS CLASSES AND BUYING BEHAVIOR ARE RELATED

The focus on kinds of goods may not seem exciting—but it is vital because the nature of goods has an effect on how buyers will accept and buy them.

This obviously has a direct bearing on the planning of the marketing mixes.

Buyers often specialize by product categories

Don't forget that an individual buyer may behave differently toward different kinds of goods. Or, in a larger company, there may be specialists buying the various goods. This can both simplify and complicate the selling process. Buying specialists may be easier to deal with—at least they are more expert and, therefore, require less educating about technical points. On the other hand, if there are many buying specialists in a company, a sales rep cannot do a good job by calling on just one.

Each buyer of each type of good should be treated as an entirely separate customer. The buyer's attitude may be entirely different when dealing with one type of good than with another. And salespeople should not expect any special consideration from one buyer just because they have sold successfully to another in the same company. The two buyers may think and act quite differently—and each may require a unique sales approach.

The organization of buyers in a large purchasing department may help illustrate these ideas. Figure 10–7 shows the layout of a centralized purchasing department for a large manufacturer with plants throughout the country. Seventeen buyers

Figure 10–7
Layout of the purchasing department of a large manufacturer

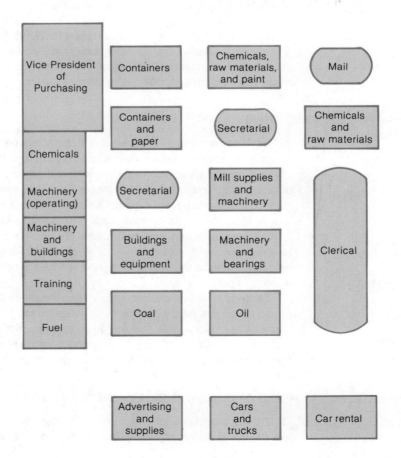

work under a vice president of purchasing. Some of these buyers (shown by rectangles in the figure) report to group supervisors (shown in offices along the left edge of the figure), who also do some buying and report directly to the vice president. As you can see, each of the buyers specializes in certain types of *industrial goods* classes that have been discussed in this chapter.

THE GROWING IMPORTANCE OF PACKAGING

Sometimes a distinction is made between packing and packaging—the former is concerned with protection and the latter with promotion. We will *not* make this distinction—because the difference is seldom clear-cut. Modern packaging involves protecting *and* promoting the product.

The amount spent is large and rising

The importance of packaging is partly shown by its cost. About $14 billion was spent on packaging *materials* alone in 1965. This total was estimated at $52 billion in 1980—and is expected to continue rising in coming years.[11] For perspective, this is roughly equal to the total amount spent on advertising. And the actual cost of packaging might be twice as high—if all costs of handling, sorting, and moving containers were included. These rising costs for packaging are due in part to a shift from an earlier emphasis on protection—to the current interest in protection *and* the promotion potential of the package.

Higher corporate status for packaging

The purchasing agent used to be in charge of packaging in many companies—when protection was the major job of the package. But now, some companies have corporate packaging staffs. And in some companies, the product manager or a specialist in packaging has taken over the job.

General Foods Corporation appointed a manager of packaging development and procurement services when it decided that packaging is an important management tool. This manager coordinates packaging activities with the various product managers. At National Biscuit Company, a vice president of packaging is chairman of the packaging committee.[12]

This new-found status for packaging occurred in part because of the growing competitiveness in many markets. This status also reflects the costliness of packaging errors—and the difficulty of correcting them. A poor package could have long-term effects—killing the product for customers who try it—and creating bad will among middlemen. In other words, packaging can have great strategic importance. Packaging is definitely an important part of the marketing mix.

THE STRATEGIC IMPORTANCE OF PACKAGING

May improve or create a "new" product

A new package can make *the* important difference in a new marketing strategy—by improving the product. A better box, wrapper, can, or bottle may even let a relatively small, unknown firm compete successfully with established competitors. Carter Products Co.—new to the men's toiletries field—introduced its first product, Rise shaving cream, in aerosol cans and was able to compete effectively against the usual tubes and cartons.

A package change often creates a "new" product—by giving customers a

Good packaging can cut cost by protecting products and making handling easier.

Mary McCarthy

more desirable quantity. Packaging frozen vegetables in 1-pound packages—instead of 10-ounce packages—served larger families better. The smaller packages held too little for them—while two packages held too much.

Multiple packs can be the basis of a new marketing strategy, too. Consumer surveys showed that some customers were buying several units at a time of products like soft drinks, beer, and frozen orange juice. This suggested a "new" market. Manufacturers tried packaging in 4-, 6-, and 8-packs—and have been very successful.

May lower total distribution costs

Better protective packaging is especially important to manufacturers and wholesalers. They often have to pay the cost of goods damaged in shipment. There are also costs for settling such claims—and getting them settled is a nuisance. Goods damaged in shipment also may delay production or cause lost sales.

Retailers need good packaging too. Packaging which provides better protection can reduce store costs by cutting breakage, preventing discoloration, and stopping theft. Packages that are easier to handle can cut costs by speeding price marking, improving handling and display, and saving space.

Promotion-oriented packaging may be "better" than advertising

Packaged goods are regularly seen in retail stores. They may actually be seen by many more potential customers than the company's advertising. A good package sometimes gives a firm more promotion effect than it could possibly afford with advertising. An attractive package may speed turnover so much that total costs will decline as a percentage of sales.

Or . . . may raise total costs

In other cases, total distribution costs may rise because of packaging. But customers may be satisfied because the packaging improves the product—perhaps by offering much greater convenience or reducing waste.

Packaging costs as a percentage of a manufacturer's selling price vary widely—

ranging from 1 to 70 percent. Let's look at sugar as an example. In 100-pound bags, the cost of packaging sugar is only 1 percent of the selling price. In 2- and 5-pound cartons, it is 25–30 percent. And for individual serving packages, it is 50 percent. Most customers don't want to haul a 100-pound bag home—and are quite willing to pay for more convenient packages. Restaurants use one-serving envelopes of sugar—finding that they reduce the cost of filling and washing sugar bowls, and that customers prefer the more sanitary little packages. In both cases, packaging adds value to the product. Actually, it creates new products and new marketing strategies.

WHAT MAKES A GOOD PACKAGE DESIGN?

The right packaging is just enough packaging

Experience shows that a specific package must be designed for each product. The package must safely transport its contents, serve in a specific climate (especially if the product is to be exported), and last for a specific time. To provide such packaging, the manufacturer must know the product, the target customers, and how the product will be delivered to them. Underpackaging costs money—for damage claims or poor sales. But overpackaging also costs money—because dollars are spent for no benefit. Glassware, for example, needs to be protected from even relatively light blows that might smash it. Heavy-duty machinery doesn't need protection from blows—but may need protection from moisture.

Packaging suppliers can offer suggestions

Packaging suppliers know the importance of packaging—and their sales people are usually highly trained to help customers. Typically, they will insist on knowing about the needs of the potential customers and the middlemen who are likely to be handling the packages. With this kind of information, they suggest how to blend the package into the whole marketing strategy.

WHAT IS SOCIALLY RESPONSIBLE PACKAGING?

Some consumers say that some package designs are misleading—perhaps on purpose. Others feel that the great variety of package designs makes it hard for consumers to compare values. And some are concerned about whether they are environmentally safe—and whether they are biodegradable, or recyclable.

Federal law tries to help

Consumer criticism finally led to the passage of the *Federal Fair Packaging and Labeling Act* (of 1966)—which requires that consumer goods be clearly labeled in understandable terms—to give the customer more information. The law also calls upon government agencies and industry to try to reduce the number of package sizes. The Food and Drug Administration is made responsible for foods, nonprescription drugs, and cosmetics. The Federal Trade Commission is responsible for nonfood items. And the Commerce Department is expected to seek voluntary agreements by industry groups with respect to the large number and size of packages—and proper labeling.

The Commerce Department wants consumer goods manufacturers to come up with tags answering such basic questions as: How long a particular vacuum bottle will keep its contents hot; how much usable storage space a refrigerator contains; and how effectively a vacuum cleaner picks up dirt. Industry participation is still voluntary—but some firms are moving to supply this information.[13]

And some progress has been made in reducing the number of package sizes. Industry representatives reduced the number of toothpaste sizes from 57 to 5— and the number of paper-towel packages from 33 to 8. But major problem areas still exist with products such as hair sprays, deodorants, mouthwashes, and after-shave lotions. Producers of these products have not shown much interest. They feel consumers are more concerned with how products feel, smell, or look— than with price comparisons.

Food products must now have labels showing nutrients—as well as weight or volume. But there is some question whether many consumers understand this information—or what to do with it—or even whether this is the information they are seeking. At the same time, it may be difficult or impossible to provide the kind of information they do want—for example, regarding taste, color, and texture.[14]

Unit-pricing—a possible help

Weight and volume are not completely irrelevant, however. There is continuing interest in unit-pricing—which involves placing the price per ounce (or some other standard measure) on or near the product. This makes comparison shopping easier—using weight and volume. Some large supermarket chains have voluntarily adopted unit-pricing—many consumers do appreciate this service.[15]

Universal product codes may lead to less price information

To "automate" the handling of foods and drugs, government and industry representatives have developed a universal product code—which identifies each product with marks that can be "read" by electronic scanners and related to prices by computers. Figure 10–8 shows a universal product code mark.

Figure 10–8
An illustration of a universal product code for a ballpoint pen

Large supermarket chains have been eager to use these codes because this could lower operating expenses, and perhaps prices. Using the codes speeds the checkout process—and gets rid of the need for marking the price on every item in the store. Prices are shown near the product—but not on each individual item.

Some consumers don't like the codes, however, because they can't compare prices later—either in the store or at home. These complaints have made the code idea less attractive. But probably more electronic checkout systems will be installed—whether the prices are marked on each item or not—because it does speed the checkout process, improves inventory control, and lowers costs.

BRANDING HAS STRATEGIC IMPORTANCE, TOO

There are so many brands—and we're so used to seeing them—that we take them for granted. In the grocery products area alone, there are about 38,000 brands. Many of these brands are of great importance to their owners—because they help identify a tangible part of the company's marketing mix—and help consumers recognize the firm's products and advertising. This is an important area which is ignored by many business people. So we will treat it in some depth.

What is branding, brand name, and trademark?

Branding means the use of a name, term, symbol, or design—or a combination of these—to identify a product. It includes the use of brand names, trademarks, and practically all other means of product identification.

Brand name has a narrower meaning. A brand name is a word, letter, or a group of words or letters.

Trademark is a legal term. A trademark includes only those words, symbols, or marks that the law says are trademarks.

The word Buick can be used to explain these differences. The Buick car is *branded* under the *brand name* "Buick" (whether it is spoken or printed in any manner). When "Buick" is printed in a certain kind of script, however, it becomes a *trademark*. A trademark need not be attached to the product. It need not even be a word. A symbol can be used.

These differences may seem technical. But they are very important to business firms that spend much money to protect their brands.

BRANDING—WHY IT DEVELOPED

Brands meet needs

Branding started during the Middle Ages—when craft guilds (similar to labor unions) and merchant guilds formed to control the quantity and quality of production. Each producer had to mark his goods, so output could be cut back when necessary. This also meant that poor quality—which might reflect unfavorably on other guild products and discourage future trade—could be traced back to the guilty producer. Early trademarks were also a protection to the buyer—who could now know the source of the product.

Not restriction but identification

More recently, brands have been used mainly for identification.

The earliest and most aggressive brand promoters in America were the patent medicine companies. They were joined by the food manufacturers—who grew in size after the Civil War. Some of the brands started in the 1860s and 1870s (and still going strong) are Dr. Lyon's Tooth Powder, Borden's Condensed Milk, Quaker Oats, Pillsbury's Best Flour, and Ivory Soap.[16]

Customers are willing to buy by brand—without inspection—when they are sure of quality. In many countries, however, the consumer doesn't feel so sure. In India, for example, inspecting the product is common—because there is little faith in packaged goods and brands. There is good reason for this. Foods are often mixed with sawdust, husks, and colored earth—which may be 10–50 percent of the weight of packaged or prepared foods. And an Indian car battery manufacturer has had great success with its brand by correctly advertising "the battery you don't have to test."

Soviets adopted brands

The importance of brands in a nation's economy can be seen clearly in the Soviet experience. The USSR evolved toward an enthusiastic use of branding—after economic disaster forced it on them.

Several Russian factories were manufacturing supposedly identical 17-inch TV sets—but actually one of the plants was shipping "lemons." When customers became aware of this, many stopped buying any 17-inch set—because they could not identify the bad ones. This obviously caused inventory problems for the central planners. It also caused public discontent with the Soviet system. Shortly thereafter, factory numbers on products were required—to help the planners identify the production source. Subsequently, consumers discovered the factory numbers—and plants that were producing poorer-quality products began to have difficulties meeting their economic plans. Soviet consumers rather than planners forced the plants to pay more attention to quality. Before long, there were more than 25 state-sponsored advertising agencies—to tell people about the "quality" of various factories. Now, advertising courses are even offered in Russian universities.[17]

The important thing to note here is that the "brands" were created by the customers—rather than the planners. The factory identification numbers had been added to help the planners—but the consumers quickly adapted them to their own use.

WHY BRANDING IS ADVANTAGEOUS TO CUSTOMERS

Makes shopping feasible and more efficient

Well-recognized brands make shopping possible in a modern economy. Think of the problem of buying groceries, for example, if you had to consider seriously the advantages and disadvantages of each of 10,000 items every time you went to a supermarket.

Assures regular satisfaction

Many customers are willing to buy new things—but having gambled and won, they like to buy a "sure thing" the next time. Customers may even be willing to pay a premium for brands that they like. One study showed that customers were willing to pay about 13 percent more for well-known food brands.[18]

Dependable guides to quality

There is much evidence that if consumers used well-known brands rather than high prices as an indication of good quality, they might be further ahead. One study of grocery products found that the known brands usually had fairly consistent quality—but there was little assurance that a high price meant high quality.[19]

Branding makes shopping easier.

Mary McCarthy

Branded drug products may also be better than unbranded ones which meet the same minimum specifications. This is an important political and social matter—because some branded drug products are prescribed by doctors and are priced higher than unbranded ones in the same generic class. Business critics have been very vocal here. Industry representatives argue that there are differences. And some tests suggest that this is true. In other cases, there is not even agreement about which test should be used—or if it is possible to measure effectiveness.[20]

May satisfy status need

Some lower-class customers may buy well-recognized manufacturers' brands—not for status—but for assurance of quality within their narrowly perceived range of choices.[21] Other customers, however, seem to be less concerned with the physical characteristics of the product and more concerned with the symbolic value. They seem to get psychic satisfaction from the use of well-known brands—perhaps because they feel some of the status or prestige of the product may rub off on them.

WHY BRANDING IS ADVANTAGEOUS TO BRANDERS

Encourages repeat buying and lowers costs

Brands obviously would not be used so aggressively by companies if target customers did not respond to them. Many advantages of brand promotion to the branders are related to the advantages to customers. A good brand speeds up shopping for the customer—and so reduces the marketer's selling time and effort. When a customer repeats purchases by brand, promotion costs are reduced and sales volume is increased.

May develop loyal customers

Another important advantage of successful branding is that the brander may be able to carve out a market of loyal customers. Whether the brander is a manufacturer, wholesaler, or retailer, this brand loyalty protects against competition.

May build corporate image

Good brands can improve the company's image—speeding acceptance of new products marketed under the same name. The idea of improving the company's image—as well as its brands—has been growing. When customers think a company is big and successful, they often have a better impression of it and its products. The U.S. Steel Corporation, with its many large subsidiaries, found that industrial customers who were aware of the relationship of U.S. Steel to its subsidiaries viewed the subsidiaries more favorably. This was important in their choice of supplier—especially when competing products were basically similar. For this reason, U.S. Steel redesigned its trademark and began to identify all the subsidiaries with it.

Growing acceptance of the idea that a good customer image is important has led some companies to change their corporate name—so that the name is more descriptive of the firm's activities. U.S. Rubber, with many foreign subsidiaries, adopted the Uniroyal name and trademark—because it felt that the new name was more accurate. And the Bankamericard companies changed their name to VISA to have a common name.

CONDITIONS FAVORABLE TO BRANDING

Most marketing managers accept branding—and are concerned with seeing that their brand succeeds.

The following conditions would be favorable to successful branding:

1. The demand for the general product class should be large.
2. The demand should be strong enough so that the market price can be high enough to make the effort profitable.
3. There should be economies of scale. If the branding is really successful, the cost of production should drop and profits should increase.
4. The product quality should be the best for the price—that is, the "value" for the price. And the quality should be easily maintained.
5. The product should be easy to identify by brand or trademark.
6. Dependable and widespread availability should be possible. When customers start using a brand, they want to be able to continue finding it in their stores.
7. Favorable shelf locations or display space in stores will help. This is something retailers can control when they brand their own products. Manufacturers must use aggressive sales forces to get favorable positioning.

ACHIEVING BRAND FAMILIARITY IS NOT EASY

Brand acceptance must be earned with a good product and regular promotion. **Brand familiarity** means how well customers recognize and accept a company's brand. There are many brands which—for practical purposes—have no value because they have no meaning to customers. And there are others which have actually been rejected by potential customers.

There are five levels of brand familiarity

Five levels of brand familiarity are useful for strategic planning: (1) rejection, (2) nonrecognition, (3) recognition, (4) preference, and (5) insistence.

Some brands have been tried and found wanting. **Rejection** means the potential customers won't buy a brand—unless its current image is changed. Rejection may suggest a change in the product—or perhaps only a shift to target customers who have a better image of the brand. Overcoming negative images is difficult—and can be very expensive.

Some products are seen as basically the same. **Nonrecognition** means a brand is not recognized by final consumers at all—even though middlemen may use the brand name for identification and inventory control. Examples here are: school supplies, novelties, inexpensive dinnerware, and similar goods found in discount stores.

Brand recognition means that customers have heard of and remember the brand. This can be a big advantage if there are many "nothing" brands on the market.

Most branders would like to win **brand preference**—which means target customers will generally choose the brand over other brands—perhaps because of habit or past experience. Here the firm has achieved a favorable position in a monopolistic competition situation.

Brand insistence means customers insist upon a firm's branded product and

When a product has reached the brand preference or insistence stage, a customer buys it with little thought.

Mary McCarthy

would be willing to search for it. This is the goal of many target marketers. Here, the firm may enjoy a very inelastic demand curve.

Knowing how well you're known may take research

While the level of brand familiarity will affect the development of a marketing mix, marketing research may be needed to find out exactly how well the firm is known—and in which target markets. Sometimes, managers feel their products have a higher level of brand familiarity than they really do—and they develop their marketing mixes accordingly. This mistake puts too much stress on the other Ps. Studies show that some brands don't reach even the brand recognition level. One study, for example, showed that two out of every five homemakers couldn't name the brand of furniture they owned.[22]

CHOOSING A BRAND NAME

Although research can help, brand name selection is still an art—because it is difficult to define what is a good brand name. Some successful brand names seem to break all the rules. Many of these names, however, got started when there was less competition.

A good brand name can make a difference—helping to tell something important about the company or its product. Just using the company's name or a family member's name is no longer enough. See Figure 10–9 for the characteristics of a good brand name.

PROTECTING BRAND NAMES AND TRADEMARKS

Common law assures the rights of the true originators and users of trademarks and brand names—stating that ownership of brand names and trademarks is established by continued usage without abandonment. Clearly, by now Morton Salt, Coca-Cola, and Saran-Wrap are unmistakably identified with particular products.

The exact procedure for protecting trademarks and what could be protected were not clear, however, until the passage of the federal *Lanham Act* in 1946.

Figure 10–9
Characteristics of a good brand name

Short and simple.

Easy to spell and read.

Easy to recognize and remember.

Pleasing when read or heard—and easy to pronounce.

Pronounceable in only one way.

Pronounceable in all languages (for goods to be exported).

Always timely (does not get out of date).

Adaptable to packaging or labeling needs.

Legally available for use (not in use by another firm).

Not offensive, obscene, or negative.

Suggestive of product benefits.

Adaptable to any advertising medium (especially billboards and television).

This act specifies what types of marks (including brand names) can be protected by law—and provides for registration records. It applies to goods shipped in interstate or foreign commerce.

You must protect your own brands and trademarks

The Lanham Act does not force registration. Further, the government does not police the use of brand names and trademarks. Each brander must protect his own. This means that the brand must continually be in use—and the company should maintain evidence to this effect. Further, it must monitor how the brand is being used—that it is being used only to identify its own product—not a broad generic class. Further, the brander must watch that others are not using his brand—and bring suit against any infringers. You can see that much legal work is involved in protecting one's brand and trademark.

A trademark can be a real asset to a company. So each firm should try to see that it doesn't become a common descriptive term for its kind of product. When this happens, the brand name or trademark becomes public property— the owner loses all rights to it. This happened with the names cellophane, aspirin, shredded wheat, and kerosene. There was concern that "Teflon" and "Scotch Tape" might become public property—and Miller Brewing Co. tried unsuccessfully to protect its "Lite" beer by suing brewers that wanted to use the word "light."[23]

Registering for foreign trade

A good reason for registering under the Lanham Act is to protect a trademark to be used in foreign markets. Before a trademark can be protected in a foreign country, some nations require that it be registered in its home country.

WHAT KIND OF BRAND TO USE?

Keep it in the family

Branders who manufacture or handle more than one item must decide whether they are going to use a family brand—the same brand name for several products—or individual brands for each product.

The use of the same brand for many products makes sense if all are similar in type and quality. The goodwill attached to one or two products may help the others—which cuts promotion costs. It also tends to build loyalty to the family brand—and makes it easier to introduce new products.

Examples of family brands are the Heinz "57" food products, and three A&P brands (Ann Page, Sultana, and Iona) and Sears' "Craftsman" tools and "Kenmore" appliances.

Individual brands for outside and inside competition

Individual brands —separate brand names for each product—are used by a manufacturer when its products are of varying quality or type. If the products are really different—such as meat products and glue—individual brands are better. Or an individual brand may be better if the quality and higher price of one of the company's well-known brands is to be protected while another brand (perhaps identifying a lower-priced line) is used as a **fighting brand** —an individual brand which is used to meet competition. Individual brands are preferred, too, if there is any risk of failure of one product—thereby damaging the reputation of others in the product line.

Sometimes firms use individual brands to encourage competition within the organization. Each brand is the responsibility of a different group. Management feels that internal competition keeps everyone alert. The theory is that—if anyone is going to take business away from them—it ought to be their own brand. This kind of competition is found among General Motors' brands. Chevrolet, Pontiac, Oldsmobile, Buick, and even Cadillac compete with each other in some markets.

Generic brands at lower prices

Products which are seen by consumers as "commodities" may be difficult to brand meaningfully. Recently, some manufacturers and middlemen have faced up to this problem and come out with **generic products** —products which have no brand other than the identification of their contents. For example, some supermarkets offer the following generic products: corn flakes, macaroni, beans, noodles, and dog food. Typically, these are offered in plain packages at lower prices. Some have been well accepted by consumers—because they appear to be just as good as the "commodities" which are offered at higher prices in fancier packages.

Producers and advertisers of "me too" products should worry about this development—if it continues to spread.[24]

Generic brands offer lower prices.

Mary McCarthy

WHO SHOULD DO THE BRANDING?

Manufacturer brands versus dealer brands

Manufacturer brands are brands which are created by manufacturers. These are sometimes called "national brands"—because manufacturers often promote these brands all across the country or in large regions. Such brands include Kellogg's, Stokely, Whirlpool, International Harvester, and IBM.

Dealer brands are brands created by middlemen. These are sometimes called "private brands." Examples of dealer brands include the brands of Kroger, A&P, Sears Roebuck, and Montgomery Ward. Some of these are advertised and distributed more widely than many "national brands."

So far we have been focusing on the value of branding in general, but branding has some special advantages and disadvantages for middlemen. This affects whether they should use manufacturers' brands or develop their own dealer brands. These advantages and disadvantages are discussed below.

Advantages of manufacturers' brands— more prestige, less inventory

The major advantage of selling a popular manufacturer's brand is that the product already is presold to some target customers. It may bring in new customers. It can encourage higher turnover with reduced selling cost—and some of the prestige of the manufacturer's brand may rub off on the dealers. And in case the manufacturer doesn't maintain his quality, *he* receives the blame, not the dealer. The customer can be shifted to another manufacturer's brand or a dealer brand. The dealer does not lose *his* customer.

Since manufacturers' brands usually are readily available at wholesalers' or manufacturers' warehouses, the dealer can carry less inventory. Another advantage for some retailers is that the retailer can advertise special prices on items which are carried in other stores—calling attention to his store as a source of bargains.

Disadvantages of manufacturers' brands— lost products, lost customers

The major disadvantage of manufacturers' brands is that manufacturers normally offer a lower gross margin than the dealer might be able to earn with its own brands. This, however, may be offset by higher turnover.

Another disadvantage is that the manufacturer maintains control of his brand—and may withdraw it from the dealer at any time. Wholesalers are especially vulnerable. If customers become loyal to a manufacturer's brand and the wholesaler does not or cannot carry the product, then the customers may go elsewhere. Here, loyalty may be tied to the brand—rather than to the dealer.

Advantages of dealer brands—loyal sales reps, the best shelves

The advantages of dealer brands are—roughly—the converse of the disadvantages of manufacturers' brands. The dealer may be able to buy products at lower prices—and so be able to obtain higher gross margins, even with lower retail prices. He can have greater price flexibility with his own brands—because (1) price comparisons are not as easy as with manufacturer's brands and (2) there is no manufacturer to dictate pricing policy.

Another advantage of dealer brands is that middlemen can easily change from one supplier to another—if any one firm can't offer the quality and price needed. By using their own brands, dealers may be able to protect themselves from the arbitrary action of manufacturers.

Dealer brands protect wholesalers from the defection of their sales reps—and their customer following—to other wholesaling firms. Why? Dealer brands give the wholesaler—rather than the sales force—a claim to customer loyalty.

Since the dealer's own brand ties customers to him, he may be able to estimate demand and buy more effectively. His salespeople may also control the point of sale—and be able to give their products special shelf position or displays.

Disadvantages of dealer brands—taking the blame, buying big quantities

Dealer branders must stimulate their own demand. This may be costly, especially if turnover is typically slow in the lines being considered. Also, they must take the blame for inferior quality. They may have difficulty getting consistently good quality at low prices—especially during times of short supply. And dealers must buy in fairly large quantities from suppliers—assuming the risk and cost of carrying inventory.

Dealer brands have a chance if . . .

Branding by dealers begins to move them into the traditional role of a manufacturer. They must assume all of the marketing responsibilities of a manufacturer—and plan their marketing strategies accordingly. Therefore, the decision to go into dealer branding should not be made lightly. The chances of a dealer brand being successful are helped if a number of conditions exist:

1. If there are several manufacturers' brands in the market, none should be strongly established.
2. A dependable quality and quantity of ingredients or raw materials for the dealer brand should be available at a reasonable price—to ensure a good margin in case the brand is accepted.
3. It helps if manufacturers' brands are overpriced—so the dealer brand can be priced under them, yet with a larger-than-normal gross margin—to cover higher promotion costs.
4. Although the dealer's brand must be promoted, the promotion should not be so expensive as to use up the extra gross margin.
5. There should be an adequate, well-established market—dealers may find it expensive to pioneer the introduction of new products.
6. Product quality should be easily and economically determined by inspection or use—customers will be more willing to experiment if a dealer's brand does not present too much of a risk.
7. If the dealer brand is lower priced, depressed business conditions may help its sale—customers are more price conscious then.

Dealer brands in the food and drug lines usually are offered at slightly lower prices than manufacturers' brands. Dealer brands, however, are not always priced lower. Sometimes dealers—having analyzed their target market—offer a prestige-laden, higher-quality product and price it even higher than major manufacturers' brands.

THE BATTLE OF THE BRANDS—WHO'S WINNING?

The battle of the brands is the competition between dealer brands and manu-

*Manufacturers brands are "luxuries"
for some younger households.*

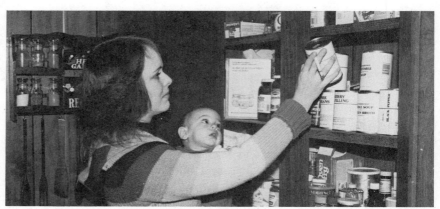

Mary McCarthy

facturer brands. The "battle" is just a question of whose brands are to be more popular—and who is to be in control.

Some research suggests (for food products at least) that manufacturers' brands may be losing the fight. In 1951, manufacturers' brands were preferred by 2 or 3 to 1. Even higher prices were accepted. This strong preference has continued to go down. By 1970, almost half of the consumers had shifted to dealer brands. Younger and more educated households may be leading here.[25]

One of the reasons for this shift is that some of the manufacturers' brands are thought of as luxuries—while the dealer-branded chain store products are seen as necessities.[26] Also, the chains' dealer-branded products are more likely to be in stock—because the chains control the channel of distribution.

Another reason for the growth of dealer branding is that established stores needed a competitive weapon against retail price cutters—who promoted "discounts" on well-known manufacturer brands. Department stores, supermarkets, service stations, clothing stores, appliance dealers, and drugstores are all doing more dealer branding.

Manufacturers may become only manufacturers

The battle of the brands is far from over—but the former dominance of manufacturers' brands may have ended. Some retailers are becoming so large that dealer brands frequently sell in large volume and are nationally advertised. And some wholesalers have extremely strong brands—and ties to regional chains with hundreds of stores.

In the future, retailer-controlled brands may seek broader distribution amcng other retailers and perhaps wholesalers, too. It seems logical that as retailers begin to advertise nationally—but have only a limited number of outlets—they may find it profitable to permit others to carry their brands. This might be a serious challenge to manufacturers' brands.

If this trend continues, manufacturers could become just that—only the manufacturing arms of middlemen. Retailers and wholesalers might come to dominate marketing. Certainly, the latter are closer to final consumers—and can have greater control of the final sale.[27]

WARRANTIES ARE IMPORTANT TOO

Warranty should mean something

Common law says that producers must stand behind their products. And now federal law (Magnuson-Moss Act of 1975) says that producers must provide a clearly written warranty if they choose to offer any warranty. A **warranty** explains what the seller guarantees about its product. It is important to recognize that the warranty does not have to be strong. But Federal Trade Commission (FTC) guidelines try to make sure that warranties are not "deceptive" or "unfair." Basically, the FTC wants to be sure the warranty is clear and definite. Some firms used to say their products were "fully warranted" or "absolutely guaranteed." The time period was not stated. And the meaning of the guarantee was not spelled out.

Now, the company has to make clear whether it's offering a "full" or "limited" warranty—and the law spells out what a "full warranty" must include. Also, the warranty must be available for inspection before the purchase. Some firms just guarantee their products against "defects of material or workmanship" for 30 to 90 days. Others are trying to design more quality into their products—they offer longer and stronger warranties. Some companies—for example, Sears Roebuck—have gone even further by providing a one-year replacement—not just repair—guarantee on some small appliances.

Customers might like a strong warranty, but it can be very expensive. It might even be economically impossible for small producers. Some customers abuse products—and demand a lot of service on warranties. Backing up warranties can be a problem too. Although manufacturers may be responsible, they may have to depend upon reluctant or poorly skilled middlemen to do the job—or set up their own service companies. This can make it hard for a small firm to compete with larger firms that have many service centers. Foreign auto producers and small U.S. auto producers, for example, can't match the number of Chevrolet or Ford service locations.

Deciding on the warranty is clearly a strategic matter. Specific decisions should be made about what the warranty will cover—and then it should be communicated clearly to the target customers. In some cases, the warranty may make the difference between success and failure for a whole strategy.

CONCLUSION

In this chapter, we looked at Product very broadly. A Product may not be a physical good at all. It may be a service. Or it may be some combination—like a meal at a restaurant.

A firm's Product is what satisfies the needs of its target market. This *may* be a physical good—but also could include a package, brand, installation, repair service, and so on—whatever is needed to satisfy target customers.

Consumer goods and industrial goods classes were introduced to simplify your study of marketing—and help in planning marketing mixes. The consumer goods classes are based on consumers' buying behavior. Industrial goods classes are based on how buyers see the products—and how they are used.

Knowing these goods classes—and learning how marketers handle specific products within these classes—will speed the development of your "marketing sense."

The fact that different people may view the same product as different goods helps explain why firms may use very different marketing mixes—quite successfully.

Packaging and branding can create new and more satisfying products. Variations in packaging can make a product salable in various target markets. A specific package must be developed for each strategy. Both under-packaging and over-packaging can be expensive.

To customers, the main value of brands is as a guarantee of quality. This leads to repeat purchasing. For marketers, such "routine" buying means lower promotion costs and higher sales.

Should brands be stressed? The decision depends on whether the costs of brand promotion and honoring the brand guarantee can be more than covered by a higher price or more rapid turnover—or both. The cost of branding may reduce other costs—by reducing pressure on the other three Ps.

In recent years, the strength of manufacturers' brands has declined and dealer brands have become more important. The dealer-labeled products may win in the battle of the brands—because dealers are closer to customers and can emphasize their own brands.

Branding gives marketing managers choice. They can add brands and use individual or family brands. In the end, however, customers express their approval or disapproval of the whole product (including the brand). The degree of brand familiarity is a measure of management's ability to carve out a separate market—and affects Place, Price, and Promotion decisions.

Warranties are also important strategic matters. A warranty need not be strong—it just has to be clearly stated. But some customers find strong warranties attractive.

So, it should be clear that Product is concerned with much more than a physical good or service. The marketing manager must also be concerned about packaging, branding, and warranties—if he is to help his firm succeed in our increasingly competitive marketplaces.

QUESTIONS AND PROBLEMS

1. Define, in your own words, what a Product is.

2. Explain how the addition of guarantees, service, and credit can improve a "product." Cite a specific case where this has been done and explain how customers viewed this new "product."

3. What "products" are being offered by an exclusive men's shop? By a nightclub? By a soda fountain? By a supermarket?

4. What kinds of consumer goods are the following: (a) fountain pens, (b) men's shirts, (c) cosmetics? Explain

your reasoning and draw a picture of the market in each case to help illustrate your thinking.

5. Some goods seem to be treated perpetually as unsought goods by their producers. Give an example and explain why.

6. How would the marketing mix for a staple convenience good differ from the one for a homogeneous shopping good? How would the mix for a specialty good differ from the mix for a heterogeneous shopping good? Use examples.

7. Which of the Ps would receive the greatest emphasis in the marketing mix for a new unsought good? Explain why, using an example.

8. In what types of stores would you expect to find: *(a)* convenience goods, *(b)* shopping goods, *(c)* specialty goods, and *(d)* unsought goods?

9. Cite two examples of industrial goods which require a substantial amount of service in order to make them useful "products."

10. Would you expect to find any wholesalers selling the various types of industrial goods? Are retail stores required (or something like retail stores)?

11. What kinds of industrial goods are the following?
    a. Nails and screws.
    b. Paint.
    c. Dust-collecting and ventilating systems.
    d. An electric lift truck.
    Explain your reasoning.

12. What impact does the fact that demand for industrial goods is derived and fairly inelastic have upon the development of industrial goods marketing mixes? Use examples.

13. How do farm product raw materials differ from other raw materials or other industrial goods? Do the differences have any impact on their marketing mixes? If so, what, specifically?

14. For the kinds of industrial goods described in this chapter, complete the table at the top of the next column (use one or a few *well-chosen* words).

15. Explain the increasing interest in packaging, not only for consumer goods but also for industrial goods. Is this likely to continue?

16. Suggest an example where packaging costs probably: *(a)* lower total distribution costs, and *(b)* raise total distribution costs.

17. Is there any difference between a brand name and a trademark? If so, why is this difference important?

18. Is a well-known brand valuable only to the owner of the brand?

19. Would it be profitable for a firm to expend large sums of money to establish a brand for any type product in

Goods	1	2	3
Installations			
Buildings and land rights			
Major equipment			
Standard			
Custom made			
Accessory equipment			
Raw materials			
Farm products			
Natural products			
Components			
Parts			
Materials			
Supplies			
Operating supplies			
Maintenance and small operating supplies			
Services			

1—Kind of distribution facility(ies) needed and functions they will provide.
2—Caliber of salespeople required.
3—Kind of advertising required.

any competitive situation? Why, or why not? If the answer is no, suggest examples.

20. Evaluate the suitability of the following brand names: *(a)* Star (sausage), *(b)* Pleasing (books), *(c)* Rugged (shoes), *(d)* Shiny (shoe polish), *(e)* Lord Jim (ties).

21. Explain family brands. Sears Roebuck and A&P use family brands but they have several different family brands. If the idea is a good one, why don't they have just one brand?

22. What is the "battle of the brands"? Who do you think will win and why?

23. What does the degree of brand familiarity imply about previous promotion efforts and the future promotional task? Also, how does the degree of brand familiarity affect the Place and Price variables?

24. If you have been operating a small supermarket with emphasis on manufacturers' brands and have barely been breaking even, how should you evaluate the proposal of a large wholesaler who offers a full line of dealer-branded groceries at substantially lower prices? Specify any assumptions necessary to obtain a definite answer.

SUGGESTED CASES

9 Annie's Floral
10 Byron Pharmaceutical Company

12 Ski Haus Sports Shop

NOTES

1. Stanley C. Hollander, "Is There a Generic Demand for Services?" *MSU Business Topics,* Spring 1979, pp. 41–46; John M. Rathmell, "What Is Meant by Services?" *Journal of Marketing,* October 1966, pp. 32–36; T. Levitt, "The Industrialization of Service," *Harvard Business Review,* September–October 1976, pp. 63–74; R. W. Obenberger and S. W. Brown, "A Marketing Alternative: Consumer Leasing and Renting," *Business Horizons,* October 1976, pp. 82–86; Richard B. Chase, "Where Does the Customer Fit in a Service Operation?" *Harvard Business Review,* November–December 1978, pp. 137–42; Dan R. E. Thomas, "Strategy is Different in Service Industries," *Harvard Business Review,* July–August 1978, pp. 158–65; Paul F. Anderson and William Lazer, "Industrial Lease Marketing," *Journal of Marketing,* January 1978, pp. 71–79; Robert E. Sabath, "How Much Service Do Customers Really Want?" *Business Horizons,* April 1978, pp. 26–32; "Sony's U.S. Operation Goes in for Repairs," *Business Week,* March 13, 1978, pp. 31–32; and Bernard Wysocki, Jr., "Branching Out: Major Retailers Offer Varied Services to Lure Customers, Lift Profits," *The Wall Street Journal,* June 12, 1978, pp. 1, 21.

2. Robert C. Blattberg, Peter Peacock, and S. K. Sen, "Purchasing Strategies across Product Categories," *Consumer Research,* December 1976, pp. 143–54; J. B. Mason and M. L. Mayer "Empirical Observations of Consumer Behavior as Related to Goods Classification and Retail Strategy," *Journal of Retailing,* Fall 1972, pp. 17–31; Arno K. Kleinenhagen, "Shopping, Specialty, or Convenience Goods?" *Journal of Retailing,* Winter 1966–67, pp. 32–39 ff; Louis P. Bucklin, "Testing Propensities to Shop," *Journal of Marketing,* January 1966, pp. 22–27; William P. Dommermuth, "The Shopping Matrix and Marketing Strategy," *Journal of Marketing Research,* May 1965, pp. 128–32; Richard H. Holton, "The Distinction Between Convenience Goods, Shopping Goods, and Specialty Goods," *Journal of Marketing,* July 1958, pp. 53–56; Perry Bliss, "Supply Considerations and Shopper Convenience," *Journal of Marketing,* July 1966, pp. 43–45; S. Kaish, "Cognitive Dissonance and the Classification of Consumer Goods," and W. P. Dommermuth and E. W. Cundiff, "Shopping Goods, Shopping Centers, and Selling Strategies," *Journal of Marketing,* October 1967, pp. 28–36; Edward M. Tauber, "Why Do People Shop?" *Journal of Marketing,* October 1972, pp. 46–49; and Fred D. Reynolds and William R. Darden, "Intermarket Patronage: A Psychographic Study of Consumer Outshoppers," *Journal of Marketing,* October 1972, pp. 50–54.

3. David T. Kollat and Ronald P. Willett, "Customer Impulse Purchasing Behavior," *Journal of Marketing Research,* February 1967, pp. 21–31. See also David T. Kollat and Ronald P. Willett, "Is Impulse Purchasing Really a Useful Concept for Marketing Decisions?" *Journal of Marketing,* January 1969, pp. 79–83.

4. M. Alexis, L. Simon, and K. Smith, "Some Determinants of Food Buying Behavior," in *Empirical Foundations of Marketing: Research Findings in the Behavioral and Applied Sciences,* ed. M. Alexis, R. Hancock, and R. J. Holloway (Skokie, Ill.: Rand McNally & Co., 1969).

5. L. P. Feldman, "Prediction of the Spatial Pattern of Shopping Behavior," *Journal of Retailing,* Spring 1967, pp. 25–30 f.

6. "If You Don't Give the Lady What She Wants, She'll Go Elsewhere," *Marketing News,* January 1, 1968, p. 11.

7. Many of the ideas presented in this section are based on R. S. Alexander, "Goods for the Market: Industrial Goods," in *Marketing by Manufacturers,* ed. C. F. Phillips (Homewood, Ill.: Richard D. Irwin, Inc., 1950), pp. 34–60.

8. "Switching the Charge on Batteries," *Business Week,* March 13, 1965, pp. 132–34.

9. "Will Tiny Cells Power Big Sales," *Business Week,* January 14, 1967, pp. 60–64.

10. Warren J. Wittreich, "How to Buy/Sell Professional Services," *Harvard Business Review,* March–April 1966, pp. 127–38.

11. "Containers and Packaging" (chap. 7), *U.S. Industrial Outlook 1980,* p. 75; "Bullish '77: Packagers to Fight Price Hikes," *Modern Packaging,* January 1977, pp. 22–28.

12. "The New Power of Packaging: Management Takes Control," *Printers' Ink,* November 21, 1958, pp. 21–27.

13. *Money,* September 1976, p. 108.

14. W. A. French and L. O. Schroeder, "Package Information Legislation: Trends and Viewpoints," *MSU Business Topics,* Summer 1972, pp. 39–42. See also J. A. Miller, D. G. Topel, and R. E. Rust, "USDA Beef Grading: A Failure in Consumer Information?" *Journal of Marketing,* January 1976, pp. 25–31.

15. J. E. Russo, "The Value of Unit Price Information," *Journal of Marketing Research,* May 1977, pp. 193–201; and K. B. Monroe and P. J. LaPlaca, "What Are the Benefits of Unit Pricing?" *Journal of Marketing,* July 1972, pp. 16–22.

16. Frank Presbrey, *The History and Development of Advertising* (New York: Doubleday & Co., Inc., 1929).

17. T. Levitt, "Branding on Trial," *Harvard Business Review,* March–April 1966, pp. 28–32.

18. J. O. Peckham, *Planning Your Marketing Operations for 1959 . . . and the Years Ahead* (Chicago: A. C. Nielsen Co., 1958), p. 15.

19. Robert H. Cole. "The Battle of Brands in Canned Goods," in *Frontiers in Marketing Thought,* ed. S. H. Rewoldt (Bloomington: Bureau of Business Research, Indiana University, 1955), pp. 153–59.

20. "Just How Good?" *Time,* July 7, 1967, pp. 66–67; and "FDA Has Doubts on Generic Names," *Business Week,* January 13, 1968, p. 36.

21. James A. Carman, *The Application of Social Class in Market Segmentation* (Berkeley: Institute of Business and Economic Research, University of California, 1965), p. 28.

22. *Business Week,* February 20, 1960, p. 71. See also Kent B. Monroe, "The Influence of Price Differences and Brand Familiarity on Brand Preferences," *Consumer Research,* June 1976, pp. 42–49.

23. "DuPont's Teflon Trademark Survives Attack," *Advertising Age,* July 14, 1975, p. 93; and George Miaoulis and Nancy D'Amato, "Consumer Confusion and Trademark Infringement," *Journal of Marketing,* April 1978, pp. 48–55.

24. "Generic Products Are Winning Noticeable Shares of Market from National Brands, Private Labels," *The Wall Street Journal,* August 10, 1979, p. 6; and Betsy D. Gelb, " 'No Name' Products: A Step Toward 'No-Name' Retailing," *Business Horizons,* June 1980, pp. 9–13.

25. *Marketing Communications,* August 1970, p. 13; "Is the Private Label Battle Heating up?" *Grey Matter,* vol. 44, no. 7 (July 1973); Zarrel V. Lambert; Paul L. Doering; Eric Goldstein; and William C. McCormick, "Predisposition Toward Generic Drug Acceptance," *Consumer Research,* June 1980, pp. 14–23; "Private-Label Firms Aided by Inflation, Expected to Post Healthy Growth in 1980," *The Wall Street Journal,* March 31, 1980, p. 20; and "Generic Products in Supermarkets—Some New Perspectives," *The Nielsen Researcher,* No. 3, 1979, pp. 2–9.

26. E. Dichter, "Brand Loyalty and Motivation Research," *Food Business,* January–February 1956.

27. "Private Label Products Gain Increased Space on Many Retailers' Shelves," *The Wall Street Journal,* February 11, 1971, p. 1; "A&P's Own Brand of Consumerism," *Business Week,* April 11, 1970, p. 32; Victor J. Cook and T. F. Schutte, *Brand Policy Determination* (Boston: Allyn & Bacon, Inc., 1967); Arthur I. Co-

hen and Ana Loud Jones, "Brand Marketing in the New Retail Environment," *Harvard Business Review,* September–October 1978, pp. 141–48; "The Drugmaker's Rx for Living with Gener-ics," *Business Week,* November 6, 1978, pp. 205–8; and "No-Name Goods Catching On with Grocers," *Detroit Free Press,* April 9, 1978, p. 16D.

Milt & Joan Mann

1. Understand how product life cycles should affect strategy planning.
2. Understand product positioning.
3. Know what is involved in designing new products and what "new products" really are.
4. Understand a new-product development process.
5. Understand the need for product or brand managers.
6. Recognize the important new terms (shown in red).

11

Product management and new-product development

Product management is a dynamic, full-time job for product managers.

In this chapter, we will talk about product management and new-product planning. Developing a good new product is not easy. Not only are customer needs and attitudes changing, but competition continually makes current products obsolete. In some lines of business, new-product development is so rapid that 50 percent or more of the products made by a firm were not even in the planning stages five to ten years earlier.

Products go through product life cycles. So we will talk about managing products over their cycles. We will also discuss (1) some analytical aids to product management, (2) the importance of an organized new-product development effort to ensure that the company continues to produce successful products, and (3) the role of product managers.

MANAGEMENT OF PRODUCTS OVER THEIR LIFE CYCLES

Products—like consumers—have life cycles. So product and marketing mix planning is important. Competitors are always developing and copying ideas and products—making existing products out-of-date more quickly than ever.

Industry sales and profits don't move together

The **product life cycle** is the stages a new product goes through from beginning to end. It is divided into four major stages: market introduction, market growth, market maturity, and sales decline.

A particular firm's marketing mix for a product usually must change during these stages for several reasons. Customers' attitudes and needs may change

307

through the course of the product's life cycle. Entirely different target markets may be appealed to at different stages in the life cycle. And, the nature of competition moves toward pure competition or oligopoly.

Further, the total sales of the product—by all competitors in the industry—vary in each of its four stages. And more importantly, the profit picture changes. It is important to see that the two do not move together. *Industry profits decline—while industry sales are still rising.* Their general relationships can be seen in Figure 11–1.

Market introduction—investing in the future

In the **market introduction** stage a new idea is being introduced to a market. Customers aren't looking for the product. They don't even know about it. Informative Promotion is needed to tell potential customers about the new product—its advantages and uses.

Even though a firm promotes its new product, it takes time for customers to learn that the product is available. The introductory stage usually is marked by losses—with much money spent for Promotion, Product, and Place development. Money is being invested in the hope of future profits.

Market growth—many competing products and best profits

In the **market growth** stage industry sales are growing fast—but profits rise and then start falling. The innovator begins to make big profits, but competitors start coming into the market—each trying to develop a better product design. There is much product variety. But some competitors copy the most successful products. Monopolistic competition—with down-sloping demand curves—is typical of the market growth stage.

During this stage, the sales of the industry are rising fairly fast—as more and more customers buy. This second stage may last from several days to several years—depending on whether the product is hula hoops, credit card service, or color television sets. This is the time of biggest profits—*for the industry. But* it is *also the beginning of the decline of industry profits*—as competition increases. See Figure 11–1. Some firms have made strategic mistakes and try to patch them up with price cuts and more promotion. Some *firms* even lose money in this stage.

Market maturity—sales level off, profits down

The **market maturity** stage is when industry sales level off—and competition gets tougher. Many competitors have entered the race for profits—except in oligopolies. Competition becomes more aggressive. Industry profits go down throughout the market maturity stage—because promotion costs rise and some

Figure 11–1
Life cycle of a typical product

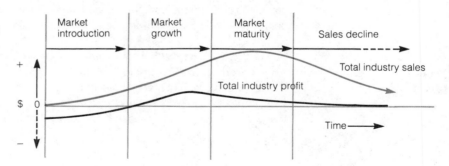

Microwave ovens have been selling well, but probably haven't reached the market maturity stage.

THE NORELCO MICROWAVE OVEN
We took the buttons off. We kept the features on.

Norelco ends the mystery of microwave cooking. With a microwave oven that has no complicated buttons. Just 3 easy-to-use dials. Temperature Control lets you cook by temperature, instead of time. And keeps the food hot until you're ready to enjoy it. Power Level Control gives you a choice of 10 cooking speeds, from "Warm" to "Full Power." The Digital Timer helps you set cooking time with accuracy and ease.

The Norelco Microwave Oven also features an exclusive "Hands Full" door release.

So get the microwave designed simply for you. The Norelco Microwave Oven. It has everything you need. Except the buttons. And confusion.

Norelco ® © 1980 North American Philips Corporation, 100 East 42nd Street, New York, N.Y. 10017

Courtesy North American Philips Corp.

competitors cut prices to attract business. Even in oligopoly situations, there is a long-run downward pressure on prices.

New firms may still enter the market at this stage—increasing competition even more. Note that late entries do skip the early stages—including the profitable market growth stage! And they must try to take a share of the market from established firms—which is difficult and expensive to do.

Persuasive promotion becomes more important during the market maturity stage. Products differ only slightly—if at all. Most competitors have discovered the most effective appeals—or copied the leaders. Although each firm may still have its own demand curve, the curves are becoming increasingly elastic—as the various products become almost the same in the minds of potential consumers.

Some markets move quickly to market maturity—if there are fast copiers or the buyers insist on several sources of supply. This is especially common in industrial goods markets—where buyers buy by specification and want to have several sources of supply. This often leads to oligopoly conditions in market maturity.

In the United States, the markets for most automobiles, boats, many household appliances, most groceries, television sets, and tobacco products are in market maturity.[1] This stage may continue for many years—until a basically new product idea comes along. This is true although different brands or models may come and go. Gasoline-powered automobiles, for example, replaced horse-drawn carriages. Eventually they may be replaced by some other method of transportation—electric autos or high-speed mass transit.

Sales decline—a time of replacement

During the sales decline stage new products replace the old. Price competition from dying products may become more vigorous—but firms with strong brands may make profits almost till the end. These firms will have down-sloping demand curves—because they have successfuly differentiated their products.

As the new products go through their introductory stage, the old ones may keep some sales—by appealing to the most loyal target customers. And some customers accept new ideas more easily than others. The former would "discover" the new product. More conserative buyers might switch later—smoothing the sales decline.

Product life cycles are getting shorter

The total length of the cycle may vary from 90 days—in the case of hula hoops—to possibly 90 years for automobiles. In general, however, product life cycles are shortening.

In the highly competitive grocery products industry, they are down to 12–18 months for really new ideas. Simple variations of such a new idea may have even shorter life cycles. Competitors may copy flavor or packaging changes in a matter of weeks or months.

Large manufacturers—even in industrial goods markets—face product life cycles too. A top Du Pont manager said: "Lead time is gone . . . there's no company so outstanding technically today that it can expect a long lead time in a new discovery."[2] Du Pont had nylon to itself for 15 years. But in just two years a major competitor—Celanese Corporation—came out with something very competitive to Delrin—another synthetic fiber discovery that Du Pont hoped would be as important as nylon. Similarly, six months after U.S. Steel came out with a new "thin tin" plate, competitors were out with even better products.

Even copying products is not uncommon. And this speeds up the cycle. Westinghouse found a company copying its new hair dryer and instruction book almost exactly.[3] And patents may not be much protection. The product's life may be over before a case would get through the courts. The copier might be out of business by then.

The early bird makes the profits

The increasing speed of the product life cycle means that firms must be developing new products all the time. Further, they must try to have marketing mixes that will make the most of the market growth stage—when profits are highest. But it is important to recognize that the profits do not necessarily go to the original innovator. Sometimes fast copiers of the basic concept will share in the market growth stage. Other times, fast adapters of the original concept will be able to zero in more exactly on the market's needs. This emphasizes the importance of being flexible *but also* correctly understanding the needs and attitudes of target markets. Some firms spend a lot of research money monitoring competitors' market tests—and evaluating competitive offerings. Progressive firms are well aware of the attractiveness of the market growth stage—and are willing to spend money to be "early birds" in such markets.

PRODUCT LIFE CYCLES SHOULD BE RELATED TO MARKET AREAS

Each market area should be carefully defined

To fully understand the *why* of a product life cycle, we should carefully define the market area we are considering. The way we define a market makes a difference in the way we see product life cycles—and who the competitors are. If a market is defined very generally, then there may be many competitors—and the market may appear to be in market maturity. On the other hand, if we focus on a narrow area—and a particular way of satisfying specific needs—then we might see much shorter product life cycles, as improved products come along to replace the old. For example, there may be an ongoing general market demand for copies of letters, term papers, and book pages. If we add the annual sales of all the copying machines which have come on the market during the last few decades and treat them as the sales of one product, the industry seems to be in the market growth stage. If we think of individual kinds of machines applying different technical principles, however, we see relatively short life cycles—as new generations of machines come along.[4] In this case, "wet copy" machines have already gone through the sales decline stage and disappeared from the market—while some "dry copy" machines are still fighting it out.

Each market segment has its own product life cycle

Too narrow a view of a market may lead to misreading the nature of competition—and the speed of the relevant product life cycle. A firm producing exercise machines, for example, could focus only on the "exercise machine" market. But this narrow view may lead it to compete only with other exercise machine producers, when it might be more sensible to compete in the "fitness" market. Certainly, it should not ignore competitors' machines, but even tougher competition may come from health clubs—and suppliers of jogging suits, athletic shoes, and other fitness-related goods. Perhaps there should be one strategy for the people who are already interested in exercise machines, and a different strategy for potential customers who still have to be encouraged to think of exercise machines as a way of satisfying their "fitness" needs. In other words, there may be two markets and life cycles to work with—the exercise machine market and the fitness market. It is important to see that focusing on only the exercise machine market might cause the managers to feel they are in the market maturity stage—especially if some panicky competitor starts cutting prices—when actually there is much upside potential in the "fitness" market. If all the exercise machine firms start cutting prices, however, there may be little money left for developing

A producer of exercise bikes should decide what his market is.

the fitness market. And this could lead to retailers dropping the product—and an untimely shortening of the product's life.[5]

Individual products don't have product life cycles

It is important to see that product life cycles describe *industry* sales and profits within a particular product-market—*not* the sales and profits of an *individual* product or brand. Individual products or brands may be introduced or withdrawn during any stage of the product life cycle. Further, their sales and profits may fluctuate up and down throughout the life cycle—sometimes moving in the opposite direction of industry sales and profits.

A "me-too" product introduced during the market growth stage, for example, might reach its peak and start to decline even before the market maturity stage begins—or it may never get any sales at all and suffer a quick death. Other "me-too" products may enter the market in the market maturity stage and have a difficult time trying to capture a share of the market from established competitors. Market leaders may enjoy high profits during the market maturity stage—even though industry profits are declining. Weaker products, on the other hand, may not earn any profit during any stage of the product life cycle.

What this discussion suggests, therefore, is that the sales of *individual* products do not follow any general pattern—and studying past sales patterns can be misleading for strategy planning purposes. It's the life cycle for the whole product-market—including all current or potential competitors—that marketing managers must consider when planning their strategies. In fact, it might be more sensible to think in terms of "market life cycles" or "product-market life cycles" rather than product life cycles—but we will use the term *product life cycle* because it is commonly accepted and widely used.

PLANNING FOR DIFFERENT STAGES OF THE PRODUCT LIFE CYCLE

Length of cycle affects strategy planning

The probable length of the cycle affects strategy planning—realistic plans must be made for the later stages. In fact, where a product is in its life cycle—and how fast it's moving to the next stage—should affect strategy planning. Figure 11–2 shows the relation of the product life cycle to various marketing variables. The technical terms in this figure are discussed later in the book.

Introducing new products

Figure 11–2 shows that a marketer has a lot of work to do introducing a really new product—and this should be reflected in the strategy planning. The product may be unique—but this doesn't mean that everyone will immediately come running to the producer's door. The firm will have to build channels of distribution—perhaps offering special incentives to win cooperation. Promotion will have to build demand for the whole idea—not just try to sell a specific brand. All of this is expensive—and losses can be expected in the market introduction stage of the product life cycle. This may lead the marketer to try to "skim" the market—charge a relatively high price to help pay for the introductory costs.

What is the correct strategy, however, depends on how fast the product life cycle is likely to move—that is, how quickly the new idea will be accepted by customers—and how quickly competitors will follow with their own version of the product. Also relevant is how quickly the firm can change its strategy as

Figure 11–2
Typical changes in marketing variables over the course of the product life cycle

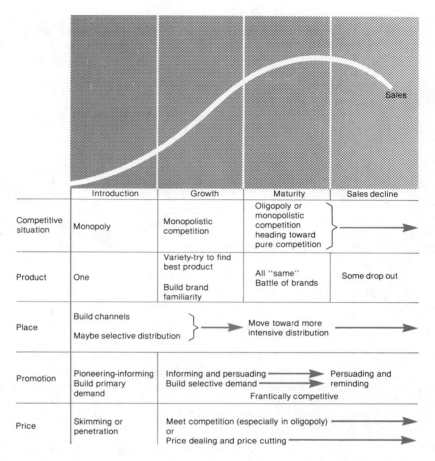

	Introduction	Growth	Maturity	Sales decline
Competitive situation	Monopoly	Monopolistic competition	Oligopoly or monopolistic competition heading toward pure competition	
Product	One	Variety-try to find best product Build brand familiarity	All "same" Battle of brands	Some drop out
Place	Build channels Maybe selective distribution	Move toward more intensive distribution		
Promotion	Pioneering-informing Build primary demand	Informing and persuading Build selective demand Frantically competitive	Persuading and reminding	
Price	Skimming or penetration	Meet competition (especially in oligopoly) or Price dealing and price cutting		

the life cycle moves on. Some firms are very flexible—and may be able to compete effectively with larger, less flexible competitors by adjusting their strategies more frequently.

Managing maturing products

Product life cycles keep moving, but a company does not have to sit by and watch its products go through a complete product life cycle. It has choices. It can improve the product—for the same or a different market—and let it start off on a different cycle. Or it can withdraw it before it completes the cycle. These two choices are shown in Figure 11–3. Of great relevance here is whether there is some differential advantage which the firm has developed. As we move into market maturity, even small differences make a big difference—and some firms do very well by careful management of maturing products. They may be able to capitalize on a slightly better product—or perhaps lower production and/or marketing costs. Or they may simply be more successful at promotion—enabling them to successfully differentiate their more or less homogeneous product from that of their competitors.

An important point to remember here, however, is that industry profits are

Figure 11–3
Significantly improved product starts a new cycle, but maybe with short introductory stage

Profit-oriented firm dropping out of market during market maturity stage

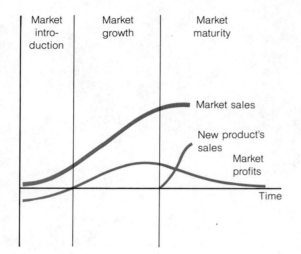

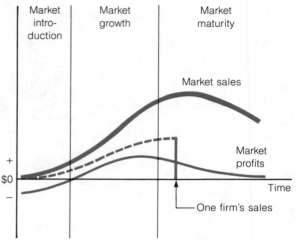

declining in market maturity. Financially oriented top management must be made to see this—or they will continue to expect the attractive profits of the market growth stage. This is simply not possible here—and everyone must understand the situation, or impossible burdens will be placed on the marketing department—causing marketing managers to begin to think about collusion with competitors, deceptive advertising, or some other desperate way of reaching impossible objectives.

Top management must be led to see that there is an upper limit in any product-market. The product life cycle concept has been very useful in communicating this unhappy message. It is one of the powerful tools of marketing which is turning up in the finance and top management literature—because it does affect overall corporate planning and objective setting.

Product life cycles can be extended

When a firm's product wins the position of "the product that meets my needs," its life may last as long as it continues to meet these needs. If the needs change, the product may have to change—but the consumers will continue to buy it if it does meet their needs. An outstanding example is Procter & Gamble's *Tide*. Introduced in 1947, this synthetic detergent gave consumers a significantly cleaner wash than they were able to obtain before—because it eliminated soap film. Tide led to a whole new generation of laundry products—because it produced better cleaning with fewer suds. Since 1947, consumers' needs have changed, washing machines have changed, and fabrics have changed—so the Tide sold today is much different than the one sold in 1947. In fact, there were 55 modifications during its first 29 years of life. But the product continues to sell well—because it continues to meet consumers' needs.[6]

Do the kinds of product modifications made on Tide create a wholly new product which should have its own product life cycle—or are they simply technical adjustments of the original product concept? We will take the latter position—focusing on the product *concept* rather than chemical ingredients. Detergents did permit a new standard of cleaning. Customers desiring cleanliness shifted quite rapidly to detergent products—causing sales decline for the traditional soaps. As detergents were gaining acceptance, they went through the early stages of the product life cycle—and now may continue in market maturity, with various modifications, until a wholly new concept—say, ultrasonic cleaning—comes along. Therefore—for strategic planning purposes new brands of detergents must be seen as immediately entering the market maturity stage—not market introduction.

Phasing out dying products

Not all strategies have to be "exciting" growth strategies. If prospects are poor in some product-market, then a "phase-out" strategy may be needed. The need for phasing out may become increasingly obvious as the sales decline stage arrives. But even in market maturity, it may be clear that a particular product is not going to be profitable enough to reach the company's objectives. Then, the appropriate action is to develop a strategy which helps the firm get out of the product-market as quickly as possible—even before the sales decline stage sets in—while minimizing possible losses.

Strategic plans are implemented as "ongoing" strategies—with sales people making calls, inventory moving in the channel, advertising scheduled for several months into the future, and so on. So usually it is not possible to abruptly end a plan without some losses. It may be better to phase out the product. This might involve selective materials ordering—so that production can end with a minimum of unused inventory. Salespeople might be shifted to other jobs (or laid off). The advertising and other promotion efforts might be cancelled or phased out as quickly as possible—since there is no point in promoting for the long run anymore. These various actions will obviously affect morale within the company—and may cause channel members to pull back also. So it may be necessary to offer price inducements in the channels. The company's people should be reassured that a phase-out strategy is being implemented—and that they will be shifted to other jobs as the plan is completed.

Obviously, there are some difficult implementation problems here, but it should be clear that a phase-out strategy is also a *strategy*—and it should be market-oriented, to minimize losses. In fact, it may even be possible to "milk out" a dying product for some time if competitors move out more quickly. There still is ongoing demand—although it is declining—and some customers may be willing to pay attractive prices to obtain their "old favorite." Further, there may be an ongoing need for repair parts and service—which may help sustain the overall profitability of the phase-out strategy. Alternately, a new strategy could handle just the repairs and service—even as the basic product is being phased out.

So you can see that whole product life cycles should be planned—for each strategy. And for a company with many strategies, it will be necessary to plan for many product life cycles. You can see that the product life cycle concept will add depth to the portfolio management analysis which we discussed in Chapter 4. There we were concerned with planning and evaluating the prospects for various kinds of opportunities. Now we can see that these opportunities will have different product life cycles—and the product life cycle should be taken into consideration when estimating the attractiveness of alternative opportunities.

STYLE AND FASHION CYCLES CAN HELP STRATEGY PLANNING, TOO

The concept of the product life cycle applies generally to most products, but a special kind—a *fashion cycle*—can be seen clearly in markets where style or fashion is important to consumers.

The short happy life of fads

The words "style" or "fashion" mean the same thing to most consumers. Technically, however, they are different.

Style is a "characteristic or distinctive mode or method of expression, presentation, or conception in the field of art."[7] Various home styles such as colonial, Cape Cod, ranch, and modern have been popular during certain periods of history.

Fashion is the *currently* accepted or popular style in a given field. A particular style of house—such as a ranch house or A-frame—may be in fashion for a time and then lose its popularity. Or a certain color and style of women's dresses—such as mini-skirts—may be in fashion one year, then outdated the next. It is still a style—but no longer a fashion.

A **fad** is a particular fashion that seems fashionable only to certain groups who are enthusiastic about it—but so fickle that it is short-lived as a fashion. Some teenagers' music tastes are fads.

Fashion cycles have stages, too

Consumer acceptance of fashions usually goes through a **fashion cycle** consisting of three stages: the *distinctiveness, emulation,* and *economic emulation* stages—which roughly parallel the product life cycle stages.

During the **distinctiveness stage** some consumers seek—and are willing to pay for—products different from those satsifying the majority. They have products

Fads are short-lived fashions, but can be profitable.

Mike Jaeggi

custom-made or patronize manufacturers or middlemen who offer products in small quantities and/or in "distinctive" places.

If a particular style catches on with a number of style leaders, then other consumers—because of their desire to emulate—may copy them. This is the **emulation stage** when many more consumers want to buy what is satisfying the original users. Emulation is easier as manufacturers begin to make larger quantities of the products that seem to be catching on. This stage is similar to the early market growth stage of the product life cycle.

In the **economic emulation stage** many consumers want the currently popular fashion—but at a lower price. When this happens, manufacturers mass produce large quantities of the product at low cost—and we move quickly through the market growth stage and maybe through the market maturity stage into sales decline.

Perhaps in the second stage—and certainly in the third stage—the style that began as the private fling of the few becomes less attractive to these original style leaders. They already are trying other styles—which eventually may become fashions and run through another cycle.[8]

It's not really clear how a particular fashion gets started. Most present fashions are adaptations or revivals of previously popular styles. Designers and business firms are always looking for styles that will satisfy consumers who crave distinctiveness.

Predicting what will sell is not easy. Fortunes can be lost in the fashion business by guessing wrong about consumer behavior. Ambrose Bierce once wrote, "Fashion is a despot whom the wise ridicule—and obey." And Thoreau commented, "Every generation laughs at the old fashions but follows religiously the new."

In spite of the chancy nature of any fashion-oriented business, companies keep trying to find new fashions.[9] It is mostly "trial and error," but there are a few generalizations which are relevant to marketing.

1. Fashions cannot be forced—but many styles can be presented, and when one becomes fashionable, its cycle may be shortened by aggressive promotion.
2. A higher standard of living—and greater mobility—encourage a greater interest in fashions.
3. The speed of communication affects the rate of change or acceptance of fashions.
4. Speed in change of fashions increases the cost of producing and marketing products. There are losses due to trial and error in finding acceptable styles, then producing them on a limited basis because of uncertainty about the length of the cycle. These increased costs are not always charged directly to the consumer—since some firms lose their investment and go out of business. But in total, fashion changes cost consumers money.

PRODUCT POSITIONING AIDS PRODUCT MANAGEMENT

A new aid to product planning—**product positioning**—shows where proposed and/or present brands are located in a market—as seen by customers. It requires some formal marketing research. The results are usually plotted on graphs to help see where the products are "positioned" in relation to competitors. Usually, the products' positions are related to two product features which are important to the target customers.

Assuming the picture is reasonably accurate, the managers have to decide whether they want to leave their product (and marketing mix) alone—or reposition the product. This might mean *physical changes* in the product—or simply *image changes*. For example, with respect to beers, most people can't pick out their "favorite" brand in a blind test—so physical changes might not be necessary (and might not even work) to reposition a beer brand.

Product positioning techniques—sometimes called "clustering techniques"—are beyond the scope of this text. But the results of one such analysis—for the beer industry—shows the possibilities. In this case, besides plotting the customers' views of current beers in relation to two product attributes, the respondents were also asked to evaluate their "ideal" beer.

Figure 11–4 shows the product space for various beers using two dimensions—price and lightness. This data was obtained by asking beer drinkers to rate several beers on various scales—and then computer programs averaged these ratings and plotted the results as shown. Note that the "name" brands are seen as high priced, that is, as the "premium" beers. But not all the premium beers are direct competitors with respect to lightness.

The circles on Figure 11–4 show consumers clustered near their "ideal" beer preferences. These clusters were obtained by asking the respondents to rate their ideal beer on the same scales, plotting the results, and then subjectively drawing circles around apparent customer concentrations.

Ideal clusters 1 and 2 are the largest and are close to two large-selling brands—

Figure 11–4.
Product space for the Chicago beer market

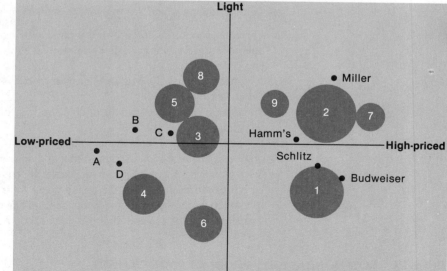

Source: Adapted from Richard M. Johnson, "Market Segmentation: A Strategic Management Tool," *Journal of Marketing Research*, February 1971, p. 160.

Taste, price, and packaging are some ways of positioning products.

Mary McCarthy

Budweiser and Schlitz. It appears that customers in cluster 1 might like to see both Schlitz and Budweiser a little "heavier." However, exactly what these brands should do about lightness requires some soul searching. Perhaps both of these brands should leave their products alone—but emphasize lightness more in their promotion, to make a stronger appeal to those who want lighter beer.

Hamm's beer does not appear to satisfy any of the "ideal clusters" very well. Therefore, some attempt probably should be made to reposition Hamm's—either through physical or image changes. However, management must make some strategic decisions here. Should Hamm's aim for cluster 1, for example, and compete head-on with Schlitz and Budweiser? Or should it compete with Miller for cluster 2? Or maybe try to capture the smaller cluster 9 all by itself—and minimize direct competition?

Note that there are several ideal clusters which are not near any of the present brands. This might suggest an opportunity for introducing new products—both heavier and lighter beers, at lower prices. If some firm chose to follow this approach, we would think of it as a segmenting effort.

Combining versus segmenting

Product positioning analysis might lead a firm to combining—rather than segmenting—if the managers see that they may be able to make several general appeals to different parts of a "combined" market. For example, by varying its promotion Miller might try to appeal to clusters 2, 7, and 9 with one product. On the other hand, there may be clearly defined sub-markets—and some parts of the market may be "owned" by one product or brand. This may make it practical to think of segmenting efforts—moving the firm's own product into another segment of the general market area, where competition is weaker. This might require modifying the product—or simply changing the promotion appeal to make the product's image fit more closely with the desires of those customers.

The major value of product positioning is to help managers see how customers see their market—it is a visual aid to understanding a market. But product positioning usually focuses on specific product features—that is, it is very product-oriented. There is the risk that important customer-related dimensions—including needs and attitudes—may be overlooked. But as part of a broader analysis of target markets, product positioning can be very useful. The first time such an analysis is done, the managers may be shocked to see how much customers' perceptions of a market differ from their own. For this reason alone, product positioning may continue to be useful.

Premature emphasis on product features can be dangerous, however, and it is easy to do if you start with a product-oriented definition of a market—as in the Chicago "beer market" example. This leads to positioning beers against beers. This can be useful—but it also can cause a firm to miss more basic shifts in markets. For example, the beer industry has been losing some customers to white wine and Perrier water. Such shifts would not be seen by only looking at alternative brands of beer. The focus would just be too narrow. Similarly, studying only alternative luxury cars might be too narrow—if potential customers were considering spending their money not only on luxury cars but also on foreign vacations, summer cottages, and other products in the status symbol market we discussed in Chapter 4—see Figure 4–2. Focusing on the physical characteristics of alternative luxury cars might completely miss the relevant competition—and what should be emphasized in the promotion effort.

As we have emphasized throughout the text, it *is* necessary to understand potential needs and attitudes when planning products and marketing strategies. And if the customers are treating quite different products as substitutes, then those are the products which a firm must position itself against. Great care must be used to avoid focusing on physical product characteristics which are not the determining dimensions of the target market.

NEW-PRODUCT PLANNING

Competition is so strong and dynamic in most markets, that it is absolutely essential for a firm to keep developing new products—as well as modifying its current products—to meet changing customer needs and competitors' actions. Not having an active product development process means that consciously—or subconsciously—the firm has decided to "milk" its current products and go out of business. New-product planning is not an optional matter—it has to be done—just to survive in our dynamic marketplaces.

What is a new product—lemons?

A **new product** is one that is new *in any way* for the company concerned. A "new product" can become "new" in many ways. A new idea can be turned into a new item or service. Small changes in an existing product also can make it "new." Or an existing product may be offered to new markets as a "new" product. Lemons are a good example.

In the marketing of lemons by one company, no physical changes were made—but much promotion created many "new" products. The same old lemons were promoted successfully for lemonade, mixed drinks, diet supplements, cold remedies, lemon cream pies, a salad dressing, sauce for fish, and many other uses.[10] Note: several—not just one—product life cycles are involved here. For each of these markets, the product had to go through the early stages of its own product life cycle.

Physical changes aren't necessary to create new products.

More, perhaps, than you care to know about Sunkist lemons.

Courtesy Sunkist Growers Inc.

This broad approach to what is a new product deserves additional emphasis because one or more of the other Ps may have to be revised when no physical changes are made in the product. The experience of an office machine manufacturer is a good example. Its normal target markets were office managers and efficiency experts. But the dictating machines had less appeal to the much larger potential market of general business executives, although the products were technically good.

Motivation research revealed several facts. One was that the promotion appeals being used—speed, economy, and efficiency—were psychologically unattractive to the executive. He felt he might lose prestige by using such a machine because it might reduce or eliminate the need for *his* secretary. The research also showed that secretaries believed that machines might set up a wall between them and their bosses, and that they might become nothing but "slaves to machines." As a result, management was afraid to order the machines for fear that employees would quit.

The solution here—which in effect created a new product—was to explain that the machines speeded up work and made the secretary, manager, and machines a happy team. This was done by advertisements stressing "no more staying at the office after hours . . . time to relax . . . secretary free to be a real assistant . . . I can get ahead and still be a real father . . . home while the kids are still awake." The close interrelation of two Ps—Product and Promotion—should be noted.

How new should it be?

A product can be called "new" for only a limited time. Six months is the longest time that a product should be called new—according to the Federal Trade Commission (FTC)—the federal government agency which polices antimonopoly laws. To be called new—says the FTC—a product must be entirely new or changed in "a functionally significant or substantial respect.[11] While six months may seem a very short time for production-oriented managers, it may be reasonable, given the short life cycles of many products.

Some marketers have been preoccupied with relatively minor changes to make products "new." But such minor changes may not lead to long-lived strategies. These strategies require finding ways of satisfying needs in a substantially better way. The needs might have been there all along—just not seen in the way that the firm now sees them—but a "good" marketing mix would try to satisfy these needs "very well." This might even require a good deal of education—promotion—to explain that this "really new" product is available—and how it will better satisfy their needs. This is obviously a more difficult job than emphasizing trivial differences—but it may lead to the breakthrough opportunities we have been talking about.

Find out what the customers and middlemen want

Everyone who handles, sells, or uses a product must be considered when developing a new product. Of course, the product should reflect the needs and attitudes of the target customers. The relevant product-oriented dimensions—obtained during the segmenting process—should be helpful in deciding what product features to emphasize. And, obviously, the product should have all the core features that consumers would expect.

The product designers must not only think about final customers—but intermediate customers, too. There may be special packaging or handling needs. The shelf height in supermarkets, for example, might limit package size. Shipping or handling problems—in the warehouse or on carriers—might call for different types of packaging or package sizes—to keep damage down or make the package easier to handle.

Design long-term "goodness" into products if possible

Socially responsible firms are becoming aware that they should consider consumers' *long-term* interests—as well as their short-term interests—when designing products. Consumer groups are helping to force this awareness on more firms.

The firm's final choice in product design should fit with the company's overall objectives—and make good use of the firm's resources. But it would also be desirable to create a need-satisfying product which will appeal to consumers—not only in the short run but also in the long run. These kinds of new-product opportunities are shown in Figure 11–5. Obviously, a socially responsible firm would try to find "desirable" opportunities—rather than "deficient" ones. This may not be as easy as it sounds, however. Some consumers may want "pleasing

**Figure 11–5
Types of new-product
opportunities**

Immediate satisfaction

Source: Adapted from Philip Kotler, "What Consumerism Means for Marketers," *Harvard Business Review,* May–June 1972, pp. 55–56.

products"—instead of "desirable products." That is, the consumers may emphasize immediate satisfaction and give little thought to their own long-term welfare. And some competitors may be very willing to offer what consumers want in the short run. Being "socially responsible" will challenge new-product planners.

Safety should also be considered in product design

Real acceptance of the marketing concept would certainly lead to the design of safety into products. But some inherently risky products may be purchased because they do provide thrills and excitement—for example, bicycles, skis, and hang gliders. Even so, safety features can usually be added—and they are desired by some potential customers.

The *Consumer Product Safety Act* of 1972 set up the Consumer Product Safety Commission to encourage more awareness of safety in product design—and better quality control. The commission has a great deal of power. It can set safety standards for products—and it can order costly repairs or return of "unsafe products." And it can back up its orders with fines and jail sentences. The Food and Drug Administration has similar powers for foods and drugs.

Product safety complicates strategy planning because not all customers—including some who want better safety features—are willing to pay more for safer products. And some features cost a lot to add—and may increase prices considerably.

Product liability must be taken seriously

Another factor must be considered regarding safety—product liability. **Product liability** means the legal obligation of sellers to pay damages to individuals who are injured by defective products or unsafely designed products. Some firms are finding their product liability insurance costs rising astronomically—to the point where they have to "self-insure"—take the risk themselves—or go out of business. Nissen Corporation, for example, recently was offered a product liability insurance policy costing $400,000 to cover $300,000 worth of protection (because of uncertainty about the size of court settlements) on its gym equipment! This is an extreme example—but machine tool makers have seen their insurance

"Unsafe" products will be sold as long as consumers want them.

Mike Jaeggi

premiums increase drastically in recent years. The major reason for these rising premiums is a growing number of claims, law suits, *and* settlements. And the potential for more suits is great. Recently, a paper-making machinery manufacturer was notified of claims by users of two of its presses for damages arising out of industrial accidents. One of the presses was built in 1895, and the other in 1897![12]

It is clear that the uncontrollable environment has changed—especially regarding safety. Safety is one of the four basic needs—and people seem to feel quite strongly about it. Whether some law suits or government agencies go "too far"— for example, the Food and Drug Administration's proposal to ban saccharin—is not at issue here. Obviously, the uncontrollable environment has changed—and it is more important than ever to take new-product planning—and in particular the safety of products—seriously. Production-oriented managers must become more market oriented—or they may be driven out of business.

Keeping score on product design

An analysis of present and/or potential customers' needs and attitudes—as well as the need of channel members—is obviously important in product development. Ignoring these influences—as is typical with production-oriented managers—helps contribute to the relevantly high failure rate on new—as well as existing products. It is important to note that firms are regularly dropping—or should be dropping—present products and product lines. And the failure rate on new products which are actually placed in the market may be as high as 50 percent.[13]

Most of these "failures" are due to inadequate analysis of market demands to begin with—or changing market demands *and* competitive moves. Therefore, it is extremely important that the marketing manager continue to evaluate present products—as well as carefully studying possible new ones. The checklist in Figure 11–6 can help in this ongoing monitoring. This checklist is useful because it usually is safer to make 13 separate small judgments—than one large "yes" or "no" judgment.

On this checklist, a yes on 11–13 questions would indicate a good design; 9 or 10 points, a fair design (with "no" answers indicating weak spots to be corrected); and below 9 points, a poor design—probably indicating that profits will be reduced through lost sales and possibly through high manufacturing costs. This list is suitable for all manufactured products—except high-fashion women's apparel—which is a world of its own. Adaptations must be made for services.

Design examples

Successes. Several examples illustrate how careful customer analysis—especially of the different demands in different segments of a market—can lead to successful product design. When the Powers Regulator Company wanted to enter the home-building market with a shower control, it found it had to redesign the product it was already selling to schools, hotels, and hospitals. Research found this product "too severe and institutional" to win the acceptance of the new target market—builders and homeowners. Powers developed a more suitable—and successful—product for home use.

Elgin had a different problem with its outboard motors—which were designed with controls in various places. Market research showed that customers found this confusing. The controls were redesigned into one panel—and the same market was served more effectively.

Failures. Two failures tell the other side of the design story. In one case, a large manufacturer of food machinery and equipment completed the design of a large citrus juicer without making an adequate study of the citrus industry. Management went ahead with engineering development confident that the machine would find a market. After spending nearly $1 million on the design and engineering work, the company learned that the machine had been built for the top of the market rather than for the bulk of potential users—the smaller processors. The machine was too big and expensive—only a few concerns could afford it. If a few thousand dollars had been spent on determining how many citrus processors there were by size and groups, types of machines used and wanted, and related facts, the company might have avoided its costly mistake.

In a second case, a manufacturer of small firearms decided to produce forged-steel hand tools. This was a new line for the company—yet it engineered the product with no study of user preferences, customs, and practices. The tools—although well designed—were given a rust-proofing treatment which left a dull finish rather than the popular, shiny steel finish. The company—certain that sales

Figure 11–6
Good design: Does your product have it?

	Yes	No
1. Does the product's present design reflect quality?	____	____
2. Is the present design economical to manufacture?	____	____
3. Is the design well accepted by wholesalers, retailers, sales people and customers?	____	____
4. Is the design in tune with current design trends?	____	____
5. Does the design have a comparatively long life?	____	____
6. Are the details of the product well designed?	____	____
7. Does the design contribute to the product's usefulness, safety, and convenience?	____	____
8. Are the materials used practical for product's end use?	____	____
9. Is the color right for use and environment?	____	____
10. Is the size right for best use?	____	____
11. Is the weight right for best use?	____	____
12. Does the design stand up well with competition?	____	____
13. Does the design meet environmental requirements?	____	____

Figure 11–7
Decay of new-product ideas during an organized new-product development process

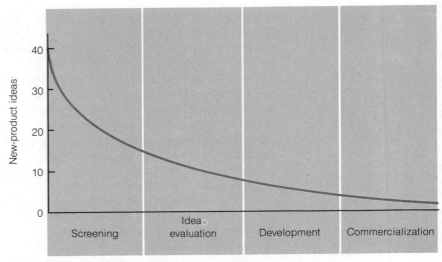

Source: Adapted from Management Research Department, Booz, Allen, and Hamilton, Inc.

would go well—undertook a full-scale development and marketing effort—but the tools did not move from the retailers' shelves. Craftsmen did not like the dull finish and would not buy them. Because this company ignored user preferences, thousands of dollars were wasted in development, tooling, and inventories. Worse yet, the company gave retailers a bad impression of its products and management ability.[14]

AN ORGANIZED NEW-PRODUCT DEVELOPMENT PROCESS IS DESIRABLE

The failures discussed above suggest that not all new products are successes. This is true. The failure rate of new product *ideas* is even higher. Figure 11–7 illustrates the decay of new product ideas—as the process moves from screening ideas to commercialization. It is estimated that out of each 40 new ideas, only one is left after the ideas have passed through an organized development process of the type described below. The rate of rejection varies among industries and companies—but the general shape of this decay curve seems to be typical. An especially conservative company might have even more rejects, of course.

Five-step process is logical

New-product development demands much time and talent—and still the risk and costs of failure are high. To improve this effort, it is useful to follow an organized new-product development process. The following pages describe such a process—moving logically through five steps: (1) idea generation, (2) screening, (3) idea evaluation, (4) development (of product and marketing mix) and (5) commercialization.[15] See Figure 11–8.

The general process is similar for both consumer markets and industrial markets. But there are significant detailed differences. We will emphasize the similarities in the following discussion.

Process tries to kill new ideas—economically

An important element in the new-product development process for both markets is continued evaluation of the likely profitability and return on investment of new ideas. In fact, it is desirable to apply the hypothesis-testing approach discussed in Chapter 5 to new-product development. The hypothesis which is tested is that the new idea will *not* be profitable. This puts the burden on the new idea to prove itself—or be rejected. This may seem harsh, but experience shows that most new ideas have some flaw which will lead to subsequent problems—and even substantial losses. This process tries to discover those flaws early—and either see a remedy or eliminate the idea from further consideration. Applying this process requires much analysis of the idea—both within the firm and outside—*before* any money is spent by research and development (R&D)—or engineering to develop a physical item. This is a major departure from the usual production-oriented approach—which develops a product and then asks sales to "get rid of the product."

Idea generation step

New ideas might come from a company's own sales or production staff, middlemen, competitors, consumer surveys, or miscellaneous sources—such as trade associations, advertising agencies, or government agencies. Imaginative exploration of different views of the company's markets may help spot opportunities

**Figure 11–8
New-product development process**

Industrial markets	Consumer markets
1. Idea generation	1. Idea generation

2. Screening
    Rough ROI estimate
	2. Screening
	    Rough ROI estimate

3. Idea evaluation
    Exploratory
        Rough ROI verification
    Qualitative
    Quantitative
        ROI estimate
	3. Idea evaluation
	    Concept testing
	        Rough ROI verification

4. Development
    R&D
    Build model
    Engineering test
    Test in market
        ROI estimate
	4. Development
	    R&D
	    Engineering
	    Build model(s)
	    Test in market
	        ROI estimate
	    Revise product specifications
	    Pilot production
	    Production and quality
	        control test
	    Market testing
	    Product variations
	    Variations of marketing mix
	        ROI estimates

5. Commercialization
    Finalize production model
    Finalize marketing mix (plan)
        Final ROI estimate
    Start full-scale production
        and marketing plan
	5. Commercialization
	    Finalize product
	    Finalize marketing mix (plan)
	        Final ROI estimate
	    Start full-scale production
	        and marketing plan

Source: Adapted from Frank R. Bacon, Jr. and Thomas W. Butler, Jr., *Planned Innovation,* rev. ed. (The University of Michigan, Ann Arbor: Institute of Science and Technology, 1980).

which have not yet occurred to competitors—or perhaps even to potential customers. Basic studies of present consumer behavior might point up opportunities, too.

When looking for ideas, the consumer's viewpoint is all-important. It may be helpful to consider the image that potential customers have of the firm. If some potential customers think of a firm as a food manufacturer—rather than just a flour miller—then many products become logical additions to the line. If customers think of a toaster manufacturer as a maker of electrical appliances—then it may be easy to expand into other appliance markets. And, going a step further, if they think of the electrical appliance manufacturer as a producer of convenience items for the home, then the horizon becomes even broader. The company might even be able to sell expandable tables, for example.

This line of thinking led the Maryland Cup Corporation—the world's largest manufacturer of paper drinking straws and a leading manufacturer of paper drinking cups—to produce plastic food containers of all types. Customers had identified them with the "disposable container" business—rather than just the straw and cup business. Similarly, S. C. Johnson & Son, Inc., expanded from a line of paste waxes to many other household products. Some camera manufacturers have expanded into photographic equipment and supplies of all kinds.

It probably is desirable to establish a formal procedure for seeking new ideas. The lists of considerations and checkpoints discussed above—as well as the hierarchy of needs and other behavioral considerations discussed earlier—should be reviewed regularly to assure that there is a continual flow of new—but sound—ideas. The importance of a continual flow is obvious. Later steps will eliminate many ideas. Yet a company must have some which succeed in the market—if it is to survive.

Screening step

Screening involves running the new ideas by the product-market screening criteria which were described in Chapter 4. Recall that these criteria include the combined output of a resource (strengths and weaknesses) analysis, a long-run trends analysis, and the objectives of the company. See Figure 4–6. The criteria should include quantitative statements of objectives—as well as qualitative statements about the nature of the business the company would like to be in—and businesses or markets they would not like to be in. Further, the qualitative part of the criteria should include statements which will help select ideas which will enable the company to lead from its strengths and avoid its weaknesses. Ideally, a company should match its resources to the size of its opportunities. A "good" new idea should eventually lead to a product (and marketing mix) which will give the firm a competitive differential advantage—and hopefully a lasting competitive differential advantage.

Who does the screening—and how it is done—is very important. Very conservative managers could kill all new ideas. A case in point is a company noted for *one* really successful product in its whole history. The head of new-product development there said "fortunately not enough good ideas come along to cause us trouble." The obvious solution to this problem is a whole-hearted commitment by top management to the new-product development process. If this is not there,

A new product idea can be killed by negative consumer response.

Peter Le Grand

it is very likely that many "really good ideas" will be killed—and in the extreme *all* of them will be.

Getting by the product-market criteria will not guarantee success for the new idea—but it will show that at least the new idea is "in the right ballpark"—*for this firm.* If many ideas pass the screening criteria, then it is necessary to set priorities for which ones go on to the next step in the process. This can be done by comparing the ROI (return on investment) for each idea—assuming the firm is ROI-oriented. The most attractive alternatives will be pursued first.

Idea evaluation step

Once an idea has moved past screening, the basic concept must be evaluated more carefully. It is important to recognize that no tangible product has yet been developed—and this handicaps concept testing from the start. Final consumers, especially, have difficulty visualizing "ideas" or "concepts." Nevertheless, this kind of research can help guide the next step—where we actually develop models.

Concept testing involves market research—anywhere from informal focus groups to formal surveys of potential customers' attitudes towards the idea. Even informal focus groups may be very useful—especially if they show that potential users aren't excited about the new idea. It may even be possible to make a rough ROI estimate after this type of research. And if the results are very discouraging, it may be desirable to kill the idea at this stage. Remember, we are testing the hypothesis that an idea is *not* a good opportunity for this firm. So, any (serious) negative evidence should be the grounds for accepting the hypothesis—and rejecting the idea.

Idea evaluation can be more elaborate in industrial markets. Here potential customers are more informed about their needs—and their buying is nomic and less emotional. Further, given the derived nature of deman markets, most needs are already being satisfied in some way. So, are "substitutes" for existing ways of doing things. This means th small number of interviews with knowledgeable people can whether there is an opportunity—and the range of variation in

**Figure 11–9
Information requirements to
develop new products**

Information requirements

	1 How is basic function performed now?	2 What do present methods cost?	3 What's wrong with present methods?	4 What value improvements have?
A. Physical need	_____ _____ _____	_____ _____ _____	_____ _____ _____	_____ _____ _____
B. Technical product design (R&D)	_____ _____ _____	_____ _____ _____	_____ _____ _____	_____ _____ _____
C. Production methods	_____ _____ _____	_____ _____ _____	_____ _____ _____	_____ _____ _____
D. Marketing and distribution methods	_____ _____ _____	_____ _____ _____	_____ _____ _____	_____ _____ _____
E. Economic cost and value consideration				

Source: Adapted from Frank R. Bacon, Jr., and Thomas W. Butler, Jr., *Planned Innovation*, rev. ed. (Ann Arbor: The University of Michigan, Institute of Science and Technology, 1980).

ments. A form similar to Figure 11–9 can be helpful in gathering the kind of information which will be useful in deciding whether there is an opportunity—and whether it fits with the firm's resources—*and* whether there is a basis for developing a competitive advantage. With such information, it is possible to estimate likely ROI in the various market segments—and decide whether to continue the new product development process.

Development step

Product ideas which have survived the screening and idea evaluation steps must now be analyzed further. Usually, this involves some research and development (R&D) and engineering—to develop the physical part of the product. Input from the earlier efforts will help guide this technical work. But it is still desirable to test the models and early versions of the product in the market. There may have to be several cycles of the process—building a model, testing it, revising product specifications based on the tests, and so on—*before* pilot plant production—to test whether engineering and production can actually produce the item in quantity.

With actual models, it is possible to show potential customers how the idea has been converted into a tangible product. Using small focus groups, panels, and larger surveys, it is possible to get their reaction to specific features and the whole product idea. This can lead to revision of product specifications—for different markets. Months or even years of research may be necessary to focus in precisely on what some market segments will find acceptable. It took Procter & Gamble over ten years and $80 million to develop Pringles Potato Chips!

After testing the tangible product, then production should begin—to be sure that the desired product can be produced—economically. This product then goes into the market for testing—perhaps testing product variations if there are still questions—as well as variations in the marketing mix. For example, alternative brands, prices, or advertising copy might be tested. Test marketing is risky, because it not only tests ideas for the company—but also give information to competition. But not testing can be dangerous, too. Fortunately, if this new product development procedure has been used carefully, it is likely that the market tests will provide a lot more information to the firm than to its competitors. Presumably it will be testing specific variables—rather than just vaguely testing whether a new idea will "sell." After the market test, an estimate of likely ROI for various strategies will determine whether the idea moves on to commercialization.

Sometimes, a market test is not run because it is not practical. In fashion goods, for example, speed is extremely important and products are usually just tried in the market. And durable goods—which have very high fixed production costs and long production lead times—may have to go directly to the market. In these cases, it is especially important that the early steps are done carefully— to reduce the chances for failure in the marketplace.

Commercialization

A product idea which has survived this far must finally be placed on the market. First, it may be necessary to decide exactly which product form or line will be sold. Then, it is necessary to complete the marketing mix—really the whole strategic plan. And an estimate of the likely ROI for this plan would have to get final approval from top management before implementation. Then, the product idea will finally emerge from the new-product development process and success will require the cooperation of the whole company.

Actually putting a product on the market is expensive—because manufacturing facilities have to be set up and enough product has to be produced to fill the channels of distribution. Further, introductory promotion can be expensive. This is especially true if new channels of distribution must be developed.

After an idea is accepted by potential consumers, it goes to R&D.

Because of the size of the job, some firms introduce their products city by city or region by region—in a gradual "roll out"—until they obtain complete market coverage. This also permits more market testing—but that is not the purpose of the roll out. All implementation efforts should be controlled—to be sure the strategic plans are still on target.

Eventually, the "new" product is no longer "new"—and it becomes just another product. About this time, the "new-product people" turn the product over to the regular operating people—and go on to developing other new products.

NEW-PRODUCT DEVELOPMENT: A TOTAL COMPANY EFFORT

Top-level support is vital

New-product development must have the enthusiastic support of top management. New products tend to disrupt the old routines that managers of established products often try to subtle but effective ways to maintain. So someone should be responsible for new-product development. The specific organization arrangement may not be too important—as long as new-product development has top-level support.[16]

Some organization helps

Rather than just leaving new-product development to anyone who may be interested—perhaps in engineering, R&D, or sales—it probably will be desirable to put someone in charge of new-product development. This could be a person, a department, or a committee.

A new-product development department or committee helps make sure that new ideas are carefully evaluated—and good ones profitably marketed. Delays may lead to late introduction—and give competitors a head start. A delay of even six months may make the difference between a product's success or failure.

A well-organized development process might even make it possible for a firm to copy others' attractive innovations—quickly and profitably. This possibility should not be overlooked. No one company can hope to be first always—with the best.[17]

A complicated, integrated effort is needed

Developing new products should be a total company effort. The whole process—involving people in management, research, production, promotion, packaging, and branding—must move in steps from an early exploration of ideas to development of the product. Even with a careful development process, many new products do fail. Usually this happens, however, when the process has been hurried—or some steps have been skipped. It is always tempting to do this when some part of the process seems to indicate that the company has a "really good idea." But the process moves in steps—gathering different kinds of information along the way—and skipping some of the steps may lead to missing an important aspect that will make a whole strategic plan less profitable—or actually cause failure.

NEED FOR PRODUCT MANAGERS

~duct variety leads to ~t managers

When a firm has only one or a few related products, everyone is interested in them. But when new products are being developed, someone may be put in charge of new-product planning—to be sure it is not neglected. Similarly, when a firm has several different kinds of products, it may decide to put someone in charge of each kind—or even each brand—to be sure they are not lost in the rush of everyday business. **Product managers** or **brand managers** manage specific products—often taking over the jobs formerly handled by an advertising manager. That gives a clue to what is often their major responsibility—Promotion—given that the products have already been developed by the "new product" people.

Product managers are especially common in large companies which produce many kinds of products. There may be several product managers serving under a marketing manager. Sometimes these product managers are responsible for the profitable operation of the whole marketing effort for a particular product. Then, they have to coordinate their efforts with others—including the sales manager, advertising agencies, and production and research people.

In some companies, the product manager has much power and profit responsibility. He has difficulties, however, because although he has profit responsibility, he usually has no authority over other functional areas whose efforts he is expected to direct and coordinate!

In other companies, the product manager may serve primarily as a "product champion"—concerned with planning and getting the promotion effort implemented. Product managers vary considerably in their activities—depending on their experience and aggressiveness—and the company's organizational philosophy. More emphasis is now being placed on marketing *experience*—as it becomes clearer that this important job takes more than academic training and enthusiasm. But it is clear that someone must be responsible for developing and implementing product-related plans when a company has many products.[18]

CONCLUSION

Product planning is an increasingly important activity in a modern economy—because it is no longer very profitable to sell just "commodities." Product positioning was described as an aid to product planning—helping to see where products and brands are positioned in a market.

The product life cycle concept is especially important to marketing strategy planning because it shows that different marketing mixes—and even strategies—are needed as a product moves through its cycle. This is an important point, because profits change during the life cycle—with most of the profits going to the innovators or fast copiers.

We pointed out that a new product is not limited to physical newness. We will call a product "new" if it is new in any way—to any target market.

New products are so important to the survival of firms in our ̲ ̲ ̲ ̲ ̲ ̲ ̲ ̲ ̲ ̲ economy that some organized method for developing them is needed ̲ ̲ ̲ ̲ approach was discussed—but it is obvious that is must be a total co ̲ ̲ ̲ ̲ to be successful.

The failure rate of new products is high—but it is lower for lar ̲ ̲ ̲ managed firms that have recognized product development and r ̲ ̲ ̲ ̲ vital processes. Some firms have appointed product managers to ̲ ̲ ̲ ual product lines—and new-product committees to assure that the process is carried out successfully.

QUESTIONS AND PROBLEMS

1. Explain how market sales and market profits behave over the product life cycle.

2. Cite two examples of products which you feel are currently in each of the product life-cycle stages.

3. Explain how different conclusions might be reached with respect to the correct product life-cycle stage(s) in the automobile market, especially if different views of the market are held.

4. Can product life cycles be extended? Illustrate your answer for a specific product.

5. Discuss the life cycle of a product in terms of its probable impact on a manufacturer's marketing mix. Illustrate using battery-operated toothbrushes.

6. Distinguish among a fad, style, and fashion. How should a retailer adapt to them? Some people maintain that fads or fashions can be created by businesses. Can you give an example of any business firm that has *consistently* created successful fads or fashions? *Consistently* is important, because anyone can be lucky a few times; the successes are publicized but the failures are not.

7. Explain how product positioning differs from segmenting markets. Is target marketing involved in product positioning?

8. What is a new product? Illustrate your answer.

9. Discuss how the checklist "Good design: Does your product have it?" (Figure 11–6) could be used to evaluate: *(a)* a can opener, *(b)* a baby stroller, *(c)* men's hats (fedoras), *(d)* a coffeemaker.

10. Explain the importance of an organized new-product development process and illustrate how it might be used for: *(a)* an improved phonograph, *(b)* new frozen-food items, *(c)* a new children's toy.

11. Explain the role of product or brand managers. Are they usually put in charge of new-product development work?

12. Discuss the social value of new-product development activities which seem to encourage people to discard products which are not "all worn out." Is this an economic waste? How worn out is "all worn out?" Must a shirt have holes in it? How big?

SUGGESTED CASES

11 Bing Corporation

18 Billing Sports Company

NOTES

1. "RCA to Cut Prices on Eight Color TVs in Promotion Effort," *The Wall Street Journal,* December 31, 1976, p. 16; "Decline in Color TV Sales Brings Worry That More Makers May Fall by Wayside," *The Wall Street Journal,* April 2, 1974, p. 36; "Sales of Major Appliances, TV Sets Gain; But Profits Fail to Keep Up. Gap May Widen," *The Wall Street Journal,* August 21, 1972, p. 22; "What Do You Do When Snowmobiles Go on a Steep Slide?" *The Wall Street Journal,* March 8, 1978, pp. 1, 33; "Price of a Home Videotape Recorder Cut to $795 as U.S. Sales Efforts Accelerate," *The Wall Street Journal,* September 26, 1977, p. 8; "IBM Announces 2 New Processors for Big Systems," *The Wall Street Journal,* October 7, 1977, p. 4; "After Their Slow Year, Fast-Food Chains Use Ploys to Speed Up Sales," *The Wall Street Journal,* April 4, 1980, p. 1 f; "Home Smoke Detectors

Fall On Hard Times as Sales Apparently Peaked," *The Wall Street Journal,* April 3, 1980, p. 1; "As Once Bright Market for CAT Scanners Dims, Smaller Makers of the X-ray Devices Fade Out," *The Wall Street Journal,* May 6, 1980, p. 40; and "Imports Fuzz the Future of Color TV Makers," *Business Week,* May 26, 1980, p. 51.

2. "The Short Happy Life," *Time,* March 29, 1963, p. 83.

3. Ibid.

4. "Xerox Unveils First of 'New Generation' of Copying Machines," *The Wall Street Journal,* May 20, 1970, p. 11.

5. "Getting Fat by Making Others Slim," *Business Week,* March 22, 1969, pp. 140–44.

6. " 'Good Products Don't Die,' P&G Chairman Declares," *Advertising Age,* November 1, 1976, p. 8. See also, "Detroit Brings Back the Fast, Flashy Auto to Aid Sluggish Sales," *The Wall Street Journal,* December 9, 1976, p. 1 f.

7. P. H. Nystrom, *Economics of Fashion* (New York: Ronald Press Co., 1958), p. 3; and "Fad, Fashion, or Style?" *Saturday Review,* February 5, 1977, pp. 52–53.

8. M. T. Copeland, *Principles of Merchandising* (New York: A. W. Shaw Co., 1942), p. 167; and Claude R. Martin, Jr., "What Consumers of Fashion Want to Know," *Journal of Retailing;* Winter 1971–72, pp. 65–71.

9. Alfred H. Daniels, "Fashion Merchandising," *Harvard Business Review,* May 1951, pp. 51–60. See also Chester R. Wasson, "How Predictable Are Fashion and Other Product Life Cycles?" *Journal of Marketing,* July 1968, pp. 36–43; and "Troubled Industry (Apparel)" and "Durable Denims," *The Wall Street Journal,* January 11, 1977, p. 1, and February 7, 1977, p. 1.; Dwight E. Robinson, "Style Changes: Cyclical, Inexorable, and Foreseeable," *Harvard Business Review,* November–December 1975, pp. 121–131; and "Playtex: Buying Its Way from Function to Fashion," *Business Week,* July 7, 1980, pp. 40–41.

10. Chester R. Wasson, "What is 'New' About New Products?" *Journal of Marketing,* July 1960, pp. 52–56; Patrick M. Dunne, "What Realy Are New Products?" *Journal of Business,* December 1974, pp. 20–25; and S. H. Britt and V. M. Nelson, "The Marketing Importance of the 'Just Noticeable Difference,' " *Business Horizons,* August 1976, pp. 38–40.

11. *Business Week,* April 22, 1967, p. 120.

12. "Inflation in Product Liability," *Business Week,* May 31, 1976, p. 60; Jane Mallor, "In Brief: Recent Products Liability Cases," *Business Horizons,* October 1979, pp. 47–49; and William L. Trombetta; "Products Liability: What New Court Ruling Means for Management," *Business Horizons,* August 1979, pp. 67–72.

13. *Marketing News,* February 8, 1980; C. Merle Crawford, "Marketing Research and the New-Product Failure Rate," *Journal of Marketing,* April 1977, pp. 51–61.

14. Gustav E. Larson, and Marshall N. Poteat, *Selling the United States Market,* U.S. Department of Commerce, Domestic Commerce Series no. 29 (new series) (Washington, D.C.: U.S. Government Printing Office, 1951), p. 20–21.

15. Adapted from Frank R. Bacon, Jr., and Thomas W. Butler, Jr., *Planned Innovation,* rev. ed. (Ann Arbor, Mich.: Institute of Science and Technology, The University of Michigan, 1980).

16. Bacon and Butler, *Planned Innovation;* Edgar A. Pessemier, *Managing Innovation and New Product Development,* Marketing Science Institute Report No. 75–122. December 1975: Phillip R. McDonald and Joseph O. Eastlack, Jr., "Top Management Involvement with New Products," *Business Horizons,* December 1971, pp. 23–31; William A. Bours III, "Imagination Wears Many Hats," *Journal of Marketing,* October 1966, pp. 59–61; John H. Murphy, "New Products Need Special Management," *Journal of Marketing,* October 1962, pp. 46–49; and E. J. McCarthy, "Organization for New-Product Development?" *Journal of Business of the University of Chicago,* April 1959, 128–32.

17. See T. Levitt, "Innovation Imitation," *Harvard Business Review,* September–October 1966, pp. 63–70.

18. Richard T. Hise and J. Patrick Kelly, "Product Management on Trial," *Journal of Marketing,* October 1978, pp. 28–33; Victor P. Buell, "The Changing Role of the Product Manager in Consumer Goods Companies," *Journal of Marketing,* July 1975, pp. 3–11.

Milt & Joan Mann

12

Place and the development of channel systems

You may build a "better mousetrap" but if it's not in the right place at the right time, it won't do anyone any good.

In the next four chapters, we will look at some of the activities and specialists needed to provide "Place"—and build **channels of distribution:** any series of firms or individuals who participate in the flow of goods and services from producer to final user or consumer.

Place is concerned with building channels of distribution. It involves the selection and use of marketing specialists—middlemen and facilitators—to provide target customers with time, place, and possession utilities. A marketing manager's decisions on Place have long-run effects. They are harder to change than Product, Price, and Promotion decisions. It's hard to move retail stores and wholesale facilities once leases have been signed—and customer movement patterns are settled. And effective working arrangements with middlemen may take several years—and a good deal of money to develop.

Place decisions are important strategic decisions. See Figure 12–1 for a "picture" of the strategic areas we will discuss in the next four chapters. In this chapter, we will briefly discuss Place objectives—and whether direct or indirect channels should be used. But most of the chapter will be concerned with the development and management of indirect channels of distribution.

"IDEAL" PLACE OBJECTIVES SUGGESTED BY GOODS CLASSES

The needs and attitudes of potential target markets should obviously be considered when developing Place. Presumably, people in a particular target market would have similar attitudes and, therefore, could be satisfied with a similar Place system. Their attitudes about urgency to have needs satisfied and willingness

Figure 12–1
Strategic decision areas in
Place

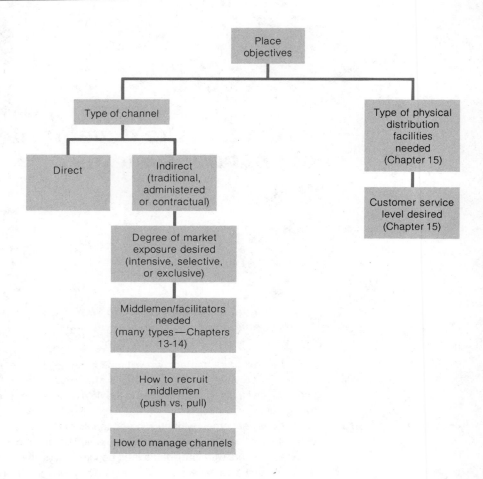

to shop have already been summarized in the goods classes. Now we should be able to use these goods classes to suggest how Place should be handled.

The relationship between goods classes and *ideal place objective* was shown in Figure 10–3 for consumer goods and Figure 10–5 for industrial goods. These figures should be studied carefully—since they set the framework for solving the whole Place problem.

Place system is not automatic

Just as there are no automatic classifications of products, we cannot automatically determine the one best Place arrangement. If there are two or three market segments holding different views of the product, then different Place arrangements may be required as well. Further, Place depends on both (1) what customers would like best and (2) what channel members can provide profitably.

DIRECT CHANNEL SYSTEMS MAY BE BEST, SOMETIMES

Many producers would prefer to handle the whole distribution job themselves. They may have a desire to control large organizations or perhaps it is simply a case of, "If you want a job done right, do it yourself." In any case, there are real advantages in selling directly to the final user or consumer.

When the producer is close to target customers, marketing research is easier. The firm is more sensitive to changes in customer attitudes—and is in a better position to promptly adjust its marketing mix. If aggressive selling effort or special technical service is needed, management can be sure that the sales force receives the necessary training and motivation.

Some products typically have short channels of distribution—and a *direct-to-user channel* is not uncommon. It is not always necessary to use middlemen. On the other hand, it is not always best to "go direct" either.

SPECIALISTS AND CHANNEL SYSTEMS DEVELOP TO ADJUST DISCREPANCIES[1]

Discrepancies require channel specialists

All producers want to be sure that their products reach the final customer. But the assortment and quantity of goods wanted by customers may be different than the assortment and quantity of goods normally produced. Specialists have developed to adjust these discrepancies. Remember that we discussed this briefly in Chapter 1. Now we need to go into more detail—so you will be able to help plan all kinds of channels of distribution.

Discrepancy of quantity—only a few golf balls are wanted

It is economically sensible for a firm to specialize and offer those products that it can produce most efficiently—given its resources and objectives. This specialization usually causes a manufacturer to create a *discrepancy of quantity*. **Discrepancy of quantity** means the difference between the quantity of goods it is economical for a producer to make and the quantity normally wanted by final users or consumers. For example, most manufacturers of golf balls produce large quantities—200,000 to 500,000—in a given time period. See Figure 12–2. The average golfer, however, is interested only in a few balls at a time. For a golf ball manufacturer to deal directly with thousands of golfers would be a big job. Each individual order would have to be mailed to the customer's home (unless he lived right around the street). And then there would be a question of credit.

Some producers want to handle the whole distribution process.

Peter Le Grand

Figure 12–2
Movement of golf balls from manufacturer to consumers (showing discrepancy of quantity produced, and handled by wholesalers and retailers, and desired by consumers*)

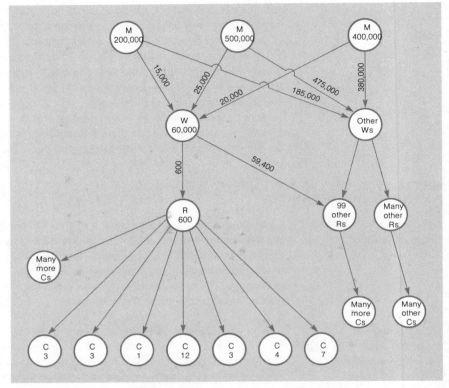

*Number in a circle indicates quantity of golf balls produced, handled, or desired: M = Manufacturer; W = Wholesaler; R = Retailer; C = Consumer.

The solution to this problem would be a local specialist—a retailer—who could fill the various needs of individual consumers for a product—and ease the manufacturer's headaches. We now have one link in a channel of distribution.

But there still might be a great discrepancy between the quantity the manufacturer produced and the quantity each retailer wanted. The solution to this problem would be wholesalers. They could serve perhaps 100 retailers each—another link in our channel of distribution.

If we limit our discussion to the golf ball example alone, however, we only partially explain the development of specialists. Why doesn't the producer simply open wholesale branches and retail outlets—to adjust for these discrepancies in quantity?

Discrepancy of assortment—clubs, bags, and shoes are wanted, too

The typical consumer usually doesn't want a large quantity of each item—but rather an assortment of products. The typical golfer, for example, needs more than golf balls. Golfers want golf shoes, gloves, clubs, a bag, and so forth. Probably they would prefer not to shop around for each item.

While the typical consumer wants an assortment, the typical producer specializes by product—and therefore another discrepancy develops. **Discrepancy of** assortment means the difference between the lines the typical producer makes and the assortment wanted by final consumers or users. It is the job of specialists—wholesalers and retailers—to adjust the discrepancy of assortment—by assembling assortments for their target customers. If retailers offer a wide assortment, they may sell enough so each one's total purchases from wholesalers may be large enough to be an economical transaction for wholesalers. Along with orders for golf balls, for example, they might also place orders for other golf supplies—for delivery at the same time. The wholesalers, in turn, while assembling attractive size orders for their manufacturers, are also able to run profitable businesses—because of the large total sales volumes they get by selling for many manufacturers. See Figure 12–3.

In actual practice, bringing goods to customers is not as simple as in the golf example. Specializing only in golfing products may not achieve all the economies possible in a channel of distribution. Sporting goods retailers usually carry even wider assortments of goods. And they may buy from a variety of wholesalers who specialize by product line. Some of these wholesalers may be supplied by other wholesalers. These complications will be discussed later. The important thing to remember is that discrepancies in quantity *and* assortment cause distribution problems for manufacturers—and explain why specialists develop.

CHANNEL SPECIALISTS ADJUST DISCREPANCIES BY REGROUPING ACTIVITY

It is not always necessary to overcome discrepancies of quantity and assortment, but if it is, *regrouping activities* will be needed.

Figure 12–3
Movement of golf supplies to consumers

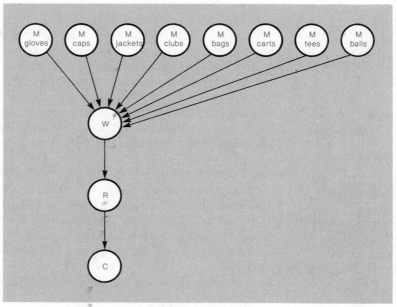

M = Manufacturer; W = Wholesaler; R =Retailer; C = Consumer.

Accumulation helps adjust discrepancies of quantity.

E. Jerome McCarthy

Channel specialists adjust discrepancies with regrouping activities

Regrouping activities involve adjusting the quantities and/or assortments of goods handled at each level in a channel of distribution.

There are four regrouping activities: accumulation, allocation, sorting-out, and assorting. When one or more of these activities is required, a marketing specialist might develop to fill this need.

Adjusting quantity discrepancies by accumulating and allocating

The **accumulation process** involves collecting products from many small producers. This is common for agricultural products—because they are often produced in relatively small quantities. Collecting larger quantities of such products is necessary so that the products can be handled economically further along in the channel. It is especially important for obtaining the lowest transportation rate—by accumulating and shipping goods in truckload or carload quantities.

The **allocation process** involves breaking bulk—that is, breaking carload or truckload shipments into smaller quantities as goods get closer to the final market. Sometimes this even starts at the manufacturer's level—as in our golf example. This process may involve several middlemen. Wholesalers may sell smaller quantities to other wholesalers—or directly to retailers. Retailers continue the allocation process as they "break bulk" to their customers.

Adjusting assortment discrepancies by sorting-out and assorting

Different types of specialists are needed to adjust assortment discrepancies. Two types of regrouping activities may be needed: sorting-out and assorting.

The **sorting-out process** means grading or sorting products. This is a common process for agricultural products. Nature produces what it wants and these products must be sorted into the grades and qualities desired by different target markets.

Sorting-out may create assortments the producers or middlemen won't want. They may be of lower quality—or may not fit into the company's product line at all—and must be distributed to entirely different target markets. Minor defects

Mary McCarthy

in clothing, tires, and sporting goods, for example, may require the marketing manager to offer them—perhaps at little profit—as "seconds" in regular or special outlets.

The **assorting process** means putting together a variety of products to give a target market what it wants. Here, instead of nature producing a mixed assortment which must be sorted out, marketing specialists put together an assortment to satisfy some target market. This usually is done by those close to the final consumer or user—retailers or wholesalers who try to supply a wide assortment of products for the convenience of their customers. An electrical goods wholesaler, for example, may take on a line of lawnmowers or garden products for the convenience of hardware-retailer customers.

Watch for changes

Sometimes, these discrepancies are adjusted badly—especially when there have been rapid shifts in buying habits and preferences. Some producers and marketing specialists continue to offer the same marketing mixes. When this happens, marketing opportunities may open up for new firms—or breakthrough opportunities can occur if a marketing specialist is able to see a "better way." This might include eliminating some specialists. Specialists should develop to adjust discrepancies—*if they must be adjusted*. But there is no point in having middlemen just because "that's the way it has always been done." Start watching for such opportunities.

Figure 12–4
Sales of paperback books are made through many kinds of wholesalers and retailers

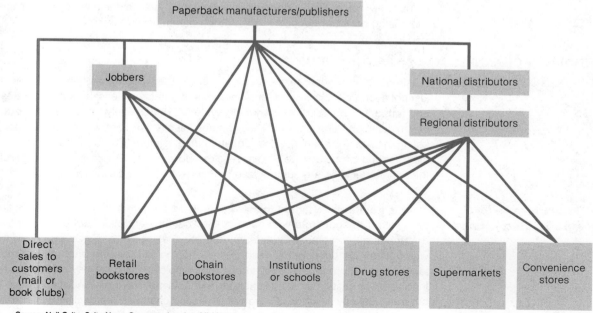

Source: Neil Suits, Suits News Company, Lansing, Michigan.

Channel systems can be complex

Adjusting discrepancies can lead to complex channels of distribution. The possibility for competition between different channels is shown in Figure 12–4. This figure shows the many channels used by manufacturers of paperback books. These can be both consumer goods and industrial goods. This helps explain why some channels would develop. But note that the books go through wholesalers and retailers—independent and chain bookstores, schools, drug stores, supermarkets, and convenience stores. This can cause problems—because these wholesalers supply retailers who are used to different markups. This increases competition—including price competition. And the different markups may lead to open price wars—especially on well-known and branded products.

Dual distribution occurs when a manufacturer uses several competing channels to reach the same target market—perhaps using several middlemen and selling directly himself. This is resented by some established middlemen because they do not appreciate *any* competition—especially competition set up by their own suppliers. But manufacturers often are forced to use dual distribution—because their present channels are doing a poor job or aren't reaching some potential customers.

Sometimes there's not much choice

The paperback example seems to suggest that there are plenty of middlemen around to form almost any kind of channel system. But this isn't true. Sometimes there is only one key middleman serving a market. To reach this market, producers may have no choice—but to use this one middleman.

In other cases, there are no middlemen at all! Then a producer may try to go directly to target customers. If this isn't possible, the product may die because it can't be distributed economically. Some products are not wanted in big enough volume and/or at high enough prices to justify any middlemen providing the regrouping activities needed to reach the potential customers.

INDIRECT CHANNELS MAY BE BEST, SOMETIMES

Although a producer might prefer to handle the whole distribution job, this is just not economically feasible for many kinds of goods—unless the firm integrates and forms its own "vertical marketing system." But typically, producers have to use middlemen—like it or not. They join administered or contractual vertical marketing systems—or simply a traditional channel system. The survival of the firm may depend on what type it joins—or develops. These kinds of systems and their characteristics are summarized in Figure 12–5 and discussed below.

Traditional channel systems are common

In a **traditional channel system**—the various channel members make little or no effort to cooperate with each other. They buy and sell from each other—and that's all. In some very independent channels, buyers may even prefer to wait until sellers desperately need to sell—hoping to force the price down. This leads to erratic production, inventory, and employment patterns that can only increase total costs. Traditional channel members may have their independence—but they may pay for it too. As we will see, such channels are declining in importance—with good reason. But they are still typical in some industries.

Figure 12–5
Types of channel systems

	Traditional	Vertical marketing systems		
		Administered	Contractual	Corporate
Amount of cooperation	Little or none	Some to good	Fairly good to good	Complete
Control maintained by	None	Economic power and leadership	Contracts	Ownership by one company
Examples	Typical channel of "independents"	General Electric, Miller's Beer, O.M. Scott & Sons (lawn products)	McDonald's, Holiday Inn, IGA, Ace Hardware, Super Valu, Coca-Cola, Chevrolet	Florsheim Shoes, Firestone Tire

Corporate channel systems—shorten channels

Some corporations develop their own vertically integrated channel systems. With corporate ownership all along the channel, we can say that the firm is "going direct"—but actually it may be handling manufacturing, wholesaling, *and* retailing—and it is more meaningful to think of it as running a vertical marketing system.

Horizontal integration may be needed

At first, it might seem that **horizontal integration**—the acquiring of firms at the same level of activity—would have little to do with channels of distribution— which are usually shown as vertical. But discrepancies of quantity and assortment must be considered, too. For these reasons, horizontal integration can make sense in a channel discussion.

To have enough sales volume to integrate vertically, a firm might have to integrate horizontally—or expand its horizontal operations by internal expansion. Woolworth's, Kmart, A&P, Safeway Stores, Kroger, Florsheim Shoes, Genesco, and J. C. Penney have expanded or integrated horizontally at the retail level. General Motors Corporation is integrated horizontally at the producer level—with plants and divisions around the country and the world.

Vertical integration is at different levels

Vertical integration is acquiring firms at different levels of activity—for example, two or more successive stages of production or distribution. A retailer might go into wholesaling and perhaps even manufacturing. Some companies are integrated both horizontally and vertically. A&P, Kroger, Genesco, Florsheim Shoes, and J. C. Penney are wholesalers or manufacturers—as well as retailers. A&P, for example, has fish-canning plants. Genesco and Florsheim make their own shoes—and J. C. Penney controls textile plants. Firestone Tire and Rubber Co. has rubber plantations in Liberia, tire plants in Akron, Ohio, and Firestone-label wholesale and retail outlets all over the United States.

There are many possible advantages to vertical integration—stability of operations, assurance of materials and supplies, better control of distribution, better quality control, larger research facilities, greater buying power, and lower executive

Horizontal integration can cut the cost of adjusting quantity and assortment discrepancies.

Mike Voss

overhead. Provided that the discrepancies of quantity and assortment are not too great at each level in a channel—that is, the firms fit together well—vertical integration may be extremely efficient and profitable.[2]

The economies of vertical integration may benefit the consumer, too, through lower prices and better products. Vertical integration brings smooth, routine operation—and can cut costs. Business transactions that once required negotiations between separate firms now are routine requisitions, acknowledgements, and internal accounting transactions.

Administered and contractual systems may work well

The natural advantages of an integrated system have been understood by some progressive marketers. But instead of integrating corporately, they have developed administered or contractual channel systems. In **administered channel systems**—the various channel members informally agree to cooperate with each other. This could include agreements to routinize ordering, standardize accounting, and coordinate promotion efforts. In **contractual channel systems**—the various channel members agree by contract to cooperate with each other. With both of these systems, the members achieve some of the advantages of corporate integration—while retaining some of the flexibility of a traditional channel system.

Norge Division of Borg-Warner Corporation, for example, developed an informal arrangement in an administered channel system—with its independent wholesalers to provide them automatically and continually with a six weeks' inventory of appliances—based on current inventory and sales, plus projected sales. Every week, Norge makes a thorough item-by-item analysis of 125,000–130,000 major appliance units valued at around $18 million. These units are located in many warehouses operated by 87 wholesalers throughout the country. Each week, all this data is analyzed by the president and the managers of distribution, sales, and marketing research (as well as the manufacturing heads)—and plans for production and sales activities for the following weeks are set.

Similar systems have been developed and coordinated by middlemen in the grocery, hardware, and drug industries. In fact, a retailer in these lines almost has to be a member of such a system to survive.

Vertical marketing systems—new wave in the marketplace

In addition to their other virtues, smoothly operating channel systems also appear to be competitively superior.

In the consumer goods field, corporate chains that are at least partially vertically integrated account for about 26 percent of total retail sales; firms aligned with other vertical systems account for an additional 37.5 percent. This gives vertical systems in the consumer goods area a healthy majority of retail sales. Importantly, it appears that such systems will continue to increase their share in the future. The inevitable conclusion is that vertical marketing systems are becoming the major competitive units in the U.S. distribution system.[3]

THE BEST CHANNEL SYSTEM SHOULD ACHIEVE IDEAL MARKET EXPOSURE

The best Place system does not happen automatically. Someone must plan the system—and the Place objectives suggest the kind of system that should be developed as well as how much market exposure will be needed in each geographic area. Although it might seem that all marketing managers would want their products to have maximum exposure to potential customers, this is not true. Some goods classes require much less market exposure than others.

Generally, the **ideal market exposure** should make a product widely enough available to satisfy target customers' needs—but not exceed them. Too much exposure would only increase the total marketing cost.

Three degrees of market exposure may be ideal

We will discuss three degrees of market exposure: *intensive distribution, selective distribution,* and *exclusive distribution.* As we move from intensive to exclusive distribution, we give up exposure in return for some other advantage—including, but not limited to, lower cost.

Intensive distribution is selling a product through all responsible and suitable wholesalers or retailers who will stock and/or sell the product. **Selective distribution** is selling through only those middlemen who will give the product special attention. **Exclusive distribution** is selling through only one middleman in a particular geographic area.

In practice, this means that cigarettes are handled—through *intensive distribution*—by at least a million U.S. outlets, while Rolls Royces or expensive chinaware are handled—through *exclusive distribution*—by only a limited number of middlemen across the country.

Intensive distribution— sell it where they buy it

Intensive distribution is commonly needed for convenience goods and for industrial supplies—such as pencils, paper clips, and typing paper—used by all plants or offices. Customers want such goods nearby.

Manufacturers of new unsought goods that must compete with convenience goods want to achieve intensive distribution. They may not be able to get this degree of exposure, because customers aren't demanding their products and so the channel isn't willing to carry them. Nevertheless, these manufacturers have an intensive distribution policy.

The seller's *intent* is important here. Intensive distribution refers to the *desire* to sell through *all* responsible and suitable outlets. What this means depends on customer habits and preferences. If target customers normally buy a certain product at a certain type of outlet, ideally, we would specify this type of outlet in our Place policies. If customers prefer to buy hardware items only at hardware stores, we would try to sell all hardware stores to achieve intensive distribution. If, however—as it seems today—many customers will buy certain hardware items at any convenient outlet—including drugstores and food stores—an intensive distribution policy logically requires use of these outlets—and more than one channel to reach one target market.

Selective distribution—
sell it where it sells best

Selective distribution covers the broad band of market exposure between intensive and exclusive distribution. It may be suitable for all categories of products. Only the better middlemen—chosen on some basis—are used here. The usual reason for going to selective distribution is to gain some of the advantages of exclusive distribution—while still achieving fairly widespread market coverage.

A selective policy might be used to avoid selling to wholesalers or retailers who (1) have a poor credit rating, (2) have a reputation for making too many returns or requesting too much service, (3) place orders that are too small to justify making calls or providing service, or (4) are not in a position to do a satisfactory marketing job.

Selective distribution is growing in popularity—over intensive distribution—as firms see it is no longer necessary to have 100-percent coverage of the market to justify or support national advertising. Often, the majority of sales come from relatively few customers—while a large number are clearly unprofitable to serve.

Selective distribution may produce greater profits for all channel members—because of the closer cooperation among them. Transactions become more routine—requiring less negotiation in the buying and selling process. Wholesalers and retailers may be more willing to give aggressive promotion to products—if they know they are going to obtain the majority of sales produced through their own efforts. They may carry more stock, wider lines, do more promotion, and provide more service—all of which contribute to increased sales.

Many fashion designers use selective distribution.

Mary McCarthy

Selective distribution makes sense for shopping and specialty goods—and for those industrial goods that need special efforts from channel members. It reduces interchannel competition—and gives each of the members a greater opportunity for profit.

When selective distribution is used by manufacturers, fewer sales contacts have to be made—and fewer wholesalers may be needed. In fact—as in the garment industry—a manufacturer may be able to contact retailers directly if selective distribution is suitable at the retail level.

In the early part of the life cycle of a new unsought good, a manufacturer's marketing manager may have to use selective distribution to encourage enough middlemen to handle the product. The manager wants to get the product out of the unsought category as soon as possible—but can't as long as it lacks distribution. Well-known middlemen may have the power to get such a product introduced—but sometimes on their own terms, which often includes limiting the number of competing wholesalers and retailers.

Exclusive distribution sometimes makes sense

Exclusive distribution is just an extreme case of selective distribution—only one middleman is selected in each geographic area. Besides the various advantages of selective distribution, manufacturers might want to use exclusive distribution to help control prices—and the service offered in a channel.

Unlike selective distribution, exclusive distribution arrangements probably would involve a verbal or written agreement stating that channel members will buy all or most of a given kind of product or product line from a particular firm. In return, these middlemen would be granted the exclusive rights to that product in their territory. Many middlemen are so anxious to get a manufacturer's exclusive franchise that they will do practically anything to satisfy the manufacturer's demands. For example, retailers of shopping goods and specialty goods often try to get exclusive distribution rights in their territories.

But is limiting market exposure legal?

Exclusive distribution is not specifically illegal in the antimonopoly laws. But current interpretation of these laws by the courts gives the impression that almost any exclusive distribution arrangement *could be* interpreted as an injury to some competitor somewhere.

Horizontal arrangements are definitely illegal

The Supreme Court has consistently ruled that horizontal arrangements—among competing retailers, wholesalers, or manufacturers—to limit sales by customer or territory are illegal.

Vertical arrangements may or may not be legal

The legality of vertical arrangements—between producers and middlemen—is not as clear-cut. A 1977 Supreme Court decision reversed its 1967 ruling that vertical relationships that would limit territories or customers were always illegal. Now, possible good effects can be weighed against possible restrictions on competition. It seems likely that vertical relationships will be changing in the future—to ensure that channels work better. There may be less price competition and more service competition—because manufacturers may be able to control their channels, and choose to control price. Under the previous rule, the price-cutting "maverick" who came in after the introductory work had been done could not be controlled. Now that may be changed, as long as some good reasons can be shown for limiting distribution—such as building stronger retailers who can and will offer advertising and sales support and better repair services. Major changes may be seen in the following lines: appliances, television sets, oil, tires, bicycles, hearing aids, beer, and auto accessories.[4]

Caution is suggested

In spite of the recent Supreme Court ruling, it seems that firms should be extremely cautious about entering into any exclusive-dealing arrangements. The antimonopoly rules still apply. The courts can force a change in expensively developed relationships. And, perhaps—even worse—triple damages might be imposed if the courts rule that competition has been hurt. Apparently the law will allow some exclusive arrangements—to permit the introduction of a new product or to enable a new company to enter a market—but these arrangements probably should be short term.

The same cautions probably apply to selective distribution. Here, however, less formal arrangements are typical—and the possible impact on competition is more remote. It now may be more acceptable to carefully select channel members when building a channel system. Refusing to sell to some middlemen, however, should be part of a logical plan which has longer-term benefits. It probably should not be used *only* to control price-cutting middlemen—who seek to buy popular items just when the middlemen who helped build their popularity would like to reap some of the rewards. These situations should be handled when planning channel strategy.

HOW TO RECRUIT MIDDLEMEN

A producer has a special challenge with respect to channel systems: How to ensure that the product reaches the end of the channel. Middlemen—especially retailers—don't have this problem, since they already control that end of the channel.

The two basic methods of recruiting middlemen are *pushing* and *pulling*.

Pushing policy—get a hand from the firm in the channel

Pushing a product through the channels means using normal promotion effort—personal selling and advertising—to help sell the whole marketing mix to possible channel members. This method is common—since these sales transactions are usually between rational, presumably profit-oriented buyers and sellers. The approach emphasizes the importance of building a channel—and securing the whole-hearted cooperation of channel members. The producer—in effect—tries to develop a team that will work well together to get the product to the user.

Pulling policy—makes them reach for it out there

By contrast, **pulling** means getting consumers to ask middlemen for the product. This usually involves highly aggressive promotion to final consumers or users—perhaps using coupons or samples—and temporary bypassing of middle-

"Pushing" a product requires getting cooperation in the channel.

Mary McCarthy

men. If the promotion works, the middlemen are forced to carry the product—to satisfy their customers.

This method—common in the soap industry—may be necessary if many products are already competing in all desired outlets. The channel members will be reluctant to handle a new product. But they should be told about the pulling effort before hand—so they can be ready if the promotion is successful.

Sell the whole mix to channel members

Regardless of how channel cooperation is won, potential channel members must be convinced that the producer knows what is to be accomplished and why. The marketing manager's sales representatives must be able to tell prospective channel members what is expected of them—and how much competition they may get from other channels. And it may be a good idea to spell out how the firm and channel will react to probable competitive marketing mixes. In other words, Place policies must be integrated with the rest of the marketing mix if the whole effort is to be effective.

HOW TO MANAGE CHANNELS

Managing conflict in channels

There are many good reasons for cooperation within a channel system. But there are also reasons why conflicts can arise—and these are and should be anticipated and managed, if possible. There could be horizontal conflicts, for example. Middlemen's territories may overlap—and they may argue over taking each other's business or "predatory pricing." Careful administration of selective or even exclusive distribution policies can be helpful here. But problems should be expected—and we see middlemen forming their own "dealer councils" to discuss their own problems—as well as potential vertical conflicts with their suppliers.

Vertical conflicts can occur also—because policies which may be "good" for the producer—perhaps expanding *his* sales by lowering suggested retail prices (by reducing the middlemen's margins)—may not be quite as "good" for the middlemen. And dual distribution conflicts can easily happen unless channel systems are planned very carefully. This leads us to the channel captain concept.

Channel captain can guide channel planning

We can now see that it is logical that each channel system should act as a unit—perhaps directed by a **channel captain**—a manager who would help direct the activities of a whole channel and try to avoid or solve channel conflicts. But given that there are several firms and marketing managers in a single distribution channel, a big question is: Which marketing manager should be the captain? Also: Is it necessary to have a recognized channel captain?

The concept of a single channel captain is useful—but we must recognize that some channels, including most traditional channels, do not have a recognized captain—since the various firms are not acting as a system. The reason may be lack of leadership. Or members of the system may not understand their interrelationship. Many managers—more concerned with those firms immediately above and below them—seem almost unaware that they are part of a channel.[5]

But, like it or not, firms are interrelated—even if poorly—by their policies. And there is potential for conflict in the buyer-seller relationship. So, it makes sense to try to avoid channel conflicts by planning for channel relations.

Manufacturer or middleman?

In the United States, manufacturers frequently take the initiative in channel relations. Middlemen wait to see what the manufacturer intends to do—and what it wants done. After the manufacturer sets price, promotion, and place policies, middlemen decide whether their roles will be profitable—and whether they want to join in the manufacturer's plans. Middlemen may not play an active role in building the channel—but they must be considered by manufacturers in their planning, if only because the middlemen have the power to say *no.*

Some middlemen dominate their channels

There are large or strategically located middlemen who do take the initiative—especially in foreign markets where there are fewer large manufacturers. Such middlemen may determine the types of products their customers want and then seek out manufacturers—perhaps small ones—who can provide these products at reasonable prices.

Such middlemen may develop their own dealer brands. Or they may handle

Strong middlemen can become channel captains.

Mary McCarthy

manufacturers' brands—but on their own terms. These strong middlemen can even become—in effect—manufacturers. They specify the whole marketing mix for a product and merely delegate production to a factory.

Large middlemen are closer to the final user or consumer—and are in an ideal position to assume the channel captain role. It is even possible that middlemen—especially retailers—may dominate the marketing structure of the future.

Our captain, the producer—for convenience only

We cannot overemphasize the importance of a whole channel system viewing itself in competition with other systems. Without this view, one firm might adopt policies clearly unfavorable to another member of the same system. In the short run, a stronger firm might succeed in forcing its policies by sheer weight of market power. Yet—in the long run—this might lead to the failure, not only of a weaker channel member but of the whole team.

A good example of how *not* to act as channel captain is the manufacturer who loads retailers with excessive inventory. The manufacturer may make money in the short run—but will not be welcomed back by the overloaded firms.

The person or firm that helps direct an integrated system of action is the leader. We will consider that person our channel captain. Identity may change from time to time—depending on the success of product development or promotion efforts, financial reserves, or management personalities—but this does not change the concept or its impact on marketing.

For convenience, we will assume that the channel captain is a producer. Remember, though, that a middleman may play this role, too.[6]

Product-market commitment can guide strategy

It helps to think of the members of a vertical marketing system having a *product-market commitment*—with all members focusing on the same target market at the end of the channel—sharing the various functions in appropriate ways.

The job of the channel captain is to arrange for the performance of the necessary functions in the most effective way. This might be done as shown in Figure 12–6 in a manufacturer-dominated channel system. Here, the manufacturer has

Figure 12–6
How channel strategy might be handled in a manufacturer-dominated system

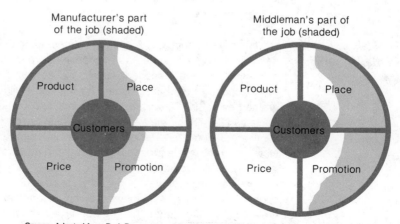

Manufacturer's part of the job (shaded)

Middleman's part of the job (shaded)

Product · Place · Customers · Price · Promotion

Product · Place · Customers · Price · Promotion

Source: Adapted from D. J. Bowersox and E. J. McCarthy, "Strategic Development of Planned Vertical Marketing Systems," in *Vertical Marketing Systems,* ed. Louis Bucklin (Glenview, Ill.: Scott, Foresman & Co., 1970).

selected the target market and developed the product, set the price structure, done some consumer promotion and promotion in the channels, and developed the Place setup. Middlemen are then expected to finish the promotion job in their respective places.

In a middleman-dominated channel system, we would see quite different diagrams. In the extreme, in a channel similar to that dominated by Sears Roebuck, the middleman circle would be almost completely shaded for some products. Manufacturers would be almost solely concerned with manufacturing the product to meet Sears specifications.

New and better ways of organizing channel systems might evolve out of this way of thinking. By rearranging who does what functions, unnecessary and costly duplication may be avoided—and the flow of information and physical goods smoothed and speeded. Franchising organizations—like McDonalds—have grown rapidly in recent years by developing systems in which the members have the same product-market commitment. In the fast-food franchise industry, for example, a successful franchiser will have a training program to teach prospective franchise holders how to carry out the strategy effectively. The importance of not deviating from the basic strategy may be stressed—or even required by contract. If the franchiser shares profits with the franchise holder, it will feel even more strongly about the franchisee carrying out the channel strategy.[7]

A coordinated channel system can help everyone

A channel system in which the members have accepted a common product-market commitment can work very well—even though not everyone in the channel system is strongly market-oriented. As long as someone, say, the channel captain, is market-oriented, it may be possible to win the confidence and support of production-oriented firms—and make the whole channel work effectively.

Small production-oriented producers in Japan or Hong Kong, for example, may become part of an effective channel reaching the U.S. market—if there is a middleman who correctly analyzes market needs and relays them clearly to the producers. The producers may not even know where their products are going—but the system still can be competitive with other systems and profitable to the members.

The channel system may shift and share functions

Ultimately, a successful *channel system* must deliver the goods and services desired by target customers—at reasonable prices. Regardless of whether the marketing manager uses long or short channels, the channels must provide all the functions of marketing. Some buying and selling are required. Transporting, grading or sorting, financing, risk taking, and market information functions are necessary in all channels. These functions can be shifted and shared—but not eliminated. Note that the customer can participate in this shifting and sharing. How costly the whole process is depends on how well the functions are combined *and* how much work has to be done.

If a manufacturer has been very successful in differentiating its mix in the minds of customers, there may not be much for other channel members to contribute—and the manufacturer might not have to offer channel members very attractive returns for their efforts. Auto and appliance manufacturers, for instance,

Channels can be short, but marketing functions can't be eliminated.

H. Armstrong Roberts

offer retailers a lower margin on fast-selling, lower-priced models than on less popular, top-of-the-line models.

Even if a producer takes goods directly to the user, the channel functions are not eliminated. The direct-to-user route may reduce the number of times the functions are performed—but it does not eliminate them. It *may* or *may not* reduce the cost—depending on the situation and the Place objectives. As explained earlier in the chapter, middlemen may be more efficient at performing the regrouping activities—as well as other marketing functions. Middlemen may have some economies of scale which enable them to operate at lower cost. Or they simply may have regular and friendly contacts with the target customers—which will speed the promotion job, while "going direct" might be very difficult. In summary, planning who should do the marketing functions in the channel is an important strategic matter—which should be decided not only on the basis of costs but also on how well Place will fit in with the rest of the marketing strategy.

CONCLUSION

This chapter has discussed the role of Place—and noted that Place decisions are especially important because they may be difficult to change.

Marketing specialists and channel systems develop to adjust discrepancies of quantity and assortment. Their regrouping activities are basic in any economic system—and adjusting discrepancies provides opportunities for creative marketers.

The importance of planning channel systems was discussed—along with the role of a channel captain. It was stressed that channel systems compete with each other—and that vertical marketing systems seem to be winning out in the marketplace.

Channel planning requires deciding on the degree of market exposure desired.

The legality of limiting market exposures should also be considered—to avoid jail or having to undo an expensively developed channel system.

It is channel systems which compete with each other. The "battle of the brands," for example, can be seen in a broader context as only a skirmish in the battle between various channel systems. And, it should be emphasized that producers are not necessarily channel captains. Often, middlemen control or even dominate channels of distribution. The degree of this control must be considered by producers when they decide whether they should try to push or pull their product through a channel system.

QUESTIONS AND PROBLEMS

1. Explain "discrepancies of quantity and assortment," using the clothing business as an example. How does the application of the concept of discrepancies change when coal for sale to the steel industry is considered rather than clothing? What impact does this have on the number and kinds of marketing specialists required?

2. Explain the four steps in the regrouping process with an example from the building supply industry (nails, paint, flooring, plumbing fixtures, etc.). Would you expect many specialists to develop in this industry or would the manufacturers handle the job themselves? What kind of marketing channels would you expect to find in this industry and what functions would be provided by various channel members?

3. In view of the Place objectives suggested for convenience goods, what kinds of specialized marketing institutions would the manufacturer hope to find when he went into the market to implement the objectives? What kinds for shopping goods? For unsought goods? For industrial goods? (In your answer, don't be concerned with whether there are any such institutions, just indicate ideally what you would like to find.)

4. Discuss the Place objectives and distribution arrangements which might be appropriate for the following products (indicate any special assumptions required to obtain a definite answer):
   a. A postal scale for products weighing up to two pounds.
   b. Children's toys: (1) electric train sets costing $20 or more, (2) balloons.
   c. Pneumatic nut tighteners for factory production lines.
   d. Caustic soda used in making paper.

5. If a manufacturer has five different markets to reach, how many channels is he likely to use? If only one, why? If more than one, what sort of problems will this raise?

6. Find an example of horizontal integration within your city. Do there appear to be any particular advantages from this horizontal integration? If so, what are they? If there are no such advantages, how do you explain the integration?

7. Explain how a "channel captain" could help traditional independent firms compete with a corporate (integrated) channel system.

8. Discuss the possibility of retailer-organized integrated channels (either formally integrated or administered) dominating consumer goods marketing.

9. Relate the nature of the product to the degree of market exposure desired.

10. Why would middlemen seek to be exclusive distributors for a product? Why would producers seek exclusive distributors? Would middlemen be equally anxious to obtain exclusive distribution for any type of product? Why or why not? Explain with reference to the following products: cornflakes, razor blades, golf clubs, golf balls, steak knives, hi-fi equipment, and industrial woodworking machinery.

11. Explain the present legal status of exclusive distribution. Describe a situation where exclusive distribution is almost assured to be legal. Describe the nature and size of competitors and the industry, as well as the nature of the exclusive arrangement. Would the exclusive arrangement so described be of any value to the producer or middleman?

12. Discuss the promotion a grocery products manufacturer would need in order to develop appropriate channels and move goods through these channels. Would the

nature of this job change at all for a dress manufacturer? How about for a small producer of installations?

13. Discuss the advantages and disadvantages of either a pushing or pulling policy for a very small manufacturer who is just getting into the candy business with a line of inexpensive candy bars. Which policy would probably be most appropriate? State any assumptions you need to obtain a definite answser.

SUGGESTED CASES

14. **Deller Company.**

15. **Watson Sales Company.**

NOTES

1. Wroe Alderson, "Factors Governing the Development of Marketing Channels," in *Marketing Channels for Manufactured Goods,* ed. Richard M. Clewett (Homewood, Ill.: Richard D. Irwin, 1954), p. 7–9. © 1954 by Richard D. Irwin, Inc.

2. This discussion is based on the advantages and disadvantages discussed in *Vertical Integration in Marketing,* Bulletin 74, ed. Nugent Wedding (Urbana: Bureau of Economic and Business Research, University of Illinois, 1952), pp. 11–12, 30.

3. Bert C. McCammon, Jr., "The Emergence and Growth of Contractually Integrated Channels in the American Economy," a paper presented at the Fall Conference of the American Marketing Association, Washington, D.C., September 2, 1965.

4. "The Court Switches Franchise Signals," *Business Week,* July 11, 1977, pp. 30–31. See also James R. Burley, "Territorial Restriction and Distribution Systems: Current Legal Developments," *Journal of Marketing,* October 1975, pp. 52–56; Louis W. Stern et al., "Territorial Restrictions and Distribution: A Case Analysis," *Journal of Marketing,* April 1976, pp. 69–75; "Soft-Drink Bottlers Choke on FTC Ruling against Exclusive-Territory Restrictions," *The Wall Street Journal,* April 25, 1978, p. 6; Michael B. Metzger, "Schwinn's Swan Song," *Business Horizons,* April 1978, pp. 52–56; and "Justice Takes Aim at Dual Distribution," *Business Week,* July 7, 1980, p. 24–25.

5. Phillip McVey, "Are Channels of Distribution What the Textbooks Say?" *Journal of Marketing,* January 1960, pp. 61–65; but awareness of channel thinking may help spot opportunities. See Bruce Mallen, "Functional Spin-Off: A Key to Anticipating Change in Distribution Structure," *Journal of Marketing,* July 1973, pp. 18–25.

6. Michael Etgar, "Selection of an Effective Channel Control Mix," *Journal of Marketing,* July 1978, pp. 53–58; Michael Etgar, "Intrachannel Conflict and Use of Power," *Journal of Marketing Research,* May 1978, pp. 273–74; and Robert F. Lusch, "Intrachannel Conflict and Use of Power; A Reply," *Journal of Marketing Research,* May 1978, pp. 275–76. For further discussion on channel control, see Robert F. Lusch, "Sources of Power: Their Impact on Intrachannel Conflict," *Journal of Marketing Research,* November 1976, pp. 382–90; William P. Dommermuth, "Profiting from Distribution Conflicts," *Business Horizons,* December 1976, pp. 4–13; Shelby D. Hunt and John R. Nevin, "Power in a Channel of Distribution: Sources and Consequences," *Journal of Marketing Research,* May 1974, pp. 186–93; Louis P. Bucklin, "A Theory of Channel Control," *Journal of Marketing,* January 1973, pp. 39–47; Ronald D. Michman and Stanley D. Sibley, second edition, *Marketing Channels and Strategies,* (Columbus, Ohio: Grid Publishing, Inc.). 1980; and Joseph B. Mason, "Power and Channel Conflicts in Shopping Center Development," *Journal of Marketing,* April 1975, pp. 28–35.

7. Shelby D. Hunt and John R. Nevin, "Full Disclosure Laws in Franchising: An Empirical Investigation," *Journal of Marketing,* April 1976, pp. 53–62; S. D. Hunt and J. R. Nevin, "Tying Agreements and Franchising," *Journal of Marketing,* July 1975, pp. 20–26; Shelby D. Hunt, "The Socioeconomic Consequences of the Franchise System of Distribution," *Journal of Marketing,* July 1972, pp. 32–38; P. Ronald Stephenson and Robert G. House, "A Perspective on Franchising," *Business Horizons,* August 1971, pp. 35–42; and Bruce J. Walker and Michael J. Etzel, "The Internationalization of U.S. Franchise Systems: Progress and Procedures," *Journal of Marketing,* April 1973, pp. 38–46; "Supreme Court Declines Review of Franchise Suit," *The Wall Street Journal,* October 30, 1979, p. 4.

Mike Voss

When you finish this chapter, you should:	1. Understand about retailers planning their own marketing strategies.
	2. Know about the many kinds of retailers which might become members of producers' or wholesalers' channel systems.
	3. Understand the differences among the conventional retailers, and the nonconventional retailers, including those who have accepted the mass merchandising concept.
	4. Understand scrambled merchandising and the "wheel of retailing."
	5. Recognize the important new terms (shown in red).

358

13

Retailing

If the goods aren't sold, nobody makes any money.

Not only retailers—but marketing managers of consumer goods at all channel levels—must understand **retailing**—it covers all of the activities involved in the sale of goods and/or services to final consumers. If the retailing effort is not effective, some products may not be sold at all—and everyone in the related channel system will suffer.

Retailing consists mainly of buying a satisfying assortment of products for some market segments, making these products available at a reasonable price, and often persuading the target customers that the products will satisfy them. The term *merchandising* is often used in retailing circles to cover all these activities.

Note that retailing is *not* concerned with industrial goods—nor the sale of consumer goods in the channels. Retailing is concerned with final consumers.

Place decisions by retailers may determine the success or failure of a product. Therefore, let's look at retailer strategy planning, the nature and development of different kinds of retailers, and likely future trends. We will not cover the promotion and pricing aspects of retailing here, however. These problems are similar for all firms—and are discussed in later chapters.

PLANNING A RETAILER'S STRATEGY

A retailer must plan strategy just like any other marketing manager. He must identify one or more target markets and develop a marketing mix(es) to satisfy his customers. In fact, retailers are so close to final consumers that their strategy planning must be effective—or they will not survive. Unlike manufacturers or wholesalers—who have a chance to "load" middlemen with goods that do not sell—a retailer must be guided by an old maxim: "Goods well bought are half sold."

Figure 13–1 shows some of the strategic decision areas for a retailer. Usually, a retailer is selling more than just one or a few individual goods and services. A whole assortment is offered. So it often is useful to think of the retailer's whole offering as a product. In the case of a service—lawn care or pet grooming, for example—the retailer may even have to "produce" the "product" himself. This provides form utility—which is usually thought of as a function of a manufacturer. So, as you can see, most of what we said in the Product area applies here—and we can extend our thinking beyond why people buy specific products to why they select particular stores. Fortunately, the same line of reasoning discussed earlier applies to why consumers pick retailers.

CONSUMERS HAVE REASONS FOR BUYING IN PARTICULAR STORES

It may seem unnecessary to note that different consumers prefer particular kinds of retailers—but why they do is often ignored by retailers. Retail strategy planners should study customer behavior—and select specific target market(s) when planning their strategies. Just renting an empty store and assuming that customers will come running is all too common among beginning small retailers—and the failure rate is very high. More than three fourths of new retailing ventures die a slow and costly death during the first year.[1] To avoid this fate, a new retailer—or one trying to adjust to changing conditions—should carefully identify target markets and try to understand why they buy where they do.

Economic needs—which store has the lowest price?

The needs listed below are similar to the economic needs for products—and help explain why consumers choose a particular retailer.

1. Convenience.
2. Variety of selection.
3. Quality of products—freshness, purity, craftsmanship, and so on.
4. Courtesy of salespeople.
5. Integrity—reputation for fairness in dealings.
6. Services offered—delivery, credit, returned-goods privileges.
7. Value offered.

Figure 13–1
Strategic decision areas for a retailer

Target customer			
Product	Place	Promotion	Price
Assortment	Location		
Customer service	Facilities		
Hours	Size		
Credit	Layout		

Ignoring customers' needs can lead to failure.

Customers patronize stores that offer the conveniences and services they want—at the lowest prices consistent with all the service they want. Some consumers want a great deal of service—and are willing to pay for it. The conventional thinking in retailing, however, tends to emphasize economic needs—especially the value offered or, more narrowly, low prices.

Emotional needs—the importance of social class

There may also be important emotional reasons for patronizing particular retailers. Some people visit a store because they may meet friends there. Others feel certain stores are distinctive—and wear their labels with pride. As a result, others may patronize these same stores to emulate the leaders. By contrast, they might not patronize another store—because they would be embarrassed to carry home packages bearing the brand of an obviously "inferior" store.

Social class seems to be especially important in consumers' selection of stores. In one study, it was found that a lower-class woman thinks that if she goes into a higher-class store, the clerks and the other customers in the store may "punish" her in various subtle ways. "The clerks treat you like a crumb," one woman said.[2]

Others get an ego boost from shopping in a "prestigious" store. Different stores do seem to attract different classes of customers. Ignorance about relevant dimensions—including the social class dimensions—could lead to serious errors in marketing strategy planning. There is no one "right" answer as to whom a store should appeal. In fact, not all stores have, or want, a distinct image. Some try to avoid creating a class image—because they want to appeal to a wide audience. Macy's, in New York and elsewhere, for example, tries to create a fairly universal appeal. John Wanamaker, in Philadelphia, thinks of itself as a family store with a friendly atmosphere. As a result, it (like Macy's) has departments that carry some very expensive merchandise—and others that handle goods for the masses.

Goods classes help understand store types

Retail strategy planning can be simplified by recalling our earlier discussion of consumer behavior and the consumer goods classes—convenience goods, shopping goods, and specialty goods.

We can define three types of stores: *convenience* stores, *shopping* stores, and *specialty* stores. But it is very important to see that these classifications refer to the *customer's* image of the store.

A **convenience store** is a convenient place to shop—either centrally located "downtown" or "in the neighborhood." Such stores attract many customers because they are so handy.

Shopping stores attract customers from greater distances because of the width and depth of their assortments. Stores selling clothing, furniture, or household appliances are usually thought of as shopping stores.

Specialty stores are those for which customers have developed a strong attraction. For whatever reasons—service, selection, or reputation—some customers will consistently buy convenience, shopping, and specialty goods at these stores.

Store type sets strategy guidelines

A retailer's strategy planning must consider potential customers' attitudes toward both the product and the store. Classifying stores by type of product—as shown in Figure 13–2 helps to understand this complete view. It is important to see, however, that different market segments might see or use a particular store differently. Also, a specific store might try to satisfy the people in two or more boxes. A supermarket, for example, might try to be a convenience store for convenience goods—by adding a fast checkout line. Further, some specific stores are hard to classify because the managers have not focused their efforts—trying instead to cater to "everyone."

When a retailer is planning a new strategy—or trying to fine-tune a store's present strategy—he will obtain a deeper understanding of the market by estimat-

Figure 13–2
How customers view store-product combinations

Product type \ Store type	Convenience	Shopping	Specialty
Convenience	Will buy any brand at most accessible store	Shop around to find better service and/or lower prices	Prefer store. Brand may be important
Shopping	Want some selection but will settle for assortment at most accessible store	Want to compare both products and store mixes	Prefer store but insist on adequate assortment
Specialty	Prefer particular product but like place convenience too	Prefer particular product but still seeking best total product and mix	Prefer both store and product

Source: Adapted from Louis Bucklin, "Retail Strategy and the Classification of Consumer Goods," *Journal of Marketing,* January 1963, pp. 50–55.

Convenience stores are located downtown or in the heart of neighborhoods.

Peter Le Grand

ing the relative size of each of the boxes shown in Figure 13–2. And by identifying which competitors are satisfying which market segments, the retailer may see that some boxes are already filled. In fact, the manager may find that both he and his competitors are all charging head-on for the same customers—and completely ignoring others. He may see an opportunity for building a new strategy—as Liz Gray did.

Liz Gray opens a convenience store for shopping goods

Liz Gray—a buyer in a local department store—is considering opening her own women's clothing shop. She finds most of the competitors are shopping or specialty stores—carrying the kinds of shopping goods Liz is considering offering. On further analysis, she finds that the convenience store–shopping goods market has been neglected by her competitors. Finding an opening in a small shopping center where no competitors are located, Liz decides to avoid competing directly in the other markets. She chooses to offer a reasonable selection of shopping goods items—at her convenient location. Prices will have to be reasonable. But since there will be no direct competition, a "sale" atmosphere will not be necessary. Further, she won't have to carry deep assortments of high-fashion items. Instead, a selection of smart—but not "faddy"—blouses, skirts, sweaters, and accessories will meet the needs of this market segment. Of course, the demographics of the nearby area will have to be considered when selecting particular items—but the store-goods classes helped set the guidelines for her strategy.

The store-goods classes are also important to manufacturers and wholesalers. If, for example, the majority of a manufacturer's target customers patronize convenience stores, then intensive distribution may be necessary. Similarly, if a large group of customers treat particular stores or a chain as specialty stores, manufacturers will have to be in those stores if they want to reach those customers. Unfortunately, if those stores happen to use dealer brands, the manufacturers may be blocked from those customers. Some customers see Sears Roebuck as a specialty store, for example, and regularly buy their paint, hardware, and major appliances at Sears—without shopping at other stores. Competing manu-

facturers simply have to accept the Sears' position—and cater to other markets.
While our store classes can help guide strategy planning, other dimensions of retailers are useful too. So let's go on to see what kinds of retailers are already competing in the marketplace—and how they have developed.

NUMBER AND SIZE OF RETAILERS ALREADY COMPETING

There are lots of retailers—in part because it is easy to enter retailing. Kids can open and close a lemonade stand in one day. A more serious retailer can rent an empty store and be in business with relatively little capital in a week or two. In 1977 there were about 1.9 million retailers compared to about 380,000 wholesalers and 360,000 manufacturers.

Lots of small retailers, but . . .

The large number of retailers might suggest that retailing is a field of small businesses. To an extent, this is true. In 1977, the date of the last census, 45.8 percent of the nation's retailers accounted for only 4.2 percent of total retail sales—grossing less than $100,000 each annually.

Yet in total, retailing is big business. Retail sales in 1977 totaled $723 billion—making retailing a key element in the U.S. economy. The larger retail stores—those selling more than $1 million annually—such as supermarkets—do most of this business. Only 7.4 percent of the retail stores are this big, yet they account for almost 62 percent of all retail sales. See Table 13–1.

The many small retailers can't be ignored—especially because they frequently cause difficult problems for producers and wholesalers. Their large number—and relatively small sales volume—make working with them expensive. They often require separate marketing mixes. Yet these stores do reach many consumers—and often are valuable channel members.

Table 13–1
Retail trade, sales by size of establishment (United States, 1977)

Sales size of establishments	Establishments			Sales volume		
	Number (000)	Percent	Cumulative percent	Sales ($000,000)	Percent	Cumulative percent
Total, all establishments..........................	1,885			723,134		
Total, establishments operated for the entire year	1,582	100.0		683,340	100.0	
Annual sales of:						
$5,000,000 or more...........................	22	1.4	1.4	216,753	31.7	31.7
$2,000,000 to $4,999,999	40	2.5	3.9	126,553	18.5	50.2
$1,000,000 to $1,999,999	56	3.5	7.4	77,868	11.4	61.6
$ 500,000 to $ 999,999	127	8.0	15.4	87,619	12.8	74.4
$ 300,000 to $ 499,999	171	10.8	26.2	65,854	9.6	84.0
$ 100,000 to $ 299,999	443	28.0	54.2	80,917	11.8	95.8
$ 50,000 to $ 99,999	246	15.5	69.7	17,722	2.6	98.4
$ 30,000 to $ 49,999	143	9.0	78.7	5,607	0.8	99.2
$ 20,000 to $ 29,999	88	5.6	84.3	2,145	0.3	99.5
$ 10,000 to $ 19,999	110	7.0	91.4	1,562	0.2	99.8
Less than $10,000	134	8.5	100.0	742	0.1	100.0

Source: *1977 Census of Retail Trade*, Table 1, p. 1–8.

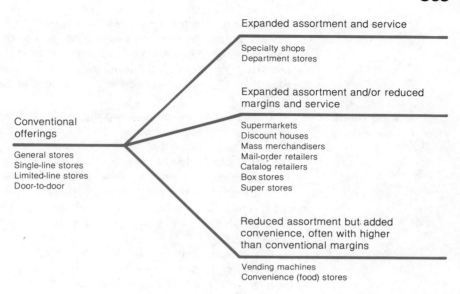

Figure 13–3
Types of retailers and the
nature of their offerings

Expanded assortment and service

Specialty shops
Department stores

Expanded assortment and/or reduced
margins and service

Conventional
offerings

General stores
Single-line stores
Limited-line stores
Door-to-door

Supermarkets
Discount houses
Mass merchandisers
Mail-order retailers
Catalog retailers
Box stores
Super stores

Reduced assortment but added
convenience, often with higher
than conventional margins

Vending machines
Convenience (food) stores

EVOLUTION OF CONVENTIONAL RETAILERS

A variety of retail institutions has developed over the years—to meet customer needs. In the following sections, we will discuss why and how present retailers have evolved—and why there are so many stores—especially so many small stores.

Actually, there is constant change in the retailing area. So a solid understanding of the *why* of various kinds of retailers will help you plan better marketing strategies now—and in the future.

To get an accurate feel for the various kinds of retailers, try to picture their profit and loss statements. To survive, retailers must consistently show at least some profit—and it is not trivial to note that typical net profit margins on sales are very slim—from 0 to 5 percent. This is a competitive area which seems to be getting even more competitive—and less profitable. This means that retailers should develop their marketing strategies carefully.

Conventional retailers
are a durable lot

Figure 13–3 names some types of retailers which have evolved and survived—by finding a niche in our competitive marketplace. We will start by discussing the conventional retailers—and then go on to show that other types have developed by modifying their offerings.

It is important to see that conventional retailers have been around for a long time—and are still with us. They are a durable lot—and clearly satisfy some people's needs. Usually these conventional retailers start with one person or family running the operation. The breadth of assortment is limited by their capital—and ability to control the whole operation by themselves. Usually such retailers focus on a single or limited line of merchandise—so they can carry the minimum assortment which will satisfy their potential customers. If they face much competition, however, they may expand assortment—or specialize further—trying to keep costs down and prices up by avoiding competition on identical products. These conventional retailers are found in every community—but they face continuing pressure from retailers who have modified their mixes in the various ways suggested in Figure 13–3. Let's have a closer look at these conventional retailers.

Door-to-door retailers—effective for unsought goods

Door-to-door selling means going directly to the consumer's home. It is an old—but still effective—method inherited from the Yankee peddler. It accounts for less than 1 percent of retail sales—but it may be especially useful during the introductory stage of the product life cycle, for sales of unsought goods, or during a recession—when goods need a special push.

This is an expensive method of selling. Markups range from 30 to 50 percent—often higher. Overhead costs are lower—because the door-to-door retailer has no store—but travel is costly and the number of personal contacts possible in a day is limited.

Great success is possible with this method—if it meets the needs of some segments of the market. Vacuum cleaners may be an unsought good for some people, for example, and no store type will reach them. If a demonstration is needed to show how a vacuum cleaner will meet a household's needs, then door-to-door selling can do it. Electrolux has sold vacuum cleaners door-to-door since its introduction from Sweden decades ago. And it still claims the top position in the vacuum cleaner business—selling all its cleaners at list price! Fuller Brush and most encyclopedia companies use this approach successfully. And is there anyone who hasn't heard Avon ring the doorbell?

General stores were popular in the country

General stores sell anything the local consumers will buy in enough volume to justify carrying it. Before the Civil War, they were the main type of retailer in this country.

The main advantage of the general store is its convenient location for some target customers. It sometimes serves, too, as a social center and a collecting point for agricultural produce.

Such stores are still found at rural crossroads and in some small towns—carrying mainly food and other convenience goods—but there are so few now that the U.S. Bureau of Census no longer reports them as a separate category.

Single-line, limited-line stores are being squeezed

Single-line or limited-line stores specialize in certain lines rather than the broad assortment carried by general stores. They became common after the Civil War—when the continuing expansion in the volume and variety of consumer goods began to make it impossible for the general store to offer depth and breadth in all its traditional lines. Some stores began specializing in dry goods, apparel, furniture, or groceries. Some stores specialize not only in a single line—such as food—but also in a *limited line* within the broader line. For example, within the food line a store might carry *only* meat, staples, fresh produce, or bakery goods.

Most retail stores are single- and limited-line stores—specializing in groceries, or hardware, or gasoline, or clothing, or sporting goods—and this probably will continue as long as customer demands are varied and large enough to support

Kenneth Yee

these stores. The main advantage of a single-line—and especially a limited-line—store is that it can satisfy some target markets better. Perhaps it can achieve a specialty-store status, by adjusting its marketing mix—including store hours, credit, and product assortment—to suit certain customers.

Such stores face a major disadvantage in having to stock in depth some slow-moving items that must be carried to satisfy each store's target market. Further, many of these stores have the disadvantage of being small—with high expenses relative to sales. Stores of this type have traditionally applied the retailing philosophy of "buying low and selling high." They are the "conventional" retailers who have been—and probably will continue to be—squeezed by newer forms of retailing.

Convenience (food) stores must have the right assortment

Convenience (food) stores are a variation of the conventional limited-line food stores. Instead of expanding their assortment, convenience stores severely limit the assortment to those "pick-up" or "fill-in" items like bread, milk, ice cream, or beer. Stores such as 7–11 or Majik Markets fill needs between major shopping trips to a supermarket. They are offering convenience—not assortment—and often charge prices 10–20 percent higher than those charged at nearby supermarkets. Apparently this price differential is more than offset by the convenience offered—because these stores continue to spread all over the country. Further, the higher margins—coupled with faster turnover of a narrow assortment—makes them much more profitable than supermarkets. They net approximately 4 percent on sales—rather than 1 percent earned by supermarkets! This helps explain why the number of such stores increased from 2,500 in 1960 to 33,000 in 1980.[3]

Speciality shops usually sell shopping goods

A **specialty shop**—a type of limited-line store—usually is small, with a distinct "personality." It aims at a carefully defined market segment by offering a unique product assortment, knowledgeable sales clerks, and better service. For example, a small chain of specialty shops has developed to satisfy the growing market of "joggers." The clerks are runners themselves. They know the sport—and are eager to explain the advantages of different types of running shoes to their customers. These stores also carry a selection of books on running—as well as clothes for the jogger. They even offer a discount to customers who are members of local track teams.

Usually specialty shops deal in special types of shopping goods—such as high-quality sporting goods, exclusive men's clothing, high-fashion dresses, clothes in special sizes, and women's shoes.[4]

Using the term "specialty" should not cause us to confuse specialty *shops,* specialty *stores,* and specialty *goods.* A successful specialty shop might achieve a specialty-store status among a small group of target customers—but the owner probably would be more satisfied to be well known among a larger group for the distinctiveness of its line and the special services offered. Similarly, a specialty shop might carry specialty goods—but only if those goods fit into its narrow line and they could benefit by the additional service and display the specialty shop offers. For example, "The Kitchen Korner"—a specialty *shop*—might become a specialty *store* for some gourmet-cook customers. And the owner of

Mary McCarthy

"The Kitchen Korner" might be willing—because it fits into "The Kitchen Korner's" line—to carry a well-respected brand of pots and pans which are considered specialty *goods* by the gourmet-cook customers.

The specialty shop's major advantage is that it caters to certain types of customers whom the management and sales people come to know well. This familiarity simplifies buying, speeds turnover, and cuts the costs due to obsolescence and style changes.

Specialty shops probably will continue to be a part of the retailing scene as long as customers have varied tastes—and the money to satisfy them.

Department stores are many limited-line stores and specialty shops

Department stores are larger stores—organized into separate departments. They usually handle a wide variety of products—such as women's ready-to-wear and accessories, men's and boys' wear, textiles, housewares, and house furnishings.

The distinguishing characteristic of department stores is that they are organized into separate departments—which are limited-line stores and specialty shops—for promotion, service, and control.

Some specialty shops—grown large and departmentalized—appear to be department stores—and we will treat them as such. As a rule, however, specialty shops do not carry complete lines. They frequently omit housewares, house furnishings, and furniture—and prefer instead to emphasize depth of line and distinctiveness in the lines they do choose to carry. Neiman-Marcus of Dallas, for example, is departmentalized—but insists it is a specialty shop.[5]

Department stores generally try to cater to customers seeking shopping goods. Originally, they were downtown—close to other department stores—and convenient to many potential customers. Historically, this close grouping developed at the intersection of major railroad and streetcar routes—the main forms of urban public transportation in the 19th century, when the major U.S. department stores began.

Since World War II, many downtown department stores have opened suburban branches—usually in shopping centers—to serve the middle- and upper-income groups who moved to the suburbs.

The downtown stores have suffered—but some are making efforts to renew the appeal of their traditional downtown locations by (1) carrying wide lines in the major shopping goods items for which they have long been famous; (2) attracting the trade of conventioneers and tourists; and (3) appealing to low-income groups remaining in the residential neighborhoods near the downtown area. New urban trends—including downtown apartment units, urban redevelopment, and improved mass transit—may save some of the big downtown stores.[6]

Department stores are often looked to as the retailing leaders in a community. Leaders, first, because they seem to be so generous with customer services—including credit, merchandise return, delivery, fashion shows, and Christmas displays. And leaders also because of their size. In 1977, the annual sales volume of U.S. department stores averaged about $9 million—compared to about $390,000 for the average retail store. The biggest—Macy's, May Company and Dayton-Hudson—each top $500 million in sales annually. Although department stores account for less than 1 percent (8,807) of the total number of retail stores, they had almost 11 percent of total retail sales in 1977.

Certain department stores have a strong grip on their market. Some market segments can be reached *only* through particular department stores. These stores have achieved a strong specialty-store status—and their buyers can make it tough on suppliers. In other words, instead of playing the role of channel captain—because of their strength—they simply demand all the concessions they can get. These might include restricting suppliers from selling preferred lines to the store's competitors—although this is illegal under the antimonopoly laws.[7]

Mail-order retailing reaches out

Mail-order retailing—allows "shopping by mail"—using mail-order catalogs to let customers "see" the offerings, and delivering the purchases by mail or truck. It can be very useful for reaching widely scattered markets—with products that otherwise might be unsought. Some mail-order houses aim at narrow target markets—selling only electronic components, phonograph records, or health foods. Others—such as the big mail-order houses—offer both convenience goods and shopping goods. These houses have continued to grow with the U.S. economy—numbering almost 11,000 firms in 1977. Yet they have never achieved more than 1.3 percent of total U.S. sales—and in 1977, they were down to about 1 percent.

Some of the early mail-order houses—including Sears Roebuck and Montgomery Ward—were started after the Civil War, as railroads and postal service expanded. They were so successful with their low prices and wide variety that some conventional retailers sought laws to restrict them.

Today, mail-order selling isn't what it used to be. The emphasis is no longer only on low-price selling by mail. There is an increasing emphasis on high-fashion women's and girls' wear—and luxury items. Some companies offer catalog *stores,* telephone service, convenient pickup depots, and delivery—to make it easier

Courtesy Spiegel, Inc.

to buy from their catalogs. The big mail-order houses started all this—but now department stores and limited-line stores are seeing the profit possibility and selling by mail, too. Not only can they get additional business this way—but costs may be lower because they can use warehouse-type buildings and limited sales help. They may even be able to offer wider selections—at lower prices—than conventional retailers. Sears' mail-order and catalog operation typically undersells its own retail stores.

Vending machines are convenient

Automatic vending is selling and delivering products through vending machines. Although vending machine growth has been spectacular, automatic vending sales are only about 1.5 percent of total U.S. retail sales. But in certain lines, the vending machine is an important factor—16 percent of all cigarettes sold in the United States, 20 percent of the candy bars, and 25 percent of the bottled soft drinks are sold through machines.[8] For some target markets, this retailing method cannot be ignored.

The major stumbling block in automatic vending is high cost of operation. The machines are relatively expensive for the volume they sell—and they require much stocking time and repair labor. Marketers of similar nonvended products can operate profitably on a margin of about 20 percent—while the vending industry requires about 41 percent to break even. So they must charge higher prices.[9] If costs come down—and consumers' desire for convenience rises—we may see more growth in this method of retailing.

EVOLUTION OF NEW, MASS MERCHANDISING RETAILERS

Mass merchandising is different than conventional retailing

So far we have been describing retailers primarily in terms of the *number of lines carried* and their *physical facilities.* This is conventional thinking about retailing. But there are some important kinds of retailers that cannot be adequately described this way. Supermarkets and discount houses, for example, can be shoved into the single-line or limited-line category. But by so doing, we would miss their essence—just as some conventional retailers did when these stores first appeared.

Automatic vendors have to charge higher prices to break even, but consumers are willing to pay for the convenience.

Kenneth Yee

Conventional retailers believe in a fixed demand for a territory and have a "buy low and sell high" philosophy. Some modern retailers reject these notions. They have accepted the **mass merchandising concept**—which says that retailers should offer low prices to get faster turnover and greater sales volumes—by appealing to larger markets. Some mass merchandising retailers were started by nonretailers willing to depart from the conventional wisdom of existing retailers. To better understand what mass merchandising is, let's look at its evolution from the development of supermarkets and discounters to the modern mass merchandisers—like Kmart.

Supermarkets started the move to mass merchandising

A **supermarket** is a large store specializing in groceries—with self-service and wide assortments. As late as 1930, most food stores were relatively small single- or limited-line operations. In the early depression years, some innovators felt that price appeals could move goods in volume. Their early experiments in vacant warehouses were an immediate success. Conventional retailers—both independents and chains—quickly copied the innovators—emphasizing lower prices and self-service.[10]

According to the Food Marketing Institute, $1 million is considered the minimum annual sales volume for a store to be called a supermarket. In 1980, there were over 33,000 supermarkets—about 13 percent of all food stores—and they handled about 73 percent of total food store sales. Today, supermarkets are beginning to reach the saturation level—yet new ones still do well when they are wisely located.[11]

Supermarkets sell convenience goods—but in quantity. Their target customers don't want to shop for groceries every day—as was common in presupermarket times. To make volume shopping easier, supermarkets generally offer free parking facilities.

Present-day supermarkets are planned for maximum efficiency. Some carefully analyze the sales and profit of each item—and allocate space accordingly. This approach helps sell more goods in less time, reduces the investment in inventory, makes stocking easier, and reduces the cost of handling goods. Such efficiency is essential. Grocery competition is keen—and net profits after taxes in grocery supermarkets usually run a thin 1 percent of sales—*or less!*

Box stores reduce assortment and prices

A recent development in the food industry is the **box store**—a small-supermarket-sized store which carries a reduced assortment of staples—selling them out of shipping boxes—at much lower prices. These are relatively bare, plain stores—catering to the price-conscious. They don't offer a full assortment of groceries or all the popular brands. In fact, they may have few or no nationally known brands. Usually the products are fast moving canned and boxed "commodities" which some supermarkets are now offering as generic brands.

The box stores do not carry perishable merchandise, fresh fruits and vegetables, meats, milk or any other items which require special facilities or care. In other words, this is a "bare bones" low-overhead type of operation. The early supermarkets started this way during the Great Depression of the 1930s. But they soon expanded beyond basic canned and boxed goods. Now, the box store

Box stores offer little variety but much lower prices.

Mary McCarthy

seems to be a well-planned attempt to take *some* of their "commodity" business—moving large volumes at low prices.[12]

Catalog showroom retailers preceded discount houses

Catalog showroom retailers sell several lines out of a catalog and display showroom—with backup inventories. Before 1940, these retailers were usually wholesalers who also sold at retail to friends and members of groups—such as labor unions or church groups. In the 1970s, however, these operations expanded rapidly. Using catalogs intended for consumer use and large showrooms with backup inventories, the average catalog retailer can offer lower prices and deliver almost all the items in its catalog from its backroom warehouse. Price is the important variable here—and big price savings can be had in jewelry, gifts, luggage, and the small-appliance areas where these retailers have tended to specialize.[13]

The early catalog operations did not bother the conventional retailers—because they were not well publicized and accounted for a small portion of total retail sales. If they had moved ahead aggressively—as the current catalog retailers are doing—the retailing scene might be different. But, instead, discount houses developed.

Discount houses upset some conventional retailers

Right after World War II, some retailers moved aggressively beyond offering discounts to selected customers—or those who happened to hear about their catalog operations. These **discount houses** offered "hard goods" (cameras, TVs, appliances) at substantial price cuts—to customers who would go to the discounter's low-rent store, pay cash, and take care of any service or repair problems. They were much more open about their operations. Some even advertised widely in newspapers—and on radio and television. These retailers sold at perhaps 20–30 percent off the list price being charged by conventional retailers—for similar or the same nationally advertised brands. The emphasis in these discount houses was on cutting prices to get fast turnover.

In the early 1950s—with war shortages finally over—manufacturers' brands became more available and a buyers' market developed. The discount houses were able to get any brands they wanted—and to offer fuller assortments. At this stage, many discounters "turned respectable"—moving to better locations and offering more services and guarantees. They began to act more like regular retailers—but kept their prices lower than conventional outlets, to keep turnover high.

Conventional retailers fight back by cutting prices

The discount house strategy was a new approach to retailing. Faced with discount house competition, some conventional hard goods retailers resorted to price cutting on highly competitive items. But these purely defensive tactics are just that—price cutting—while discounters make a standard practice of selling everything with lower than usual markups.

More than simple price cutting is involved in a successful discount house, however. Careful buying with the firm's target markets in mind is essential—to assure high turnover. A major discounter's first venture into apparel sales flopped, for instance, because its buyers were appliance experts—who knew nothing about fashions. The discount approach worked only after they hired experienced fashion buyers from department stores.

Mass merchandisers are more than discounters

The **mass merchandisers** are large, self-service stores with many departments—which emphasize "soft goods" (housewares, clothing, and fabrics) but still follow the discount house's emphasis on lower margins to get faster turnover. Mass merchandisers—for example, Kmart and Woolco—have checkout counters in the front of the store and little or no sales help on the floor. This is in contrast to more conventional retailers—such as Sears and Penney's—who still offer some service and have sales stations and cash registers in each department. The more conventional retailer may try to replenish sizes and stocks in lines it carries, whereas some mass merchandisers make little effort in this regard. They want to move merchandise—fast—and are less concerned with continuity of lines and assortment.

Recently, some of the mass merchandisers have moved into groceries. These "discount" stores are a real threat to their competitors. They are selling more food—among other things—per store than the chain supermarkets!

There are over 5,000 of these mass merchandisers. The average one has nearly 60,000 square feet of floor space. This is three to four times the size of the average supermarket.[14]

The mass merchandisers are usually operated as chains. Some were started by relative newcomers to retailing. Two important competitors, however, are Kmart and Woolco. Kmarts are 100,000-square-foot, full-line department stores that sell top-quality manufacturers' and dealer brands at moderate prices.

The mass merchandisers may have already reached saturation levels in many markets. Profits are declining and some have gone bankrupt. The number expanded so rapidly in some areas that they were no longer taking customers from conventional retailers—but from each other.[15]

Seeing the declining potential in major metropolitan areas, Kmart has started moving into smaller towns with a slightly smaller Kmart. This has really upset some small-town merchants who felt they were safe from the competitive "rat-race" that their big-city cousins had to contend with.

Consumers appreciate mass merchandisers

The success of mass merchandisers shows that at least some customers weren't fully satisfied with the conventional retailers' strategies—clearly, there is a demand for this kind of store. Mass merchandisers probably will continue to use their present methods—because they see these methods as "conventional" for their type of operation.

Super-stores meet all routine needs

Some supermarkets and mass merchandisers have moved toward becoming **super-stores**—very large stores that try to carry not only foods, but all goods and services which the consumer purchases *routinely*. Such a store may *look* like a mass merchandiser, but it is different in concept. A super-store—or "hyper-market"—is trying to meet *all* the customer's routine needs—at a low price.

The super-store concept is much bigger than the supermarket or mass merchandiser concept. The super-store has to carry not only foods—but also personal care products, alcoholic beverages, some apparel products, some lawn and garden products, gasoline—and services such as laundry, dry cleaning, shoe repair, check cashing, and bill paying. Some firms have already moved in this direction—and it is estimated that if the trend continues, the food-oriented supermarkets may suffer badly. Their present buildings and parking lots are not large enough to convert to super-stores. Super-stores could make half of the present supermarkets obsolete in the near future.[16]

WILL SCRAMBLED MERCHANDISING CONTINUE?

Who's selling what to whom?

Conventional retailers tend to specialize by product line. But current retailing can be called **scrambled merchandising**—retailers carrying *any* product lines which they feel they can sell profitably. Mass merchandisers are selling groceries—while supermarkets and "drug stores" are selling anything they can move in volume.

The wheel of retailing keeps rolling

What is behind this scrambled merchandising? The **wheel of retailing theory** says that new types of retailers enter the market as low-status, low-margin, low-price operators and then—if they are successful—evolve into more conventional retailers offering more services—with resulting higher operating costs and higher prices. Then they are threatened by new low-status, low-margin, low-price retailers—and the wheel turns again.

Early department stores began this way. Then they became higher priced—and built basement departments to serve the more price-conscious customers. The 5-and-10-cent store and the mail-order house were developed on a price basis—as were the food chains, economy apparel chains, drug chains, and the automotive accessory chains which developed during the 1920s. The supermarket, in turn, was started with low prices and little service.

*Some innovators start
with high margins*

The wheel theory, however, does not explain all major retailing developments. Vending machines entered retailing as high-cost, high-margin operations. Convenience food stores are high-priced. The branch trend of the department stores—and shopping centers—have not been low-price oriented. On the contrary, they sometimes have been high-price operations. Nor have all innovations been immediate successes. Some of the first department stores failed—while vending machine history is filled with failures.

The probable cause of these exceptions has been summarized very well by Hollander:

> . . . retailers are constantly probing the empty sectors of competitive strategy with many failures until someone uses exactly the right technique at the right time. In at least some cases, the merchant prince's skill may have been in judging opportunities rather than in originating techniques.[17]

*Customers' needs and
preferences help explain
scrambled
merchandising*

A clearer view of the present retailing scene is presented in Figure 13–4—which suggests that three consumer-oriented dimensions affect the types of retailers customers choose. The dimensions are: (1) width of assortment desired; (2) depth of assortment desired, and (3) a price/service combination. Within this three-dimensional market, it is possible to position most existing retailers.

Figure 13–4, for example, suggests the *why* of vending machines. Some people—in the front upper left-hand corner—have a strong need for a specific item—and are *not* interested in the width of assortment, the depth of assortment, *or* the price.

On the other hand, some people have very specific needs and would like to be able to select from a very deep assortment—and a range of price alternatives

Figure 13–4
A three-dimensional view of the market for retail facilities and the probable position of some present offerings

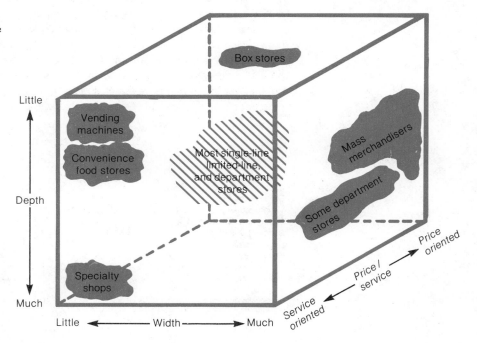

as well. Various kinds of specialty shops fill these needs. This market can be seen in the lower left front corner of Figure 13–4.

At another extreme, if a customer wanted to shop for a broad assortment of items with reasonable depth, he might choose a large department store or a mass merchandiser—depending upon his price/service preferences.

Drawing a three-dimensional picture is easy—but it does not guarantee that all parts of the market have the same number of people to be satisfied. In fact, it is quite possible that some parts would be almost empty. This emphasizes the importance of retailers focusing on market needs *before* developing their offerings.

Product life-cycle concept helps, too

People's needs and preferences help explain why the various kinds of retailers developed. But we have to apply the product life-cycle concept to retailers to understand fully the evolutionary process. The merchant prince may exploit new opportunities for a while—but if his judgment is correct, he can count on fairly prompt imitation and a squeeze on his profits.

Some conventional retailers are far along in their cycle. Some have already declined—while current innovators are still in the market growth stage. See Figure 13–5.

The retailers who are confused by the scrambling going on around them don't see this evolutionary process—and don't understand that some of their more successful competitors are aiming at different market segments—rather than just selling products. These product-oriented retailers can get away with focusing on their internal problems during the early stages of the life cycle of particular kinds of retail firm. But as each market gets saturated with that particular kind of retailer, market maturity sets in and profits are squeezed. Then they, too, may blindly scramble for more profitable opportunities.

It's no surprise to find that some modern success stories in retailing are among firms which aim at needs along the edges of the market shown in Figure 13–4. The convenience food store and box stores, for example, don't just sell food—but deliberately sell a particular assortment-service combination to meet special needs. The same can be said for specialty shops as well as some of the mass merchandisers and department store chains.[18]

**Figure 13–5
Retailer life-cycle positions**

Retailers	Early growth	Maturity	Approximate time required to reach maturity
Department stores	Mid-1860s	Mid-1960s	100 years
Variety stores	Early 1900s	Early 1960s	60 years
Supermarkets	Mid-1930s	Mid-1960s	30 years
Discount department stores	Mid-1950s	Mid-1970s	20 years
Fast-food outlets	Early 1960s	Mid-1970s	15 years
Home improvement centers	Mid-1960s	Late1970s	15 years
Furniture warehouse showrooms	Late1960s	Late 1970s	10 years
Catalog showrooms	Late 1960s	Late 1970s	10 years

Source: Adapted from Bert C. McCammon, Jr., "The Future of Catalog Showrooms: Growth and Its Challenges to Management," Marketing Science Institute Working Paper (1973), p. 3.

Table 13–2
Gross margins in selected retail trades for recent years

Gross margin ranges	Retail trades
50 percent or more	Custom tailors, monuments, florists and nurseries, bakery shops, furs
40–50 percent	Garages, jewelry, restaurants, eating places, furniture, and undertaking
35–40 percent	Musical instruments, house furnishings, dairy and poultry products, gifts, novelties, souvenirs, books, furniture, drinking places, taverns, bars, office equipment and supplies, floor coverings, shoes (family stores), electric and gas household appliances
30–35 percent	Paint, wallpaper, glass, confectionery, drugs, women's accessory and specialty stores, men's clothing, stationery, men's furnishings, women's ready-to-wear, limited-price variety, automobile accessories and parts, family clothing, coal and other fuel
20–30 percent	Hardware, sporting goods, dry goods, general merchandise, lumber, cigar stores and stands, filling stations, meats, hardware and farm implements
Less than 20 percent	Alcoholic beverage package stores, farm implements, motor vehicles, groceries and meats, groceries

Source: Dun & Bradstreet.

Will retailers keep scrambling for profits?

Scrambled merchandising may continue into the future. There are still many rigidities in our marketing system—including the inflexibility of the traditional retailers' pricing policies. Pricing will be discussed in detail later, but it should be noted here that many conventional retailers have traditionally used fixed percentage markups for *all* items—regardless of the rate of turnover. The fast-moving items contributed nicely to profit—while the slow-moving items tended to reduce profits. If a firm were looking for opportunities, it would sell these fast-moving, high-profit items. And it is exactly these items that are crossing traditional lines and appearing in unexpected places.

Table 13–2 shows the ranges of gross margins conventional retailers have found necessary—to assure staying in business and making *some* profit. *Some* is emphasized because usually the net profit—the difference between a seemingly big gross margin and apparently necessary expenses—is only 1 or a few percent.

Mass merchandisers and discounters like to operate on gross margins and markups of 15–30 percent but—as shown in this table—conventional retailers usually need much higher percentages. This table should give you a better idea of the *why* of scrambled merchandising—and suggest possible directions it will take. This table shows, for example, why scramblers want to sell bakery goods, jewelry, appliances, refreshments, and gifts. Try to analyze why some of the conventional retailers have such high gross margins—and why other types of retailers can operate more economically.

RETAILER SIZE AND CHANNEL SYSTEM THINKING

Mass production is not the only source of economies of scale. These economies also apply to retailing and help explain why some retailers have grown—and why channel system thinking is so important.

*Some small retailers can operate only
because the whole family works
without pay.*

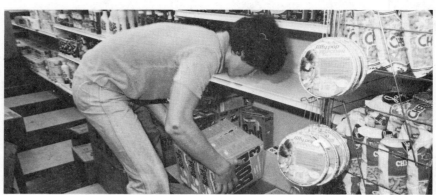

Peter Le Grand

*Small size may be hard
to overcome*

A small independent retailer may satisfy his psychic needs—by being his own boss. And he can be very helpful to some target customers—because of his flexibility. But the store may only *seem* profitable because some of the costs of doing business are ignored. He may not be allowing for depreciation—or for family members working without pay. Sometimes, he can keep the doors open only because he has a full-time job elsewhere. About 475,000 small retailers gross less than $50,000 in sales annually—which, after expenses, leaves hardly enough to support one person.

Even the average retail store is too small to gain economies of scale. Annual sales for the average store of only $390,000 is not very impressive—especially considering that net profits as a percentage of sales range from 1 to 5 percent. We gain some perspective on size when we realize that a grocery supermarket sells more than $1 million worth of goods per year!

But although larger stores may be able to buy in quantity at lower prices, take advantage of mass advertising, and hire specialists—larger size alone doesn't guarantee more efficient operation. A large department store may be made up of many small-scale specialty shops and limited-line stores that require special management skills. Leasing of some departments—optical goods and restaurants—may be necessary if specialized skill is required to operate them. Moreover, the departments in a department store might not be any larger than independent limited-line stores—and so there may be little possibility for volume buying.

*Being in a chain may
help*

The disadvantages of small size—even among large department stores—has led to the growth of chains—to obtain the benefits of large-scale operations.

A (corporate) **chain store** is one of several stores owned and managed by the same corporation. Chains grew slowly until after World War I—then spurted ahead during the 1920s. The first Census of Distribution in 1929—designed in part to determine the importance of chains—found that more than 7,000 chain organizations controlled about 21 percent of all retail sales—and a much larger share in certain lines. This discovery caused a number of states to pass anti–

chain store legislation. The Robinson-Patman Act of 1936 was intended, in part, to stop certain chain store practices—especially demanding and getting lower prices because of size.

Chains have done even better in certain lines. Variety store chains—such as Woolworth's—have 81 percent of sales in that field. Department store chains have 95 percent of that business. Sears, Montgomery Ward, and J. C. Penney are in this category. And supermarket chains have 57 percent of the grocery sales.

Independents form chains, too

The growth of corporate chains has encouraged the development of both cooperative chains and voluntary chains.

Cooperative chains are retailer-sponsored groups—formed by independent retailers—to run their own buying organization and conduct joint promotion efforts. Sales of cooperative chains have been rising as they have learned how to meet the corporate chain competition. Examples include Associated Grocers, Certified Grocers, and True Value.

Voluntary chains are wholesaler-sponsored groups which work with "independent" retailers. Some are linked by contracts stating common operating procedures—and the use of common store front designs, store name, and joint promotion efforts. The wholesaler-sponsor often provides training programs, computer and accounting assistance, and dealer brands. Examples include IGA and Super Valu in groceries, ACE in hardware, and Western Auto in auto supplies.

Franchising is similar

Franchise operations are like voluntary chains—with the franchiser developing a good marketing strategy and the franchise holders carrying out the strategy in their own units. Examples include McDonald's, Burger King, Wendy's, and automobile (new) dealerships. The voluntary chains have tended to work with existing retailers, while some franchisers like to work with newcomers—whom they train and get started. Sometimes they will locate the site—as well as supervise building and the initial promotion and opening.[19]

Co-ops try—but usually in vain

Cooperative and voluntary chains should not be confused with **consumer cooperatives**—which are groups of *consumers* who buy together. These groups usually operate on a nonprofit basis—with voluntary or poorly paid management. Consumer cooperatives have never made much of an impact in the United States. Their high point was 1 percent of retail sales in 1954.

Consumer cooperatives have been more successful in Europe—where most retailers have been high priced and inefficient. Most U.S. markets, on the other hand, have been so competitive that customers have not been willing to go to the typically out-of-the-way location for the (sometimes) unknown or co-op dealer brands—which may or may not be offered at lower prices.

The fate of consumer cooperatives is further evidence that size or good-will alone do not make an efficient channel system. Economies of scale may be possible, but it takes some hard-headed business decisions to link the members of a channel system efficiently. As always, the final test is consumer approval. Some large horizontal and vertical systems seem to be getting this approval.

Downtown shopping strips are relatively unplanned and offer mainly shopping goods.

Kenneth Yee

LOCATION OF RETAIL FACILITIES

Evolution of downtowns and shopping strips

Conventional retailers have usually chosen convenient locations—for themselves and their customers. Some early stores were a combination home and store. As cities grew larger, convenience stores might be sprinkled farther from the downtown—where all the stores were located when the city was small.

When all of a city's stores are downtown, there does appear to be some plan. Actually, however, the location of individual stores is more an accident of time—who wants to start a store now—and availability. As time goes on, the cost of rent downtown forces less profitable stores away from the busiest streets. Further, some streets may begin to specialize by product line—because new retailers want to be close to others who are already attracting customers.

As cities grow, strips of convenience stores develop along major roads. Generally, they emphasize convenience goods. But if the population in the neighborhood is large enough, then a variety of single-line and limited-line stores may enter too. Many of these continually have difficulty, however, because although real estate developers have stores available, there is not enough demand nearby. Eventually, however, most cities develop a pattern of a "central business district" downtown—offering primarily shopping goods—and outlying "shopping strips"— offering a variety of convenience and shopping goods. All of these retail areas are more or less unplanned—except that city planners sometimes restrict some commercial development. They certainly are not the planned shopping centers which have developed in the last 30 years.

Planned shopping centers—not just a group of stores

Planned shopping centers are a group of stores planned as a unit—to satisfy some market needs. Usually, free parking is provided. Many centers are enclosed to make shopping more pleasant. The centers are made up of several independent retailers—who sometimes act together for Promotion purposes.

Neighborhood shopping centers consist of several convenience stores. These centers usually include a supermarket, drug store, hardware store, beauty shop, laundry, dry cleaner, gas station, and perhaps others—such as a bakery or appliance shop. They normally must serve 7,500 to 40,000 people living within 6–10 minutes driving distance.

Community shopping centers are larger and offer some shopping stores as well as the convenience stores found in neighborhood shopping centers. They usually include a small department store which carries shopping goods (clothing and home furnishings). But most sales in these centers are convenience goods. These centers must serve 40,000 to 150,000 people within a radius of 3–4 miles.

Regional shopping centers are the largest centers and emphasize shopping stores and shopping goods. They include one or more large department stores—and as many as 200 smaller stores. Stores that feature convenience goods are often placed at the edge of the center—so they won't get in the way of customers primarily interested in shopping.

Regional centers must serve 150,000 or more persons within a radius of 5–6 miles. They are like downtown shopping districts of larger cities. Regional centers usually are found near suburban areas.

WHAT DOES THE FUTURE LOOK LIKE?

The changes in retailing in the last 30 years have been rapid—and seem to be continuing. Scrambled merchandising may become more scrambled. Some people are forecasting larger stores—while others are predicting smaller ones.

More customer-oriented retailing may be coming

Any effort to forecast trends in such a situation is risky—but our three-dimensional picture of the retailing market (Figure 13–4) can be helpful. Those who suggest bigger and bigger stores may be primarily concerned with the center of the market. Those who look for more small stores and specialty shops may be anticipating more small—but increasingly wealthy—target markets able to afford higher prices for special products.

To serve small but wealthy markets, convenience food grocery stores continue to spread. And sales by vending machines—even with their higher operating costs and prices—may grow. Certainly, some customers are getting tired of the large supermarkets that take so much of their time. Logically, convenience goods should be offered at the customer's—rather than the retailer's—convenience. For example, some retailers still fight night and weekend hours—hours when it is most convenient for many families to shop.

In-home shopping will become more popular

Telephone shopping may become more popular also. The mail-order houses and department stores already find phone business attractive. Telephone supermarkets—now a reality—sell only by phone and deliver all orders. Linking the phone to closed-circuit TV would let the customer see the products at home—while hearing well-prepared sales presentations. The customer could place an order through a small computer system—which would also handle the billing and delivery.

We now have far greater electronic capabilities than we are using. There seems to be no reason why the customer couldn't shop in the home—saving time and gasoline. Such automated retailing could take over a large share of the convenience goods and homogeneous shopping goods business.[20]

Retailers becoming manufacturers and vice versa

We also may see more horizontal and vertical arrangements in channel systems. This would certainly affect present manufacturers—who already see retailers developing their own brands—and using manufacturers mainly as production arms.

The large manufacturers themselves may go into retailing in the future—for self-protection. Rexall Corporation, Sherwin-Williams, B. F. Goodrich, Van Heusen, and others already control or own retail outlets.

The function of retailing will continue to be needed. But the role of individual retailers—and even the concept of a retail store—may have to undergo much change. There will always be customers' needs—and they will probably want to satisfy these needs with combinations of goods and services. But retail stores are not necessarily the only way of accomplishing this.

Renting may eliminate buying

Just as builders of tract homes shifted some home appliance sales from retailers, the builders of new cities may sell completely furnished homes—and eliminate the need for retail home furnishing stores. And apartment builders catering to the mobile young, may rent furnished apartments—or offer assortments of furniture for rent from a selection owned by the management. This may fit the need of a mobile population better than *owning* goods. But it will also have a direct impact on present retailers. Some won't be needed at all!

Retailers must face the challenge

One thing is certain—change in retailing is inevitable. For years conventional retailers' profits have declined. Even some of the newer discounters—like the warehouse furniture retailers—and shopping centers have had disappointing records. Department stores, and food and drug chains have seen profit declines. The old variety stores have done even worse. Some are shifting into mass merchandising operations—and that picture is less attractive now as limited-line stores try to "meet competition" with lower margins.

A few firms—especially Kmart—have avoided this general profit squeeze. But, the future does not look too bright for retailers who stick with the status quo. New technological developments—like automatic checkout counters—require capital to save labor costs. But the developments are available to all competitors. In our competitive markets, the benefits are passed on to the consumers—but the firms are stuck with higher fixed costs. Further, unionization is increasing labor costs in the traditionally nonunionized retailing sector.

No easy way for more profit

In fact, it appears that the "fat" has been squeezed out of the retailing sector—and there is no easy route to greater profitability. Instead, careful strategy planning—and great care in implementation—will be needed for success in the future. This means more careful market segmenting to find unsatisfied needs which (1) have a long life expectancy and (2) can be satisfied with low levels of investment. This is a big order. But it is safe to say that the imaginative marketing planner will find more profitable opportunities than the conventional retailer who doesn't know that the product life cycle is moving along—and is just "hoping for the best."[21]

CONCLUSION

Modern retailing is scrambled—and we will probably see more changes in the future. In such a dynamic environment, a producer's marketing manager must choose among the available kinds of retailers very carefully. Retailers must plan their offering with their target customers' needs in mind—while at the same time trying to be part of an effective channel system.

We described many kinds of retailers—and saw that each has its advantages and disadvantages. We also saw that modern retailers have discarded conventional practices. The old "buy low and sell high" philosophy is no longer a safe guide. Lower margins for faster turnover seems to be the modern philosophy—as retailers move from discounting into mass merchandising. But even this is no guarantee of success—as retailers' product life cycles move on.

Scrambled merchandising will probably continue as retailing evolves to meet changing consumer demands. But important breakthroughs are still possible—because it seems unlikely that consumers will continue to want all the conventional retail services. Convenience goods, for example, may be made more conveniently available by some combination of electronic ordering and home delivery or vending. The big, all-purpose department store may not be able to satisfy anyone's needs exactly. Again, some combination of mail-order and electronic ordering might make a larger assortment of goods available to more people—to better meet their particular needs.

In the face of declining profit margins, new approaches will be tried. Our society needs a retailing function, but it is not certain that all the present retailers are needed. It is safe to say that the future retail scene will offer the marketing manager new challenges and opportunities.

QUESTIONS AND PROBLEMS

1. Identify a specialty store selling convenience goods in your city. Explain why you feel it is that kind of a store and why an awareness of this status would be important to a manufacturer. Does it give the retailer any particular advantage? If so, with whom?

2. What sort of a "product" are specialty shops offering? What are the prospects for organizing a chain of specialty shops?

3. A department store consists of many departments. Is this horizontal integration? Are all of the advantages of horizontal integration achieved in a department store operation?

4. Many department stores have a bargain basement. Does the basement represent just another department, like the hat department or the luggage department, for example, or is some whole new concept involved?

5. Distinguish among discount houses, discount selling, and mass merchandising. Forecast the future of low-price selling in food, clothing, and appliances.

6. In view of the wide range of gross margins (and expenses) in various lines of trade, suggest what the supermarket or scrambled merchandising outlet of the future may be like. Use care here. Are products with high gross margins necessarily highly profitable?

7. List five products which seem suitable for automatic vending and yet are not normally sold in this manner. Generally, what characteristics are required?

8. Apply the "Wheel of Retailing" theory to your local community. What changes seem likely? Does it seem likely that established retailers will see the need for change or will entirely new firms have to develop?

9. Discuss the kinds of markets served by the three types

of shopping centers. Are they directly competitive? Do they contain the same kinds of stores? Is the long-run outlook for all of them similar?

10. Explain the growth and decline of various retailers and

shopping centers in your own community. Use the text's three-dimensional drawing (Figure 13–4) and the product life cycle concept. Also, treat each retailers' whole offering as a "product."

SUGGESTED CASES

13 Andrews Photo Inc.

16 The Donell Company

NOTES

1. *Client's Monthly Alert*, June 1977, p. 3.

2. P. Martineau, "The Pattern of Social Classes," in *Marketing's Role in Scientific Management*, ed. R. L. Clewett (Chicago: American Marketing Association, 1957), p. 234.

3. "Convenience Stores: A $7.4 Billion Mushroom," *Business Week*, March 21, 1977, pp. 61–64; "Convenience Stores Battle Lagging Sales by Adding Items and Cleaning Up Image," *The Wall Street Journal*, March 28, 1980, p. 16; and "Arco Takes on Convenience Stores," *Advertising Age*, December 17, 1979, p. 1 f.

4. "Bonwit's Turns Up the Heat," *Business Week*, October 11, 1976, pp. 120–22.

5. "The Merchant Prince of Dallas," *Business Week*, October 21, 1967, pp. 115–18 f.

6. "Why Profits Shrink at a Grand Old Name" (Marshall Field), *Business Week*, April 11, 1977, pp. 66–78; Louis H. Grossman, "Merchandising Strategies of a Department Store Facing Change," *MSU Business Topics*, Winter 1970, pp. 31–42; and "Suburban Malls Go Downtown," *Business Week*, November 10, 1973, pp. 90–94; "Smaller Cities, With No End to Suburbanization," *Business Week*, September 3, 1979, pp. 204–6.

7. "Anti-Trust Verdict Rocks the Stores," *Business Week*, July 26, 1969, p. 29.

8. "Vendors Pull Out All Stops," *Business Week*, August 15, 1970, pp. 52–54.

9. Douglas J. Dalrymple, "Will Automatic Vending Topple Retail Precedence?" *Journal of Retailing*, Spring 1963, pp. 27–31.

10. David Appel, "The Supermarket: Early Development of an Institutional Innovation," *Journal of Retailing*, Spring 1972, pp. 39–53.

11. "Supermarkets Eye the Sunbelt," *Business Week*, September 27, 1976, pp. 61–62; "Safeway: Selling Nongrocery Items to Cure the Supermarket Blahs," *Business Week*, March 7, 1977, pp. 52–58; and "How a Long Price War Dragged on and Hurt Chicago Food Chains," *The Wall Street Journal*, July 19, 1976, pp. 1 f.; Gilbert D. Harrell and Michael D. Hutt, "Crowding in Retail Stores," *MSU Business Topics*, Winter 1976, pp. 33–39.

12. Jonathan N. Goodrich and Jo Ann Hoffman, "Warehouse Retailing: The Trend of the Future?" *Business Horizons*, April 1979, pp. 45–50; and "Kmart Corp. Gives Up on No-Frill Food Store," *The Wall Street Journal*, November 30, 1979, p. 35.

13. "Discount Catalogs: A New Way To Sell," *Business Week*, April 29, 1972, pp. 72–74; and "Catalog Discounting Is a Small Man's Game," *Business Week*, October 13, 1973, pp. 70–76.

14. "Mass Merchandisers Move toward Stability," *The Nielsen Researcher*, no. 3, 1976, pp. 19–25.

15. "Those 1,215 K's Stand for Kresge, Kmart's, and the Key to Success," *The Wall Street Journal*, March 8, 1977, p. 1 f.; Where Kmart Goes Next Now That It's No. 2," *Business Week*, June 2, 1980, pp. 109–14.

16. Walter J. Salmon, Robert D. Buzzell, and Stanton G. Cort, "Today the Shopping Center, Tomorrow the Superstore," *Harvard Business Review*, January–February 1974, pp. 89–98; "Super-stores May Suit Customers to a T—a T-Shirt or a T-Bone," *The Wall Street Journal*, March 13, 1973, p. 1 f; and *The Super-Store—Strategic Implications For the Seventies* (Cambridge, Mass.: The Marketing Science Institute, 1972).

17. Stanley C. Hollander, "Retailing: Cause or Effect?" in *Emerging Concepts in Marketing*, ed. William F. Decker (Chicago: American Marketing Association, December 1962), pp. 220–30.

18. For more discussion on segmenting of retail markets, see "Fast-Food Franchisers Invade the City," *Business Week*, April 22, 1974, pp. 92–93; "Korvettes Tries for a Little Chic," *Business Week*, May 12, 1973, pp. 124–26; Philip D. Cooper, "Will Success Produce Problems for the Convenience Store?" *MSU Business Topics*, Winter 1972, pp. 39–43; "Levitz: The Hot Name in 'Instant' Furniture," *Business Week*, December 4, 1971, pp. 90–93; David L. Appel, "Market Segmentation—A Response to Retail Innovation," *Journal of Marketing*, April 1970, pp. 64–67; Steven R. Flaster, "A Consumer Approach to the Specialty Store," *Journal of Retailing*, Spring 1969, pp. 21–31; and A. Coskun Samli, "Segmentation and Carving a Niche in the Market Place," *Journal of Retailing*, Summer 1968, pp. 35–49.

19. E. H. Lewis and R. Hancock, *The Franchise System of Distribution* (Minneapolis: University of Minnesota Press, 1963). See also, the special issue on franchising in the *Journal of Retailing*, Winter 1968–69.

20. Larry J. Rosenberg and Elizabeth C. Herschman, "Retailing Without Stores," *Harvard Business Review*, July–August 1980, pp. 103–12.

21. Albert D. Bates, "The Troubled Future of Retailing," *Business Horizons*, August 1976, pp. 22–28; William R. Davidson, Albert D. Bates, and Stephen J. Bass, "Retail Life Cycle," *Harvard Business Review*, November–December 1976, pp. 89–96; "Investigating the Collapse of W. T. Grant," *Business Week*, July 19, 1976, pp. 60–62; "Shopping Center Boom Appears to Be Fading Due to Overbuilding," *The Wall Street Journal*, September 7, 1976, pp. 1 f; and "Jewel Co. Discloses Operations Review in Search of a More Successful Strategy," *The Wall Street Journal*, March 23, 1977, p. 12; Ronald D. Michman, "Changing Patterns in Retailing," *Business Horizons*, October 1979, pp. 33–38; "The Discount Twist in Suburban Shopping Malls," *Business Week*, July 7, 1980, pp. 95–96; and "Sears Mulls Test of Catalog Sales via Warner Cable," *Advertising Age*, February 18, 1980, p. 1 f.

<table>
<tr><td>When you
finish this
chapter, you
should:</td><td>
1. Understand what wholesalers are and the wholesaling functions they may provide for others in channel systems.
</td></tr>
</table>

*When you
finish this
chapter, you
should:*

1. Understand what wholesalers are and the wholesaling functions they *may* provide for others in channel systems.

2. Know the various kinds of merchant wholesalers and agent middlemen.

3. Understand when and where the various kinds of merchant wholesalers and agent middlemen would be most useful to channel planners.

4. Understand why wholesalers have lasted.

5. Recognize the important new terms (shown in red).

14

Wholesaling

"I can get it for you wholesale," the man said. But could he? Would it be a good deal?

Wholesaling is important in the marketing process. Wholesalers are a vital link in many channel systems. To understand their role better, you should look at wholesalers primarily as members of channels—rather than as separate business firms.

In this chapter, you will learn how wholesalers have evolved, how they fit into various channels, why they are used, and what functions they perform.

WHAT IS A WHOLESALER?

This question is hard to answer exactly, but one way to get at the definition is to find out why a given firm wants to be considered a wholesaler rather than a retailer. There are several reasons.

How to tell a wholesaler from a retailer

First—in some channels—manufacturers sell only to wholesalers. The wholesalers, in turn, are expected to sell only to other middlemen, or producers—but *not* to final consumers. Exactly which firms will be permitted to buy from the manufacturer depends on how the manufacturer defines a wholesaler.

Second—and related to the first point—is the amount of discount granted. If retailers in a certain line normally expect a 30-percent discount off the suggested retail list price, then the wholesalers supplying them may be given a 45-percent discount off retail list. They, in turn, are expected to pass on a 30-percent discount to their retailers. In practice, this can be much more complicated.

Some manufacturers set up a scale of wholesale discounts depending on the size of the wholesaler—and the services offered. These "trade discounts" are discussed further in the pricing chapters. Correctly determining which firms are entitled to what trade discounts is a serious matter—because of the possibility of violating the price discrimination laws.

Third, some cities and states have retail sales taxes—or taxes on inventories or gross receipts—that apply only to retailers. These taxes require record keeping—and out-of-pocket costs when the retailer fails to collect the tax from the consumer. It is natural therefore, that some firms should try to avoid classification as a retailer.

Any of these three points explains why a firm might wish to be labeled a wholesaler rather than a retailer. The *fourth* point operates in reverse. Some retailers—but not wholesalers—are exempt from federal minimum wage legislation.[1]

A wholesaler—by any other name—is still a middleman

Despite the apparent difficulty in writing a single, hard definition of wholesaling, the *main* source of confusion is the wide variation in the way wholesale firms operate, the functions performed, the cost of operations, and the operating policies followed.

Many wholesalers perform more functions than we usually associate with the term. Some wholesalers engage in all four regrouping steps—and some of their sorting-out and accumulation activities may even seem like manufacturing. As a result, we find some firms calling themselves "manufacturer and jobber," or "manufacturer and dealer." In addition, some use general terms such as merchant, dealer, distributor, or jobber—because their actual operations are flexible—and they don't wish to be narrowly classified.

To avoid a prolonged technical and semantic discussion, we will use the U.S. Bureau of Census definition. This is basically:

> **Wholesaling** is concerned with the activities of those persons or establishments which sell to retailers and other merchants, and/or to industrial, institutional, and commercial users, but who do not sell in large amounts to final consumers.

So, **wholesalers** are firms whose main function is providing wholesaling activities.

It should be noted that producers who take over wholesaling activities are not considered wholesalers. However, if separate establishments—such as branch warehouses—are set up, those facilities are counted as wholesalers by the U.S. Bureau of Census.

Wholesaling is a middleman activity. When a manufacturer goes direct, it still must assume the marketing functions that an independent wholesaler might provide. This is important from a channel standpoint. Wholesaling functions usually must be performed by some channel member—whether a wholesaler or the manufacturer.

POSSIBLE WHOLESALING FUNCTIONS

Wholesalers may perform certain functions for both their own customers and

Wholesalers sell in large quantities to intermediate customers.

Milt & Joan Mann

their suppliers—in short, for those above and below them in a channel. These *wholesaling functions* really are variations of the basic marketing functions—buying, selling, grading, storing, transporting, financing, risk taking, and gathering market information. These wholesaling functions are basic to the following discussion and should be studied carefully now. But *keep in mind that these functions are provided by some, but not all, wholesalers.*

What a wholesaler might do for customers

1. *Anticipate needs*—forecast customers' demands, and buy accordingly.
2. *Regroup goods*—provide at least one and sometimes all four regrouping activities—to provide the assortment wanted by customers at the lowest possible cost.
3. *Carry stocks*—carry inventory so customers don't have to store a large inventory.
4. *Deliver goods*—provide prompt delivery at low cost.
5. *Grant credit*—give credit to customers, perhaps supplying their working capital. Note: This financing function may be *very* important to small customers—and is sometimes the main reason why they use wholesalers—rather than buying directly from manufacturers.
6. Provide information and advisory service—supply price and technical information as well as suggestions on how to install and sell products. Note: The wholesaler's sales force may be experts in the products they sell.
7. Provide part of buying function—offer products to potential customers so they don't have to hunt for supply sources.
8. Own and transfer title to goods—permits completing a sale without the need for other middlemen—speeding the whole buying and selling process.

What a wholesaler might do for producer-suppliers

1. *Provide part of producer's selling function*—by going to producer-suppliers, instead of waiting for their sales reps to call.
2. *Store inventory*—this reduces a producer's need to carry large stocks—and cuts his warehousing expenses.

3. *Supply capital*—this reduces a producer's need for working capital by buying his output and carrying it in inventory until it is sold.
4. *Reduce credit risk*—by selling to customers the wholesaler knows—and taking the loss if these customers don't pay. Note: A producer's customers—retailers and other producers—may be numerous. And some may be poor credit risks. It is expensive for a small producer, especially one far distant, to evaluate all these potential credit risks when selling only one or a few products. The wholesaler who sells these customers many products is in a better position to evaluate their credit status. Also, if the wholesaler is a source of supply for many products, the customer may be more likely to pay a helpful wholesaler than a producer from whom he may not reorder.
5. *Provide market information*—as an informed buyer and seller closer to the market, the wholesaler reduces the producer's need for market research.

KINDS AND COSTS OF AVAILABLE WHOLESALERS

Table 14–1 lists the types, number, sales volume, and operating expenses of wholesalers operating in 1977. The differences in operating expenses suggest that each of these types performs—or does not perform—certain wholesaling functions. But which ones and why?

Why, for example, do manufacturers use merchant wholesalers costing 12.7 percent of sales when manufacturers' branches with stock cost only 8.9 percent?

Table 14–1
Wholesale trade by type of operation (United States, 1977)

Type of operation	Number of establishments	Sales ($000)	Operating expenses (including payroll) percent of sales
United States total	382,837	1,258,400,268	9.4
Merchant wholesalers	307,264	676,057,580	12.7
Wholesale distributors and jobbers	283,390	516,958,819	14.7
Importers	9,541	65,876,465	8.4
Exporters	3,762	47,768,454	3.2
Terminal grain elevators	223	7,636,441	2.0
Country grain elevators	6,233	21,259,407	6.1
Assemblers of farm products, except country grain elevators	4,115	16,557,994	7.8
Manufacturers' sales branches and offices, total	40,521	451,854,912	6.0
Sales branches (with stock)	26,892	221,527,038	8.9
Sales offices (without stock)	13,629	230,327,874	3.1
Agents, brokers, and commission merchants, total	35,052	130,487,776	4.6
Auction companies	1,743	10,825,776	3.0
Brokers (representing buyers or sellers)	4,820	30,584,574	3.2
Commission merchants	7,481	27,966,084	4.8
Import agents	319	3,920,058	2.4
Export agents	710	8,822,234	1.9
Manufacturers' agents	19,979	48,369,050	6.6

Source: *1977 Census of Wholesale Trade.*

**Figure 14–1
Types of wholesalers**

Merchant wholesalers (Own the goods)		Agent middlemen (Don't own the goods, emphasize selling)
Service (All the functions)	Limited function (Some of the functions)	
General merchandise wholesalers (or mill supply houses)	Cash-and-carry wholesalers	Auction companies
	Drop-shippers	Brokers
	Truck wholesalers	Commission merchants
Single-line or general-line wholesalers	Mail-order wholesalers	Manufacturers' agents
	Producers' cooperatives	Food brokers
Specialty wholesalers	Rack jobbers	Selling agents

Why use either when brokers cost only 3.2 percent?

Is the use of wholesalers with higher operating expenses the reason why marketing costs are high—if, in fact, they are?

To answer these questions we must understand what these wholesalers do—and don't do. Figure 14–1 gives a big-picture view of the wholesalers described in more detail below. Note that a major difference is whether they *own* goods they sell. Also, some historical background will help answer these questions.

Each wholesaler found a niche

In this text, we are emphasizing the evolutionary nature of change in our marketing system—and this applies fully to wholesaling. America has transformed itself from a colonial territory—dependent on England for its finished goods in exchange for its raw materials—into an industrial nation. As output grew, so did the need for middlemen to handle it.

To serve the retail general stores of earlier times, wholesalers carried a wide line of merchandise. They were called "general merchandise" wholesalers—because their merchandise was so varied. We already have seen that the general store developed into a single- or limited-line store—as towns grew and more goods became available. To serve these stores, "single-line" wholesalers developed. Those specializing in very narrow lines were called "specialty" wholesalers. Single-line wholesalers were well-established in the Eastern grocery and dry goods fields by the early 1800s. This same evolution took place a little later in the markets farther west.

Since wholesaling developed to distribute the greater production of the factories to an expanding population, wholesalers served not only retailers and final consumers—but also manufacturers. Many manufacturers were so small that it was hard for them to contact the growing number of wholesalers or other manufacturer customers, so special wholesalers—called agents and brokers—developed to make these contacts. In general, specialized needs arose—and specialized wholesalers developed to meet them.

Learn the pure to understand the real

One of the wholesaler's principal assets is his customer list. He tries to offer a unique service to certain customers and may be the only one who does this particular job. The manufacturer who wants to reach the market segment served by this wholesaler *may have to use him.* Who each possible wholesaler serves should be one of the first questions asked by a channel planner.

The next important question would be: what functions does a particular wholesaler provide? Wholesalers typically specialize by product line—a fact which should please product-oriented manufacturers! But they do provide different functions.

To get a clear understanding of wholesaling, we will identify and analyze—as pure types—several specific kinds of wholesalers. In practice, it may be difficult to find examples of these pure types—because many wholesalers are mixtures. Further, the names commonly used in a particular trade may be misleading. Some so-called "brokers" actually behave as limited-function merchant wholesalers—and some "manufacturers' agents" operate as full-service wholesalers. This casual use of terminology makes it all the more important for you to thoroughly understand the pure types before trying to understand the blends—and the names they go under in the business world. Similarly, a manufacturer's or retailer's marketing manager should understand these differences *and* clearly specify *his* Place objectives—before trying to select suitable wholesalers.

In the following pages, we will discuss the major types of wholesalers which have been identified by the U.S. Bureau of Census—to guide its data collection. Remember, detailed data is available by kind of business, by product line, and by geographic territory. Among other things, such detailed data can be valuable in strategic planning—especially in determining if there are potential channel members serving a target market—and the sales volumes achieved by the present middlemen.

In international markets, we find the same kinds of wholesalers as in the United States—although good data may be lacking. In addition, different names may be used. And this again emphasizes the importance of understanding the pure types.

MERCHANT WHOLESALERS ARE THE MOST NUMEROUS

Merchant wholesalers own (take title to) the goods they sell. They also provide some—or all—of the wholesaling functions. There are two basic kinds of merchant wholesalers: (1) service—sometimes called full-service—wholesalers, and (2) limited-function or limited-service wholesalers. Their names explain their difference.

More than three fourths of all wholesaling establishments are merchant wholesalers—but they handle only about half of wholesale sales. Why?

Service wholesalers provide all the functions

Service wholesalers provide all the wholesaling functions. Within this basic group are three types: (1) *general merchandise,* (2) *single line,* and (3) *specialty.*

General merchandise wholesalers carry a wide variety of nonperishable staple items such as hardware, electrical supplies, plumbing supplies, furniture, drugs, cosmetics, and automobile equipment. With this broad line of convenience and shopping goods, they serve general stores, hardware stores, drugstores, electric appliance shops, and small department stores. In the industrial goods field, the *mill supply house* operates in a similar way. Somewhat like a hardware store, the mill supply house carries a broad variety of accessories and supplies for industrial customers.

Single-line (or general-line) wholesalers carry a narrower line of merchandise than general merchandise wholesalers. For example, they might carry only groceries or wearing apparel, or certain types of industrial tools or supplies. In consumer goods, they service the single- and limited-line stores. In industrial goods, they cover a wider geographic area and offer more specialized service.

Specialty wholesalers carry a very narrow range of products. A *consumer goods* specialty wholesaler might carry only health foods or Oriental foods—instead of a full line of groceries. Or the specialty house might carry only automotive items—selling exclusively to mass merchandisers. One wholesaler, for example, is willing to arrange and stock mass merchandisers' shelves—an important service to these retailers because their customers' behavior seems to vary according to geography. Final consumers in northern Indiana, for instance, respond to different shelf arrangements and products from those in southern Indiana. The specialty wholesalers' task is to learn these differences, and adjust stocks and displays accordingly. In this effort, they go further than most merchant wholesalers—providing some of the customers' selling functions—since displays do most of the selling in mass merchandising outlets.

For industrial goods, a specialty wholesaler might limit itself to fields requiring technical knowledge or service—perhaps electronics or plastics.

The Cadillac Plastic and Chemical Co., in Detroit, became a specialty wholesaler serving the needs of plastics makers and users alike—because neither the large plastics manufacturers nor the merchant wholesalers with wide lines were in a position to give individual advice to the many customers (who often have little knowledge of which product would be best for them). Cadillac carries 10,000 items and sells to 25,000 customers—ranging in size from very small firms to General Motors.

Limited-function wholesalers provide certain functions

Limited-function wholesalers provide only *some* wholesaling functions. Table 14–2 shows the functions typically provided—and not provided. In the following paragraphs, the main features of these wholesalers will be discussed. Some

Speciality wholesalers carry a narrow range of products.

Kenneth Yee

Table 14–2
Functions provided by limited-function merchant wholesalers

Functions	Cash-and-carry	Drop-shipper	Truck	Mail-order	Cooperatives	Rack jobbers
For customer:						
Anticipates needs	X		X	X	X	X
"Regroups" goods (one or more of four steps)	X		X	X	X	X
Carries stocks	X		X	X	X	X
Delivers goods			X		X	X
Grants credit		X	Maybe	Maybe	Maybe	Consignment (in some cases)
Provides information and advisory services		X	Some	Some	X	
Provides buying function		X	X	X	Some	X
Owns and transfers title to goods	X	X	X	X	X	X
For producers:						
Provides producer's selling function	X	X	X	X	X	X
Stores inventory	X		X	X	X	X
Helps finance by owning stocks	X		X	X	X	X
Reduces credit risk	X	X	X	X	X	X
Provides market information	X	X	Some	X	X	Some

are not very numerous. In fact, they are not counted separately by the U.S. Census Bureau. Nevertheless, these wholesalers are very important for some products.

Cash-and-carry wholesalers want cash

Cash-and-carry wholesalers operate like service wholesalers—except that the customer must pay cash.

Many small retailers—especially small grocers and garages—are too small to be served profitably by a service wholesaler. Discovering this fact, service wholesalers set a minimum charge or merely refuse to handle certain customers' business. Or, they may set up a *cash-and-carry department* to give the small retailer the products needed in exchange for cash on the counter. This works like a retail store—but for small retailers. It can operate at lower cost—because the retailers take over many wholesaling functions. And using cash-and-carry outlets may allow the small retailer to stay in business.

Drop-shipper does not handle the goods

Drop-shippers own the goods they sell—but do not actually handle, stock, or deliver them. These wholesalers are mainly involved in selling. They get orders—from wholesalers, retailers, or industrial users—and pass these orders on to producers. Then the orders are shipped directly to the customers. Because drop-shippers do not have to handle the goods, their operating costs are lower.

Drop-shippers commonly sell products which are so bulky that additional handling would be expensive—and possibly damaging. Also, the quantities they usually sell are so large that there is little need for regrouping—for example, rail carload shipments of coal, lumber, oil, or chemical products.

Truck wholesalers deliver—at a cost

Truck wholesalers specialize in delivering goods which they stock in their own trucks. Handling perishable products in general demand—tobacco, candy, potato chips, and salad dressings—truck wholesalers may provide almost the same functions as full-service wholesalers. Their big advantage is that they deliver perishable products that regular wholesalers prefer not to carry. Also, they may call on many small service stations and "back-alley" garages—providing local delivery of the many small items these customers often forget to pick up from a service wholesaler. Truck wholesalers' operating costs are relatively high—because they provide a lot of service for the little they sell.

Mail-order wholesalers reach outlying stores

Mail-order wholesalers sell out of a catalog which may be distributed widely to smaller industrial customers or retailers. These wholesalers operate in the hardware, jewelry, sporting goods, and general merchandise lines. Their markets are often small industrial or retailer customers who might not be called on by other middlemen.

Producers' cooperatives do sorting-out

Producers' cooperatives operate almost as full-service wholesalers—with the "profits" going to the cooperative's customer-members—in the form of "patronage dividends." They develop in agricultural markets—where there are many small producers.

The successful producers' cooperatives have emphasized the sorting-out process—to improve the quality of farm products offered to the market. Some have also branded these improved products—and then promoted the brands. Farmers' cooperatives have sometimes had success in restricting output and increasing price—by taking advantage of the normally inelastic demand for agricultural commodities.

Examples of such organizations are the California Fruit Growers Exchange (citrus fruits), Sunmaid Raisin Growers Association, The California Almond Exchange, and Land O'Lakes Creameries, Inc.

Rack jobbers sell hard-to-handle assortments

Rack jobbers specialize in nonfood items which are sold through grocery stores and supermarkets—and they often display them on their own wire racks. Many grocers don't want to bother with reordering and maintaining displays of nonfood items (housewares, hardware items, and health and beauty aids) because they sell small quantities of so many different kinds of goods. And regular wholesalers handling such items are not too interested in this business either—because opening up this new channel might strain relations with their present customers. While many wholesalers specialize by product lines, the rack jobber must handle a scrambled assortment because this is what customers want.

Rack jobbers are almost service wholesalers—except that they usually are paid cash for the amount of stock sold or delivered. This is a relatively expensive operation—with operating costs of about 18 percent of sales. The large volume of nonfood sales from these racks has encouraged some large chains to experiment with handling such items themselves. But they often find that rack jobbers can provide this service as well as—or better than—they can themselves.

MANUFACTURERS' SALES BRANCHES PROVIDE WHOLESALING FUNCTIONS, TOO

The drive toward horizontal and vertical integration that began in the late 1880s had its effect in wholesaling, too. Many manufacturers set up their own sales branches whenever the sales volume—or the nature of their products—justified it.

Manufacturers' sales branches are separate businesses which manufacturers set up away from their factories. For example, computer manufacturers such as IBM set up local branches to provide service, display equipment, and handle sales. About 11 percent of wholesale businesses are owned by manufacturers—but they handle 36 percent of total wholesale sales. One reason the sales per branch are so high is that they are usually placed in the best market areas. This also helps explain why their operating costs are often lower. But cost comparisons between various channels can be misleading, since sometimes the cost of selling is not charged to the branch. If all the expenses of the manufacturers' sales branches were charged to them, they probably would turn out to be more costly than they seem now.

The U.S. Bureau of Census collects extensive data showing the number, kind, location, and operating expenses of manufacturers' sales branches. Such data can help manufacturers determine competitors' distribution systems and probable costs. If many competitors are going direct, it may mean that there are no good specialists available—or at least none who can provide the functions needed.

AGENT MIDDLEMEN ARE STRONG ON SELLING

They don't own the goods

Agent middlemen *do not own* the goods they sell. Their main purpose is to help in buying and selling. They usually provide even fewer functions than the limited-function wholesalers. In certain trades, however, they are extremely valuable. They may operate at relatively low cost, too—sometimes 2–6 percent of selling price.

Agent middlemen—like merchant wholesalers—normally specialize by customer type—and by product or product lines—and so it is important to determine exactly what each one does.

In the following paragraphs, only the most important points about each type will be mentioned. See Table 14–3 for details on the functions provided by each. It is obvious from the number of empty spaces in Table 14–3 that agent middlemen provide fewer functions than merchant wholesalers.

Auction companies— display the goods

Auction companies provide a place where buyers and sellers can come together and complete a transaction. Auction companies are not numerous (see Table 14–1)—but they are important in certain lines—such as fruit, livestock, fur, tobacco, and used cars. For these products, demand and supply conditions change rapidly—and the product must be seen to be evaluated. Buyers and sellers, therefore, are brought together by the auction company—and demand and supply interact to determine the price while the goods are being inspected.

Facilities can be plain—keeping overhead costs low. Frequently, auction sheds are close to transportation so that the commodities can be reshipped quickly. The auction company charges a set fee or commission for the use of its facilities and services.

Brokers—provide information

Brokers bring buyers and sellers together. Unlike the auction company, physical facilities are not crucial. Brokers may not even have a separate office. They may operate out of their homes—perhaps with the aid of an answering service. Their "product" is information about what buyers need—and what supplies are available. They aid in buyer-seller negotiation. If the transaction is completed, they earn a commission from whichever party hired them.

Usually, some kind of broker will develop whenever and wherever market information is inadequate. Brokers are especially useful for selling seasonal products. For example, they could represent a small food canner during the canning season—then go on to other activities.

Brokers are also active in used machinery, real estate, and even ships. These products are not similar, but the needed marketing functions are. In each case, buyers don't come into the market often. Someone with knowledge of available products is needed to help both buyers and sellers complete the transaction quickly and inexpensively.

Commission merchants handle and sell goods in distant markets

Commission merchants handle goods shipped to them by sellers, complete the sale, and send the money—minus their commission—to each seller.

Commission merchants are common in agricultural markets where farmers

Table 14–3
Functions provided by agent middlemen

Functions	Auction companies	Brokers	Commission merchants	Manufacturers' agents and food brokers	Selling agents
For customers:					
Anticipates needs		Some		Sometimes	
"Regroups" goods (one or more of four steps)	X		X	Some	
Carries stocks	Sometimes		X	Sometimes	
Delivers goods			X	Sometimes	
Grants credit	Some		Sometimes		X
Provides information and advisory services		X	X	X	X
Provides buying function	X	Some	X	X	X
Owns and transfers title to goods	Transfers only		Transfers only		
For producer:					
Provides selling function	X	Some	X	X	X
Stores inventory	X		X	Sometimes	
Helps finance by owning stocks					
Reduces credit risk....................	Some				X
Provides market information		X	X	X	X

must ship to big-city central markets. They need someone to handle the goods there as well as to sell them—since the farmer cannot go with each shipment. Although commission merchants do not own the goods, they generally are allowed to sell them at the market price—or the best price above some stated minimum. Prices in these markets usually are published in newspapers, so the producer-seller has a check on the commission merchant. Usually costs are low because commission merchants handle large volumes of goods—and buyers usually come to them.

Commission merchants are sometimes used in other trades, too—such as textiles. Here, many small producers wish to reach buyers in a central market—without having to maintain their own sales forces.

Manufacturers' agents—
free-wheeling sales reps

A **manufacturers' agent** sells similar products for several noncompeting manufacturers—for a commission on what is actually sold. Such agents work almost as members of each company's sales force—but they are really independent middlemen. They may cover one city or several states.

Their big "plus" is that they already call on a group of customers and can add another product line at relatively low cost. If the sales potential in an area is low, a manufacturers' agent may be used instead of a company's own sales rep because he can do the job at lower cost. A small producer often has to use agents everywhere—because its sales volume is too small to support a sales force anywhere.

Manufacturers' agents are very useful in fields where there are many small manufacturers who need to contact customers. These agents are often used in the sale of machinery and equipment, electrical goods, automobile products, clothing and apparel accessories, and some food products.

The agent's main job is selling. The agent—or his customer—sends the orders to the producer. The agent, of course, gets credit for the sale. Agents seldom have any part in setting prices—or deciding on the producer's policies. Basically, they are independent, aggressive sales people.

Agents can be especially useful in introducing new products. For this service, they may earn 10 to 15 percent commission. (By contrast, their commission on large-volume established goods may be quite low—perhaps only 2 percent.) The

Manufacturers' agents help small producers contact customers.

higher rates for new products often come to be the agent's major disadvantage for the manufacturer. The 10 to 15 percent commission rate may have seemed small when the product was new—and sales volume was low. Once the product is selling well, the rate seems high. At about this time, the producer often begins using its own sales reps—and the manufacturers' agents must look for other new products to develop. Agents are well aware of this possibility. Most try to work for many manufacturers—so they are not dependent on only one or a few lines.

Food brokers—fill a gap

Food brokers are manufacturers' agents who specialize in grocery distribution. More than half of the processed goods handled by grocery stores is sold by these brokers.

Food brokers call on grocery wholesalers and large retailers for their manufacturer clients. Some aggressive food brokers have become quite involved with their client's marketing strategy planning—more than the typical manufacturers' agent. They may even work closely with the producer's advertising agency.[2] They are consulted for these roles because they are so familiar with their territory.

For the usual commision of 5 percent of sales, these firms may take over the entire selling function for the manufacturer. Some even suggest what prices and advertising allowances should be offered to particular retailers. For a small manufacturer, they can perform a vital service. For large firms with many small divisions, they can be equally helpful.

Food brokers specialize by geographic area. A manufacturer could achieve national distribution with between 70 and 100 food brokers.

The food broker fills a gap in the sales efforts of many manufacturers. The brokers generally have an effective sales force—because they pay their salespeople well and keep them in the field. In contrast, manufacturers often use their sales territories as training grounds—and promote good salespeople to larger territories or home offices as soon as (and sometimes before) they have really become effective in their sales areas.

Selling agents—almost marketing managers

Selling agents take over the whole marketing job of manufacturers—not just the selling function. A selling agent may handle the entire output of one or more producers—even competing producers—with almost complete control of pricing, selling, and advertising. In effect, the agent becomes each producer's marketing manager.

Financial trouble is one of the main reasons a producer calls in a selling agent. The selling agent may provide working capital—but also may take over the affairs of the business.

Selling agents have been especially common in highly competitive fields, like textiles and coal. They also have been used for marketing lumber, certain food products, clothing items, and some metal products. In all these industries, marketing is much more important than production for the survival of firms. The selling agent provides the necessary financial assistance and marketing know-how.

International marketing is not so different

We find agent middlemen in international trade, too. Most operate much like those just described. **Export or import agents** are basically manufacturers' agents. **Export or import commission houses** and **export or import brokers** are really brokers. A **combination export manager** is a blend of a manufacturers' agent and a selling agent—handling the entire export function for several manufacturers of similar but noncompeting lines. As with domestic agent middlemen, it is necessary to determine exactly what functions each one provides before deciding to use it in a channel system.

Agent middlemen are more common in international trade because of the critical problem of financing. Many markets include only a few well-financed merchant wholesalers. The best many manufacturers can do is get local representation through agents—and then arrange financing through banks which specialize in international trade.

OTHER SPECIALIZED MIDDLEMEN—FACILITATORS—FILL UNIQUE ROLES

Factors—like a credit department

Factors are wholesalers of credit—who buy their clients' accounts receivable. Usually they specialize in certain lines of trade—and are willing to extend credit for longer periods than commercial banks. Sometimes, factors provide management assistance—and almost become selling agents. In fact, some are former selling agents who have concentrated on financing rather than selling. Like selling agents, factors are especially common in the highly competitive textile industry.

In buying accounts receivable, factors provide their clients with working capital. The factors' lending charge varies from 6 to 18 percent—depending on interest rates and whether the factor has any recourse to the seller for collection in case of nonpayment. He may charge extra for advice on customer selection and collection—perhaps 1 to 3 percent of the invoice face value. In effect, the factor may assume the function of a credit department—relieving clients of this expense.

Usually factors have many clients in a given line—such as textiles—and so are able to spread their risks over many customers. By specializing in a certain line, they get to know most of the buyers in the trade—and are better able to evaluate the credit risks. One result is that while a buyer might be willing to delay payment to a single seller, he might hesitate to delay when he owes money to a factor. The factor might seriously hurt his credit rating, or even cut off all future credit—probably closing the business.

Field warehousing— cash for goods on hand

Another specialist in financing is the **field warehouser**—a firm which segregates some of a company's finished goods on its own property and issues warehouse receipts which can be used to borrow money. If a firm has accounts receivable, it can use a factor or even borrow at a bank. But if it has financial problems and its good are not yet sold, then borrowing may be more difficult. One solution is to move the goods to a public warehouse and obtain a warehouse receipt—which can then be used as collateral for borrowing at a bank. But moving goods can be expensive.

In field warehousing, the selling company's own warehouse is used, but an area is formally segregated by the field warehouser. The seller retains title to the goods, but control of them passes to the field warehouser. He in turn issues a warehouse receipt which can be used as collateral in borrowing. These field

Factors offer advice and credit in a given field because they know the business and the people in it.

Mary McCarthy

warehousing organizations usually know capital sources—and may be able to arrange loans at lower cost than is possible locally.

Using this method, large stocks can be maintained at various distribution points—in anticipation of future needs. Or economical production runs can be made—and then stored at the factory against future needs.

Sales finance companies—do floor planning

Some **sales finance companies** finance inventories. **Floor planning** is the financing of display stocks for auto and appliance retailers. Many auto dealers, for example, do not own outright any of the cars on their display floors. They may have only a 10 percent interest in each of them—the other 90 percent belonging to a sales finance company. The auto dealer has physical possession. But the finance company owns the cars—and the proceeds from sales may go directly to it.

In effect, these companies are providing part of the dealer's financing function. But because the goods are usually well branded—and therefore easily resold—there is relatively little risk. The charge to the dealer for these services may be as low as 10 percent a year—just a little above the finance company's cost of borrowing money.

WHOLESALERS TEND TO CONCENTRATE TOGETHER

Different wholesalers are found in different places

Some wholesalers—such as grain elevator operators—are located close to producers. But most of wholesaling is done in or near large cities. Over forty percent of all wholesale sales in 1977 were made in the 15 largest Standard Metropolitan Statistical Areas.

This heavy concentration of wholesale sales in large cities is caused, in part, by the concentration of manufacturers' sales offices and branches in these attractive markets. It also is caused by the tendency of agent middlemen to locate in these large cities—near the many large wholesalers and industrial buyers. Some large manufacturers buy for many plants through one purchasing department located in the general offices in these cities. And large general merchandise wholesalers often are located in these transportation and commerce centers.

The prominent role played by the New York area should be especially noted—11 percent of all wholesale sales. This results partly from the concentration of much of the U.S. wholesale clothing and jewelry industries in this one market. But it also points up the important role played by large commercial cities. This is true not only in the United States—but also in world markets. Wholesalers tend to concentrate together—near transporting, storing, and financing facilities—as well as a large population.

COMEBACK AND FUTURE OF WHOLESALERS

In the 1800s, wholesalers held a dominant position in marketing. The many small producers and small retailers needed their services. As producers became larger, some bypassed the wholesalers—by setting up their own sales organizations or by selling directly to industrial customers. When retailers also began to grow larger—especially during the 1920s when chain stores began to spread rapidly—many predicted a gloomy future for wholesalers. Chain stores normally assume the wholesaling functions—and it was thought that the days of independent wholesalers were numbered.

Not fat and lazy, but enduring

Some analysts and critics felt that the decline of wholesalers might be desirable from the social point of view—because many wholesalers had apparently grown "fat and lazy," contributing little more than breaking bulk. Their sales people often were only order takers. The selling function was neglected. High-caliber management was not attracted to the wholesaling industry. It became a domain of vested interests which many persons felt should be eliminated.

Our review here, however, has shown that wholesaling functions *are* necessary—and wholesalers have not been eliminated. True, their sales volume declined from 1929 to 1939, but wholesalers have since made a comeback. By 1954, they had regained the same relative importance they had in 1929—and they have continued to hold their own since then.[3]

Producing profits, not chasing orders

Wholesalers have held their own, in part, because of new management and new techniques. To be sure, there are still many operating in the old ways—and wholesaling has had nothing comparable to the rapid changes in retailing. Yet progressive wholesale firms have become more concerned with their customers—and with channel systems. Some are offering more services to their independent customers—and others are developing voluntary chains that bind them more closely to their customers. Some of this ordering is done routinely by mail or telephone—or directly by telephone to computer.

Today's *progressive* wholesaler is no longer a passive order taker. As part of the new look in wholesaling, many sales representatives have been eliminated. In place of the old order takers, wholesalers are now using order slips similar to those used between a chain warehouse and chain retail stores.

Some modern wholesalers no longer require all customers to pay for all the services offered—simply because certain customers use them. This traditional

Wholesalers are being more selective about the size of their customers so they can provide better, more economical service.

Milt & Joan Mann

practice had the effect of encouraging limited-function wholesalers and direct channels. Now, some wholesalers are making a basic service available at a minimum cost—then charging additional fees for any special services required. In the grocery field, for instance, the basic servicing of a store might cost the store 3 to 4 percent of wholesale sales. Then promotion assistance and other aids are offered at extra cost.

Modern wholesalers also are becoming more selective in picking customers— as cost analysis shows that many of their smaller customers are clearly unprofitable. With these less desirable customers gone, wholesalers can give even more attention to more profitable customers. In this way, they are helping to promote healthy retailers—who are able to compete in any market.

Some wholesalers have renamed their salespeople "store advisers" or "supervisors" to reflect their new roles. These representatives provide many management advisory services—including location analysis, store design and modernization, legal assistance on new leases or adjustments in old leases, store-opening services, sales training and merchandising assistance, and advertising help. Such sales people—really acting as management consultants—must be more competent than the mere order takers of other days.

Progress—or fail

Training a modern wholesaler's salespeople is not easy—and it is sometimes beyond the management in small wholesale firms. In some fields—such as the plumbing industry—wholesaler trade associations have taken over the job. They organize training schools designed to show the wholesaler's salespeople how they, in turn, can help retailers manage their businesses and promote sales. These schools give instructions in bookkeeping, figuring a markup, collecting accounts receivable, advertising, and selling—all in an effort to train the wholesalers' salespeople to improve retailers' effectiveness as channel members.[4]

Many wholesalers are now using electronic data processing systems to control inventory. And some are modernizing their warehouses and physical handling facilities.

Some wholesalers are offering central bookkeeping facilities for their retailers— realizing that their own survival is linked to their customers' survival. In this sense, some wholesalers are becoming more channel system minded—no longer trying to overload retailers' shelves. Now they are trying to clear the merchandise *off* the retailers' shelves. They follow the adage, "Nothing is really sold until it is sold at retail."[5]

Perhaps good-bye to some

Despite these changes, however, not all wholesalers today are progressive. Many still follow outmoded practices. Some of the smaller, less efficient ones may have difficulty in the future. While the average operating expense ratio is 12.7 percent for merchant wholesalers, some small wholesalers have expense ratios of 20–30 percent.

Low cost, however, is not the only criterion for success. The higher operating expenses for some smaller wholesalers may be a reflection of the special services they offer to some market segments. Truck distributors are usually small—and have high operating costs—yet some customers are willing to pay the higher cost of this service. Some of the apparently expensive, older, full-service wholesalers probably will continue operating—because they offer the services and contacts needed by some small manufacturers. And, of course, some goods and some markets traditionally have slow turnover. Wholesalers may be the best choice—even though they have high operating expenses.

Even making these allowances, though, it is clear that the smaller wholesalers—and the larger, less progressive ones—face future difficulty unless each has carved out a specific market for itself. Profit margins are not large in wholesaling—typically ranging from less than 1 percent to 2 percent. And they have been declining in recent years—as the competitive squeeze has become tighter.

In short, the institution of wholesaling certainly will survive—but weaker, less progressive wholesale firms may not.

CONCLUSION

Wholesalers can provide functions for those both above and below them in a channel of distribution. These services are closely related to the basic marketing functions. There are many types of wholesalers. Some provide all the wholesaling functions—while others specialize in only a few. Eliminating wholesalers would not eliminate the need for the functions they provide. And we cannot assume that direct channels will be more efficient.

Merchant wholesalers are the most numerous and account for just over half of wholesale sales. Their distinguishing characteristic is that they take title—and often physical possession—of goods. Agent middlemen, on the other hand, act more like sales representatives for sellers or buyers—and usually they do not take title or possession.

Despite various predictions of the end of wholesalers, they continue to exist. And the more progressive ones have adapted to a changing environment. No such revolutions as we saw in retailing have yet taken place in the wholesaling area—and none seem likely. But it is probable that some smaller—and less progressive—wholesalers will fail, while larger and more market-oriented wholesalers will continue to provide these necessary functions.

QUESTIONS AND PROBLEMS

1. Discuss the evolution of wholesaling in relation to the evolution of retailing.

2. What risks do merchant wholesalers assume by taking title to goods? Is the size of this risk about constant for all merchant wholesalers?

3. Why would a manufacturer set up its own sales branches if established wholesalers were already available?

4. What is an agent middleman's marketing mix? Why don't manufacturers use their own salespeople instead of agent middlemen?

5. Discuss the future growth and nature of wholesaling if low-margin retailing and scrambled merchandising become more important. How will wholesalers have to adjust their mixes if retail establishments become larger and the retail managers more professional? Might the wholesalers be eliminated? If not, what wholesaling functions would be most important? Are there any particular lines of trade where wholesalers may have increasing difficulty?

6. Which types of wholesalers would be most appropriate for the following products? If more than one type of wholesaler could be used, provide the specifications for the situation in each case. For example, if size or financial strength of a company has a bearing, then so indicate. If several wholesalers could be used in this same channel, explain this also.
   a. Fresh tomatoes.
   b. Paper-stapling machines.
   c. Auto mechanics' tools.
   d. Canned tomatoes.
   e. Men's shoes.
   f. An industrial accessory machine.
   g. Ballpoint pens.
   h. Shoelaces.

7. Would a drop-shipper be desirable for the following products: coal, lumber, iron ore, sand and gravel, steel, furniture, or tractors? Why, or why not? What channels might be used for each of these products if drop-shippers were not used?

8. Explain how factors differ from commercial banks and why factors developed.

9. Explain how field warehousing could help a marketing manager.

10. Which types of wholesalers are likely to become more important in the next 25 years? Why?

SUGGESTED CASES

14 Deller Company

15 Watson Sales Company

NOTES

1. For a detailed discussion of the definition of wholesaling and the operation and management of a wholesale business, see T. N. Beckman, N. H. Engle, and R. D. Buzzell, *Wholesaling,* 3rd ed. (New York: Ronald Press Co., 1959).

2. "Food Brokers: A Comprehensive Study of Their Growing Role in Marketing." *Grocery Manufacture,* December 1969. This and others available from the National Food Brokers Association, 1916 M Street, N.W., Washington, D.C. 20036.

3. Paul D. Converse, "Twenty-Five Years in Wholesaling: A Revolu-tion in Food Wholesaling," *Journal of Marketing,* July 1957, pp. 40–41; and Richard S. Lopata, "Faster Pace in Wholesaling," *Harvard Business Review,* July–August 1969, pp. 130–43.

4. *Dealer Development Institute* (Chicago: Central Supply Association).

5. For more discussion, see F. E. Webster, Jr., "The Role of the Industrial Distributor in Marketing Strategy," *Journal of Marketing,* July 1976, pp. 10–16; and "Wetterau: A Maverick Grocery Wholesaler," *Business Week,* February 14, 1977, pp. 121–22.

E. J. McCarthy

1. Understand why physical distribution is such an important part of Place *and* marketing.

2. Know about the advantages and disadvantages of the various transporting methods.

3. Know what storing possibilities a marketing manager can use.

4. Understand the distribution center concept.

5. Understand the total cost approach to physical distribution.

6. Understand customer service level as a strategic variable.

7. Recognize the important new terms (shown in red).

15

Physical distribution

If it got to you, it probably came at least part way by truck.

Physical distribution (PD) is the transporting and storing of physical goods within individual firms and along channel systems. Nearly half the cost of marketing is spent on physical distribution.

PD is very important to the firm—and the macro-marketing system—since goods that remain in the factory or on the farm really have no "use" at all. And *possession* utility is not possible until *time* and *place* utility have been provided. This usually requires the transporting and storing functions that are part of physical distribution.

Deciding who will haul and store is strategic

As any marketing manager develops the Place part of a strategy, it is important to decide how transporting and storing functions can and should be divided within the channel. Who will store and transport the goods—and who will pay for these services? Just deciding to use certain types of wholesalers or retailers does not automatically—or completely—answer these questions. A wholesaler may use its own trucks to haul goods from a producer to its warehouse—and from there to retailers—but only because the manufacturer gives a transportation allowance. Another wholesaler may want the goods delivered.

When developing a marketing strategy, the marketing manager must decide how these functions are to be shared—since this will affect the other three Ps—and especially Price. The truth is, however, that there is no ideal sharing arrangement. Physical distribution can be varied endlessly in a marketing mix—and in a channel system.

These are important strategic decisions—because they can make or break a strategy. Wise PD decisions may help attract new customers by providing better service—or by cutting PD costs and lowering prices. And effective management of PD will help assure that the "right" *Product* actually is in the "right" *Place* when the customer wants to buy. Providing *time, place,* and *possession utilities* is not a small matter—sales are often lost just because the product is not available.

In this chapter, we will discuss physical distribution possibilities—and also some important new ideas, including the distribution center, the total cost approach, and customer service level.

THE TRANSPORTING FUNCTION

From backpacks to cargo planes

Transporting is the marketing function of moving goods. It provides time and place utilities. Before the coming of powered vehicles, transporting was slow and the movement of goods was limited to what a person could carry on his back or haul in a wagon. People lived where the goods were—on self-sufficient farms—and traded their surpluses in nearby markets.

Early societies developed along seacoasts or rivers partly because transportation of goods by water was easier than by land. Yet, most commercial river transportation was still one way—downstream.

The introduction of the steamboat in the early 1800s—and the first practical steam locomotive in 1829—opened a whole new era. In the United States, the railroad made it possible to ship midwestern farm products to the eastern industrial area—lowering food prices considerably. Later, motor trucks and highways brought even small towns and remote farms closer to the markets.

Today, the marketing manager generally has several carriers in one or more modes competing for the firm's transportation business. There are five basic modes of freight movement: railroads, trucks, waterways, pipelines, and airplanes.

Table 15–1 shows the annual volume of intercity freight moved in the United States by each mode. Ton-miles carried is the most common method of measuring the importance of various methods of transportation. A **ton-mile** means the movement of a ton of goods one mile. If, for example, 10 tons of sand were carried 10 miles, the total movement would be a 100 ton-miles.

Using this measure makes it obvious that railways are the backbone of the U.S. transportation system. Following in importance are trucks, pipelines, and barges. Relatively speaking, airplanes don't move much freight as yet.

The numbers in the table do not tell the whole story, however—since they do not show the tons shipped. Information on this subject is sketchy, but probably at least 75 percent of all freight moves by trucks—at least part of the way—from producer to user. Railroads may carry goods for long distances—but trucks

Table 15–1
Intercity freight movement in the United States (1977)

	Ton-miles carried (in billions)	Percent of total
Railways	832	36.1
Motor vehicles	555	24.1
Pipelines	546	23.7
Inland waterways	368	16.0
Airways	4	0.2
Total	2,305	100.0

Source: *Statistical Abstract of the United States, 1979,* p. 635.

Almost everything travels by truck at least part of the way from producer to consumer.

Kenneth Yee

haul the bulk of the short-haul movement. The trucking industry slogan, "If you have it, it came by truck," is certainly true for consumer goods—although many industrial goods are still delivered by railroads or other transportation modes.

The point to remember is that without transportation, there could be no mass distribution with its regrouping activities—or any urban life as we know it today. We understand this most clearly during a major rail or truck strike.

TRANSPORTING CAN BE COSTLY

Can you afford to get to the target?

The cost of shipping an average product by rail is about 5 percent of wholesale cost.[1] For many bulky or low-value products, however, the percentage is much higher. Transporting sand and gravel, for example, costs about 55 percent of its value; bituminous coal, 42 percent; cabbage, 38 percent; watermelons, 38 percent; and iron ore, 20 percent. At the other extreme are lighter or more valuable commodities—such as copper and office machines—transported for less than 1 percent of wholesale cost; and cigarettes and butter for less than 2 percent.[2]

Transportation costs may limit the target markets that a marketing manager can consider. Shipping costs increase delivered cost—and this is what really interests the customer. High costs for goods in outlying areas—caused by higher transportation costs—encourage local production. The high costs of shipping sand and gravel mean that these materials must be sold in the limited geographic areas near the pits where they are extracted.

Different transporters charge different rates

Common carriers—such as the railroads and major truck lines—are transporters which maintain regular schedules and accept goods from any shipper. They charge rates which are fixed for all users by government regulators. **Contract carriers** are transporters who are willing to work for anyone for an agreed sum—and for any length of time. They are less strictly regulated. **Private carriers** are company-owned transportation facilities. "Do-it-yourself" transporting is al-

*Contract carriers will take a cargo
wherever it has to go for an agreed
amount.*

Peter Le Grand

ways a possibility—but it often isn't economical because the contract or common carriers can make fuller use of their facilities and, therefore, charge less.

Common carriers provide a dependable transportation service for the many producers and middlemen who make small shipments in various directions. Contract carriers, on the other hand, are a more free-wheeling group—going wherever goods have to be moved.

SHOULD YOU DO IT YOURSELF?

To cut transporting costs, some marketing managers do their own transporting—rather than buy from specialists. Trucking has made it easier to "do-it-yourself." Some large manufacturers own thousands of cars and trucks. And there are iron ore, gypsum rock, and petroleum producers who have their own ships.

*It depends on
discrepancies of
quantity and shipment
consistency*

The concept of discrepancy of quantity is important here. If there is a great difference between the quantity a firm normally ships and the quantity that common carriers find most economical, the firm may have to ship via common carrier. But if a company normally ships in the same quantities that common carriers find economical, it may save money by using its own trucks. This avoids the cost that common carriers must charge for maintaining a regular schedule—or that contract carriers must charge against future uncertainties.

If a marketing manager is fairly certain of the firm's future plans, do-it-yourself transporting may be good business. A wine wholesaler in New Orleans found that it cost much more to ship wine by rail from California than if a tank truck and driver were hired for the California run. Because this was a regular and frequent shipment, the firm bought a truck—and operated it at a large saving.

DEVELOPMENT OF THE TRANSPORTING RATE STRUCTURE

In our discussion of transporting rates, we will concentrate on *rail common carrier rates,* since they set a competitive standard. Most other rate structures have similar characteristics.

The development of the railroad rate structure was guided by government regulatory commissions. The thinking underlying the rate structure was that the railways could carry the heavy and bulky items—such as sand and gravel—at a relatively low charge per ton; carry the more valuable, less bulky items at higher rates per ton; and then balance the low charges against the high charges—to show a profit. As we will see, however, this hasn't worked out as planned. The railroads have been carrying the heavy bulky items at low rates—but trucks and airlines have been taking the high-rate business—and many railroads have gone bankrupt.

There are three basic types of rates: (1) class, (2) commodity, and (3) exception. These three kinds of rates are quoted for carloads (CL, 60,000–100,000 pounds), truckloads (TL, 15,000 pounds or more), less than carloads (LCL), and less than truckloads (LTL).

Rates on less than full carloads and truckloads vary but are often twice as high as those on full loads. These rate differentials are another reason for the development of wholesalers, who buy in larger quantities than most users need—to get the advantage of full-load rates—and then sell in the smaller quantities the users *do* need.

Class rates—higher rates for smaller volume

The railroads handle so many different products that they have had to develop a freight classification system covering more than 10,000 different articles or groups of articles. Each class is assigned rates—based on the cost and value of the service, the size of the shipment, and the distance shipped.

Class rates are the rates charged for general manufactured products that are shipped in amounts too small to justify much negotiation by shippers. Between 2 and 4 percent of the volume shipped by rail comes under these rates—and these are the rates which were supposed to offset the low rates on bulky, low-value items.

Special commodity rates are set for bulky products that are shipped regularly.

William S. Nawrocki

Commodity rates—
lower rates for big bulk

In many instances, there is no provision within the 10,000 class-rate classifications for the specific characteristics of certain commodities—especially bulky or low-value items. Commodity rates are the rates set for transporting specific commodities between specific points or over specific routes. These rates frequently develop out of negotiation between shippers and railroads.

There are special commodity rates for most bulky items—such as wheat, iron ore, coal, lumber, or any products shipped regularly in large volume. Some of the negotiated commodity rates are called "blanket rates"—because the same rate is applied over a large geographic area, regardless of the distance between specific points within that area. Fresh fruits and vegetables, for example, can be shipped from the West Coast to almost any place on the East Coast for the same rate. Approximately 90 percent of the rail carload traffic moves under commodity rates.

Exception rates—
special rates for special
conditions

Exception rates are special low rates set to meet competition. If a certain producer needs lower rates to compete in other markets—or if competition from other methods of transportation is especially strong—the carriers sometimes are forced to set special rates.

Railways grant exception rates on many items—to meet truck competition. But less than 10 percent of carload traffic moves under these rates.[3]

Correct rate not easy to
determine

The large number of rate classes—and the many exceptions—make traffic management a difficult job. A carrier frequently charges a higher rate when a lower rate should apply. Some companies find it profitable to audit all freight bills before payment. There are even private firms specializing in this kind of work—earning a share of the savings.

It is not that carriers are deliberately overcharging—but rather that the freight agents who determine the appropriate rates must choose from a large number of possible routes, rates, and rate combinations. Planning the best routing for the lowest rate gets more complex each year—since more than 150,000 rate changes are made annually.[4] And the basic rate books do not show cross-references to all these new rates. Because of this complexity—and the possibility of error—some channel members prefer to have prices quoted on a delivered basis.

MARKETING MANAGER MAY AFFECT RATES

Present rate structure
not permanently fixed

There is nothing final about the present rate structure. Since it is man-made, it could be changed. If it were changed, it might lead to a vastly different—perhaps more efficient or fairer—transportation system. In some other countries, for instance, the rate differentials are much smaller—or nonexistent. As a result, goods are shipped in much smaller quantities, freight cars are smaller, and wholesalers and retailers handle smaller quantities.

Carriers can and do make changes—and if no one objects—the new rates usually go into effect. Rate changes can be made relatively quickly (1 to 30 days) and easily—as indicated by those 150,000 changes made each year.

Capitalize on carrier competition

Most rates are based originally on supply factors, that is, the cost of providing necessary services—loading, product liability, regular scheduled service even though it is not used, special equipment such as refrigerated cars, and so on. But supply factors do not determine the final rates. Rather, they determine the rate the carrier *would like to charge.* The rates actually charged are determined by competition among the various carriers—*and* alternate methods of transportation. By taking advantage of these factors, an aggressive marketing manager can reduce the cost of transporting.

Carriers are usually interested in stimulating business in their areas. If the marketing manager can show that business could expand if lower rates were granted into certain territories, the carriers may be willing to grant these lower rates. In fact, much adjustment has taken place—so that now distance traveled and total transportation costs are often only weakly related. New England railroads, for example, have long charged the same rates from New England as from New York on shipments going west. This allows their New England customers to compete on equal terms with respect to transportation costs. Similarly, southern railroads reduced their rates on finished cotton goods—so southern mills could sell in northern territories in competition with New England mills.[5] Note the behavior here of competing channel systems—with the railroads as part of the channel.

Creative marketing managers—by bargaining for rate changes—can help their channel system members with the transporting function. In fact, some manufacturers and middlemen have *traffic departments* staffed by ten or more employees to deal with carriers. These departments can be a big help—not only to their own firm but also to their suppliers and customers—finding the best routes and lowest rates.

WHICH TRANSPORTING ALTERNATIVE IS BEST

Lowest cost alternative may not be best

The best transporting alternative should not only be as low in cost as possible—but also provide the level of service (for example, speed and dependability) required. Obviously, the transporting function should fit into the whole marketing strategy. Therefore, the marketing manager should fully understand the advantages and disadvantages of the various transportation modes discussed below. See Figure 15–1. It is important to see from the beginning that lowest transporting cost is *not* the only criterion for selecting the best method.

Figure 15–1
Transportation modes ranked according to various criteria (1 = highest rank)

	Speed (door-to-door)	Frequency (scheduled shipments)	Dependability (meeting schedules)	Capability (ability to handle variety)	Availability (number of points served)	Cost (per ton-mile)
Rail	3	4	3	2	2	3
Water	4	5	4	1	4	1
Truck	2	2	2	3	1	4
Pipeline	5	1	1	5	5	2
Air	1	3	5	4	3	5

Source: Adapted from James L. Heskett, Robert J. Ivie, and Nicholas A. Glaskowsky, *Business Logistics* (New York: Ronald Press, 1964), pp. 71n.

Railroads—workhorse of the nation

The *railroad*—the workhorse of U.S. transportation—has been important mainly for carrying heavy and bulky freight such as coal, sand, and steel. By handling large quantities of such commodities, the railroads are able to transport at relatively low cost. But railroads have had profit difficulties in recent years—in part because trucking firms have set their rates low enough to compete for the more profitable, less bulky items that the railroads were counting on to offset the low rates on the bulky commodities.

Competiton has forced railroads to innovate

The railroads have taken various steps to bring their profits up. Computerization and automation of rail facilities have helped. Catering more specifically to the needs of some target customers has helped too. By introducing triple-deck carriers for automobiles, the rails were able to win back from trucks a large share of new-car transports. And now, specially designed railcars can carry 30 small automobiles—twice as many as the triple-deck carriers—by stacking them vertically rather than horizontally. The design of special refrigerator cars, tank cars, hopper cars, and cars especially suited for loading and unloading livestock also has helped attract and hold business.[6]

Rails now offer more special services

To be more competitive, the railroads have offered a variety of special services and shipping alternatives. Some of these are discussed below.

Piggy-back service loads truck trailers on rail cars to provide both speed and flexibility. Operating with the apparent philosophy, "If you can't beat them, haul them," truck trailers are picked up at the producer's location, loaded onto specially designed rail flatcars, hauled as close to the customer as rail lines run, then picked up by a truck tractor and delivered to the buyer's door. Such service provides all the flexibility of trucking—and on some routes it costs even less. A loaded truck trailer can be shipped piggy-back from the Midwest to the West Coast for approximately half the cost of sending it over the highways.

Fast freight service provides special faster trains. Many of the goods shipped

Piggyback service cuts cost and provides flexibility for producers.

Mary McCarthy

by rail are not particularly perishable or in urgent demand—and as a result, much railroad freight moves more slowly than truck shipments. But when speed is needed, a train can really move.

Some railroads offer a fast freight service for perishable or high-value items. Such trains—highballing at 60 miles per hour and stopping only to change crews and load water and ice—can be competitive in speed with trucks—provided shippers and receivers are located near rail lines.

Pool car service allows several shippers to pool their like goods as a full car. Railroads are most efficient at handling full carloads of goods. Less-than-carload (LCL) shipments take a lot of handling and rehandling. They usually move slowly—and at a higher price per 100 pounds than carload shipments.

To offset the shortcomings of low speed and high cost—and still encourage the business of small shippers—some railroads encourage groups of shippers to pool their shipments into a full car. This service also permits a producer to ship to several small-quantity buyers in a single area at greater speed and under the lower carload rates. If buyers are not located in the same area, the goods may be shipped in a pool car at the carload rate to the first buyer—and then broken up for further shipment at LCL rates.

Sometimes local retailers buying from a single area—such as New York City—consolidate their shipments in single cars. Local truckers deliver the goods when they arrive. When different commodities are shipped in the same car, it is called a *mixed car* rather than a pool car—and the highest rate for any of the commodities applies to the whole shipment.

The **diversion in transit service** allows redirection of carloads already in transit. A carload of California oranges could be shipped toward Chicago—or simply eastward toward no specific destination—and as market demand and supply conditions change, the shipper could change or specify the destination. The railroad would then reroute the car for a small fee.

This diversion in transit service lets a marketing manager get the goods rolling—but still stay flexible about target market selection.

Transit privilege service allows for processing of goods in transit. Some agricultural and industrial raw materials must be processed at another location on the way to users. To aid this regrouping and processing, some railroads permit shippers to move the raw materials toward the market, stop along the way for processing, and then reship them to the final destination at the "through" rate—as long as the same general direction is maintained. This *transit privilege* is especially important in the flour milling industry—where the service is called *milling in transit*.

The **transloading privilege** allows for combining several smaller shipments into a carload for part of the distance. It speeds delivery of parts of an original carload shipment to two or more destinations. When goods are to be shipped in a car cross-country to customers at several destinations, the railroad does not pull the car from city to city—unloading it bit by bit, here and there. Instead, it moves a full carload of goods to the point closest to the various customers, then reloads parts of the shipment into other cars for the remaining distance.

Since the transloading privilege makes LCL size deliveries feasible, customers can maintain a smaller inventory—shifting the storing function back to the manufacturer or wholesaler. Like other special services, transloading gives channel members more freedom in planning marketing strategies—and sharing channel functions.

Trucks are flexible, fast, dependable, and indispensable

The flexibility of *trucks* makes them especially suitable for moving small quantities of goods for short distances. They can travel on almost any road. They are not limited to where the rails go—and can give extremely fast service. The way truckers compete with railroads for these high-charge items is somewhat like the way retailers compete in "scrambled merchandising." Going after such business is logical for the truckers—because it is these smaller, high-charge items that trucks are best able to handle. And the recent deregulation of trucking is likely to increase this "scrambling."

Trucking has opened many new markets—and permitted decentralization—by bringing fast, dependable transport to outlying urban areas, smaller towns, and rural areas. Although trucks may congest traffic and damage highways, it is a fact that trucks are essential to our present macro-marketing system.

Waterways are slow and seasonal, but inexpensive

Water transportation is the lowest-cost method—but it is also the slowest and most seasonal. *Barges* on the inland waterways are used mostly for bulky, nonperishable products—such as iron ore, grain, steel, petroleum products, cement, gravel, sand, coal, and coke. When winter ice closes fresh water harbors, alternate transportation must be used. Some shippers—such as those dealing in iron ore—ship their total annual supply during the summer months and store it near their production facilities for winter use. Here, low-cost transporting combined with storing reduces *total cost.*

The St. Lawrence waterway system—and a combination of rivers, canals, and locks—make ocean transport available to the vast industrial and agricultural regions of inland United States. Foreign ships regularly move on the Great Lakes. And ocean-going barges can reach as far north as Minneapolis–St. Paul—and deep into Arkansas.

A recent advance in coastal and transoceanic shipping is the redesign of ships to handle large standard-size containers and truck trailers. Now ships, combined with trucks, can offer a **fishy-back service**—similar to rail piggy-back ser-

Distribution by waterways is the slowest but most economical for many products.

Milt & Joan Mann

vice—only using ships and trucks. Door-to-door service is now offered between the United States and European cities.

Pipelines are used primarily by the petroleum industry

In the United States, *pipelines* are used primarily by the petroleum industry— to move oil and natural gas. Extensive lines—especially in the Southwest—bring oil from the fields to refineries. From there, the more flexible railroads, trucks, and ships usually transport refined products to customers.

Airplanes are fast and expensive

The most expensive means of cargo transportation yet developed is by airplane—but it also is fast! Airfreight rates normally are at least twice as high as trucking rates—but the greater speed may more than justify the added cost. Trucks took the cream of the railroads' traffic. Now airplanes are taking the cream of the cream. They also are creating new transporting business by carrying—across continents and oceans—perishable commodities that simply could not be moved before. Tropical flowers from Hawaii, for example, now are jet-flown to points all over the United States. California's strawberries are flown to the Midwest and East all through the year. Brazilian manufacturers sell goods throughout South America by air.

The bulk of airfreight so far has been fashions, perishable commodities, and high-value industrial parts for the electronics and metal-working industries.

But airplanes may cut the total cost of distribution

An important advantage of using airplanes is that the cost of packing, unpacking, and preparing the goods for sale may be reduced or eliminated. One Los Angeles manufacturer of electronic products—who makes all deliveries beyond 150 miles by air—merely wraps the complex 600-pound machines in heavy wrapping paper. The increased transporting costs are more than offset by the lower packaging costs—and the firm is now competing for business nationally. The speedy service at lower costs has improved the company's marketing mix—and market position.

Planes may help a firm reduce its inventory costs—by eliminating outlying warehouses. And, valuable by-products of airfreight's speed are less spoilage, theft, and damage. With less time from shipper to customer, goods are exposed to fewer hazards.

Although the *transporting cost* of air shipments may be higher, the *total cost of distribution* may be lower.

FREIGHT FORWARDERS ARE TRANSPORTING WHOLESALERS

They accumulate economical shipping quantities

Freight forwarders combine the small shipments of many shippers into more economical shipping quantities. Many marketing managers use freight forwarders regularly to make optimum use of available transporting facilities. They are especially good for the many small shipments that may have to move by varied transportation services.

Freight forwarders do not own their own transporting facilities—except perhaps for delivery trucks. Rather, they wholesale air, ship, railroad, and truck space. Accumulating small shipments from many shippers, they reship in larger quantities to obtain lower transportation rates. Their profits mainly come out of the difference in freight rates between small- and large-quantity shipments—though they some-times make special service charges.

They help exporters

Freight forwarders can be especially helpful to the marketing manager who ships many small shipments to foreign markets. They handle an estimated 75 percent of the general cargo shipped from U.S. ports to foreign countries. More than 90 percent of all exporters—including companies with large shipping departments—use their services. An important reason is that the forwarders are located right at the exporting point—and can more easily process all the complicated paper work necessary in overseas shipments.[7]

THE STORING FUNCTION

Store it and smooth out sales, increase profits and consumer satisfaction

Storing is the marketing function of holding goods. It provides time utility.

Storing is necessary because production doesn't always match consumption. Some products—such as agricultural commodities—are produced seasonally al-though they are in demand year-round. If crops could not be stored when they mature or ripen, all of the crop would be thrown onto the market—and prices might drop sharply. Consumers might benefit temporarily from this "surplus," but later in the year—when supplies were scarce and prices high—they would suffer. Storing, therefore, helps stabilize prices during the consumption period—although prices usually do rise slightly over time to cover storing costs.

Planning to store, some buyers purchase in large enough quantities to get quantity discounts. Also, goods are sometimes stored as a hedge against future price rises, strikes, shipping interruptions, and other disruptions.

Finally, storing allows manufacturers and middlemen to keep stocks at convenient locations—ready to meet customers' needs. In fact, storing is one of the major activities of some middlemen.

Storing varies the channel system

Most channel members provide the storing function for varying lengths of time. Even final consumers store some things for their future needs. Since storing can be provided anywhere along the channel, the storing function offers several ways to vary a firm's marketing mix—and its channel system—by: (1) adjusting

Storing perishables keeps prices more stable throughout the year.

Mary McCarthy

the time goods are held, (2) sharing the storing costs, and (3) delegating the job to a specialized storing facility. This latter variation would mean adding another member—a facilitator—to the distribution channel.

Which channel members store the product—and for how long—affects the behavior of all channel members. If a manufacturer of groceries, for example, had a large local stock, wholesalers probably would carry smaller inventories—since they would be sure of dependable local supplies.

SPECIALIZED STORING FACILITIES CAN BE VERY HELPFUL

Private warehouses are common

Private warehouses are storing facilities owned by companies for their own use. Most manufacturers, wholesalers, and retailers have some storing facilities—either in their main buildings or in a warehouse district. Management of a manufacturer's finished-goods warehouse is often the responsibility of a sales manager—especially at sales branches located away from the factory. In retailing, storing is so closely tied to selling that the buyers may control this function.

Private warehouses are used when a large volume of goods must be stored regularly. Owning warehouse space can be expensive, however. If the need changes, the extra space may be hard—or impossible—to rent to others. See Figure 15–2 for a comparison of private warehouses and public warehouses.

Public warehouses fill special needs

Public warehouses are independent storing facilities. The company that does not need permanent warehouse space may find public warehouses useful. The customer pays only for the space used—and may purchase a variety of additional services. Public warehouses are useful to manufacturers who must maintain stocks in many locations—including foreign countries.

Some public warehouses provide all the services that could be obtained in the company's own branch warehouse—or from most wholesalers. These warehouses will receive goods in carload quantities, unload and store them, and later reship them in any size lots ordered by the company or its customers. They will inspect goods, package them, and even invoice customers. They will facilitate the financing function—by issuing warehouse receipts that can be used as collateral when borrowing from banks. Some public warehouses will provide

Figure 15–2
A comparison of private warehouses and public warehouses

	Type of warehouse	
	Private	*Public*
1. Fixed investment	Very high	No fixed investment
2. Unit cost	High, if volume is low. Very low, if volume is very high	Low; charges are made only for space needed
3. Control	High	Low managerial control
4. Adequacy for product line	Highly adequate	May not be convenient
5. Flexibility	Low; fixed costs have already been committed	High; easy to end arrangement

Source: Adapted from Louis W. Stern and Abel I. Elsary, *Marketing Channels* (Englewood Cliffs, N.J.: Prentice-Hall, Inc., 1977), p. 150.

desk space and telephone service for a company's salespeople. The public warehouse is responsible for the risk of damage or the loss of the product in the warehouse.

Public warehouses are located in all major metropolitan areas—and many smaller cities. Rural areas also have public warehouses for locally produced agricultural commodities.

General merchandise and bonded warehouses

General merchandise warehouses are public warehouses which store almost every kind of manufactured goods. A special form of public warehouse is the **bonded warehouse**—which specializes in storing imported goods or other goods (such as liquors or cigarettes) on which a tax must be paid before the goods are released for sale. If a long storing period is needed—say, to age liquor—then these warehouses may lower costs by delaying payment of taxes or duties until the goods are removed. Private bonded warehouses also can provide this latter feature.

Commodity and cold-storage warehouses

Commodity warehouses and **cold-storage warehouses** are public warehouses that are designed for storing perishable or easily spoiled products—such as apples, butter, and furs. Grain is stored in huge elevators which move the grain around to keep it cool.

Warehousing facilities have modernized

The cost of physical handling is a major storing cost. The goods must be handled once when put into storage—and again when removed to be sold. In older, multistoried warehouses—located in congested areas—these operations take many hours of high-cost labor. Difficult parking, crowded storage areas, and slow freight elevators delay the process—increasing the cost of distribution.

Today, modern, one-story buildings are replacing the old multistory buildings. These new designs eliminate the need for elevators—and permit the use of power-operated lift trucks, battery-operated motor scooters, roller-skating order pickers, electric hoists for heavy items, and hydraulic ramps to speed loading and unloading. Some grocery warehouses even have radio-controlled tractors that order pickers drive by remote control. Most of these new warehouses use lift trucks and pallets (wooden "trays" which carry many cases) for vertical storage—and better use of cube space.

THE DISTRIBUTION CENTER—A DIFFERENT KIND OF WAREHOUSE

Is storing really needed?

Storing is needed only if it helps achieve time utility. Storing is *not* necessary just because there is some discrepancy of quantity or assortment between one channel level and another. If there is a discrepancy *and* time must be used, then it can make economic sense to regroup and store at the same time. But if time is not needed, then no storing should be done. This leads us to a whole new idea—the distribution center.

Don't store it, distribute it

A **distribution center** is a special kind of warehouse designed to speed the flow of goods and avoid unnecessary storing. It is a breaking-bulk operation.

Peter Le Grand

Turnover is increased—and the cost of carrying inventory is reduced. This is important—because these costs may run as high as 35 percent a year of the value of the average inventory.

The concept behind the distribution center is the same one that led to the development of discount houses and mass merchandisers: *reducing costs and increasing turnover will lead to bigger profits.*

There are many variations of the distribution center. The following example of its application in the Pillsbury Company shows it within an integrated operation. Some public warehouses offer similar services for smaller manufacturers. Eventually, it may be possible for a manufacturer to use only 10 to 15 such public distribution centers and still service the country efficiently—and at lower cost than with present methods.

Pillsbury's distribution system was overwhelmed by expanding product lines and sales

The Pillsbury Co.—a large manufacturer of baking mixes and flour—used to move its products in carload lots—directly from factory to wholesaler or large retailer. Plants were as near to customers as possible. And each plant, initially, was able to produce the whole Pillsbury line. As lines expanded, however, it became apparent that no plant could produce all the various products. When customers began to ask for mixed carload shipments and faster delivery, Pillsbury found itself adding warehouse space—and hauling goods from plant to plant. By 1955, Pillsbury had set up 100 branch warehouses—controlled by 33 sales offices. Each sales office had its own accounting, credit, and other processing operations.

Later, one Pillsbury official was to say of this old system: "Turnover was slow, warehousing costs were high, and there was no effective control over inventories." It was then taking the company one week *just to process an order.*[8]

The distribution center brings it all together

Now, Pillsbury uses distribution centers to gurantee its customers "third morning delivery" anywhere in the United States. Each manufacturing plant specializes in a few product lines—and ships in carload lots directly to the distribution centers—almost eliminating storing at the factories. The field sales organization no longer handles physical distribution or inventory. Sales is its only activity—and it has been able to expand its branches from 33 to 52. The distribution centers are controlled by four regional data processing centers—which immediately determine where and when the goods are to be shipped for that "third morning delivery." Centralized accounting speeds invoices to customers—resulting in quicker payment. And because each distribution center always has adequate inventory, it is possible to ship orders the most economical way.

Before these changes at Pillsbury, neither the production nor the sales departments had responsibility for what happened to goods between manufacture and sale. Now, the entire physical distribution effort is treated as one system—under a director of distribution who is equal in rank to the heads of manufacturing and sales.

Pillsbury sales people have something extra to sell—better and faster service. Costs have been reduced and profits increased.

PHYSICAL DISTRIBUTION CONCEPT FOCUSES ON THE WHOLE DISTRIBUTION SYSTEM

We have been looking at the transporting and storing functions as separate activities—partly because this simplifies discussion, but also because it is the traditional approach. In recent years, however, attention has turned to the *whole* physical distribution function—not just transporting and storing. This sometimes affects production, too—since these activities are interdependent. We just saw this in the Pillsbury case.

Physical distribution—a new idea whose time may come

The **physical distribution (PD) concept** says that all transporting and storing activities of a business and a channel system should be thought of as part of one system—which should seek to minimize the cost of distribution for a given level of customer service. It may be hard to see this as a startling development. But until just a few years ago, even the most progressive companies treated PD functions as separate—and quite unrelated—activities. And they didn't worry about the total cost of physical distribution—because these costs were spread among various departments—and sometimes not calculated separately. And planning for a customer service level was almost unheard of—the idea was to "get the goods out the door." Unfortunately, this is still the situation in most firms.

In some firms, the production department is responsible for storing and shipping—and it builds inventories related to its production activities—rather than market needs. In other companies, storing may be a separate activity. If those in charge of inventory put little faith in sales forecasts, they may simply carry large stocks.

This naïve focusing on individual functional activities may actually increase a firm's and channel's total distribution costs. Therefore, those who accept the PD concept usually study the total cost of alternative physical distribution systems—applying the *total cost approach*.

EVALUATE ALTERNATIVE PD SYSTEMS WITH TOTAL COST APPROACH

Searching for the lowest total cost

The total cost approach.—to selecting a PD system—evaluates *all* costs of various possible PD systems. This means that all costs—including those which are sometimes ignored—should be considered. Inventory carrying costs, for example, are often ignored—because these costs may be buried in "overhead costs." Yet, they may be 10 to 35 percent of the value of average inventory.

The tools of cost accounting and economics are used with this approach. Sometimes, total cost analyses reveal that unconventional physical distribution methods will yield service as good as or better than conventional means—and at lower cost. The following simple example illustrates the approach.

Evaluating rail/ warehouse versus airfreight

Table 15–2 shows the result of a comparative cost analysis of two alternatives: airfreight with no warehouse versus rail with warehouse. The comparison was based on the distribution of 1,000 tons of a particular commodity during a definite period of time.

Comparing the final totals showed that using airfreight would be less expensive than the rail-warehouse combination, even though airfreight itself was much more expensive than rail.

In any total cost analysis of this kind, all practical alternatives should be evaluated and compared. Sometimes, alternatives are so numerous or complicated that advanced mathematical and statistical techniques—and perhaps a computer—are needed for their analysis.[9] For evaluating many alternatives, some companies have found it desirable to do simulation with a computer. In simulation, the characteristics and costs of the many alternatives are described as carefully as possible, and then the computer tests the alternatives—using a trial-and-error

Table 15–2
Comparative costs of airplane versus rail and warehouse

	Total cost	Cost per ton
Rail and warehouse		
*Interest on inventory, 30-day cycle, 360-day interest year at 6% on $1,500,000 of inventory	$ 90,000.00	$ 90.00
*Taxes on inventory	40,000.00	40.00
*Warehouse cost	55,200.00	55.20
†Transport expense (rail carload)	58,000.00	58.00
Cost via rail and warehouse	$243,200.00	$243.20
Airfreight		
*Interest on investment in inventory, 10-day cycle, 360-day interest year at 6% on $500,000 inventory	$ 30,000.00	$ 30.00
†Airfreight	120,000.00	120.00
†Local delivery	10,000.00	10.00
Cost via airfreight	$160,000.00	$160.00

Note: Total sales = 1,000,000 units or 1,000 tons
* indicates fixed and variable expense; † indicates variable expense only.

Source: Reprinted with permission of the publisher from p. 76 of *Physical Distribution Management* by E. W. Smykay, D. J. Bowersox, and F. H. Mossman. Copyright 1961 by the Macmillan Co.

Some firms are using total cost analysis, simulation, and other means to find the most efficient physical distribution methods.

Milt & Joan Mann

technique. Typically, however, the straight-forward total cost analysis discussed above is practicable—and will show whether there is need for a more sophisticated analytical approach.

PHYSICAL DISTRIBUTION PLANNING AS PART OF A COMPANY'S STRATEGY PLANNING

Physical distribution not just cost-oriented

Early physical distribution efforts emphasized lowering costs. Now, there is more attention given to making physical distribution planning a part of the company's strategy planning. Sometimes, by increasing physical distribution cost somewhat, the customer service level can be increased so much that, in effect, a new and better marketing mix is created.

Decide what level of service to offer

Customer service level is a measure of how rapidly and dependably a firm can deliver what customers want. Figure 15–3 shows the typical relation between physical distribution costs and customer service level. When a firm decides to minimize total cost, it may also be settling for a lower customer service level. By increasing the number of distribution points, the firm might be able to serve more customers within a specified time period. Transporting costs would be reduced—but warehousing and inventory costs would be increased. The higher service level, however, might greatly improve the company's strategy. Clearly, the marketing manager has a strategic decision about what service level to offer. Minimizing cost is not always the right answer.

Higher service level may cost more and sell more

Increasing service levels may be very profitable in highly competitive situations where the firm has relatively little to differentiate its marketing mix—for example, in close to pure competition or oligopoly. Here, simply increasing the service level—perhaps through faster delivery or wider stocks—may allow the firm to make headway in the market without changing product, price, or promotion. In fact, improved service levels can put a marketing mix across—and competitors

Figure 15–3
Higher customer service levels
are obtained at a cost

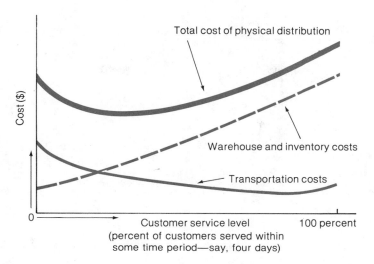

Figure 15–3
Higher customer service levels
are obtained at a cost

may not fully realize what has happened. Industrial buyers usually must have several sources of supply—but each buyer has some option as to how much he buys from whom. A higher service level might lead a buyer to forget about splitting orders equally among three suppliers—to reward the one offering much better service. He has to buy from someone—so adjusting shares does not affect him. But see what happens if the supplier with the better marketing mix were given one half of the business—rather than the usual one third. Without affecting the buyer—except that he gets better service—the seller would see a 50 percent increase in sales![10]

NEED FOR A PHYSICAL DISTRIBUTION MANAGER

An integrator is needed

Basic company reorganization may be needed for full acceptance of the physical distribution concept. It is even less accepted than the marketing concept. Just adding a "distribution manager" or a "manager of physical distribution"— or simply giving the traffic manager or warehouse manager a new title—will not do the job. What is really needed is the merging of producing, storing, transporting, and selling into one integrated system. Such far-reaching changes may be a long time coming. Not only will typically production-oriented departments resist such moves, but many sales and marketing managers still have not recognized their responsibility for physical distribution. One survey found that in 43 percent of the firms the top marketing executive did not assume any responsibility for physical distribution. In 35 percent of the firms, he was not involved in discussions about this important part of marketing.[11]

A real **physical distribution manager** is concerned not only with physical product flows—but also the location of place facilities through which the flows move. This is a big job. In some companies, it might be good to have a separate distribution manager—co-equal with the marketing manager—with centralized control of all physical distribution activities. There is much ferment and controversy

A physical distribution manager should work with the marketing manager to integrate production and distribution.

Mary McCarthy

in this area—because a "total system" is involved. But it is clear that major changes will be required in many companies if the marketing concept and the physical distribution concept are wholeheartedly adopted.

FUTURE PHYSICAL DISTRIBUTION PROBLEMS AND OPPORTUNITIES

Getting ready for an age of planning—and more costly fuel

New approaches must be found to mass transportation and urban living. Already, the federal government is subsidizing urban mass transportation systems. There are some attempts at developing new residential and commercial building arrangements. England, France, and Sweden have experimented with communities combining residential, working, and recreation facilities in the same center.

Deregulation or adjustments in transportation rate structures may lead to drastic changes in physical movement patterns—and where and what goods are produced and sold. The railroads have seen more and more of their most profitable business go to competitors. But if rates were adjusted on a grand scale, the changes might have a profound impact on the whole economy.

Suppose, for example, that the low rail rates charged on bulk commodities such as lumber were raised sharply. A lumber company in the Northwest might suffer. Contractors might shift to other types of building materials. Such a rate increase might even force the whole construction industry to change its methods and materials.

Similarly, higher fuel costs and pollution controls may increase the cost of truck and air movements—and make the rails more appealing. Lower speed limits on trucks may make the railroads look even better. The energy "crisis" may force even more radical changes—such as limiting the use of private cars or even banning them from city streets.

What will such regulations do to our car- and truck-oriented society? How will you and your community change? Such shifts will affect where people live and work—and what they produce and consume—and where and how they buy. In other words, these changes will have an impact on our whole macro-marketing system—and an alert marketing manager should try to anticipate and plan for this future.[12]

CONCLUSION

This chapter has dealt with transporting and storing—providing *time* and *place* utility. We discussed various modes of transporting—and their advantages and disadvantages. The railroad rate structure, particularly, seems in need of a drastic overhauling—and this might have a big impact on our present marketing system.

Storing—the second part of physical distribution—was considered, together with the types of warehousing now available. Examples were given of modern techniques which can cut storing and handling costs.

Although we discussed transporting and storing separately, it was emphasized that both are related. The distribution center—a new approach to PD—is an attempt to integrate these two functions to speed turnover and lower costs. The physical distribution concept is concerned with integrating all the storing and transporting activities into a smoothly working system.

Although cost is important in evaluating physical distribution alternatives, service level must also be considered—along with its strategic implications. Management often wants to improve service—and may select a higher-cost alternative to improve its marketing mix. Or the total cost approach might reveal that it is possible *both* to reduce costs and to improve service—perhaps by eliminating warehouses and using airplanes to speed delivery.

New organization structures—including the addition of a physical distribution manager—may be needed to achieve the potential benefits of integrating physical distribution activities.

Effective marketing managers make important strategic decisions about physical distribution arrangements. But acceptance of the physical distribution concept probably will continue to be slow. Many marketing managers do not even see physical distribution as part of their job—even though it accounts for half the cost of marketing.

But rising energy costs—and rising transporting costs—may encourage more marketing managers to coordinate storing and transporting in their planning. Creative marketing managers may be able to cut costs—while maintaining or improving service levels—and production-oriented competitors may not even understand what is being done.

QUESTIONS AND PROBLEMS

1. Discuss the relative advantages and disadvantages of railroads, trucks, and airlines as transporting methods.

2. Describe how your college town would be changed if there were no incoming or outgoing transportation except by foot, horseback, or horse-drawn covered wagon.

3. Distinguish between common carriers and contract carriers. What role do the contract carriers play in our economic system? How would our economy be different if there were no common carriers?

4. Distinguish among the following types of railroad rates:

class, commodity, and exception rates. If all three rates might apply in a particular situation, which one would probably be the lowest?

5. Explain which transportation method would probably be most suitable for shipment of goods to a large Chicago department store:
   a. A 10,000-lb. shipment of dishes from Japan.
   b. 15 lbs. of screwdrivers from New York.
   c. Three couches from High Point, N.C.
   d. 500 high-fashion dresses from the garment district in New York City.

e. 300 lbs. of Maine lobsters.

f. 600,000 lbs. of various appliances from Evansville, Indiana.

How would your answers change if this department store were the only one in a large factory town in Ohio?

6. Indicate the nearest location where you would expect to find substantial storage facilities. What kinds of products would be stored there and why are they stored there instead of some other place?

7. Indicate when a producer or middleman would find it desirable to use a public warehouse rather than a private warehouse. Illustrate, using a specific product or situation.

8. Discuss the distribution center concept. Is this likely to eliminate the storing function of conventional wholesalers? Is it applicable to all products? If not, cite several examples.

9. Clearly differentiate between a warehouse and a distribution center. Explain how a specific product would be handled differently by these marketing institutions.

10. Explain the total cost approach and why it may be necessary to have a physical distribution manager to implement the concept.

11. How would a distribution manager differ from a transportation manager? Would he really be any different than a marketing manager?

12. Explain how adjusting the customer service level could improve a marketing mix. Illustrate.

SUGGESTED CASES

15 Watson Sales Company

25 Valley View Company

NOTES

1. D. Philip Locklin, *Economics of Transportation,* 4th ed. (Homewood, Ill.: Richard D. Irwin, 1954), p. 35. © 1972 by Richard D. Irwin, Inc.

2. D. Philip Locklin, *Economics of Transportation,* 7th ed. (Homewood, Ill.: Richard D. Irwin, 1972), p. 57. © 1972 by Richard D. Irwin, Inc.

3. F. M. Cushman, *Transportation for Management* (New York: Prentice-Hall, Inc., 1953), pp. 173–74; and R. J. Sampson and M. T. Farris, *Domestic Transportation,* 2d ed. (Boston: Houghton-Mifflin, 1971), p. 55.

4. C. A. Taff, *Traffic Management,* 3d ed. (Homewood, Ill.: Richard D. Irwin, 1964), p. 248. © 1964 by Richard D. Irwin, Inc.

5. Locklin, *Economics of Transportation,* 6th ed. p. 54.

6. "Railcars Haul Vegas Vertically," *Detroit Free Press,* August 6, 1970, p. 8-D; "High-Mountain Railroad with Profits to Match," *Business Week,* June 10, 1967, pp. 174–80.

7. Paul V. Horn and Henry Gomez, *International Trade Principles and Practices,* 4th ed. (Englewood Cliffs, N.J.: Prentice-Hall, Inc., 1959), p. 521.

8. "New-fangled Routes Deliver the Goods—Faster and Cheaper," *Business Week,* November 4, 1959, pp. 108–10.

9. Arthur M. Geoffrion, "Better Distribution Planning with Computer Models," *Harvard Business Review,* July–August 1976, pp. 92–99. See also Donald J. Bowersox, *Logistical Management* (New York: Macmillan Publishing Co., Inc., 1974); Kenneth B. Ackerman and Bernard J. LaLonde, "Making Warehousing More Efficient," *Harvard Business Review,* March–April 1980, pp. 94–102; and David P. Herron, "Managing Physical Distribution for Profit," *Harvard Business Review,* May–June 1979, pp. 121–132.

10. For more discussion on this point, see William D. Perreault and Frederick A. Russ, "Physical Distribution Service in Industrial Purchase Decisions," *Journal of Marketing,* April 1976, pp. 3–10, and see also William D. Perreault and Frederick R. Russ, "Physical Distribution Service: A Neglected Aspect of Marketing Management," *MSU Business Topics,* Summer 1974, pp. 37–46; Douglas M. Lambert and James R. Stock, "Physical Distribution and Consumer Demands," *MSU Business Topics,* Spring 1978, pp. 49–56; Harvey N. Shycon and Christopher R. Sprague, "Put a Price Tag on Your Customer Servicing Levels," *Harvard Business Review,* July–August 1979, pp. 71–78; and Richard A. Matteis, "The New Back Office Focuses on Customer Service," *Harvard Business Review,* March–April 1979, pp. 146–159.

11. Robert E. Weigand, *Business Topics,* Summer 1962, pp. 70–71. See also James A. Constantin, Ronald D. Anderson, and Roger E. Jerman, "Views of Physical Distribution Managers," *Business Horizons,* April 1977, pp. 82–86.

12. R. F. Lusch, J. G. Udell, and G. R. Laczniak, "The Future of Marketing Strategy," *Business Horizons,* December 1976, pp. 65–74. See also "A Dark Tunnel Ahead for Mass Transit," *Business Week,* April 18, 1977, pp. 121–23; and Walter F. Friedman, "Physical Distribution: The Concept of Shared Services," *Harvard Business Review,* March–April 1975, pp. 24–26.; "Back to Railroading for a New Era," *Business Week,* July 14, 1980, pp. 64–69 (Union Pacific Railroad); and "A Sickly Conrail Heads for Radical Surgery," *Business Week,* July 28, 1980, p. 78.

Kenneth Yee

16
Promotion—introduction

"People won't buy your product if they've never heard of it."

Promotion—one of the four major variables with which the marketing manager works—is communicating information between seller and buyer—to influence attitudes and behavior. The marketing manager's promotion job is to tell target customers that the right Product is available at the right Place at the right Price.

What the marketing manager communicates is basically determined when the target customer's needs and attitudes are known.

How the appropriate messages are communicated depends on what blend of the following promotion methods are chosen: personal selling, mass selling, and sales promotion.

Promotion planning is only part of marketing strategy planning—but it is an important part because it links the seller with potential buyers—hopefully convincing them that the seller has the product they need.

In this chapter, we will discuss basic promotion methods, promotion objectives and methods of implementing them, and how these methods can be blended for effective promotion. The next two chapters will cover personal selling and mass selling—two important promotion methods.

SEVERAL PROMOTION METHODS ARE AVAILABLE

The marketing manager has several promotion methods to choose from. These include personal selling, mass selling, and sales promotion (see Figure 16–1).

Figure 16–1
Basic promotion methods and strategy planning

Personal selling—flexibility is the biggest asset

Personal selling involves direct face-to-face communication between sellers and potential customers. Salespeople can be very important parts of a marketing mix—because they are able to adapt the company's marketing mix to the needs of each target market—and, in the extreme, to each potential customer. Face-to-face selling also provides immediate feedback—which helps salespeople to adapt effectively. Salespeople are included in most marketing mixes, but their services come at a price. Sometimes personal selling is very expensive—and it is desirable to supplement this effort with mass selling and sales promotion.

Mass selling—reaching millions at a price or even free

Mass selling is communicating with large numbers of customers at the same time. It is less flexible than personal selling. But when the target market is large and scattered—mass selling is less expensive.

Advertising is the main form of mass selling. **Advertising** is any paid form of nonpersonal presentation of ideas, goods, or services by an identified sponsor. It includes the use of such media as magazines, newspapers, radio and TV, signs, and direct mail. While advertising must be paid for, another form of mass selling—publicity—is "free."

Publicity is "free"

Publicity is any *unpaid* form of nonpersonal presentation of ideas, goods, or services. Although, of course, publicity people get paid, they try to attract attention to the firm and its offerings *without having to pay media costs.*

If the firm has a "new" message, publicity may be more effective than advertising. Trade magazines, for example, may carry articles featuring the newsworthy products of regular advertisers—in part because they *are* regular advertisers. This publicity may raise more interest than the company's paid advertising. The publicity people probably would write the basic copy—and then "sell" its use to the magazine editors.

Large firms have specialists to handle this job. Usually though, it is treated as just another kind of advertising—and often it isn't used as effectively as it could be. Much more attention needs to be paid to publicity in the future.[1]

Sales promotion tries to complement

Sales promotion refers to those promotion activities which complement personal and mass selling. See Table 16–1.

It's hard to generalize about sales promotion—because it includes such a wide variety of activities. Also, its objective usually is to complement mass selling and personal selling—which are often seen as the basic—or strategic—methods, while sales promotion is seen as tactical—or short-run oriented. And given that the sales manager may be responsible for short-run price adjustments, "price dealing" may come to be thought of as sales promotion. He may be expected to decide whether the money which might be "lost" on a price deal might be used instead for special advertising allowances, contests, or other activities which are usually called "sales promotion."

THREE TYPES OF SALES PROMOTION

There are three types of sales promotion—those aimed at: (1) final consumers or users, (2) middlemen, and (3) the company's own sales force. The three types make it clear that sales promotion complements the other promotion methods. Sales promotion specialists are needed because the personal selling and mass selling people may be too busy with their own functions to have the time to develop the skill to handle the "fill-in" activities which are usually handled by sales promotion. Sales promotion specialists must be flexible—working in areas that most need improvement.

Sales promotion for final consumers or users

Sales promotion aimed at final consumers or users usually is trying to increase demand or speed up the time of purchase. Such promotion might involve developing materials to be displayed in retailers' stores—including banners and streamers, sample packages, calendars, and various point-of-purchase materials. The sales promotion people might also develop the aisle displays for supermarkets. They might be responsible for "jackpot" and "sweepstakes" contests—as well as coupons designed to get customers to try a product. All of these efforts would be aimed at specific promotion objectives.

Table 16–1
Examples of sales promotion activities

Aimed at final consumers or users	Aimed at middlemen	Aimed at company's own sales force
Banners	Price deals	Contests
Streamers	Promotion allowances	Bonuses
Samples	Sales contests	Meetings
Calendars	Calendars	Portfolios
Point-of-purchase materials	Gifts	Displays
Aisle displays	Trade shows	Sales aids
Contests	Meetings	Training materials
Coupons	Catalogues	
Trade shows	Merchandising aids	
Trading stamps		

Sales promotion may try to attract attention and increase demand.

Peter Le Grand

Sales promotion directed at industrial goods customers might use some of the ideas we just mentioned. In addition, the sales promotion people might set up and staff trade show exhibits. These activities would be especially important in international marketing. Here, attractive models are often used to try to encourage economically oriented buyers to look over a particular firm's product—especially when it is displayed near other similar products in a circus-like atmosphere.

Sales promotion for middlemen

Sales promotion aimed at middlemen—sometimes called *trade promotion*—stresses price-related matters—because the objective assigned to sales promotion may be to encourage stocking new items, or buying in larger quantity, or buying early. The tools used here are price and/or merchandise allowances, promotion allowances, and perhaps sales contests to encourage retailers or wholesalers to sell specific items—or the company's whole line. Offering to send contest winners to Hawaii, for example, may increase sales greatly.

Sales promotion for own sales force

Sales promotion aimed at the company's own sales force might try to encourage getting new customers, selling a new product, or generally stimulating sales of the company's whole line. Depending on the objectives, the tools might be contests, bonuses on sales or number of new accounts, and holding sales meetings at fancy resorts to raise everyone's spirits.

Ongoing sales promotion work might also be aimed at the sales force—to help sales management. Sales promotion might be responsible for preparing sales portfolios, displays, and other sales aids. They might develop the sales training material which the salespeople could use in working with customers—and other channel members. They might develop special racks for product displays—which the sales rep could sell or give to retailers. Rather than expecting each individual salesperson—or the sales manager—to develop these sales aids, sales promotion might be given this responsibility.

Sales promotion is a weak spot in marketing

Sales promotion—like publicity—is currently a weak spot in marketing. Sales promotion includes such a wide variety of activities—each of which may be custom-designed and used only once—that little skill can be developed within the firm. Further, the personal or mass selling managers may be responsible for specific sales promotion activities—but they often treat them as "stepchildren" to whom money is allocated if there is any "left over," or a crisis develops. Many companies—even large ones—don't have a separate budget for sales promotion—or even know what it costs in total.

This neglected method is bigger than advertising

This neglect of the sales promotion area is most unfortunate, however. In total, sales promotion expenditures are estimated to be much larger than the total amount that firms spend on advertising. This means they deserve more attention—and perhaps separate status within the marketing organization.[2]

The spending on sales promotion is large and growing—sometimes at the expense of other promotion methods. There are several reasons for this growth in sales promotion activities. They have proved successful in an increasingly competitive market. Sales promotion can usually be implemented quickly—and get results sooner than advertising. Sales promotion activities may help the product manager win support from an already overworked sales force. The sales force may be especially receptive to sales promotion—including promotion in the channels—because competition has been growing and middlemen respond to sales promotion.[3]

Creative sales promotion can be very effective, but making sales promotion work is a learned skill—not a sideline for amateurs. It isn't something that should be delegated to a sales trainee. In fact, specialists in sales promotion have developed—both inside firms and as outside consultants. Some are extremely creative—and might be willing to take over the whole promotion job. But it's the marketing manager's responsibility to set promotion objectives and policies which will fit in with the rest of the marketing strategy.[4]

Sales promotion may work faster than advertising.

Mary McCarthy

WHICH METHODS TO USE DEPENDS ON PROMOTION OBJECTIVES

Basic objective is to shift demand curve

Good marketers are not interested in just "communicating." They want to communicate information which will lead to decisions favorable to the firm. They know that if they have a better offering for some target market, informed customers are more likely to buy. Therefore, they are interested in (1) reinforcing present attitudes that are likely to lead to favorable behavior, or (2) actually changing the attitudes and behavior of the firm's target market. In demand curve terms, promotion may help the firm make its present demand curve more inelastic—or shift the demand curve to the right—or both. These possibilities are shown in Figure 16-2.

The buyer behavior model introduced in Chapter 7 showed the many influences on buying behavior. You should see that changing behavior is a difficult job—but, nevertheless, it is the main objective of Promotion.

Informing, persuading, and reminding are promotion objectives

If a firm's promotion is to be effective, agreeing on and defining promotion objectives is critical—because the right promotion blend depends on what the firm wants to accomplish. Three broad *promotion objectives* are useful—to *inform, persuade,* and *remind* target customers about the company and its marketing mix. All are concerned with providing more information.

A more specific set of promotion objectives that state *exactly who* we would want to inform, persuade, or remind, and *why,* is even more useful—but this is unique to each company's strategy—and too detailed to discuss here. Instead, we will limit ourselves to the three general promotion objectives—and how we might reach them.

Informing is educating

We know that potential customers must know something about a product offering if they are to buy at all. Therefore, *informing* may be the most important objective.

A firm with a distinctly new product may not have to do anything but *inform* consumers about it—and show how it works better than all existing products. Newness and uniqueness in a product can simplify the promotion process. It may even get free publicity for the seller.

Persuading usually becomes necessary

When competitors are offering similar products, however, the firm must not only inform the customers that its product is available—but also persuade them

Figure 16-2
Basic promotion objective is to shift the demand curve

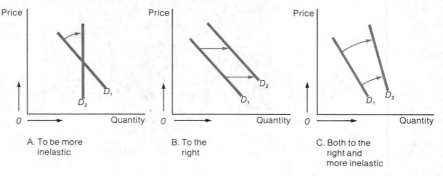

A. To be more inelastic

B. To the right

C. Both to the right and more inelastic

to buy it. A *persuading* objective means the firm would try to develop or reinforce a favorable set of attitudes—in the hope of affecting buying behavior. Here, comparative information could be supplied.

Reminding may be enough, sometimes

If target customers already have positive attitudes about—or actually prefer—the firm's product, then a *reminding* objective might be suitable. It would try to reinforce previously satisfactory behavior—by keeping cues in front of the customer. This objective can be extremely important in some cases. Even though customers have been attracted and sold once, they are still open to competitive influences. Reminding them of their past satisfaction may keep them from shifting their purchases to a competitor.

PROMOTION REQUIRES EFFECTIVE COMMUNICATION

Promotion obviously must get the attention of the target audience—or it is wasted effort. What is obvious, however, is not always easy to do. Much promotion doesn't really communicate. Behavioral science studies indicate that the communication process is very complicated.

The same message may be interpreted differently

Researchers have found that an audience evaluates not only the message—but also the source of the message—in terms of trustworthiness and credibility. Studies have also shown that some people are more easily persuaded than others. Persuasibility seems to be related to feelings of inadequacy and social inhibitions—but it does not seem to be related to the level of general intelligence.[5]

Different audiences see the same message in different ways—and interpret the same words differently. Such differences are often found in international marketing—when translation is a problem. The Parker Pen Company, for example, once blanketed Latin America with an ad campaign that suggested that its new ink would help prevent unwanted pregnancies. And General Motors had trouble in Puerto Rico with its Nova automobile until it discovered that—while Nova means "star" in Spanish—when it is spoken it sounds like "no va," which means "it doesn't go." The company quickly changed the car's name to "Caribe"—and it sold well.[6]

Semantic problems in the same language may not be so obvious—and yet they must be recognized and solved to avoid giving offense. This is an especially sensitive matter now—to make sure that advertising does not offend any minority groups. Blacks and women have been especially vocal in this regard—but other minorities are becoming increasingly sensitive. These may seem like small differences, but it is such subtleties that make a target audience tune out a message—wasting the whole promotion effort. Marketing research and greater sensitivity will help prevent the *selective processes* discussed in Chapter 7 from blocking the communication effort.

The communication process needs feedback

The **communication process** shows how a source tries to reach a receiver with a message. Figure 16–3 illustrates this. There we see that a **source**—the sender of a message—is trying to deliver a message to a **receiver**—a potential customer. A source can deliver a message by many message channels. The

Figure 16–3
The communication process

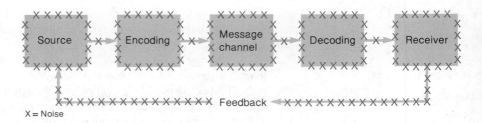

X = Noise

personal salesperson does it with voice and action. Advertising must do it with mass media—magazines, newspapers, radio, and TV.

A major advantage of personal selling is that the source—the seller—can get immediate feedback from the receiver. The source can judge how the message is being received—and change it if necessary. This is a real advantage to personal selling. Mass sellers must depend on marketing research or total sales figures to measure success.

The **noise** shown in Figure 16–3 is any factor which reduces the effectiveness of the communication process. Perhaps the source can't agree on what should be said and how—and settles for a general message. Or the receiver—perhaps a parent—may be distracted by children when the message comes out of the radio. Or other advertisers or salespeople may be saying the same things—and the receiver may become confused and ignore everyone.

Encoding and decoding depend on common frame of reference

The basic difficulty in the communication process occurs during encoding and decoding. **Encoding** is the source deciding what it wants to say and translating it into words that will have the same meaning to the receiver. **Decoding** is the receiver translating the message. This process can be very tricky—because the meanings of various words and symbols may differ, depending on the attitudes and experiences of the two groups. See Figure 16–4.

Noise in the channel can block the communication process.

Mary McCarthy

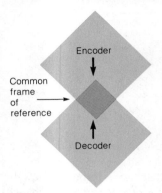

**Figure 16–4
Encoding and decoding depend
on common frame of reference**

Encoder

Common
frame
of
reference

Decoder

Average car drivers, for example, might think of the Ford Mustang as a sports car. If they are the target market, they want to hear about ease of handling, acceleration, and racing symbols—such as wide tires. Auto engineers and sports car fanatics, however, don't consider the Mustang a real sports car. So, if they are writing—or approving—copy, they might encode the message in regular "small-car" terms. Errors could be minimized by knowing the relevant market dimensions—in terms of the needs and attitudes of potential customers. This data should be available for strategy planning anyway—and it would be especially useful here.

Whether the message should emphasize only the positive features (one-sided arguments) or both positive and negative features (two-sided arguments) depends on the attitudes of the target market. Sometimes accenting the positive is desirable—it's less confusing. But if the potential customers already know something of the pros and cons, a two-sided approach may be more effective. The marketing manager must realize that such details may affect the effectiveness of communication—and be sure that they are considered during the implementation process.

**Message channel is
important, too**

The communication process is complicated even more because the receiver is aware that the message is not only coming from a source but also coming through some **message channel**—the carrier of the message. The receiver may attach more value to a product if the message comes in a well-respected newspaper or magazine, rather than over the radio. Similarly, information from the president of a company might be more impressive than from a junior sales representative.

ADOPTION PROCESSES CAN GUIDE PROMOTION PLANNING

The adoption process discussed in Chapter 7 is related to effective communication and promotion planning. You learned that there were six steps in that adoption process: awareness, interest, evaluation, trial, decision, and confirmation. Further, in Chapter 7 we saw consumer buying as a problem-solving process in which buyers go through these several steps on the way to adopting (or rejecting) an idea or product. Now we will see that the basic promotion objectives can be related to these various steps—to show what is needed to achieve the objectives. See Figure 16–5.

Informing and persuading may be needed to affect the potential customer's knowledge and attitudes about a product—and then bring about its adoption. Later, promotion can simply remind the customer about that favorable experience—aiming to confirm the adoption decision.

**The AIDA model is a
practical approach**

The basic adoption process fits very neatly with another action-oriented model—called AIDA—which we will use in this and the next two chapters to guide some of our discussion.

The **AIDA model** consists of four promotion jobs—(1) to get *Attention*, (2) to hold *Interest*, (3) to arouse *Desire*, and (4) to obtain *Action*.[7] (As a memory aid, note that the first letters of the four key words spell AIDA—the well-known opera.)

Figure 16–5
Relation of promotion
objectives, adoption process,
and AIDA model

Promotion objectives	Adoption process (Chapter 7)	AIDA model
Informing	Awareness	Attention
	Interest	Interest
	Evaluation ⎫	Desire
Persuading	Trial ⎭	
	Decision ⎫	Action
Reminding	Confirmation ⎭	

The relationship of the adoption process to the AIDA tasks can be seen in Figure 16–5.

Getting attention is necessary if the potential customer is to become aware of the company's offering. Holding interest gives the communication a chance to really build the prospect's interest in the product. Arousing desire affects the evaluation process—perhaps building preference. And obtaining action includes obtaining trial—which then may lead to a purchase decision. Continuing promotion is needed to confirm the decision—and encourage continuing action.

GOOD COMMUNICATION VARIES PROMOTION BLENDS ALONG ADOPTION CURVE

The communication and adoption processes discussed above look at individuals. This emphasis on individuals helps us understand how people behave. But it also is useful to look at markets as a whole. Different customers within a market may behave differently—with some taking the lead in accepting products and, in turn, influencing others.

Adoption curve focuses on market segments, not individuals

Research on how markets accept new ideas has led to the adoption-curve. The adoption curve shows when different groups accept ideas. It shows the need to change the promotion effort as time passes. It also emphasizes the relations among groups. It shows that some groups act as leaders in accepting a new idea.

Promotion must vary for different adopter groups

The adoption curve for a typical successful product is shown in Figure 16–6. Some of the important characteristics of each of these customer groups are discussed below. Which one are you?

Innovators—venturesome

The innovators are the first to adopt. They are eager to try new ideas and willing to take risks. Innovators tend to be young and—at the same time—high in social and economic status. They are mobile and sophisticated—with many contacts outside their own local social group and community. They are also able to understand and apply complex technical information.

Business firms in the innovator class usually are large and rather specialized.

For promotion purposes, an important characteristic of innovators is that they rely on impersonal and scientific information sources—or other innovators—rather than personal salespeople. They often read articles in technical publications—or informative advertisements in sophisticated magazines or newspapers.

Early adopters—respectable

Early adopters are relatively high in social status—well-respected by their peers and usually high in opinion leadership. They may be younger, more mobile, and more creative than later adopters. But, unlike innovators, they have few contacts outside their own social group or community.

Business firms in this category also tend to be specialized.

This group tends to have the greatest contact—of all the groups—with salespeople. Mass media are important information sources, too.

Early majority—deliberate

The early majority are those with above average social status. They usually will not consider a new idea until many early adopters have tried it. In other words, the early majority may deliberate for some time before completely adopting a new idea.

Average-sized business firms with less specialization would fit in this category.

The early majority have a lot of contact with mass media, salespeople *and* early adopters. They interact a lot with their peers, but usually are not opinion leaders.

Late majority—skeptical

The late majority tend to be below average in social status and income. They are skeptical and cautious about new ideas. And, they are less likely to follow opinion leaders and early adopters. In fact, strong social pressure from their own peer group may be needed before they adopt a new product.

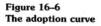

Figure 16–6
The adoption curve

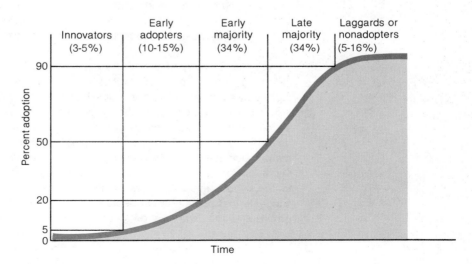

Kenneth Yee

Business firms in this group tend to be smaller-sized firms with little specialization.

The late majority make little use of mass media or salespeople. They tend to be oriented more to other late adopters—than to outside sources of information.

Laggards or nonadopters—traditional

The laggards or nonadopters tend to be low in social status and income. They prefer to do things the way they have been done in the past—and are very suspicious of new ideas.

The smallest businesses with the least specialization are often in this category.

Laggards tend to be "loners" and have almost no opinion leadership. The main source of information for laggards is other laggards. This certainly is bad news for marketers who want to reach a whole market quickly—or want to use only one promotion method. In fact, it may not pay to bother with this group. By the time they finally adopt a new product, the firm has probably started marketing even newer products to innovators and early adopters.[8]

PROMOTION MUST REACH OPINION LEADERS TO BE EFFECTIVE

Adoption curve research reinforces our earlier discussion in Chapter 7 of the importance of *opinion leaders*—people who influence other people's attitudes and behavior.

Are consumers helpless victims of the mass media?

The role that opinion leaders play in the communication process was not recognized until the early 1940s. Prior to that time, communication theorists believed in the hypodermic needle model of mass communication—which assumed that the mass media had direct, immediate, and powerful effects on people (receivers). It was felt that exposing people to the mass media was like sticking a big hypodermic needle into their arms—the people were helpless victims whose attitudes and behavior were influenced by whatever messages the mass media forced upon them. It was also assumed that people were not influenced very much by word-of-mouth communication with their peers.

Or are opinion leaders more important than the mass media?

However, a study of the 1940 Presidential election surprised researchers by indicating that the political choices of voters were much more influenced by face-to-face contact with other people than by the mass media. The study revealed that information flowed from the mass media to opinion leaders who then influenced the attitudes and behavior of the rest of the population. This finding gave rise to the two-step flow model of mass communication—which assumed that mass media messages flow mainly to opinion leaders who react to these messages and then relay them to the people with whom they interact. Compared to the hypodermic needle model (See Figure 16–7), the two-step flow model suggests that mass media effects on people are not as direct, immediate, and powerful as they were once thought to be.

Today the multistep flow model is used

Current research suggests that neither the hypodermic needle model nor the two-step flow model is entirely correct. Rather, mass communication seems to

Figure 16–7
Models of mass communication flows

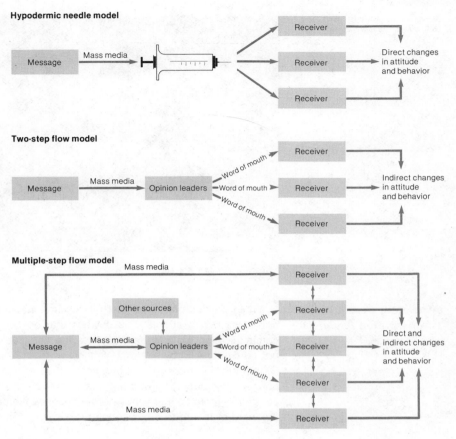

occur through a **multistep flow model**—which assumes that there are a variety of ways that messages can flow from the mass media (or other sources) to people in the mass audience. In some cases, the mass media may have direct effects on people. In other cases, mass media messages may flow to opinion leaders and then from opinion leaders to the people with whom they interact. And in some cases, messages may flow through a whole series of opinion leaders and interacting people—that is, there may be more than two steps in the communication process.

The multistep flow model also recognizes that opinion leaders do not rely exclusively on the mass media as a source of information. Early adopters, for example, have a lot of contact with salespeople. Further, people are not always passive receivers of information forced upon them by the mass media or opinion leaders. Instead, people often seek out information from the mass media or opinion leaders. Further, people use the selective processes we discussed in Chapter 7—selective exposure, selective perception, and selective retention—to keep themselves from becoming helpless victims of the mass media or any other message source.

Marketers should try to reach the early adopter opinion leaders.

Mary McCarthy

Marketers should try to reach opinion leaders

While we don't know all there is to know about the communication process and mass media effects, it is obvious that opinion leaders and word-of-mouth communication are important parts of the communication process. They should not be overlooked by strategy planners in their Promotion decisions.

In particular, marketers should focus their efforts on reaching *early adopters,* because this adopter group has the highest degree of opinion leadership. Early adopters—more so than innovators—influence the early majority and help spread the word of mouth to other adopter groups.

Opinion leaders may accept or reject new ideas

It is important for marketers to keep in mind that opinion leaders do not always accept new ideas—they reject them sometimes, too! Some degree of opinion leadership exists among all of the adopter groups, and opinion leaders among the late majority and the laggards may be extremely resistant to new ideas.

Therefore, if the early adopter groups reject a new product, it will probably never get off the ground. But if the early adopter groups accept the new product, then opinion leaders in those groups will help spread the word of mouth—and may create enough social pressure to force the later adopter groups to accept the new product. Thus, the "web of word of mouth"—rather than the firm's mass selling and personal selling efforts—may do the real selling job in the marketplace.

Who are the opinion leaders?

All this points up the importance of trying to reach the opinion leaders in various social groups. But as you may recall from Chapter 7—opinion leaders are often hard to identify. A person can be an opinion leader for some products but not for others. For example, you might ask a friend who is a serious photographer for some advice about buying a camera—but he might come to you for advice about buying a component stereo system. In this case, you would both be opinion leaders—but not all of the time and not for all products.

Because of the difficulty of identifying opinion leaders, marketers usually have to rely on a variety of promotion messages and media to reach them—and try to spread the word of mouth.

We know less about the adoption process in industrial goods markets. It seems likely that the same general process is at work—but one study suggests that there is little word-of-mouth communication in these markets. This points up the importance of both personal selling and mass selling in communicating with industrial buyers *and* the multiple buying influences.[9]

MAY NEED A DIFFERENT BLEND FOR EACH MARKET SEGMENT

Each unique market segment may need a separate marketing mix—and a different promotion blend. This is mentioned here because some mass selling specialists have missed this point. They think mainly in "mass marketing"—rather than "target marketing"—terms. Aiming at large markets may be desirable in some situations, but unfortunately, promotion aimed at everyone can end up hitting no one. In the Promotion area, we should be especially careful about slipping into a "shotgun" approach when what is really needed is a "rifle" approach—with more careful aiming.

SUCCESSFUL PROMOTION MAY BE AN ECONOMICAL BLEND

Once promotion objectives for a product-market have been set, a marketing manager may decide to use a blend of promotion methods—since some jobs can be done more economically one way than another. This can be seen most clearly in the industrial goods market. While personal selling dominates most industrial goods promotion budgets, mass selling is necessary, too. Personal sales representatives nearly always have to complete the sale, but it is seldom practical for them to carry the whole promotion load. The cost of an industrial sales call is estimated to be over $100.[10] This relatively high cost is because salespeople have only limited time and much of what they do is spent on nonselling activities—traveling, paper work, sales meetings, and strictly service calls. Only 42 percent of their time is available for actual selling.

The job of reaching all the buying influences is made more costly and difficult by the constant turnover of buyers and influences. An industrial salesperson may be responsible for several hundred customers and prospects—with about four buying influences per company. They don't have enough time to get the company's whole message across to every potential customer. The problem is pictured in the classic McGraw-Hill advertisement shown in Figure 16–8. As the ad suggests, too much has been invested in a salesperson to use his time and skill to answer questions that could be better handled through mass selling. Mass selling can do the ground work. The salesperson should concentrate on answering specific questions—and closing the sale. These mass selling "sales calls" can be made at a fraction of the cost of a personal call. One McGraw-Hill study found a mass selling "call" costing 1/645th the cost of a personal call.[11]

Figure 16–8

"I don't know who you are.
I don't know your company.
I don't know your company's product.
I don't know what your company stands for.
I don't know your company's customers.
I don't know your company's record.
I don't know your company's reputation.
Now—what was it you wanted to sell me?"

MORAL: Sales start **before** your salesman calls—with business publication advertising.

McGRAW-HILL MAGAZINES
BUSINESS • PROFESSIONAL • TECHNICAL

"That guy's probably been asking the same questions
for fifty years.
Man, am I glad to hear he's retiring."

"I don't know who you are.
I don't know your company.
I don't know your company's product.
I don't know what your company stands for.
I don't know your company's customers.
I don't know your company's record.
I don't know your company's reputation.
Now—what was it you wanted to sell me?"

MORAL: Sales start **before** your salesman calls—with business publication advertising.

McGRAW-HILL MAGAZINES
BUSINESS • PROFESSIONAL • TECHNICAL

"Oh, no!"

One generation passeth away,
and another generation cometh . . .
There is no new thing under the sun.
(Ecclesiastes)

FACTORS AFFECTING THE SELECTION OF A PROMOTION BLEND

Most business firms develop a *promotion blend* of some kind—because the various methods complement each other. But what blend is right in a particular situation?

Wholesalers rely on personal selling—perhaps with good reason. Some retailers do, too—while other retailers advertise aggressively.

At the same time, a food products manufacturer may develop a promotion blend with 10 parts advertising to 1 part personal selling. A lawn seed producer might emphasize advertising 4 to 1—while a paint manufacturer might reverse the ratio. Is there some logical pattern to these differences?

Each promotion blend should be designed to achieve the firm's overall objectives. But the particular blend selected depends on a number of factors—including (1) the promotion budget available, (2) stage of product in its life cycle, (3) nature of competition, (4) target of the promotion, and (5) nature of the product.

Size of promotion budget affects promotion efficiency

There are some economies of scale in Promotion. Network radio or television may reach more people more economically than local media. City-wide radio, TV, and newspapers may be more economical than neighborhood newspapers or direct personal contact. But the minimum charge for some "mass media" may force small firms—or those with small promotion budgets—to use the less economical alternative, in terms of cost per contact. For example, a small retailer might like to use local television, but all he can afford are handbills and perhaps ads in church and school bulletins. Similarly, a small manufacturer might see personal selling as his only choice—because a personal salesperson can be hired for $10,000 to $15,000 a year plus expenses, while a single hour of network television can cost from $50,000 to $400,000—depending on whether it is a daytime soap opera or a prime-time show like "Dallas." The TV show might bring the firm's message to more people for less per person—but its total cost might be too high for a small firm.

A small budget doesn't limit a firm to personal selling, however. Sales promotion and direct mail are attractive possibilities. A small tire manufacturer wanted to tell potential retailers about its product—but couldn't afford to compete with the big tiremakers' promotion campaigns. It decided instead to use direct mail. A carefully targeted campaign was extremely successful—yielding $196 in new business for every dollar invested.[12] A direct-mail expenditure of $1,681 brought in 101 new retailers—and more than $360,000 of new business.

Stage of product in its life cycle

A new product seldom becomes a spectacular success overnight. The adoption curve helps explain why. Further, the product must go through the product life-cycle stages described in Chapter 11—market introduction, market growth, market maturity, and sales decline. During these stages, promotion blends may change—to achieve different promotion objectives.

Market introduction stage—"this new idea is good"

During market introduction, the basic objective is to inform. If the product is an entirely new idea, the promotion must build primary demand—that is, demand for a product idea—electric cars, or microwave ovens—not just the company's own brand. There may be few potential innovators during the introductory stage and personal selling can help find them. Salespeople also are needed to select good channel members—and then persuade them to carry the new product.

Since there are few competitors at this stage, mass selling can concentrate on the basic informing job. Initial advertisements may try to get inquiries.

Market growth stage—"our brand is best"

In the market growth stage, competitors begin entering the market—and promotion emphasis must shift from building primary demand to stimulating selective demand—that is, demand for a company's own brand. The main job is to persuade customers to buy—and stay with the company's own product.

Now that more potential customers are trying and adopting the product—mass selling may become more economical. But personal salespeople must still work in the channels—expanding the number of outlets.

Market maturity stage—"our brand is better, really"

In the market maturity stage, more competitors have entered the market. Promotion must become more persuasive.

At this stage, mass selling may dominate the promotion blends of consumer products manufacturers. Industrial products might require more aggressive personal selling—perhaps supplemented by more advertising. The total dollars allocated to promotion may rise—as the competitive pressure rises.

Firms that have strong brands are able to use reminder-type advertising—to remind customers of the product name. This may be much less expensive than persuasive efforts.

Sales decline stage—let's tell those who still want our product

During the sales decline stage, the total amount spent on promotion may decrease—as firms try to cut costs to remain profitable. Since the product may still be acceptable to some people, more targeted promotion is needed to reach these customers.

Nature of competition requires different promotion

Firms in monopolistic competition may favor mass selling—because they have differentiated their marketing mix—and have something to talk about. As a market tends toward pure competition—or oligopoly—it is difficult to predict what will happen. Competitors in some markets try to "out-promote" each other. The only way for a competitor to stay in this kind of market is to match rivals' promotion efforts—unless the whole marketing mix can be improved in some other way. We see such competitive advertising in our daily newspapers.

In markets that are drifting toward pure competition, some companies resort to price cutting. This *may* increase the number of units sold—temporarily—but it may also reduce total revenue and the amount available for promotion *per unit*. And competitive retaliation may reduce the temporary sales gains—and drag price levels down faster. The cash flowing into the business may decline—and all promotion will have to be cut back.

Once a firm is in pure competition, there would seem to be little reason to promote the product. But someone has to get the business—and using persuasive

In monopolistic competition mass selling is common.

Peter Le Grand

personal salespeople can be the way to get it. For the customer's part, he must buy needed products someplace—and often prefers to buy from friendly salespeople who call regularly. This is also true in oligopoly situations. Only here, there may be enough profit to support more promotion—including entertaining and business gift-giving.

Target of promotion helps set the blend

Promotion can be directed to four different groups: final consumers, industrial customers, retailers, and wholesalers. The right promotion blend for each group can be slightly different.

Promotion to final consumers

The large number of potential customers almost forces consumer goods manufacturers and retailers to emphasize mass selling. Effective mass selling may even win enough brand familiarity so that little personal selling is needed—as in self-service and discount operations.

Mass selling may even be the best way to supply information to consumers who seek it. The innovators and early adopters—and opinion leaders within social groups—are widely scattered—and it isn't possible to identify and approach each one individually.

Personal selling can be effective too. Some retailers—in particular specialty shops—rely heavily on well-informed salespeople. Some door-to-door retailers have been very successful. But aggressive personal selling to final consumers usually is found only in relatively expensive channel systems.

Promotion to industrial customers

Industrial customers are much less numerous than final consumers—and there is more reason to emphasize personal selling. Industrial customers may have technical questions—or need adjustments in the marketing mix. Manufacturers' or wholesalers' salespeople can be more flexible in adjusting their companies' appeals to suit each customer. They also are able to call back later—and provide confirmation and additional information. Personal selling becomes more practical

Personal selling is dominate in promotion to middlemen.

Mary McCarthy

as the size of each purchase increases—and larger unit purchases are more typical in industrial goods markets.

Promotion to retailers

As with industrial buyers, the relatively small number of retailers makes it practical for manufacturers and wholesalers to emphasize personal selling. Sales promotion and some mass selling in trade magazines and newspapers can be valuable. But most of the promotion is by personal salespeople—who can answer retailers' questions about what promotion will be directed toward the final consumer, the retailers' own part in selling the product, and important details concerning price, markups, and promotion assistance and allowances.

In other words, promotion to retailers is primarily informative. But since the manufacturer's or wholesaler's sales reps cannot *guarantee* the retailer a profit, the promotion must also be persuasive. The sales rep must convince the retailer that demand for the product exists—and that making a profit will be easy. Further, he must establish and maintain good channel relationships. The retailer must be convinced that the manufacturer or wholesaler has his interest at heart. A channel is a human system and depends on the mutual trust and understanding of channel members. This can be built only by personal relations.

Another reason personal selling is so important in dealing with retailers is that marketing mixes may have to be adjusted drastically from one geographic territory to another—to meet competitive situations. The mixes in highly competitive urban areas, for example, may emphasize price more than those in outlying areas. Personal salespeople have to judge these conditions. We already saw the development of a specialist—the food broker—to assist producers' sales reps in the extremely competitive grocery industry.

Promotion to wholesalers

Promotion to wholesalers is very similar to promotion to retailers—except that wholesalers are less numerous—and perhaps even more aware of demand and cost. They respond to economic arguments. They may want to know about the promotion which the producer intends to direct at retailers and final consumers. And personal sales reps are needed to cement the relationship between producer and wholesaler.

Nature of the product makes a big difference

The target customers' view of the product is the common thread tying together all the variables that must be combined into a marketing mix. Their view of the product affects the promotion blend, too. The goods classes introduced in Chapter 10 had a direct bearing on the Place objectives. These goods classes have a bearing on the development of promotion blends, too. The way all these factors interact will be discussed in Chapter 21. Here, however, we should consider the impact of some general product characteristics on promotion blends.

Technical nature of product

An extremely technical industrial product may require a heavy emphasis on personal selling—preferably by technically trained salespeople. This is the only sure way to make the product understood—and get feedback on how industry can use it. The technical sales rep can meet with engineers, plant people, purchasing agents, and top managers—and adjust the sales message to the needs of these various influences.

Mass selling, on the other hand, is practical for many consumer goods—because there is no technical story to be told. Or, if there are some technical details—for example, with cars or appliances—they can be offered to interested customers—perhaps in sales promotion materials at the retailer's showroom.

Degree of brand familiarity

If a product has already won brand preference or insistence—perhaps after years of satisfactory service—there may be no need for aggressive personal selling. Reminder-type advertising may be all that's needed. Hershey Chocolate long prided itself on not having to do any advertising! Recently, however, it did begin some advertising and sales promotion—to counter increasing competition in the United States. But in Canada—where it is not well established—Hershey has advertised aggressively.[13]

If a manufacturer has not differentiated its product, and does not plan to invest in building a brand name—perhaps because its product is not different—then much heavier emphasis on personal selling is sensible. The objective would be to build good channel relations. Rather than spending—perhaps uselessly—to build a brand name, a firm would invest in Place.

HOW TYPICAL PROMOTION BUDGETS ARE BLENDED

There is no one right blend

There is no one *right* promotion blend for all situations. Each must be developed as part of a marketing mix. But to round out our discussion of promotion blends, let's look at ways different manufacturers have allocated their promotion budgets. They do vary considerably—depending on the various factors discussed above. Retailers' blends vary widely also. Wholesalers—on the other hand—use personal selling almost exclusively.

Figure 16–9 shows how manufacturers have allocated their promotion budgets.

It shows the ratios of advertising expenditures to personal selling which might be expected in various situations. It's common to find the ratios of advertising to personal selling varying from 10 to 1 to 1 to 10. Note, here we are referring to ratios—not actual expenditures. A 1-to-1 ratio would mean that the expenditures for advertising and personal selling were roughly equal.

Figure 16–9 shows that manufacturers of well-branded consumer goods (such as cars, breakfast cereals, and nonprescription drugs)—and especially those which are seeking to build brand familiarity—will tend to have heavier ratios in favor of advertising. The ratio might be even higher if the firm had already built its channel of distribution.

At the other extreme, smaller companies—even those with new consumer products—use more personal selling—especially if the products are relatively undifferentiated. Middlemen and industrial buyers want several sources of supply—so personal selling is quite important to assure that the firm continues to satisfy—and remain on the supplier list.

A balanced blend of personal selling and advertising might be expected where a firm sells both consumer and industrial goods. Now we are considering a blend for the whole company—not an individual product. The heavier emphasis on advertising which might be expected with consumer goods might be offset by a heavier emphasis on personal selling for industrial goods.[14]

Personal selling usually is dominant

The relatively heavier emphasis on personal selling which you might have assumed from the figure is correct. As we will see in the next two chapters—for the economy as a whole—far more is spent on personal selling than on advertising. The many advertisements one sees in magazines and newspapers—and on television—are impressive and costly. But you should be aware that most retail sales are completed by salesclerks—and that behind the scenes much personal selling goes on in the channels. In total, personal selling is several times more expensive than advertising.

SOMEONE MUST PLAN AND MANAGE THE PROMOTION BLEND

Selecting a promotion blend is a strategic decision which should fit with the rest of the marketing strategy. Once the outlines of the promotion blend are set, then more detailed plans for the parts of the blend must be developed and implemented. This may be the job of specialists—such as the sales and advertising managers.

Figure 16–9
Typical promotion blends of manufacturers (ratio of advertising to personal selling)

10:1	5:1	1:1	1:5	1:10
	← Advertising emphasis →		← Personal selling emphasis →	
	Firms with well-branded consumer goods (with established channels)	Blend of consumer and industrial goods	Smaller companies and any firms offering relatively undifferentiated consumer goods or industrial goods	

Personal selling accounts for the largest share of promotion.

Mary McCarthy

Sales managers manage salespeople

Sales managers are concerned with managing personal selling. The sales manager is also responsible for building good distribution channels and implementing Place policies. In smaller companies, he often acts as the marketing manager. Since most sales managers have come up through sales, they usually have great confidence in the power of personal contact. This can be both a strength and a weakness. They may believe in—and be able to develop and motivate an effective sales force—but they may have less interest in—and respect for—developing a whole promotion blend.

Advertising managers work with ads and agencies

Advertising managers manage their company's mass selling effort—in television, newspapers, magazines, and other media. Their job is choosing the right media for each purpose—and developing the ads. An advertising department within their own firms may help in these efforts—especially if they are in retailing—or they may use outside advertising agencies. They—or their agencies—may handle publicity also. Or it may be handled by whoever handles **public relations**—communication with noncustomers—including labor, consumerists, stockholders, and the government.

Advertising managers usually come up through advertising—and have an exaggerated view of the potential power of advertising. They may feel that advertising can do the whole promotion job—or, that advertising *is* promotion.

Sales promotion managers need many talents

Sales promotion managers manage their company's sales promotion effort. They fill the gaps between the sales and advertising managers—increasing their effectiveness. Nearly everything the sales promotion department does *could* be done by the sales or advertising departments. But sales promotion activities are so varied that specialists tend to develop. In some companies, the sales promotion managers work for the sales managers. In others, they are moving toward independent status—with responsibility to the marketing manager. If sales promotion expenses exceed those for advertising, it would seem logical to have a separate sales promotion manager.

Marketing manager talks to all, blends all

Because of differences in outlook and experience—the advertising, sales, and sales promotion managers may have difficulty working with each other as partners or equals—especially when each feels that his approach is the most important. It is the marketing manager's job to weigh the pros and cons of the various approaches. Then he must come up with an effective promotion blend—fitting the various departments and personalities into it—and coordinating their efforts.

Deciding on the right promotion blend is a difficult job—because it must fit together with the rest of the marketing mix. And this is why it cannot be left to one or another of the promotion specialists. It requires balancing the alternative use of scarce resources among the various elements of a *marketing mix*—not just in the promotion area. This is why we hold the marketing manager responsible for developing the promotion blend.

Note that all these jobs might be carried by one person in a small company—perhaps with the title of sales manager. In this case, *that person* is responsible for planning and implementing an effective promotion blend.

CONCLUSION

Promotion is an important part of any marketing mix. Most consumers and intermediate customers can choose from among many products. To be successful, a manufacturer must not only offer a good product at a reasonable price, but also let potential customers know about the product—and where they can buy it. Further, producers must tell wholesalers and retailers in the channel about their product—and their marketing mix. These middlemen, in turn, must use promotion to reach their customers.

The promotion blend should fit logically into the strategy which is being developed to satisfy a particular target market. *What* should be communicated to them—an how—should be stated as part of the strategy planning.

The main promotion objective is affecting buying behavior—but basic promotion objectives include informing, persuading, and reminding.

Various promotion methods can be used to reach these objectives. How the promotion methods are combined to achieve effective communication can be guided by behavioral science findings. In particular, we know something about the communications process, and how individuals and groups adopt new products.

An action-oriented framework called AIDA will help guide strategic planning of promotion blends—but finally the marketing manager is responsible for blending the promotion methods into one promotion effort for each marketing mix. Special considerations which may affect the promotion blend are the size of the promotion budget, stage of product in its life cycle, the particular target customers who must be reached, the nature of competition, and the nature of the product.

In this chapter, we have considered some basic ideas. In the next two chapters we will treat personal and mass selling in more detail. Sales promotion will not be treated anymore—because it is difficult to generalize about all the possibilities. Further, the fact that most sales promotion activities are short-run "tactical" efforts—which must be specially tailored—means that sales promotion will probably continue to be a "stepchild"—even though sales promotion costs more than advertising. Marketers must find a better way of handling this important decision area.

QUESTIONS AND PROBLEMS

1. Briefly explain the nature of the three basic promotion methods which are available to a marketing manager. Explain why sales promotion is currently a "weak spot" in marketing and suggest what might be done about it.

2. Relate the three basic promotion objectives to the four tasks (AIDA) of the promotion job, using a specific example.

3. Discuss the communication process in relation to a manufacturer's promotion of an accessory good, say, a portable air hammer used for breaking up concrete pavement.

4. Explain how an understanding of the way individuals adopt new ideas or products (the adoption process) would be helpful in developing a promotion blend. In particular, explain how it might be desirable to change a promotion blend during the course of the adoption process. To make this more concrete, discuss it in relation to the acceptance of a new men's sportcoat style.

5. Explain how opinion leaders should affect a firm's promotion planning. Be sure to refer to the two-step flow model and the multistep flow model.

6. Discuss how our understanding of the adoption curve should be applied to planning the promotion blend(s) for a new, small (personal) electric car.

7. Discuss the nature of the promotion job in relation to the life cycle of a product. Illustrate, using household dishwashing machines.

8. Promotion has been the target of considerable criticism. What specific types of promotion are probably the object of this criticism?

9. Might promotion be successful in expanding the general demand for: *(a)* oranges, *(b)* automobiles, *(c)* tennis rackets, *(d)* cashmere sweaters, *(e)* iron ore, *(f)* steel, *(g)* cement? Explain why or why not in each case.

10. Indicate the promotion blend which might be most appropriate for manufacturers of the following established products (assume average- to large-sized firms in each case) and support your answer:

    a. Candy bars
    b. Men's T-shirts.
    c. Castings for automobile engines.
    d. Car batteries.
    e. Industrial fire insurance.
    f. Inexpensive plastic raincoats.
    g. A camera which has achieved a specialty-goods status.

11. Discuss the potential conflict among the various promotion managers. How might this be reduced?

SUGGESTED CASES

17 Spears National Bank

18 Billing Sports Company

NOTES

1. Robert S. Mason, "What's a PR Director For, Anyway?," *Harvard Business Review,* September–October 1974, pp. 120–26; "Top Flacks Want Nobodies, Where the Power, Prestige and Big Bucks Are at More Firms," *The Wall Street Journal,* March 4, 1980, p. 1; and Raymond Simon, *Public Relations: Concepts and Practices,* 2d ed., (Columbus, Ohio: Grid Publishing, Inc., 1980).

2. Roger A. Strang, "Sales Promotion—Fast Growth, Faulty Management," *Harvard Business Review,* July–August 1976, pp. 115–24; "Now the Battling Airlines Try Mass Marketing," *Business Week,* April 18, 1980, p. 104; and Michel Chevalier, "Increase in Sales Due to In-Store Display," *Journal of Marketing Research,* November 1975, pp. 426–31.

3. Ibid., pp. 116–19.

4. For more discussion on sales promotion activities, see Alfred Gross, *Sales Promotion,* various editions (New York: The Ronald Press Co.); and Ovid Riso, *Sales Promotion Handbook,* 6th ed (Chicago: Dartnell, Inc.)

5. Abe Shuchman and Michael Perry, "Self-Confidence and Persuasibility in Marketing: A Reappraisal," *Journal of Marketing Research,* May 1969, pp. 146–55; and *Personality and Persuasibility,* ed. Carl I. Hovland and Irving L. Janis (New Haven, Conn.: Yale University Press, 1959), pp. 229–40.

6. "More Firms Turn to Translation Experts to Avoid Costly Embarrassing Mistakes," *The Wall Street Journal,* January 13, 1977, p. 32.

7. M. S. Heidingsfield and A. B. Blankenship, *Marketing* (New York: Barnes & Noble, Inc., 1957), p. 149.

8. For further discussion, see Gerald Zaltman, *Marketing: Contributions from the Behavioral Sciences,* (New York: Harcourt, Brace & World, Inc., 1965), pp. 45–56 and 23–37; Everett M. Rogers, *The Diffusion of Innovations* (New York: Free Press, 1962); Kenneth Uhl, Roman Andrus, and Lance Poulsen, "How Are Laggards Different? An Empirical Inquiry," *Journal of Marketing Research,* February 1970, pp. 51–54; see also C. W. King and J. O. Summers, "Overlap of Opinion Leadership Across Consumer Product Categories," *Journal of Marketing Research,* February 1970, pp. 43–50; Joseph R. Mancuso, "Why Not Create Opinion Leaders for New Product Introductions?" *Journal of Marketing,* July 1969, pp. 20–25; and Thomas S. Robertson, "The Process of Innovation and the Diffusion of Innovation," *Journal of Marketing,* January 1967, pp. 14–19; Robert A. Westbrook and Claes Fornel, "Patterns of Information Source Usage among Durable Goods Buyers," *Journal of Marketing Research,* August 1979, pp. 303–312; V. Mahajan and E. Muller, "Innovation Diffusion and New Products," *Journal of Marketing,* Fall 1979, pp.

55–68; L. E. Ostlund, "Perceived Innovation Attributes As Predictors of Innovativeness," *Consumer Research,* September 1974, pp. 23–29; Richard W. Olshavsky, "Time and the Rate of Adoption of Innovations," *Consumer Research,* March 1980, pp. 425–28; and Thomas S. Robertson and Yoram Wind, "Organizational Psychographics and Innovativeness," *Consumer Research,* June 1980, pp. 24–31.

9. Everett M. Rogers and F. Floyd Shoemaker, *Communication of Innovations: A Cross-Cultural Approach,* (New York: Free Press) 1971, pp. 203–09; Frederick E. Webster, Jr., "Informal Communication in Industrial Markets," *Journal of Marketing Research,* May 1970, pp. 186–90; Leon G. Schiffman and Vincent Gaccione, "Opinion Leaders in Institutional Markets," *Journal of Marketing,* April 1974, pp. 49–53; John A. Czepiel, "Word-of-Mouth Processes in the Diffusion of a Major Technological Innovation," *Journal of Marketing Research,* May 1974, pp. 172–80; and John A. Martilla, "Word-of-Mouth Communication in the Industrial Adoption Process," *Journal of Marketing Research,* May 1971, pp. 173–78.

10. *Sales & Marketing Management,* February 21, 1977, p. 30; *Business Week,* November 19, 1979, p. 199, and *Sales and Marketing Management,* February 25, 1980.

11. *The Mathematics of Selling* (New York: McGraw-Hill Book Co.).

12. "Direct Mail Puts Jack with Giants," *Printers' Ink,* November 10, 1961, pp. 49–50.

13. "Hershey's Sweet Tooth Starts Aching," *Business Week,* February 7, 1970, pp. 98–104; and "Big Chocolate Maker, Beset by Profit Slide, Gets More Aggressive," *Wall Street Journal,* February 18, 1970, pp. 1 f.

14. Edwin H. Lewis, "Sales Promotion Decisions," *Business News Notes* (Minneapolis: School of Business Administration, University of Minnesota, November 1954).

Brent Jones

1. Understand the importance and nature of personal selling.
2. Know the three basic sales tasks and what the various kinds of sales people can be expected to do.
3. Understand when and where the three types of sales presentations should be used.
4. Know what a sales manager must do to carry out the job assigned to personal selling.
5. Recognize the important new terms (shown in red).

17

Personal selling

"Today, many salespeople are problem-solving professionals."

Promotion is communicating with potential customers—and personal selling is often the best way to do it. While face-to-face with prospects, salespeople can get more attention than an advertisement or a display. Further, they can adjust the presentation as they move along—and stay in tune with the prospect's feedback. If—and when—the prospect says that "this might be a good idea," the salespeople are there to close the sale—and take the order.

Marketing managers must decide how much—and what kind of—personal selling effort is needed in each marketing mix. Specifically, as part of their strategy planning, they must decide: (1) how many salespeople will be needed, (2) what kind of salespeople are needed, (3) what kind of sales presentation should be used, (4) how salespeople should be selected and trained, and (5) how they should be motivated. The sales manager would provide inputs into these strategic decisions—and once they are made, it would be his job to implement the personal selling part of the marketing strategy. These strategic decisions can be seen more clearly in Figure 17–1.

In this chapter, we will discuss the importance and nature of personal selling—so you will be able to understand the strategic decisions which face sales managers and marketing managers.

THE IMPORTANCE AND ROLE OF PERSONAL SELLING

We have already seen that personal selling is important in some promotion blends—and absolutely essential in others. Some of its supporters feel that personal selling is the dynamic element which keeps our economy going. You would have a better appreciation for the importance of personal selling if you regularly

460

Figure 17–1
Strategy planning for personal selling

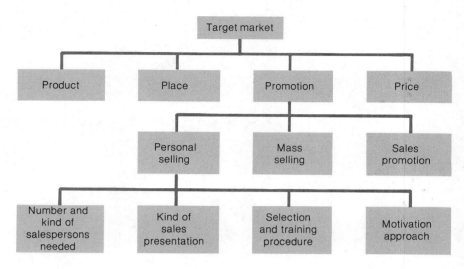

had to meet payrolls, and somehow—almost miraculously—your salespeople kept coming in with orders just in time to keep the business from closing. This helps explain why personal selling is often the largest single operating expense item.

Obviously, our economy does need and use many salespeople. U.S. Census Bureau statistics show that almost 10 percent of the total U.S. labor force is in sales work. Keeping in mind that the Bureau is inclined to place many persons who are primarily personal salespeople into other classifications, it is likely that *at least* 10 percent of the nation's labor force—or over 8 million people—are in personal selling. Contrast this with less than half a million people working in advertising. Any activity that employs so many people—and is so important to the economy—deserves study.

Death of a salesman?

Personal selling is vital to the survival of most businesses—but the role of personal selling has come in for much criticism. The aggressive and sometimes dishonest methods of some salespeople—especially some door-to-door "peddlers" and the hucksters involved in county or street fairs—have soured some prospective salespeople. The grinning "glad-hander" Willie Loman—in the play *Death of a Salesman*—set a pathetic stereotype in some peoples' minds. There also has been criticism about the salesperson's effectiveness—especially at the retail level. Many people have had bad experiences with incompetent retail clerks—who couldn't care less about customers and their needs.

The poor image of personal selling—coupled with the ineffectiveness of many salespeople—led some prophets to predict that personal selling would decline in importance. And this has happened in retailing—resulting in an increase in self-service.

Rebirth of professional salespeople

Personal salespeople are far from dead. Their role is simply being redefined and upgraded—as different sales jobs are needed. Modern sales and marketing management have gone far toward redefining what needs to be done—and then selecting, training, and motivating salespeople to perform effectively—while also providing them with personal satisfaction. In some cases, sales work is becoming a profession. Many high-caliber salespeople sincerely believe in the value of personal selling—and some subscribe to codes of ethics.

It's more than "get rid of the product"

While discussing selling—from the standpoint of marketing strategy planning—we will assume that the rest of the marketing mix the salespeople have to sell is reasonably good. But in fairness to salespeople, this is not always true. A salesperson should not be expected to make up for his firm's failings—but production-oriented managers often feel that it is the salesperson's job to "get rid of the product"—good or not. If the salespeople can see that they don't have much to sell, it is easy to understand why their morale might slip—and the whole promotion job suffer.

Helping to buy is good selling

Increasingly, good salespeople don't try to *sell* the customer. Rather, they try to *help him buy*—by presenting both the advantages and disadvantages of their products—and showing how they will satisfy needs. They find that this helpfulness results in satisfied customers—and long-term relationships. This new approach recognizes the growing sophistication of buyers—especially industrial buyers.

The old-time salesman with the funny story and the engaging grin is being replaced by salespeople who have something definite to contribute. The smiling "bag of wind"—with the big expense account—is headed toward extinction.

Salespeople represent the whole company

Increasingly, the salesperson is seen as a representative of the whole company—responsible for explaining its total effort to target customers—rather than just moving products. As evidence of this change in thinking, some companies now give their salespeople such titles as field manager, market specialist, account representative, or sales engineer.

A salesperson is both transmitter and receiver

A salesperson is expected to do much more than just bring in new business—though this certainly is an important part of the job. The salesperson should also gather feedback—to help the company to do a better job in its planning. Recall that feedback is an essential part of both the communications process *and* the basic management process of planning, implementing, and control.

The modern salesperson not only communicates the company's story to customers—but also feeds back customer reaction to the company. He is a vital link in both the communication and marketing processes.

Salespeople can be strategy planners, too

Some salespeople are expected to be marketing managers in their own geographic territories. Or, some may become marketing managers by default—because their own manager or top management has not provided any strategic guidelines. In this case, the salesperson must fill the gap—that is, develop his own marketing mix or even his own strategy. He may be given a geographic territory—but exactly who his customers are may be vague. He may have to start from scratch in his strategy planning—the only restrictions being the general product line which he is expected to sell and probably the price structure. He

Some salespeople are only given a
territory and a product and have to
develop their own strategy.

Mary McCarthy

may have his own choice as to (1) whom he aims at, (2) which particular products
in the whole line he will push aggressively, (3) which middlemen he will call on
or work hard with, (4) how he will use any promotion money that he controls—
and his own time, of course, and (5) how he will adjust prices—to the extent
that he has latitude there.

A salesperson who can put together profitable strategies—and implement
them well—can rise very rapidly. If a strategy will work in his territory, it may
work elsewhere. And it is very likely that he will become responsible for larger
and larger territories. The opportunity is there—for those who are prepared and
willing to work.

Even the starting job may offer great opportunities. Some beginning salespeople—especially those working for manufacturers or wholesalers—are responsible
for larger sales volumes than are achieved by many retail stores. This is a responsibility which must be taken seriously—and should be prepared for.

Further, the sales job is often used as an entry-level position—to evaluate a
person. Success in this job can lead to rapid promotion to higher-level sales
and marketing jobs—and more money and security.

BASIC SALES TASKS MAY BE SPLIT

One of the difficulties of discussing selling is that every sales job is different.
While the engineer or accountant can look forward to fairly specific duties, the
salesperson's job is constantly changing.

*Selling is divided into
three tasks*

The three **basic sales tasks** are *order getting, order taking,* and *supporting.*
For convenience we will describe salespeople by these terms—referring to their
primary task—although one person might have to do all three tasks in some
situations.

As the names imply, order getters and order takers are interested in obtaining orders for their company. In contrast, supporting salespeople are not directly interested in orders. Their function is to help the order-oriented salespeople. With this variety, you can see that there is a place in personal selling for nearly everyone.

ORDER GETTERS DEVELOP NEW BUSINESS

Order getters are concerned with getting new business. **Order getting** means aggressively seeking out possible buyers with a well-organized sales presentation designed to sell a product, service, or idea. Order getters may be interested in selling the advantages of buying from one company rather than from another— or shifting a larger share of purchases to their own company—or finding completely new customers and even entirely new markets.

Order getters must have complete confidence in their abilities, company, and product—since their attitudes show through to customers. They must also know what they are talking about—not be just a personal contact.

Order-getting salespeople work for manufacturers, wholesalers, and retailers. They normally are well paid—many earning more than $25,000 per year.

Manufacturers' order getters—find new opportunities

Manufacturers of all kinds of goods—but especially industrial goods—have a great need for order getters. They are needed to locate new prospects, open new accounts, visualize new opportunities, and help establish and build channel relationships.

High-caliber order getters are essential in sales of installations and accessory equipment—where large sums are involved—and top-level management participates in the buying decision.

Top-level customers are more interested in ways to save or make more money than in technical details—and good order getters cater to this interest. They sell concepts and ideas—rather than physical products. The products are merely the means of achieving the ends desired by the customer.

In selling other industrial goods—such as raw materials, components, supplies, and services—skilled order getters also are necessary, but perhaps only for initial contacts. Since many competitors offer nearly the same product, the salesperson's crucial selling job here is getting the company's name "on the list." Persuasion of the highest order—and sometimes deliberate social cultivation of top-executive prospects may be needed.

Industrial goods order getters need the "know-how" to help solve their customer's problems. To have technically competent order getters, firms often give special technical training to business-trained college graduates. Such salespeople then can deal intelligently with their specialist customers. In fact, they may be more technically competent in their narrow specialty than anyone they are likely to encounter—and so may be able to provide a unique service.

Wholesalers' order getters—hand it to the customer, almost

Progressive wholesalers are developing into counselors and store advisors— rather than just order takers. Such order getters are almost "partners" of retailers in the job of moving goods from the wholesale warehouse through the retail store to consumers. These order getters almost become a part of the retailer's staff—helping to check stock, write orders, conduct demonstrations—and plan advertising, special promotions, and other retailing activities.

Agent middlemen often are order getters—particularly the more aggressive manufacturers' agents and brokers. They face the same tasks as manufacturers' order getters.

Retail order getters— visionaries at the storm window

Order getters are needed for unsought goods—and desirable for some shopping goods.

Unsought goods need order getters

Convincing customers of the merits of products they haven't seriously considered takes a high degree of personal selling ability. Encyclopedia sales reps, for example, must convince prospects that $400 to $800 is a small price for a lifetime of literacy and enjoyment.

Order getters may have to visualize how a particular product will satisfy needs now being filled by something else. Early order getters for aluminum storm windows and other aluminum and plastic home improvements faced the difficult task of convincing skeptical prospects that these materials were not only durable—but also would save money and require less maintenance in the long run. Similar problems were faced by early refrigerator salesmen in the 1920s—and air-conditioning salesmen in the 1930s. Encyclopedia salespeople will probably face them forever.

Without order getters, many of the products we now accept as part of our standard of living—such as refrigerators and window air-conditioners—might have died in the introduction stage. Most people reject new ideas or wait for others to accept them first. It is the visionary order getter who helps bring products out of the introduction stage—into the market growth and market maturity stages. It is the order getter who sells enough customers to get the web-of-word-of-mouth going. Without sales and profits in the early stages, the product may fail and never be offered again.

They help sell shopping goods

Order getters are helpful for selling *heterogeneous* shopping goods. Consumers shop for many of these items on the basis of price *and* quality. They welcome useful information. Automobiles, furniture and furnishings, cameras and photographic supplies, and fashion items can be sold effectively by an aggreessive, helpful order getter. Friendly advice—based on thorough knowledge of the product and its alternatives, may really help consumers—and bring profits to the salesperson and retailers.

Many specialty shops and limited-line stores have developed a following because of the help offered by the stores' sales clerks. Some notify their regular customers when they have special offerings. They often will advise a customer *not* to buy a particular product because it will not fit his needs—even though they do not have a suitable substitute. The store may lose an immediate sale—but this kind of service is profitable to retailers seeking loyal customers and repeat business.

ORDER TAKERS—KEEP THE BUSINESS COMING

Order takers sell the regular or typical customers. Order takers complete most sales transactions. After the customer becomes interested in the products of a specific firm—from an order getter or a supporting salesperson or through advertising or sales promotion—an order taker usually is needed to answer any final questions and complete the sale. **Order taking** is the routine completion of sales made regularly to the target customers.

Sometimes sales managers or customers will use the term "order taker" as a "put down" when referring to unaggressive salespeople. While a particular salesperson may perform so poorly that criticism of him is justified, it is a mistake to downgrade the function of order taking. Order taking is extremely important—whether handled by human hands or machines. Many sales are lost just because no one ever took the order—and closed the sale!

Manufacturers' order takers—responsible for training and explaining

After order getters open up industrial, wholesale, or retail accounts, regular follow-up is necessary. Someone has to explain details, make adjustments, handle complaints, explain or negotiate new prices and terms, place sales promotion materials, and keep customers informed on new developments. It may also be necessary to train the customers' employees to use machines or products. In sales to middlemen, it may be necessary to train wholesalers' or retailers' salespeople. All these activities are part of the order taker's job.

Usually these salespeople have a regular route with many calls—which they may make at fixed times. To handle these calls well, they must have energy, persistence, enthusiasm, and a friendly personality that wears well over time.

Sometimes jobs that are basically order taking are used to train potential order getters and managers—since they may offer some order-getting possibilities. This can be seen in the following description of his job by a young Colgate salesperson, who moved rapidly into the ranks of sales management:

Order takers close most sales.

Mike Voss

Over many months, I worked carefully with Gromer's Super Market. It was an aggressive young store. After a few calls, I felt I had built up a warm friendship with the store personnel. They came to trust me and, more frequently than not, after I straightened shelves, checked out-of-stocks, and did the usual dusting and rearranging, I gave them an order blank already filled in.

It got to be a joke with big, husky Paul Gromer, the owner, and his hard-working manager-brother. They kept asking, "Well, what did we buy today?" and they signed the order book without checking.

Naturally, I worked at the order like it was my own business, making certain that they were never stuck with dead stock or over-orders. They were making continual progress, though nothing sensational.

Finally, Colgate came out with a good deal. I knew it was right for Gromer's and I thought the store ought to double its weekly order to 400 cases. I talked to Paul Gromer about it and, without any reason that I'm able to think of today, I said, "Paul, this is a hot deal and I think you're ready for a carload order."

He looked at me for just a moment. I braced myself for an argument. Then he said, "Sure, why not? You've always been right before. Just ship it."

It was the biggest order of soap Gromer's had ever taken—and the store soon became a regular carload buyer.[1]

Wholesalers' order takers—not getting order, but keeping them

While manufacturers' order takers handle relatively few items—and sometimes even a single item—wholesalers' order takers may sell 125,000 items or more. Most wholesale order takers just sell out of their catalog. They have so many items that they can't possibly give aggressive sales effort to many—except perhaps newer or more profitable items. Once a new product has been featured, the order taker probably won't give it much attention for some time. He just has too many items to single any out for special attention. The order taker's strength is his wide assortment—rather than detailed knowledge of individual products. Even if shown how to greatly increase sales of particular items, he probably would not and should not do it.

The wholesale order taker's main job is to maintain close contact with his customers—perhaps once a week—and fill any needs that develop. Sometimes such an order taker gets very close to industrial customers or retailers. Some retailers let him take inventory—and write up his own order. Obviously, this position of trust cannot be abused. After writing up the order, this order taker normally checks to be sure his company fills the order promptly—and accurately. He also handles any adjustments or complaints—and generally acts as a liaison between his company and customers.

Such salespeople are usually of the low-pressure type—friendly and easygoing. Usually these jobs are not as high paying as the order-getting variety—but are attractive to many because they are not as physically taxing. Relatively little traveling is required—and there is little or no pressure to get new accounts.

Retail order takers— often they are poor sales clerks

Order taking may be almost mechanical at the retail level—for example, at the supermarket checkout counter. For many products, not much is needed— except to fill the customers' order, wrap it, and make change. As a result, retail clerks often are expected to concentrate on setting up and arranging stock— and sometimes they seem to be annoyed by having to complete sales. Many are downright rude. This is most unfortunate because order taking *is* a vital function. They may be poor order takers, however, because they are not paid very well—often at the minimum wage. But—they may be paid little because they do little. In any case, order taking at the retail level appears to be declining in quality. And it is likely that there will be far fewer such jobs in the future—as more marketers make adjustments in their mixes and turn to self-service selling.

SUPPORTING SALES FORCE—INFORMS AND PROMOTES IN THE CHANNEL

Supporting salespeople help the order-oriented salespeople—but don't try to get orders themselves. Their activities are aimed at getting sales in the long run. For the short run, however, they are ambassadors of goodwill who provide specialized services. Almost all supporting salespeople work for manufacturers—or middlemen who do this supporting work for manufacturers. There are two types of supporting salespeople: *missionary salespeople* and *technical specialists*.

Missionary salespeople can increase sales

Missionary salespeople work for manufacturers—calling on their middlemen and their customers. They try to develop goodwill and stimulate demand, help the middlemen train their salespeople to do so, and often take orders for delivery by the middlemen.

Missionary salespeople are sometimes called *merchandisers* or *detailers*.[2] They may be necessary if a manufacturer uses the typical merchant wholesaler to obtain widespread distribution—and yet knows that the retailers will need promotion help. These salespeople may be able to give an occasional "shot in the arm" to the company's regular wholesalers and retailers. Or, they may work regularly with these middlemen—setting up displays, arranging special promotions, and, in general, implementing the sales promotion plans.

An imaginative missionary salesperson may double or triple sales. Naturally, this doesn't go unnoticed—and missionary sales jobs are often a route to order-oriented jobs. In fact, this position is often used as a training ground for new salespeople.

Supporting salespeople build awareness, interest, and goodwill in channels.

John Penzari

*Technical specialists
help order-oriented
people*

Technical specialists provide technical assistance to order-oriented sales people. They are usually scientists or engineers who have little interest in sales. Instead, they have technical know-how—plus the ability to explain the advantages of the company's product. Since they usually talk to the customer's technical people, there is little need for much sales ability. Before the specialist's visit, an order getter probably has stimulated interest. The technical specialist provides the details. The order getter probably will complete the sale—but only after the customer's technical people give at least tentative approval. Some of these technical specialists eventually become fine order getters, but most are more interested in showing the technical excellence of their product than persuading customers to buy it.

*Most selling requires a
blend of all three*

We have described three sales tasks—order getting, order taking, and supporting. You should understand, however, that a particular salesperson might be given at least two of these tasks—and perhaps all three. Ten percent of a particular job may be order getting, 80 percent order taking, and the additional 10 percent supporting. Another sales person may have the same title—but a very different blend of sales tasks.

The type of person needed for a given sales job—and the level of compensation—will depend largely on which sales tasks are required—and in what combination. This is why job descriptions are so important.

*Job descriptions are
needed*

A **job description** shows what a salesperson is expected to do. It might list 10 to 20 specific tasks—as well as the routine prospecting and sales report writing. Each company must write its own job specifications—but when they are written, they should provide clear guidelines as to the kind of sales people who should be selected—and how they should be trained and motivated. These strategic details are discussed later in the chapter.

NATURE OF THE PERSONAL SELLING JOB

*Good salespeople are
trained, not born*

The idea that good salespeople are born has some truth in it—but it isn't the whole story. A *born* salesperson—if that term refers to a gregarious, aggressive kind of individual—may not do nearly as well—when the going gets rough—as a less extroverted co-worker who has had solid, specialized training. Experiments have shown that it is possible to train any alert person to be a good salesperson.

Much of this training is grounded on basic steps which each salesperson should follow—including prospecting, planning sales presentations, making sales presentations, and following up after the sale. See Figure 17–2 for a diagram

**Figure 17–2
Personal selling is a
communication process**

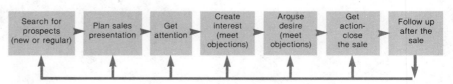

Salespeople need training and practice.

Peter Le Grand

which shows that the personal salesperson is just carrying out the communications process discussed in the last chapter.

While these basic steps may seem logical—and even obvious—what is obvious in theory isn't always practiced. Many salespeople fail—or are mediocre in performance—because they don't follow the basic steps. Others have never even been taught them. Many orders are lost simply because the salesperson doesn't have enough information about the product—or doesn't ask for the order.

New salespeople often are hired and immediately sent out on the road—or retail selling floor—with no grounding in the basic steps and no information about the product or the customer—just a price list and a pat on the back. This isn't enough!

It is up to sales and marketing management to be sure that the salespeople know what they are supposed to do—and how to do it.

Finding prospects—the big buyer who wasn't there

Finding "live" prospects isn't as easy as it sounds. Although the marketing strategy should specify the target market, we have already seen that some people within a target market may be innovators, while others are late adopters.

Basically, **prospecting** involves following down all the "leads" in the target market. But this only identifies which kinds of people or companies *may* be prospects—not which ones are currently "live" and will help make the buying decision. In the industrial goods area, for example, about two thirds of industrial calls are made on the wrong person—because of multiple-buying influences and the fact that companies often rearrange their organization structures and buying responsibilities. This means that constant, detailed customer analysis is needed—requiring many personal calls and telephone calls.

Priority system guides prospecting

Another part of prospecting is deciding how much time to spend on which prospects. Here, the potential sales volume—as well as the likelihood of a sale—must be weighed. If many competitors are concentrating on a few accounts, the probability of any one of them making the sale may be low. It may be more sensible for the salesperson to shift to other prospects. This obviously requires judgment—but well-organized salespeople usually develop some priority system. Attractive accounts may be labeled "A"—and the salesperson may plan to call on them weekly until the sale is made or they are placed in a lower category. "B" customers might offer somewhat lower potential—and be called upon monthly. "C" accounts might be called on only once a year—unless they happen to contact the salesperson. And "D" accounts might be ignored—unless the customer takes the initiative.

Some such system is needed to guide prospecting—because most salespeople have too many prospects. They cannot afford to "wine and dine" all of them. Some may deserve only a phone call. Taking them to lunch would be a waste of the salesperson's precious time. There are only a few hours each business day for personal sales calls—this time must be used carefully if the salesperson is to succeed. You can see that effective prospecting is important to success—in fact, it may be more important than making a good sales representation, especially if the company's marketing mix is basically strong.

Three kinds of sales presentations may be useful[3]

Once a promising prospect has been located, it is necessary to make a **sales presentation**—a salesperson's effort to make a sale. But someone has to plan the kind of sales presentation to be made. This is a strategic matter. The kind of presentation should be set before the salesperson is sent prospecting. Or, in situations where the customer comes to the salesperson—for example, in a retail store—the planners have to make sure that prospects are brought together with salespeople. Eventually, then, the planned sales presentation must be made.

The marketing manager can choose among three basically different sales presentations: the *black box* approach, the *selling formula* approach, and the *need-satisfaction* approach. Each has its place.

The black box approach

The **black box approach** uses a "canned" or prepared sales presentation—building on the black box (stimulus-response) model discussed in Chapter 7. This model says that a customer faced with a particular stimulus will give the desired response—in this case, a "yes" answer to the salesperson's request for an order. In applying the black box approach, the salesperson usually does not have a very good idea about what goes on in the consumer's mind. So he tries various appeals which he has been taught—one after the other—hoping to get the desired response.

The use of these prepared sales presentations is shown in Figure 17–3. Basically, the salesperson does most of the talking—see the shaded area in Figure 17–3—only occasionally letting the customer talk when the salesperson attempts to close. If one closing attempt does not work, another prepared presentation is tried—and another attempt at closing. This can go on for some time—until either the salesperson runs out of material—or the customer either buys or decides to leave.

This approach can be effective and practical. It is commonly used when the prospective sale is low in value—and only a short presentation is practical. This is true, for example, for many convenience goods in food stores, drug stores,

Figure 17–3
Black box approach to sales presentations

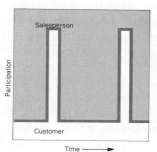

With the black box approach a salesperson tries different "canned" presentations.

Mary McCarthy

and department stores. The presentation might be as simple as: "That's very nice, should I wrap it up?" or "That looks nice on you, would you like to take it?" or "Would you like to try it on?" or "Would you like a carton instead of a package?" or "Should I fill'er up?" Each can be effective for some customers—and all the situation demands.

This approach treats all potential customers the same. It may work for some and not for others—and the salespeople probably won't know why. Moreover, they don't improve with more experience—because they are just mechanically trying standard presentations. This approach may be suitable for simple order taking—but it is no longer considered good selling for complicated situations.

Selling formula approach

The **selling formula approach** uses a prepared outline—also building on the black box (stimulus-response) model—taking the customers through some logical steps to a final close. The steps are logical because here we assume that we know something about the target customers' needs and attitudes.

The selling formula approach is illustrated in Figure 17–4. A salesperson does most of the talking at the beginning of the presentation—because he knows exactly what he wants to say. It even may have been prepared as part of the marketing strategy. As the sales presentation moves along, however, the salesperson brings the customer into the discussion—to help clarify just what needs this customer has. In other words, the strategy planners may know that the target customers may have several needs. The salesperson's job is to discover the needs of a particular customer—so that he will know how to proceed. Once he knows which kind of customer he is talking to, the salesperson comes back to show how his product satisfies the person's specific needs. Then he goes on to close the sale.

**Figure 17–4
Selling formula approach to sales presentations**

This approach can be useful for both order-getting and order-taking situations—where potential customers are similar, and relatively untrained salespeople must be used. This is similar to using mass selling—where only one general presentation must be tailored to a large audience—only here several preplanned presentations are possible. And, of course, they are made face-to-face. Some of the office equipment and computer manufacturers, for example, have used this approach—because they know the kinds of situations that their salespeople meet—and roughly what they want them to say. Using this approach speeds the training process and makes the sales force productive sooner.

Need-satisfaction approach

The **need-satisfaction approach** involves developing a good understanding of the prospective customer's needs before trying to close the sale. Here, after making some general benefit statement—to get the customer's attention and interest—the salesperson leads the customer to do most of the talking—to help the salesperson pinpoint the customer's needs. See Figure 17–5. After the salesperson feels that he understands what the customer needs, he begins to enter into the sales presentation more—trying to help the customer understand his own needs. Once they agree on needs, the seller tries to show how his product fills those needs—and closes the sale.

The need-satisfaction approach can be useful if there are many subtle differences among the various customers in one target market. The salesperson's job is to decide which of the many potentially relevant dimensions describe a particular person, and then to help the customer understand what his needs are. In the extreme, each customer may be thought of as a separate target market—with the salesperson trying to adapt to each one's needs and attitudes. This kind of sales presentation obviously takes more skill—and also more time. So this approach might be used when the sale is large.

With this approach, the salesperson is much more on his own—and should have not only a good grounding in the company's product and policies, but also much empathy for people and situations. Further, some knowledge of the behavioral science theories which we have discussed would be useful. In particular, a good understanding of the "hierarchy of needs" would help a salesperson to (1) analyze what motivates a particular customer and (2) think of ways to show how the company's offering would help the customer satisfy those needs.

Need-satisfaction selling provides great satisfaction for some salespeople—causing them to move toward a professional status. Some become so deeply involved with satisfying their customers' needs that they see themselves as representatives of their *customers* in dealings with their own firms.

Figure 17–5
Need-satisfaction approach to sales presentations

AIDA helps plan sales presentations

AIDA—Attention, Interest, Desire, Action. Each presentation—except for some simple black box types—follows this AIDA sequence. The "how-to-do-it" might even be set as part of the marketing strategy. The time spent with each of the steps might vary, depending on the situation—and the selling approach being used—but it is still necessary to begin a presentation by getting the prospect's *attention,* and hopefully, moving him to *action* through a close. Let's look at some ways in which these steps might be carried out.

Attention

There is no sure way to get a prospect's attention. Much depends on the salesperson's instincts and originality—as well as knowledge of his customers. If a salesperson calls on the same customers frequently, he will want to use a new approach each time. If each call is on a new prospect, a few successful attention getters will be enough.

At the beginning of a meeting with a customer, a salesperson's objective is to distract the potential customer from his current thoughts and begin a conversation. The seller could do this by just introducing himself—or saying, "Hello, can I help you?" as a retail clerk might. Or a statement about the plans of the prospect's competitors—or outstanding benefits being offered by his firm—might get attention.

Whatever method is used, the attention getter should be casual—not elaborate—so the presentation can move quickly, naturally, and logically into the next step—creating interest. Otherwise, attention may be followed by a letdown.

Interest

Creating interest takes more time. The best way is to look for the customer's basic needs or problems—especially those which the salesperson might help to solve. A furniture store salesclerk should not make a prepared speech about rugs every time a customer comes in—some might want lamps, sofas, and so on. Getting the customer to talk helps to give the salesperson the all-important feedback which guides later effort. Because, it is hoped, he has selected prospects from among the target customers of the marketing strategy or strategies he is implementing, he should know roughly what they want—and have a marketing mix designed specifically for them. His job is to show how and why it fits their needs—and close the sale.

If the salesperson has correctly selected his prospect, he may be able to use some visual aids which were specifically designed to hold interest—and avoid having the presentation cut short. A slide or movie projector might communicate what the salesperson's company sells or does. Or the potential customer's senses might be appealed to with a product to handle or a sample to taste.

Desire

Arousing desire requires an even more persuasive effort. In this step, the salesperson has to discover exactly what the prospect's needs and attitudes are. This allows the seller to show how his product fits the need, answer any objections, and prepare to close the sale. This feedback is important to the sales presentation—and is a big advantage of personal selling.

Knowing the prospect's special needs, the seller can explain *specifically* how

Once a salesperson has gotten attention he should try to understand the customer's needs and move toward action.

Mary McCarthy

the product could be used in the customer's factory—or how it would be purchased by the buyer's customers.

One objective in this step is to encourage the prospect to make a "mental trial" of the product—to see how it could fill his needs. For example, the sales rep might show a grocer some statistics or testimonials on the success of the product in other stores.

Action

Finally, the salesperson will try to summarize the important points, tailor arguments to the customer's needs and attitudes, and try to close the sale—that is, affect the prospect's behavior. You may be surprised to learn that one of the most frequent reasons for losing a sale is that the salesperson never *asks* for the order! Perhaps this is because he doesn't want to be refused. He's afraid that a direct request for the order is too easily answered with a no.

There are ways, however, to avoid this awful word. Without asking for a direct yes or no the experienced salesperson may just assume that, "of course," the customer will buy. He may begin to write up the order—or ask which of various delivery dates would be preferable—or what quantity the customer would like to try in a new display. This may lead the customer into taking action without consciously having to make a direct decision—a difficult step for some people.

SALES MANAGEMENT MUST BE PLANNED, TOO

Marketing strategies must include some sales management guidelines—about how the personal selling job will be carried out—including selecting, training, and motivating salespeople.

Besides helping the marketing manager set these guidelines, the sales manager must allocate territories, set quotas, and evaluate and control the whole process. We can't cover all the details of sales management here—but you should see that they are done within the strategic guidelines set by the marketing strategy. The more that is known about the needs and attitudes of the target market, the easier it will be for the sales manager to plan. This emphasizes, again, the importance of marketing strategy planning—and knowing as much as possible about the firm's target markets.[4]

Selecting good salespeople takes judgment, plus

It is important to hire *good, well-qualified* salespeople. But the selection of salespeople in most companies is a hit-or-miss affair—usually done without any job description—or serious thought about exactly what kind of person is needed. Friends and relations—or people who are available—may be hired because many feel that the only qualifications for sales jobs are a friendly personality and "looking good." This approach has led to poor sales—and high personnel turnover—for many companies.

Progressive companies try to use more scientific procedures in hiring—including multiple interviews with various executives, and psychological tests. Unfortunately, these techniques can't guarantee success—but experiments have shown that using some kind of selection method results in a better sales force than using no selection aids at all.

Research has found that people sell best to others who are like them.

Mary McCarthy

Dyads affect strategies

The company's target market may have to be given more consideration when choosing salespeople. Behavioral science research seems to indicate that the effectiveness of a sales force depends on the kinds and personalities of the company's customers. Greater sales result when the **dyad**—the relationship between the customer and the salesperson—is positive. Insurance salespeople, for example, seem to be more successful when dealing with individuals similar to themselves—in age, height, income, religious affiliation, education, politics, and even smoking habits![5]

Logically, this would mean that the sales manager should learn as much as possible about his various target markets before choosing salespeople. He may need to hire different kinds of people—to meet different kinds of customers. Insurance companies, for example, probably make a mistake when they hire only college graduate athletes from middle-class backgrounds to sell for them. The former athlete may be very good for some potential customers—but totally wrong for others. In contrast, women's clothing stores—like Lane Bryant—that cater to larger sizes, try to hire saleswomen who also wear those sizes. They seem to be able to relate better to their customers than a more petite salesperson might.

Training salespeople

It is not possible to have a successful sales force unless the people are told what is expected of them—and how to accomplish these objectives. A job description is helpful in telling the salespeople what they are expected to do. But showing them how to get the job done is harder—as people may be hired with different backgrounds, skills, and levels of intelligence.

From an experience standpoint, new salespeople may be divided into the following categories:

People have to be trained to be good representatives of a company.

Ellis Herwig—Stock, Boston

1. The salesperson who is new to sales as well as to the company's products.
2. The salesperson with previous selling experience—but no knowledge of the company or its products.
3. The salesperson with knowledge of the company's products but no previous selling experience—who has transferred from the production or warehouse department to the sales department.
4. The salesperson with previous selling experience with the company's type of products.

The kind of sales training should be modified for each group. This might mean skipping certain parts of a complete training program for trainees with better qualifications or backgrounds.

The company's sales training program should cover at least the following areas: (1) company policies and practices, (2) product information, and (3) selling techniques.

Company policies and practices

As the salesperson may be the only company representative that a customer ever sees, he ought to be thoroughly familiar with the company's policies with respect to credit, size of orders, dating of invoices, delivery, transportation costs, returned goods privileges, and pricing. The salesperson must be familiar with the procedures concerning reports expected of him, expenses and their control, attendance at sales meetings, and other requirements. As far as company practices are concerned, the salesperson should understand internal procedures—so he can help his customers by speeding up orders, securing adjustments, and generally making it easier for them to deal with his company.

Product information

The amount of product information a salesperson needs depends on the type of job he will fill—and the variety, extent, and technical complexity of the product line. We have looked at some of these problems in this chapter—as well as throughout the book where the goods classes and customer-buying behavior have been discussed. The important thing is that the salesperson have enough information to be able to satisfy his customers—much information for some accessory and shopping goods, for example, and less for convenience goods. Ideally, the salesperson would also know a lot about competitors and their products, too.

Selling techniques

The importance of planning an effective sales presentation has already been discussed.

In most companies, unfortunately, training in selling techniques has been neglected because of the feeling that selling techniques are something everyone has—or at least anyone hired for a sales job. More progressive companies are finding that salesmanship can be taught very effectively by observing senior salespeople, making trial demonstrations and sales presentations, and by analyzing why present customers buy from the company, why former customers now buy from competitors, and why some prospects remain only prospects. This training is started in the classroom and often supplemented by on-the-job coaching from district managers and supervisors.

Length of training period

How long the initial training period should be depends almost directly on the difficulty of the salesperson's job—as shown by the job description. Some go on as long as three years. Sales training, however, should go on indefinitely. Many companies use weekly sales meetings or work sessions, annual or semiannual conventions or conferences, and regular weekly or biweekly newsletters—as well as normal sales supervision. Many salespeople get set in their ways and profit greatly by—and often welcome the chance for—additional training.

Compensating and motivating salespeople

Most companies use financial motivation—but public recognition, sales contests, and simple personal recognition for a job well done, may be highly effective in encouraging greater sales effort.[6] Our main emphasis here, however, will be upon financial stimulation.

Two basic decisions must be made in developing a compensation plan: (1) determine the level of the compensation and (2) decide how to provide this level of compensation.

Level of compensation

The first step is to write a job description to determine what is to be done. This forces a careful evaluation of the salesperson's role in the total marketing mix. This description will show whether any special skills or responsibilities are required that would command higher pay levels. The next step then is to determine how valuable such a salesperson will be to the company. An order getter may be worth $50,000 to $100,000 to a large organization, but only $5,000 to $10,000 to a smaller company—simply because it does not have enough to sell to justify the higher salary. In some cases, though, smaller companies pay order getters more than they might get in a larger company—because these people carry almost the whole promotion burden—and because their efforts are so necessary to the firm's success.

Most companies must at least meet the going market wage for salespeople of a particular skill level. Conditions in the market will usually set the minimum salary for each kind of job. Order getters earn the highest levels—and then the pay scale works on down to some of the supporting salespeople and eventually to the order takers. Some retail store clerks—basically low-level order takers—may not even be paid the federal minimum wage.

If there are particularly difficult aspects to a job—such as extensive traveling, aggressive pioneering, or contacts with more difficult customers—the level of compensation may have to be increased. It must be kept in mind, however, that the salesperson's compensation level should correspond at least roughly with the pay scale of the rest of the firm. Normally salespeople will be paid more than the office or production force, but seldom more than top management.

Methods of paying the level

Once the general level of compensation has been decided, then the method of payment must be decided. There are three basic methods of payment: (1) *straight salary,* (2) *straight commission,* or (3) *a combination plan.* Straight salary normally supplies the most security for the salesperson, and straight commission the most incentive. Because these two represent extremes—and most companies want to offer their salespeople some balance between incentive and security— the most popular method of payment is a combination plan which includes some salary and some commission. Bonuses, profit sharing, pensions, insurance, and other fringe benefits may be included too. Still, some blend of salary and commission provides the basis for most combination plans.

What determines the choice of the pay plan? Four standards should be applied: control, incentive, flexibility, and simplicity.

Control. A sales manager's control over a salesperson varies directly with

Salespeople on straight salary should have more direction.

Mary McCarthy

what proportion of his compensation is in the form of salary. The straight salary plan permits the maximum amount of supervision—since the person on commission tends to be his own boss. The salesperson on straight salary earns the same amount regardless of how he spends his time—or which product he pushes. If the sales manager wishes the salesperson to spend much time on order taking, supporting sales activities, repair work or delivery services, then the salaried salesperson can be expected to do these activities without complaining. The company is paying for the use of his services for a set period of time—and he should expect to work as needed.

It should be noted that straight salary or a large salary element in the compensation plan increases the amount of sales supervision needed. The control is maintained only if the sales manager supervises the salesperson. If such personal supervision would be difficult, better control might be obtained by a compensation plan which included some commission—or even a straight commission with built-in direction.

A poorly designed commission plan can lead to lack of control however. A manufacturer of industrial fabrics which paid its salespeople a straight commission found its plant was swamped with a large quantity of small yardage orders. Furthermore, the plant was receiving many requests for bids on highly competitive low-margin items. This was disappointing—since the company's objective was the development of new markets, not obtaining immediate business. In this case, the sales compensation plan was directing the salespeople toward the wrong objective.[7]

Incentive. An incentive plan can range anywhere from an indirect incentive (a modest sharing of company profits) to very direct incentive where a salesperson's income is strictly a commission on his sales. The incentive should be large only if there is a direct relationship between the salesperson's effort and results. If the relationship is less direct, as when a number of people are involved in the sale—engineers, top management, or supporting salespeople—then each one's contribution is less obvious and greater emphasis on salary may make more sense.

Strong incentives are normally offered order-getting salespeople when a company wants to expand sales rapidly. Strong incentives may be used, too, when the company's objectives are shifting or varied. In this way, the salesperson's activities and efforts can be directed and shifted as needed. One trucking company, for example, has a sales incentive plan that pays commissions on business needed to balance the freight movement—depending on how heavily traffic has been moving in one direction or another. At any one time, commissions are paid only on traffic moving in one direction.

A poor incentive plan may cause the company's level of compensation to get out of line with competitive firms. Such situations can cause dissatisfaction among the company's salespeople and actually reduce the company's sales. In one situation, a number of companies were offering large office machines. One salesperson could make $40,000 commission on a particular machine, but his competitor would only make $3,000. In this situation, the first salesperson offered the other a third of his $40,000 commission to help him make the sale!

Obviously, such situations cause problems and dissatisfaction. In this case, the second company was in a peculiar position; it was the industry leader. It had formerly paid such high commissions—but had given them up when it found that the incentive was too great and the salespeople "oversold" their customers—damaging the company's long-run reputation. In the short-run however, its salespeople were unhappy about the lower commission rates—especially when competitors still were earning the high rates.

Flexibility. Flexibility is probably the most difficult aspect to achieve. One major reason that combination plans have become more popular is that they offer a way to meet varying situations. Four major kinds of flexibility will be considered:

1. Flexibility in selling costs. This is important for most small companies. With limited working capital and uncertain markets, small companies like the fixed selling costs (as a percent of sales) aspect of straight commission—or combination plans with a large commission element. This is similar to using manufacturers' agents who have to be paid only if they deliver sales. When sales drop off, costs do too. This feature often dominates in selecting a method of sales compensation.
2. Flexibility among territories. Different sales territories present different potentials. Unless the pay plan allows for this fact, the salesperson in a growing territory might have rapidly increasing earnings for the same amount of work—while the salesperson in a poor area will have little to show for his effort. Such a situation is not fair—and can lead to high turnover and much dissatisfaction. The star salesperson may be the one who through luck or a family relationship has managed to get the best territory.
3. Flexibility among people. Most companies use salespeople at varying stages of their development. Trainees and new salespeople usually require a special pay plan with emphasis on salary. This provides at least some stability of earnings.
4. Flexibility among products. Most companies make several different products with different profit potentials. Unless this fact is recognized, the salespeople may emphasize the sale of those products which sell easiest—ignoring overall company profit. A flexible commission system may more easily adjust to changing profit potentials as demand conditions warrant.

Simplicity. A final consideration is the need for simplicity. Complicated plans are hard for salespeople to understand—and costly for the accounting department to administer. Much dissatisfaction will result if salespeople can't see a direct relationship between their effort and their income.

Simplicity is best achieved with straight commission. In practice, however, it is usually better to sacrifice some simplicity to gain some flexibility, incentive, or control. The actual combination of these factors must depend on the job description and the company's objectives. Figure 17–6 shows the general relation between personal selling expenses—for the basic alternatives—and sales volume. It also shows why firms switch from agents to their own sales forces as sales increase.

Figure 17-6
Relation between personal selling expenses and sales volume—for basic personal selling compensation alternatives

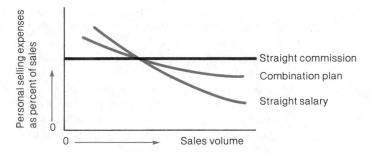

Source: This figure suggested by Prof. A. A. Brogowicz, Western Michigan University.

Sales management must plan, implement, and control

There are, unfortunately, no easy answers to the compensation problem. It is up to the sales manager—in cooperation with the marketing manager—to develop a good compensation plan. The sales manager's efforts must be coordinated with the whole marketing plan—because he can accomplish his objectives only if enough money is allocated for this job.

As you have seen, it is the marketing manager's job to balance the promotion blend. The expected cost and performance of the sales force are only two of the many variables he has to consider in making the final decision. To make these judgments, the marketing manager has to know what a sales force should consist of, what its objectives should be, and what it should cost.

Once the sales manager's basic plan and budget have been set, his job is to implement the plan—including directing and controlling the sales force. This would include assigning sales territories, and controlling performance.

More is said on controlling in Chapter 22—but you can see now that the sales manager has more to do than fly about the country, sipping martinis and entertaining customers. A sales manager is deeply involved with the basic management tasks of planning and control—as well as ongoing implementing of the personal selling effort.

CONCLUSION

In this chapter, we have discussed the importance and nature of personal selling. Selling is much more than just "getting rid of the product." In fact, a salesperson who is not provided with strategy guidelines may have to become his own strategic planner. Ideally, however, the sales manager and marketing manager should work together to set some strategic guidelines: the number and kind of salespersons needed, the kind of sales presentation, and selection, training, and motivation approaches.

Three *basic* sales tasks were discussed: (1) order getting, (2) order taking, and (3) supporting. Most sales jobs are a combination of at least two of these three tasks. The nature of the job—and the level and method of compensation—

depend on the blend of these tasks. A job description should be developed for each sales job. This, in turn, provides guidelines for selecting, training, and compensating salespeople.

Three kinds of sales presentations were identified. Each has its place—but the need-satisfaction approach seems most applicable for higher-level sales jobs. It is in these kinds of jobs that personal selling is achieving a new, professional status—because of the competence and degree of personal responsibility required of the salesperson. The day of the old-time "glad-hander" is passing in favor of the specialist who is creative, industrious, persuasive, knowledgeable, highly trained—and, therefore, able to help the buyer. This type of salesperson always has been—and probably always will be—in short supply. And the demand for high-level salespeople is growing.

QUESTIONS AND PROBLEMS

1. Identify the strategic planning decisions which are needed in the personal selling area and explain why they should be treated as strategic decisions to be made by the marketing manager.

2. What kind of salesperson (or what blend of the basic sales tasks) is required to sell the following products? If there are several selling jobs in the channel for each product, then indicate the kinds of sales people required. (Specify any assumptions necessary to give definite answers).
   a. Soya bean oil.
   b. Costume jewelry.
   c. Nuts and bolts.
   d. Handkerchiefs.
   e. Mattresses.
   f. Corn.
   g. Cigarettes.

3. Distinguish among the jobs of manufacturers', wholesalers', and retailers' order-getting salespeople. If one order getter is needed, must all the salespeople in a channel be order getters? Illustrate.

4. Discuss the role of the manufacturers' agent in the marketing manager's promotion plans. What kind of salesperson is he?

5. Discuss the future of the specialty shop if manufacturers place greater emphasis on mass selling because of the inadequacy of retail order taking.

6. Explain the sequential nature of the personal selling job.

7. Cite an actual local example of each of the three kinds of sales presentations discussed in the chapter. Explain for each situation whether a different type of presentation would have been better.

8. Describe a need-satisfaction sales presentation which you have experienced recently and explain how it might have been improved by fuller use of the AIDA framework.

9. Explain how a straight commission system might provide flexibility in the sale of a line of women's clothing products which continually vary in profitability.

10. Explain how a compensation system could be developed to provide incentives for older sales people and yet make some provision for trainees who have not yet learned their job.

11. Describe the operation of our economy if personal salespeople were outlawed. Could the economy work? If so, how; if not, what is the minimum personal selling effort necessary? Could this minimum personal selling effort be controlled effectively by law?

SUGGESTED CASES

NOTES

1. F. A. Russell and F. H. Beach. *Textbook of Salesmanship,* 6th ed. (New York: McGraw-Hill Book Co., 1951), pp. 113–14.

2. "Making Sure the Goods Get on the Shelves," *Business Week,* July 22, 1972, pp. 46–47.

3. Adapted from Harold C. Cash and W. J. E. Crissy. "Ways of Looking at Selling," *Psychology of Selling,* 1957.

4. Franklin B. Evans, "Selling is a Dyadic Relationship—A New Approach," *American Behavioral Scientist,* May 1963, p. 79; see also James Holbert and Noel Capon, "Interpersonal Communication in Marketing," *Journal of Marketing Research,* February 1972, pp. 27–32; Paul Busch and David T. Wilson, "An Experimental Analysis of a Salesman's Expert and Referent Bases of Social Power in the Buyer-Seller Dyad," *Journal of Marketing Research,* February 1976, pp. 3–11.

5. For further treatment, see W. J. Stanton and R. H. Buskirk, *Management of the Sales Force,* 4th ed. (Homewood, Ill.: Richard D. Irwin, Inc., 1973). See also A. F. Doody and W. G. Nickels, "Structuring Organizations for Strategic Selling," *MSU Business Topics,* Autumn 1972, pp. 27–34; Davis Fogg and Josef W. Rokus, "A Quantitative Method for Structuring a Profitable Sales Force," *Journal of Marketing,* July 1973, pp. 8–17; Leonard M. Lodish, " 'Vaguely Right' Approach to Sales Force Allocations," *Harvard Business Review,* January–February 1974, pp. 119–124; Porter Henry, "Manage Your Sales Force as a System," *Harvard Business Review.* March–April 1975, pp. 85–94; Charles A. Beswick and David W. Cravens, "A Multistage Decision Model for Salesforce Management," *Journal of Marketing,* May 1977, pp. 135–44; and Michael S. Herschel, "Effective Sales Territory Development," *Journal of Marketing,* April 1977, pp. 39–43; Stephen X. Doyle and Benson P. Shapiro, "What Counts Most in Motivating Your Sales Force," *Harvard Business Review,* May–June 1980, pp. 133–140; P. Ronald Stephenson, William L. Cron, and Gary L. Frazier, "Delegating Pricing Authority to the Sales Force: The Effects on Sales and Profit Performance," *Journal of Marketing,*

Spring 1979, pp. 21–24; and Kenneth Lawyer, *Training Salesmen to Serve Industrial Markets* (Washington, D.C.: Small Business Management Series No. 36, Small Business Administration, 1975).

6. For further discussion, see *The Conference Board, Incentives for Salesmen,* Experiences in Marketing Management, no. 14 (New York: National Industrial Conference Board, 1967): Richard C. Smyth, "Financial Incentives for Salesmen," *Harvard Business Review,* January–February 1968, pp. 109–17; H. O. Pruden, W. H. Cunningham, and W. D. English, "Nonfinancial Incentives for Salesmen," *Journal of Marketing,* October 1972, pp. 55–59; O. C. Walker, Jr., G. A. Churchill, and N. M. Ford, "Motivation and Performance in Industrial Selling: Present Knowledge and Needed Research," *Journal of Marketing Research,* May 1977, pp. 156–68; R. Y. Darmon, "Salesmen's Responses to Financial Incentives: An Empirical Study," *Journal of Marketing Research,* November 1974, pp. 418–26; James H. Donnelly, Jr., and John M. Ivancevich, "Role Clarity and the Salesman," *Journal of Marketing,* January 1975, pp. 71–74; and Henry C. Lucas, Jr., Charles B. Weinberg, and Kenneth W. Clowes, "Sales Response as a Function of Territorial Potential and Sales Representative Workload," *Journal of Marketing Research,* August 1975, pp. 298–305.

7. For more discussion, see F. E. Webster, Jr., "Rationalizing Salesmen's Compensation Plans," *Journal of Marketing,* January 1966, pp. 55–58; R. L. Day and P. D. Bennett, "Should Salesmen's Compensation Be Geared to Profits?" *Journal of Marketing,* October 1962, pp. 6–9; John P. Steinbrink, "How to Pay Your Sales Force," *Harvard Business Review,* July–August 1978, pp. 111–22; D. Wilson, "Common Characteristics of Compensation Plans for Industrial Salesmen," in R. L. Clewitt (ed.) *Marketing's Role in Scientific Management* (Chicago: American Marketing Association, 1957), p. 168; and "Managers on Compensation Plans: There Has to Be a Better Way," *Sales and Marketing Management,* November 12, 1979, pp. 41–43.

H. Armstrong Roberts

When you finish this chapter, you should:

1. Understand when the various kinds of advertising are needed.
2. Understand how to go about choosing the "best" medium.
3. Understand how to plan the "best" message—that is, the copy thrust.
4. Understand what advertising agencies do and how they are paid.
5. Understand how to advertise legally.
6. Recognize the important new terms (shown in red).

18

Mass selling

To reach a lot of people quickly and cheaply, you can use mass selling.

Mass selling makes widespread distribution possible. Although a marketing manager might prefer to use personal selling only, it can be expensive on a per-contact or per-sale basis. Mass selling is a way around this problem. It is not as pinpointed as personal selling, but it does permit communication to large numbers of potential customers at the same time. Today, most promotion blends contain both personal and mass selling.

Marketing managers have strategic decisions to make about mass selling. Working with advertising managers, they must decide: (1) who is to be aimed at, (2) what kind of advertising is to be used, (3) how customers are to be reached (via which types of media), (4) what is to said to them (the copy thrust), and (5) by whom (that is, the firm's own advertising department or advertising agencies) (see Figure 18–1). We'll talk about these questions in this chapter. We'll also consider measurement of advertising effectiveness—and how to advertise legally in an increasingly hostile environment.

THE IMPORTANCE OF ADVERTISING

$55 billion in ads in 1980

Advertising can get results in a promotion blend. Good advertising results cost money, of course. In the United States, expenditures for advertising have been growing continuously since World War II—and more growth is expected. In 1946, they were slightly more than $3 billion and they topped $55 billion in 1980.[1]

**Figure 18–1
Strategy planning for
advertising**

It's all done by less than
half a million people

While total advertising expenditures are large, the advertising industry itself employs relatively few people. The major expense is for media time and space. And in the United States, the largest share of this—29 percent—goes for newspaper space. Television takes about 21 percent of the total, and direct mail, about 14 percent.[2]

Fewer than 500,000 people work directly in the U.S. advertising industry. This includes all people who help create or sell advertising or advertising media (such as radio and television stations, newspapers, and magazines) as well as those in advertising agencies—and those working for retailers, wholesalers, and manufacturers. The sometimes glamorous and often criticized 4,800 U.S. advertising agencies employ only about 200,000 of those persons. Most agencies are small—employing less than ten persons. They are highly concentrated in New York and Chicago.[3]

Advertisers aren't really
spending that much

U.S. corporations spend an average of only about 1.5 percent of their sales dollar on advertising. This is relatively small compared to the total cost of marketing—perhaps 50 percent of the consumer's dollar—and the 20 to 50 percent markups we have seen in the channels of distribution.

Some spend more than
others

Some industries spend a much larger percentage of sales for advertising than the average of 1.5 percent.[4] Soap and drug manufacturers may spend in the 5 to 10 percent range. At the other extreme, some industrial goods companies—those who depend on personal selling—may spend less than 1/10 of 1 percent. And wholesalers and retailers may spend about 1 percent. See Table 18–1 for the top ten national advertisers in 1979.

Clearly, advertising is an important factor in certain markets—especially the consumer goods markets. Nevertheless, we must keep in mind that in total it costs much less than personal selling—and less than sales promotion.

ADVERTISING OBJECTIVES ARE SET BY MARKETING STRATEGY

Every advertisement and every advertising campaign should have clearly defined objectives. These should grow out of the overall marketing strategy—and the jobs assigned to advertising. It is not enough for the marketing manager to say just—"Promote the product." The marketing manager should decide exactly what advertising should do—although specifying what should be accomplished in each individual advertisement isn't necessary. Such detailed objectives should be set by the advertising manager—to guide his own efforts.

Advertising may be assigned specific objectives

An advertising manager might be given one or more of the following specific objectives—along with the budget to accomplish them:

1. Aid in the introduction of new products to specific target markets.
2. Help obtain desirable outlets.
3. Prepare the way for salespeople—by presenting the company's name and the merits of its products.
4. Provide ongoing contact with target customers—even when the salesperson isn't available.
5. Get immediate buying action.
6. Help buyers confirm their purchasing decisions.

If you want half the market, say so!

The objectives listed above are not as specific as they could be. The advertising manager might want to sharpen them for his own purposes—or encourage the marketing manager to set more specific objectives. If a marketing manager really wants specific results, then he should state what he wants. A general objective: "To help in the expansion of market share," could be rephrased more specifically: "To increase traffic in our cooperating retail outlets by 25 percent during the next three months."

Such specific objectives would obviously affect implementation. Advertising that might be right for building a good image among opinion leaders might be all wrong for getting customers into the retailers' stores. Instead, a combination

Table 18–1
Top 10 U.S. national advertisers in 1979

Rank	Company name	Total advertising dollars—1979 ($ million)
1	Procter & Gamble Co.	$614.9
2	General Foods Corp.	393.0
3	Sears, Roebuck & Co.	379.3
4	General Motors Corp.	323.4
5	Philip Morris Inc.	291.2
6	K mart Corp.	287.1
7	R. J. Reynolds Industries	258.1
8	Warner-Lambert Co.	220.2
9	American Telephone & Telegraph Co.	219.8
10	Ford Motor Co.	215.0

Source: *Advertising Age,* September 11, 1980, p. 1.

of advertising and sales promotion—perhaps contests or tie-in sales—might be used. Media would be selected to help particular retailers—perhaps using local newspapers and billboards, rather than national consumer magazines.[5]

Even more specific objectives might be needed in some cases. For new products, for example, the majority of the target market may have to be brought through the early stages of the adoption process. This might mean that the advertising manager would want to use "teaser" campaigns or announcements—along with informative ads. On the other hand, for more established products, advertising's job might be to build brand preference—as well as help purchasers confirm their decisions. This, too, would lead to different kinds of advertising—as shown in Figure 18–2.

Advertising objectives should be very specific—much more so than personal selling objectives. One of the advantages of personal selling is that the salespeople can shift their presentations to meet customers' needs. Each advertisement, however, is a specific communication that must be effective, not just for one customer, but for thousands—or millions—of target customers. This means that specific objectives should be set for each advertisement—as well as a whole advertising campaign. If specific objectives are not set, one should not be surprised to find a creative advertising staff pursuing its own objectives. The group may set some reasonable objective like "selling the product" and then begin to plan campaigns that may win artistic awards within the advertising industry—but fail to do the advertising job hoped for.

Figure 18–2
Advertising should vary for adoption process stages

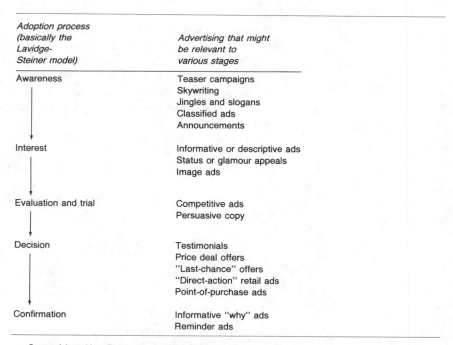

Adoption process (basically the Lavidge-Steiner model)	Advertising that might be relevant to various stages
Awareness	Teaser campaigns Skywriting Jingles and slogans Classified ads Announcements
Interest	Informative or descriptive ads Status or glamour appeals Image ads
Evaluation and trial	Competitive ads Persuasive copy
Decision	Testimonials Price deal offers "Last-chance" offers "Direct-action" retail ads Point-of-purchase ads
Confirmation	Informative "why" ads Reminder ads

Source: Adapted from R. J. Lavidge and G. A. Steiner, "A Model for Predictive Measurements of Advertising Effectiveness," *Journal of Marketing,* October 1961, p. 61.

The American Egg Board tries to develop primary demand rather than selective demand.

Courtesy American Egg Board

OBJECTIVES DETERMINE THE KINDS OF ADVERTISING NEEDED

The advertising objectives will largely determine which of two basic types of advertising to use—*institutional* or *product.*

Institutional advertising tries to develop goodwill for a company or even an industry—instead of a specific product. Its objective is to improve sales—and relations with the various groups with whom the company deals. This includes not only consumers—but also current and prospective channel members, suppliers, shareholders, and so on.

Product advertising— meet us, like us, remember us

Product advertising falls into three categories: pioneering, competitive, and reminder advertising.

Pioneering advertising—builds primary demand

Pioneering advertising tries to develop **primary demand**—demand for a product category rather than a specific brand. It is needed in the early stages of the adoption process—to inform potential customers about a new product.

Pioneering advertising is used in the introductory stage of the product life cycle—and can be used with several specific advertising objectives (objectives 1, 2, and 3 given above, for example). Its basic job is to inform—not persuade.

Pioneering advertising doesn't have to mention the brand or specific company at all. The California olive industry promoted olives as olives—not certain brands. This was so successful that after only five years of promotion, the industry's surpluses had become shortages. Then it diverted promotion funds to horticultural research—to increase production.

Competitive advertising—emphasizes selective demand

Competitive advertising tries to develop **selective demand**—demand for a specific brand rather than a product category. A firm can be forced into competi-

Can you spot the difference between these twins?

This twin was made by a Xerox 2300 copier costing $3,695.   *This twin was made by a Toshiba BD 3201 copier with a suggested manufacturer's retail price of $2,995.*

In case you haven't spotted it, the big difference is the price.

The Toshiba BD 3201 dry plain-paper copier is proof that you don't have to pay a higher price for high-quality copies.

Before we could prove it to you, we had to prove it to ourselves. We made two copies. One on a Xerox 2300 copier. One on a Toshiba BD 3201 copier.

Both made excellent copies. Ours costs less.

But don't just take us at face value. You can spot all the benefits you look for in a compact copier.

Our 1-99 digital counter with auto reset helps prevent copy mistakes. Our adjustable cassette handles both standard and legal-size paper. There's even a clear/stop key.

And if all that isn't enough, the BD 3201 boasts an international record of success.

So if you thought you had to spend $3,695 for a compact copier with similar features, start thinking differently.

TOSHIBA
Toshiba America, Inc.,
82 Totowa Road, Wayne, NJ 07470 Tel.(201) 628-8000

Xerox® is a trademark of Xerox Corporation. *Published price July 8, 1980.

Comparative advertising says that one brand is better than others.

Courtesy Toshiba America Co., Inc.

tive advertising as the product life cycle moves along—to hold its own against competitors' products and promotion. The United Fruit Company gave up a 20-year pioneering effort to promote bananas—in favor of advertising its own "Chiquita" brand. The reason was simple. While United Fruit was single-handedly promoting bananas, it slowly lost market share to competitors. The competitive advertising campaign was launched to avoid further losses.

Competitive advertising may be either direct or indirect. The **direct type** aims for immediate buying action. The **indirect type** points out product advantages—to affect future buying decisions.

Much airline advertising is of the competitive variety. Each airline is trying for sales, either immediately—in which case the ads are the *direct type* with price, timetables, and phone numbers to call for reservations—or eventually—in which case the ads are of the *indirect type,* suggesting that you mention their name when talking to your travel agent.

Comparative advertising is even rougher. **Comparative advertising** means making specific brand comparisons—using actual product names. The competitive frenzy caused by comparative advertising has been rising since the Federal Trade Commission encouraged these kinds of ads a few years ago. But this approach has led to legal as well as ethical problems—and some advertisers and their agencies have backed away from it. Supposedly, research evidence should support superiority claims, but the guidelines aren't clear here. Some firms just keep running tests until they get the results they want. Others talk about minor differences that don't reflect the overall benefits of a product. This may make consumers less—rather than more—informed. Some comparative ads leave consumers confused—or even angry if the product they are using has been criticized. And, in at least one instance, comparative ads appear to have benefited the competitive product (Tylenol) more than the advertisers' products (Datril, Anacin, and Bayer aspirin).[6]

Comparative advertising may be "a can of worms" which some advertisers wish had not been opened. But since it has been, it is likely that the approach will be continued by some advertisers—and encouraged by the government—as long as the ad copy is not obviously false.[7]

Reminder advertising—reinforces early promotion

Reminder advertising tries to keep the product's name before the public. It may be useful when the product has achieved brand preference or insistence—perhaps in the market maturity or sales decline stages. Here, the advertiser mainly wants to keep the product's name before the public. It may use "soft-sell" ads that just mention the name—as a reminder. Much Coca-Cola advertising has been of this variety. See Figure 18–3.

Institutional advertising—remember our name in Dallas, Seattle, Boston

Institutional advertising focuses only on the name and prestige of a company or industry. It may seek to inform, persuade, or remind.

A persuading kind of promotion is sometimes used by large companies with several divisions. General Motors Corporation, for example, does much institutional advertising of the GM name—emphasizing the quality and research behind *all* GM products. (See Figure 18–4).

Courtesy The Coca-Cola Company

Some large companies—such as General Motors and Du Pont—use institutional ads to emphasize the value of large corporations. Their long-run objective is developing a favorable political and legal environment in which to work.

Sometimes an advertising campaign may have both product and institutional aspects—because the federal government has taken an increasingly dim view of institutional advertising. The Internal Revenue Service has limited tax deductions for some institutional advertising. And defense contractors are specifically barred from including advertising expenditures as a cost of doing business with the government.[8]

COOPERATIVE ADVERTISING MAY BUY MORE

Vertical cooperation—
advertising allowances,
cooperative advertising

So far, our discussion might suggest that only producers do product or institutional advertising. This is not true, of course, but producers can affect the advertising done by others. Sometimes a manufacturer knows what promotion job or

**Figure 18–4
An example of institutional
advertising**

GM takes a giant step
forward in engine
control technology.

COMPUTER COMMAND CONTROL

FOR 1981 GM CARS

**It can
talk to you, too.**
Even the most
reliable of sys-
tems can some-
times require
service. So just
in case, Com-
puter Command
Control is pro-
grammed to tell
you if something
needs attention.
First, an indi-
cator light on the
instrument panel
tells you to
"check engine." But that's not all.
One of the most dramatic features of the system is its ability
to send a coded message to your
service technician indicating
which circuit in the system to
check.

**From now on you'll
activate a computer
when you step on the gas.**
For 1981, all standard and most
optional gasoline engines* from
Chevrolet, Pontiac, Oldsmobile,
Buick and Cadillac will have
GM's new Computer Command
Control system.
It allows GM to achieve the
highest Corporate Average Fuel
Economy (CAFE) in GM history,
while also reducing automobile
exhaust emissions to the *lowest*
in GM history. CAFE, as you
probably know, is the federal
government's measure of a car
company's overall annual fuel
economy.

Brain Power Plus.
In its simplest form, a solid-state
electronic control module (ECM)
monitors oxygen in the exhaust,
engine speed and engine coolant
temperature through three highly
specialized sensors.

**GM-built engines are produced by
various divisions. Ask your dealer for
details.*

Digital Dexterity.
Analyzing this information at
thousands of calculations per
second, it then adjusts the
air/fuel mixture in the carburetor
(or fuel-injection system in some
models) to optimize combustion.
The exhaust gases then pass
through GM's new dual-bed cata-
lytic converter to be cleaned up
before entering the atmosphere
—mostly as water vapor and
harmless CO_2.

Space Age Reliability.
Computer Command Control is
built by our Delco Electronics
Division, the same people who
build inertial guidance naviga-
tion systems for many of today's
jetliners. And it has been tested
over millions of miles of both on-
highway and test-track evaluation. In fact, Computer Command
Control, together with the rest of
the emissions control system, is
covered by a 5-year/50,000-mile
warranty. Ask your GM dealer for
details.

Important benefits.
In this day of greater concern for
the world we live in, plus the reality of our dwindling natural resources, we think Computer
Command Control offers solid
proof of our ongoing commitment to design and build cars for
a changing world.
Quite simply, the system helps
us clean the air while
giving good fuel
economy.

GM MARK OF EXCELLENCE

*Designing and engineering
cars for a changing world.*

Chevrolet·Pontiac
Oldsmobile·Buick
Cadillac

*Courtesy General Motors Corp. and
D'Arcy, MacManus & Masius*

advertising job he wants done—but finds that it can be done more effectively
or more economically by someone further along in the channel. In this case,
he may offer **advertising allowances**—price reductions to firms further along
in the channel to encourage them to advertise or otherwise promote the firm's
products locally.

Cooperative advertising may get more cooperation

Cooperative advertising involves middlemen and producers sharing in the
cost of ads. It helps the manufacturer get more promotion for the advertising
dollar—because media rate structures usually give local advertisers lower rates
than national firms. In addition, the retailer is more likely to follow through when
he is paying a share of the cost.

Cooperative advertising and advertising allowances are subject to abuse, however, because allowances can be given to retailers with little expectation that they will be used for ads. This may become a disguised price concession—and result in price discrimination. The Federal Trade Commission has become more interested in this problem—and some manufacturers have pulled back from cooperative advertising. To avoid legal problems, intelligent producers insist on proof of use.

Horizontal cooperation may be good, too

Some retailers—particularly those in shopping centers—may get together for join promotion efforts. Similarly, the manufacturers of complementary products—such as house furnishings—may find it desirable to join forces. Generally, the objective is the same as in vertical cooperation—to get more for the promotion dollar.

CHOOSING THE "BEST" MEDIUM—HOW TO DELIVER THE MESSAGE

For effective promotion, specific target customers must be reached. Unfortunately, not all potential customers read all newspapers, magazines, or other printed media—or listen to all radio and television programs. So not all media are equally effective.

There is no simple answer to the question—"What is the best medium?" Effectiveness depends on how well it fits with the rest of a marketing strategy—that is, it depends on (1) your promotion objectives, (2) what target markets you want to reach, (3) the funds available for advertising, and (4) the nature of the media—including who they *reach,* with what *frequency,* with what *impact,* at what *cost.* Table 18–2 shows some of the pros and cons of major kinds of media—and some illustrative costs.

Specify promotion objectives

Before a firm can choose the best medium, it must decide on its promotion objectives. For example, if the objective is to inform—telling a long story with precise detail—and if pictures are desired, then the print media—including magazines and newspapers—may be better. Jockey switched its annual budget of more than $1 million to magazines from television when it decided to show the variety of colors, patterns, and styles that Jockey briefs offer. They felt that it was too hard to show this in a 30-second TV spot. Further, it is not the kind of product that can be worn on television—the same problem that manufacturers of women's undergarments face! Jockey ads were run in men's magazines—such as *Sports Illustrated, Outdoor Life, Field and Stream, Esquire,* and *Playboy.* But, aware that women buy over 80 percent of men's ordinary underwear—and 50 percent of fashion styles—they also placed the ads in *TV Guide, New Yorker, People, Money, Time,* and *Newsweek.* And a page of scantily clad males was run in *Cosmopolitan.*[9]

When timeliness is not too important, then weekly or monthly magazines may be practical. But if demonstrations are needed, then TV may become desirable—or necessary.

If your objective is to provide technical information to a particular group, you might have to choose specialized journals. Remember, you pay for the audience

Table 18–2
Relative size and costs, and advantages and disadvantages of major kinds of media

Kinds of media	Sales volume—1980 ($billions)	Typical costs— 1980	Advantages	Disadvantages
Newspaper	$15.9	$9,117.96 for one page weekday, Cleveland (ADI Network)	Flexible Timely Local market Credible source	May be expensive Short life No "pass-along"
Television	12.4	$2,800 for a 30-second spot, prime time, Cleveland	Offers sight, sound, and motion Good attention Wide reach	Expensive in total "Clutter" Short exposure Less selective audience
Direct mail	7.6	$13,500 for listing of 450,000 engineers	Selected audience Flexible Can personalize	Relatively expensive per contact "Junk mail"—hard to retain attention
Radio	3.8	$187 for one minute prime time, Cleveland (WERE)	Wide reach Segmented audiences Inexpensive	Offers audio only Weak attention Many different rates Short exposure
Magazine	3.4	$34,624 for one page, 4-color in U.S. News & World Report	Very segmented audiences Credible source Good reproduction Long life Good "pass-along"	Inflexible Long lead times
Outdoor	0.6	$1,400 for prime billboard, 30–60-day showings, Cleveland	Flexible Repeat exposure Inexpensive	"Mass market" Very short exposure

Source: Data from Standard Rate and Data Service and estimates based on *Advertising Age* data.

the media delivers—which may (or may not) be your target audience. The use of men's magazines such as *Esquire* and *True* to reach doctors would be highly inefficient. Medical journals and direct mail are the most effective advertising media for telling doctors about new drugs.

Match your market with the media

To guarantee good media selection, the advertiser first must *clearly* specify its target market—a step necessary for all marketing strategy planning. Then, media can be chosen that are heard, read, or seen by *those* target customers.

Matching target customers and media is the major problem in effective media selection—because it is not always certain who sees or hears what. Most of the major media use marketing research to develop profiles of the people who buy their publications—or live in their broadcasting area. But they cannot be as definite about who actually reads each page or sees or hears each show. And, they seldom tailor their marketing research to gather information on the market dimensions which *each* advertiser may think important. Generally, media research focuses on demographic characteristics. But what if the really important dimen-

With all the alternatives available, a manager has to analyze and choose his media carefully.

Mary McCarthy

sions are concerned with behavioral needs or attitudes which are difficult to measure—or unique to a particular product-market?

The difficulty of evaluating alternative media has led some media analysts to focus excessively on objective measures—such as cost in relation to audience size or circulation. But preoccupation with keeping these costs down may lead to ignoring the relevant dimensions—and slipping into "mass marketing." The media buyer may become hypnotized by the relatively low cost of "mass media" when, in fact, a more specialized medium might be a much better buy. Its audience might have more interest in the product—or more money to spend—or more willingness to buy.

Specialized media help zero in on target markets

Media are now directing more attention to reaching smaller, more defined target markets. National media may offer regional editions. *Time* magazine, for example, offers not only several regional and metropolitan editions, but also special editions for college students, educators, doctors, and business managers.

Large metropolitan newspapers usually have several editions—to cater to city and suburban areas. Where these outlying areas are not adequately covered, however, suburban newspapers are prospering—catering to the desire for a "small town" newspaper.[10]

Many magazines serve only special-interest groups—such as fishermen, radio and television fans, homemakers, religious groups, and professional groups. In fact, the most profitable magazines seem to be the ones aiming at clearly defined markets—*Playboy, Car Craft, Skiing, Bride's Magazine,* and *Southern Living* have been doing well.

There are trade magazines in many fields—such as chemical engineering, electrical wholesaling, farming, and the defense market. *Standard Rate and Data* provides a guide to the thousands of magazines now available.

Radio suffered at first from the inroads of television. But now—like some magazines and newspapers—it has become a more specialized medium. Some stations cater to particular nationality, racial, and religious groups—such as Puerto Ricans, blacks, and Catholics—while others emphasize country, rock, or classical music.

Perhaps the most specific medium is **direct-mail advertising**—selling directly to the customer via his mailbox. The method is to send a specific message to a carefully selected list of names. Some firms specialize in providing mailing lists—ranging in number from hundreds to millions of names. The diversity of these lists is shown in Table 18–3—and shows the importance of knowing your target market.[11]

"Must buys" may use up available funds

Selecting which media to use is still pretty much an art. The media buyer may start with a budgeted amount and try to buy the best blend to reach the target audience. There may be some media that are obvious must buys—such as *the* local newspaper for a retailer in a small or medium-sized town. Such "must buys" may even use up the available funds. If not, then the media buyer must begin to think of the relative advantages and disadvantages of the alternatives—and recognize that trade-offs must be made. Typically, media that have several advantages—for example, television which permits visual and audio presentations along with movement—are more expensive. So the buyer might want to select a media blend which included some "expensive" media as well as some less expensive ones. This may allow him to reach additional customers—or reinforce the presentation from a different angle.

Ideally, the first media choice would reach a large part of the target audience. Then, any other choices (if any more can be afforded) would reach fewer who had not already been covered. Figure 18–5 illustrates the concept for four equally costly magazines. Here, the first choice reaches 60 percent of the target audience. The second choice adds only 20 percent who were not reached before. The third choice adds 10 percent—and the fourth 5 percent. Five percent cannot be reached at all with only these four magazines.

PLANNING THE "BEST" MESSAGE—WHAT IS TO BE COMMUNICATED

Specifying the copy thrust

Once it has been decided *how* the messages are to reach the target audience, then it is necessary to decide on the **copy thrust** —*what* is to be communicated

Table 18–3
Examples of available mailing lists

Quantity of names	Name of list
425	Small Business Advisors
40,000	Social Register of Canada
5,000	Society of American Bacteriologists
500	South Carolina Engineering Society
2,000	South Dakota State Pharmaceutical Association
250	Southern California Academy of Science
12,000	Texas Manufacturing Executives
720	Trailer Coach Association
1,200	United Community Funds of America
50,000	University of Utah Alumni
19,000	Veterinarians

Figure 18–5
Increase in audience coverage as additional magazine ads are purchased

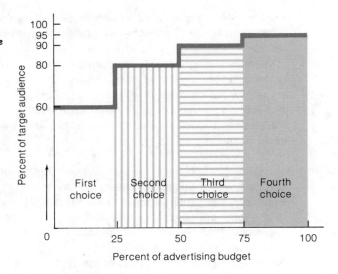

by the written copy and illustrations. This should flow from the promotion objectives—and the specific jobs assigned to advertising. Although the overall *promotion* objective is to affect the target customer's attitudes *and* behavior, a particular advertisement may have the specific objective of informing target customers that the firm's prices have dropped 10 percent. Or, it might have the more difficult job of persuading customers that a product with a 10-percent price premium is really a "good buy."

Carrying out the copy thrust is the job of advertising specialists. But the advertising manager and the marketing manager should have an understanding of the process—to be sure that the job is done effectively.

Communication process is relevant to message planning

Message planning should be guided by a sound understanding of the communication process. As we saw in Chapter 16, common frames of reference and experience are needed for good communication. This is not a small matter in advertising—because advertising professionals are often far removed from their target audiences. Much advertising comes from agencies in New York City—and one advertising manager deplored advertising "conditioned by our New York sophistication." His experience has taught him that "New York's price for being New York is loss of perspective; New York is not America."[12]

Some advertisers realize the complexity of the communication process and use marketing research to help them as much as possible. At the very least, research may give clues about perceived needs—and the words or ideas that can communicate with potential customers in the company's product-market.

Other advertisers depend almost entirely on their own "creative genius." This is at the root of many poor campaigns. Some are brilliant—and others are miserable failures—and they don't know why.

There are relatively few tried-and-true rules in message construction. Everything we see—and every new way we see it—changes us in some way. An idea that may have worked a year ago can fail today. A highly successful advertising campaign for beer in the New York area flopped in Los Angeles—and one industrial advertiser received more inquiries when it *reduced* the *size* of its ads.[13]

Behavioral science research does provide some help, however. The concepts of needs, learning, and perception discussed in Chapter 7 are certainly relevant here. We know, for example, that consumers have a fantastic ability for selectively "tuning out" messages or ideas which are not of current interest. Just think of how much of the daily newspaper you actually "see" as you page through it. We don't see everything the advertisers want us to see—or learn all they would like us to learn.

Let AIDA help guide message planning

Basically, the overall marketing strategy should determine *what* should be said in the message. Then management judgment—perhaps aided by marketing research—can help decide how this content can be encoded so it will be decoded as intended.

As a guide to message planning, we can make use of the AIDA concept: getting Attention, holding Interest, arousing Desire, and obtaining Action.

Getting attention

Getting attention is the first job of an advertisement. If this is not done, it doesn't matter how many people can or do see it. Many readers leaf through magazines and newspapers without paying attention to any of the advertisements. Many listeners or viewers do chores—or get snacks—during commercials on radio and television.

There are many devices for catching the customer's attention. A large headline, newsy or shocking statements, pictures of pretty girls, babies, cartoon characters—or anything that is "different" or eye-catching—may do the trick. But . . . the attention-getting device must not distract from the next step—holding interest.

Holding interest

Holding interest is another matter. A pretty girl may get attention—but once you've seen her, then what? A man may pause to appreciate her. Women may evaluate her. But if there is no relation between the girl and the product, observers of both sexes will move on.

More is known about holding interest than getting attention. The tone and language of the advertisement must be compatible with the field of experience and attitudes of target customers—and their reference groups. A good advertisement featuring fox hunters in riding costumes, for example, might be noted but passed over by many potential customers who do not ride to the hounds.

In addition to speaking the target customer's language, the advertising layouts should look "right" to the customer. Print illustrations and copy should be arranged so that the eye is encouraged to move smoothly through the ad—perhaps from the upper left-hand corner to the signature or brand name at the lower right-hand corner. Advertisements having this natural flowing characteristic are said to encourage *gaze motion*.[14]

Arousing desire

Arousing desire to own or use a particular product is one of the most difficult

An attention getting picture with good gaze motion "leads" readers to see the copy.

Courtesy Calvin Klein

jobs of an advertisement. The advertiser must be successful in communicating with the customer. To communicate effectively, the advertiser should understand how target customers think, behave, and make decisions.

To be successful, an advertisement must convince the customer that the product can meet his needs. Pioneering advertising may be useful to develop primary demand—and show how the whole product category would satisfy needs. Later, in the market growth and market maturity stages, competitive advertising can show how a particular brand satisfies a particular want—better.

An advertisement may also have the objective—especially during the market growth and market maturity stages—of supplying words that the customer can use for rationalizing a desire to buy. Although products may satisfy certain emotional needs, many consumers find it necessary to justify their purchases on an economic or even moral basis. Desire may develop around emotional needs, but economic reasons must also be reinforced.

Obtaining action

Getting action is the final requirement—and not an easy one. We now know—from communications research—that the potential customer should be encouraged to try the product. The prospective customer must be led beyond considering how the product might fit into his life—to actually trying it or letting the company's sales rep come in and show how it works.

Strongly felt customer needs might be pinpointed in the ads to communicate more effectively. Careful research on the attitudes in the target market may help uncover such strongly felt unsatisfied needs.

Appealing to these needs can get more action—and also provide the kind of information the buyer needs to confirm his decision. Post-purchase dissonance may set in—and obtaining confirmation may be one of the important advertising objectives. Some customers seem to read more advertising *after* the purchase than before. What is communicated to them may be very important if satisfied customers are to start—or keep—the web-of-word-of-mouth going. The ad may reassure them about the correctness of their decision—and also supply the words they use to tell others about the product.

ADVERTISING MANAGER DIRECTS MASS SELLING

An advertising manager manages a company's mass selling effort. Many advertising managers—especially those working for retailers—have their own advertising departments that plan the specific advertising campaigns—and carry out the details. Others delegate much of the advertising work to specialists—the advertising agencies. See Table 18–4 for a list of the top ten U.S. advertising agencies.

ADVERTISING AGENCIES OFTEN DO THE WORK

Ad agencies are specialists

Advertising agencies are specialists in planning and handling mass selling details for advertisers. Agencies play a useful role—because they are independent

Table 18–4
Top 10 advertising agencies in 1979 (U.S. billings)

		1979 ($ millions)
1.	Young and Rubicam	$1,157.5
2.	J. Walter Thompson	788.0
3.	Ogilvy and Mather International	712.1
4.	Ted Bates and Company	652.7
5.	Foote, Cone, and Belding	639.9
6.	Leo Burnett Company	639.8
7.	BBDO International	625.6
8.	McCann-Erickson	463.2
9.	D'Arcy-MacManus and Masius	382.5
10.	SSC and B, Inc.	222.4

Source: *Advertising Age*, April 30, 1979.

of the advertiser—and have an outside viewpoint. They bring experience to the individual client's problems, because they work for many other clients. Further, as specialists they often can do the job more economically than a company's own department.

Agencies sometimes handle overall marketing strategy planning—as well as marketing research, product and package development, and sales promotion. Some agencies make good marketing partners and almost assume the role of the firm's marketing department.

One of the ad agency's advantages is that the advertiser is free to cancel the arrangement at any time. This provides extreme flexibility for the advertiser. Some companies even use their advertising agency as a scapegoat. Whenever anything goes wrong—it's the advertising agency's fault—and the advertiser shops around for a new one.

Are they paid too much?

The major users of advertising agencies are manufacturers or national middlemen—because of the media rate structure. Normally, media have two prices: one for national advertisers—and a lower rate for local advertisers, such as retailers. The advertising agency gets a 15 percent discount only on national rates. This makes it worthwhile for national advertisers to use agencies. The national firm would have to pay the higher media rate, anyway. So it makes sense to let the agency experts do the work—and earn their discount. Local retailers— allowed the lower media rate—seldom use agencies.

There is a growing resistance to the traditional method of paying agencies. The chief complaints are (1) that the agencies receive the flat 15 percent commission—regardless of work performed, and (2) that the commission system makes it hard for the agencies to be completely objective about low-cost media—or promotion campaigns that use little space or time.

Not all agencies are satisfied with the present arrangement either. Some would like to charge additional fees—as they see costs rising and advertisers demanding more services.

The fixed commission system is most favored by accounts—such as producers of industrial goods—that need a lot of service but buy relatively little advertising. These are the firms the agencies would like to—and sometimes do—charge additional fees.

The fixed commission system is generally opposed by very large consumer goods advertisers who do much of their own advertising research and planning. They need only basic services from their agencies. Some of these accounts can be very profitable for agencies. Naturally, these agencies would prefer the fixed-commission system.

Fifteen percent is not required

The Federal Trade Commission worked for many years to change the method of advertising agency compensation. Finally, in 1956, the American Association of Advertising Agencies agreed they would no longer require the 15 percent commission system. This opened the way to discounts and fee increases.

Du Pont recently reported that it was paying agencies an average of 21 percent of billings on industrial accounts and 14 percent on consumer goods accounts. Other companies report very different arrangements with their agencies—but most take off from the 15 percent base. Some use a sliding scale of commissions—which decline with increasing advertising volume (e.g., Gillette and Lorillard). Others pay a reduced commission for limited agency services—running from 7.5 percent to 10 percent (e.g., American Home Products, Carter Products, and Lipton). And others manage the spending of the 15 percent commission—paying for agency services on a fee basis and perhaps using some of the funds for outside suppliers or even in-house operations (e.g., Best Foods).[15]

Agency arrangements are changing

The advertising agency business has seen much change and profit squeezes in recent years. Some agencies have given up the full-service approach (for 15 percent) and become more specialized—for example, in media buying or creative functions. Other agencies have gone out of business—some have been purchased by advertisers. Many of the changes probably can be traced to the work of the less efficient agencies who—under the umbrella of the 15 percent commission—were able to get business primarily through social contacts, rather than business ability.

Internal conflict causes changes

Some of the changes in the advertising business are due to internal struggles between the creative and the business types—with the latter winning many of the battles because the very survival of the agencies is involved. Some of the creative types might properly be called "production-oriented."[16]

At the root of this tension is the fact that the advertiser's product manager or brand manager may be personally responsible for the success of a particular product—and feels that he has some right to direct and even veto the work of the creative people. This has resulted in confrontations in which the agency often loses—because the advertiser is paying the bills. One agency woman–turned–client said she had lost patience with the "ego-dominated creative type who is blindly in love with his own efforts." She feels the yardstick of successful advertising is whether advertising communicates what it's supposed to communicate to its target audience.[17] Advertisers such as this woman have been partly responsible for the changes occurring in the agency business.

MEASURING ADVERTISING EFFECTIVENESS IS NOT EASY

Success depends on the total marketing mix

It would be convenient if we could measure the results of advertising by looking at sales. Unfortunately, this is not possible—although the advertising literature is filled with success stories that "prove" advertising has increased sales. The total marketing mix—not just promotion generally, or advertising specifically—is responsible for the sales result. The one exception to this rule is direct-mail advertising. If it doesn't produce immediate results, it is considered a failure.

Research and testing can improve the odds

Ideally, advertisers should pretest advertising before it is run—rather than relying solely on the judgment of creative people or advertising "experts." They

Direct mail is the only advertising medium whose performance can be measured by sales.

Mary McCarthy

too often judge only on the basis of originality—or cleverness of the copy and illustrations. And advertisers may be no better—if as good—at deciding how "good" an ad will be.

Some progressive advertisers now demand laboratory or market tests to evaluate the effectiveness of ads. In addition, before ads are run generally, attitude research is sometimes used. Researchers try to evaluate consumers' reaction to particular advertisements—or parts of advertisements—sometimes using laboratory-type devices which measure skin moisture or eye reaction. Split runs on cable TV also are being used to experiment with alternative ads.

Hindsight may lead to foresight

After the advertisements have been run, researchers may try to measure how much is recalled about specific products or advertisements. Inquiries from customers may be used as a measure of the effectiveness of particular ads. The response to radio or television commercials—or magazine readership—can be estimated using various survey techniques to check the size and composition of audiences (the Nielsen and Starch reports are produced routinely) with the implied assumption that larger audiences lead directly to greater purchases.

While advertising research techniques are far from foolproof, they are probably far better than relying on pure judgment by advertising "experts." Until more effective advertising research tools are developed, moreover, the present methods—carefully defining specific advertising objectives, choosing media and messages to accomplish these objectives, testing plans, and then evaluating the results of actual advertisements—would seem most productive.

HOW TO AVOID DECEPTIVE ADVERTISING

FTC is getting tougher about unfair practices

The Federal Trade Commission now has the power to control unfair or deceptive business practices—including "deceptive advertising." The FTC has been policing deceptive advertising for many years. And they may be getting results—now that advertising agencies as well as advertisers must share equal responsibility of large financial penalties and/or the need to pay for new ads—to correct past "mistakes." The FTC's tougher attitude has caused more agencies and advertisers to stay well within the law—rather than just going along the edge.

The FTC would like to move more aggressively against what it feels may be "unfair" practices—as it concludes that there are few outright deceptive ads in national campaigns. Some in the FTC feel it is unfair for children to be a target for advertising. Going further, some feel a case could be made against promotion that "encourages materialism"—by persuading consumers to buy things that they otherwise would not purchase. An FTC lawyer recently created a stir by criticizing electric hair dryers. His feeling was "that if you wait 15 minutes, your hair gets dry anyway." And there is a question whether food and drug advertising should be controlled to protect "vulnerable" groups such as the aged, poor, non-English-speaking, and, apparently, less-educated adults. For example, a question was raised as to whether obesity among low-income women might be caused by ads for high-calorie foods.

Not everyone agrees with the FTC thrust, however. In 1980, Congress specifically limited FTC rule-making for three years. It said that any rule would have to be based on whether the advertising is *deceptive* rather than *unfair.*[18] It is important to note, however, that while the FTC is prohibited from using "unfairness" in a rule affecting a whole industry, "unfairness" can still be used against an individual company. So advertisers *do* have to worry about being "unfair!"

What is unfair or deceptive is changing

What is unfair and deceptive is a difficult topic which marketing managers will have to wrestle with for years. It is clear that the social and political environment has changed. Practices considered acceptable some years ago are now questioned—or actually considered deceptive.

This is a serious matter, because if the FTC decides that a particular practice is unfair or deceptive, it has the power to require affirmative disclosures—such as the health warnings on cigarettes, or **corrective advertising**—ads to correct deceptive advertising. Industry groups have made some efforts at self-regulation—but the offenders usually are not members of such groups. So there probably will be an ongoing need for some government regulation.

In the long run, however, the safest way to avoid "unfair" and "deceptive" criticisms will be to stop the typical production-oriented efforts to differentiate "me-too" product offerings. A little "puffing" has always been—and probably always will be—acceptable. But trying to pass off "me-too" products as really new probably should be avoided in the future. Already, some advertising agencies will not take on such jobs.

Supporting ad claims is a fuzzy area

Supporting ad claims is a vague area—with no clear guidelines. There are many ways to "lie with statistics"—and unethical and/or desperate advertisers of "me-too" products have tried many of them. They may rig the sampling, show only satisfied testimonials, or focus on minor—even irrelevant—product characteristics.

Clarifying the rules on what research support is needed to back up advertising

The FTC already requires some manufacturers to provide warnings about their products—to protect consumers.

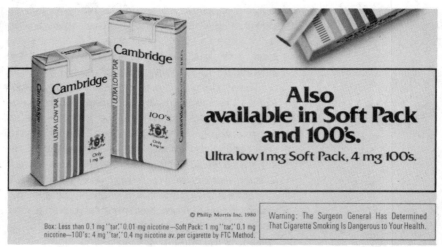

Box: Less than 0.1 mg "tar," 0.01 mg nicotine—Soft Pack: 1 mg "tar," 0.1 mg nicotine—100's: 4 mg "tar," 0.4 mg nicotine av. per cigarette by FTC Method.

Warning: The Surgeon General Has Determined That Cigarette Smoking Is Dangerous to Your Health.

Courtesy Philip Morris Inc.

claims might reduce unfair or deceptive advertising. But, ultimately, it may be necessary to add criminal penalties to reach the hard-core few who are willing to grab at any chance to "make a buck." And, unfortunately, only one or a few such competitors in an industry can cause major shifts in market share—and affect the nature of competition in that market. Most members of the industry may have good intentions—but an old cliché may be relevant here: "One bad apple can spoil a whole barrel." Those in favor of self-regulation are well aware of this situation. This is why they have organized and have worked cooperatively with the government—and probably will have to continue to do so.

CONCLUSION

Theoretically, it may seem simple to develop a mass selling campaign. Just pick the media and develop a message. But this isn't so simple. Effectiveness depends upon using the "best" medium and the "best" message, considering: (1) promotion objectives, (2) the target markets, and (3) the funds available for advertising.

The specific advertising objectives will determine what kind of advertising to use—product or institutional. If product advertising is needed, then the particular type must be decided—pioneering, competitive (direct or indirect), or reminder. And advertising allowances and cooperative advertising may be helpful.

Many technical details are involved in mass selling, and specialists—advertising agencies—handle some of these tasks. But specific objectives must be set for them—or their advertising may have little direction and be almost impossible to evaluate.

Ultimately, effective advertising should affect sales. But the whole marketing mix affects sales—and the results of advertising can't be measured by sales changes alone. Advertising is only a part of promotion—and promotion is only a part of the total marketing mix that the marketing manager must develop to satisfy target customers.

QUESTIONS AND PROBLEMS

1. Identify the strategic decisions a marketing manager must make in the mass selling area.

2. Discuss the relation of advertising objectives to marketing strategy planning and the kinds of advertising actually needed. Illustrate.

3. Present three examples where advertising to middlemen might be necessary. What would be the objective(s) of such moves?

4. What does it mean to say that "money is invested in advertising"? Is all advertising an investment? Illustrate.

5. Find advertisements to final consumers which illustrate the following types of advertising: (a) institutional, (b) pioneering, (c) competitive, (d) reminder. What objective(s) does each of these ads have? List the needs utilized in each of these advertisements.

6. Describe the type of media which might be most suitable for promoting: (a) tomato soup, (b) greeting cards, (c) an industrial component material, (d) playground equipment. Specify any assumptions necessary to obtain a definite answer.

7. Discuss the use of testimonials in advertising. Which of the four AIDA steps might testimonials accomplish? Would they be suitable for all types of products? If not, for which types would they be most suitable?

8. Find an advertisement which seeks to accomplish all four AIDA steps and explain how you feel this advertisement is accomplishing each of these steps.

9. Discuss the future of independent advertising agencies now that the 15 percent commission system is not required.

10. Does mass selling cost too much? How can this be measured?

11. How would retailing promotion be affected if all local advertising via mass media such as radio, television, and newspapers were prohibited? Would there be any impact on total sales? If so, would it probably affect all goods and stores equally?

12. Is it "unfair" to advertise to children? Is it "unfair" to advertise to less educated or less experienced people of any age? Is it "unfair" to advertise for "unnecessary" products?

SUGGESTED CASES

17 Spears National Bank

18 Billing Sports Company

NOTES

1. *Advertising Age,* November 13, 1980, p. 14.

2. *Advertising Age,* July 18, 1977, p. 31, and *Ibid.*

3. Exact data on this industry are elusive. But see "Showing Ad Agencies How to Grow," *Business Week,* June 1, 1974, p. 50–56; and "How Many People Work in Advertising?" *Printers' Ink,* December 6, 1957, p. 88.

4. *Advertising Age,* September 18, 1967, pp. 77–78.

5. For further discussion on this, see Russell H. Colley, *Defining Advertising Goals for Measured Advertising Results* (New York: Association of National Advertisers, Inc., 1961), Part 2, and *Setting Advertising Objectives,* Studies in Business Policy, no. 118 (New York: National Industrial Conference Board, 1966); and S. H. Britt, "Are So-Called Successful Advertising Campaigns

Really Successful?" *Journal of Advertising Research,* June 1969, pp. 3–9.

6. "A Pained Bayer Cries 'Foul,' " *Business Week,* July 25, 1977, p. 142.

7. "Product Pitches That Knock the Competition Creates New Troubles," *The Wall Street Journal,* April 16, 1976, p. 1 f; "The FTC Broadens Its Attack on Ads," *Business Week,* June 20, 1977, pp. 27–28; William L. Wilkie and Paul W. Farris, "Comparison Advertising: Problems and Potential," *Journal of Marketing,* October 1975, pp. 7–15; and V. K. Prasad, "Communications Effectiveness of Comparative Advertising: A Laboratory Analysis," *Journal of Marketing Research,* May 1976, pp. 128–37; Murphy A. Seawall and Michael H. Goldstein, "The Comparative Advertising Controversy: Consumer Perceptions of Catalog Showroom

Reference Prices," *Journal of Marketing,* Summer 1979, pp. 85–92; Linda L. Golden, "Consumer Reactions to Explicit Brand Comparisons in Advertisements," *Journal of Marketing Research,* November 1979, pp. 517–32; Stephen Goodwin and Michael Edgar, "An Experimental Investigation of Comparative Advertising: Impact of Message Appeal, Information Load and Utility of Product Class," *Journal of Marketing Research,* May 1980, pp. 187–202; and "Should an Ad Identify Brand X?" *Business Week,* September 24, 1979, pp. 156–61.

8. "Will Defense-Contractor Ads Run into New Snags in Washington?" *Printers' Ink,* January 4, 1963, p. 7; and Nugent Wedding, "Advertising, Mass Communication, and Tax Deduction," *Journal of Marketing,* April 1960, pp. 17–22.

9. "Why Jockey Switched Its Ads from TV to Print," *Business Week,* July 26, 1976, pp. 140–42.

10. J. M. Kramer, "Benefits and Use of Suburban Press for Large Metropolitan Buys," *Journal of Marketing,* January 1977, pp. 68–70.

11. "Mailing-List Brokers Sell More Than Names to Their Many Clients," *The Wall Street Journal,* February 19, 1974, p. 1 f.

12. *Advertising Age,* May 27, 1963, p. 90.

13. "More Than Ads Sell Rheingold," *Business Week,* September 21, 1957, p. 70; "How to Advertise *Not* by The Book," *Printers' Ink,* September 6, 1963, pp. 47–48.

14. See Otto Kleppner, *Advertising Procedure,* 5th ed. (New York: Prentice-Hall, Inc., 1966).

15. "How Agencies Should Get Paid: Trend is to 'Managed' Systems," *Advertising Age,* January 17, 1977, pp. 41–42.

16. "The days of fun and games are over," *Business Week,* November 10, 1973, p. 84

17. Helen Van Slyke, Vice President, Advertising, Helena Rubenstein, Inc., New York, in a speech to the meeting of the American Association of Advertising Agencies, April 25, 1970.

18. "The FTC Starts a New Life," *Consumer Reports,* August 1980, p. 504; "The FTC Broadens Its Attack on Ads," *Business Week,* June 20, 1977, pp. 27–28; "FTC Tells Sears to Use Reliable Test Results in Ads for Appliances," *The Wall Street Journal,* May 19, 1980, p. 3; Dorothy Cohen, "The FTC's Advertising Substantiation Program," *Journal of Marketing,* Winter 1980, pp. 26–35; and Gary M. Armstrong, Metin N. Gurol, and Frederick A. Russ, "Detecting and Correcting Deceptive Advertising," *Consumer Research,* December 1979, pp. 237–46.

Kenneth Yee

1. Understand how pricing objectives should affect pricing.
2. Understand the choices the marketing manager must make about—price flexibility, price level, and pricing over the product life cycle.
3. Understand the legality of price level and price flexibility policies.
4. Understand the many possible variables of a price structure, including discounts, allowances, and who pays the transportation costs.
5. Recognize the important new terms (shown in red).

510

19

Pricing objectives and policies

Deciding what price to charge can be agonizing.

Price is one of the four major variables the marketing manager controls. Price decisions affect both the firm's sales and profits—so they are very important decisions.

Guided by the company's objectives, marketing managers must develop a set of pricing objectives and policies. They must spell out what price situations the firm will face and how it will handle them. These policies should explain: (1) how flexible prices will be, (2) at what level they will be set, (3) how pricing will be handled during the course of a product life cycle, (4) how transportation costs will be handled, and (5) to whom and when discounts and allowances will be given. These strategic pricing decision areas are shown in Figure 19–1.

PRICE HAS MANY DIMENSIONS

It is not easy to define price in real-life situations. Price has many dimensions—and not understanding these could lead to big mistakes. For example, if you were offered a current-model Ford station wagon for $3,000, would this be a good price for an automobile that normally sells for over $6,000? Or if you were offered a 21-inch television set for $100—when they normally sell for $200— would this be a good buy?

In each case, the first reaction might be an enthusiastic "Yes!" But wait a minute. It might be wiser to look further. The $3000 for the Ford station wagon might be the price of a wreck worth only a few hundred dollars at a scrap yard. And the $100 for the TV set might be a reasonable price for all of its components in a parts bin at the factory. If you wanted these assembled, you would have

Figure 19–1
Strategy planning for Price

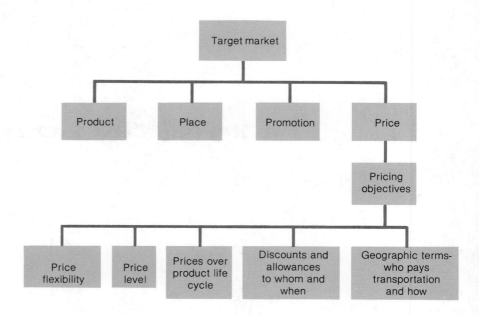

to pay $25 extra. If you were interested in buying the cabinet, it might be $25 more. And if you wanted a quality guarantee, there might be an added charge of $50.

The price equation:
Price equals Something

These examples emphasize that when a price is quoted, it is related to *some* assortment of goods and/or services. So, **Price** is what is charged for "something." *Any business transaction in our modern economy can be thought of as an exchange of money—the money being the Price—for Something.*

This description of Price is similar to our broad definition of Product. The *Something* can be a physical product in various stages of completion, with or without the services normally provided, with or without quality guarantees, and so on. Or it could be service—dry cleaning, medical care, and so on.

If the product is made available to channel members instead of final consumers or users, the price should be set so that each channel member has a chance to cover his costs and make a profit.

The nature and extent of this *Something* will determine the amount of money to be exchanged. Some consumers may pay list price. Others may obtain large discounts or allowances—because something is *not* provided. The possible variations are summarized in Figure 19–2 for consumers or users and in Figure 19–3 for channel members. Some of these variations will be discussed more fully below. But here it should be clear that the price variable has many dimensions.

PRICING OBJECTIVES SHOULD GUIDE PRICING

Pricing objectives should flow from—and fit in with—company-level and marketing objectives. Sometimes price-related topics are included in the marketing

**Figure 19–2
Price as seen by consumers or
users**

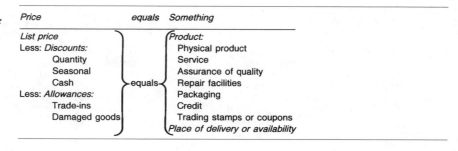

**Figure 19–3
Price as seen by channel
members**

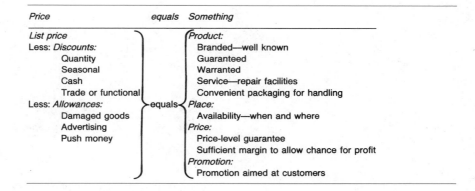

or even the company-level objectives—because pricing is so important. But here they should be *explicitly stated*—because they have a direct effect on pricing policies as well as the methods used to determine prices.

The various types of pricing objectives we will discuss are diagrammed in Figure 19–4.

*Profit-oriented
objectives*

Target returns provide specific guidelines

A **target return objective** sets a specific profit-related goal. Seeking a target return is a common profit-oriented objective. The firm's "target" may be a certain percentage return on sales—perhaps a 1 percent return on sales, as in the supermarket industry. Or a large producer might aim for a 25-percent return on investment. A small family-run firm might want a fixed dollar amount of profit to cover living expenses.

Common long-run targets are somewhere between 10- and 30-percent return on investment after taxes. The actual size may depend partly on industry or market practice—and partly on competition. Some companies set a relatively moderate objective to discourage potential competitors. Others—expecting relatively little competition—set extremely high targets for the short run.

A target return objective has administrative advantages in a large company. It simplifies measuring and controlling the performance of the many divisions and departments—all of which are using capital. Some companies will eliminate divisions or drop products not yielding the target rate of return on investment.

**Figure 19–4
Possible pricing objectives**

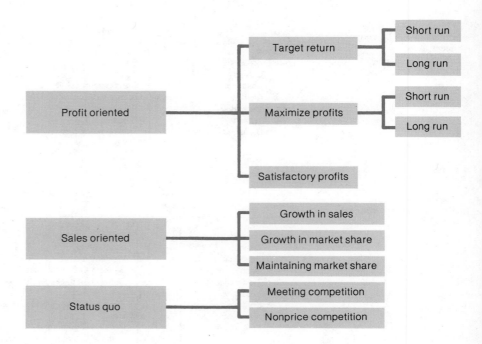

Naturally, then, managers use target return pricing—trying to hit this desired figure. This is not easy. Too large a return may invite government action. Too small a return may put the division out of business.

Long-run targets are used by companies that have carved out markets for themselves or that are, at least, leaders in their fields—such as Alcoa, Du Pont and General Motors.

For such companies, a long-run target return objective makes some sense. These companies are almost like public utilities. They are well aware that the public and the government are keeping an eye on them. They often play the role of price leaders and wage setters. And the public seems to expect them to follow a policy that is popularly thought of as being "in the public interest."

Profit maximization can be socially responsible

A **profit maximization objective** states that the firm seeks to get as much profit as it can. It might be stated as a desire for a rapid return on investment. Or—more bluntly—to earn "all the traffic will bear."

Profit maximization objectives seem to be more common among small firms—small retailers and manufacturers—who are out of the public eye.[1] Large firms, on the other hand, might avoid a profit maximization objective.

The public—and many business executives—link profit maximization with high prices and monopolies. They feel that anyone trying to maximize profits is not operating in the public interest.

Economic theory does not support this idea. *Profit maximization doesn't always lead to high prices.* True, demand and supply *may* bring extremely high prices if competition can't offer good substitutes. But this happens *if and only if* demand is highly inelastic. If demand is very elastic, it might be in a monopolist's interest to charge relatively low prices—so sales will increase.

Profit maximization can have desirable results for both business and consumers. Profit can be viewed as a reward for efficiency. If the customers are served poorly, there may be no profit at all. If they are served better, profits may be larger. Competitors will see the company's high profits and want to copy it. In this way, competition—even the monopolistic variety—will eventually reduce profits (and probably prices, too). We saw this process at work in Chapter 11 in the rise and fall of profits during the life cycle of a product. Contrary to common belief, a profit maximization objective may be socially responsible.

Some just want satisfactory profits

Some managers aim for only "satisfactory" profits. They may work for profits. But they aren't nearly as aggressive as they might be if they were trying to maximize profits. They just want to show stockholders they're "doing a good job." And they also want to be sure of the firm's survival. As long as profits are "good enough," they feel that they have reached their objective.[2]

Sales-oriented objectives

A **sales-oriented objective** states that the firm seeks to get some level of sales or share of market—without referring to profit.

Sales growth does not mean big profits

Some managers seem more concerned about sales growth than profits. This is probably because many feel sales growth always means big profits. This belief is dying, however. Major corporations have faced a continuing profit squeeze over the last 20 years—while sales have grown. More attention is now being paid to profits—along with sales.[3]

Another reason for the popularity of sales growth–oriented objectives is that a manager's salary may be more closely tied to sales than to profits.[4] Here, compensation systems have affected the selection of objectives—rather than vice versa!

Some managers feel that greater sales always lead to greater profits.

Kenneth Yee

Maintaining market share may be enough

Just maintaining market share—the percentage of the market you are "entitled" to because of your size and reputation—seems to be very important to some managers. This is partly because market share is easier to measure than whether profits are being maximized. It is fairly easy to measure whether a company has maintained its percentage of a market. So, as long as some profit is earned, the managers may prefer stressing market share instead—especially if job promotions are based on market share.

How about increasing market share?

Aggressive companies often aim to increase market share—or even to control a market. In some businesses, economies of scale encourage a firm to seek increased market share—and probably greater profits. Sometimes, however, firms blindly follow the market growth goal. This leads to pricing almost at cost to get more of the market. Sales growth objectives sometimes lead to profitless prosperity—where slight errors lead to bankruptcy.

Status quo objectives

Don't rock the boat objectives

Status quo objectives are "don't-rock-the-*pricing*-boat" objectives—and are fairly common. They may be stated as "meeting competition" or "avoiding competition" or "stabilizing prices."

Often, a status quo objective is held by conservative managers who want to reduce the risk of loss. They prefer instead a comfortable way of life and some guarantee of profit. Maintaining stable prices may discourage price competition and remove the need for hard decisions. The managers may have more time for golf!

Kenneth Yee

Or stress nonprice competition instead

On the other hand, a status quo *pricing* objective can be part of an extremely aggressive marketing strategy. The pricing objective may seem conservative, but the aim could be to avoid price competition in favor of nonprice competition—aggressive action on one or more of the Ps other than Price.

MOST FIRMS SET SPECIFIC PRICING POLICIES—TO REACH OBJECTIVES

Specific pricing policies are vital for any firm. Otherwise, the marketing manager has to re-think the strategy every time a customer asks for a price. This not only would be a drain on manager time, but customer goodwill could be lost if quoted prices do not appear to follow a logical pattern.

Price policies usually lead to administered prices—consciously set prices—aimed at reaching the firm's objectives. In other words, instead of letting daily market forces decide their prices, most firms (including *all* of those in monopolistic competition) set their own prices. They may even hold them steady for long periods of time.

Some firms, however, handle pricing rather mechanically—simply "meeting competition," or worse, marking up their costs with little thought of demand.

Manufacturers suggest list prices from which adjustments are made.

MODEL PRICES . . . Compact and Mid-Size Models											
Model	Model Code	MSRP a	Dest Chg	Total	Local Price	Model	Model Code	MSRP a	Dest Chg	Total	Local Price
OMEGA Coupe Sedan	B37 B69	$6343.49 $6514.49				CUTLASS SUPREME BROUGHAM Coupe	M47	$7969.44			
OMEGA BROUGHAM Coupe Sedan	E37 E69	$6700.49 $6855.49				CUTLASS BROUGHAM Sedan	M69	$8100.44			
CUTLASS Sedan	G69	$6955.24				CUTLASS CALAIS Coupe	K47	$8004.44			
CUTLASS SUPREME Coupe	R47	$7484.44				CUTLASS CRUISER 2-Seat Wagon	G35	$7416.88			
CUTLASS LS Sedan	R69	$7652.44				CUTLASS CRUISER BROUGHAM 2-Seat Wagon	H35	$7725.88			

a—Manufacturer's Suggested Retail Price. Includes reimbursement for New Vehicle Preparation Charges

Courtesy Oldsmobile Division, General Motors, Corp.

Remember that price has many dimensions. Managers do have many options. They *should* administer their prices. And they should do it carefully—because finally, it is these prices which customers must decide to pay before a whole marketing mix is a success. In the rest of this chapter, we will talk about policies a marketing manager must set to do an effective job of administering Price.

Price starts with a list price

Most price structures are built around list prices. How these list prices are set is discussed in the next chapter. For now, however, we must see that there may be several list prices. Then, we will go on to see the many variations from list.

Basic list prices—are "list prices"

Basic list prices are the prices that final customers or users are normally asked to pay for products. Unless noted otherwise, "list price" refers to "basic list price" in this book.

Unchanging list prices—an administrative convenience

Unchanging list prices are published prices that remain the same for long periods of time—perhaps years—but the actual price is adjusted upward or downward by add-ons or discounts. This method of changing prices is often used where frequent price changes are necessary. It avoids many catalog revisions. Rather than printing a complete new catalog, the seller can just publish a new list of add-ons or discounts.

Phony list prices for "bargain hunters"

Phony list prices are prices that customers can be shown to suggest that the price they are to pay has been discounted from "list." Some customers, in fact, seem more interested in the size of the supposed discount than the list price itself. And they can end up paying more than the competitive market price.

Most businesses, Better Business Bureaus, and government agencies frown on phony prices. And the FTC tries to stop such pricing—using the **Wheeler-Lea Amendment**—which bans "unfair or deceptive acts in commerce."

The FTC says that firms "must in every case act honestly and in good faith on advertising a list price, and not with the intention of establishing a basis . . . for a deceptive comparison in any local . . . trade area.[5]

The FTC has had some court success. But deception is difficult to define. Sometimes "two-for-one" and "1-cent" sales are real offers appealing to the price-conscious.[6]

There is also some question whether customers are really deceived by "high" list prices from which they bargain. Do the list prices from which "discounts" are offered on cars fool anyone? The FTC thinks so. But auto industry managers feel that consumers understand the meaning of the sticker price—as a starting price from which to begin bargaining. What do you think?

PRICE FLEXIBILITY POLICIES

One of the first decisions any marketing manager has to make is about price flexibility. Should he have a one-price or a flexible-price policy?

One-price policy—the same price for everyone

A **one-price policy** means offering the *same price to all customers* who purchase goods under essentially the same conditions and in the same quantities. The majority of U.S. firms use a one-price policy—mainly for administrative convenience and to maintain goodwill among customers. Most food stores, department stores, and even the modern discount houses and mass merchandisers use a one-price policy.

A one-price policy makes pricing easier. But the marketing manager must be careful to avoid a rigid one-price policy. This could amount to broadcasting a price which competitors could undercut—especially if the price is somewhat high. One reason for the growth of discount houses is that conventional retailers applied traditional margins and rigidly stuck to them.

Flexible-price policy—different prices for different customers

A **flexible-price policy** means offering the same product and quantities to different customers at different prices. What price is offered may depend on the customer's bargaining ability or relationship with the seller.[7]

Flexible pricing was most common when businesses were small, products were not standardized, and bargaining was typical. These conditions still exist in many countries.

Flexible pricing does have advantages, however. It is often used in the channels, in direct sales of industrial goods, and at retail for more expensive items and homogeneous shopping goods. It allows a sales rep to make adjustments for competitive conditions—rather than having to turn down an order. An aggressive seller might first emphasize product quality rather than price. He may charge a higher price to those customers who will pay it—and cut the price for those who won't.

Flexible prices can cause legal difficulties—as we will see later in this chapter. A flexible pricing policy has other disadvantages, too. The customer who finds that others have paid lower prices for the same marketing mix is not going to be happy. The time needed for bargaining may increase—and the cost of selling may rise as buyers become aware that this could be profitable to them. Finally, some sales reps may let price cutting become a habit. This could eliminate price as a competitive tool and lead—instead—to a lower price level.

PRICE-LEVEL POLICIES

When marketing managers administer prices—as most do—they must consciously set their price-level policy: Will the price be set below the market, at the same level as competition, or above the market? If the firm is in pure competition, of course, no policy is really necessary. To offer goods above or below the market price would be foolish. We will be concerned, therefore, with those less than purely competitive situations in which the marketing manager does have a choice. Further, we will assume that the firm is seeking at least some profits. Other objectives might lead to thinking of price level policies in quite a different way. A very sales-oriented marketing manager, for example, might set "below the market" prices with the hope of expanding sales.

Is it below, at, or above the market?

Some firms seem to emphasize below-the-market prices in their marketing mixes. Retail discounters and mass merchandisers offer goods below the prices charged by conventional retailers. And some manufacturers—such as Honda—sell products which appear to be offered below the market. At the other extreme, manufacturers such as Zenith Radio Corporation proudly claimed that their prices started well above those of competing models. They felt that one of the reasons for many successful sales years was that—while other companies cut prices and skimped on quality—Zenith consistently maintained high quality.

The question is: Do these various strategies contain prices which are above or below the market—or are they really different prices in different market segments? Perhaps *some* target customers *do* see important differences in the physical product, or in convenience of location, or in the whole marketing mix. Then

One strategy is to sell "below the market."

what we are talking about are different marketing strategies—not different price levels. The seemingly "below-the-market" prices are merely lower prices in different markets. The retail discounters, for example, may have lower prices than conventional retailers. But they may not be direct competitors. Economic shoppers may be comparing prices between discounters—a fact which some discounters are beginning to discover to their dismay.

Obviously, target marketing is relevant here. If some market segment was not already satisfied, a more attractive marketing mix might be offered with a higher price. That price probably should not be thought of as "above the market," but rather a new price which is part of a new marketing mix. Similarly, a "lower" price may not automatically cause the firm to be "below the market." It may be the price needed to make a good mix and compete with similar "low-price" mixes—that is, it is "at the market" against these mixes.[8]

Meeting competition may be best in oligopoly—conscious parallel action

In oligopoly situations, pricing "at the market"—that is, meeting competition—may be the only sensible policy. To raise prices might lead to a large loss in sales—unless competitors follow the price rise. And cutting the price would probably lead to competitors cutting prices too—downward along an inelastic industry demand curve. This can only lead to a decrease in total revenue for the industry and probably for each of the firms. Therefore, a meeting-competition policy may make sense for each firm—and price stability may develop without any conspiracy (although some critics call this pricing behavior "conscious parallel action"—and imply that it's the same as conspiracy).

PRICING OVER THE PRODUCT LIFE CYCLE

The product life cycle should be considered when the original price level for a new product is set. That price will affect how fast the product moves through the cycle. A high price, for example, may lead to attractive profits—but also to competition and a faster cycle. With this in mind, should a firm's original price be a skimming or a penetration price?

Skimming pricing— feeling out demand at a good price

A **skimming pricing policy** tries to get the "cream" of a market (the top of a demand curve) at a high price before aiming at the more price-sensitive segments of that market. Skimming often is used to maximize profits on new products—particularly in the market introduction stage when demand is fairly inelastic, at least in the upper price ranges.

Skimming is useful for feeling out demand—for getting a better understanding of the shape of the demand curve. It is easier to start with a high price that customers can refuse—and then reduce it—than to start with a low price and then try to raise it.

A skimming policy can lead to a slow reduction of the price in a stepdown or "cascading" process. It is important to realize that as prices are lowered, new target markets are probably being sought. So, new *Place* and *Promotion* policies may be needed, too. In short, a skimming pricing policy may involve changing prices through a series of marketing strategies—during the course of the product life cycle.

Penetration pricing—
get the business at a low
price

A **penetration pricing policy** tries to sell the whole market at one low price. A penetration pricing policy is the opposite of a skimming policy. The intention is to try to sell all the market at one price—that is, at a low price on the firm's demand curve where the quantity demanded is larger. This policy might be wise where there is no "elite" market—where the whole demand curve is fairly elastic—even in the early stages of the product life cycle.

A penetration policy will be even more attractive if: (1) as volume expands, economies of scale reduce costs greatly, or (2) the firm seriously expects strong competition *very* soon after introduction. A *low* penetration price may be called a "stay out" price—since it is intended to discourage competitors from entering the market.

Introductory price
dealing—temporary
price cuts

Price cuts do attract customers. Therefore, marketers often use **introductory price dealing**—temporary price cuts—to speed new products into a market. These *temporary* price cuts should not be confused with low penetration prices, however. The plan here is to raise prices as soon as the introductory offer is over.

Established competitors often choose not to meet introductory price dealing—as long as the introductory period is not too long or too successful. But knowing that customers may shift their loyalties if they try competitors' products, some aggressive competitors do meet such introductory price cuts.

Once price dealing gets started in a market, it may continue for some time. So an introductory dealing policy must be chosen with care.[9]

DISCOUNT POLICIES—OFF LIST PRICES

Discounts are reductions from list price that are given by a seller to a buyer who either gives up some marketing function or provides the function for himself. Discounts can be useful in marketing strategy planning.

In the following discussion, think about what function the buyers are giving up or providing when they get each of these discounts.

Quantity discounts
encourage volume
buying

Quantity discounts are discounts offered to encourage customers to buy in larger amounts. This lets a seller get more of a buyer's business, or shifts some of the storing function to the buyer, or reduces shipping and selling costs—or all of these. Such discounts are of two kinds: cumulative and noncumulative.

Cumulative quantity discounts apply to purchases over a given period—such as a year—and normally increase as the amount purchased increases. Cumulative discounts are intended to encourage buying from a single company by reducing the price for additional purchases.

Noncumulative quantity discounts apply only to individual orders. Such discounts encourage larger orders—but do not tie a buyer to the seller after that one purchase.

Quantity discounts may be based on the dollar value of the entire order, or on the number of units purchased, or on the size of the package purchased. While quantity discounts are usually given as price cuts, sometimes they are given as "free" or "bonus" goods. Customers may receive one or more units "free" with the purchase of some quantity.

Quantity discounts can be a very useful tool for the marketing manager. Some customers are eager to get them. But marketing managers must use quantity discounts carefully—offering them to all customers on equal terms to avoid price discrimination.

Seasonal discounts— buy sooner and store

Seasonal discounts are discounts offered to encourage buyers to stock earlier than present demand requires. If used by producers, this discount tends to shift the storing function further along in the channel. It also tends to even out sales over the year and, therefore, permit year-round operation. If seasonal discounts are large, channel members may pass them along to their customers. In coal sales, for example, seasonal discounts are given in the spring and summer all the way through the channel to final consumers and users.

Payment terms and cash discounts set payment dates

Most sales to channel members and final users are made on credit. The seller issues a bill (invoice)—and the buyer sends it through the accounting department for payment. Many channel members come to depend on other members for temporary working capital. Therefore, it is very important for both sides to clearly state the terms of payment—including the availability of cash discounts. The following terms of payment are commonly used.

Net means that payment for the face value of the invoice is due immediately. These terms are sometimes changed to "net 10" or "net 30"—which mean payment is due within 10 to 30 days of the date on the invoice.

1/10 net 30 means that a 1 percent discount off the face value of the invoice is allowed if the invoice is paid within 10 days. Otherwise, the full face value is due within 30 days. And it usually is understood that an interest charge will be made after the 30-day free credit period.

Servco, Inc.

1475 LAKE LANSING ROAD
LANSING, MICHIGAN 48912

(517) 482-2270

N° 1522

| | | DATE |
| | | 10-20-80 |

Sold To JONES SUPPLY COMPANY

220 COMMERCIAL AVENUE

SOUTH GATE, CALIFORNIA

CUSTOMER'S ORDER
#179642

SALESMAN
Miller

TERMS
Net 30

Shipped To Jones Supply Co., 623 Kensington,
Portland, Oregon

F.O.B.
Lansing

SHIPPED VIA
Truck

| 200 | Smoke Alarms, #263 - A | 12. | 00 | 2400. | 00 |

Thank You.

An invoice shows the terms of the sale.

Courtesy Servco, Inc.

Why cash discounts are given and should be taken

Cash discounts are reductions in the price to encourage buyers to pay their bills quickly. Smart buyers take advantage of them. A discount of 2/10, net 30 may not look like very much. But any company that passes it up is missing a good chance to save money.

The 2 percent discount is earned for paying the invoice just 20 days sooner than it would have to be paid anyway. And if it is not taken, the company—in effect—is borrowing at an annual rate of 36 percent. That is, assuming a 360-day year and dividing by 20 days, there are 18 periods during which the firm could earn 2 percent—and 18 times 2 equals 36 percent a year.

While the marketing manager can often use the cash discount as a marketing variable, a specific cash discount may be so firmly established in his industry that he cannot change it or use it to suit his needs. He must give the usual terms—even if he has no need for cash. Purchasing agents are aware of the value of cash discounts and will insist that the marketing manager offer the same terms offered by competitors. In fact, some buyers automatically deduct the accepted cash discount from their invoice—regardless of the seller's invoice terms.

Trade discounts often are set by tradition

A **trade (functional) discount** is a list price reduction given to channel members for the job they are going to do.

A manufacturer, for example, might allow retailers a 30 percent trade discount from the suggested retail list price—to cover the cost of the retailing function and their profit. Similarly, the manufacturer might allow wholesalers a chain discount of 30 percent and 10 percent off the suggested retail price. In this case, the wholesalers would be expected to pass the 30 percent discount on to retailers.

Trade discounts seem to offer a manufacturer's or wholesaler's marketing manager great flexibility in varying a marketing mix. In fact, however, they may limit him greatly. The customary trade discounts can be so well established that he has to accept them in setting his prices.

ALLOWANCE POLICIES—OFF LIST PRICES

Allowances—like discounts—are given to final consumers, customers, or channel members for doing "something" or accepting less of "something."

Bring in the old, ring up the new—with trade-ins

A **trade-in allowance** is a price reduction given for used goods when similar new goods are bought.

Trade-ins give the marketing manager an easy way to lower the price without reducing list price. Proper handling of trade-ins is important when selling durable goods. Customers buying machinery or buildings, for example, buy long-term satisfaction in terms of more manufacturing capacity. If the list price less the trade-in allowance does not offer greater satisfaction—as the customer sees it—then no sales will be made.

Many firms replace machinery slowly—perhaps too slowly—because they value their old equipment above market value. This also applies to new cars. Customers want higher trade-ins for their old cars than the current market value.

This encourages the use of high, perhaps "phony," list prices so that high trade-in allowance can be given.

Advertising allowances—something for something

Advertising allowances are price reductions given to firms further along in a channel to encourage them to advertise or otherwise promote the firm's products locally. Channel system thinking is involved here. General Electric has given a 1.5 percent allowance to its wholesalers of housewares and radios. They, in turn, are expected to provide something—in this case, local advertising.

PMs—push for cash

Push Money (or Prize Money) allowances—sometimes called "PMs" or "spiffs"—are given to retailers by manufacturers or wholesalers to pass on to the retailers' salesclerks—for aggressively selling particular items. PM allowances are used for new merchandise, slower moving items, or higher margin items. They are especially common in the furniture and clothing industries. A salesclerk, for example, might earn an additional $5 for each mattress of a new type sold.

SOME CUSTOMERS GET EXTRA SOMETHINGS

Trading stamps— something for nothing?

Trading stamps are free stamps (like "Green Stamps") given by some retailers with every purchase.

Retailers can buy trading stamps from trading-stamp companies or set up their own plans. In either case, customers can trade stamps for merchandise premiums or cash or goods at the retailer's own store or at stamp redemption centers.

Some retailers offer trading stamps to their customers to differentiate their offering. Some customers seem to be attracted by trading stamps. They feel they are getting something for nothing. And, sometimes they are—if competitive pressures don't allow the retailers to pass the cost of the stamps (2 to 3 percent of sales) along to customers. Also, lower promotion costs or a large increase in sales may make up for the increased cost of the stamps.[10]

Some shoppers shop where trading stamps are given because they feel they're getting something for nothing.

Mike Kelly

The early users of stamps in a community seem to gain a competitive advantage. But when competitors start offering stamps, the advantage can disappear. This is similar to competition in the product life cycle—where new ideas are copied and profits are squeezed.

There was much interest in trading stamps in the 1950s and 1960s. Then their use declined—especially in grocery retailing. There, food discounters cut into the appeal of seemingly "higher cost" stamp givers.

Now that some of the enthusiasm for stamp plans is dying down, perhaps they can be seen for what they really are. They are a potential addition to a marketing mix—perhaps instead of a price reduction. In some situations, stamp plans may be very effective—especially if half of a market wants stamps.[11] So we may see them used more in the future.

Clipping coupons brings other extras

Many manufacturers and retailers are offering discounts (or free items) through the use of coupons found in packages, mailings, newspapers and magazine advertising—or at the store. By presenting a coupon to a retailer, the consumer is given "10 cents off" or may be given the product at no charge. This plan is especially effective in the food business. Supermarkets are filled with customers clutching handfuls of coupons.[12] In fact, coupon saving has become so popular that a book has been put out to explain how to make the most of coupons.

LIST PRICE MAY DEPEND ON GEOGRAPHIC PRICING POLICIES

Retail list prices often include free delivery. Or free delivery may be offered to some customers as an aid to closing the sale. In short, what is included (or not included) in the retail list price may not be formally published. This helps the retailer adjust its marketing mix—depending on the needs (and attitudes or bargaining ability) of each customer.

Deciding who is going to pay the freight is more important on sales to intermediate customers than to final consumers, because more money may be involved. Usually purchase orders specify place, time, method of delivery, freight costs, insurance, handling, and other charges. There are many possible variations here for an imaginative marketing manager. Some specialized terms have developed. A few are discussed in the following paragraphs.

F.O.B. pricing is easy

A commonly used transportation term is F.O.B. F.O.B. means "free on board" some vehicle at some place. Typically, it is used with the place named—often the location of the seller's factory or warehouse—as in "F.O.B. Detroit," "F.O.B. Houston," or "F.O.B. mill." It means that the seller pays the cost of loading the goods onto some vehicle—usually a common carrier such as a truck, railroad car, or ship. At the point of loading, title to the goods passes to the buyer. Then the buyer pays the freight and takes responsibility for damage in transit—except as covered by the transportation company.

Variations are made easily—by changing the place part of the term. If the marketing manager wanted to pay the freight for the convenience of customers, he could use: "F.O.B. delivered" or "F.O.B. buyer's factory" (or warehouse). In this case, title would not pass until the goods were delivered. If he did want title to pass immediately—but still wanted to pay the freight (and then include it in the invoice)—he could use "F.O.B. seller's factory–freight prepaid."

F.O.B. "shipping point" pricing simplifies the seller's pricing—but it may narrow his market. Since the delivered cost of goods will vary depending on the buyer's location, a customer located farther from the seller must pay more and might buy from closer suppliers.

Zone pricing smoothes delivered prices

Zone pricing means making an average freight charge to all buyers within specific geographic areas. The seller pays the actual freight charges and then bills the customer for an average charge. The United States might be divided into five zones, for example, and all buyers within each zone would pay the same freight charge.

Zone pricing reduces the wide variation in delivered prices which result from an F.O.B. shipping point pricing policy. It also simplifies charging for transportation.

This approach often is used by manufacturers of hardware and food items—both to lower the chance of price competition in the channels and to simplify figuring transportation charges for the thousands of wholesalers and retailers they serve.

Uniform delivered pricing—one price to all

Uniform delivered pricing means making an average freight charge to all buyers. It is an extension of zone pricing. An entire country may be considered as one zone—and the average cost of delivery is included in the price. It is most often used when (1) transportation costs are relatively low and (2) the seller wishes to sell in all geographic areas at one price—perhaps a nationally advertised price.

Freight-absorption pricing—competing on equal grounds in another territory

When all the firms in an industry use F.O.B. shipping point pricing, a firm usually does well near its shipping point but not so well farther away. As sales reps look for business farther away, delivered prices rise. They find themselves priced out of the market. This problem can be solved with freight absorption.

Freight-absorption pricing means absorbing freight cost so that a firm's delivered price meets the nearest competitor's. This amounts to cutting list price to appeal to new market segments.

With freight absorption pricing, the only limit on the size of a firm's territory is the amount of freight cost it is willing to absorb. These absorbed costs cut net return on each sale, but the new business may raise total profit.

LEGALITY OF PRICING POLICIES

Even very high prices may be OK—if they are not fixed

From our general discussion of legislation in Chapter 3, you might think that companies have little freedom in pricing—or may even need government approval for their prices. Generally speaking, this is not true. They can charge what they want—even "outrageously high" prices—as long as they don't conspire with their competitors or discriminate against some of their customers.

The first step to understanding pricing legislation is to know the thinking of legislators and the courts. Ideally, they try to help the economy operate more

Different geographic pricing policies may be needed to expand into new territories.

Milt & Joan Mann

effectively—in the consumers' interest. In practice, this doesn't always work out as neatly as planned. But generally their intentions are good. And if we take this view, we get a better idea of the "why" of legislation. This helps us to anticipate future rulings. We will look at U.S. legislation here, but other countries have similar laws on pricing.[13]

Price fixing is illegal— you can go to jail

There are some restrictions on pricing, however. Difficulties with pricing—and perhaps violation of price legislation—usually occur only when competing marketing mixes are quite similar. When the success of an entire marketing strategy depends upon price, there is pressure (and temptation) to make agreements with competitors (conspire). And **price fixing**—competitors getting together to raise, lower, or stabilize prices—is common and relatively easy. But it is also completely illegal. It is "conspiracy" under the Sherman Act and the Federal Trade Commission Act. Fixing prices can be dangerous. Some business managers have already gone to jail! And governments are getting tougher on price fixing—especially by smaller companies.

Unfair trade practice acts control some minimum prices

The **unfair trade practice acts** put a floor under prices, especially at the wholesale and retail levels. They have been passed in more than half the states. Selling below cost in these states is illegal. Wholesalers and retailers are usually required to take a certain minimum percentage markup over their merchandise-plus-transportation costs. The most common markup figures are six percent at retail and two percent at wholesale.

If a specific wholesaler or retailer can show that operating costs are lower than the minimum required figure, offering lower prices may be permitted. But conclusive proof of lower costs must be shown. And in most cases, this is almost impossible.

Most retailers know enough about their costs to set larger markups than these minimums. The practical effect of these laws is to protect certain limited-line food retailers—such as dairy stores—from the kind of "ruinous" competition that

Levi-Strauss has tried to control "price-cutting" in the channels.

Milt & Joan Mann

full-line stores might offer if they sold milk as a "leader"—offering it below cost—for a long time.

Some price fixing was permitted with "fair trade"

Price fixing is generally prohibited under the Sherman Act and the Federal Trade Commission Act. From the 1930s to 1975, however, some price fixing was specifically permitted by *fair trade* or *resale price maintenance* legislation.

The laws allowing price fixing grew out of the great depression of the 1930s—when drastic price cutting was used to stimulate sales. This was especially hard on many small retailers. So they banded together to get government protection from this aggressive price cutting. At one time, 45 states had laws allowing some price fixing. But discounters and legislators who were more sympathetic with price-oriented competition continued to test the laws in courts and repeal them in state legislatures. Some federal legislation permitted this state-by-state price fixing. But finally, in 1975 all such agreements were made illegal.[14]

The decline of pricing-fixing legislation occurred in part because some manufacturers did not feel that it was fair to consumers—its main purpose was to stabilize or increase the price level. This was certainly not in tune with 1970s thinking about running a more efficient macro-marketing system. As a sign of how times had changed, it is interesting to note that not even one of fair trade's former supporters showed up for the final hearings at the national level.

Price-fixing arrangements are found in other countries. Probably the outstanding example in recent times is the OPEC cartel for fixing world oil prices.

Fair trade had some pluses

It is only fair to the former supporters of fair trade legislation to note that there are situations where fixing the retail price might be beneficial to all the firms in the channel *and* to the target customers. When, for example, consumers need much information or service, it may not be supplied if retailers are allowed to cut prices as they wish. Discounters may provide only a place for the product, and emphasize price—while ignoring promotion and service. In other words, they might only use three of the four Ps, skimming the "cream" by dealing only with customers who are presold or easily sold—and ignoring the balance of the market. Marketing managers faced with this kind of a situation are going to have to find a new approach—or decide that it is not possible to develop an effective marketing mix to reach the "harder-to-sell"—given the nature of competition and our laws.

Antimonopoly legislation bans price discrimination unless . . .

Price level and price flexibility policies can lead to price discrimination. The **Robinson-Patman Act** (of 1936) makes illegal any **price discrimination**—selling the same goods to different buyers at different prices—which injures competition. This law does permit some price differences—but they must be based on (1) cost differences or (2) the need to meet competition. Both buyers and sellers are guilty if they know they are entering into discriminatory agreements. This is a serious matter—price discrimination suits are common.

What does "like grade and quality" mean?

The Robinson-Patman Act allows a marketing manager to charge different prices for similar products if they are *not* of "like grade and quality." But the problem is: How similar can products be without being considered to be of "like grade and quality"? The FTC position is that if the physical characteristics of a product are similar, then they are of like grade and quality. The FTC's view was upheld in a 1966 U.S. Supreme Court ruling against the Borden Company. The Court held that a well-known label *alone* does not make a product different from the one with an unknown label. The issue was rather clear-cut in the Borden case—the company agreed that the physical characteristics of the canned milk it sold at different prices under different labels were basically the same.

The FTC's "victory" in the *Borden* case was not complete, however. Although the U.S. Supreme Court agreed with the FTC in the *Borden* case—with respect to like grade and quality—it sent the case back to the U.S. Court of Appeals to determine whether the price difference actually injured competition—which is also required by the law. In 1967, this court found no evidence of injury and

Many of Borden's products have "recognized consumer appeal."

Courtesy Borden, Inc.

further noted that there could be no injury unless Borden's price differential exceeded the "recognized consumer appeal of the Borden label." How "consumer appeal" is to be measured was not spelled out and may lead to additional suits.[15] Eventually, what the consumer thinks about the product may be the determining factor. For now, however, it would appear safer for producers who want to sell several brands or dealer brands at lower prices than their main brand to offer physical differences—and differences that are genuinely useful, not merely decorative or trivial. Another possibility for differentiation that has won some support in the courts is packaging differences.[16]

Can cost analysis justify price differences?

The Robinson-Patman Act allows price differences if there are cost differences—say for larger quantity shipments or because middlemen take over some of the physical distribution functions. Justifying cost differences is a difficult job, however. Costs usually must be allocated to several products—perhaps using logical assumptions. It is easy, then, for the FTC to raise objections to whatever allocation method is used. Such objections often are raised—in part because there can be differences of opinion about how to allocate costs. But perhaps more basically, it is because the FTC has been especially concerned about the impact of price differences on competition—and on small competitors in particular. The FTC has even sought to control the size of quantity discounts on the grounds that big discounts—although justified on a cost basis—may be unfair to small competitors.[17]

Can you legally meet price cuts?

Meeting competition is permitted as a defense in price discrimination cases—under the Robinson-Patman Act—although the FTC normally has taken a dim view of this argument.

In a significant 5–4 decision in 1956, the U.S. Supreme Court said that "meeting competition" in "good faith" is a permissible defense if it can be shown that the price discrimination occurred as a *defensive* rather than an offensive action. The dissenting justices saw the implications and suggested that this ruling "crippled the enforcement of the act." They added that if price cutting should begin generally, the majority decision could permit a great deal of price cutting—*perhaps harming the less efficient outlets.*[18]

A major objective of antitrust legislation is to protect competition—not competitors—and "meeting competiton" in "good faith" still seems to be legal—even if it is large firms which meet the lower prices of small firms.

Are functional discounts discriminatory?

Can functional (trade) discounts be considered price discrimination? The laws are not completely clear on this issue, but court decisions appear to have settled the matter—with emphasis on functions provided.[19] At the root of the problem is the distinction between wholesalers and retailers—since wholesalers are entitled to certain discounts from producers to provide wholesaling functions.

Generally, the courts have felt that the identification of a firm as a wholesaler or a retailer depends not on the quantity bought or handled, but on the nature of the functions provided. A producer could legally refuse to give a wholesale discount to a large retail grocery chain—although the chain might handle a much larger volume than small wholesalers. The justification is that functional discounts are necessary if the small wholesaler is to cover costs and still sell to retailers at prices low enough to permit the retailers to be competitive.

A retail chain probably would not have to pay the same price offered a small retailer, however, because a special functional discount would be set up for chain stores. As long as a functional discount seems to reflect the nature of the job required in the channel, the courts probably would consider it legal.

"Brokerage allowance" may be illegal

Regular brokers are paid commissions for their services. But sometimes large organizations—such as grocery chains—act as their own brokers and request the broker's commission in the form of a **brokerage allowance**—a discount to buyers for performing the broker functions. Under the Robinson-Patman Act, such brokerage allowances for buyers or buyers' representatives are *illegal*. In highly competitive fields, however, the marketing manager may feel forced to grant such an allowance—perhaps calling it an advertising allowance, but without expecting additional promotion. In effect, competitive pressures are pushing prices downward. This has been seen in the low-profit-margin grocery retailing industry. There, the buyer's ability to win extra allowances and favorable cash discounts may make the difference between profit and loss for the whole business. But they still are illegal!

Special promotion allowances might not be allowed

Some firms have violated the Robinson-Patman Act by providing PMs (Push Money), demonstrations, advertising allowances, or other promotion aids to some customers and not others. The act specifically prohibits such special allowances— *unless they are made available to all customers on "proportionately equal" terms.* No proof of injury to competition is necessary. And the FTC has been fairly successful in prosecuting such cases.

The need for such a rule is clear—once price regulation begins. Allowances for promotion aid could be granted to retailers or wholesalers without expecting that any promotion would actually be done. This plainly would be price discrimination in disguise.

The law does work hardships, however. Sometimes it is difficult to provide allowances on "proportionately equal" terms to both large and small customers.

A retail chain may get a special functional discount.

Kenneth Yee

The Robinson-Patman Act does not state clearly whether a small store should be allowed the same dollar advertising allowance as a large one or an allowance in proportion to sales. But the latter probably would not buy the same promotion impact.

It may also be difficult to determine exactly who are competing customers. The FTC might define a relevant list of competitors much more broadly than either the seller or the competing buyers. Supermarket operators might only be concerned about other supermarkets and the food discounters. But the FTC might feel small drugstores were also competitors for health and beauty aids.[20]

In 1969, the FTC issued guidelines for advertising and promotion allowances—including requirements for informing all competitive customers that deals were available. As a result, there has been some move away from cooperative advertising and promotion allowances—to avoid possible legal problems.[21]

Present legal status of geographic pricing

There are two points of view on what is geographic price discrimination under the Robinson-Patman Act. According to one view, the *delivered* price should be the same to all buyers. According to the other, the *factory* price should be the same to all buyers.

The first view would permit freight absorption to enable sellers to broaden their territory—perhaps allowing them to expand their factories and operate at more efficient levels (assuming that economies of scale are possible).

The second view, by contrast, insists on F.O.B. shipping point pricing—on the assumption that it is improper for outlying customers to pay less than the "full cost." But without freight absorption, sellers might not be able to obtain this additional business, and their basic costs and prices could actually rise. In addition, strict F.O.B. shipping point pricing might encourage the development of monopoly areas around each firm's plant or warehouse.

This second view is a logical extension of antitrust legislation designed to block price discrimination which would force some customers to pay more than others. This view has long been favored by the FTC and is gaining acceptance in the courts. Currently, however, freight absorption systems which enable firms to reach more distant markets are not considered illegal—unless the members of an industry arrive at a common method through conspiracy.

How to avoid discriminating

One way to avoid discriminating is to avoid price differences. Until price discrimination law is clarified, many business managers probably will continue to deemphasize price as a marketing variable. They have concluded that the safest course is to offer few or no quantity discounts—and to offer the same cost-based prices to *all* customers.

CONCLUSION

The Price variable offers an alert marketing manager many possibilities for varying marketing mixes. What pricing policies will be used depends on the pricing objectives. We looked at profit-oriented, sales-oriented, and status quo–oriented objectives.

A marketing manager must set policies about price flexibility, price level, prices over the product life cycle, who will pay the freight, and who will get discounts and allowances. While doing this, the manager should be aware of pricing legislation affecting these policies.

In most cases, a marketing manager must set prices—that is, administer prices. Starting with a list price, a variety of discounts and allowances may be offered to adjust for the "Something" being offered in the marketing mix.

Throughout this chapter, we have assumed that a list price had already been set. We have emphasized what may be included (or excluded) in the "Something"—and what objectives a firm might set to guide its pricing policies. Price setting itself was not discussed. It will be covered in the next chapter—showing ways of carrying out the various pricing objectives and policies.

QUESTIONS AND PROBLEMS

1. Identify the strategic decisions a marketing manager must make in the Price area. Illustrate your answer for a local retailer.

2. How should the acceptance of a profit-oriented, a sales-oriented, or a status quo–oriented pricing objective affect the development of a company's marketing strategy? Illustrate for each.

3. Distinguish between one-price and flexible-price policies. Which would be most appropriate for a supermarket? Why?

4. Cite two examples of continuously selling above the market price. Describe the situations.

5. Explain the types of competitive situations which might lead to a "meeting competition" pricing policy.

6. What pricing objective(s) would a skimming pricing policy most likely be implementing? Could the same be true for a penetration pricing policy? Which policy would probably be most appropriate for each of the following products: (a) a new type of home lawn-sprinkling system, (b) a new low-cost meat substitute, (c) a new type of children's toy, (b) a faster computer.

7. Discuss unfair trade practices acts. To whom are they "unfair"?

8. How would our marketing structure be changed if manufacturers were required to specify fair trade prices on all products sold at retail and all retailers were required to use these prices? Would this place greater or lesser importance on the development of the manufacturer's marketing mix? What kind of an operation would retailing

be in this situation? Would consumers receive more or less service?

9. Would price discrimination be involved if a large oil company sold gasoline to taxicab associations for resale to individual taxi cab operators for 2½ cents a gallon less than charged to retail service stations? What happens if the cab associations resell gasoline not only to taxicab operators, but to the general public as well?

10. Indicate what the final consumer really obtains when paying the list price for the following "products": (a) an automobile, (b) a portable radio, (c) a package of frozen peas, and (d) a lipstick in a jeweled case.

11. Are seasonal discounts appropriate in agricultural businesses (which are certainly seasonal)?

12. What are the "effective" annual interest rates for the following cash discount terms: (a) 1/10 net 60, (b) 1/5 net 10, (c) net 30?

13. Explain how a marketing manager might change his F.O.B. terms to make his otherwise competitive marketing mix more attractive.

14. What type of geographic pricing policy would seem most appropriate for the following products (specify any assumptions necessary to obtain a definite answer): (a) a chemical by-product, (b) nationally advertised candy bars, (c) rebuilt auto parts, (d) tricycles?

15. Explain how the prohibition of freight absorption (that is, requiring F.O.B. factory pricing) might affect a producer with substantial economies of scale in production.

SUGGESTED CASES

23 Ace Photofinishing Company   **24 The Schmidt Manufacturing Company**

NOTES

1. W. Warren Haynes, *Pricing Decisions in Small Business* (Lexington: University of Kentucky Press, 1962); and Alan Reynolds, "A Kind Word for 'Cream Skimming,'" *Harvard Business Review*, November–December 1974, pp. 113–20.

2. For more discussion of the behavior of satisficers, see Herbert A. Simon, *Administrative Behavior*, 2d ed., (New York: Macmillan Publishing Co., Inc. 1961).

3. "Squeeze on Product Lines," *Business Week*, January 5, 1974, p. 50 f; and "Pricing Strategy in an Inflation Economy," *Business Week*, April 6, 1974, pp. 43–49.

4. Joseph W. McGuire, John S. Y. Chiu, and Alvar O. Elving, "Executive Incomes, Sales and Profits," *American Economic Review*, September 1962, pp. 753–61; "For the Chief, Sales Sets the Pay," *Business Week*, September 30, 1967, p. 174; and Alfred Rappaport, "Executive Incentives versus Corporate Growth," *Harvard Business Review*, July–August 1978, pp. 81–88.

5. "Guides against Deceptive Pricing," Federal Trade Commission, October 10, 1958, and January 8, 1964.

6. *FTC* v. *Mary Carter Paint Co.* 382 U.S. 46, 1965.

7. For an interesting discussion of the many variations from a one-price system in retailing, see Stanley C. Hollander, "The 'One-Price' System—Fact or Fiction?" *Journal of Retailing*, Fall 1955, pp. 127–44.

8. See, for example, "The Airline that Thrives on Discounting," *Business Week*, July 24, 1971, pp. 68–70; see also Zarrel V. Lambert, "Product Perception: An Important Variable in Pricing Strategy," *Journal of Marketing*, October 1970, pp. 68–76; and "Price and Choice Behavior," *Journal of Marketing Research*, February 1972, pp. 35–40.

9. For more discussion on price dealing, see Charles L. Hinkle, "The Strategy of Price Deals," *Harvard Business Review*, July–August 1965, pp. 75–85.

10. A. Haring and W. O. Yoder (eds.), *Trading Stamps Practice and Pricing Policy*, Indiana Business Report no. 27, Bureau of Business Research (Bloomington: Indiana University, 1958), p. 301.

11. "Buyer's Choice: Stamps or Savings," *Business Week*, February 7, 1970, p. 106; and "Sharp Drop in Gas-Station Business Brings Trading-Stamp Industry More Profit Woes," *The Wall Street Journal*, March 1, 1974, p. 26.

12. "Grocery Coupons Are Seen Threatened by Growth of Fraudulent Redemptions," *The Wall Street Journal*, April 12, 1976, p. 26.

13. For discussion concerning European countries, see *Market Power and the Law* (Washington, D.C.: Organization for Economic Cooperation and Development Publication Center, 1970), 206 pp.

14. James C. Johnson and Louis E. Boone, "Farewell to Fair Trade," *MSU Business Topics*, Spring 1976, pp. 22–30.

15. Morris L. Mayer, Joseph B. Mason, and E. A. Orbeck, "The Borden Case—A Legal Basis for Private Brand Price Discrimination," *MSU Business Topics*, Winter 1970, pp. 56–63; and Jacky Knopp, Jr., "What Are 'Commodities of Like Grade and Quality'?" *Journal of Marketing*, July 1963, p. 63.

16. T. F. Schutte, V. J. Cook, Jr., and R. Hemsley, "What Management Can Learn from the Borden Case," *Business Horizons*, Winter 1966, pp. 23–30.

17. Peter G. Peterson, "Quantity Discounts in the Morton Salt Case," *Journal of Business of the University of Chicago*, April 1952, pp. 109–20; "Is the Cost Defense Workable," *Journal of Marketing*, January 1965, pp. 37–42; and B. J. Linder and Allan H. Savage, "Price Discrimination and Cost Defense—Change Ahead?" *MSU Business Topics*, Summer 1971, pp. 21–26.

18. *Business Week*, February 1, 1958, p. 53.

19. *FTC* v. *The Mennen Company*, and *National Biscuit Company* v. *FTC*.

20. Lawrence X. Tarpey, Sr., "Who Is a Competing Customer?" *Journal of Retailing*, Spring 1969, pp. 46–58; and John R. Davidson, "FTC, Robinson-Patman and Cooperative Promotion Activities," *Journal of Marketing*, January 1968, pp. 14–18.

21. "The FTC Gets Tough on 'Promo' Payments," *Business Week*, November 24, 1973, p. 30; and L. X. Tarpey, Sr., "Buyer Liability under the Robinson-Patman Act: A Current Appraisal," *Journal of Marketing*, January 1972, pp. 38–42.

Appendix B

Marketing arithmetic

The beginning business student must become familiar with the essentials of the "language of business." Business people commonly use accounting language when discussing costs, prices, and profit. So you need to understand this terminology. Using accounting data is a practical tool in analyzing marketing problems.

The following discussion introduces the basic ideas underlying the operating statement, some commonly used ratios related to the operating statement, markups, the markdown ratio, and ROI and ROA ratios. Other analytical techniques are discussed in various parts of the text—and are not treated separately here.

THE OPERATING STATEMENT

An operating statement for a wholesale or retail business—commonly referred to as a profit and loss statement—is presented in Figure B–1. A complete and detailed statement is presented so you will see the framework throughout the discussion—but the amount of detail on an operating statement is not standardized. Many companies use financial statements with much less detail than this one. Their emphasis is on clarity and readability—rather than detail. To understand an operating statement, however, you must know about its parts.

The operating statement is a simple summary of the financial results of the operations of a company over a specified period of time. Some beginning students may feel that the operating statement is complex—but as we shall see, this really isn't true. *The main purpose of the operating statement is determining the net profit figure—and presenting data to support that figure.*

535

Figure B-1
An operating statement (profit
and loss statement)

XYZ COMPANY
Operating Statement
For the Year Ended December 31, 198X

Gross sales			$54,000
Less: Returns and allowances			4,000
Net sales			$50,000
Cost of goods sold			
Beginning inventory at cost		$ 8,000	
Purchases at billed cost	$31,000		
Less: Purchase discounts	4,000		
Purchases at net cost	$27,000		
Plus freight-in	2,000		
Net cost of delivered purchases		29,000	
Cost of goods available for sale		$37,000	
Less: Ending inventory at cost		7,000	
Cost of goods sold			30,000
Gross margin (gross profit)			$20,000
Expenses			
Selling expenses			
Sales salaries	$ 6,000		
Advertising expense	2,000		
Delivery expense	2,000		
Total selling expense		$10,000	
Administrative expense			
Office salaries	$ 3,000		
Office supplies	1,000		
Miscellaneous administrative expense	500		
Total administrative expense		4,500	
General expense			
Rent expense	$ 1,000		
Miscellaneous general expenses	500		
Total general expense		1,500	
Total expenses			16,000
Net profit from operation			$ 4,000

Only three basic components

The basic components of an operating statement are *sales*—which come from the sale of goods or services; *costs*—which come from the making and selling process; and the balance—called *profit or loss*—which is merely the difference between sales and costs. So there are only three basic components in the statement: *sales, costs,* and *profit.*

Time period covered may vary

There is no one time period which an operating statement covers. Rather, statements are prepared to satisfy the needs of a particular business. This may be at the end of each day—or at the end of each week. Usually, however, an operating statement summarizes results for one month, three months, six months, or a full fiscal year. Since the time period does vary, this information is included in the heading of the statement as follows:

XYZ Company
Operating Statement
For the (Period) Ended (Date)

Also, see Figure B-1.

Management uses of operating statements

Before going on to a more detailed discussion of the components of our operating statement, note some of the uses for such a statement. A glance at Figure B–1 reveals that a wealth of information is presented in a clear and concise manner. With this information, management can easily find the relation of its net sales to the cost of goods sold, the gross margin, expenses, and net profit. Opening and closing inventory figures are available—as is the amount spent during the period for the purchase of goods for resale. The total expenses are listed to make it easier to compare them with previous statements—and to help control these expenses.

All of this information is important to the management of a company. Assume that a particular company prepared monthly operating statements. It should be obvious that a series of these statements would be a valuable tool for the direction and control of the business. By comparing results from one month to the next, management can uncover unfavorable trends in the sales, expense, or profit areas of the business—and take the needed action.

A skeleton statement gets down to essential details

Let's refer to Figure B–1 and begin to analyze this seemingly detailed statement. The intention at this point is to get first-hand knowledge of the components of the operating statement.

As a first step, suppose we take all the items that have dollar amounts extended to the third, or right-hand, column. Using these items only, the operating statement looks like this:

Gross sales	$54,000
Less: Returns and allowances	4,000
Net sales	$50,000
Less: Cost of goods sold	30,000
Gross margin	$20,000
Less: Total expenses	16,000
Net profit (loss)	$ 4,000

Is this a complete operating statement? The answer is yes. This skeleton statement differs from Figure B–1 only in supporting detail. All the basic components are included. In fact, the only items we *must* list to have a *complete* operating statement are:

Net sales	$50,000
Less: Costs	46,000
Net profit (loss)	$ 4,000

These three items are the *essence* of an operating statement. All other subdivisions or details are just useful additions.

Meaning of "sales"

Now let's define and explore the meaning of the terms that are used in the skeleton statement.

The first item is "sales." What do we mean by sales? The term **gross sales** is the total amount charged to all customers during some time period. It is certain, however, that there will be some customer dissatisfaction—or just plain errors in ordering and shipping goods. This results in returns and allowances which reduce gross sales.

A **return** occurs when a customer sends back purchased products. The company either refunds the purchase price or allows the customer dollar credit on other purchases.

An **allowance** occurs when a customer is not satisfied with a purchase for some reason. The company gives a price reduction on the original invoice (bill) but the customer keeps the goods or services.

These refunds and reductions must be considered when the sales figure for the period is computed. Really, we are only interested in the revenue which the company manages to keep. This is **net sales**—the actual sales dollars the company will receive. Therefore, all reductions, refunds, cancellations, and so forth—made because of returns and allowances—are deducted from the original total (gross sales) to get net sales. This is shown below:

```
Gross sales ........................ $54,000
        Less: Returns and allowances ......    4,000
Net sales .......................... $50,000
```

Meaning of "cost of goods sold"

The next item in the operating statement—**cost of goods sold**—is the total value (at cost) of all the goods sold during the period. We will discuss its computation later. Meanwhile, merely note that after the cost of goods sold figure is obtained, it is subtracted from the net sales figure to get the gross margin.

Meaning of "gross margin" and "expenses"

Gross margin (gross profit) is the money left to cover the cost of selling the products and managing the business. The hope is that a profit will be left after subtracting these expenses.

Selling expense commonly is the major expense below the gross margin. Note that in Figure B–1, all **expenses** are subtracted from the gross margin to get the net profit. The expenses in this case are the selling, administrative, and general expenses. (Note that the cost of purchases and cost of goods sold are not included in this total expense figure—they were subtracted from net sales earlier to get the gross margin.)

Net profit—at the bottom of the statement—is what the company has earned from its operations during a particular period. It is the amount left after the cost of goods sold and the expenses have been subtracted from net sales.

DETAILED ANALYSIS OF SECTIONS OF THE OPERATING STATEMENT

Cost of goods sold for a wholesale or retail company

The cost-of-goods sold section includes details which are used to find the "cost of goods sold" ($30,000 in our example).

In Figure B–1, it is obvious that beginning and ending inventory, purchases, purchase discounts, and freight-in are all necessary in calculating costs of goods sold. If we pull the cost of goods sold section from the operating statement, it looks like this:

Cost of goods sold

Beginning inventory at cost		$ 8,000
Purchases at billed cost	$31,000	
Less: Purchase discounts	4,000	
Purchases at net cost	$27,000	
Plus: Freight-in	2,000	
Net cost of delivered purchases		29,000
Cost of goods available for sale		$37,000
Less: Ending inventory at cost		7,000
Cost of goods sold...................		$30,000

"Cost of goods sold" is the cost value of goods sold—that is, actually removed from the company's control—and not the cost value of goods on hand at any given time.

The inventory figures merely show the cost of merchandise on hand at the beginning and end of the period the statement covers. These figures may be obtained by a physical count of the merchandise on hand on these dates—or they may be estimated through a system of perpetual inventory bookkeeping which would show the inventory balance at any given time. The methods used in determining the inventory should be as accurate as possible—since these figures affect the cost of goods sold during the period, and net profit.

The net cost of delivered purchases must include freight charges and purchase discounts received—since these items affect the money actually spent to buy goods and bring them to the place of business. A **purchase discount** is a reduction of the original invoice amount for some business reason. For example, a cash discount may be given for prompt payment of the amount due. The total of such discounts is subtracted from the original invoice cost of purchases to get the *net* cost of purchases. To this figure we add the freight charges for bringing the goods to the place of business. This gives the net cost of *delivered* purchases. When the net cost of delivered purchases is added to the beginning inventory at cost, we have the total cost of goods available for sale during the period. If we now subtract the ending inventory at cost from the cost of the goods available for sale, we finally get the cost of goods sold.

One important point should be noted about cost of goods sold. The way the value of inventory is calculated varies from one company to another—and different methods can cause big differences on the operating statement. See any basic accounting textbook for how the various inventory valuation methods work.

Cost of goods sold for a manufacturing company

Figure B–1 illustrates the way the manager of a wholesale or retail business would arrive at the cost of goods sold. Such a business would *purchase* finished goods and resell them. In a manufacturing company, the purchases section of this operating statement would be replaced by a section called "cost of goods manufactured." This section would include purchases of raw materials and parts, direct and indirect labor costs, and factory overhead charges (such as heat, light, and power)—which are necessary to produce finished goods. The cost of goods manufactured is added to the beginning finished-goods inventory to arrive at the cost of goods available for sale. Often, a separate cost of goods manufactured statement is prepared—and only the total cost of production is shown in

Figure B–2
Cost-of-goods-sold section of
an operating statement for a
manufacturing firm

Cost of goods sold			
Finished goods inventory (beginning)		$ 20,000	
Cost of goods manufactured (Schedule 1)		100,000	
Total cost of finished goods available for sale		$120,000	
Less: Finished goods inventory (ending)		30,000	
Cost of goods sold			$ 90,000

Schedule 1, Schedule of cost of goods manufactured			
Beginning work in process inventory			$ 15,000
Raw materials			
Beginning raw materials inventory		$ 10,000	
Net cost of delivered purchases		80,000	
Total cost of materials available for use		$ 90,000	
Less: Ending raw materials inventory		15,000	
Cost of materials placed in production		$ 75,000	
Direct labor		20,000	
Manufacturing expenses			
Indirect labor	$4,000		
Maintenance and repairs	3,000		
Factory supplies	1,000		
Heat, light, and power	2,000		
Total manufacturing expenses		10,000	
Total manufacturing costs			105,000
Total work in process during period			$120,000
Less: Ending work in process inventory			20,000
Cost of goods manufactured			$100,000

Note: The last item, cost of goods manufactured, is used in the operating statement to determine the cost of goods sold, as above.

the operating statement. See Figure B–2 for an illustration of the cost-of-goods-sold section of an operating statement for a manufacturing company.

"Expenses" go below the gross margin. They usually include the costs of selling, and administering the business. They do not include the cost of goods—either purchased or produced.

There is no "right" method for classifying the expense accounts or arranging them on the operating statement. They might just as easily have been arranged alphabetically—or according to amount, with the largest placed at the top, and so on down the line. In a business of any size, though, it is desirable to group the expenses in some way—and to use subtotals by groups for analysis and control purposes. This was done in Figure B–1.

The statement presented in Figure B–1 contains all the major categories in an operating statement—together with a normal amount of supporting detail. Further detail could be added to the statement under any of the major categories—without changing the nature of the statement. The amount of detail normally is determined by the use to which the statement will be put. A stockholder may be given a sketchy operating statement—while the one prepared for internal company use may have a great amount of detail.

We have already seen that eliminating some of the detail in Figure B–1 did not affect the essential elements of the statement—net sales, costs, and net profit. Whatever further detail is added to the statement, its purpose is to help the reader to see how these three figures were determined. A very detailed statement could easily run to several single-spaced pages—yet the nature of the operating statement would be the same.

COMPUTING THE STOCKTURN RATE

A detailed operating statement can provide the data needed to compute the stockturn rate—a measure of the number of times the average inventory is sold during a year. Note, the stockturn rate is related to the *turnover during a year*—not the length of time covered by a particular operating statement.

The stockturn rate is a very important measure—because it shows how rapidly the firm's inventory is moving. Some businesses typically have slower turnover than others—but a decrease in the rate of turnover in a particular business can be very alarming. For one thing, it may mean that the firm's assortment of products is no longer as attractive as it was. Also, it may mean that more working capital will be needed to handle the same volume of sales. Most businesses pay a lot of attention to the stockturn rate—trying to get faster turnover.

Three methods—all basically similar—can be used to compute the stockturn rate. Which method is used depends on the data which are available. These three methods are shown below and usually give approximately the same results.*

(1)
$$\frac{\text{Cost of goods sold}}{\text{Average inventory at cost}}$$

(2)
$$\frac{\text{Net sales}}{\text{Average inventory at selling price}}$$

(3)
$$\frac{\text{Sales in units}}{\text{Average inventory in units}}$$

Computing the stockturn rate will be illustrated only for Formula 1—since all are similar. The only difference is that the cost figures used in Formula 1 are changed to a selling price or numerical count basis in Formulas 2 and 3. It is necessary—regardless of the method used—to have both the numerator and denominator of the formula in the same terms.

Using Formula 1, the average inventory at cost is computed by adding the beginning and ending inventories at cost—and dividing by 2. This average inventory figure is then divided *into* the cost of goods sold (in cost terms) to get the stockturn rate.

For example, suppose that the cost of goods sold for one year was $100,000. Beginning inventory was $25,000 and ending inventory $15,000. Adding the two inventory figures and dividing by 2, we get an average inventory of $20,000. We next divide the cost of goods sold by the average inventory ($100,000 divided by $20,000) and get a stockturn rate of 5.

Further discussion of the use of the stockturn rate is found in Chapter 20.

---

* Differences will occur because of varied markups and non-homogeneous product assortments. In an assortment of tires, for example, those with high markups might have sold much better than those with small markups—but with Formula 3 all tires would be treated equally.

OPERATING RATIOS HELP ANALYZE THE BUSINESS

The operating statement is also used for a number of other purposes. In particular, many business people calculate operating ratios—the ratio of items on the operating statement to net sales—and compare these ratios from one time period to another. They can also compare their own operating ratios with those of competitors. Such competitive data is often available through trade associations. Each firm may report its results to the trade association—and then summary results are distributed to the members. These ratios help management to control their operations. If some expense ratios are rising, for example, those particular costs are singled out for special attention.

Operating ratios are computed by dividing net sales into the various operating statement items which appear below the net sales level in the statement. Net sales is used as the denominator in the operating ratio—because it is this figure with which the business manager is most concerned—that is, the revenue actually received by the business.

We can see the relation of operating ratios to the operating statement if we think of there being an additional column to the right of the dollar figures in an operating statement. This additional column would contain percentage figures—using net sales as 100 percent. This can be seen below:

Gross sales	$540.00	
Less: Returns and allowances	40.00	
Net sales	$500.00	100%
Cost of goods sold	350.00	70
Gross margin	$150.00	30%
Expenses	100.00	20
Net profit	$ 50.00	10%

The 30-percent ratio of gross margin to net sales in the above illustration shows that 30 percent of the net sales dollar is available to cover sales expenses and the administration of the business—and provide a profit. Note that the ratio of expenses to sales added to the ratio of profit to sales equals the 30-percent gross margin ratio. The net profit ratio of 10 percent shows that 10 percent of the net sales dollar is left for profit.

The usefulness of percentage ratios should be obvious. The percentages are easily figured—and much easier to work with than large dollar figures. With net sales as the base figure, they provide a useful means of comparison and control.

Note that because of the interrelationship of these various categories, only a few pieces of information are necessary to figure the others. In this case, for example, knowing the gross margin percent and net profit percent makes it possible to figure the expense and cost of goods sold percentages. Further, knowing a single dollar amount would let you figure all the other dollar amounts.

MARKUPS

A markup is the dollar amount added to the cost of goods to get the selling price. The markup is similar to the gross margin. Gross margin and the idea of markups are related because the amount added onto the unit cost of a product by a retailer or wholesaler is expected to cover the selling and administrative expenses—and to provide a profit.

The markup approach to pricing is discussed in Chapter 20—so it will not be discussed at length here. A simple example will illustrate the idea, however. If a retailer bought an article which cost $1 when delivered to his store, then obviously he must sell it for more than this cost if he hopes to make a profit. He might add 50 cents onto the cost of the article in order to cover his selling and other costs and, hopefully, to provide a profit. The 50 cents would be the markup.

It would also be the gross margin or gross profit on that item *if* it is sold— but note that it is *not* the net profit. His selling expenses might amount to 35 cents, 45 cents, or even 55 cents. In other words, there is no assurance that the markup will cover his costs. Further, there is no assurance that the customers will buy at the marked-up price. This may require markdowns—which are discussed later in this appendix.

Markup conversions

Sometimes it is convenient to talk in terms of markups on cost, while at other times markups on selling price are useful. To have some agreement, *markup* (without any explanation) will mean percentage of selling price. By this definition, the 50 cents markup on the $1.50 selling price is a markup of 33-⅓ percent.

Some retailers and wholesalers have developed markup conversion tables— so they can easily convert from cost to selling price—depending on the markup on selling price they want. To see the interrelation, look at the two formulas below. They can be used to convert either type of markup to the other.

(4) $$\text{Percentage markup on selling price} = \frac{\text{Percent markup on cost}}{100\% + \text{Percentage markup on cost}}$$

(5) $$\text{Percentage markup on cost} = \frac{\text{Percent markup on selling price}}{100\% - \text{Percentage markup on selling price}}$$

In the previous example, we had a cost of $1, a markup of 50 cents, and a selling price of $1.50. We saw that the markup on selling price was 33 ⅓ percent— and on cost, it was 50 percent. Let's substitute these percentage figures into Formulas 4 and 5 to see how to convert from one basis to the other. Assume first of all that we only know the markup on selling price, and want to convert to markup on cost. Using Formula 5 we obtain:

$$\text{Percentage markup on cost} = \frac{33\tfrac{1}{3}\%}{100\% - 33\tfrac{1}{3}\%} = \frac{33\tfrac{1}{3}}{66\tfrac{2}{3}} = 50\%$$

If we know, on the other hand, only the percentage markup on cost, we could convert to markup on selling price as follows:

$$\text{Percentage markup on selling price} = \frac{50\%}{100\% + 50\%} = \frac{50\%}{150\%} = 33\tfrac{1}{3}\%$$

These results can be proved and summarized as follows:

Markup $0.50 = 50%$ of cost, or $33\frac{1}{3}\%$ of selling price
plus Cost $1.00 = 100%$ of cost, or $66\frac{2}{3}\%$ of selling price
───
Selling price $1.50 = 150%$ of cost, or 100% of selling price

It is important to see that only the percentage figures changed—while the money amounts of cost, markup, and selling price stayed the same. Notice, too, that when selling price is the base for the computation (100 percent), then the cost percentage plus the markup percentage equal 100 percent. But when the cost of the product is used as the base figure (100 percent), it is obvious that the selling price percentage must be greater than 100 percent—by the markup on cost.

MARKDOWN RATIOS HELP CONTROL RETAIL OPERATIONS

The ratios we discussed above were concerned with figures on the operating statement. Another important ratio, the markdown ratio—is a tool used by many retailers to measure the efficiency of various departments and their whole business. But note—it is *not directly related to the operating statement*. It requires special calculations.

A markdown is a retail price reduction which is required because the customers will not buy some item at the originally marked-up price. This refusal to buy may be due to a variety of reasons—soiling, style changes, fading, damage caused by handling, or an original markup which was too high. To get rid of these products, the retailer offers them at a lower price.

Markdowns are generally considered to be due to "business errors"—perhaps because of poor buying, too high original markups, and other reasons. Regardless of the cause, however, markdowns are reductions in the original price—and are important to managers who want to measure the effectiveness of their operations.

Markdowns are similar to allowances—because price reductions are made. Thus, in computing a markdown ratio, markdowns and allowances are usually added together and then divided by net sales. The markdown ratio is computed as follows:

$$\text{Markdown \%} = \frac{\$ \text{ Markdowns} + \$ \text{ Allowances}}{\$ \text{ Net sales}} \times 100$$

The 100 is multiplied times the fraction to get rid of decimal points.

Returns are *not* included when figuring the markdown ratio. Returns are treated as "consumer errors"—not business errors—and therefore are *not* included in this measure of business efficiency.

Retailers who use markdown ratios keep a record of the amount of markdowns and allowances in each department—and then divide the total by the net sales in each department. Over a period of time, these ratios give management a measure of the efficiency of the buyers and salespersons in the various departments.

It should be stressed again that the markdown ratio is not calculated directly from data on the operating statement—since the markdowns take place before the products are sold. In fact, some products may be marked down and still not sold. Even if the marked-down items are not sold, the markdowns—that is, the reevaluations of their value—are included in the calculations in the time period when they are taken.

The markdown ratio is calculated for a whole department (or profit center)—*not* individual items. What we are seeking is a measure of the effectiveness of a whole department—not how well the department did on individual items.

RETURN ON INVESTMENT (ROI) REFLECTS ASSET USE

Another "off the operating statement" ratio is **return on investment (ROI)**—the ratio of net profit (after taxes) to the investment used to make the net profit—multiplied by 100 to get rid of decimals. "Investment" is not shown on the operating statement—but it would be on the **balance sheet** (statement of financial condition)—another accounting statement—which shows the assets, liabilities, and net worth of a company. It might take some "digging" or special analysis, however.

"Investment" means the dollar resources the firm has "invested" in a project or business. For example, a new product might require $400,000 in new money—for inventory, accounts receivable, promotion, and so on—and its attractiveness might be judged by its likely ROI. If the net profit (after taxes) for this new product was expected to be $100,000 in the first year, then the ROI would be 25%—that is ($100,000 ÷ $400,000) × 100.

There are two ways to figure ROI. The *direct* way is:

$$\text{ROI (in \%)} = \frac{\text{Net profit (after taxes)}}{\text{Investment}} \times 100$$

The *indirect* way is:

$$\text{ROI (in \%)} = \frac{\text{Net profit (after taxes)}}{\text{Sales}} \times \frac{\text{Sales}}{\text{Investment}} \times 100$$

This way is concerned with net profit margin and turnover—that is:

$$\text{ROI (in \%)} = \text{Net profit margin} \times \text{Turnover} \times 100$$

This indirect way makes it clearer how to *increase* ROI. There are three ways:

1. Increase profit margin.
2. Increase sales.
3. Decrease investment.

Effective marketing strategy planning and implementation are ways of increasing profit margin and/or sales. And careful asset management can decrease investment.

ROI is a revealing measure of managerial effectiveness. Most companies have alternative uses for their funds. If the returns in the business aren't at least as high as outside uses, then the money probably should be shifted to the more profitable uses. Further, many companies must borrow to finance some of their operation. So the ROI should be higher than the cost of money—or the company should cut back until it can operate more profitably.

Some firms borrow more than others to make "investments." In other words, they invest less of their own money to acquire assets—what we have called "investments." If ROI calculations use only the firm's own "investment," this gives higher ROI figures to those who borrow a lot—which is called leveraging. To adjust for different borrowing proportions—to make comparisons among projects, departments, divisions, and companies easier—another ratio (ROA) has come into use. **Return on assets (ROA)** is the ratio of net profit (after taxes) to the assets used to make the net profit—times 100.

Both ROI and ROA measures are trying to get at the same thing—how effectively is the company using resources. These measures have become increasingly popular recently—as profit rates have dropped and it becomes more obvious that increasing sales does not necessarily lead to higher profits—or ROI—or ROA. Further, inflation and higher costs for borrowed funds force more concern for ROI and ROA. Marketers must include these measures in their thinking—or top managers are likely to ignore their plans and requests for financial resources.

QUESTIONS AND PROBLEMS

1. Distinguish between the following pairs of items which appear on operating statements:

   a. Gross sales and net sales.
   b. Purchases at billed cost and purchases at net cost.
   c. Cost of goods available for sale and cost of goods sold.

2. How does gross margin differ from gross profit? From net profit?

3. Explain the similarity between markups and gross margin. What connection do markdowns have with the operating statement?

4. Compute the net profit for a company with the following data:

Beginning inventory (cost)	$ 15,000
Purchases at billed cost	33,000
Sales returns and allowances	25,000
Rent	6,000
Salaries	40,000
Heat and light	18,000
Ending inventory (cost)	25,000
Freight cost (inbound)	9,000
Gross sales	130,000

5. Construct an operating statement from the following data:

Returns and allowances	$ 15,000
Expenses	20%
Closing inventory at cost	60,000

Markdowns	2%
Inward transportation	3,000
Purchases	100,000
Net profit (5%)	30,000

6. Data given:

Markdowns	$ 10,000
Gross sales	100,000
Returns	8,000
Allowances	12,000

Compute net sales and percent of markdowns.

7. (a) What percentage markups on cost are equivalent to the following percentage markups on selling price: 20, 37½, 50, and 66⅔ (b) What percentage markups on selling price are equivalent to the following percentage markups on cost: 33⅓, 20, 40, and 50?

8. What net sales volume is required to secure a stockturn rate of 20 times a year on an average inventory at cost of $100,000, with a gross margin of 30 percent?

9. Explain how the general manager of a department store might use the markdown ratios computed for his various departments? Would this be a fair measure? Of what?

10. Compare and contrast return on investment (ROI) and return on assets (ROA) measures. Which would be best for a retailer with no bank borrowing or other outside sources of funds, i.e., the retailer has put up all the money that is needed in the business?

H. Armstrong Roberts

When you finish this chapter, you should:

1. Understand how most wholesalers and retailers set their prices—using markups.

2. Understand why turnover is so important in pricing.

3. Understand the advantages and disadvantages of average cost pricing.

4. Know how to use break-even analysis to evaluate possible prices.

5. Know how to find the most profitable price and quantity—using marginal analysis, and total revenue and total cost.

6. Know the many ways that price setters use demand estimates in their pricing.

7. Recognize the important new terms (shown in red).

20

Price setting in the real world

"How should I price this product?" is a common problem facing marketing managers.

In the last chapter, we accepted the idea of a list price and went on to discuss variations from this list price. Now, we will see how the basic list price might be set in the first place. In practice, there are many ways of arriving at the list price. But these can be reduced—for simplicity—to two basic methods: *cost-oriented* and *demand-oriented* price setting.

Cost-oriented pricing is typical in business. We will see, however, that cost-oriented pricing is not as easy or foolproof as some people think. Ideally, a marketing manager should consider potential customers' demand as well as his own costs when setting prices. But let's begin by looking at how most firms—including wholesalers and retailers—set cost-oriented prices.

PRICING BY WHOLESALERS AND RETAILERS

Why use traditional markups?

Most retail and wholesale prices are set by using the markups which are commonly used in a particular line of business. A markup is the dollar amount added to the cost of goods to get the selling price. For example, retailers usually add a markup to their cost of goods to get their own selling price.

The markup is usually large enough to cover the middleman's operating expenses—and to provide some profit. It is usually the same as the trade (functional) discount which was allowed for by the manufacturer in the suggested list price. So, these traditional markups are often applied automatically. Some middlemen, in fact, use the same markup for all of their goods. This makes pricing easier for them!

When you think of the large number of items the average retailer and wholesaler carries—and the small sales volume of any one item—this cost-oriented approach makes sense. Spending the time to find the "best" price to charge on every item in stock (day-to-day or week-to week) probably wouldn't pay.

Should you mark up on cost or selling price?

Suppose that a retailer buys an article for $1. To make a profit, the retailer obviously must sell this article for more than $1. If the retailer adds 50 cents to cover operating expenses and provide a profit—we say that he is marking up the item 50 cents.

Markups, however, usually are stated as percentages rather than dollar amounts. And this is where the difficulty begins. Is a markup of 50 cents on a cost of $1 a markup of 50 percent? Or should the markup be figured as a percentage of the selling price—$1.50—and therefore be 33⅓ percent? A clear definition is necessary.

Markup on selling price—is a convenient rule

Unless otherwise stated, markup (percent) *means percentage of selling price* which is added to the cost to get the selling price. So, the 50-cent markup on the $1.50 selling price is a markup of 33⅓ percent.

Markups are related to selling price for convenience. For one thing, the markup on selling price is roughly equal to the gross margin (and the trade discount). Most business managers understand the idea of gross margin. They always see gross margin data on their profit and loss statements. (See Appendix B on Marketing Arithmetic—it follows Chapter 19—if you are unfamiliar with these ideas.) They know that unless there is a large enough gross margin, there won't be any profit. For this reason, they accept traditional markups that are close to their usual gross margins.

There is nothing wrong, however, with the idea of markup on cost. The important thing is to state clearly which markup we are using—to avoid confusion.

Retailers often need to change a markup on cost to one based on selling price—or vice versa. Conversion tables are available for this purpose. But they aren't necessary—because the calculations are simple. (See the section on "Markup Conversion" in Appendix B on Marketing Arithmetic.)

Markup chain may be used in channel pricing

A markup chain can set the price structure in a whole channel. A markup is figured on the *selling price* at each level of the channel. The producer's selling price becomes the wholesaler's cost—the wholesaler's selling price becomes the retailer's cost—and this cost plus a retail markup becomes the retail selling price. Each markup should cover the costs of selling, running the business—and leave a profit. Figure 20–1 shows how a markup might be used at each level of a channel system.

Figure 20–1 starts with a production cost (factory cost) of $21.60. In this case, the producer is taking a 10-percent markup and sells the goods for $24. The markup is 10 percent of $24 or $2.40. The producer's selling price now becomes the wholesaler's cost—$24. If the wholesaler is used to taking a 20-

Figure 20–1
Example of a markup chain and channel pricing

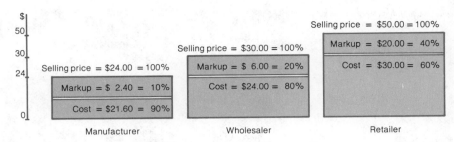

percent markup on selling price, the markup is $6—and the selling price becomes $30. The wholesaler's selling price of $30 now becomes the retailer's cost. And if the retailer is used to a 40 percent markup, he adds $20 and the retail selling price becomes $50.

High markups don't always mean big profits

Some people—including many retailers—link high markups with high profits. But this often is not true. Some kinds of business just have high operating expenses and need high markups. In other cases, high markups may lower sales and lead to low profits—or even losses.

The problem with trying to get high profits with high markups can be seen by an extreme example. A 90-percent markup on selling price may not be nearly as profitable as a 10-percent markup on selling price! This is easy to understand if we assume that *no* units are sold at the high markup, but a very large number are sold at the low one. The key is "turnover." You can't earn much if you don't sell much—no matter how high your markup. But many retailers and wholesalers seem more concerned with the size of their markup than total profit.

Lower markups can speed turnover—and the stockturn rate

Some retailers and wholesalers, however, are trying to speed turnover to increase profit—even if this means reducing the markup. They see themselves in a business that is running up costs over time. If they can sell a much greater amount in the same time period, they may be able to take a lower markup—and still have a higher profit at the end of the period.

An important idea here is the **stockturn rate**—the number of times the average inventory is sold in a year. Various methods of figuring stockturn rates are used—but they all measure how many times the average inventory is sold in a year. (See the section "Computing the Stockturn Rate" in Appendix B.) If the stockturn rate is low, this may be bad for profits.

At the very least, a low stockturn will increase cost by tying up working capital. If the stockturn were 1 (once per year) instead of 5, selling goods costing $100,000 would require $100,000 rather than $20,000 in working capital—just to carry the needed inventory.

Whether stockturn is high or low depends on the industry. An annual rate of 1 or 2 might be expected in the retail jewelry industry—while 40 to 50 would be typical for fresh fruits and vegetables.

Grocers run in fast company

Supermarket operators know the importance of fast turnover. They put low markups on fast-selling items like sugar, shortening, soaps, detergents, canned

Mary McCarthy

milk, soups, desserts, beverages, baby foods, pet foods, bleaches, flour, and canned vegetables. Sugar, for example, may carry a markup of 8 percent; shortening, 9 to 10 percent, soaps and detergents, 10 to 11 percent.

Since supermarket operating expenses are 16–20 percent of sales, it looks like many of these items are carried at a loss! But since such figures are store-wide averages, this need not be true.

Fast-moving goods usually are less expensive to stock and sell. They take up valuable space for shorter periods, are damaged less, and tie up less working capital. Lower markups will cover the costs of these items and make a profit too. With lower markups, the goods may sell even faster—and a small profit per unit will be earned more often.

These fast-moving goods may be more profitable per item—in spite of the low margins—because of the higher turnover. The average turnover in one study was 14 times a year. Yet sugar turned over 31 times, beverages 28 times, shortening 23 times, and soups 21 times.

Note that the high-margin items were not all unprofitable. They simply were not as profitable *per item* as some of the low-margin items.[1]

Discounters are running faster

The modern food discounter and mass merchandisers carry the fast turnover idea of the supermarket even further. By pricing food even lower—and attracting customers from wider areas who purchase in large quantities—they are able to operate profitably on even smaller margins.

PRICING BY PRODUCERS

It's up to the producer to set the list price

Some markups eventually become customary in a trade. Most of the channel members will tend to follow a similar process—adding a certain percentage to the previous price. Who sets price in the first place?

The basic list price usually is decided by the producer and/or brander of the product—a large retailer, a large wholesaler, or most often, the producer. Now, we'll look at the pricing approaches of such firms. For convenience, we will call them "producers."

Customary formulas are common

Producers commonly use a cost-oriented approach. They may start with a dollar-cost-per-unit figure and add a markup—perhaps a customary percentage—to obtain the selling price. Or they may use a rule-of-thumb formula such as: *Production cost* × 3 = *Selling price.*

Each producer usually develops rules and markups in the light of its own costs and objectives. Yet even the first step of selecting the appropriate cost per unit to build on isn't easy. Let's discuss several approaches to see how cost-oriented price setting really works.

AVERAGE-COST PRICING IS COMMON AND DANGEROUS

Average-cost pricing consists of adding a "reasonable" markup to the average cost of a product. The average cost per unit is usually found by studying past records. The total cost for the last year is divided by all the units produced and sold in that period to get the average cost per unit. If the total cost were $5,000 for labor and materials and $5,000 for fixed overhead expenses—such as selling expenses, rent, and manager salaries—then total cost would be $10,000. If the company produced 10,000 items in that time period, the average cost would be $1 per unit. To get the price, the producer would decide how

Figure 20–2
Results of average-cost pricing

Calculation of planned profit if 10,000 items are sold		Calculation of actual profit if only 5,000 items are sold	
Calculation of costs:		Calculation of costs:	
Fixed overhead expenses	$ 5,000	Fixed overhead expenses	$5,000
Labor and materials	5,000	Labor and materials	2,500
Total costs	$10,000	Total costs	$7,500
"Reasonable" profit	1,000		
Total costs and planned profit	$11,000		

Calculation of "reasonable" price for both possibilities:

$$\frac{\text{Total costs and planned profit}}{\text{Planned number of items to be sold}} = \frac{\$11,000}{10,000} = \$1.10 = \text{``Reasonable'' price}$$

Calculation of profit or (loss):		Calculation of profit or (loss):	
Actual unit sales (10,000) times price		Actual unit sales (5,000) times price	
($1.10) =	$11,000	($1.10) =	$5,500
Minus: Total costs	10,000	Minus: Total costs	7,500
Profit (loss)	$ 1,000	Profit (loss)	($2,000)
Therefore: Planned ("reasonable") profit of $1,000 is earned if 10,000 items are sold at $1.10 each.		Therefore: Planned ("reasonable") profit of $1,000 is not earned. Instead, $2,000 loss results if 5,000 items are sold at $1.10 each.	

Figure 20–3
Typical shape of average cost
curve

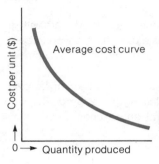

much profit per unit seems "reasonable." This would be added to the cost per unit. If 10 cents were considered a reasonable profit for each unit, then the new price would be set at $1.10. See Figure 20–2.

It does not make allowances for cost variations as output changes

This approach is simple. But it also can be dangerous. It's easy to lose money with average-cost pricing. To see why, let's follow this example further.

If, in the next year, only 5,000 units are produced and sold, the firm may be in trouble. Five thousand units sold at $1.10 each would yield a total revenue of $5,500. The overhead would still be fixed at $5,000. And the variable material and labor cost would drop in half to $2,500—for a total of $7,500. This would mean a loss of $2,000 or 40 cents a unit. The method that was supposed to allow a profit of 10 cents a unit actually causes a loss of 40 cents a unit! See Figure 20–2.

The basic problem is that this method did not allow for cost variations at different levels of output. In a typical situation, average costs per unit are high when only a few units are produced. Average costs continually drop as the quantity produced increases. This is shown in Figure 20–3. This typical decline in the average cost curve occurs because of *economies of scale*. This is why mass production and mass distribution often make sense. And this behavior of cost must be considered when setting prices.

MARKETING MANAGER MUST CONSIDER VARIOUS KINDS OF COST

Average-cost pricing may fail because total cost includes a variety of costs. And each of these costs changes in a different way as output changes. Any pricing method that uses cost must consider these changes. To understand why, however, we need to define *six types of costs*. Differences among these costs help explain why many companies have problems with pricing.

There are three kinds of total cost

1. **Total fixed cost** is the sum of those costs that are fixed in total—no matter how much is produced. Among these fixed costs are rent, depreciation,

Fixed costs still have to be covered even though nothing is being produced.

Mike Voss

managers' salaries, property taxes, and insurance. Such costs must be paid even if production stops temporarily.

2. **Total variable cost,** on the other hand, is the sum of those changing expenses that are closely related to output—expenses for parts, wages, packaging, materials, outgoing freight, and sales commissions.

At zero output, total variable cost is zero. As output increases, so do variable costs. If a dress manufacturer doubles the output of dresses in a year, the total cost of cloth would also (roughly) double.

3. **Total cost** is the sum of total fixed and total variable costs. The growth of total cost depends upon the increase in total variable cost—since total fixed cost is already fixed.

There are three kinds of average cost

The pricing manager usually is more interested in cost per unit than total cost—because prices are usually quoted per unit. Costs per unit are called "average costs."

1. **Average cost** is obtained by dividing total cost by the related quantity (that is, the total quantity which causes the total cost). See Table 20–1.
2. **Average fixed cost** is obtained by dividing total fixed cost by the related quantity. See Table 20–1.
3. **Average variable cost** is obtained by dividing total variable cost by the related quantity. See Table 20–1.

An example illustrates cost relations

Table 20–1 shows typical cost data for one firm. Here we assume that average variable cost is the same for each unit. Notice how average fixed cost goes down steadily as the quantity increases. Notice also how total variable cost increases when quantity increases, although the average variable cost remains the same. Average cost decreases continually too. This is because average varia-

Table 20–1
Cost structure of a firm

Quantity (Q)	Total fixed costs (TFC)	Average fixed costs (AFC)	Average variable costs (AVC)	Total variable costs (TVC)	Total cost (TC)	Average cost (AC)
0	$30,000	—	—	—	$ 30,000	—
10,000	30,000	$3.00	$0.80	$ 8,000	38,000	$3.80
20,000	30,000	1.50	0.80	16,000	46,000	2.30
30,000	30,000	1.00	0.80	24,000	54,000	1.80
40,000	30,000	0.75	0.80	32,000	62,000	1.51
50,000	30,000	0.60	0.80	40,000	70,000	1.40
60,000	30,000	0.50	0.80	48,000	78,000	1.30
70,000	30,000	0.43	0.80	56,000	86,000	1.23
80,000	30,000	0.38	0.80	64,000	94,000	1.18
90,000	30,000	0.33	0.80	72,000	102,000	1.13
100,000	30,000	0.30	0.80	80,000	110,000	1.10

$$\begin{bmatrix} 110,000 \text{ (TC)} \\ -80,000 \text{ (TVC)} \\ \hline 30,000 \text{ (TFC)} \end{bmatrix} \quad (Q)\,100,000\,\overline{\begin{vmatrix}0.30 \text{ (AFC)} \\ 30,000 \text{ (TFC)}\end{vmatrix}} \quad \begin{bmatrix} 100,000 \text{ (Q)} \\ \times 0.80 \text{ (AVC)} \\ \hline 80,000 \text{ (TVC)} \end{bmatrix} \quad \begin{bmatrix} 30,000 \text{ (TFC)} \\ +80,000 \text{ (TVC)} \\ \hline 110,000 \text{ (TC)} \end{bmatrix} \quad (Q)\,100,000\,\overline{\begin{vmatrix}1.10 \text{ (AC)} \\ 110,000 \text{ (TC)}\end{vmatrix}}$$

Figure 20–4
Typical shape of cost (per unit) curves when AVC is assumed constant per unit

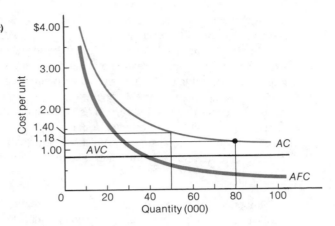

ble cost is the same and average fixed cost is decreasing. Figure 20–4 graphs the three average-cost curves.

Ignoring demand is major weakness of average-cost pricing

Average-cost pricing works well if the firm actually sells the quantity which was used in setting the average cost price. Losses may result, however, if actual sales are *much lower* than were expected. On the other hand, if sales are much higher than expected, then profits may be very good. But this will only be by accident—that is, because the firm's demand is much larger than expected.

To use average-cost pricing, a marketing manager must make *some* estimate of the quantity to be sold in the coming period. But unless this quantity is related to price—that is, unless the firm's demand curve is considered—the marketing manager may set a price that doesn't even cover a firm's total cost! This can be seen in a simple illustration for a firm with the cost curves shown in Figure 20–4. This firm's demand curve is shown in Figure 20–5. It is important to see that customers' demands (and their demand curve) are still important—whether management takes time to analyze the demand curve or not.

Figure 20–5
Evaluation of various prices along a firm's demand curve

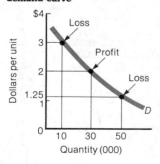

In this example, whether management sets the price at a high $3 or a low $1.25, it will have a loss. At $3, only 10,000 units will be sold for a total revenue of $30,000. But total cost will be $38,000—for a loss of $8,000. At the $1.25 price, 50,000 units will be sold—for a loss of $7,500. If management tried to estimate the demand curve—however roughly—the price probably would be set in the middle of the range—say at $2—where a profit of $6,000 would be earned. See Figure 20–5.

In short, average-cost pricing is simple in theory—but often fails in practice. In stable situations, prices set by this method may yield profits—but not necessarily maximum profits. And note that such cost-based prices might be higher than a price that would be more profitable for the firm—as shown in Figure 20–5. When demand conditions are changing, average-cost pricing may be even more risky.

Experience curve pricing is even riskier

In recent years, some aggressive marketers—including Texas Instruments—have used a variation of average-cost pricing—called experience curve pricing. **Experience curve pricing** is average-cost pricing using an estimate of future average costs. This approach to pricing grew out of the electronics industry—where added experience with greater quantities led to substantially lower costs—year after year. In a bid to increase market share—and beat out competition—some aggressive marketers set average-cost prices where they expected costs to be when the products were actually produced—rather than where they were at the time the strategy was set. As long as costs continue to drop, this approach works fairly well—but it has the same deficiency of regular average-cost pricing—unless demand is included in the price setting. At the least, this means that the price-setter would have to estimate what quantity will be sold—to be able to read off the "right" experience curve price.[2]

THE TARGET RETURN METHOD

Target return pricing scores . . . sometimes

Target return pricing—adding a "target return" to the cost of a product—has become popular in recent years. With this approach, the price setter seeks to obtain (1) a percentage return (say 10 percent per year) on the investment or (2) a specific total dollar return.

The method is basically the same as the average-cost method—since the desired target return is added into total cost. An example illustrates the method: 12,000 units were sold last year. And it is hoped the same quantity will be sold this year. Manager salaries, general administrative overhead, and other fixed expenses total $600,000. Total investment is $300,000. The target return is a 10 percent return on this investment—$30,000.

Therefore . . . *total fixed cost*—including the 10 percent target return—is $630,000.

This total, divided by 12,000 units, yields a fixed cost and target return per unit figure of $52.50. If the variable cost per unit is $40, the price that apparently should be set to bring a 10-percent return on investment is $92.50—that is, $52.50 plus $40.00 = $92.50.

This approach suffers from the same problem of average-cost pricing. If the quantity that actually is sold (in the relevant time period) is less than the quantity used in setting the price, then the target return is not earned—even though it seems to be part of the price structure. To see more clearly how this happens, look at the results when either 10,000 or 20,000 units are sold (see Table 20–2).

Table 20–2
Results of target return pricing

	10,000 units sold		20,000 units sold	
Total revenue		$ 925,000		$1,850,000
Total cost				
Total fixed cost	$600,000		$600,000	
Total variable cost	400,000		800,000	
		1,000,000		1,400,000
Profit (loss)		($75,000)		$ 450,000
Return on investment $\left\{\frac{-75,000}{300,000}\right\} = -25\%$			$\left\{\frac{450,000}{300,000}\right\} = 150\%$	

If only 10,000 units are sold, there is a 25 percent *loss* on investment instead of a 10-percent return. If 20,000 units are sold, there is a 150-percent return on investment—instead of only a 10-percent target return. Target return pricing clearly does not guarantee that the target will be hit.

THE LONG-RUN TARGET RETURN METHOD

Hitting the target in the long run

Managers in some larger firms—wanting to achieve a long-run target return objective—have used another cost-oriented pricing approach—*long-run* target return pricing. Instead of estimating the quantity they expect to produce in any one year, they assume that during several years' time their plants will produce at, say, 80 percent of capacity. They use that quantity in their pricing.

No reference at all is made to current demand when setting current prices. Demand was estimated when the plant was built. Some demand and cost factors had to be considered at that time. In fact, it was the decision to build a plant of a certain size that determines subsequent long-run target return prices.

Companies taking this longer-run view assume that there will be recession years when sales drop below 80 percent of capacity. Then, the target return won't be earned. But there will also be other years when the plant operates at a higher level and betters the target return. Over the long run, they expect that the target return will be achieved.

This long-run approach to target return pricing sounds simple. But like pricing in general, it cannot be used mechanically. For example, "capacity" is a rather flexible concept—perhaps referring to a five-day, single-shift operation or to a seven-day, three-shift operation. So, long-run target return pricing need not lead to a unique price or a stable price. Typically, however, companies using long-run target return pricing tend to have more stable prices.

BREAK-EVEN ANALYSIS CAN EVALUATE POSSIBLE PRICES

Some price setters use break-even analysis to bring likely revenue (and perhaps demand) into pricing. They already know their costs fairly well. Now they are concerned with what price to set. Perhaps they are trying to decide among several prices which are somewhere close to competition.

Break-even analysis analyzes whether the firm would be able to break even—that is, cover all its costs—with a particular price. This is important, because a business firm must cover all costs in the long run—or there is not much point to being in business. This method focuses on the **break-even point (BEP)**—the quantity where the firm's total costs will just equal its total revenue (that is, total sales.)

Break-even charts help find the BEP

Break-even analysis usually uses charts with straight-line total cost and total revenue curves. One line shows the total revenue which would be received when various quantities of units are sold at *an (one) assumed price*. This total revenue curve intersects the total cost curve (also a straight line) to show the break-even point (BEP)—where the company would break even. The BEP is the quantity at which total revenue and total cost are equal. Beyond this, if more units are

Figure 20–6
Break-even chart for a
particular situation

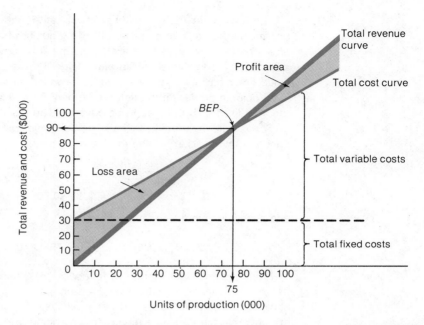

sold, the company will begin to make a profit on each unit. Below the BEP, the company will have a loss. Figure 20–6 is a break-even chart and shows these profit and loss areas.

Each price has its own break-even point

To consider several alternative prices—and break-even points—a chart can be made for each assumed price. The marketing manager can then evaluate each chart and consider how customers may respond to price. If the break-even quantity for a particular price is very low, that assumed price may be too high. Clearly, likely demand must be considered by managers when they are studying alternative prices.

Break-even analysis can be very useful if used properly. The big question is: Will break-even analysis help find the right price? Before answering this question, let us look at the details of break-even analysis.

How to compute a break-even point

In most break-even analysis, we make a few simplifying assumptions to speed the analysis. First, we assume that any quantity can be sold at the same price. This permits us to draw a straight-line total revenue curve. Similarly, we assume that average variable cost *(AVC)* is the same per unit. Graphing the total revenue and total cost (*TFC* plus *TVC*) lines will yield the *BEP*—at the intersection of the two lines.

Finding the break-even point in units

The BEP may be computed in terms of units or dollar value of units. In units, the BEP can be found by using the following formula:

$$BEP \text{ (in units)} = \frac{TFC}{FC \text{ contribution per unit}}$$

The **fixed-cost** *(FC)* **contribution per unit** is the assumed selling price per unit minus the variable cost per unit. This number is used here because if we are to break even, then total fixed costs must be covered. Therefore, we must calculate the contribution which each unit will make to coverning the total fixed costs (after paying for the variable costs which must be covered first or there is no point in producing the item), and then divide this per-unit contribution into the total fixed cost that has to be covered. The result is the *BEP* (in units).

To illustrate the formula, let's use the following cost data and assume a selling price per unit of $1.20. Using the following data:

$$
\begin{array}{lr}
\text{Total fixed cost} & = \$30,000 \\
\text{Variable cost per unit} & = \$0.80 \\
FC \text{ contribution } (\$1.20 - \$0.80) = & \$0.40
\end{array}
$$

and substituting in the formula:

$$BEP = \frac{30,000}{0.40} = 75,000 \text{ units}$$

From this it is clear that if this firm sells 75,000 units, it will exactly cover all its fixed and variable costs. If even one more unit is sold, then it will begin to show a profit—in this case, 40 cents per unit. Note that once the fixed costs are covered, the part of revenue formerly going to cover fixed costs is now all profit.

Finding the break-even point in dollars*

The BEP can also be figured in dollars:

$$BEP \text{ (in dollars)} = \frac{TFC}{1 - \dfrac{VC/\text{Unit}}{\text{Selling price}/\text{Unit}}}$$

Using the figures above, we obtain:

$$\frac{\$30,000}{1 - \dfrac{\$0.80}{\$1.20}} = \$90,000$$

To check our result, we can multiply the selling price ($1.20) times the BEP in units (75,000): $1.20 times 75,000 equals $90,000—the BEP in dollars.

Break-even analysis is helpful—but not a pricing solution

The results of the above analyses are graphed in Figure 20–6. The definiteness of this graph—and the ease with which it is understood by cost-oriented managers—have made it popular. But it is too often misunderstood. The fact that a

---

* Students familiar with algebra may find the following approach more meaningful—where x equals *BEP* in quantity, and we solve for the intersection of the *TR* and *TC* lines.

$$
\begin{array}{rl}
(\text{Price}) \ (x) = & TFC + VC(x) \\
1.20x = & 30,000 + 0.80x \\
0.40x = & 30,000 \\
x = & 75,000 \text{ units}
\end{array}
$$

and $1.20 (75,000) = $90,000, or *BEP* in dollars.

price is *assumed* is often forgotten. And the "Alice in Wonderland" quality of the ever-widening profit area is ignored. It is just too tempting to production-oriented managers—who think of economies of scale and want to increase output.

Although the graph—with its straight-line total revenue curve—makes it seem that any quantity might be sold at the assumed price, this usually is not true. *It is the same as assuming a perfectly horizontal demand curve at that price.* In fact, most managers must work with down-sloping demand situations. And their total revenue curves *do not* keep going up—see the next section.

Break-even analysis can be useful for comparing pricing alternatives—providing managers with alternative break-even points to consider against market reality. Break-even analysis is especially useful for quickly eliminating obviously ridiculous pricing alternatives. But for really zeroing in on the most profitable price, marketers would be better off trying to estimate the demand curve more explicitly—and then using "marginal analysis," which is discussed next.

TRADITIONAL DEMAND AND SUPPLY ANALYSIS SHOWS HOW TO MAXIMIZE PROFITS

Most demand curves are down-sloping and most supply curves are upsloping. The intersection of these demand and supply curves would seem to determine price—and, therefore, take care of demand-oriented pricing. Unfortunately, reality is not quite that simple. Although such analysis may be suitable for whole industries, some refinements are necessary when applying it to an individual firm seeking to maximize profits.

We are seeking the biggest profit

In the following pages, we will discuss these refinements—concentrating on price setting in the large majority of situations in which demand curves are down-sloping—that is, in monopolistic competition situations. In these situations, the firm has carved out a little market for itself and does have a pricing decision to make. By contrast, in pure or nearly pure competition, marketing managers have

A manager should know that the price which is set will affect the quantities that will be sold.

Brent Jones

little difficulty with the pricing decision. They simply use the market price. The special case of oligopoly will be treated later in the chapter.

Our discussion will focus on how to *maximize* profits—not just to seek *some* profits. This has been the traditional approach of economic analysis. And it is a reasonable one. If you know how to make the biggest profit, you can always adjust to pursue other objectives—while knowing how much profit you are giving up!

*Marginal analysis—
helps find the one best
price*

In monopolistic competition, marketing managers face a down-sloping demand curve. They must pick a price on that curve—and generally must offer that price to all potential buyers (to avoid price discrimination under the Robinson-Patman Act). Therefore, they should consider the effect on total revenue of the alternative prices being considered.

If a lower price is chosen, the demand curve shows that additional units will be sold. But *all* customers would be offered this lower price—and the impact on total revenue should be calculated. Or, if a higher price is chosen, less will be sold. What will be the impact on revenue—both total and marginal? The important point to see here is that the marketing manager usually does *not* have the choice of selling individual items at different prices. Instead he must make one decision about price and quantity—and then live with it for the length of the plan.

Marginal analysis can help one make the best pricing decision. Marginal analysis *focuses on the last unit which would be sold and equates marginal revenue and marginal cost to find the most profitable price and quantity*. This is a very useful—but technical—idea. It is treated more fully in the next several pages. Be sure to study the tables and figures.

*Marginal revenue helps
decide—can be negative*

Marginal revenue *is the change in total revenue which results from the sale of one additional unit of product*. Since the firm's demand curve is down-sloping, this extra unit can be sold only by reducing the price of *all* items.

Table 20–3 shows the relationship between price, quantity, total revenue, and marginal revenue in a situation with a straight-line down-sloping demand curve.

If four units could be sold for a total revenue of $420 and five units for $460,

**Table 20–3
Marginal revenue and price**

(1) Quantity q	(2) Price p	(3) Total revenue (1) × (2) = TR	(4) Marginal revenue MR
0	$150	$ 0	
1	140	140	$140
2	130	260	120
3	117	351	91
4	105	420	69
5	92	460	40
6	79	474	14
7	66	462	−12
8	53	424	−38
9	42	378	−46
10	31	310	−68

Figure 20-7
A plotting of the demand and marginal revenue data in Table 20-3

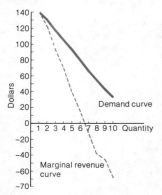

Marginal cost is needed, too

then marginal revenue for the fifth unit is $40. Considering only revenue, it would be desirable to sell this extra unit. But would this continue if more units were sold at lower prices? No! Table 20-3 shows that negative marginal revenues occur at lower price levels. Obviously, this would not be an attractive area for the firm! (Note: the *total* revenue that would be obtained if price were cut might still be positive, but the *marginal* revenue—the *extra* revenue gained—*might be positive or negative.*)

Marginal revenue curve and demand curve are different

The marginal revenue curve is always below a down-sloping demand curve because the price of each "last unit" must be lower to sell more. This can be seen in Figure 20-7—where the data in Table 20-3 is plotted. The fact that the demand curve and the marginal revenue curves are different in monpolistic competition is quite significant. We will use both of them when finding the best price and quantity.†

As we have already seen, various kinds of costs behave differently. Further, there is an important kind of cost which is similar to marginal revenue: marginal cost. This cost is vital to marginal analysis.

Marginal cost *is the change in total cost that results from producing an extra unit.* If it costs $275 to produce nine units of a product and $280 to produce ten units, then marginal cost is $5 for the tenth unit. In other words, marginal cost contrasted to average cost per unit is the additional cost of producing one more *specific unit,* while average cost is the average for *all units.*

Cost structure example

Table 20-4 shows how these costs could vary for a typical firm. *You should fill in the missing numbers on this table.* Notice that variable cost no longer is assumed constant per unit in Table 20-4. Here, we use the more realistic assumption that variable costs will go down for a while and then rise.

In Table 20-4, several important points should be noted. *First,* total fixed costs do not change over the entire range of output—but total variable costs increase continually, as more and more units are produced. It is obvious, then, that total costs—the sum of total fixed costs and total variable costs—will increase as total quantity increases.

Second, average costs will decrease over most of the range of production—since average costs are the sum of average fixed costs and average variable costs, and total fixed costs are divided by more and more units as output increases.

---

† The data for drawing a marginal revenue curve always can be derived by calculating changes in the total revenue curve, but a simple graphical shortcut is available if straight-line demand curves are being used. Although the demand curve within the relevant range normally may not extend all the way to the horizontal and vertical axes, it can be extended to these axes. The marginal revenue curve is then obtained by drawing a line running from the intersection of the demand curve with the vertical (price) axis down to the point on the quantity axis bisecting the segment from 0 to the point where the demand curve extension intersects that axis. This marginal revenue curve also can be extended below the quantity axis—to obtain the negative marginal revenue values. The only relevant part of the marginal revenue curve is that part directly below the relevant range of the demand curve. When working with curved demand curves, tangents to the curve can be drawn at several places to obtain the general shape of the *MR* curve. Readers familiar with calculus probably will recognize that the marginal revenue curve is simply the derivative of the total revenue curve, and they can use this approach in finding the marginal revenue curve.

Table 20–4
Cost structure for individual firm

(1) Quantity Q	(2) Total fixed cost TFC	(3) Average fixed cost AFC	(4) Total variable cost TVC	(5) Average variable cost AVC	(6) Total cost (TFC+TVC=TC) TC	(7) Average cost (AC=TC÷Q) AC	(8) Marginal cost (per unit) MC
0	$200	$ 0	$ 0	$ 0	$200	Infinity	
1	200	200	96	96	296	$296	$ 96
2	200	100	116	58	316		20
3	200				331	110.33	
4	200	50			344		
5	200	40	155	31		71	11
6	200		168			61.33	13
7			183				15
8			223				
9			307		507	56.33	
10		20	510	51	710	71	203

For example—given a total fixed cost of $200—at a production level of four units, the average fixed cost is $50. At a production level of five units, the average fixed cost is $40.

Third, average costs in this table start rising for the last two units—because average variable costs have been increasing faster than average fixed costs have been decreasing. The firm may have been forced to use less efficient facilities and workers, to go into overtime work, or to pay higher prices for the materials it needed. This turn-up of the average cost curve is common—after the economies of scale run out.

The marginal cost of just one more is important

The *marginal cost* column in Table 20–4 is the most important column for our purposes. It shows what each extra unit costs—and suggests the minimum extra revenue we should get for each additional unit. Like average cost, marginal cost drops, but it begins to rise again at a *lower level of output* than average cost does.

Although average cost per unit is going down over most of the quantity range, marginal cost *starts up earlier*—at five units. Figure 20–8 shows the behavior of the *average cost, average variable cost,* and *marginal cost* curves. Note that the marginal cost curve intersects the average variable cost and average cost curves from below *at their low points,* and then rises rapidly. This is how this curve typically behaves.

How to find the most profitable price and the quantity to produce

Given that a manager must choose only *one* price level (for a time period), the problem is which one to choose. This price will determine the quantity that will be sold. To maximize profit, we now see that a manager should be willing to supply more units if he can obtain a marginal revenue at least equal to the marginal cost of extra units. From this we get the following **rule for maximizing profit:** *The firm should produce that output where marginal cost is just less than or equal to marginal revenue.*‡

‡ This rule applies in the typical situations where the curves are shaped similarly to those discussed here. Technically, however, we should add the following to the rule for maximizing profit: *The marginal cost must be increasing, or decreasing at a lesser rate than marginal revenue.*

Figure 20–8
Per-unit cost curves (for data in Table 20–4)

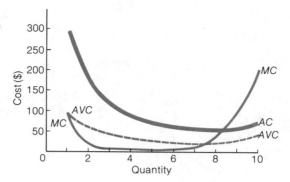

The selling price for this optimum quanitity is found by referring to the demand curve—which shows what price customers are willing to pay for the optimum quantity. Note: *the optimum price is not found on the marginal revenue curve.*

This method of finding the most profitable price and quantity is a useful tool for the marketing manager. To make sure you understand it, study the following example carefully. To make doubly sure that this approach is fully explained, we will calculate the most profitable price and quantity using total revenue and total cost curves first, and then show that the same answer is obtained with marginal curves. This will give you a check of the method—as well as perspective on how the marginal-revenue–marginal-cost method works.

Profit maximization with total revenue and total cost curves

Table 20–5 provides data on total revenue, total cost, and total profit for a firm. Figure 20–9 graphs the total revenue, total cost, and total profit relationships. It is clear from the graph of the total profit curve that the most profitable quantity is six—this is the quantity where we find the greatest vertical distance between the *TR* curve and the *TC* curve. Table 20–5 shows that the most profitable price is $79 and a quantity of six will be sold.

It is clear that beyond a quantity of six, the total profit curve declines. A

Table 20–5
Revenue, cost, and profit for an individual firm

(1) Quantity q	(2) Price p	(3) Total revenue TR	(4) Total cost TC	(5) Profit (TR − TC)	(6) Marginal revenue MR	(7) Marginal cost MC	(8) Marginal profit (MR − MC)
0	$150	$ 0	$200	$−200			
1	140	140	296	−156	$140	$ 96	$+ 44
2	130	260	316	− 56	120	20	+100
3	117	351	331	+ 20	91	15	+ 76
4	105	420	344	+ 76	69	13	+ 56
5	92	460	355	+105	40	11	+ 29
6	79	474	368	+106	14	13	+ 1
7	66	462	383	+ 79	−12	15	− 27
8	53	424	423	+ 1	−38	40	− 78
9	42	378	507	−129	−46	84	−130
10	31	310	710	−400	−68	203	−271

Figure 20–9
Graphic determination of the
output giving the greatest total
profit for a firm

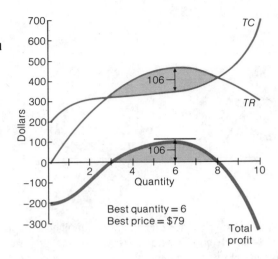

Best quantity = 6
Best price = $79

profit-oriented marketing manager should not be interested in selling more than this number.

Profit maximization using marginal curves

Now we can apply the rule for maximizing profit using marginal curves. The same best quantity and price—six at $79—are obtained. See Figure 20–10—which is based on the data for marginal revenue and marginal cost in Table 20–5.

In Figure 20–10, the intersection of the marginal cost and marginal revenue curves occurs at a quantity of six. This is the most profitable quantity. But the best price must be obtained by going up to the demand curve and then over to the vertical axis—*not* by going from the MR = MC intersection over to the vertical axis. Again, the best price is $79.

Figure 20–10
Alternate determination of the
most profitable output and
price for a firm

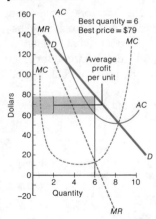

Best quantity = 6
Best price = $79

Average profit per unit

The graphic interpretation is supported by the data in Table 20–5. At a quantity of six, marginal revenue equals $14 and marginal cost is $13. There is a marginal profit of $1—and this suggests that it might be profitable to offer seven rather than six units. This is not the case, however. The marginal cost of the seventh unit is $15 while its marginal revenue is actually negative. Offering to sell seven units (instead of only six) will reduce total profit by $27.

It is important to realize that *total* profit is *not* near zero when *MR* equals *MC*. Marginal profit—the extra profit on the last unit—is near zero. But that is exactly why the quantity obtained at the *MR-MC* intersection is the most profitable. Marginal analysis shows that when the firm is finding the best price to charge, it should be willing to increase the quantity it will sell as long as the last unit it considers offering will yield *extra* profits.

Again, the marketing manager finally will choose only *one* price. Marginal analysis is useful in helping to set the best price to charge for all that will be sold. It might help to think of the demand curve as an "iffy" curve—*if* a price is selected, *then* a related quantity will be sold. Before the price is set, all these *if-then* combinations can be evaluated for profitability. But once a particular price is set, the results follow.

A profit range is reassuring

We have been trying to find the most profitable price and quantity. But in a changing world, this is an elusive goal. Fortunately, this optimum point is surrounded by a profitable range.

Note that in Figure 20–9 there are *two* break-even points rather than a single point—which was the case when we were discussing break-even analysis. The second break-even point falls farther to the right—because total costs turn up and total revenue turns down.

These two break-even points are important to note—they show the range of profitable operations. Although we are seeking the point of maximum profit, we know that this point is an ideal goal rather than a realistic possibility. So it is essential that the marketing manager knows there is a range of profit around the optimum—it is not just a lone point. This means that pursuing the optimum is a wise policy.

How to lose less, if you must

The marginal approach to finding the most profitable output also will find the output which will be least unprofitable—when market conditions are so poor that the firm must operate at a loss.

If sales are slow, the marketing manager may even have to consider stopping operation. When making this decision, fixed costs should be ignored—since these will continue regardless. Some fixed costs may even involve items that are so "sunk" in the business that they cannot be sold for anything near the cost shown on the company's records. The special-purpose buildings and machines of an unsuccessful company may be next to worthless to anyone else.

Marginal costs are another matter. If the firm cannot recover the marginal cost of the last unit (or more generally the variable cost of the units being considered), it should stop operations temporarily or go out of business. The only exceptions involve social or humanitarian considerations—or the fact that the marginal costs of closing temporarily are high and stronger demand is expected *soon*. But if marginal costs can be covered in the short run—even though all fixed costs cannot—the firm should stay in operation.

Marginal analysis helps get the most in pure competition

Marketing managers caught in pure competition also can apply marginal methods. They do not have price decisions—but they do have output decisions. The demand curves facing them are flat. This means that the marginal revenue curves are also flat at the same level. They could use that marginal revenue curve, therefore, with their own unique marginal cost curves to determine the most profitable (or least unprofitable) output level. See Figure 20–11. Not incidentally, this approach usually leads to a different (and more profitable) output decision than the average-cost approach favored by "common sense" managers.

MARGINAL ANALYSIS APPLIES IN OLIGOPOLY, TOO

Marginal analysis can be used whenever a firm can estimate its demand and

Figure 20–11
Finding the most profitable (or least unprofitable) price and quantity in pure competition (in the short run)

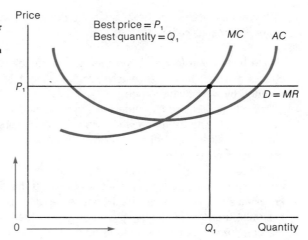

cost curves. The special kinked nature of the oligopoly demand curve is no problem.

When demand kinks, marginal revenue drops fast

As we saw in Chapter 3, individual competitors in an oligopoly face a kinked demand curve. We said then that the tendency in such situations is to avoid the use of Price—to avoid disastrous price cutting. Marginal analysis now helps us understand this situation better.

Figure 20–12
Marginal revenue drops fast in an oligopoly

The dashed marginal revenue line in Figure 20–12 shows that marginal revenue drops steeply at the kinked point. This is a technical but important matter. It helps explain why prices are relatively sticky at the kinked point. Even if costs change—and, therefore, each firm's supply curve were to move up or down—the MC curve still might cross the MR curve someplace along this vertical drop. In this case, even though costs are changing and there might seem to be a reason for changing the price, each firm may hold its price at the kinked price level—to maximize its profits!

A price leader usually sets the price

Most of the firms in an oligopoly are aware of the economics of the situation—at least intuitively. Usually, a **price leader** sets a price for all to follow—perhaps to maximize profits or to get a certain target return on investment—and (without any collusion) other members of the industry follow. This price may be maintained for a long time—or at least as long as all members of the industry continue to make a reasonable profit.

The price leader must take this responsibility seriously. If the followers are not able to make a reasonable profit at the market price, then they may try secret price cuts to expand sales. If very much of this happens, the price leader will lose business. And the situation may turn into a violent price war. Or there may be a temptation to collude—which is done, although it is illegal. Lacking an effective leader, the market may be unstable. And severe price cutting may be a continual threat.

A price leader may try to lead others to higher price levels if industry conditions seem to justify it—say, if labor costs have increased. Or the leader may try to get the industry price back up to former levels after a long period of price cutting. But this must be done carefully. The competitors may not play the game. And the leader may lose heavily before being forced to retreat. The National Gypsum Company, for example, once tried to return industry prices to list price levels and was "chopped up" during its two-month effort. As a result, the firm vowed not to try to lead the industry in price actions again. Its managers said that in the future, they were "going to be absolutely convinced in the marketplace by the actions of our competitors before doing anything." Furthermore, "If they demonstrate statesmanship, our participation will go with them. But if we see them being cute, we will react differently."[3]

Price leader should know costs and demand

A price leader should have a good understanding of its own and its competitors' cost structures—as well as an estimate of the industry demand curve. Setting too high a price may look attractive in the short run, but it may attract more competitors to the market and lead to trouble later—when capacity has expanded. Setting too low a price, on the other hand, can lead to action from antitrust officials who become concerned about small competitors. An optimal price may be one which is just high enough to support the marginal firm—the least efficient company whose production would be needed to meet peak long-run demands.[4]

If the price leader chooses a price that others can accept profitably, they may follow without any need for agreement. This "conscious parallel action" is deplored by the FTC and the Justice Department, but it still has not been declared illegal. Indeed, it is hard to see how it could be. Each firm *must* administer its prices, and meeting competition is certainly legal. In fact, basically the same behavior is found in pure competition. So—as long as conspiracy is avoided—meeting competition in any market situation probably will continue to be acceptable.

High profits will attract competitors.

Kenneth Yee

SOME PRICE SETTERS DO ESTIMATE DEMAND

Cost-oriented pricing is relatively simple and practical. But it is also clear that most cost-oriented approaches require some estimate of the likely demand. And, as we have seen, estimating the demand curve might help avoid mistakes in pricing.

Actual use of demand curves is not very common in the real world. Yet we do find marketers setting prices as though they believe certain types of demand curves are present. (And pricing research indicates they are.) It is clear that some prestige, odd-even, and psychological pricing efforts do consider demand. And some retailers do adjust their markups in the light of their feelings about demand.

The following sections discuss various examples of demand-related pricing. Some may be only intuitive adjustments of cost-based prices—but it is clear that demand is being considered.

Prestige pricing—make it high and not too low

Prestige pricing is setting a rather high price to suggest high quality or high status. Some target customers seem to want the "best." If prices are dropped a little below this "high" level, they may see a bargain. But if the prices begin to appear "cheap," they may become worried about quality and stop buying.[5]

Target customers who respond to prestige pricing give the marketing manager an unusual demand curve. Instead of a normal down-sloping, the curve goes down for a while and then bends back to the left again. See Figure 20–13. Marketing managers faced with this kind of demand—such as jewelry and fur retailers and some night club owners—typically set "high" prices.

Leader pricing—make it low to attract customers

Leader pricing is setting some very low prices—real bargains—to get customers into retail stores. Certain products are picked for their promotion value and priced low—but above cost. In food stores, the leader prices are the "specials" that are advertised regularly to give an image of low prices.

Leader pricing usually is limited to well-known, widely-used items which customers don't stock heavily—milk, butter, eggs, or coffee—but on which they will recognize a real price cut. The idea is to attract customers—not to sell large quantities of the leaders. To avoid hurting the firm's own profits, items may be used that are not directly competitive with major lines—as when bargain-priced cigarettes are sold at a gasoline station.

Bait pricing—offer a "steal," but sell under protest

Bait pricing is setting some very low prices to attract customers—but not to sell products. It's something like leader pricing. But here the seller *doesn't* plan to sell much at the low price.

This approach is used by some furniture retailers. To attract customers, a store will offer an extremely low price on an item. Once customers are in the store, the salespeople are expected to point out the disadvantages of the lower-quality item and sell customers higher-quality, more expensive products instead. Customers can buy the bait items—but only with great difficulty!

This policy tries to attract bargain hunters—or customers on the very low end of the demand curve who are not usually part of the market. If bait pricing is successful, customers may be "traded up"—and the demand for higher-quality

Figure 20–13
Demand curve showing a
prestige price situation

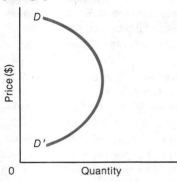

Figure 20–14
Demand curve when odd-even
pricing is appropriate

Figure 20–15
Demand curve when psychological
pricing is appropriate

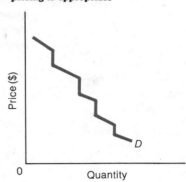

products will expand. But extremely aggressive and sometimes dishonest bait-pricing advertising has given this method a bad reputation. The Federal Trade Commission considers bait pricing a deceptive act—and has banned its use in interstate commerce. But some retailers who operate only within one state continue to advertise bait prices.

Odd-even pricing

Odd-even pricing is setting prices which end in certain numbers. Some marketers do this because they feel that consumers react better to these prices.

For goods selling under $50, prices ending with 95—such as $5.95, $6.95, and so on—are common. In general, prices ending in nine are most popular, followed by prices ending in five and three. For products selling over $50, prices that are $1 or $2 below the even-dollar figure are the most popular.[6]

Marketers using these prices seem to assume that they have a rather jagged demand curve—that consumers will buy less for a while as prices are lowered and then more as each "magic" price is reached. This kind of demand curve is shown in Figure 20–14.

Odd-even prices were used long ago by some retailers to force their clerks to make change. Then they had to record the sale and could not pocket the money. Today, however, it is not always clear why these prices are used—and whether they really work. Perhaps consumers have learned to expect better buys at certain prices and they do work. Or perhaps it is done simply because "everyone else does it."

Psychological pricing—
some prices just seem
right

Psychological pricing is setting prices which have special appeal to target customers. Some people feel there are whole ranges of prices which potential customers see as the same. Price cuts in these ranges would not increase the quantity sold. But just below this range, customers may buy more. Then, at even lower prices the quantity demanded would stay the same again. And so on.

The kind of demand curve that leads to psychological pricing is shown in Figure 20–15. Vertical drops mark the price ranges which customers see as the same. Pricing research shows that there are such demand curves.[7]

PRICING A FULL LINE

Our emphasis has been—and will continue to be—on the problem of pricing a single item—mainly because this makes our discussion clearer. But most marketing managers are responsible for more than one product. In fact, their "product" may be the whole company line! So we will discuss this matter briefly.

*Full-line pricing—
market- or firm-
oriented?*

Full-line pricing is setting prices for a whole line of products. How to do this depends on which of two basic strategies a firm is using. In one case, all products in the company's line are aimed at the same general target market—which makes it important for all prices to be related to one another.

In other cases, the different products in the line are aimed at entirely different target markets—and so there doesn't have to be any relation between the various prices. A chemical manufacturer of a wide variety of products with several target markets, for example, probably should price each product separately.

Examples of a full line being offered to the same target market are a TV manufacturer selling a whole line to retailers, or a forklift truck producer offering various sizes to large manufacturers, or a grocery retailer with thousands of items. Here the firm has to think of the customers' reaction to its full line of prices.

Usually the marketing manager attempts to price products in a full line so that the prices will appear logically related and make sense to potential customers. Most customers—especially industrial customers—feel that prices should be related to cost. And this must be considered in setting prices. Customers usually realize that small production runs or handling small quantities is likely to cost more. And they may be willing to pay higher prices for items which they know have a small market.

*Cost is not much help in
full-line pricing*

The marketing manager must try to recover all costs on the whole line—perhaps by pricing quite low on competitive items and much higher on less competitive items. But costs are not much help to the marketing manager in full-line pricing. There is no one "right" way to assign a company's fixed costs to each of the products. And if any method is carried through without considering demand, it may lead to very unrealistic prices. The marketing manager should judge demand for the whole line—as well as demand for each individual product in each target market—to avoid mistakes.

As an aid to full-line pricing, the marketing manager can assemble directly variable costs on the many items in the line—for calculating a floor under which prices will not be lowered. To this can be added a "reasonable" markup based on the quality of the product, the strength of the demand for the product, and the degree of competition. But finally, the image projected by the full line must be evaluated.

*Price lining—a few
prices cover the field*

Price lining is like full-line pricing. But here the focus is on how prices look at the retail level.

Price lining is setting a few price levels for a product class and then marking all items at these prices.

Most customers will pay between $5 and $15 for a necktie. In price lining, there will not be many prices in this range. There will be only a few. Ties will not be priced at $5.00, $5.50, $6.00, and so on. They might be priced at four levels—$5.00, $7.50, $10.00, and $15.00.

The main advantage of price lining is simplicity—for both clerks and customers. It is less confusing than a big variety of prices. Some customers may consider items in only one price class. Their big decision, then, is which item(s) to choose at that price. Price is no longer a question—unless the products at that price are not satisfactory. Then, perhaps the customer can be "traded up" to the next price level.

For retailers, price lining has several advantages. Sales may increase because (1) they can offer a bigger variety in each price line and (2) it is easier to get customers to make decisions within one price line. Stock planning is simpler—because demand is larger at the relatively few prices. Price lining also can reduce costs because inventory needs are lower—even though large stocks are carried in each line. In summary, price lining results in faster turnover, fewer markdowns, quicker sales, and simplified buying.

Demand-backward pricing aids price lining

Demand-backward pricing starts with an acceptable final consumer price and works backward to what a producer can charge. It is commonly used by producers of final consumer products—especially shopping goods, such as women's and children's clothing and shoes. It is also used for toys or gifts for which customers will spend a specific amount—because they are seeking a "five-dollar" or a "ten-dollar" gift. Here, a reverse cost-plus pricing process is used. This method has been called "market-minus" pricing.

The producer starts with the retail price for a particular item and then works backward—substracting the typical margins which channel members expect. This gives the approximate price that he can charge. Then, he subtracts from this price the average or planned marketing expenses to find how much can be spent producing the item.

Don Smetzer

Demand estimates are necessary if demand-backward pricing is to be successful. The quantity which will be demanded affects production costs—that is, where the firm will be on its average cost curve. Also, since competitors can be expected to make the best product possible, it is important to know customer needs—to set the best amount to be spent on manufacturing costs. By increasing costs a little, the product might be so improved in consumers' eyes that the firm would sell many more units. But if consumers only want novelty, additional quality might not increase the quantity demanded—and shouldn't be offered.

BID PRICING DEPENDS HEAVILY ON COSTS

A new price for every job

Bid pricing is offering a specific price for each possible job—rather than setting a price that applies for all potential customers. Building contractors, for example, must bid on possible projects. And many companies selling services (like cleaning or data processing) must submit bids for jobs they would like to have.

The big problem in bid pricing is collecting all the costs that apply to each

All costs must be considered when bidding on a job.

Peter Le Grand

job. This may sound easy, but thousands of cost components may have to go into a complicated bid. Further, management must include an overhead charge and a charge for profit.

Demand must be considered too

It is when adding in overhead and profit that demand and competition must be considered. Usually, the customer will get several bids and accept the lowest one. So, unthinking addition of overhead and profit should be avoided. Some bidders use the same overhead and profit rates on all jobs—regardless of competition—and then are surprised when they don't get some jobs.

Bidding can be expensive. So a firm might want to be selective about which jobs it bids on—and select those where they feel they have the greatest chance of success.[8] Thousands or even millions of dollars have been spent just developing bids for large industrial or government orders.

Sometimes bids are bargained

Some buying situations (including much government buying) require the use of bids—and the purchasing agent must take the lowest bid. In other cases, however, bids may be called for and then the company submitting the *most attractive* bid—not necessarily the lowest—will be singled out for further bargaining. This may include price adjustments—but it also may be concerned with how additions to the job will be priced, what guarantees will be provided, and the quality of labor and supervisors who will do the job. Some projects—such as construction projects—are hard to define exactly. So it is important that the buyer be satisfied about the whole marketing mix—not just the price. Obviously, effective personal selling can be important here.

CONCLUSION

In this chapter, we discussed various approaches to price setting. Generally, retailers and wholesalers use traditional markups. Some use the same markups for all their items. Others have found that varying the markups may increase turnover and profit. In other words, demand is considered!

Cost-oriented pricing seems to make sense for middlemen—because they handle small quantities of many items. Producers must take price setting more seriously. They are the ones that set the "list price" to which others apply markups.

Producers commonly use average cost curves to help set their prices. But this approach sometimes ignores demand completely. A more realistic approach to average cost pricing requires a sales forecast. This may just mean assuming that sales in the next period will be roughly the same as in the last period. This *will* enable the marketing manager to set a price—but this price *may or may not* cover all costs and earn the desired profit.

Break-even analysis can be useful for evaluating alternative prices. But management judgment must be used to evaluate the likelihood of reaching alternative break-even points. It does provide a rough and ready tool for eliminating obviously unworkable prices.

Traditional demand and supply analysis can be a useful tool for finding the most profitable price and quantity to produce. The most profitable quantity is found at the intersection of the marginal revenue and marginal cost curves. To determine the *most profitable* price, the manager takes the most profitable quantity to the firm's demand curve—to find what price target customers will be willing to pay for this quantity.

The major difficulty with demand-oriented pricing is estimating the demand curve. But experienced managers—aided perhaps by marketing research—can make estimates of the nature of demand for their products. Such estimates—even if they aren't exact—are useful. They get one in the right "ballpark." Sometimes, when all that is needed is a decision about raising or lowering price, demand estimates can be very revealing. Further, it is important to recognize that a firm's demand curve does not cease to exist simply because it is ignored. Some information is better than none at all. And it appears that some marketers do consider demand in their pricing. We saw this with prestige pricing, leader pricing, bait pricing, odd-even pricing, psychological pricing, full-line pricing, and even bid pricing.

We have stressed throughout the book that the customer must be considered before anything is done. This certainly applies to pricing. It means that when managers are setting a price, they have to consider what customers will be willing to pay. This isn't always easy, but it is nice to know that there is a profit range around the "best" price. Therefore, even "guesstimates" about what potential customers will buy at various prices will probably lead to a better price than mechanical use of traditional markups or cost-oriented formulas.

QUESTIONS AND PROBLEMS

1. Why do department stores seek a markup of about 40 percent when some discount houses operate on a 20-percent markup?

2. A manufacturer of household appliances distributed its products through wholesalers and retailers. The retail selling price was $250, and the manufacturing cost to the company was $100. The retail markup was 40 percent and the wholesale markup 25 percent.
   a. What was the cost to the wholesaler? To the retailer?
   b. What percentage markup did the manufacturer take?

3. Relate the concept of stock turnover to the rise of discounters. Use a simple example in your answer.

4. If total fixed costs are $100,000 and total variable costs are $200,000 at an output of 10,000 units, what are the probable total fixed costs and total variable costs at an output of 20,000 units? What are the average fixed costs, average variable costs, and average costs at these two output levels? Determine the price which should be charged. (Make any simplifying assumptions necessary to obtain a definite answer.)

5. Explain how target return pricing differs from average cost pricing.

6. Construct an example showing that mechanical use of a very large or very small markup might still lead to unprofitable operation while some intermediate price would be profitable. Draw a graph and show the break-even point(s).

7. The Smith Company's fixed costs for the year are estimated at $100,000. The variable costs are usually about 70 percent of sales. Sales for the coming year are expected to reach $380,000. What is the break-even point? Expected profit? If sales were forecast at only $200,000, should the Smith Company shut down operations? Why?

8. Distinguish among marginal revenue, average revenue, and price.

9. Draw a graph showing a demand and supply situation where marginal analysis would correctly indicate that the firm should continue producing even though the profit and loss statement shows a loss.

10. Discuss the idea of drawing separate demand curves for different market segments. It seems logical because each target market should have its own marketing mix. But won't this lead to a considerable number of demand curves and possibly prices? And what will this mean with respect to functional discounts and varying prices in the marketplace? Would this be legal? Would it be practical?

11. Brown Bean Co. has been enjoying a profitable year. Their product sells to wholesalers for 20 cents a can. After careful study, it has been decided that a 60-percent gross margin should be maintained. Their manufacturing costs are divided in this manner: material, 50 percent of cost; labor, 40 percent of cost; and 10 percent of cost for overhead. Both material and labor costs experienced a 10-percent increase. Determine the new price per can based on their present pricing methods. Is it wise to hold fast to a 60-percent margin, if a *price increase* would mean lost customers? Answer, using graphs and *MC-MR* analysis. Show a situation where it would be most profitable to *(a)* raise price, *(b)* leave price alone, *(c)* reduce price.

12. How would a prestige pricing policy fit into a marketing mix? Would exclusive distribution be necessary?

13. Cite a local example of the use of odd-even pricing and then evaluate whether you feel it makes sense.

14. Cite a local example of the use of psychological pricing and then evaluate whether you feel it makes sense.

15. Distinguish between leader pricing and bait pricing. What do they have in common? How can their use affect a marketing mix?

16. Is a full-line pricing policy available only to producers? Cite local examples of full-line pricing. Why is full-line pricing important?

SUGGESTED CASES

NOTES

1. Super-Valu Study (New York: Progressive Grocer, 1957), p. S-4-7.

2. "Selling Business a Theory of Economics," *Business Week,* September 8, 1973, pp. 85–90.

3. "National Gypsum Vows Not to Lead Industry Again in Price Actions," *The Wall Street Journal,* July 17, 1970, p. 11; and "Gypsum Makers Move to Stop Sharp Discounts," *The Wall Street Journal,* December 3, 1969, p. 6. See also (re cigarette industry) Marvin A. Jolson and Noel B. Zabriskie, "Nonprice Parallelism in Oligopolistic Industries," *MSU Business Topics,* Autumn 1971, pp. 33–41.

4. See J. Howard Westing and Jon G. Udell, "Pricing and the Antitrust Laws," *Michigan Business Review,* November 1962, pp. 6–11.

5. John J. Wheatley and John S. Y. Chiu, "The Effects of Price, Store Image, and Product and Respondent Characteristics on Perceptions of Quality," *Journal of Marketing Research,* May 1977, pp. 181–86; Arthur G. Bedeian, "Consumer Perception of Price as an Indicator of Product Quality," *MSU Business Topics,* Summer 1971, pp. 59–65; David M. Gardner, "An Experimental Investigation of the Price/Quality Relationship," *Journal of Retailing,* Fall 1970, pp. 25–41; Kent B. Monroe, "Buyers' Subjective Perceptions of Price," *Journal of Marketing Research,* February 1973, pp. 70–80; and N. D. French, J. J. Williams, and W. A. Chance, "A Shopping Experiment on Price-Quality Relationships," *Journal of Retailing,* Fall 1972, pp. 3–16; Michael R. Hagerty, "Model Testing Techniques and Price-Quality Tradeoffs," *Consumer Research,* December 1978, pp. 194–205; Peter C. Riesz, "A Major Price-Perceived Quality Study Reexamined," *Journal of Marketing Research,* May 1980, pp. 259–62; and J. Douglas McConnell, "Comment on 'A Major Price-Perceived Quality Study Reexamined,'" *Journal of Marketing Research,* May 1980, pp. 263–64.

6. Dik W. Twedt, "Does the '9 Fixation in Retailing Really Promote Sales?" *Journal of Marketing,* October 1965, pp. 54–55; and H. J. Rudolph, "Pricing and Today's Market," *Printers' Ink,* May 29, 1954, pp. 22–24; "Strategic Mix of Odd, Even Prices Can Lead to Increased Retail Profits," *Marketing News,* March 7, 1980, p. 24.

7. E. R. Hawkins, "Price Policies and Theory," *Journal of Marketing,* January 1954, p. 236; see also B. P. Shapiro, "The Psychology of Pricing," *Harvard Business Review,* July–August 1968, pp. 14–25; C. Davis Fogg and Kent H. Kohnken, "Price-Cost Planning," *Journal of Marketing,* April 1978, pp. 97–106; and Benson P. Shapiro and Barbara B. Jackson, "Industrial Pricing to Meet Consumer Needs," *Harvard Business Review,* November–December 1978, pp. 119–27.

8. Stephen Paranka, "Competitive Bidding Strategy," *Business Horizons,* June 1971, pp. 39–43; Wayne J. Morse, "Probabilistic Bidding Models; A Synthesis," *Business Horizons,* April 1975, pp. 67–74; and Kenneth Simmonds and Stuart Slatter, "The Number of Estimators: A Critical Decision for Marketing under Competitive Bidding," *Journal of Marketing Research,* May 1978, pp. 203–13.

PART FOUR

Planning, implementing, and controlling marketing activities

This part is concerned with tying together and extending much of the material we have been discussing throughout the book. Chapter 21 reemphasizes the need for focusing on target markets when planning marketing mixes—and shows how knowing about target markets as well as the goods classes can help you develop effective—and perhaps even breakthrough—strategies. Ways of developing and selecting such strategic plans are discussed—starting with "typical" marketing mixes and then adjusting them to the needs and preferences of the target markets—in the light of competitors' actions and the company's own resources and objectives.

Controlling marketing plans and programs is the subject of Chapter 22. The interrelation of controlling and later planning is emphasized—because the marketing management process is continuous—involving planning, implementing, and control—which leads to feedback to make better plans for the future.

Chapter 23 applies the material you have studied to international marketing. We will discuss the need to deal with even more uncontrollable and less familiar environments. This should not discourage an aggressive marketer, because the potential rewards are great—and working in international markets can be very exciting and challenging.

Kenneth Yee

When you	1.	Know that strategy planning is much more than assembling the four Ps.
finish this		
chapter, you	2.	Know how response functions can help plan marketing strategies.
should:	3.	Understand why typical mixes are a good starting point for planning.
	4.	Understand how marketing mixes are related to goods classes.
	5.	Know the content and differences among strategic plans and a marketing program.
	6.	Know about allocating budgets for marketing plans.
	7.	Know about some graphical aids for implementing marketing programs.
	8.	Recognize the important new terms (shown in red).

21

Planning and implementing marketing programs

More than strategies must be planned.

In this chapter we will finish our discussion of strategy planning. We will emphasize *why* an individual firm should see each of its internal activities as part of a whole—and why a marketing manager must plan whole marketing mixes to satisfy target markets, rather than looking at only one or another of the four Ps.

Further, we will see that marketing managers must go beyond just developing strategies. They must develop strategic *plans* and then a whole marketing *program*—a set of strategic plans. Then, a marketing manager must carry out this program—perhaps with the aid of some flow charting procedures discussed at the end of the chapter.

STRATEGIC PLANNING IS MORE THAN ASSEMBLING THE FOUR Ps

They must be blended together

Strategic planning involves much more than assembling the four parts of a marketing mix. The four Ps must be *blended* together in a creative way—so that the "best" mix is developed for the firm's target market. This may mean that the proposed plans of some specialists—the product manager, sales manager, physical distribution manager, and so on—may have to be adjusted to improve the whole mix.

Throughout the text, we have given the job of integrating the four Ps to the marketing manager. But now we should formally recognize the need for this integrating role. It is easy for specialists to focus on their own area—and expect the rest of the company to work for or around them. This is especially true in larger firms—where specialists are needed—just because the size of the whole marketing job is too much for one person.

Need plans and program

Marketing managers must plan strategies, strategic plans, and finally, a whole marketing program. As explained in Chapter 2, a strategy is a "grand design" of what a firm will do in some market—while a strategic plan includes the time-related details for that strategy—and a marketing program is a combination of the firm's strategic plans.

By now, it should be clear that each strategy which gets implemented must be carried out over a period of time. Some time schedule is implicit in any strategy. A strategic plan simply spells out this time period and the time-related details. Usually, we think in terms of some reasonable length of time, such as six months, a year, or a few years. But it might be only a month or two in some cases—especially when style and fashion are important factors. Or, a strategy might be implemented over several years—perhaps the length of a product life cycle or at least the early stages of the life of the product.

Clearly, strategy planning is a creative process—but it also is a logical process. It requires blending many of the ideas which we have discussed already in this book. So this chapter might be thought of as a review. Figure 21–1 shows the strategic decision areas which we have been talking about throughout the book. Now these must be integrated into logical marketing mixes, marketing strategies, strategic plans, and a marketing program.

BLENDING THE FOUR Ps TAKES UNDERSTANDING OF A TARGET MARKET

The marketing concept emphasizes that all of a firm's activities should be focused on its target markets. It logically follows, therefore, that if one fully understands the needs and attitudes of a target market, then combining the four Ps should be "easy." There are three gaps in this line of reasoning, however: (1) we don't always know as much as we would like to about the needs and attitudes of our target markets; (2) competitors are also trying to satisfy these or similar

Figure 21–1
Strategic decision areas

Product	Place	Promotion	Price
Features	Objectives	Objectives	Objectives
Accessories	Channels	Promotion blend	Flexibility
Installation	Market exposure	Sales people	Level
Instructions	Kinds of middlemen	Kind	Changes over product
Service	Kinds and location	Number	life cycle
Warranty	of stores	Selection	Geographic terms
Product lines	Who handles	Training	Discounts
Packaging	transporting	Motivation	Allowances
Branding	and storing	Advertising	
	Service levels	Targets	
		Kind of ads	
		Media type	
		Copy thrust	
		Prepared by whom	
		Sales promotion	
		Publicity	

Marketing managers should consider the uncontrollable variables when developing their marketing mixes.

Mary McCarthy

needs—and their efforts may force shifts of a firm's marketing mix; and (3) the other uncontrollable variables may be changing—and require more changes in marketing mixes.

Understanding leads to profitable mixes—maybe

A clear understanding of the needs and attitudes of the firm's target market can make the development of a marketing mix "relatively" easy—even in the face of competition. Kodak, for example, has had continued success in the "consumer film market" by stressing good quality and convenience. It has prospered by following George Eastman's original philosophy: "You press the button, we do the rest." As segmenters, Kodak offered good film, made it conveniently available, and arranged for high-quality, rapid processing all over the world.

Kodak's successful marketing mix did not satisfy everyone however—particularly those who wanted their pictures *immediately*. Polaroid came along to satisfy this market segment with a different marketing mix—including "instant pictures." They may not be as good as the pictures a production-oriented chemical engineer would like to deliver. But they are delivered fast (providing time utility)—and the speed makes up for the lower quality and higher price, at least for some customers. Polaroid's strategy was extremely profitable. To compete in this market, Kodak came out with its own "fast delivery" system in 1976—30 years after Kodak had rejected the Polaroid approach as "frivolous."

Kodak's move into the "instant picture" market may put it in the role of imitator. On the other hand, market research showed that Polaroid was not satisfying everyone in the "instant picture" market. Even people who already owned a Polaroid said they might be interested in buying another kind of instant camera—if conditions were right. Desired features were: no need for timing, better color, no peeling, no waste paper, and no use of chemicals. As Kodak saw it, some customers wanted greater convenience in use—and better quality in their instant pictures. Kodak hopes to satisfy these needs better than Polaroid has. If its research is correct, it may be able to capture a large share of the "instant picture" market.[1]

Superior mixes may be breakthrough opportunities

When marketing managers fully understand their target markets, they may be able to develop marketing mixes which are obviously superior to "competitive mixes." Such understanding may provide breakthrough opportunities—until their competitors reach the same understanding of the market and decide to meet them "head on." Taking advantage of these kinds of opportunities can lead to substantial sales and profit growth. This is why we have continually stressed the importance of looking for breakthrough opportunities—rather than merely trying to patch up or improve present mixes.

Inferior mixes are easy to reject

Just as some mixes are clearly superior, some mixes are clearly inferior or unsuitable. For example, a national TV advertising campaign might make sense for a large company—while being completely out of the question for a small manufacturer offering a new product on the East Coast.

In-between mixes are harder to develop

Where competitors are hitting each other "head on," it is even more important to understand the target market—and how it is likely to respond to alternative marketing mixes. Here, we have more need for estimating response functions.

RESPONSE FUNCTIONS MAY HELP PLAN BETTER STRATEGIES

A response function shows (mathematically and/or graphically) how the firm's target market is expected to react to changes in marketing variables. So, trying to estimate relevant response functions can be a real aid in developing better marketing mixes.

Response functions usually are plotted as curves showing how sales and profit will vary at different levels of marketing expenditures—but other relationships may be helpful, too. Possibilities include how sales and profits will vary if (1) prices are changed or (2) different promotion blends are used.

To deepen your understanding about response functions—and to show how they might be useful—we will first focus on response functions for each of the four Ps. See Figure 21–2, where possible response functions are graphed for each of the four Ps. The response function for the whole marketing mix will be discussed a little later.

These are just examples of the general shape of the curves which *might* be found in the real world. A particular company aiming at a particular target market and facing a particular group of competitors might have quite different response functions. And these functions might lead a marketing manager to select very different mixes than competitors'—or than similar companies operating in other markets. Again, the response functions illustrated here should be seen as examples only—*not* as typical responses.

The shape of such response functions is obviously critical to the selection of the "best" blend for each particular P and for a whole marketing mix. Yet, we do not know much about the precise shapes of the functions. Worse, there is no published source of empirically verified response functions for varying situations. The manager usually must develop his own response functions—using past experience and judgment, perhaps aided by marketing research. As difficult as such estimating may be, it is still necessary if a careful evaluation of alternatives

Figure 21–2
Four "illustrative only"
response functions

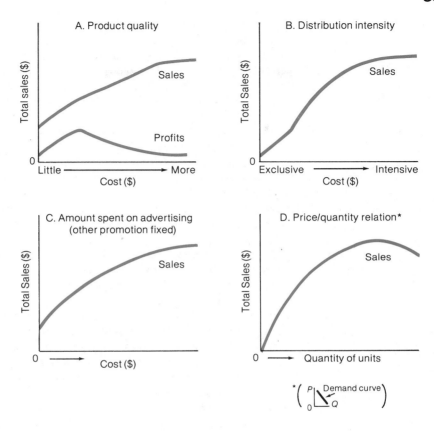

is desired. Response functions do not "go away" if they are ignored—and decisions made without them may be just crude guesses.

Product quality
response function

A response function for product quality might show that adding more quality (and features) would increase sales (perhaps even continuously up to a point)—but it may also increase costs and, therefore, result in a profit response function which reaches a high point and then declines. This "maximum point" is the "best" level for product quality (depending upon the firm's objectives, of course!) (see Figure 21–2A).

Place—distribution
intensity response
function

A Place-related response function which focuses on the degree of market exposure desired (ranging from exclusive to intensive) might look like the response function shown in Figure 21–2B. The reason sales level off near the extreme of intensive distribution is that when most outlets already carry the product, little increase in sales can be expected from the last few, perhaps marginal, outlets.

Promotion—advertising
response function

Figure 21–2C illustrates a possible response function for advertising. This figure suggests that even with no advertising, personal selling (and other promotion efforts) would obtain some sales results. But sales would be higher with some advertising. On the extreme right of the response function, the curve starts to level off—showing declining results from extra advertising. (Although picking the best level is beyond the scope of this text, it is important to note that the best point may not be at the highest sales level. Marginal analysis can be used here to show that as the response function begins to flatten out, the marginal return of sales to advertising dollar begins to decline.)

Price—demand curve response function

The Price-oriented response function shown in Figure 21–2D illustrates the impact on sales and quantity sold of price level variations. This figure is simply another way of illustrating the down-sloping demand curve which we have discussed in various parts of the text. Note that a down-sloping demand curve does mean that total sales will start declining at some quantity (recall that marginal revenue can go negative and this means that total revenue is declining). It is not possible to expand total dollar sales indefinitely with price cuts!

A manager must estimate own response functions

Estimating response functions is not easy. They are probably changing all the time. Further, there will be different response functions for each target market. Nevertheless, each marketing manager should make some estimate about the response of customers to the various ingredients he controls. This is where past experience and careful analysis of how the same or similar customers are responding to competitors' mixes is useful. If one firm has already tried a 10-percent price cut to encourage retailers to sell more by cutting their prices, for example, and the retailers simply absorb the extra margin, then the response function for this kind of price cutting is not attractive. But another competitor may have increased the number of calls made on each retailer—with great results. Some marketing research might help a manager decide whether he also has such a response function—and whether increasing sales effort would be equally successful for his firm.

Estimating general marketing effort response functions

Besides trying to estimate response functions for each of the four Ps, it would be desirable to estimate the general response function for all marketing effort in one marketing mix. Then, different response functions for alternative mixes

A manager has to use experience, judgment, and market research to estimate his own response functions.

Milt & Joan Mann

Figure 21–3
A marketing effort response
function for one marketing mix

could be compared when seeking the "best" mix for any particular target market. Such a generalized marketing response function is presented in Figure 21–3—showing the relation between marketing effort (in dollars) and sales (or profits) for one marketing mix.

A threshold effort is needed to get any sales

The shape of this response function probably is typical of the alternatives facing marketing managers. This response function shows that a higher level of marketing expenditures *may* yield a higher level of sales (or profits). But just spending more and more money for marketing won't guarantee better profits. Further, there is not a straight-line relationship between marketing expenditures and sales (or profits). Instead, some expenditure may be necessary to get any sales at all. This is called the threshold expenditure level—the minimum expenditure level needed just to be in a market. After this level, small increases in expenditures may result in large increases in sales (as the curve rises rapidly)—after which, additional expenditures may lead to little or no increase in sales (where the sales curve flattens out) but a decline in profits.

The response function for a whole marketing mix would be the result of the interaction of all the mix ingredients. There are techniques for estimating these functions—if we know the shape of all the mix ingredient functions. But this topic is beyond our scope.[2]

For our purposes, we'll have to be satisfied to know that it is possible to "roughly" estimate response functions for alternative mixes and that, therefore, it would be possible to select the best one—given the firm's resources and objectives. Figure 21–4 illustrates three estimated response functions for three different mixes. If the marketing manager's budget were fixed at the level shown in Figure 21–4—and he wanted to maximize sales in the short run—then Mix A is clearly best.

If a manager didn't want to estimate whole functions, it would be useful to estimate the sales and costs of "reasonable" alternative marketing mixes and compare them for profitability. Table 21–1 illustrates such a comparison for a small appliance which is currently selling for $15—Line 1 in the example. Here, the marketing manager simply estimated the costs and likely results of four "reasonable" alternatives. And, assuming profitability is the objective *and* there are

Figure 21–4
Response functions for three different marketing mixes for next year

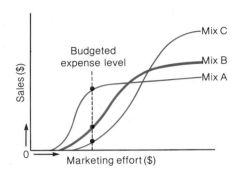

Table 21–1
Comparing the estimated sales, costs, and profits of four "reasonable" alternative marketing mixes.*

Marketing mix	Price	Selling cost	Advertising cost	Total units	Sales	Total cost	Total profit
A	$15	$20,000	$ 5,000	5,000	$ 75,000	$ 70,000	$ 5,000
B	15	20,000	20,000	7,000	105,000	95,000	10,000
C	20	30,000	30,000	7,000	140,000	115,000	25,000
D	25	40,000	40,000	5,000	125,000	125,000	0

* For the same target market, assuming product costs per unit are $5 and fixed (overhead) costs are $20,000.

adequate resources to consider each of the alternatives, then marketing Mix C is obviously the best alternative.

Typical mixes are a good starting point for marketing mix planning

Typical mixes are a good starting point for developing alternative marketing mixes—and estimating their response functions. What others have done in similar situations must have satisfied someone—and can serve as a guide. And, if actual sales and cost data are available or can be estimated, then at least a few points on response functions can be estimated. Beyond this, judgment or some marketing research will be needed. In this way, one can make use of past experience—while not relying blindly on it.

We will discuss typical marketing mixes in the next section. They will serve as a good starting point for developing unique marketing mixes—knowing the firm's own target market and its own objectives, resources, and competition.

During this discussion, try to develop a feel for which mix ingredients seem "most important." These will probably be the ones which have the most steeply rising response functions over reasonable cost levels—that's why they are typically used. For example, if personal selling is very important in a particular mix, this probably means that the personal selling response function is more attractive than the alternatives. Even so, a marketing manager would want to evaluate how good personal selling is (over a range of expenditures) before naïvely spending all his promotion money on personal selling or (maybe worse) all his marketing money on this one ingredient.

TYPICAL MARKETING MIXES RELATED TO GOODS CLASSES

Ideally, the ingredients of a good marketing mix will flow logically from all the relevant dimensions of a target market. Table 21–2 shows the kinds of market dimensions we might like to know—and their effect on the strategic decision areas. Usually, however, we do not or cannot know all that we would like to about a potential target market. We may know enough, however, to decide whether the product is a consumer good or an industrial good—and which goods class is most relevant.

The relevant goods classes have a direct bearing on marketing mix planning—because they are based on how potential customers view and buy the product—not on the characteristics of the products themselves. So, if we don't know as much as we might like to about the potential customers' needs and attitudes, at least knowing how they would classify the company's product can give us a head start on developing a marketing mix. Further, it is reassuring to see that goods classes do summarize some of what we would like to know about target markets—as seen in Table 21–2.

A first step, then, would be to put each product into the proper goods class. This will simplify the selection of Place and Promotion—since goods classes suggest how and why various products are typically distributed and promoted.

Now, let's tie together what we know about goods classes with a description of how and why various products typically are distributed and promoted. The major emphasis will be on how Place and Promotion are usually handled, although packaging and branding will be referred to when relevant.

Price will be more or less ignored in this discussion of typical behavior because, generally, Price is badly handled. Also, goods classes are not as relevant for pricing—except when they suggest inelasticity of demand, for example, as with impulse, emergency, specialty, and repair goods. After a manager has considered a mix that he might develop based on goods classes, he probably should spend a good deal more time considering what would be the best price—in the light of the firm's objectives. This matter has already been discussed in Chapters 19 and 20.

"Typical" is not necessarily "right"

In the following discussion, we will describe the typical Place and Promotion methods used. Try to see the "why" of typical channels and typical promotion blends—rather than memorizing "right" answers. Although these are typical, they

Table 21–2
Relation of potential target market dimensions (including ones which are related to goods classes) to marketing mix decision areas

Potential target market dimensions	Effects on decision areas
1. Geographic location and other demographic characteristics of potential customers	Affects size of *Target Markets* (economic potential) and *Place* (where products should be made available) and *Promotion* (where and to whom to advertise)
2. Behavioral needs, attitudes, and how present and potential goods or services fit into customers' consumption patterns	Affects *Product* (design, packaging, length or width of product line) and *Promotion* (what potential customers need and want to know about the product offering, and what appeals should be used)
3. Urgency to get need satisfied and desire and willingness to compare and shop	Affects *Place* (how directly products are distributed from producer to consumer, how extensively they are made available, and the level of service needed) and *Price* (how much potential customers are willing to pay)

are not necessarily right for all situations. Some very profitable marketing mixes have departed from the typical to satisfy some target markets better.

TYPICAL MIXES FOR CONSUMER GOODS

Convenience goods—get them where the customers are

Most convenience goods, especially staples, are relatively simple items—seldom requiring installation, service, or even much personal selling.

The scattered location of target customers and the typically small size of each purchase encourage the use of several middlemen—especially merchant wholesalers and retailers. Setting up their own retail outlets would be impractical for manufacturers.

Staples

Since staples are often in the market maturity stage of the product life cycle—with large potential target markets—a manufacturer's promotion blend usually emphasizes mass selling. If a producer promotes a product effectively, the merchant wholesalers and retailers may not have to do much more than handle, break bulk, and store the appropriate assortment until needed.

Retailers usually will not voluntarily provide displays or special promotion aids—except for their own dealer brands. Therefore, producers and wholesalers' sales reps have to promote each product to wholesalers and retailers—and provide any store displays and point-of-purchase aids which are needed.

Impulse goods

With impulse goods, the need for intensive distribution and point-of-purchase display at the retail level is obvious. Basically, promotion of impulse goods is aggressively aimed at the channels—relying mainly on personal selling to the retailer. Although merchant wholesalers may stock the goods, the manufacturer usually has to go directly to retailers with his own salespeople to assure well-placed displays. This usually requires highly persuasive personal selling to the retailer. Consumer advertising may not be essential—unless several similar goods are competing in the channels. Then, a producer may have to promote his product to final consumers—to impress retailers and wholesalers that his product is the best impulse item available.

Emergency goods

Since emergency goods are regarded as necessities for special circumstances, they must have wide distribution—and must be available at times when regular outlets might not be open. A variety of retailers cater to emergency business—all-night gas stations, open-till-midnight food and beverage stores, and vending machines. Intensive distribution is needed to these outlets. And this could require intensive distribution to wholesalers to reach these outlets.

Little consumer promotion is needed—except what is necessary to remind buyers of its availability when an emergency occurs. Mass selling to consumers could be used if a producer wanted to move a product from the emergency goods class—where brands are less important—to another class. Anti-freeze manufacturers, for example, advertise to try to get motorists to install *their* brand early in the fall—to avoid the last-minute rush. But despite their efforts, many drivers still wait until the first freeze warning and then pour anything available into the radiator. At this point, having widespread distribution is all-important to the producer and wholesalers.

The main promotion job for these goods is in the channels—to get distribution. A very persuasive personal selling job may be needed if competitive products are available. As with impulse goods, mass selling can be used to impress channel members with the firm's offering.

Shopping goods—the direct route if necessary

Target customers for shopping goods—like the customers for convenience goods—are widely scattered. But shopping-goods customers are willing to make more of an effort to satisfy their needs. The producer needs fewer outlets— and direct-to-retail distribution is possible. Producer-to-consumer selling is unlikely, however, because consumers generally want to compare shopping goods. Retailers play a key role here.

Homogeneous shopping goods

Homogeneous shopping goods do not require attractive surroundings or knowledgeable sales personnel. For well-known manufacturers' brands of appliances, for instance, price is very important to some consumers. They are willing to go to back-alley discount houses, if necessary, to buy them. Unbranded soft goods— such as towels and children's clothing—may be dumped into bins and customers will sort through them for the lowest-priced items.

A manufacturer of homogeneous shopping goods may decide that it is too difficult or even impossible to upgrade the consumer image of the product— especially if it is in the last stages of the product life cycle. He may then drop selective distribution efforts and try to gain intensive distribution—with as many wholesale and retail outlets as possible.

Some retailers use personal selling to try to get potential customers to see that they offer more than just low price. Others—such as the mass merchandisers—have gone to self-service and checkout counters for such products. They still advertise products, however—emphasizing low prices—to project a low-price

Price is very important for homogeneous shopping goods buyers.

Mary McCarthy

image for *all* their products. Here, the objective is to "sell" the store—not just particular items.

Heterogeneous shopping goods

Heterogeneous shopping goods are compared by consumers on more than price alone. For this reason, they require more retail display and often more personal selling—both to final consumers and to middlemen.

Producers frequently bypass wholesalers, because they *must* tell the sales story to retailers—sometimes including technical information that must be explained directly to the retail clerks. Since they must make the sales calls anyway, they feel they might as well take the orders and deliver the product themselves. Fairly direct channels are also encouraged by the willingness of retail buyers to make regular trips to central markets, say, to Chicago for furniture and New York for clothing. Resident buyers also speed the direct movement of these goods—especially for style and fashion goods.

Mass selling may be used by manufacturers or retailers—to inform customers about the different characteristics of these heterogeneous goods. Copies of national advertisements may be sent to retailers—and displayed by the retailers to show customers that they offer nationally advertised products.

Generally, brand promotion is less important for these goods. Some manufacturers do little or no advertising for clothing and house furnishings—because consumers want to compare products in the store. Manufacturers may rely more on informed retail clerks. They may be paid promotion allowances—as a $5 bonus for each new mattress sold. Personal contacts in the channels—stressing economic arguments and demonstrating effective selling techniques—are essential here.

Specialty goods—hold a favored position

Specialty goods are normally distributed through the same channels as those convenience or shopping goods they most nearly resemble. The favored status of these products makes it relatively easy to promote them to wholesalers and retailers—on the basis of profit potential.

Retailers advertising these products may use mass media—such as billboards and newspaper advertisements—simply to remind customers where they are for sale.

However, specialty goods might require continued mass selling by the manufacturer. Consumers are fickle. If similar products are being promoted aggressively, the manufacturer would not want to risk losing his brand familiarity. New customers are continually entering the market—and must be convinced that the product is a specialty good. This mass selling by producers also helps assure middlemen of continued customer acceptance.

Unsought goods—need some extra push

Unsought goods are in the introductory stage of their life cycle. All potential customers must be fully informed about them. Mass selling may be used by manufacturers to reach final consumers—but order getters may be needed to convince wholesalers and retailers of the profit potential of these products. If they are not convinced, the products might not even reach the retail level.

A large, established firm just introducing an unsought good—but one similar to the firm's other products—may be able to use the rest of its line and its brand's reputation to get distribution for the new product. The producer may still have to pay for or supply all promotion, but it *is* able to get distribution.

A smaller producer—or a larger one going into a new market—might not be so lucky. It may have to resort to the use of less efficient middlemen, mail-order selling, or house-to-house selling.

Aggressive and persuasive personal selling are needed to put these products across—especially in the channels. But to impress the channel members, it may have to be supported by mass selling—and even a pulling policy. Manufacturer's or wholesaler's salespeople may be needed to give demonstrations—and set up displays and point-of-purchase materials. Perhaps the company will need to offer pricing deals. Personal salespeople may have to adapt a company's marketing mix to each individual situation.

TYPICAL MIXES FOR INDUSTRIAL GOODS

For the industrial buyer, personal selling is important

Unlike final consumers, industrial buyers usually do not seek out the goods they need. By accepted practice, they wait for the seller to present products or ideas. If a technical story must be told, direct distribution may be desirable or even necessary.

The promotion blends of both producers and middlemen tend to emphasize personal selling because most markets are relatively limited and concentrated—and the selling job is often technical. The specific marketing mix, however, varies by goods class.

Installations—president may become the sales rep

Some installations—specific buildings or pieces of property, or custom-made machines—are unique and have special technical characteristics. Promotion must inform target customers about these products—and persuade them of the advantages. Usually, personal selling is the best method.

New installations are normally sold directly by the contractor's or manufacturer's own sales representative, since (1) customers are relatively few and geographically concentrated, (2) the potential sales volume is large, and (3) there is need for design, technical assistance, and service of a kind that middlemen

Industrial goods usually need personal selling.

Courtesy The First National Bank of Chicago

don't normally provide. Even smaller companies may sell directly. The president or executive officers often serve as the sales force.

Brokers often handle sales of used buildings and land rights—since buyers and sellers are not regularly in the market. These specialized middlemen know the market and can provide a useful service.

Accessory equipment—middlemen are often needed

With some accessory equipment, direct-to-user personal selling by the producer is common—and important (1) to convince users of the merits of buying one company's product rather than others' and (2) to give technical assistance when necessary.

For other accessories, however, potential customers are spread out and need frequent contact by experienced salespeople. For such products, large firms use manufacturers' agents or brokers in less populous areas—and smaller firms use them throughout the country. These agents provide continuous contact—and there is no cost to the producer except when a sale is completed. The cost of the agents' regular sales calls is spread over a number of products—so the producer can obtain sales coverage without the high overhead sales costs he would incur doing this job for himself for only one line.

If effective agents or brokers are not available, then merchant wholesalers—such as mill supply houses or oil field supply houses—may be used. But relatively little sales effort can be expected from them. They may simply list the items in a catalog—and sell them if customers ask about them. Typically, their salespeople are not specialists—and cannot be expected to provide a technical sales job or service.

Farm product raw materials—many small farmers

The large number of small farmers creates a real discrepancy of quantity—and perhaps of assortment. This creates many specialized middlemen. Assemblers gather farm products in rural areas—and commission merchants and merchant wholesalers handle these products in the terminal markets, as the products are brought closer to users.

There usually is no promotion for farm products—except for the routine order taking which is needed to complete a sale. Usually, farm products are homoge-

Many small firms lead to specialized middlemen

Courtesy The First National Bank of Chicago

neous commodities sold in almost pure competition—so the channel systems have evolved to routinely bring buyers and sellers together.

Some farmers' cooperatives and trade associations try to differentiate their offerings—even to the extent of branding their products and spending fairly large sums on advertising. These mass selling efforts are not done by the individual producers, however.

Natural product raw materials—a few big producers

These products are produced by fewer and larger firms. There is little or no need for assemblers. Users are not numerous—compared to final consumers. The result is that many of these producers handle distribution themselves—although smaller producers may use brokers or drop-shippers. The smaller firms need practically the same market coverage as the larger firms, but have less to sell and a smaller sales volume to cover selling costs.

Most of these products have reached the market maturity or even sales decline stages—and tend to be standardized. Prices—which usually are available in newspapers—are competitive. Promotion is not unimportant, however. Buyers still must decide from whom they will buy. There are opportunities for much persuasive personal selling by order getters. The personality of the particular salesperson—and the company image which he conveys—can be the deciding factors.

Component parts and materials—personal contact may be vital

Most components producers are specialized—and cater to a relatively small, concentrated group of users. Since technical and design assistance may be needed, these producers normally deal directly with their target customers. If potential customers are numerous and widespread, however, agents may help locate and service new business. And they may be granted exclusive territories to encourage selling effort.

Promotion for these products must inform the prospective buyers about technical details—as well as price, quality, and delivery dependability.

Personal selling is the chief means of promoting component parts and materials. Some components are custom-made for specific applications—and sales reps are vital to assure that both buyers and sellers are aware of each other's needs and capabilities. Salespeople also are important because many competitors can offer the same technical service or even identical products—so much personal persuasion is needed. As with raw materials, given essentially homogeneous products and price, the competence and personality of the salesperson play an important role.

Supplies—middlemen rank high for maintenance items

Maintenance items are used widely—and are similar to convenience goods. Customers are widely dispersed, purchases of each item are relatively small, and little technical assistance or service is required. Since this is an ideal situation for middlemen, merchant wholesalers are common in this field. Mill supply houses and office and stationery supply stores often serve as middlemen for maintenance items. They are contacted directly by larger producers in the major metropolitan areas—and by manufacturers' agents in other areas. The smaller producers may use manufacturers' agents for all contacts with these merchant wholesalers.

For these goods, the producer's main promotion job is personal selling—in the channel—to get distribution. Some mass selling might be desirable to encourage wholesalers to stock the firm's products, but personal selling is vital—to actually get the wholesalers' business. The merchant wholesalers, then, provide an order-taking role.

Repair items

Repair items are used widely and—with some exceptions—may be distributed in the same way as maintenance items. Large customers might have complete repair facilities and prefer to buy repair parts directly. Smaller manufacturers and contractors usually prefer to have wholesalers carry the parts inventory—and perhaps handle the repair service, too.

Since most repair parts come directly from the original manufacturer, the main promotion job is to inform buyers of their availability. These products have a "captive market." Persuasion is not necessary.

However, if the market is large enough to attract competitors—as with some automotive and electrical products—then persuasion must be used, too. The main promotion appeals are faster, more dependable service. Mass selling might be able to tell this story—but personal selling may have to be used anyway, to meet competition.

Operating supply items

Operating supply items—with few exceptions—are similar to maintenance items and are distributed in the same way. The exceptions are some bulky items—such as coal, lubricants, and fuel oil. Direct distribution of these supplies by the producer may be sensible because of variations in technical service needs (as for lubricants) or the large sales volume (fuel oil). Drop-shippers commonly act as middlemen for the many small coal producers—to make the sales calls without handling the coal.

Services—usually are sold directly

Most "services" do not involve physical goods. There is nothing tangible to move through a distribution system. As a result, the producers typically sell directly to their customers. Where the potential customers are scattered, however, agents may enter to provide the initial contacts. Then, the producer's own salespeople can follow up.

Since most service businesses have relatively undifferentiated products, their promotion task is persuasion—they emphasize personal selling.

When a service is new, information about price, availability, and dependability is all that is needed. But competitors usually enter a profitable field quickly, and personal selling is then needed to hold customers.

SPECIAL FACTORS MAY AFFECT THE TYPICAL MARKETING MIX

A marketing manager may have to develop a mix which is not typical because of various market realities—including special characteristics of the product, or target market, the competitive environment, and his own firm's special capabilities and limitations. It will be useful to see how some of these market realities might affect marketing mix decisions.

Not all targets look the same

Size and geographic concentration affect sales contacts needed

If the sales potential of the target market is large enough, it may be possible to go directly to retailers, consumers, or users. This is especially true if the target customers are highly concentrated—as are the customers for many industrial goods. For final consumer goods, however, potential customers usually are numerous and widely scattered—and buy in small quantities. Although the total market may be relatively large, it might be split up into small geographic segments—with too little demand in each market to support a direct approach.

Value of item and frequency and regularity of purchase

Even low-priced items such as groceries may be handled directly if they are purchased often and the total volume is large—as in the case of home-delivered milk and bread. But for products purchased infrequently—even though purchases are large—specialists such as commission merchants, agents, brokers, and other middlemen may be useful. A critical factor is the cost of regularly providing the needed marketing functions—in relation to actual sales.

Customer preferences for personal contact

Customer preferences vary even within the same goods class. Some target customers—especially some industrial customers—don't like to deal with middlemen. Even though they may want only small quantities, they prefer to buy directly from manufacturers. The manufacturers may tolerate it because the customers sometimes may buy larger quantities.

Other buyers, however, prefer the convenience of buying through a middleman—because they can telephone orders and get immediate action from a local source. Two quite different marketing mixes could be needed to fully satisfy both types of customers.

Not all products are the same

Some goods—because of their technical nature, perishability, or bulkiness—require more direct distribution than is implied by their goods class.

Mike Jaeggi

Service companies usually need persuasive personal selling.

Bulky and perishable products create special problems.

Cary Wolinksy—Stock, Boston

Technical products

Complicated products—such as conveyor systems and electronic data processing equipment—call for a high degree of technical selling knowledge and expert installation and servicing. Wholesalers usually don't want—nor are they equipped—to provide all these required services.

Perishability

Perishable items—such as cut flowers, milk, and fresh seafood—may have to be handled directly. If many small producers are clustered together, specialists may develop to handle transportation, refrigeration, and storage. Complicated terminal markets—such as those dealing in fresh produce—may develop—along with many specialized commission merchants, brokers, merchant wholesalers, and truck wholesalers.

High-fashion items also are "perishable"—and more direct distribution may be sensible to speed the flow to retailers. Sometimes retailers and final consumers even go directly to the producers—to see the latest fashion showings in New York or Paris.

Bulkiness

Transportation, handling, and storage costs rise when bulky products are moved—making it hard for middlemen to operate. If a producer can't make enough sales contacts when selling bulky items direct, he may decide to use brokers, manufacturers' agents, and especially drop-shippers. They will make the sales contacts—and the producer will ship the goods directly to the customer.

Not all channel structures are the same

The marketing manager's "ideal" channel system may not be available or even possible—due to factors discussed below.

Availability of suitable and cooperative middlemen

The kinds of middlemen the marketing manager would like to use may not even be available or willing to cooperate. This is more likely if the company has entered a market late and competitors already have tired up the best middlemen—perhaps as part of a selective or exclusive distribution policy. *Aggressive market-oriented* middlemen usually aren't just waiting for someone to use them. They *may* be receptive to good proposals—but just another "me too" mix won't interest them.

The specific customers already being reached by each proposed middleman are very important. If these do not include the marketing manager's target markets, then that middleman doesn't have much to offer. A wholesaler specializing in groceries would have a valuable customer list for the food business—but it would not be of much value in distributing electronic machinery.

Uniformity of market coverage of available middlemen

The middlemen available in large urban areas may be very effective there—but may not cover outlying areas. Two channels may be needed to reach both areas. But it may also lead to a dual distribution problem. The middlemen who might be suitable for outlying areas may also cover urban areas—but not as well. Everyone likes to work where sales are plentiful and easy to make.

Nor does distribution through national or international companies guarantee uniform coverage. For example, A&P has a much larger share of the retail grocery market in the East than in the Midwest. And Sears Roebuck has been relatively stronger in the Midwest and West than in other sections. This simply means that, in practice, every channel for every target market must be tailor-made.

Financing required in channel system

Adequate credit may be critical for smoothing the flow through a channel system. Some middlemen enter a channel mainly because they can give financial assistance to the members. This is the role of factors. But some merchant wholesalers also hold a secure position in a channel because of their strong financial condition—and willingness to meet the financial needs of other channel members. This is especially true in international markets.

Nature of the company itself—is it big, rich, and unprejudiced?

In deciding what kind of mix to offer and how to work within a channel system, each marketing manager—at any level in the system—must evaluate his company's capabilities, needs, and potential contributions to a channel. Realistically, the best course may be to join a strong system rather than try to be the channel captain.

Size of company and width of product line

A company's size affects its place in a channel system—because size affects discrepancies of quantity and assortment. A large firm already handling a wide line of food or soap products, for example, may be in a good position to take on an additional product of the same type and handle it the same way—perhaps directly. In contract, a smaller company or one with unrelated lines might suffer from a discrepancy of quantity or discrepancy of assortment—or both—and would probably find middlemen more practical.

Financial strength

A company's financial strength is relevant if its customers need financial help.

Firms not able to provide this financing may find specialized middlemen useful. Selling agents, factors, merchant wholesalers, or large retailers, may be able to finance a producer or channel members—including users or final consumers. In fact, a channel captain's strength may depend heavily on financing ability.

PLANNING MUST USE THE PRODUCT LIFE CYCLE

So far we have been emphasizing the development of a good or the "best" marketing strategy for some target market. This can be risky, however, if we forget that markets are continually changing. This means that we must plan strategies which will adjust to likely changing conditions. Although some environmental changes are completely uncontrollable—and even unpredictable—some other changes *are* more predictable. And these should be considered when developing a plan. In particular, the product life cycle should be given serious attention because, typically, marketing variables should change throughout the product's life cycle.[3]

Figure 21-5 shows some of the typical changes in marketing variables which

Figure 21-5
Typical changes in marketing variables over the course of the product life cycle

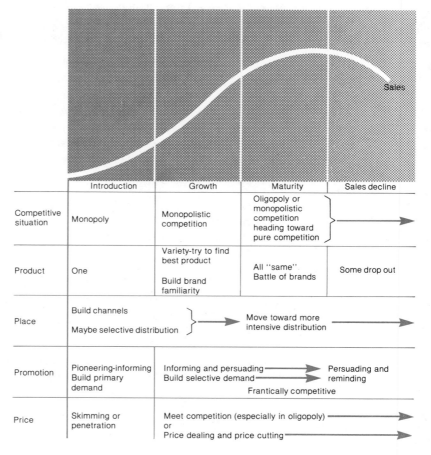

	Introduction	Growth	Maturity	Sales decline
Competitive situation	Monopoly	Monopolistic competition	Oligopoly or monopolistic competition heading toward pure competition	→
Product	One	Variety-try to find best product Build brand familiarity	All "same" Battle of brands	Some drop out
Place	Build channels Maybe selective distribution	} →	Move toward more intensive distribution	→
Promotion	Pioneering-informing Build primary demand	Informing and persuading → Build selective demand → Frantically competitive	Persuading and reminding	
Price	Skimming or penetration	Meet competition (especially in oligopoly) → or Price dealing and price cutting →		

might be needed over the course of a product life cycle. This figure should be a good review. Notice that as the product life cycle moves on, the marketing manager should *expect* to find more products entering "his" market—and pushing the market closer to pure competition or oligopoly. This means that as the cycle moves along he might want to shift from a selective to an intensive distribution policy *and* move from a skimming to a penetration pricing policy. The original strategic plan might even include these likely adjustments and the probable timing.

It is not necessary to make plans that will last for the full length of a product life cycle. A firm can drop out of a market. But it must be aware that the cycle will move on—and should make its own plans accordingly.

Long-range planning can be helpful

Our primary emphasis has been on developing marketing plans with relatively short time horizons—that is, one to five years. This fits with the reality of the fast-changing marketplace. At the same time, however, a wise marketing manager should try to think beyond this time frame. By thinking of markets in terms of changing life-styles and shifting needs and attitudes, it may be possible to see breakthrough opportunities which require only small changes in the firm's plans.

FORMS FOR EACH STRATEGY CAN MAKE PLANNING EASIER

To improve the planning process—and the communication of its results to others, including top management who may review the plans—it is helpful to use forms, such as the set shown in Figure 21–6. In this set, there are blanks for describing the target market, the nature of competition, the stage of the product life cycle, and important aspects of the proposed four Ps.

Figure 21–6 also provides a place for the time-related details—including sales, direct costs, and contribution to profit by month. There is also a place for the specific jobs to be done each month. Notice, also, that there are blanks for control purposes. Actual sales and costs would be inserted on the same planning form—and actual and cumulative differences could be calculated to determine when changes in the plan or wholly new plans are needed.

What period of time should the strategic plan cover?

Company planning for marketing, production, finance, and other functions may be done on a monthly or quarterly basis—but usually it is on an annual basis. While there is nothing basically superior about an annual period, accounting statements usually are prepared at least annually. Further, the money budgeted for the various marketing functions usually is related to time periods such as a year. And since seasons affect production and/or sales in most companies, the yearly period makes sense. As a result, marketing plans usually cover a year, or a year as part of a longer period—depending on the nature of the product, the competitive situation, and the current product life-cycle stage.

COMPANIES PLAN AND IMPLEMENT MARKETING PROGRAMS

Several plans make a program

Most companies implement more than one strategic plan at the same time. A marketing program blends all of a firm's strategic plans into one "big" plan. When the various plans in the company's program are quite different, there

Figure 21–6
Forms to plan and control each of a firm's market-oriented strategic plans—with illustrative comments and numbers for first two pages (one set of forms for each plan, number of time periods depending on length of plan)

Product identification ___McCarthy, BASIC MARKETING, 7th ed.___

Target market title ___Instructors of first marketing course___

Dimensions of target market ___All college and university level instructors interested in an integrated, analytical,___

___management-oriented approach to marketing—i.e. logical, organized, pragmatic instructors___

Competition ___Several authors trying to satisfy the same market and/or everyone (actual names___

___used in real situations)___

Nature of competition ___Monopolistic___

Product life cycle ___Market maturity___

Marketing mix

  Product characteristics

    Type ___New (revised) component part for instructor (and specialty good to students)___

    Total product ___Package of teaching materials and aids___

    Brand familiarity ___Recognition to preference___

  Place policies

    Type of channel members ___Direct to retail bookstores___

    Degree of market exposure ___Exclusive OK___

    Pulling or pushing ___Push to instructors, contact retailers___

    Physical distribution service level ___Immediate delivery to bookstores___

  Promotion thrust

    Blend type ___Heavy on personal selling, with some ads and exhibits at teachers' meetings___

    Type of salespeople ___Order getting and taking___

    Message emphasis ___Integrated analytical, etc., Package___

    Media emphasis ___Direct mail and professional journals___

  Price policies

    Flexibility ___One price___

    Level ___Meet competition___

    Geographic ___F.O.B. shipping point___

    Discounts and allowances ___20 percent of retail selling price, restricted returns___

1

may be less concern with how well they fit together—except as they compete for the firm's usually limited financial resources.

When the plans are more similar, however, the same sales force may be expected to carry out several plans. Or, the firm's advertising department may be expected to develop the publicity and advertising for several plans. In such situations, product managers will try to get enough of the common resources, say, salespeople's time, for their own plan.

Figure 21-6 *(continued)*

Time period

	Forecast	Actual	Difference	Cumulative difference
Sales	$ 0	$ 0	$ 0	$ 0
Costs (direct)	700	500	−200	−200
Contribution	$(−700)	$(−500)	$(−200)	$(−200)

Tasks to be done

Product   Be sure that all elements of package are meeting production schedule.

Place

Promotion   Prepare copy for direct mail pieces.

Prepare journal ad copy.

Prepare sales training materials.

Price   Set tentative price for text and other package elements.

Almost always, a company's resources are limited—so the marketing manager must make hard choices. He can't launch a plan to pursue every promising opportunity. Instead, limited resources force him to choose among alternative plans—while developing the program.

Find the best program by trial and error

How do you find the "best" program? There is no one best way of comparing various plans. Much reliance must be placed on management judgment. Yet some calculations are helpful, too. If a five-year planning horizon seems to be realistic for the firm's markets, then expected profits over the five-year period can be compared for each plan.

Assuming that the company has a profit-oriented objective, the more profitable plans could be looked at first—in terms of both potential profit and resources required. Also, the impact on the entire program should be evaluated. One profitable-looking alternative might be a poor first choice because it will eat up all the company's resources—and sidetrack several plans which together would be more profitable.

Some juggling among the various plans—comparing profitability versus resources needed and available—moves the company toward the *most profitable* program.

A computer program can help if a large number of alternatives must be evaluated. Actually, however, the computer would merely do the same function—trying to match potential revenues and profits against available resources.[4]

ALLOCATING BUDGETS FOR MARKETING PROGRAMS

Once the overall marketing program and five-year (or whatever) plans have been set, shorter-term plans also must be worked out. Typically, companies use annual budgets—both to plan what they are going to do and to provide control over various functions. Each department may be allowed to spend its budgeted amount—perhaps by months. As long as departments stay within their budgets, they are allowed considerable (or complete) autonomy.

Marketing managers have to set strategic plans and a marketing program.

Mary McCarthy

Budgeting for marketing—50%, 30%, or 10% is better than nothing

The most common method of budgeting for marketing expenditures is to compute a percentage of sales—either past or forecasted sales. The virtue of this method is its simplicity. A similar percentage can be used automatically each year—eliminating the need to keep evaluating the kind and amount of marketing effort needed and its probable cost. It allows those executives who aren't too tuned into the marketing concept to "write off" a certain percentage or number of dollars—while controlling the amount spent. When a company's top executives have this attitude, they often get what they expect from their marketing activities— something less than the best results.

Find the task, budget for it

Mechanically budgeting a certain percentage of past or forecasted sales leads to expanding marketing expenditures when business is good and sales are rising, and cutting back when business is poor. It may be desirable to increase marketing expenditures when business is good—but when business is poor, the most sensible approach may be to be *more,* not less, aggressive!

There are other methods of budgeting for marketing expenditures:

1. Match expenditures with competitors.
2. Set the budget as a certain number of cents or dollars per sales unit (by case, by thousand, or by ton), using the past year or estimated year ahead as a base for computation.
3. Set aside all uncommitted revenue—perhaps including budgeted profits. Companies willing to sacrifice some or all of current profits for future sales may use this approach, that is, *invest* in marketing.
4. Base the budget on the number of new customers desired or the amount required to reach a predetermined sales goal—as when entering new territories, increasing volume, or seeking other objectives. This is called the **task method**—basing the budget on the job to be done.

Task method can lead to budgeting without agony

In the light of our continuing discussion about planning marketing strategies to reach objectives, the most sensible approach to budgeting marketing expenditures would seem to be the *task method.*

The amount budgeted—using the task method—can be stated as a percentage of sales—but calculating the right amount is much more involved than picking up a past percentage. It requires a careful review of the strategic plans and the specific tasks to be accomplished this year—as part of each of these plans. The costs of these tasks, then, are totaled—to determine how much should be budgeted for marketing and the other business functions provided for in the plans. In other words, it should be possible to assemble the budgets directly from detailed strategic plans—rather than from historical patterns or ratios.

After the marketing department has received its budget for the year, it could, presumably, spend its money any way it saw fit. But if the previous planning-budgeting procedure has been followed, it would make sense to continue allocating expenditures within the marketing function according to the plans in the program.

Again, everyone in the marketing department and in the business should view the company as a total system and plan accordingly. If this is done, it will be possible to eliminate some of the traditional planning-budgeting activities which have been so agonizing—because one executive often was pitted against another and one department against another.

PROGRAM IMPLEMENTATION MUST BE PLANNED

Up to now, we have been mainly concerned with planning strategies—that is, the "big picture." Plans and programs bring this down to earth by adding the time-related details. Now we want to go a step further—illustrating graphical techniques which help marketing managers carry out their plans and programs. First, we will discuss techniques which are helpful for introducing new products or controlling special projects. Then we will consider aids for ongoing programs.

New products or projects can use PERT flowcharts

Some marketing managers find it helpful to draw flowcharts or diagrams of all the tasks that must be accomplished on schedule. In recent years, some firms have successfully applied such flowcharting techniques as CPM (critical path method) or PERT (program evaluation and review technique). These techniques were originally developed as part of the U.S. space program (NASA) to ensure that the various contractors and subcontractors' efforts would stay on schedule—and reach their goals as planned.

Detailed flowcharts are used—to describe which marketing activities must be done in sequence—and which can be done concurrently. These charts also show the time needed for various activities. By totaling the time allotments along the various chart paths, the most critical (the longest) path—as well as the most desirable starting and ending dates for the various activities—can be shown.

How flowcharting helped Diamond Alkali

The flowchart approach is credited with helping Diamond Alkali Company avoid a difficult situation when introducing a new product. By spending a few days flowcharting their plans for this product, Diamond Alkali found that they would spend about 76 weeks introducing it—although their predetermined schedule had allotted only 36 weeks for the introduction. By rearranging their plans—with the aid of the flowchart technique—they were able to squeeze the effort into 36 weeks. Now the use of flowcharts is mandatory for all Diamond Alkali new-product introductions.

Basically, a flowcharting effort follows a number of logical steps. First, a marketing strategy—better, the strategic plan—is needed. Then the various elements of the strategy which must be implemented over a period of time must be listed. Each of these elements, in turn, must be broken down into sub-elements or activities. A basic element such as sales promotion probably would include "Preparing a Sales Brochure." But this, in turn, would require detailed activities such as preparing performance charts and graphs, preparing rough copy, agency preparation of preliminary copy and layouts, and so on.

These activities are then flowcharted to pinpoint the bottlenecks.

The Diamond Alkali analysis isolated 105 activities—some of which could be done concurrently, but others which had to be done sequentially. Figure 21–7 shows the complete diagram drawn by Diamond Alkali analysts—with a

Figure 21-7
How Diamond Alkali diagrams the critical path for new-product introduction

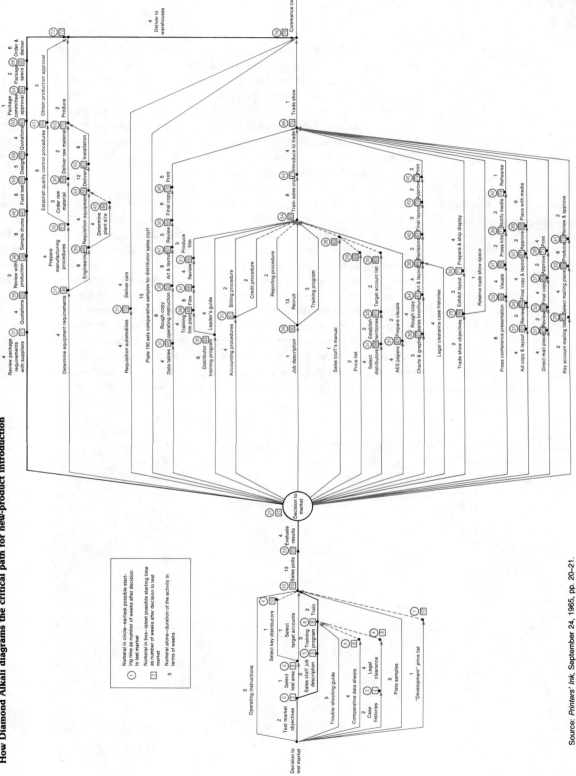

Source: *Printers' Ink*, September 24, 1965, pp. 20–21.

heavier line drawn through the critical path which would have delayed the product introduction and very likely reduced its total profitability.

It should be noted that this charting is *not* really complicated. The Diamond Alkali chart took two persons only about two days. Basically, what it requires is that all the activities—which will have to be performed anyway—be identified ahead of time and their probable duration and sequence shown on one diagram. (Nothing more than addition and subtraction is used.) Working with such information should be part of the planning function, anyway. Then the chart can be used for guiding implementation and control.

Regular plans call for monthly charts

Some marketing managers have found flowcharts helpful for keeping track of all the tasks in their ongoing plans. Each week or month in an ongoing 12-month plan, for example, can be graphed horizontally. How long each activity should take and when it should be started and completed can be seen. If it is clearly impossible to accomplish some of the jobs in the time allotted, this will become clear during the flowcharting process—and adjustments can be made. This might be necessary, for example, when several product managers had included heavy responsibilities for salespeople during the same month.

Basically, this kind of flowcharting is like the scheduling done by production planners—where wall-size graphic aids are often used. See Figure 21–8 for such a visual aid. Without such aids, it is easy to neglect some tasks—or to just wishfully presume that there will be enough time to accomplish each of the necessary tasks. By planning ahead—aided by a visual approach—one has a greater

Figure 21–8
Magnetic scheduling board showing a full year at a glance

Photo courtesy of Caddylak Systems, Inc., Westburg, N.Y., 11590.

chance of avoiding conflicts which can wreck the implementation of the company's plans and program.

CONCLUSION

This chapter has shown the importance of developing whole marketing mixes—not just policies for the individual four Ps which hopefully will fit together into some logical whole. The marketing manager is responsible for developing a worka-ble blend—integrating all of his firm's efforts into a coordinated whole—which makes effective use of its resources and guides it toward its objectives. This requires consideration of response functions—how the four Ps affect sales and profit. Ultimately, however, managers must be concerned with the market's re-sponsiveness to alternative marketing mixes. Ideally, they would know the exact shape of the alternative response functions but, in practice, they will have to rely on past experience (to some extent), marketing research if they have the time, plus a substantial amount of judgment. They also can study typical marketing mixes—and their apparent effectiveness in the marketplace—for clues about what works and how well.

As a starting place for developing new marketing mixes, a marketing manager can use the goods classes which have served as a thread through this text. Even though he may not be able to fully describe the needs and attitudes of his target markets, he may be able to make reasonable judgments about the appropriate goods class for a particular product. This, in turn, will have direct relevance for selecting the appropriate Place and Promotion.

Throughout the text we have emphasized the importance of marketing strategy planning. In this chapter, we have gone on to show that the marketing manager must develop a strategic plan for carrying out each strategy and, then, merge a set of plans into a marketing program. If this planning has been effective, the allocation of budgets to particular functions should be relatively simple.

Finally, it is the marketing manager's job to coordinate the implementation of the whole marketing program. Two types of flowcharting techniques were discussed. Both may help in this most difficult job of coordinating the activities of the firm—to better satisfy its target customers.

QUESTIONS AND PROBLEMS

1. Discuss whether Kodak was an imitator or innovative segmenter in the "instant picture" market.

2. Distinguish between competitive marketing mixes and "superior" mixes which might lead to breakthrough op-portunities.

3. Distinguish between a general marketing effort re-sponse function and a response function for one of the four Ps.

4. Explain how the use of response functions, even if they must be crudely estimated, could be helpful in develop-ing a marketing strategy.

5. Would a direct or some type of indirect channel of distri-bution be most appropriate for the following products? (Utilize the general factors discussed in this chapter and make any assumptions necessary to obtain a defi-nite answer.) *(a)* Hedge clippers, *(b)* fly swatters, *(c)* earth-moving machinery, *(d)* fingernail clippers, *(e)* mo-tor scooters, *(f)* grass seed, *(g)* picture frames, *(h)* trucks, *(i)* fresh apple cider.

6. For those products in the previous question where indirect distribution was the answer (in the light of the assumptions), indicate specifically the kinds of channels and the rest of the producer's marketing mix which might be appropriate.

7. Explain what marketing mix might be most appropriate for manufacturers of the following established products (assume average- to large-sized firms in each case and support your answer): (a) a completely new home permanent wave concept, packaged in a convenient kit; (b) a contracting service, capable of bidding on projects up to large dams; (c) lumber; (d) production tools for finishing furniture; (e) glass for window repair.

8. Distinguish clearly between strategic plans and marketing programs.

9. Consider how the job of the marketing manager becomes more complex as he must develop and plan several strategies as part of a marketing program. Be sure to discuss how he might have to handle different strategies at different stages in the product life cycle. To make this more concrete, consider the job of a marketing manager for a sporting goods manufacturer.

10. Briefly explain the task method of budgeting.

11. Discuss how a marketing manager could go about choosing among several possible marketing plans, given that he must because of limited resources. Do you feel that the job would be easier in the consumer goods or in the industrial goods area? Why?

12. Explain why the budgeting procedure is typically such an agonizing procedure, usually consisting of extending past budgets, perhaps with small modifications for current plans. How would the budgeting procedure be changed if the marketing program planning procedure discussed in the chapter were implemented?

SUGGESTED CASES

NOTES

1. "Kodak Exec Tells How the Instant Battle Strategy Shaped Up," *Detroit Free Press,* February 13, 1977, p. 1-b; and "How Kodak Will Exploit Its New Instamatic," *Business Week,* March 18, 1972, pp. 46–48.

2. David B. Montgomery and Charles B. Weinberg, "Modeling Marketing Phenomena: A Managerial Perspective," *The Journal of Contemporary Business,* Autumn 1973, pp. 17–43; J. Lámbin, "A Computer On-line Marketing Model," *Journal of Marketing Research,* May 1972, pp. 119–26; Michael L. Ray, "A Decision Sequence Analysis of Developments in Marketing Communication," *Journal of Marketing,* January 1973, pp. 29–38; and Leonard M. Lodish, "Vaguely Right" Approach to Sales Force Allocations," *Harvard Business Review,* January–February 1974, pp. 119–24; Leone P. Robert and Randall L. Schultz, "A Study of Marketing Generalizations," *Journal of Marketing,* Winter 1980, pp. 10–18; and John G. Meyers, Stephen A. Greyser, and William F. Massy, "The Effectiveness of Marketing's 'R&D' for Marketing Management: An Assessment," *Journal of Marketing,* January 1979, pp. 17–29; and Igal Ayal and Jehiel Zif, "Market Expansion Strategies in Multinational Marketing," *Journal of Marketing,* Spring 1979, pp. 84–94.

3. John E. Smallwood, "The Product Life Cycle: A Key to Strategic Marketing Planning," *MSU Business Topics,* Winter 1973, pp. 29–35; and Richard F. Savach and Laurence A. Thompson, "Resource Allocation within the Product Life Cycle," *MSU Business Topics,* Autumn 1978, pp. 35–44.

4. For further discussion on evaluating and selecting alternative plans, see W. I. Little, "The Integrated Management Approach to Marketing," *Journal of Marketing,* April 1967, pp. 32–36; Leon Winer, "A Profit-Oriented Decision System," *Journal of Marketing,* April 1966, pp. 38–44 (this article discusses discounting of cash flows for different lengths of time); see also S. M. Lee and R. E. Nicely, "Goal Programming for Marketing Decisions: A Case Study," *Journal of Marketing,* January 1974, pp. 24–32; J. Fred Weston, "ROI Planning and Control," *Business Horizons,* August 1972, pp. 35–42; Richard T. Hise and Robert H. Strawser, "Application of Capital Budgeting Techniques to Marketing Operations," *MSU Business Topics,* Summer 1970, pp. 69–76; and Louis V. Gerstner, "Can Strategic Planning Pay Off?" *Business Horizons,* December 1972, pp. 5–16.

H. Armstrong Roberts

1. Understand how sales analysis can aid strategy planning.

2. Understand the differences among sales analysis, performance analysis, and performance analysis using performance indices.

3. Understand the difference between natural accounts and functional accounts and their relevance for marketing cost analysis.

4. Know how to do a marketing cost analysis for customers or products.

5. Understand the difference between the full-cost approach and the contribution margin approach.

6. Understand how planning and control can be combined to improve the management process.

7. Understand what a marketing audit is—and when and where it should be used.

8. Recognize the important new terms (shown in red).

22

Controlling marketing plans and programs

Planning, implementing, and control—that's the basic management process.

Our primary emphasis so far has been on planning. Now, however, we must discuss **control**—the feedback process that helps the manger learn (1) how ongoing plans are working and (2) how to plan for the future.

Keeping a firmer hand on the controls

A good manager wants to know: which products' sales are highest and why; whether the products are profitable; what is selling where; and how much the marketing process is costing.

Unfortunately, the traditional accounting reports are usually of little help to the marketing manager—they are much too general. A particular company might be showing a profit, for example, while 80 percent of its business might be coming from only 20 percent of its products—or customers. The other 80 percent might be unprofitable. But without special analyses, the managers wouldn't know this. This 80/20 relationship is fairly common—and is often referred to as the *80/20 rule*.

Fortunately, it is possible for the marketing manager to get more detailed information about how the plans are progressing. This chapter discusses some of the kinds of information which can be available to the marketing manager—but only if he asks for and helps develop the necessary data.

This is an important chapter. And the techniques are not really complicated—basically requiring only arithmetic—and perhaps a computer if a large volume of adding and subtracting is required.[1]

SALES ANALYSIS SHOWS WHAT'S HAPPENING

Sales analysis—a detailed breakdown of a company's sales records—can be very informative—especially the first time it is done. Detailed data can quickly update marketing executives who have been out of touch with what is happening in the market. In addition, routine sales analyses prepared each week, month, or year may show trends—and permit managers to check their hypotheses, assumptions, and "gut feelings."[2]

Some managers resist sales analysis—or any analysis for that matter—because they don't fully appreciate how valuable it can be to them. One top executive in a large consumer products firm made no attempt to analyze his company's sales—even by geographic area. When asked why, he replied: "Why should we? We're making money!"

But today's profit is no guarantee that you'll make money tomorrow. In fact, ignoring market analysis can lead not only to poor sales forecasting but to poor decisions in general. One manufacturer did much national advertising on the assumption that the firm was, in fact, selling all over the country. A simple sales analysis, however, showed that most present customers were within a 250-mile radius of the factory! In other words, the firm did not know who and where its customers were—and was wasting most of the money it spent on national advertising.

But a marketing manager must ask for it

Detailed sales analysis is only a possibility, however, unless the manager asks for the data. Valuable sales information is regularly buried in sales invoice files—after the usual accounting functions are completed. Manual analysis of such records is so burdensome that it is seldom done.

Today—with computers—effective sales analysis can be done easily and at relatively small cost—if marketing managers decide to do it. In fact, the information desired can be obtained as a by-product of basic billing and accounts receivable procedures. The manager simply must be sure that identifying information on

A marketing manager must be sure the data he will want to analyze will be captured.

Milt & Joan Mann

important dimensions such as territory, sales reps, and so forth, are recorded in machine-processable form. Then, sales analysis and simple trend projections can easily be run.

What to ask for varies

There is no one "best" way to analyze sales data. One or several information breakdowns may be useful—depending on the nature of the company and product—and what dimensions are relevant. Typical breakdowns include:

1. Geographic region—state, county, city, sales rep's territory.
2. Product, package size, grade, or color.
3. Customer size.
4. Customer type or class of trade.
5. Price or discount class.
6. Method of sale—mail, telephone, or direct sales.
7. Financial arrangement—cash or charge.
8. Size of order.
9. Commission class.

Too much data can drown a manager

While some sales analysis is better than none—or getting data too late for action—extremely detailed sales breakdowns can easily "drown" a manager in reports. Computers can print over 1,000 lines per minute—faster than any manager can read. To avoid having to cope with mountains of data—much of which may be irrelevant—most managers move on to *performance analysis*.

PERFORMANCE ANALYSIS LOOKS FOR DIFFERENCES

Numbers are compared

Performance analysis looks for exceptions or variations from planned performance. In simple sales analysis, the figures are merely listed—without comparing them against standards. In performance analysis, comparisons are made. One territory might be compared against another, against the same territory's performance last year, or against expected performance.

The purpose of performance analysis is to improve operations. The salesperson, territory, or other factors showing poor performance can be identified—and singled out for detailed analysis and corrective action. Or, outstanding performances can be analyzed—to see if the successes can be explained and made the general rule.

Performance analysis doesn't have to be limited to sales. Other data can be analyzed, too. This data might include miles traveled, number of calls made, number of orders, or the cost of various tasks.

A performance analysis can be quite revealing—as shown in the following example.

Straight performance analysis—an illustration

A manufacturer of industrial products sold to wholesalers through five sales reps—each serving a separate territory. Total net sales for the year amounted to $2,386,000. Compensation and expenses of salespeople came to $198,000. This yielded a direct-selling expense ratio of 8.3 percent—that is, $198,000 ÷ $2,386,000 × 100.

Table 22–1
Comparative performance of
sales reps

Sales area	Total calls	Total orders	Order-call ratio	Sales by sales rep	Average sales rep order	Total customers
A............	1,900	1,140	60.0%	$ 912,000	$800	195
B............	1,500	1,000	66.7	720,000	720	160
C............	1,400	700	50.0	560,000	800	140
D............	1,030	279	27.1	132,000	478	60
E............	820	165	20.1	62,000	374	50
Total ...	6,650	3,284	49.3%	$2,386,000	$634	605

Table 22–2
Comparative cost of sales reps

Sales area	Annual compen-sation	Expense pay-ments	Total sales rep cost	Sales produced	Cost-sales ratio
A............	$ 22,800	$11,200	$ 34,000	$ 912,000	3.7%
B............	21,600	14,400	36,000	720,000	5.0
C............	20,400	11,600	32,000	560,000	5.7
D............	19,200	24,800	44,000	132,000	33.3
E............	20,000	32,000	52,000	62,000	83.8
Total ...	$104,000	$94,000	$198,000	$2,386,000	8.3%

This information—taken from a profit and loss statement—was interesting but didn't explain what was happening from one territory to another. To get a clearer picture, the manager compared the sales results with other data *from each territory* (see Tables 22–1 and 22–2).

The sales reps in Sales areas D and E obviously were not doing well. Sales were low—and marketing costs were high. Perhaps sales reps with more "push" could have done a better job—but the number of customers suggests that the potential might be low. Perhaps the whole plan needs revision.

The figures themselves, of course, do not provide the answers—but they do reveal the areas that need improvement. This is the main value of performance analysis. It is up to management to find the remedy—either by revising or changing the strategic plan.

PERFORMANCE INDICES SIMPLIFY HUMAN ANALYSIS

Comparing against "what ought to have happened"

With a straight performance analysis, the marketing manager can personally evaluate the variations among sales reps in an effort to explain the "why." This is time-consuming, however—and sometimes the "poor" performances really aren't as bad as the bare sales figures seem to indicate. There may be some uncontrollable factors in a particular territory which automatically lower the sales potential. Or, a territory just may not have good potential.

To get a better check on performance effectiveness, performance indices are used. With this approach, the marketing manager compares what did happen with "what ought to have happened."

A performance index is like a batting average

When standards have been set—that is, quantitative measures of what "ought to happen"—it is relatively simple to develop a performance index—a number—such as a baseball batting average—which shows the relation of one value to another.

Baseball batting averages are computed by dividing the actual number of hits by the number of times at bat (the possible number of times the batter could have had a hit) and then multiplying the result by 100 to get rid of decimal points. A sales performance index is computed the same way—by dividing actual sales by expected sales for an area (or sales rep, product, etc.) and then multiplying this figure by 100. If a sales rep is "batting" 82 percent, the index is 82.

A simple example shows where the problem is

Developing a performance index is shown in the following example—which assumes that population is an effective measure of sales potential.

In Table 22–3, the population of the United States is broken down by regions—as a percentage of the total population. The regions in this case are Eastern, Southern, Midwestern, Mountain, and Western.

This firm already has $1 million in sales—and now wants to evaluate performance in each region. The actual sales of $1 million—broken down in proportion to the population in the five regions—are shown in Column 2. This is what sales should have been if population were a good measure of future performance. Column 3 in Table 22–3 shows the actual sales for the year for each region. Column 4 shows measures of performance (performance indices)—Column 3 ÷ Column 2 × 100.

Population in the Eastern region was 25 percent of the population—and expected sales (based on population) were $250,000. Actual sales, however, were only $150,000. This means that the Eastern region's performance index was only 60—(150,000 ÷ 250,000) × 100—because actual sales were much lower than would be expected on the basis of population.

If population is a good basis for measuring expected sales (an important *if*), the explanation for poor sales performance will have to be traced further. Perhaps sales reps in the Eastern region are not working as hard as they should. Perhaps promotion there isn't as effective as elsewhere. Or, competitive products may have entered the market in this region.

Table 22–3
Development of a measure of sales performance (by regions)

Regions	(1) Population as percent of U.S.	(2) Expected distribution of sales based on population	(3) Actual sales	(4) Performance index
Eastern	25	$ 250,000	$ 150,000	60
Southern	20	200,000	250,000	125
Midwestern	25	250,000	300,000	120
Mountain	10	100,000	100,000	100
Western	20	200,000	200,000	100
Total	100	$1,000,000	$1,000,000	

Whatever the cause, it should be understood that performance analysis does not solve problems. It points out potential problems—and it does this well.

A SERIES OF PERFORMANCE ANALYSES MAY FIND THE REAL PROBLEM

Performance analysis allows a marketing manager to find out whether the firm's marketing plans are working properly and, if not, to correct the problems. But this may require a series of performance analyses—as shown in the following example.

To get a feel for the passage of time, follow this example carefully—one table at a time. Try to anticipate the marketing manager's decision.

The case of Stereo, Inc.

Stereo's sales manager found that sales for the Pacific Coast region were $130,000 below the quota of $14,500,000 (that is, actual sales were $14,370,000) for the January–June 1980 period. The quota was based on forecasted sales of the various types of stereo equipment which the company manufactures. Specifically, the quota was based on forecasts for each product type in each store in each sales rep's territory.

John Dexter—the sales manager—felt this difference was not too large (1.52 percent) and was inclined to forget the matter—especially since forecasts are usually in error to some extent. He thought about sending a letter, however, to all sales reps and district supervisors in the region—a letter aimed at stimulating sales effort.

The overall story of what was happening to Stereo's sales on the Pacific Coast is shown in Table 22–4. What do you think the manager should do?

Portland district had the poorest performance—but it wasn't too bad. Before writing a "let's get with it" letter to Portland and then relaxing, the sales manager decided to analyze the performance of the four sales reps in the Portland district. A breakdown of the Portland figures by sales reps is shown in Table 22–5. What conclusion or action is suggested now?

Since Ted Smith previously had been the top sales rep, the sales manager

Table 22–4
Sales performance—Pacific Coast region, January–June 1980 ($000)

District	Quota	Actual	Plus or minus	Performance to quota
Los Angeles	$ 4,675	$ 4,765	Plus $ 90	102%
San Francisco	3,625	3,675	Plus 50	101
Portland	3,000	2,800	Minus 200	93
Seattle	3,200	3,130	Minus 70	98
Total	$14,500	$14,370	Minus $130	99%

Table 22–5
Sales performance—Portland district, January–June 1980 ($000)

Sales representative	Quota	Actual	Plus or minus	Performance to quota
Jane Johnson	$ 750	$ 780	Plus $ 30	104%
Ted Smith	800	550	Minus 250	69
Bill Jones	790	840	Plus 50	106
Joe Carson	660	630	Minus 30	95
Total	$3,000	$2,800	Minus $200	93%

Table 22–6
Sales performance—selected stores of Ted Smith in Portland district, January–June 1980 ($000)

Stores	Quota	Actual	Plus or minus	Performance to quota
1	$140	$ 65	Minus $ 75	46%
2	110	70	Minus 40	69
3	105	60	Minus 45	57
4	130	65	Minus 65	50
5	205	150	Minus 55	73
Others	110	140	Plus 30	127
Total ...	$800	$550	Minus $250	69%

Table 22–7
Sales performance—Ted Smith in Portland district, January–June 1980 ($000)

Product	Quota	Actual	Plus or minus	Performance to quota
Tape recorders	$ 70	$ 80	Plus $ 10	114%
Portable phonographs	430	160	Minus 270	37
Console phonographs	150	150	0	100
Speakers	100	110	Plus 10	110
Others	50	50	0	100
Total	$800	$550	Minus $250	69%

wondered if Smith were having trouble with some of his larger customers. Before making a drastic move, he obtained an analysis of Smith's sales to the five largest customers (see Table 22–6). What action could the sales manager take now? Should Smith be fired?

Smith's sales in all the large stores were down significantly—although his sales in many small stores were holding up well. It would seem that Smith's problem was general. Perhaps he was simply not working. Before calling him, the sales manager decided to look at Smith's sales of the four major products. The data in Table 22–7 shows Smith's sales. What action is indicated now?

Smith was having real trouble with portable phonographs. Was the problem Smith or the phonographs?

Further analysis by product for the whole region showed that everyone on the Pacific Coast was having trouble with portable phonographs—because a regional competitor was cutting prices. But higher sales on other products had hidden this fact. Since phonograph sales had been doing all right nationally, the problem was only now showing up. You can see that this is *the* major problem.

Since overall company sales were going fairly well, many sales managers would not have bothered with this analysis. They might or might not have traced the problem to Smith. And without detailed sales records and performance analysis, the natural human reaction for Smith would be to blame business conditions or aggressive competition or to look for some other handy excuse.

Stay home and use the computer

This case shows that total figures can be deceiving. Marketing managers should not jump on the first plane or reach for the telephone until they have all the facts. Even worse than rushing to the scene would be a rash judgment based on incomplete information. Some students have wanted to fire Smith after the store-by-store data (Table 22–6) was given to them.

The home office should have the records and facilities to isolate problem areas—then rely on the field staff for explanations and assistance to locate the exact problem. Continuing detailed analysis usually gives better insights into problems, as this case shows. With computers, this can be done routinely and in great detail—*provided marketing managers ask for it.*

The "iceberg" principle—90 percent is below the surface

One of the most interesting conclusions to be drawn from the Stereo illustration is the iceberg principle—much good information is hidden in summary data.[3] Icebergs show only about 10 percent of their mass above water level—with the other 90 percent below water level—and not directly below, either. The submerged portion almost seems to be searching out ships that come too near.

The same is true of much business and marketing data. Since total sales may be large and company activities varied, problems in one area may be submerged below the surface. Everything looks calm and peaceful. But closer analysis may reveal jagged edges which can severely damage or even "sink" the business. The 90:10 ratio—or the 80/20 rule mentioned earlier—must not be ignored. Averaging and summarizing data can be helpful, but you should be sure that summaries don't hide more than they reveal.

MARKETING COST ANALYSIS—CONTROLLING COSTS, TOO

So far we have emphasized sales analysis. But sales come at a cost. And costs can and should be analyzed and controlled, too.

Detailed cost analysis has been very useful in the factory—but much less has been done with *marketing cost analysis.*[4] Accountants have shown little interest in the marketing process. Many think of salespeople as swingers who wine and dine the customers, play golf all afternoon, and occasionally pick up orders. In this situation, they feel it would be impossible to tie the costs of selling to particular products or customers. Many accountants feel, too, that advertising is almost a complete waste of money—that there is no way of relating it to

Managers must look beyond summaries to understand how their company is really doing.

Mary McCarthy

particular sales. They wind up treating it as a general overhead cost—and then forget about it.

Marketing costs have a purpose

Careful analysis of most marketing costs, however, shows that the money is spent for a specific purpose—either to develop or promote a *particular product* or to serve *particular customers*. It makes sense to allocate costs to specific market segments—or customers—or to specific products. In some situations, it is practical to allocate costs directly to the various market segments being served—especially when the market has been broken into geographic areas. This may permit direct analysis of the profitability of the firm's various target markets. In other cases, it may be desirable to allocate costs to specific customers—or specific products—and then add these costs for market segments—depending on how much each customer bought or the product mix of each segment.

In either case, marketing cost analysis usually requires a new way of classifying accounting data. Instead of using the natural accounts typically used for financial analysis, we have to use functional accounts.

Natural versus functional accounts—what is the purpose?

Natural accounts are the categories to which various costs are charged in the normal accounting cycle. These accounts include salaries, wages, social security, taxes, supplies, raw materials, auto, gas and oil expenses, advertising, and other such categories. These accounts are called "natural" because they have the names of their expense categories.

This is not the approach to cost analysis used in factories, however—and it is not the one we will use. In the factory, **functional accounts** show the *purpose* for which the expenditures are made. Factory functional accounts include shearing, milling, grinding, floor cleaning, maintenance, and so on. Factory cost accounting records are organized so that the cost of particular products or jobs can be calculated from them.

Marketing jobs are done for specific purposes, too. With some planning, the costs of marketing also can be assigned to specific categories—such as customers and products. Then their profitability can be calculated.

First, get costs into functional accounts

The first step in marketing cost analysis is to reclassify all the dollar cost entries in the natural accounts into functional cost accounts. For example, the many cost items in the natural *salary* account might be allocated to functional accounts with the following names: storing, inventory control, order assembly, packing and shipping, transporting, selling, advertising, order entry, billing, credit extension, and accounts receivable. The same would be true for rent, depreciation, heat, light, power, and other natural accounts.

The way natural account amounts are shifted to functional accounts depends on the method of operation of the particular firm. It might require time studies, space measurements, actual counts, and managerial estimates.

Then reallocate to evaluate profitability of profit centers

The next step is to reallocate the functional costs to those items—or customers or market segments—for which the costs were spent. The most common reallocation of functional costs is to products and to customers. After these costs are allocated, the detailed totals can be combined in any way desired—for example, by product or customer class, region, and so on.

The costs allocated to the functional accounts would equal in total those in the natural accounts. They are just organized in a different way. But instead of being used just to show total company profits, they can now be arranged to show the profitability of territories, products, customers, sales people, price classes, order sizes, methods of distribution, methods of sale, or any other breakdown desired. Each unit can be treated as a profit center.

Cost analysis finds "No-profit Jones"—tracking down the loser

These ideas can be seen more clearly in the following example. In this case, the usual accounting approach—with natural accounts—showed that the company made a profit of $938 last month (Table 22–8). When a question is raised about the profitability of the company's three customers, the profit and loss statement can't help. The managers decide to use marketing cost analysis—because they want to know whether a change in marketing methods might improve profit.

First, the costs in the five natural accounts are distributed to four functional accounts—sales, packaging, advertising, and billing and collection (see Table 22–9)—according to the functional reason for the expenses. Specifically, $1,000 of the total salary cost was for sales reps who seldom even come into the office—since their job is to call on customers; $900 of the salary cost was for packaging labor; and $600 was for office help. Assume that the office force split its time about evenly between addressing advertising material—and the billing and collection function. So the $600 is split evenly into these two functional accounts.

The $500 for rent was for the entire building—but 80 percent of the floor space was used for packaging and 20 percent for the office. Thus $400 is allocated

Table 22–8
Profit and loss statement

Sales		$17,000
Cost of goods sold		11,900
Gross margin		5,100
Expenses		
Salaries	$2,500	
Rent	500	
Wrapping supplies	1,012	
Stationery and stamps	50	
Office equipment	100	
		4,162
Net profit		$ 938

Table 22–9
Spreading natural accounts to functional accounts

Natural accounts	Sales	Packaging	Advertising	Billing and collection
Salaries	$1,000	$ 900	$300	$300
Rent		400	50	50
Wrapping supplies	1,012	1,012		
Stationery and stamps			25	25
Office equipment			50	50
Total $4,162	$1,000	$2,312	$425	$425

**Table 22–10
Basic data for cost and profit
analysis example**

Products

Products	Cost/Unit	Selling price/Unit	Number of units sold in period	Sales volume in period	Relative "bulk" per unit	Pack-aging "units"
A	$ 7	$ 10	1,000	$10,000	1	1,000
B	35	50	100	5,000	3	300
C	140	200	10	2,000	6	60
			1,110	$17,000		1,360

Customers

Customers	Number of sales calls in period	Number of orders placed in period	Number of each product ordered in period A	B	C
Smith..................	30	30	900	30	0
Jones	40	3	90	30	3
Brown	30	1	10	40	7
Total	100	34	1,000	100	10

to the packaging account. The remaining $100 is divided evenly between the advertising and billing accounts—because these functions used the office space about equally. Stationery, stamps, and office equipment charges are allocated equally to the latter two accounts for the same reason. Charges for wrapping supplies are allocated to the packaging account—because these supplies were used in packaging. In another situation, different allocations and even different accounts might be sensible—but these are workable here.

Calculating profitability of three customers

Now we can calculate the profitability of the company's three customers. But we need more information before we can allocate these functional accounts to customers or products. It is presented in Table 22–10.

Table 22–10 shows that the company's three products vary in cost, selling price, and sales volume. The products also have different "bulks"—and so the packaging costs aren't related to the selling price. For example, Product C is six times bulkier than A. When packaging costs are allocated to products, this must be considered. This is done by computing a new measure—a packaging unit—which is used to allocate the costs in the packaging account. Packaging units adjust for relative bulk and the number of each type of product sold. While only 10 units of Product C are sold, it is bulky and requires 10 times 6—or 60 packaging units. This will cause more of the costs in the packaging account to be allocated to each unit of Product C.

Table 22–10 also shows that the three customers require different amounts of sales effort, place different numbers of orders, and buy different product combinations.

Jones seems to require more sales calls. Smith places many orders which must be processed in the office—with increased billing expense. Brown seems to be a great customer—since he placed only one order—and that order was for 70 percent of the sales of high-valued Product C.

Table 22–11
Functional cost account
allocations

Sales calls	$1,000/100 calls	= $10/call
Billing	$425/34 orders	= $12.50/order
Packaging units costs	$2,312/1,360 packaging units	= $1.70/packaging unit or
		$1.70 for product A
		$5.10 for product B
		$10.20 for product C
Advertising	$425/10 units of C	= $42.50/unit of C

The computations for allocating the functional amounts to the three customers are shown in Table 22–11. There were 100 sales calls in the period. Assuming that all calls took the same amount of time, we can figure the average cost per call by dividing the $1,000 sales cost by 100 calls—giving an average cost of $10. Similar reasoning is used in breaking down the billing and packaging account totals. Advertising during this period was for the benefit of Product C only—so this cost is split among the units of C sold.

Calculating profit and loss for each customer

Now we can compute a profit and loss statement for each customer—combining his purchases and the cost of serving him. This is done in Table 22–12. A statement is prepared for each customer. And the sum of each of the four major components (sales, cost of goods sold, expenses, and profit) is the same as on the original statement (Table 22–8)—because all we've done is rearrange and rename the data.

The method is explained for customer Smith's statement in Table 22–12. Smith

Table 22–12
Profit and loss statements for customers

	Smith		Jones		Brown		Whole company
Sales							
A	$9,000		$ 900		$ 100		
B	1,500		1,500		2,000		
C			600		1,400		
Total sales		$10,500		$3,000		$3,500	$17,000
Cost of goods sold							
A	$6,300		$ 630		$ 70		
B	1,050		1,050		1,400		
C			420		980		
Total cost of goods sold		$ 7,350		$2,100		$2,450	$11,900
Gross margin		$ 3,150		$ 900		$1,050	$ 5,100
Expenses							
Sales calls ($10 each)	$ 300		$ 400.00		$ 300.00		
Order costs ($12.50 each)	375		37.50		12.50		
Packaging costs							
A	1,530		153.00		17.00		
B	153		153.00		204.00		
C			30.60		71.40		
Advertising			127.50		297.50		
		2,358		901.60		902.40	4,162
Net profit (or loss)		$ 792		$ (1.60)		$ 147.60	$ 938

bought 900 units of A at $10 each and 30 units of B at $50 each—for the respective sales totals ($9,000 and $1,500) shown in Table 22–12. Cost of goods sold is computed in the same way. Thirty sales calls cost $300. He placed 30 orders (at an average cost of $12.50 each) for a total ordering cost of $375. Total packaging costs amounted to $1,530 for A (900 units purchased times $1.70 per unit) and $153 for B (30 units purchased times $5.10 per unit). There were no packaging costs for C—because Smith did not buy any of Product C. Neither were any advertising costs charged to Smith—since all costs were spent promoting Product C—which he didn't buy.

Analyzing the results

We see now that Smith was the most profitable customer—yielding over 75 percent of the net profit.

This analysis shows that Brown was profitable, too—but not as profitable as Smith, because Smith bought three times as much. Jones was unprofitable—because he didn't buy very much and received one third more sales calls.

It is clear that the iceberg principle is operating again here. Although the company as a whole is profitable, customer Jones is not profitable. Before dropping Jones, however, the marketing manager should study the figures and the strategic plan very carefully. Perhaps Jones should be called on less frequently—or maybe he will grow into a profitable account. Now, he is at least covering some fixed costs. Dropping him might only shift those fixed costs to the other two customers—making them look less attractive. (See the discussion on contribution margin later in this chapter.)

The marketing manager may also want to analyze the advertising costs against results—since this is a heavy advertising expense against each unit of Product C. Perhaps the strategic plan should be revised.

Cost analysis is not performance analysis

Such a cost analysis is not a performance analysis, of course. If the marketing manager had budgeted costs to various jobs, it would be possible to extend this analysis to a performance analysis. This would be logical—and perhaps even desirable—but few companies have moved this far.

As the cost of computer record keeping drops, we may see more companies doing marketing cost and performance analysis. They could then compute fairly realistic profit and loss statements for individual customers—just as some factory cost accounting systems develop cost estimates for products. Then these figures could be compared with "expected" figures—to evaluate and control the plans and see how well they're working.

SHOULD ALL COSTS BE ALLOCATED

We have discussed the general principles, but allocating costs is tricky. Some costs are likely to be fixed for the near future—regardless of what decision is made. And some costs are likely to be *common* to several products or customers—making allocation difficult.

There are two basic approaches to handling this problem—the full-cost approach and the contribution-margin approach.

*Full-cost approach—
everything costs
something*

In the **full-cost approach,** all functional costs are allocated to products, cus-tomers, or other categories. Even fixed costs are allocated in some way—as are common costs. Because all costs are allocated, it is possible to subtract costs from sales and find the profitability of various customers, and so on. This *is* of interest to some managers.

The full-cost approach requires that some difficult-to-allocate costs be split on some basis. The assumption here is that the services provided for those costs are equally beneficial to customers, to products, or to whatever group they are allocated. Sometimes the allocation is done mechanically. But often logical reasoning can support the allocation—if we accept the idea that marketing costs are incurred for a purpose. For example, advertising costs not directly related to specific customers or products, *might* be allocated to *all* customers on the basis of their purchases. The theory is that advertising has helped bring in the sales.

*Contribution margin—
ignores some costs to
get results*

When we use the **contribution-margin approach,** all functional costs are not allocated in *all* situations. Why?

When various alternatives are being compared, it may be more useful to con-sider only the costs which are directly related to particular alternatives. Variables costs are particularly relevant here.

The contribution-margin approach focuses attention on variable costs—rather than on total costs. Total costs may include some fixed costs which do not change in the short run and can safely be ignored—or some common costs, which are more difficult to allocate.[5]

*The two approaches can
lead to different
decisions*

The difference between the full-cost approach and the contribution-margin approach is important. Different decisions may be suggested by the two ap-proaches—as we'll see in the following example.

Full-cost example

Table 22–13 shows a profit and loss statement—using the full-cost approach—for a department store with three operating departments. (These could be market segments or customers or products.)

The administrative expenses—which are the only fixed costs in this case—have been allocated to departments based on the sales volume of each depart-ment—a typical method of allocation. In this case, some managers argued that

**Table 22–13
Profit and loss statement by
department**

	Totals	Depart-ment 1	Depart-ment 2	Depart-ment 3
Sales	$100,000	$50,000	$30,000	$20,000
Cost of goods sold	80,000	45,000	25,000	10,000
Gross margin	$ 20,000	$ 5,000	$ 5,000	$10,000
Other expenses				
Selling expenses	5,000	2,500	1,500	1,000
Administrative expenses	6,000	3,000	1,800	1,200
Total other expenses	$ 11,000	$ 5,500	$ 3,300	$ 2,200
Net Profit or (Loss)	$ 9,000	$ (500)	$ 1,700	$ 7,800

Table 22–14
Profit and loss statement by department if Department I were eliminated

	Totals	Department 2	Department 3
Sales	$50,000	$30,000	$20,000
Cost of goods sold	35,000	25,000	10,000
Gross margin	$15,000	$ 5,000	$10,000
Other expenses			
Selling expenses	2,500	1,500	1,000
Administrative expenses	6,000	3,600	2,400
Total other expenses	$ 8,500	$ 5,100	$ 3,400
Net Profit or (Loss)	$ 6,500	$ (100)	$ 6,600

Table 22–15
Contribution-margin statement by departments

	Totals	Dept. 1	Dept. 2	Dept. 3
Sales	$100,000	$50,000	$30,000	$20,000
Variable costs				
Cost of goods sold	80,000	45,000	25,000	10,000
Selling expenses	5,000	2,500	1,500	1,000
Total variable costs	$ 85,000	$47,500	$26,500	$11,000
Contribution margin	15,000	2,500	3,500	9,000
Fixed costs				
Administrative expenses	6,000			
Net profit	$ 9,000			

Department 1 was clearly unprofitable—and should be eliminated—because it showed a net loss of $500. Were they right?

To find out, see Table 22–14—which shows what would happen if Department 1 were eliminated.

Several facts become clear right away. The overall profit of the store would be reduced if Department 1 were dropped. Fixed costs of $3,000—now being charged to Department 1—would have to be allocated to the other departments. This would reduce net profit by $2,500—since Department 1 previously covered $2,500 of the $3,000 of fixed costs. This shifting of costs would then make Department 2 unprofitable!

Contribution-margin example

A contribution margin income statement for the same department store is shown in Table 22–15. Note that each department has a positive contribution margin. Here the Department 1 contribution of $2,500 is obvious. This actually is the amount that would be lost if Department 1 were dropped. (This example assumes that the fixed administrative expenses are *truly* fixed—that none of them would be eliminated if this department were dropped.)

A contribution-margin income statement shows the contribution of each department more clearly—including its contribution to both fixed costs and profit. As long as a department has some contribution margin—and as long as there are no better uses for the resources used in it—the department should be retained.

Contribution margin versus full cost—choose your side

The full-cost approach often leads to arguments within a company. Any method of allocation can make some products or customers appear less profitable than some other allocation method.

Assigning all common advertising costs to customers based on their purchases, for example, can be supported logically. But it also can be criticized on the grounds that it may make large-volume customers appear less profitable than they really are—especially if the marketing mix aimed at the larger customers emphasizes price more than advertising.

Those in the company who want the smaller customers to look more profitable will argue *for* this allocation method—on the grounds that general advertising helps "build" good customers because it affects the overall image of the company and its products.

The argument about allocation methods can be deadly serious—because the method used may reflect on the performance of various company managers—and affect their salaries and bonuses. Product managers, for example, would be vitally interested in how the various fixed and common costs were allocated to their products. Each, in turn, might like to have costs shifted to others' products.

Arbitrary allocation of costs also may have a direct impact on sales reps' morale. If they see their variable costs loaded with additional common or fixed costs over which they have no control, they may decide—"What's the use?"

To avoid this problem, the contribution-margin approach is often used. It avoids many of the problems of arbitrarily allocating fixed or common costs. It is especially useful for evaluating alternatives—and for showing operating managers and salespeople how they're doing. The contribution-margin approach shows what they have actually contributed to covering general overhead and profit.

Top management, on the other hand, often finds full-cost analysis more useful. In the long run, some products, departments, or customers must pay for the fixed costs. Full-cost analysis has its place here.

PLANNING AND CONTROL COMBINED

We have been treating sales and cost analyses separately up to this point. But management often will combine them to keep a running check on its activi-

Deciding how to analyze cost affects the apparent profitability of areas—and employee morale.

Cornell Capa—Magnum Photos

Table 22–16
XYZ Hardware Company
planning and control chart

	Contribution to store					Store ex-pense	Op-erating profit	Cumu-lative operat-ing profit
	Dept. A	Dept. B	Dept. C	Dept. D*	Total			
January								
Planned	2,700	900	400	−100	3,900	2,400	1,500	1,500
Actual								
Variation								
February								
Planned	2,000	650	250	−100	2,800	2,400	400	1,900
Actual								
Variation								
November								
Planned	3,200	750	250	0	4,200	2,400	1,800	10,650
Actual								
Variation								
December								
Planned	6,300	1,250	400	900	8,850	3,200	5,650	16,300
Actual								
Variation								
Total								
Planned	31,600	7,000	6,900	−400	45,300	28,800	16,300	16,300
Actual								
Variation								

* The goal of minus $400 for this department was established on the same basis as the goals for the other departments, i.e., it represents the same percentage gain over last year, when Department D's loss was $420. Plans call for discontinuance of the department unless it shows marked improvement by the end of the year.

ties—to be sure the plans are working—and to see when and where new strategies are needed.

Sales + Costs + Everybody helps = $8,150

Let's see how this works at the XYZ Hardware Company—a typical hardware retailer.

This firm netted $15,500 last year. Expecting no basic change in the competitive situation—and slightly better local business conditions—Jim Smith, the owner, set this year's profit objective at $16,300—an increase of about 5 percent.

Next, he developed tentative plans to show how this higher profit could be made. He estimated the sales volumes, gross margins, and expenses—broken down by months and by departments in his store—that would be needed to net $16,300.

Table 22–16 is a planning and control chart which Jim developed to show the contribution each department should make each month. At the bottom of Table 22–16, the plan for the year is summarized. Notice that space is provided to insert the actual performance and a measure of variation—allowing both planning and control to be done with this chart.

Table 22–16 shows that XYZ's owner is focusing on the monthly contribution by each department. The purpose of monthly estimates is to get more frequent feedback—and allow faster adjustment of plans. Generally, the shorter the planning and control period, the easier it is to correct problems before they become emergencies.

In this example, a modified contribution-margin approach is being used—since some of the fixed costs can be allocated logically to particular departments. On this chart, the balance left after direct fixed and variables costs are charged to departments is called "Contribution to Store." The idea is that each department will contribute to covering *general* store expenses—such as top-management salaries and Christmas decorations—and to net profits.

In Table 22–16, we see that the whole operation is brought together when the monthly operating profit is computed. This contribution from each of the four departments is totaled—then general store expenses are subtracted to obtain the operating profit for each month.

Each department must plan and control, too

Table 22–17 shows a similar planning and control chart for a single XYZ department—Department B. In this table, actual results have been entered for the month of January. An unfavorable difference is revealed between planned and actual sales performance (−$1,400)—and gross profit (−$170).

Now the marketing manager must decide why actual sales were less than projected—and begin to make new plans. Possible hypotheses are that: (1) prices were too high; (2) promotion was ineffective; (3) the product selection was not

**Table 22–17
XYZ Hardware Company planning and control chart—Department B**

	Sales	Gross profit	Direct expense Total	Direct expense Fixed	Direct expense Variable	Contribution to store	Cumulative-contribution to store
January							
Planned	6,000	1,800	900	600	300	900	900
Actual	4,600	1,630	830	600	115	800	800
Variation	−1,400	−170	70	0	70	−100	−100
February							
Planned	5,000	1,500	850	600	250	650	1,550
Actual							
Variation							
November							
Planned	7,000	2,100	1,350	1,000	350	750	5,750
Actual							
Variation							
December							
Planned	9,000	2,700	1,450	1,000	450	1,250	7,000
Actual							
Variation							
Total							
Planned	60,000	18,000	11,000	8,000	3,000	7,000	7,000
Actual							
Variation							

satisfying the target customers; and (4) errors might have been made in marking the prices or in totaling the sales figures.

Corrective action could take either of two courses: improving tactics (or their implementation)—or developing new, more realistic strategies.

The marketing manager must take charge

Computers are commonly used for data analysis in larger companies. Increasingly, smaller companies have access to time-sharing systems offered by computer manufacturers and service bureaus.

But this kind of analysis is not possible unless the data is in machine-processable form—so it can be sorted and analyzed rapidly. Here the creative marketing manager plays a crucial role—by insisting that the necessary data is collected. If the data he wishes to analyze is not captured as it comes in, information will be difficult if not impossible to get later. The only limitation on more effective and revealing data analysis is the imagination of the marketing manager—now that machines can handle the drudgery.

THE MARKETING AUDIT

While crises pop, planning and control must go on

The analyses we have discussed so far are designed to help a firm plan and control its operations. They can help a marketing manager do a better job. Often, however, the control process tends to look at only a few critical elements— such as sales variations by product in different territories—and misses such things as the appropriateness of various marketing strategies—and the possible effectiveness of alternative mixes.

The marketing manager usually is responsible for day-to-day implementing as well as planning and control—and may not have the time to evaluate the effectiveness of the firm's efforts. Sometimes, crises are popping in several places at the same time—and attention must be focused on adjusting marketing mixes or shifting strategies in the short run.

To make sure that the whole marketing program is *regularly* evaluated—not just in times of crisis—marketing specialists have developed a new concept— the marketing audit. It is similar to the accounting audit—or the personnel audit— both of which have been accepted by business for some time.

Managers should conduct regular marketing audits.

Mary McCarthy

The **marketing audit** is a systematic, critical, and unbiased review and appraisal of the basic objectives and policies of the marketing function—and of the organization, methods, procedures, and people employed to implement the policies.[6]

A marketing audit requires a detailed look at the company's current strategic plans—to see if they are still the "best" strategic plans the firm can offer. Given that customers' needs and attitudes change—and competitors are continually developing new and better plans—plans that are more than a year or two old may be getting out of date—or may even be obsolete. Sometimes, marketing managers are so close to the "trees that they can't see the forest." An outsider can help see whether the company really has focused on some unsatisfied needs—and is offering the appropriate marketing mixes. Basically, the auditor would use our strategic planning framework—but instead of developing plans, he would work backward—and evaluate the plans which are being implemented. He would also want to evaluate the quality of the effort—looking at who is doing what and how well. This means interviewing customers, competitors, channel members, and employees. A marketing audit can be a big job—but if it helps assure that the company's strategic plans are on the right track and being implemented properly—it can be well worth the effort.

An audit shouldn't be necessary—but usually it is

A marketing audit takes a big view of the business—and evaluates the whole marketing program. It might be done by a separate department within the company—perhaps by a "marketing controller." Or to avoid bias, it might be better to have it done by an outside organization—such as a management consulting firm.

Ideally, a marketing audit should not be necessary. A good manager does his very best in planning, implementing, and control—and should be continually evaluating the effectiveness of the operation.

In practice, however, managers often become identified with certain strategies—and pursue them persistently—when other strategies might be more effective. Since an outside view can give needed perspective, we may see greater use of the marketing audit in the future.

CONCLUSION

In this chapter, we saw that sales and cost analysis can help a marketing manager control a marketing program—and that control procedures can be useful in planning. Controls lead to feedback that can aid planning.

Simple sales analysis just gives a picture of what has happened. But when sales forecasts or other data showing expected results are brought into the analysis, it is possible to evaluate performance—using performance indices.

Cost analysis also can be useful—if "natural" accounting costs are allocated to market segments, customers, products, or other categories—using functional cost breakdowns. There are two basic approaches to cost analysis—full-cost and contribution-margin. Using the full-cost approach, all costs are allocated in some way. Using the contribution-margin approach, only the variable costs are allocated. Both methods have their advantages and special uses.

Ideally, the marketing manager should arrange for a constant flow of data that can be analyzed routinely—preferably by machine—to help him to control present plans and plan new strategies. A marketing audit may help this ongoing effort. Either a separate department within the company or an outside organization might conduct this audit.

It is clear that a marketing program must be controlled. Good control helps the marketing manager locate and correct weak spots—and at the same time find strengths which he may be able to turn to his own advantage—and apply throughout his marketing program. Control works hand in hand with planning.

QUESTIONS AND PROBLEMS

1. Various breakdowns of sales are suggested for sales analysis in certain situations, depending upon the nature of the company and its product. Describe a situation (one for each) where each of the following breakdowns would yield useful information. Explain why.
   a. By geographic region.
   b. By product.
   c. By customer.
   d. By size of order.
   e. By size of sales representative's commission allowed (on each product or product group.)

2. Distinguish between a sales analysis and a performance analysis.

3. Explain carefully what the "iceberg principle" should mean to the marketing manager.

4. Explain the meaning of the comparative performance and comparative cost data in Tables 22–1 and 22–2. Why does it appear that eliminating sales areas D and E would be profitable?

5. Most sales forecasting is subject to some error (perhaps 5 to 10 percent). Is it proper to conclude then that variations in sales performance of 5 to 10 percent above or below quota are to be expected? If so, how should such variations be treated in evaluating performance?

6. Explain why there is a controversy between the advocates of the net profit approach and the contribution margin approach to cost analysis.

7. The profit and loss statement for June for the Whiting Co. is shown. If competitive conditions make price increases impossible, and management has cut costs as much as possible, should the Whiting Co. stop selling to hospitals and schools? Why?

	Retailers	Hospitals and schools	Total
Sales			
80,000 units at $0.70	$56,000		$56,000
20,000 units at $0.60		$12,000	12,000
Total	$56,000	$12,000	$68,000
Cost of goods sold	40,000	10,000	50,000
Gross margin	$16,000	$ 2,000	$18,000
Sales and administrative expenses			
Variable	$ 6,000	$ 1,500	$ 7,500
Fixed	5,600	900	6,500
Total	$11,600	$ 2,400	$14,000
Net profit (loss)	$ 4,400	$ (400)	$ 4,000

8. Explain why it is so important for the marketing manager to be directly involved in the planning of control procedures.

9. Explain why a marketing audit might be desirable even in a well-run company. Discuss who or what kind of an organization would be the best one to conduct a marketing audit. Would a marketing research firm be good? Would the present CPA firms be most suitable?

NOTES

1. James M. Hulbert and Norman E. Toy, "A Strategic Framework for Marketing Control," *Journal of Marketing,* April 1977, pp. 12–21; and Sam R. Goodman, *Techniques of Profitability Analysis* (New York: John Wiley & Sons, 1970, especially chap. 1.

2. R. I. Haley and R. Gatty, "Monitor Your Markets Continuously," *Harvard Business Review,* May—June 1968, pp. 65–69; and D. H. Robertson, "Sales Force Feedback on Competitors' Activities," *Journal of Marketing,* April 1974, pp. 69–71.

3. Richard D. Crisp, *Marketing Research* (New York: McGraw-Hill Book Co., 1957), p. 144.

4. Patrick M. Dunne and Harry I. Wolk, "Marketing Cost Analysis: A Modularized Contribution Approach," *Journal of Marketing,* July 1977, pp. 83–94; Leland L. Beik and Stephen L. Buzby, "Profitability Analysis by Market Segments," *Journal of Marketing,* July 1973, pp. 48–53; D. R. Longman and M. Schiff, *Practical Distribution Cost Analysis* (Homewood Ill.: Richard D. Irwin, Inc., 1955); Frank H. Mossman, Paul M. Fischer, and W. J. E. Crissy, "New Approaches to Analyzing Marketing Profitability," *Journal of Marketing,* April 1974, pp. 43–48; "Segmental Analysis: Key to Marketing Profitability," *MSU Business Topics,* Spring 1973, pp. 42–49; and V. H. Kirpalani and Stanley J. Shapiro. "Financial Dimensions of Marketing Management." *Journal of Marketing,* July 1973, pp. 40–47.

5. Technically, a distinction should be made between variable and direct costs, but we will use these terms interchangeably. Similarly, not all common costs are fixed costs and vice versa, but the important point here is to recognize that some costs are fairly easy to allocate, and other costs are not.

6. A. R. Oxenfeldt, "The Marketing Audit as a Total Evaluation Program," in *Analyzing and Improving Marketing Performance: Marketing Audits in Theory and Practice* (New York: American Management Association, 1959), p. 26: see also John F. Grashof, "Conducting and Using a Marketing Audit," in *Readings in Basic Marketing,* 3d ed., ed. E. J. McCarthy et al. (Homewood, Ill.: Richard D. Irwin Inc., 1981); L. M. Wooton and J. L. Tarter, "The Productivity Audit: A Key Tool for Executives, *MSU Business Topics,* Spring 1976, pp. 31–41; Frazer B. Wilde and Richard F. Vancil, "Performance Audits by Outside Directors," *Harvard Business Review,* July—August 1972, pp. 112–16; and Edward M. Mazze and John T. Thompson, Jr., "Organization Renewal: Case Study of a Marketing Department," *MSU Business Topics,* Summer 1973, pp. 39–44.

Don Smetzer

When you finish this chapter, you should:

1. Understand the various ways that businesses can get into international marketing.

2. Understand what multinational corporations are.

3. Understand the kinds of opportunities in international markets.

4. Understand the market dimensions which may be useful in segmenting international markets.

5. Recognize the important new terms (shown in red).

23

Marketing strategy planning for international markets

Did you know that more packaged spaghetti is eaten in Germany than in Italy?

Planning strategies for international markets can be even harder than for domestic markets because cultural differences are more important. Also, the uncontrollable variables may vary more. Each foreign market must be treated as a separate market—with its own sub-markets. Lumping together all people outside the United States as "foreigners"—or assuming they are just like U.S. customers—will almost guarantee failure.

There has been too much stereotype thinking about international marketing. This chapter tries to get rid of some of these misconceptions—and to suggest how strategy planning has to be adjusted when a firm goes into international marketing. We will see that a marketing manager must make several strategic decisions about international marketing: (1) whether the firm even wants to work in international markets at all and, if so, its degree of involvement, (2) in which markets, and (3) what organization arrangements should be made when it moves beyond its domestic activities. See Figure 23–1.

International markets are very important to the United States and many U.S. firms. There are many opportunities outside this country. And some U.S. firms are deeply involved—earning more abroad than in the United States. Let's look first at how important international marketing is, and then begin to consider the strategic decisions which a marketing manager must make when planning strategies for international markets.

**Figure 23–1
Strategic decisions about
international marketing**

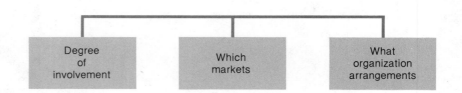

THE IMPORTANCE OF INTERNATIONAL MARKETS TO THE UNITED STATES

*As a nation grows, its
trade grows*

All countries trade to some extent—we live in an interdependent world. But you may be surprised to know that the United States is the largest exporter and importer of goods in the world. Our share of the world's foreign trade is about 12 percent. Even the United Kingdom and Japan—which have built their growth on exports and imports—are below the United States. Most of the largest traders are highly developed nations. Trade seems to expand as a country develops and industrializes.

Note, however, that while the United States is the biggest trading nation in the world, foreign trade does not dominate our economy. This is because of the large size of our national income. Our foreign trade makes up a relatively small part of our income—less than 15 percent—but the smaller part is still greater in total dollars than in other major trading countries.

DEGREES OF INVOLVEMENT IN INTERNATIONAL MARKETING

Attractive opportunities in foreign countries have led many companies into worldwide operations. The marketing concept is less understood in some foreign markets. So there are exciting opportunities for those who want to apply it abroad. There are varying degrees of involvement, however. A marketing manager can choose among six basic kinds of involvement—as shown in Figure 23–2—exporting, licensing, contract manufacturing, management contracting, joint venturing, and wholly-owned subsidiaries. Let's look at these possibilities now.

*Exporting often comes
first*

Some companies get into international marketing by just exporting the products they are now producing. Sometimes this is just a way of "getting rid of" surplus output. Other times, it comes from a real effort to look for new opportunities.

Exporting is selling some of what the firm is producing to foreign markets. Often this is tried without changing the product or even the service or instruction manuals! As a result, some early efforts are not very satisfying—to buyers or sellers.

Exporting gets a firm involved in a lot of government "red tape." Beginning exporters may build their own staffs or depend on specialized middlemen to handle these details. Export agents can handle the paper work as the goods are shipped outside the country. Then agents or merchant wholesalers can handle

**Figure 23–2
Kinds of involvement in
international marketing that a
marketing manager can choose**

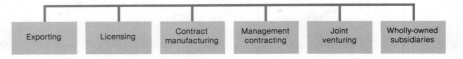

Exporting means selling present products in foreign markets.

Milt & Joan Mann

the importing details. Even large manufacturers with many foreign operations may use international middlemen for some products or markets. They know how to handle the sometimes confusing formalities and specialized functions. Even a small mistake can tie goods up at national borders for days—or months.

Export departments within firms are often treated as "stepchildren" by the regular departments. Increasingly, though, companies are aggressively pursuing foreign market prospects as they find their foreign operations becoming more profitable than domestic activities. Then, the export department's status rises—or exporting is integrated into the regular operation.

Some relationships get a firm more involved

Exporting doesn't have to involve permanent relationships. Of course, channel relationships take time to build and shouldn't be treated lightly. Sales reps' contacts in foreign countries are "investments." Nevertheless, it is relatively easy to cut back on these relationships or even drop them.

Some firms, on the other hand, develop more formal and permanent relationships with nationals in foreign countries—including licensing, contract manufacturing, management contracting, and joint venturing.

Licensing is an easy way

Licensing is a relatively easy way to enter foreign markets. **Licensing** means selling the right to use some process, trademark, patent, or other right—for a fee or royalty. The licensee takes most of the risk—because it must invest some capital to use the right.

This can be an effective way of entering a market if good partners are available. Gerber entered the Japanese baby food market in this way. But Gerber still exports to other countries.

Contract manufacturing takes care of the production problems

Contract manufacturing means turning over production to others, while retaining the marketing process. Sears, Roebuck used this approach as it opened stores in Latin America and Spain.

*Gerber entered the Japanese
market through licensing.*

Courtesy Gerber Products Co.

This approach can be especially good where labor relations are difficult or there are problems obtaining supplies and "buying" government cooperation. Growing nationalistic feelings may make this approach more attractive in the future.

*Management
contracting sells
know-how*

Management contracting means the seller provides only management skills—the production facilities are owned by others. Some mines and oil refineries are operated this way—and Hilton operates hotels all over the world for local owners. This is a relatively low-risk approach to international marketing. No commitment is made to fixed facilities—which can be taken over or damaged in riots or wars. If conditions get too bad, the key management people can fly off on the next plane and leave the nationals to manage the operation.

*Joint venturing is more
involved*

Joint venturing means a domestic firm entering into a partnership with a foreign firm. As with any partnership, there can be honest disagreements over objectives—for example, about how much profit is desired and how fast it should be paid out—and operating policies. Where a close working relationship can be developed—perhaps based on a U.S. firm's technical and marketing know-how, and the foreign partner's knowledge of the market and political connections—this approach can be very attractive to both parties. At its worst, it can be a nightmare and cause the U.S. firm to want to go into a wholly-owned operation. But the terms of the joint venture may block this for years. Or the foreign partners may acquire enough know-how to be tough competitors. And growing nationalistic feelings might block this anyway. More countries are requiring joint ventures—with nationals controlling at least 51 percent.

*Wholly-owned
subsidiaries give more
control*

When a firm feels that a foreign market looks really promising, it may want to go the final step. A **wholly-owned subsidiary** is a separate firm—owned by a parent company. This gives complete control and helps a foreign branch work more easily with the rest of the company.

Some multinational companies have gone this way. It gives them a great deal of freedom to move goods from one country to another. If it has too much capacity in a country with low production costs, for example, some production may be moved there from other plants—and then exported to countries with higher production costs. This is the same way that large firms in the United States ship goods from one area to another—depending on costs and local needs.

MULTINATIONAL CORPORATIONS EVOLVE TO MEET INTERNATIONAL CHALLENGE

Multinational corporations have a direct investment in several countries and run their businesses depending on the choices available anywhere in the world. Well-known U.S.-based multinational firms include Eastman Kodak, Warner-Lambert, Pfizer, Anaconda, Goodyear, Ford, IBM, ITT, Corn Products, 3M, National Cash Register, H. J. Heinz, and Gillette. They regularly earn over 30 percent of their total sales or profits abroad. And Coca-Cola recently moved past the halfway point—more than half of its profits come from international operations! Coca-Cola sees the day coming when as much as 75 percent of its earnings will be from abroad—because there will be more young people with money there than in aging America.[1]

Many multinational companies are American. But there are some well-known foreign-based companies such as Nestle's, Shell (Royal Dutile Shell), and Lever Brothers (Unilever). They have well-accepted "foriegn" brands—not only in the United States, but around the world. And Japanese firms producing Sony, Honda, Panasonic, and other well-known brands are operating around the globe.

Multinational operations make sense to more firms

As firms become more involved in international marketing, some reach the point where the firm sees itself as a worldwide business. As a chief executive of Abbott Laboratories—a pharmaceutical company with plants in 22 countries—said, "We are no longer just a U.S. company with interests abroad. Abbott is a worldwide enterprise and many major fundamental decisions must be made on a global basis."

A Texas Instruments manager had a similar view: "When we consider new opportunities and one is abroad and the other domestic, we can't afford to look

Multinational companies have to view the world objectively to run their companies profitably.

Ellis Herwig—Stock, Boston

upon the alternative here as an inherently superior business opportunity simply because it is in the United States. We view an overseas market just as we do our market, say, in Arizona, as one more market in the world."

A General Motors manager sees this trend as ". . . the emergence of the modern industrial corporation as an institution that is transcending national boundaries."[2]

Much of the multinational activity of the 1960s and early 1970s was U.S.-based firms expanding to other countries. As these opportunities became less attractive in the mid-1970s—due to the energy crisis, inflation, currency devaluations, labor unrest, and unstable governments—foreign multinational companies have been moving into the United States. The United States is, after all, one of the richest markets in the world.

Foreign firms are beginning to see that it may be attractive to operate in this large—if competitive—market. The Japanese "invasion" with all kinds of electronic products in well known. And they are building plants, too. For example, Sony has a TV assembly plant and a TV tube plant in southern California. And French firms (including the producers of Michelin tires) are setting up or buying facilities in the United States.[3]

One reason for the movement of some multinational firms into the United States is that labor costs in their own countries (including Japan) have been rising. Considering the total cost—including transportation costs—it may be more economical to produce products for the U.S. market here. Also, political instability in other countries is a factor. In spite of our political problems, there seems to be little doubt that businesses will not be completely hobbled or confiscated. The same cannot be said for the political environments in many foreign countries.

Multinational companies overcome national boundaries

From an international view, multinational firms do—as the GM manager said—"transcend national boundaries." They see world market opportunities and locate their production and distribution facilities for greatest effectiveness. This has upset some nationalistic business managers and politicians. But these multinational operations may be difficult to stop. They are no longer just exporting or importing. They hire local residents and build plants. They have business relationships with local business managers and politicians. These are powerful organizations which have learned to deal with nationalistic feelings and typical border barriers—treating them simply as uncontrollable variables.

We do not have "one world" politically as yet—but business is moving in that direction. We may have to develop new kinds of corporations and laws to govern multinational operations. The limitations of national boundaries on business and politics will make less and less sense in the future.[4]

IDENTIFYING DIFFERENT KINDS OF OPPORTUNITIES

Firms usually start from where they are

A multinational firm which has accepted the marketing concept will look for opportunities in the same way that we have been discussing throughout the text, that is, looking for unsatisfied needs that it might be able to satisfy—given its resources and objectives.

The typical approach—and perhaps a very practical approach, given that we're talking about going into very unfamiliar markets—is to start with the firm's current products and the needs it knows how to satisfy, and then try to find new markets—wherever they may be—with the same or similar unsatisfied needs. This approach might be combined with exporting—to "get their feet wet." Next, the firm might adapt the promotion, and then the product. Later, the firm might think about developing new products and new promotion policies. Some of these possibilities are shown in Figure 23–3. Here, the emphasis is on Product and Promotion—because Place would obviously have to be changed in new markets—and Price adjustments probably would be needed too.

The "Same-Same" box in Figure 23–3 can be illustrated with McDonald's (fast-food chain) entry into European markets. Its Director of International Marketing says, "Ronald McDonald speaks eight languages. Our target audience is the same worldwide—young families with children—and our advertising is designed to appeal to them." The basic promotion messages must be translated, of course, but the same strategy decisions which were made in the U.S. market apply. McDonald's has adapted its Product in Germany, however, by adding beer to appeal to adults who prefer beer over soft drinks. Its efforts have been extremely successful so far. Some stores are selling over $1 million (U.S.) per year—something that took many more years to do in the United States.[5]

McDonald's and other firms expanding into international markets usually move first into markets with good economic potential—such as Western Europe and Japan. But if McDonald's or some other fast-food company wanted to move into much lower-income areas, it might have to develop a whole new Product—perhaps a traveling street vendor with "hamburgers" made out of soybean prod-

Milt & Joan Mann

Figure 23–3
International marketing opportunities as seen by a U.S. firm from the viewpoint of its usual product-market in the United States

		Product	
Promotion	Same	Adaptation	New
Same	Same needs and use conditions (McDonald's usual strategy)	Basically same needs and use conditions (McDonald's strategy with beer in Germany)	Basically same needs, but different incomes and/or applications (street vendor with low-cost hamburgers)
Adaptation	Different needs but same use conditions (bicycles)	Different needs and use conditions (clothing)	Different needs and different incomes and/or applications (hand powered washing machines)

Source: Adapted from Warren Keegan, "Multinational Product Planning: Strategic Alternatives," *Journal of Marketing*, January 1969, p. 59.

Figure 23–4
Continuum of environmental
sensitivity

Insensitive		*Sensitive*
Industrial goods	Basic commodity-type consumer goods	Faddy or high-style consumer goods

ucts. This kind of opportunity is in the upper right-hand corner of Figure 23–3.

The lower left-hand box in this figure is illustrated by the different kind of promotion that is needed for just a simple bicycle. In some parts of the world, a bicycle provides basic transportation—while in the United States it is mainly a recreation vehicle. So a different promotion emphasis is needed in these different target markets.

Both product and promotion changes will be needed as one moves to the right along the bottom row of Figure 23–3. Such moves may increase the risk—and would obviously require more market knowledge.

The risk of opportunities varies by environmental sensitivity

International marketing means going into unfamiliar markets. This can increase risk. The farther one is from familiar territory, the greater the likelihood of making big mistakes. But not all products offer the same risk. It is useful to think of the risks running along a "continuum of environmental sensitivity." See Figure 23–4. Some products are relatively insensitive to the economic or cultural environment in which they are placed. These products may be accepted as is or may require just a little adaption to make them suitable for local use. Most industrial goods would be near the insensitive end of this continuum.

At the other end of the continuum, we find highly sensitive products which may be difficult or impossible to adapt to all international situations. At this end, we would find faddy or high-style consumer goods. It is sometimes difficult to understand why a particular product is well accepted in a home market—so this makes it even more difficult to know how it might be received in a different environment.

This continuum helps explain why many of the early successes in international marketing were basic commodities such as gasoline, soap, transportation vehicles, mining equipment, and agricultural machinery. It also suggests that firms producing and/or selling highly sensitive products should carefully analyze how their products will be seen and used in new environments.[6]

Evaluating opportunities in alternative international markets

Judging opportunities in international markets uses the same principles we have been discussing. Basically, each opportunity must be evaluated within the uncontrollable variables. But there may be more of these—and they may be more difficult to evaluate—in international markets. Estimating the risk involved in particular opportunities may be very difficult. Some countries are not as stable politically as the United States. Their governments and constitutions come and go. An investment that was safe under one government might become the target for a take-over under another. Further, the possibility of foreign exchange controls and tax rate changes can reduce the chance of getting profits and capital back to the home country.

Because the risks are hard to judge, it may be wise to enter international marketing by exporting first—building know-how and confidence over time. Experience and judgment are needed even more in unfamiliar areas. Allowing time to develop these skills among a firm's top management—as well as its international managers—makes sense. Then the firm will be in a better position to estimate the prospects and risks of going further into international marketing.

INTERNATIONAL MARKETING REQUIRES EVEN MORE SEGMENTING

Success in international marketing requires even more attention to segmenting. There are over 140 nations with their own unique differences! There can be big differences in language, customs, beliefs, religions, race, and even income distribution patterns from one country to another. This obviously complicates the segmenting process. But what makes it even worse is that there is less good data as one moves into international markets. While the number of variables increases, the quantity and quality of data go down. This is one reason why some multinational firms insist that local operations be handled by natives. They at least have a "feel" for their markets.

There are more dimensions—but there is a way

Segmenting international markets may require more dimensions. But a practical method adds just one step before the seven-step approach discussed in Chapter 9. See Figure 23–5. First, segment by country or region—looking at demographic, cultural, and other characteristics—including stage of economic development. This may help find reasonably similar subsets. Then—depending upon whether the firm is aiming at final consumers or intermediate customers—apply the seven-step approach discussed earlier.

Most of the discussion in the rest of this chapter will emphasize final consumer differences, because they are likely to be greater than intermediate customer differences. Also, we will consider regional groupings and stages of economic development—which can aid your segmenting. Basically, our objective is to broaden your view of international markets.

Figure 23–5
Segmenting in international markets

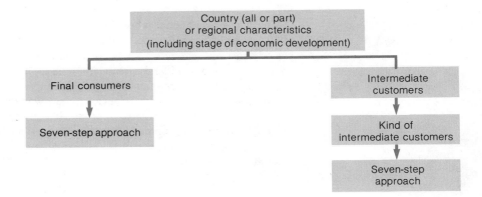

REGIONAL GROUPINGS MAY MEAN MORE THAN NATIONAL BOUNDARIES

While national boundaries are a common and logical dimension for segmenting markets, sometimes it makes more sense to treat several nearby countries with similar cultures as one region. Or, if several nations have banded together to have common economic boundaries, then these nations may be treated as a unit. The outstanding example is the European Economic Community (EEC). They have dared to abandon old ideas and nationalistic prejudices—in favor of cooperative efforts to reduce tariffs and other controls, which are commonly applied at national boundaries.

These cooperative arrangements are very important, because the taxes and restrictions at national borders can be not only annoying but may greatly reduce marketing opportunities. Tariffs—taxes on imported goods—vary, depending on whether the country is trying to raise revenue or limit trade. Restrictive tariffs often block all movement. But even revenue-producing tariffs cause red tape and discourage free movement of goods. Quotas act like restrictive tariffs. Quotas set the specific quantities of goods which can move in or out of a country. There might be great market opportunities in a country, but import quotas (or export controls applied against a specific country) may discourage outsiders from entering. The U.S. government, for example, has controlled Japan's export of TVs to the United States. (Otherwise, we might have had even more Japanese products entering the U.S. market!)

GATT works on tariff reduction

Until 1948, most countries in the world made bilateral (two-way) arrangements on trade. In 1948, most of the nations of the free world accepted the idea of multilateral negotiations—when they signed the *General Agreement on Tariffs and Trade (GATT)*. They agreed to meet every two years and negotiate for reductions in tariffs among their countries. This organization is still going strong. Several major negotiation conferences have been very effective in lowering tariffs and encouraging greater trade.

This multilateral bargaining is especially important because most major trading nations use the "most-favored-nation" clause—which says that a significant tariff reduction offered to one nation immediately will be offered to all participating nations.

Coal and Steel Community surrendered some national sovereignty

The first supranational (above-national) economic organization developed in 1952—when Belgium, France, Germany, Italy, Luxembourg, and The Netherlands signed the *Coal and Steel Community* Pact. In this agreement, some national sovereignty was surrendered to the higher body—for the purpose of establishing a free market for iron ore, steel scrap, coal, and steel.

The goal of the Coal and Steel Community was development of a regional—rather than national—pattern for the production and distribution of these products. Since none of these countries was self-sufficient in steel production, the agreement made sense. It showed that economic integration—even without political integration—was possible when it was logical and desired by the countries involved.

European Economic Community works toward full economic union

As a result of the smooth functioning of the Coal and Steel Community, these same six nations met in Rome in 1957 to sign a treaty establishing a *European Economic Community (EEC)* and a European Atomic Energy Community. They were, in effect, applying the concept behind the Coal and Steel Community to their entire economic life. These six nations formed the nucleus of the European Common Market.

By the middle 1960s, it was clear that this large free-trade market was breaking down old nationalistic and restrictionist attitudes, expanding employment and investment, reducing prices, and generally helping to raise the standard of living in these communities. So impressive were the advances made by the Common Market nations that Denmark, Ireland, and the United Kingdom joined in 1973. Over 20 other nations in Western Europe and Africa are associate members. And others have concluded free-trade agreements with the EEC—removing tariffs on industrial products. The prospects still look bright for the EEC. And it is pursuing antitrust legislation to keep the market competitive.[7]

Long term, however, the energy crisis may test the EEC concept. All the countries are dependent on foreign oil, but the impact of the crisis is falling much more heavily on some of the less-developed members of the community. There is talk in the EEC and elsewhere about setting up cartels or agreements to control the marketing of goods. We may be in for a new round of protectionism.[8]

Other groups are following the EEC

Organizations similar to the European Economic Community have formed in Eastern Europe and Latin America. The Council for Mutual Economic Assistance (CMEA) includes Bulgaria, Czechoslovakia, The German Democratic Republic, Hungary, Poland, and Romania. The Association of South East Asian Nations (ASEAN) includes Singapore, Malaysia, Thailand, The Philippines, and Indonesia. The Latin American Free Trade Association (LAFTA) includes Argentina, Brazil, Chile, Mexico, Paraguay, Peru, Uruguay, Colombia, and Ecuador. The Central American Common Market (CACM) consists of El Salvador, Guatemala, Honduras, Nicaragua, and Costa Rica.

LAFTA's main purpose was to develop a treaty to reduce tariffs among the members. Progress has been slow, however, and six countries (Bolivia, Chile, Colombia, Ecuador, Peru, and Venezuela) have formed the Andean Common Market (AnCom).

None of these groups has yet had the success of the EEC—because of border and civil wars, revolutions, and strong nationalistic and protectionist tendencies. It now appears, however, that Latin American countries may again become willing to encourage foreign investment and work together for their mutual good.[9] And the socialist states seem to be developing more interest in trade within and outside their bloc. So, strategy planning should probably include a serious consideration of these organizations.

STAGES OF ECONOMIC DEVELOPMENT HELP DEFINE MARKETS

International markets vary widely—within and between countries. Some markets are more advanced and/or growing more rapidly than others. And some

Different parts of a country may be in different development stages.

Milt & Joan Mann

countries—or parts of a country—are at different stages of economic development. This means their demands and even their marketing systems will vary.

To get some idea of the many possible differences in potential markets—and how they affect strategy planning—let's discuss six stages of economic development. These stages are helpful—but must be qualified——because they greatly oversimplify the real world for a number of reasons. In the first place, different parts of the same country may be at different stages of development—so it is not possible to identify a single country or region with only one stage. Secondly, the growing influence of multinational companies—and eager governments in some less-developed countries—has led to the skipping of one or two stages due to the infusion of outside or government capital. For example, the building of uneconomic steel mills to boost a nation's "pride"—or the coming of one or a few multinational corporations—might lead to a substantial jump in stages. This "stage-jumping" does not destroy the six-stage process. Rather, it merely explains why more rapid movements have taken place in some situations.

Stage 1—agricultural— self-supporting

In this stage, most people are subsistence farmers. There may be a simple marketing system—perhaps weekly markets—but most of the people are not even in a money economy. Some parts of Africa and New Guinea are in this stage. In a practical marketing sense, these people are not a market—they have no money to buy goods.

Stage 2—preindustrial or commercial

Some countries in Sub-Sahara Africa and the Middle East are in this second stage. During this stage, we see more market-oriented activity. Raw materials such as oil, tin, and copper are extracted and exported. Agricultural and forest crops such as sugar, rubber, and timber are grown and exported. Often this is done with the help of foreign technical skills and capital. A commercial economy may develop along with—but unrelated to—the subsistence economy. These activities may require the beginnings of a transportation system to tie the extracting or growing areas to shipping points. A money economy operates in this stage.

There are imports of industrial machinery and equipment. And huge construction projects may need many special supplies. Buying for these needs may be handled by purchasing agents in industrial countries. There is also the need for imports—including luxury goods—to meet the living standards of technical and supervisory people. These may be handled by company stores—rather than local retailers.

The relatively few large landowners and those who benefit by this business activity may develop expensive tastes. The few natives employed by these larger firms and the small business managers who serve them may develop into a small, middle-income class. But most of the population are still in the first stage—for practical purposes, they are not in the market. This total market may be so small that local importers can easily handle the demand. There is little reason for local manufacturers to try to supply it.

Stage 3—primary manufacturing

In this third stage, there is some processing of metal ores or the agricultural products that once were shipped out of the country in raw form. Sugar and rubber, for example, are both produced and processed in Indonesia. The same is true for oil on the Persian Gulf. Multinational companies may set up factories to take advantage of low-cost labor. They may export most of the output, but they do stimulate local development. More local labor becomes involved in this stage. A domestic market develops. Small local businesses are starting to handle some of the raw material processing.

Even though the local market expands in this third stage, a large part of the population is still at the subsistence level—almost entirely outside the money economy. There may still be a large foreign population of professionals and technicians needed to run the developing agricultural-industrial complex. The demands of this group and of the growing number of wealthy natives are still quite different from the needs of the lower class and the growing middle class. A domestic market among the local people begins to develop. But local manufacturers still may have trouble finding enough demand to keep them in business.

Stage 4—nondurable and semidurable consumer goods manufacturing

At this stage, small local manufacturing begins—especially in those lines that need only a small investment to get started. Often, these industries grow out of small firms that developed to supply the processors dominating the last stage. For example, plants making sulfuric acid and explosives for extracting mineral resources might expand into soap manufacturing. And recently, multinational firms have speeded development of countries in this stage with investments in promising opportunities.

Paint, drug, food and beverage, and textile industries develop in this stage. The textile industry is usually one of the first to develop. Clothing is a necessity. This early emphasis on the textile industry in developing nations is one reason the world textile market is so competitive.

Some of the small manufacturers become members of the middle- or even upper-income class. They help to expand the demand for imported goods. As this market grows, local businesses begin to see enough volume to operate profitably. So the need for imports to supply nondurable and semidurable goods is less. But consumer durables and capital goods are still imported.

Stage 5—capital goods and consumer durable goods manufacturing

In this stage, the production of capital goods and consumer durable goods begins. This includes automobiles, refrigerators, and machinery for local industries. Such manufacturing creates other demands—raw materials for the local factories, and food and fibers for clothing for the rural population entering the industrial labor force.

Industrialization has begun. But the economy still depends on exports of raw materials—either wholly unprocessed or slightly processed.

It still may be necessary to import special heavy machinery and equipment in this stage. Imports of consumer durable goods may still compete with local products. The foreign community and the status-conscious wealthy may prefer these imports.

Stage 6—exporting manufactured products

Countries that have not gone beyond the fifth stage are mainly exporters of raw materials. They import manufactured goods and equipment to build their industrial base. In the sixth stage, exporting manufactured goods becomes most important. The country specializes in certain types of manufactured goods—such as iron and steel, watches, cameras, electronic equipment, and processed food.

There are many opportunities for importing and exporting at this stage. These countries have grown richer and have needs—and the purchasing power—for a great variety of products. In fact, countries in this stage often carry on a great deal of trade with each other. Each trades those goods in which it has production advantages. In this stage, almost all consumers are in the money economy. And there may be a large middle-income class. The United States, most of the Western European countries, and Japan are at this stage.[10]

It is important to see that it is not necessary to label a whole country or geographic region as being in one stage. Certainly, different parts of the United States have developed differently and might properly be placed in different stages. It may help to understand the full implications of the stages if you try to identify geographic areas within the United States which are in each of these stages. Then, by careful thinking about the kind of public and private facilities found in these areas, you can get a better understanding about the likely character of international markets.

A large middle-income group is usually found in Stage 6.

Kenneth Yee

HOW THESE STAGES CAN BE USEFUL IN FINDING MARKET OPPORTUNITIES

A good starting point for estimating present and future market potentials in a country—or part of a country—is to estimate its present stage of economic development and how fast it is moving to another stage. Actually, the speed of movement, if any, and the possibility that stages may be skipped may suggest whether market opportunities are there—or are likely to open. But just naming the present stage can be very useful in deciding what to look at and whether there are prospects for the firm's products.

Fitting the firm to market needs

Manufacturers of automobiles, expensive cameras, or other consumer durable goods, for example, should not plan to set up a mass distribution system in an area that is in the preindustrial (Stage 2) or even the primary manufacturing (Stage 3) phase. The market would be too limited.

Among the foreign population and the wealthy landowners, nevertheless, there may be a small but very attractive market for luxury models. A simple distribution system with one or a few middlemen may be quite adequate. The market for U.S. "necessities," however—items such as canned foods or drug products—may not yet be large. Large-scale selling of these consumer items requires a large base of cash or credit customers—and so far too few are part of the money economy.

On the other hand, a market in the nondurable goods manufacturing stage has more potential—especially for durable goods producers. Incomes and the number of potential customers are growing. There is no local competition yet.

Opportunities might still be good for durable goods imports in the fifth stage—even though domestic producers are trying to get started. But more likely, the local government would raise some controls to aid local industry. Then the foreign producer might have to start licensing local producers—or building a local plant.

Pursuing that tempting inverted pyramid

Areas or countries in the final stage often are the biggest and most profitable markets. While there may be more competition, there are many more customers with higher incomes. We have already seen how income distribution shifted in the United States from a pyramid to more families with middle and upper incomes. This can be expected during the latter stages—when a "mass market" develops.

OTHER MARKET DIMENSIONS MAY SUGGEST OPPORTUNITIES, TOO

Considering country or regional differences—including stages of economic development—can be useful as a first step in segmenting international markets. After finding some possible areas (and eliminating unattractive ones) we must look at more specific market characteristics.

We discussed potential dimensions in the U.S. market. It is impossible to cover all possible dimensions in all world markets. But, some of the ideas discussed for the United States certainly apply in other countries. So, here, we will just outline some dimensions of international markets—and show some examples to emphasize that depending on half-truths about "foreigners" won't work in increasingly competitive international markets.[11]

The number of people in our world is staggering

Although our cities may seem crowded with people, the over 220 million population of the United States is less than 5 percent of the world's population—which is over 4 billion.

Numbers are important

Instead of a boring breakdown of population statistics, let's look at a map showing area in proportion to population. Figure 23–6 makes the United States look unimportant—because of our small population in relation to land area. This is also true of Latin America and Africa. In contrast, Western Europe is much larger and the Far Eastern countries are even bigger.

But people are not spread out evenly

People everywhere are moving off the farm and into industrial and urban areas. Shifts in population—combined with already dense populations—have led to extreme crowding in some parts of the world.

Figure 23–7 shows a map of the world emphasizing density of population. The darkest shading shows areas with more than 250 persons per square mile.

The urban areas in the United States show up clearly as densely populated areas. Similar areas are found in Western Europe, along the Nile River Valley in Egypt, and in many parts of Asia. In contrast, many parts of the world (like our western plains and mountain states) have few people.

Figure 23–6
Map of the world showing area in proportion to population

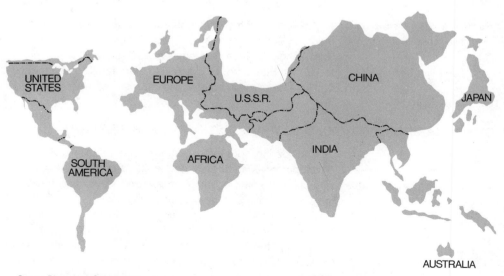

Source: Drawn by J. F. McCarthy.

Figure 23–7
Map of the world emphasizing density of population

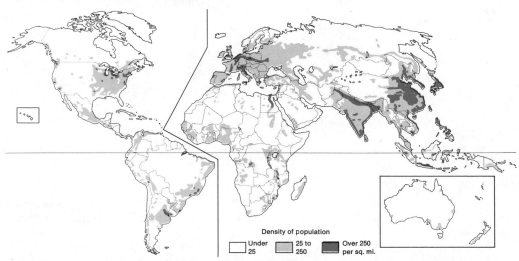

Density of population

Under 25 | 25 to 250 | Over 250 per sq. mi.

Source: Adapted from Norton Ginsberg, *Atlas of Economic Development,* by permission of the University of Chicago Press. Copyright 1961 by the University of Chicago.

Population densities are likely to increase in the near future. Birthrates in most parts of the world are high—higher in Africa, Latin America, Asia, and Oceania than in the United States—and death rates are declining as modern medicine is more widely accepted. Generally, population growth is expected in most countries. But the big questions are: How rapidly?—and—Will output increase faster than population? This is important to marketers because it affects how rapidly these countries move to higher stages of development and become new markets for different kinds of products.

You must sell where the income is

Profitable markets require income as well as people. The best available measure of income in most countries is gross national product (GNP)—the total market value of goods and services produced in a year. Unfortunately, this may not give a true picture of consumer well-being in many countries—because the method commonly used for figuring GNP may not be comparable for very different cultures and economies. For instance, do-it-yourself activities, household services, and the growing of produce or meat by family members for their own use are not usually figured as part of GNP. Since the activities of self-sufficient family units are not included, GNP can give a false picture of economic well-being in less-developed countries.

Gross national product, though, is useful and sometimes the only available measure of market potential in many countries. Table 23–1 shows the population and GNP of major regions of the world—except the USSR and mainland China. You can see that the more developed industrial regions have the biggest share

Table 23–1
Population and gross national
product of major geographic
regions of the world (1977)

Region	Population (millions)	GNP ($ billions)
North America	240	2,089
Latin America	342	429
Europe*	478	2,024
Africa	431	242
South and East Asia†	1,504	1,277
Oceania	22	120
Totals	3,017	6,181

* Except USSR.
† Except China.

Source: *Statistical Abstract of the U.S. 1979*, p. 885, and *Yearbook of National Accounts Statistics, 1979*, vol. 2 (New York: United Nations, 1980) pp. 3–9.

of the world's GNP. This is why so much trade takes place between these countries—and why many companies see them as the more important markets.

Income per person can be more helpful

GNP per person is a commonly available figure—but it can give a mistaken view of market potential. When GNP per person is used for comparison, we assume that the wealth of each country is distributed evenly among all consumers. This is seldom true. In an underdeveloped economy, 75 percent of the population may be on farms and receive 25 percent or less of the income.[12] And there may be unequal distribution along class or racial lines. In South Africa, for example, the average family income in 1970 for whites was $5,830; for Asians, $2,352; for mulattoes, $1,411; and for blacks, $538.[13]

To provide some examples, the GNP per person for several countries is shown in Table 23–2. The range is wide, from $95 (in U.S. dollars) per person per year in Ethiopia to $20,955 in the United Arab Emirates.

A business, and a human opportunity

You can see that much of the world's population lives in extreme poverty. Many of these countries are in the early stages of economic development. Most of their people work on farms and live barely within the money economy.

These people, however, have needs. And many are eager to improve themselves. But they may not be able to raise their living standards without outside help. This presents a challenge and an opportunity to the developed nations—and to their business firms.

Some companies—including American firms—are trying to help the people of less-developed countries. Corporations such as Pillsbury, Corn Products, Monsanto, and Coca-Cola have developed nutritious foods that can be sold cheaply—but still profitably—in poorer countries. One firm sells a milk-based drink—with ten grams of protein—to the Middle East and the Caribbean areas. Such a drink can make an important addition to diets. Poor people in less-developed lands usually get only 8–12 grams of protein per day in their normal diet. Sixty to 75 grams are considered necessary for an adult.[14]

Reading, writing, and marketing problems

The ability of a country's people to read and write has a direct influence on the development of the economy and on marketing strategy planning. Certainly, the degree of literacy affects the way information is delivered—which in marketing means promotion.

Literacy studies show that only about two-thirds of the world's population can read and write.[15]

Low literacy sometimes causes difficulties with product labels and with instructions—for which we normally use words. In highly illiterate countries, some manufacturers have found that placing a baby's picture on food packages is unwise. Illiterate natives believe that the product is just that—a ground-up baby! Singer Sewing Machine Co. met this lack of literacy with an instruction book that used no words.[16]

Even in Latin America—which has generally higher literacy rates than Africa or Asia—a large number of people cannot read and write. Marketers have to use symbols, colors, and other nonverbal means of communication if they want to reach the masses.

CAREFUL MARKET ANALYSIS IS VITAL

The opportunities in international marketing are exciting ones, but diversity presents a real challenge to segmenters. Careful market analysis is especially important—since there often are differences that we would not pick up unless we were aggressively seeking out all the possibilities. Our neighbor, Canada, affords an excellent example.

Table 23–2
Gross national product per capita for major regions of the world and selected countries (in 1977 U.S. dollars)

	GNP/capita for countries	GNP/capita for regions		GNP/capita for countries	GNP/capita for regions
North America		$8,720	Africa		560
United States	$ 8,731		Algeria	1,102	
Canada	8,573		Egypt	485	
Latin America		1,320	Ethiopia	95	
Argentina	1,351		Kenya	320	
Brazil	1,463		Nigeria	479	
Haiti	284		South Africa	1,427	
Mexico	1,172		Rwanda	176	
Europe		5,850	South and East Asia		780
United Kingdom	4,430		India	163	
France	7,191		Pakistan	232	
West Germany	8,396		Japan	6,094	
Italy	3,813		Indonesia	318	
Sweden	9,490		Oceania		5,470
Portugal	1,671		Australia	7,132	
Near East		2,170	New Zealand	4,781	
Israel	4,073				
United Arab Emirates	20,945				

Source: *Yearbook of National Accounts Statistics, 1979,* vol. 2 (New York: United Nations, 1980), pp. 3–9; and *Statistical Abstract of the U.S., 1979,* p. 895.

International markets require careful analysis.

Canadians are different

Some Americans think of Canadians only as our northern neighbors and as being pretty much like themselves. Actually, however, they have as much (or more) diversity as we have in the United States. The province of Quebec, for example—which has about 30 percent of Canada's population—is a unique market. Quebec is predominantly French in heritage and language. Some French-Canadians feel they have suffered at the hands of the English-speaking majority of Canada—and a strong "separatist" feeling cannot be ignored in strategy planning. These attitudes affect the marketplace—as French-Canadians support local producers, buying their goods in preference to those of firms from other parts of Canada or Great Britain or the United States.

What are you drinking?

Tastes do differ across national boundaries. French Burgundy wine going to Belgium must have a higher sugar content than the Burgundy staying in France. Burgundy going to Sweden must have still another sugar content to be sold successfully there.

Milk-drinking habits also differ greatly. Scandinavians consider milk a daily staple—while Latins feel that milk is only for children. A former French premier was able to get his picture on the front page of every Paris newspaper simply by drinking a glass of milk in public.

Who wears the makeup in France?

The great variety in international markets almost demands marketing research to learn the habits and attitudes of the many possible target markets.

The need for research to avoid common stereotypes is emphasized by the following results from a large-scale survey of European Common Market adults:

The average Frenchman uses almost twice as many cosmetics and beauty aids as his wife.

The Germans and French buy more packaged spaghetti than the Italians.

French and Italian housewives are not as interested in cooking as their counterparts in Luxembourg and Belgium.[17]

ORGANIZING FOR INTERNATIONAL MARKETING

Until a firm develops a truly worldwide view of its operations, it usually is desirable to have someone in charge of international matters. If both production and sales are involved outside the home country, then the person in charge probably should report to top management. If the activity is mainly concerned with sales, on the other hand, then reporting directly to the marketing chief might be practical. The basic concern here should be to see that the firm transfers its domestic know-how into international operations.

Organization should transfer know-how

As the firm moves beyond just a few international locations, the managers might want to develop regional groupings—clustering similar kinds of countries into groups. This smoothes the transfer of know-how among operations in similar environments. Regional groupings may also reduce the cost of supervision.

Regional groups, however, may be less useful than groups based on other relevant dimensions, such as the stage of economic development, or perhaps language. The important thing is to develop an organization which enables the local managers to control matters which require "local feel," while at the same time sharing their accumulating experience with colleagues who face similar problems.

Each national market should be thought of as a separate market. To the extent that they are really different from each other, top management will have to delegate a great deal of responsibility for strategy planning to these local managers. In extreme cases, it may not even be possible for the local managers to fully explain some parts of their strategic plans. In such cases, they can be judged only by their results. Then, the organizational setup should be such that these managers are given a great deal of freedom, but are tightly controlled against their plans. Top management need not have a deep understanding of its various national markets. Instead, it can simply insist that the various managers stick to their budgets and meet the plans which they, themselves, create. When the firm reaches this stage, it is being managed like a well-organized domestic corporation—which insists that its managers (of divisions and territories) meet their own plans, so that the whole company's program works out as planned.

CONCLUSION

The international market is large and keeps growing in population and income. Many American companies are becoming aware of the opportunities open to alert and aggressive businesses.

The great variations in stages of economic development, income, population, literacy, and other factors, however, mean that foreign markets must be treated as many separate target markets—and studied carefully. Lumping foreign nations together under the common and vague heading of "foreigners"—or, at the other extreme, assuming that they are just like U.S. customers—almost guarantees failure. So does treating them like common Hollywood stereotypes.

Involvement in international marketing usually begins with exporting. Then, a firm may become involved in joint ventures or wholly-owned subsidiaries in several countries. Companies that become this involved are called multinational corporations. Some of these corporations have a global outlook and are willing to move across national boundaries as easily as national firms move across state boundaries.

Much of what we have said about strategy planning throughout the text applies directly in international marketing. Sometimes Product adaptions or changes are needed. Promotion messages must be translated into the local languages. And, of course, new Place arrangements and Prices are needed. But blending the four Ps still requires a knowledge of the all-important customer.

The major "roadblock" to success in international marketing is an unwillingness to learn about and adjust to different peoples and cultures. To those who are willing to make these adjustments, the returns can be great.

QUESTIONS AND PROBLEMS

1. Discuss the "typical" evolution of corporate involvement in international marketing. What impact would a wholehearted acceptance of the marketing concept have on this evolutionary process?

2. Distinguish between licensing and contract manufacturing in a foreign country.

3. Distinguish between joint ventures and wholly owned subsidiaries.

4. Discuss the long-run prospects for (a) multinational marketing by U.S. firms producing in the United States only, and (b) multinational firms willing to operate anywhere.

5. Discuss how a manufacturer interested in finding new international marketing opportunities might organize its search process. What kinds of opportunities would it look for first, second, and so on?

6. Discuss how the approaches to market segmenting (which were described in Chapter 9) might have to be modified when one moves into international markets.

7. Evaluate the growth of "common markets" in relation to the phases of economic development of the members. Is this basically a movement among the developing countries which are seeking to "catch up"?

8. Discuss the prospects for a Latin American entrepreneur who is considering building a factory to produce machines which would manufacture cans for the food industry. His country happens to be in stage 4—the nondurable and semidurable consumer goods manufacturing phase. The country's population is approximately 20 million and there is some possibility of establishing sales contacts in a few nearby countries.

9. Discuss the value of gross national product per capita as a measure of market potential. Refer to specific data in your answer.

10. Discuss the possibility of a multinational marketer using essentially the same promotion campaign in the United States and in many international markets.

11. Discuss the kinds of products which you feel may become popular in Europe in the near future. Does the material on U.S. consumption behavior, discussed earlier in the text, have any relevance here?

12. Discuss the importance of careful target marketing within the European Common Market.

13. Discuss how a multinational firm might organize to develop an effective organization.

SUGGESTED CASES

30 **Canadian Foods, Limited**
31 **Modern Homes, Inc.**

32 **The Adanac Manufacturing Company**

NOTES

1. "How Coke Runs a Foreign Empire," *Business Week*, August 25, 1973, pp. 40–43.

2. "Multi-national Companies," *Business Week*, April 20, 1963, pp. 62–86; "Multi-national Firms Now Dominate Much of World's Production," *The Wall Street Journal*, April 18, 1973, p. 1 f; "ITT Europe Rings Up Profits; A Low Profile Keeps Troubles Minor," *The Wall Street Journal*, January 9, 1974, p. 1 f.; "Japanese Multinationals Covering the World with Investment," *Business Week*, June 16, 1980, pp. 92–99; David A. Heenan and Warren J. Keegan, "The Rise of Third World Multinationals," *Harvard Business Review*, January–February 1979, pp. 101–109; and Ulrich Wiechmann and Lewis G. Pringle, "Problems That Plague Multinational Marketers," *Harvard Business Review*, July–August 1979, pp. 118–124.

3. "Why So Many French Are Tackling the U.S.," *Business Week*, July 4, 1977, p. 30; and "An Appliance Maker Scouts for U.S. Sites," *Business Week*, May 30, 1977, pp. 38–39.

4. Franklin R. Root, "Public Policy Expectations of Multinational Managers," *MSU Business Topics*, Autumn 1973, pp. 5–12; "Domesticating the Multinationals," *Business Week*, May 26, 1973, p. 15; "Multinationals: The Public Gives Them Low Marks," *Business Week*, June 9, 1973, pp. 42–44; "The Unions Move Against Multinationals," *Business Week*, July 24, 1971, pp. 48–52; John Kenneth Galbraith, "The Defense of the Multinational Company," *Harvard Business Review*, March–April 1978, pp. 83–93; Lawrence G. Franko, "Multinationals: The End of U.S. Dominance," *Harvard Business Review*, November–December 1978, pp. 93–101; and Frank Meissner, "Rise of Third World 'Demands Marketing Be Stood on Its Head,'" *Marketing News*, October 6, 1978, pp. 1, 16.

5. "McDonald's Brings Hamburger (with Beer) to Hamburg," *Advertising Age*, May 30, 1977, p. 61.

6. Warren J. Keegan, "A Conceptual Framework for Multinational Marketing, *Columbia Journal of World Business*, November 1972, pp. 67–78.

7. Robert R. Jones, "Executive's Guide to Antitrust in Europe," *Harvard Business Review*, May–June 1976, pp. 106–18.

8. "Creeping Cartelization," *Business Week*, May 9, 1977, pp. 64–83; and "U.S. Firms Are Pressed to Offer Barter Terms by Overseas Customers," *The Wall Street Journal*, May 18, 1977, p. 1 f.

9. "Latin America Opens the Door to Foreign Investment Again," *Business Week*, August 9, 1976, pp. 34–50.

10. This discussion is based on William Copulsky's, "Forecasting Sales in Underdeveloped Countries," *Journal of Marketing*, July 1959, pp. 36–37. Another set of stages is interesting although less marketing oriented. See W. W. Rostow, *The Stages of Economic Growth—A Non-Communist Manifesto* (New York: Cambridge University Press, 1960).

11. The *Statistical Abstract*, and the U.S. Department of Commerce Bureau of International Commerce would be a good place to start locating current data. In its publication, *International Commerce*, the Department of Commerce issues a semiannual checklist of material it feels will be helpful to business people interested in the world market. The *Statistical Year Book* of the Statistical Office of the United Nations is also a good source of basic data.

12. Donald G. Halper, "The Environment for Marketing in Peru," *Journal of Marketing*, July 1966, pp. 42–46.

13. (Lansing, Mich.) *State Journal*, February 10, 1970, p. D–7.

14. *The Wall Street Journal*, August 8, 1968, p. 1.

15. Norton Ginsburg, *Atlas of Economic Development* (Chicago: University of Chicago Press, 1961); and *Statistical Abstract of the U.S.*, 1979, pp. 890–92.

16. Edward Marcus, "Selling the Tropical African Market," *Journal of Marketing*, July 1961, p. 30.

17. Robert L. Brown, "The Common Market: What Its New Consumer Is Like," *Printers' Ink*, May 31, 1963, pp. 23–25.

PART FIVE

Marketing Reappraised

There is only one chapter in this part—but it is an important one. It is concerned with how good a job marketing is doing—and in particular whether "marketing costs too much." The author's position is basically that marketing has been doing a pretty good job—but there is room for improvement. Further, marketing—and our whole economic system—faces very severe challenges. It is going to take some new thinking—and people with new ideas—to help our country and our business firms meet the challenges of the future. This chapter can help you see where you could make a contribution—both in some business firm (or a nonprofit organization)—as well as in our economy. This chapter does not present "answers." Rather it tries to encourage your thinking about what you're going to do with your life—and what your contribution to our society will be.

Kenneth Yee

When you finish this chapter, you should:

1. Understand why marketing must be evaluated differently at the micro and macro levels.

2. Understand why the text argues that micro-marketing costs too much.

3. Understand why the text argues that macro-marketing does not cost too much.

4. Know some of the challenges facing marketers in the future.

662

24

Marketing in a consumer-oriented society: Appraisal and challenges

Does marketing cost too much?

Does marketing cost too much? This is a fundamental question. Many people feel strongly that marketing does cost too much—that it is a waste of resources which would be better used elsewhere. In Chapter 1—and at various times throughout the text—we referred to criticisms of marketing and to the possible effects of business practices on consumer welfare. But we have *not* tried to answer the underlying question—whether marketing costs too much—believing that you needed more information before you could answer that question.

We have tried to provide the necessary background in this book. The focus has been mainly on the *micro* view of marketing—that is, marketing as seen through the eyes of the marketing manager. Now that you have a better understanding of what the marketing manager does and how he contributes to the *macro*-marketing process, you should be able to consider whether or not marketing costs too much. That's what this chapter is about.

Your answer is very important. Your own business career and the economy in which you will live will be affected by your answer.

MARKETING MUST BE EVALUATED AT TWO LEVELS

As we saw in Chapter 1, it is useful to distinguish between two levels of marketing: the *micro* level (how individual firms run) and the *macro* level (how the whole system works). Some complaints against marketing are aimed at only one of these levels at a time. In other cases, the criticism *seems* to be directed to one level but actually is aimed at the other. Some critics of specific advertise-

In the U.S. the customer is assumed to be right.

The Customer is Always Right!

Mike Kelly

ments, for example, probably would not be satisfied with *any* advertising. When evaluating marketing, we must treat each of these levels separately.

HOW SHOULD MARKETING BE EVALUATED?

Different nations have different social and economic objectives. Dictatorships, for example, may be concerned mainly with satisfying the needs of society as seen by the political elite. In a socialist state, the objective might be to satisfy society's needs as defined by government planners. In still other economies, the objective might be to build up the country militarily or economically.

Nations' objectives determine criteria

While different nations may have different objectives, each nation needs some kind of macro-marketing system to accomplish those objectives. How a macro-marketing system operates should depend on the objectives of a particular nation. Therefore, the effectiveness of any nation's macro-marketing system can only be evaluated in terms of that nation's objectives.

Consumer satisfaction is fundamental in the United States

Historically, *the basic objective of our market-directed economic system has been to satisfy consumer needs as they—the consumers—see them.* This objective implies that political freedom and economic freedom go hand in hand— and that citizens in a free society have the right to live as they choose.

This is no place for a long discussion of the merits of this objective. Economists, philosophers, politicians, and business managers have long debated the trade-offs between consumer satisfaction and efficient use of resources. Perhaps, this debate—along with changing social and economic conditions—will eventually lead to a change in our basic objective. However, this has not happened yet. And there is little evidence that the majority of American consumers are willing to give up the freedom of choice they now enjoy.

Therefore, let's try to evaluate the operation of marketing in the American economy, where the present objective is to satisfy consumer needs, *as consumers see them.* This is the essence of our system. The business firm that ignores this fact does so at its own peril.

CAN CONSUMER SATISFACTION BE MEASURED?

Since consumer satisfaction is our goal, marketing effectiveness must be measured by *the extent of this satisfaction.* Unfortunately, consumer satisfaction is hard to define and harder to measure.

Economic utility provides satisfaction, but . . .

Economists believe that consumer satisfaction is derived from the amount of economic utility—form, time, place, and possession utility—provided by various goods and services. However, no satisfactory method of measuring economic utility has been developed. Further, some consumers may consider "psychic utility" more important than economic utility for some products.

Satisfaction depends on individual aspirations

Measuring consumer satisfaction is even more difficult because satisfaction depends on one's level of aspiration or expectation—as well as one's perception or evaluation of outcomes.[1] Also, aspiration level tends to rise with repeated successes and fall with failures. Products considered satisfactory one day may be seen as unsatisfactory the next day, or vice versa. Thus, consumer satisfaction is a highly personal concept which does not provide a stable standard for evaluating marketing effectiveness.

A hierarchy of satisfaction exists

To complicate things further, consumers appear to have a hierarchy of needs. So it follows that different levels of satisfaction also exist. Thus, some consumer needs may be well satisfied, while others are not. For example, while a consumer may be very satisfied with a product that meets a lower-level need, that consumer's higher-level needs may not be satisfied at all. In fact, a consumer may be dissatisfied with life in general—and for reasons which may be quite unrelated to marketing.

Because of all these factors, it is extremely difficult to make exact quantitative estimates of consumer satisfaction.

Measuring macro-marketing must be subjective

Macro-marketing is concerned with *efficiency* (in terms of use of resources) and *fairness* (in terms of distribution of output to all parties involved)—while accomplishing the society's objectives.

If the objective is maximizing consumer satisfaction, then total satisfaction—of everyone—must be measured. But there is no quantitative way of measuring aggregate consumer satisfaction. So our evaluation of macro-marketing effectiveness will have to be subjective.

The consumer/citizens' votes can be your guide

The supreme test, probably, is whether the macro-marketing system satisfies enough individual consumer/citizens so that they vote—at the ballot box—to

A firm can't survive if it doesn't satisfy customers' needs.

Brent Jones

keep it running. So far, we have done so in the United States. But growing support for consumerism issues and more government involvement in the market suggests that support for our present system—as it is operating—is not complete. This should be of concern to supporters of our present system.

Measuring micro-marketing can be less subjective

Measuring micro-marketing effectiveness is also difficult. But it can be done. And individual business firms can and should try to measure how well their products satisfy their customers (or why their products fail). Methods which have been used include attitude research studies, unsolicited consumer responses (usually complaints), opinions of middlemen and salespeople, market test results, and profits.[2]

Satisfaction can be loosely measured by company profits

In our market-directed system, it is up to each customer to decide how effectively individual firms satisfy his or her needs. Usually, customers are willing to pay higher prices or buy more of those goods which satisfy them. Thus, efficient marketing plans can increase profits—and profits can be used as a rough measure of a firm's efficiency in satisfying customers.

Evaluating marketing effectiveness is difficult—but not impossible

Because it is difficult to measure consumer satisfaction—and, therefore, the effectiveness of micro- and macro-marketing—it is easy to see why there might be different views on the subject. If the objective of the economy is clearly defined, however—and the argument is stripped of emotion—the big questions about marketing effectiveness probably can be answered.

In this chapter we will argue that micro-marketing (how individual firms and channels operate) frequently *does* cost too much, but that macro-marketing (how the whole marketing system operates), *does not* cost too much, *given the present objective of the American economy—consumer satisfaction.* These positions should not be accepted as "gospel" but rather as points of view. In the end, you, the student of marketing, will have to make your own decision.[3]

MICRO-MARKETING OFTEN *DOES* COST TOO MUCH

Throughout the text we have been exploring what marketing managers could or should do to help their firms do a better job of satisfying customers—while achieving company objectives. Many firms are implementing highly successful marketing programs. At the same time, however, many other firms are still too production-oriented and inefficient in their operations. For the customers of these latter firms, micro-marketing often *does* cost too much.

Many consumers are discontented

While American consumers are not in a revolutionary mood, it is clear that many consumers are not happy with the marketing efforts of some firms. A recent study indicated that "helping consumers get a fair deal when shopping" ranked very high among public concerns. Only inflation, unemployment, government spending, welfare, and taxes were ranked higher. Consumers were also quite concerned about: the high price and poor quality of many products—products whose performance did not live up to advertised claims—and poor after-sale service and repairs.[4]

Many consumers are complaining

Despite the usual claim, "Satisfaction Guaranteed," there are many consumers who find reason to complain. The Better Business Bureau of Metropolitan Chicago alone receives more than 1,200 complaints and inquiries *daily* from consumers and businesses.[5] Multiply this figure by the number of Better Business Bureaus all across the United States. Add to this the complaints filed with federal, state, and local consumer protection agencies. Finally, add in the complaints made directly to businesses and nonprofit organizations. Obviously, a great many consumers are dissatisfied with a great many individual purchases.

Consumers should be encouraged to complain

To further dramatize the problem, a recent study of consumer complaints

Firms should try to satisfy customers' complaints.

Mike Kelly

found that as many as 50 percent of all serious complaints are never reported. Further, many of those that are reported never get fully resolved. The authors of the study concluded that "business should be alarmed at the amount of unresolved dissatisfaction that apparently exists in the marketplace." They advised firms to: (1) *encourage* customers to speak out when things go wrong, (2) make it more convenient for them to do so, and (3) to develop careful, speedy procedures to handle complaints. Most important, company attitudes must be changed to ensure that complaining consumers are not viewed as "the enemy."[6]

The failure rate is high

Further evidence that most firms are too production-oriented and not nearly as efficient as they could be is the fact that many new products fail. New and old businesses fail regularly, too. The main reason for such failure is poor management or just plain managerial incompetence. One survey of 15,782 failures found that more than 90 percent were caused directly by incompetent or inexperienced management.[7]

Incompetence and bad management lead to higher costs of operation and reduce the effectiveness of the business system in general. Generally speaking, marketing inefficiencies are due to one or more of three reasons:

1. Lack of interest in—or understanding of—the sometimes fickle customer.
2. Improper blending of the four Ps—caused in part by an overemphasis on production and/or internal problems as contrasted with a customer orientation.
3. Lack of understanding of—or adjustment to—uncontrollable variables.

The company can get in the way of the customer

Serving the customer is plainly the role of business. Yet some producers seem to feel that customers eagerly await any product they turn out. So they worry about internal problems instead of satisfying customer needs.

Middlemen, too, often get tied up in their own internal problems. Goods may be stocked where it is convenient for the retailer to handle them—rather than for consumers to find them. And fast-moving, hard-to-handle goods may not be stocked at all—"They are too much trouble," or "We're always running out."

Similarly, accounting and financial managers can add to the problem. Some try to cut costs by encouraging the production of standardized, "me too" products—even though this may not serve customers well.

None of these managers understand a business as a "total system" responsible for satisfying consumer needs.

The high cost of poor marketing mixes

Perhaps lack of concern for the customer is most noticeable in the ways the four Ps are combined—or forced—into a marketing mix. This can happen in many ways—as the following discussion shows.

Product—"Forget the customer, full speed ahead!"

Some production-oriented managers develop a company's product—not to meet the needs of certain target customers but rather—to satisfy some pet idea held by themselves or their friends. They sometimes produce products too high or too low in quality—or too complicated for many target markets. Or they like

Production orientation can lead to high marketing cost.

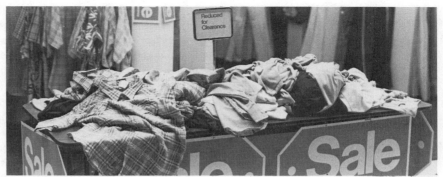

Kenneth Yee

long production runs of easy-to-make standardized products—to lower costs. Often they are not worried about quality control. Until very recently, most U.S. manufacturers lacked any quality control procedures.[8] Then, to compound these errors, the packaging people frequently put an ill-conceived product in a container that is easy to make and fill—but not really protective or appealing to the customer.

These poorly-designed, poorly-packaged products then are turned over to the sales department for unloading on the market. Sometimes these products can be moved only with overly aggressive (or even fradulent) promotion. Middle-men may join in this aggressive selling if they are given high enough markups—or additional advertising or promotion allowances.

Place—"Don't rock the boat or sell to chains"

Sales managers don't make adjustments in channels as often as they should. This is partly because of personal relationships in their channels and partly because—being human—they prefer not to "rock the boat." Yet such inflexibility can be costly—especially in view of the "scrambling" we saw in the channels of distribution.

Some old-time salesmen are so tied to the idea of small independent wholesalers and retailers that they even refuse to sell to chain stores or large firms. Their personal relationships with their old customers may make business more pleasant. But they do not necessarily contribute to efficiency and profits. The continued use of obsolete and overly expensive channels supports the charge of "too many" wholesalers and retailers.

Price—"Pick a price, any high price"

Prices often are set on a cost-plus basis. This method of pricing may ignore customer demand—and lead to unnecessarily high (*and* less profitable) prices. Many business managers consider both margin and expected volume in pricing products. But margins are fairly definite, while volume is only predictable. So they choose high margins—which may lead to high prices and reduced volume.

Promotion—"Let our advertising geniuses and star sales reps do it"

If a product is poorly designed—or if inadequate channels are employed—

or if cost-plus pricing is used—it is easy to see why promotion may be costly. Aggressive selling may be needed to try to overcome previous mistakes.

Even if a good job is done on the other three Ps, however, Promotion is sometimes inefficient and costly. As already noted, sales managers and advertising managers may not cooperate—each feeling that his own techniques are the most effective and do not need support from the other.

Until recently, the value of market research was not taken very seriously in most firms. Some advertising executives still feel that all a promotion campaign needs is their creative genius.

Sales management also has its problems. There are many types of sales jobs. Recruiting the right person for each is difficult. Further, the very nature of the sales job makes it difficult to measure sales performance.

Careful analysis and management are necessary to build a productive sales force at a reasonable cost. Unfortunately, many sales managers—although former "star" sales reps—are not up to this management job.

Company objectives may force higher-cost operation

Top-management decisions on company objectives may unnecessarily increase the cost of marketing. Seeking growth for growth's sake, for example, might lead to excessive spending for promotion. Diversification for diversification's sake could require costly new arrangements for Place. Or, if the established firms already have protected basic ideas—through patents or solid customer franchises—the firm may be forced to turn out second-rate products.

For these reasons, marketing managers must be alert to the possibility of such dangers and be involved in shaping the firm's objectives. Recognizing the importance of marketing, progressive firms have given marketing management a greater voice in determining company objectives. Unfortunately, though, in many more firms, marketing is still looked upon as the department that "gets rid of" the product.

Micro-marketing does cost too much—but things are changing

It appears that marketing does cost too much in many firms. Despite much publicity, the marketing concept has not *really* been applied in many places. Sales managers may have been renamed "marketing managers"—and vice presidents of sales called "vice presidents of marketing"—but nothing else changed. Marketing mixes were still put together by production-oriented managers in the same old ways.

But not all business firms and marketers should be criticized. Increasing numbers *are* becoming customer-oriented. And many of these are paying more attention to strategic planning—to more effectively carry out the marketing concept.

Further, some organizations have developed codes of ethics to guide members' behavior. Some of these developments are responses to the consumerism movement. But others reflect long-established company policies. Even more industry groups might be willing to get together to discuss how to do a better job (with good intentions), but they are inhibited by possible antitrust action.[9]

Competition continues to encourage the elimination of unnecessary costs *and* institutions. Distribution channels are continually shifting as better ways are found for doing the marketing job. Limited-function wholesalers have developed in many lines. Discount houses and mass merchandisers have eliminated many small, conventional retail stores—which did not recognize changing customer demands.

One encouraging sign is the end of the notion that anybody can run a business successfully. This never was true. Today, the growing complexity of business is drawing more and more professionals into business. This includes not only professional business managers but psychologists, sociologists, statisticians, and economists.

Managers who adopt the marketing concept as a way of business life do a better job. As more of these managers rise in business, we can look forward to much lower micro-marketing costs.

MACRO-MARKETING *DOES NOT* COST TOO MUCH

Many criticisms of marketing take aim at the operation of the macro-marketing system. These criticisms suggest that (1) advertising and promotion in general are socially undesirable and (2) that the macro-marketing system causes an improper allocation of resources, restricts income and employment, and leads to an unfair distribution of income. Most of these complaints imply that some micro-marketing activities should not be permitted—and because they are, macro-marketing costs too much or yields poor results.

Much of this criticism comes from those who have their own version of the ideal way to run an economy. Some of the most severe critics of our marketing system are theoretical economists who use the pure-competition model as their ideal. They want consumers and producers to have free choice in the market—but they are critical of the way the present market operates. Meanwhile, other critics would scrap our market-directed system and substitute the decisions of government planners—thus reducing freedom of choice in the marketplace. These different views should be kept in mind when evaluating criticisms of marketing.

In the following discussion, the word *business* probably could be substituted for *marketing* in most places. Marketing is the most exposed arm of business, but it is nearly impossible to separate this arm from the rest of the body. A criticism of marketing at the macro level usually: (1) implies a criticism of our entire market-directed economic system as it now exists, and (2) suggests that some modification or an entirely different system would be more effective. Let's look at some of these positions to help you form your own opinion.

Is pure competition the welfare ideal?

A major criticism of our macro-marketing system is that it permits or even encourages the allocation of too many resources for marketing activities—thus reducing consumer "welfare." This argument is concerned with how the economy's resources (land, labor, and capital) are allocated for producing and distributing goods. These critics usually feel that scarce resources could be better spent on producing goods than on marketing them. This argument assumes that marketing activities are unnecessary and do not create value. Being technical, it assumes that pure competition is the ideal for maximizing consumer welfare.

In pure competition, economists assume that consumers are "economic men," that is, that they are well informed about all available offerings and will choose rationally among the alternatives to maximize their own welfare. Therefore, these critics feel that emotional or persuasive advertising (1) discourages the economic

Marketing managers try to satisfy consumer needs—lowering the cost of marketing.

Mike Kelly

comparison required for an ideal pure-competition economy and (2) is wasteful because society does not need it.

Theoretical economic analysis can show convincingly that pure competition will provide greater consumer welfare than monopolistic competition—*provided* all the conditions and assumptions of pure competition are met. But are they?

Different people want different things

Our present knowledge of consumer behavior and peoples' desire for different products pretty well demolishes the economists' "economic man" assumption—and therefore the pure-competition ideal.[10] A pioneer in monopolistic competition analysis—E. H. Chamberlin—also argues logically against the pure-competition ideal. He observes that people, in fact, are different and that they do have different demands. He translates these differences into demands for different products. Given this type of demand (down-sloping demand curves), monopoly elements naturally develop. He concludes that "monopoly is necessarily a part of the welfare ideal . . ."[11]

Once we admit that not all consumers know everything and that they have varied demands, the need for a variety of micro-marketing activities becomes clear.

Micro-efforts expand macro-output through innovation

Some critics feel that marketing helps create monopoly, or at least monopolistic competition. Further—they feel—this leads to higher prices, restriction of output, and reduction in the national income and employment.

It is true that firms in a market-directed economy try to carve out separate monopolistic markets for themselves. This may have the short-run effect of restricting output (depending on the shape of the demand and supply curves) and raising prices on *that particular new product.*

Are customers taken advantage of, however? They do not have to buy the new product unless they feel it is a better value. The old products are still available.

ronically, the prices may even be lower on the old products to meet the new competition—yet their sales may decline because customers shift to the new product.

Over several years, the profits of the innovator may rise—but the rising profits also encourage further innovation by competitors. This leads to new investments—which contribute to economic growth and raise the level of national income and employment.

Here, the increasing profits attract competition. The profits then begin to drop as competitors enter and begin producing somewhat similar products. (Recall the rise and fall of industry profit during the product life cycle.)

It is certainly true that the performance of micro-marketing activities in monopolistic competition can lead to a different allocation of resources than would be found in a pure-competition economy. But this allocation of resources probably results in greater consumer satisfaction. Let's look at advertising, for example.

Is advertising a waste of resources?

Advertising is the most criticized of all micro-marketing activities. Indeed, many ads *are* annoying, insulting, misleading, and downright ineffective. This is one reason why micro-marketing often does cost too much. However, advertising can also make both the micro- and macro-marketing processes work better.

Advertising can result in lower prices

Advertising is a relatively economical way of informing large numbers of potential customers about a firm's products. Provided that a product satisfies customer needs and wants, advertising can increase demand for the product—resulting in economies of scale in manufacturing, distribution, and sales. Because these economies may more than offset advertising costs, advertising can actually *lower* prices to the consumer.[12] In addition, advertising can reduce the time and effort consumers must spend searching for products.[13] It may also increase competition. In recent years, for example, the Federal Trade Commission has encouraged advertising by doctors, lawyers, optometrists, and pharmacists as a means of stimulating price competition.

Advertising stimulates economic growth

At the macro level, the increased demand brought about by advertising gives producers a faster return on their investment. This in turn stimulates further investment, encourages innovation, creates jobs, raises personal incomes, and generates economic growth.

Does marketing make people buy things they don't need?

From our discussion so far it seems that the performance of micro-marketing activities aimed at satisfying consumer needs and wants does not lead to an improper allocation of resources. Giving individuals what they want, after all, is the purpose of our market-directed economic system. However, some critics feel that most firms—especially large corporations—do not really cater to the needs and wants of the consumer. Rather, they use powerful persuasive techniques—television advertising in particular—to manipulate consumers into buying whatever the firms wish to sell.

Historian Arnold Toynbee, for example, felt that American consumers have been manipulated into buying products which are not necessary to satisfy "the minimum material requirements of life." Toynbee saw American firms as mainly trying to fulfill "unwanted demand"—demand created by advertising—rather than "genuine wants." He defined genuine wants as ". . . wants that we become aware of spontaneously, without having to be told by Madison Avenue that we want something that we should never have thought of wanting if we had been left in peace to find out our wants for ourselves."[14]

What are the minimum requirements of life?

One flaw in this line of reasoning is the problem of determining "the minimum material requirements of life." Does this mean that people should go back to living in caves or in log cabins? Which products consumed today are unnecessary and therefore should be abandoned?

Obviously, some value judgments must be made to answer such questions—and few of us share the same values. One critic has suggested, for example, that Americans could and *should* do without items such as pets, newspaper comic strips, second family automobiles, motorcycles, snowmobiles, campers, recreational boats and planes, cigarettes, aerosol products, pop and beer cans, and hats.[15] You may agree with some of those. But who should determine "minimum material requirements of life"—consumers or critics?

Which wants are really "genuine"?

Another problem with Toynbee's argument is the notion that people should be "left in peace" to discover their own wants. Actually, while our basic needs may be innate, almost all our wants for need-satisfying goods and services are learned. Moreover, these wants are learned not only through advertising, but also through other sources—including our family, friends, teachers, reference groups, and so on.

For example, American consumers did not stand up and shout for refrigerators, cars, and kidney dialysis machines before they were told that such products were available. Does this mean that these products don't satisfy genuine needs and wants?

The minimum material requirements of life may differ from one household to the next.

Mike Kelly

Consumers are not puppets

The idea that firms can manipulate consumers to buy anything they choose to produce simply isn't true. A consumer who buys a can of soda pop that tastes terrible won't buy another can of that brand—regardless of how much it is advertised. In fact, many new products fail the test of the marketplace. Not even large corporations are assured of success every time they launch a new product. Consider, for example, the dismal fate of products such as Ford's Edsel, Du Pont's Corfam, Campbell's Red Kettle Soups, the "midi-skirts" that the fashion industry tried to persuade women to wear back in the 1960s, or more recently "light whiskeys" and "big cars."[16]

Satisfying needs and wants is not a static process

Consumer needs and wants are constantly changing. Few of us would care to live like our grandparents lived when they were our age—let alone like the pioneers who traveled west in covered wagons. The critics must realize that marketing's job is not just to satisfy consumer wants as they exist at any particular point in time. Rather, as Engledow has stated:

> One of marketing's most critical functions is the creative function—utilizing the capabilities of the firm *to produce a better solution to a want than any that might be envisioned by the consumer* with his limited perception of technological and marketing possibilities. (Emphasis added)[17]

Indeed, it is this continuous search for better solutions to consumer needs that makes our competitive market-directed system work so effectively.

Does marketing make people materialistic?

Along with charges of creating unwanted demand, many critics have accused marketing of distorting people's tastes and making them too materialistic. There is no doubt that marketing relies heavily on materialistic values. And some over-eager advertisers have perhaps been guilty of suggesting product-oriented solutions to all life's problems. However, there is much disagreement as to whether marketing creates materialistic values or simply appeals to already existing values.

Anthropologists have discovered that even in the most primitive societies people want to adorn themselves with trinkets and accumulate possessions. In fact, in some tribal villages a person's social status is measured by how many goats or sheep that person owns. Further, the tendency for ancient pharoahs and kings to surround themselves with wealth and treasures can hardly be attributed to the persuasive powers of the advertising agencies!

The idea that marketers create and serve "false tastes"—as defined by individual critics—has been rebutted by a well-known economist—George Stigler—who said:

> The marketplace responds to the tastes of consumers with the goods and services that are salable, whether the tastes are elevated or depraved. It is unfair to criticize the marketplace for fulfilling these desires, when clearly the defects lie in the popular tastes themselves. I consider it a cowardly concession to a false extension of the idea of democracy to make sub rosa attacks on public tastes by denouncing the people who serve them. It is like blaming the waiters in restaurants for obesity.[18]

Marketing reflects peoples' values.

Mary McCarthy

Marketing reflects our own values

Among the scholars who have studied materialism, the consensus appears to be that—in the short run—marketing reflects social values, while—in the long run—it enhances and reinforces them. And as Webster has pointed out:

> To the extent that materialism represents a consensus of opinion expressed by the public through its votes in the marketplace as well as at the polling place, it is hard to criticize it without challenging the foundation of democracy and capitalism.[19]

Material goods do improve the quality of life

In the final analysis, the issue is not really materialism versus some other alternative. Rather, it is how much materialism is "necessary." More is not always better. The quality of life should not be measured strictly in terms of quantities of material goods. But when material goods are viewed as the means to an end rather than the end itself, it is clear that material goods do make it possible to achieve higher-level needs. Modern household appliances, for example, have greatly reduced the amount of time and effort that must be spent on household duties—leaving homemakers free to pursue other interests.

Consumers ask for it, consumers pay for it

Certainly, we do not now have the economists' "ideal"—pure competition. But the monopolistic competition typical of our economy is the result of customer preferences—*not* manipulation of markets by business. Monopolistic competition may seem costly at times—when we look at micro-level situations—but it seems to work fairly well at the macro level—in serving the welfare of consumers who have many and varied demands.

All these demands add to the cost of satisfying consumers. The total cost is larger than it would be if spartan, undifferentiated products were offered at the factory door on a take-it-or-leave-it basis to long lines of buyers.

But if the role of the marketing system is to serve the consumer, then the cost of whatever services he demands cannot be considered excessive. It is merely the cost of serving the consumer the way he wants to be served.[20]

Does macro-marketing cost enough?

The question, "Does marketing cost too much?" has been answered by one well-known financial expert with another question, "Does distribution cost enough?"[21] His analysis showed that marketing is an important part of our economic system. And he suggested that perhaps even more should be spent on marketing—since "distribution is the delivery of a standard of living"—that is, the satisfaction of consumers' basic needs and wants.

The role of marketing and business in our market-directed economy is to satisfy consumers. Production cannot do this job alone—nor can marketing. It makes little sense to think of production and marketing as truly separate things. They are different sides of the same coin.

Mass production requires mass distribution—and our macro-marketing system helps make the whole market-directed economic system work well. In this sense, then, macro-marketing does not cost too much. Some of the activities of individual business firms may cost too much. And if these micro-level activities are improved, the performance of the macro system probably will improve. But regardless, our macro-marketing system performs a vital role in our economic system—and does *not* cost too much.

CHALLENGES FACING MARKETERS

We have said that our macro-marketing system does *not* cost too much—given the present objective of our economy—while admitting that the performance of many business firms leaves a lot to be desired. This presents a challenge to serious-minded students and marketers. What needs to be done—if anything?

We need better performance at the micro level

Some business executives seem to feel that in a market-directed economy they should be completely "free." They don't understand the idea that ours is a market-directed system and that the needs of consumer/citizens must be served. Instead, they focus on their own internal problems, without satisfying consumers very well.

Modern appliances leave time for other interests.

Peter Le Grand

We need better planning

Most firms are still production-oriented. Some hardly plan at all. Others simply extend this year's plans into next year. Progressive firms are beginning to realize that this doesn't work in our changing marketplaces. Strategy planning is becoming more important in many companies. More attention is being given to the product life cycle—because marketing variables should change through the product's life cycle.[22]

May need more social responsiveness

A smart business manager would put himself in the consumer's position. A useful rule to follow might be: "Do unto others as you would have others do unto you." In practice, this would mean developing satisfying marketing mixes for specific target markets. This may mean building in more quality or more safety. The consumers' long-run satisfaction should be considered, too. How will the product hold up in use? What about service guarantees?

Note, however, that this would not always mean producing the "highest quality" that could be produced or offered for sale. Low-quality, short-lived products might be acceptable in certain circumstances—as long as the target market understood what it was getting. (Recall our cost-conscious couple in the home-decorating market in Chapter 2.) Low-cost products—such as the paint in that example—might be seen as a "good value" by some market segments. In other markets, an entirely different product and/or marketing mix might be required.

Production-oriented business managers often neglect this market-oriented rule. It often is difficult—or impossible—to determine what grade or quality is being offered at what prices. Labels, salespeople, and advertising may offer no help at all. Further, the producers may not even know—because no specific customer-related quality has been built into the product. They may *feel* it is better—because higher-cost components have been installed. And these higher-cost components may result in higher prices. But they may or may not contribute to consumer satisfaction. In such cases, it is understandable why some promotion people—faced with production-oriented bosses—resort to aggressive, or even deceptive and fraudulent, promotion to "get rid of the goods."

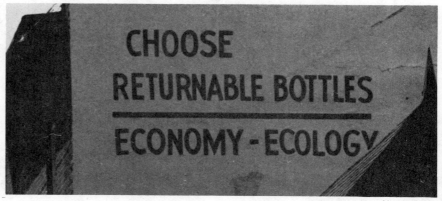

Marketing managers must be aware of environmental concerns.

Mary McCarthy

It seems doubtful that production-oriented approaches will work in the future. Tougher competition and more watchful government agencies may force the typical production-oriented business manager to change his thinking—just to survive. The "lip service" acceptance of the marketing concept in the past—or plain production-orientedness—won't do.

May need more environmental awareness

Besides focusing more on consumers' needs, marketers must be sensitive to environmental concerns. A lack of understanding of uncontrollable variables and a failure to recognize new environmental trends are major causes of marketing failure. Conditions around the world are changing rapidly—as social-economic-political systems grow more and more interdependent. Marketing managers cannot afford to conduct "business as usual."[23]

Of special concern are "environmentalists"—who are trying to protect our scarce resources by limiting their use. This movement—coupled with higher energy prices and slower population growth—will probably reduce economic growth and lead to income distribution problems. The political consequences will probably lead to more government control—and more restrictions on marketing managers.

The goal of increasing consumer satisfaction is often at odds with the environmentalists' goal of preserving the quality of our natural environment. Environmental costs have traditionally been ignored by the marketing system. Resources such as air and water have been viewed as "free commodities." Now marketers must face the fact that they will have to give greater consideration to social costs in their decision making. Perhaps they should ignore potentially profitable opportunities which are ecologically dangerous. They must give more thought to how products will be consumed over time and ultimately disposed of. Finally, marketers must contend with the higher prices that will inevitably be necessary to cover environmental costs—knowing that this will very likely reduce both sales and profits.[24]

Marketers should be looking outside the firm anyway—but now they must look farther and wider. Naïvely extending the past doesn't work any more. Correctly anticipating, or at least understanding, new developments may help their firms avoid fatal blunders or seize breakthrough opportunities.

We need better performance at the macro level

One of the advantages of a market-directed economic system is that its operation is relatively automatic. But in our version of this system, consumer/citizens provide certain constraints (laws). And these constraints can be modified at any time. So it is important for business managers to realize that they may cause new constraints—they do not have the right to do anything they want.

Need tougher enforcement of present laws

Before piling on too many new or different rules, however, it probably would be wise to enforce the ones we have. The antitrust laws, for example, have often been applied to protect competitors from each other when, in fact, they were intended to protect competition. Refocusing present constraints could make a big difference. The FTC seems to be shifting to a consumer-oriented emphasis.[25] Congress and local authorities also are taking stronger stands—for example, with respect to product safety, truth-in-lending, and deceptive advertising.

Laws should affect top management

The results of strict enforcement of present laws could be far reaching if more price fixers, fraudulent or deceptive advertisers, and others who are obviously violating existing legislation—and thereby affecting the performance of the macro-marketing system—were sent to jail or given heavy fines. A quick change in attitudes might occur if top managers—those who plan strategy—were prosecuted, rather than the salespeople or advertisers who are expected to "deliver" on weak or undifferentiated strategies.

In other words, if the government made it clear that it was serious about improving the performance of our economic system, much could be achieved within the present system—*without* adding new constraints or trying to "patch up" the present ones.

Need better-informed and politically active business leaders

Further, it probably would be desirable for business leaders to expand their understanding of—and efforts to improve—our macro system. They should take the offensive—not the defensive. More communication with legislators, government administrators, and consumer advocates could increase awareness of each others' problems, perceptions, and even use of terminology. Confusion or differences regarding the meaning of words such as: *competition, product, market, consumer needs, rationality,* and *information* can make a big difference.[26]

Need better-informed consumers

We also may need some changes to help potential customers choose among the confusing array of goods and services on the market. Legislation to ensure that consumers do have grounds for comparing products (for example, life expectancy of light bulbs and appliances) would be useful. Consumer education programs designed to teach people how to buy more effectively could also be a help.

But great care must be used here—so that the consumer's free choice *really* is preserved. If only easily measurable characteristics are used, consumers might be encouraged or even trained to use quantitative criteria, when qualitative characteristics (for example, style, taste, freshness, and fun in use) might be more important for many of them.

Need socially responsible consumers

We have been stressing the responsibility of producers to act responsibly—but consumers have responsibilities, too. This is usually ignored by consumer advocates.[27] Some consumers abuse returned-goods policies, change price tags in self-service stores, and expect attractive surroundings and courteous, well trained sales and service people—but want discount prices. Others are downright abusive to salespeople. Others think nothing of "ripping off" businesses.

Americans tend to perform their dual role of consumer/citizens with something of a split personality. We often behave one way as consumers and then take the opposite position at the ballot box. For example, while our beaches and parks lie covered with garbage and debris, we urge our political representatives to take stiff action to curb pollution. We protest sex and violence in the media and then flock to see *Jaws II, The Deer Hunter,* and other R- or X-rated movies. We complain about high energy costs and then purchase low-efficiency appliances.

Let's face it. There is a wealth of information already available to improve

People behave differently as consumers and citizens.

Mary McCarthy

consumer decision making. The consumerism movement has encouraged nutritional labeling, open dating, unit pricing, truth-in-lending, plain-language contracts and warranties, and so on. And, government agencies publish many consumer buying guides—as do organizations such as Consumers Union. Yet the majority of consumers continue to ignore most of this information.

We may need to modify our macro-marketing system

Our macro-marketing system is built on the assumption that we are trying to satisfy consumers. But with resource shortages and rising energy costs, how far should the marketing concept be allowed to go?

Should marketing managers limit consumers' freedom of choice?

Achieving a "better" macro-marketing system is certainly a desirable goal. But an important question is what role should a marketer play—in his role as a producer. As a consumer/citizen, there is no doubt that he has the right and obligation to contribute his view and vote to improve our system. But as a producer, what should he do?

This is extremely important, because some marketing managers—especially those in large corporations—might have an impact far larger than in their role as a consumer/citizen. Should they, for example, deliberately refuse to produce "energy-gobbling" appliances or cars—even though there is strong demand? Or should they be expected to install safety devices which inevitably will increase costs and which are very definitely *not* desired by potential customers?

These are very difficult questions to answer. Some things which marketing managers can do are clearly in both the firm's and consumers' interests—in that they lower costs and/or improve the options available to consumers. Other choices, however, might actually reduce consumer choice. And such decisions—therefore—would seem to be at odds with a desire to improve the effectiveness of our macro-marketing system.

Consumer/citizens should vote on the changes

It seems fair to suggest, therefore, that marketing managers should be expected to improve and expand the range of goods and services they make available to consumers—always seeking to more fully satisfy the needs and preferences of potential customers. This is the job we have assigned to business.

To the extent that pursuing this objective makes "excessive" demands on scarce resources or causes an "intolerable" level of ecological damage, then consumer/citizens have every right and responsibility to vote for laws to restrict the many individual firms which are trying to satisfy consumers' needs. This is the role which we as consumers have assigned to the government—to ensure that the macro-marketing system works effectively.

It is important to recognize that some critics of marketing are really interested in basic changes in our macro-marketing system. And some basic changes *might* be accomplished by *seemingly minor* modifications in our present system. Allowing some government agency (for example, the FDA or Consumer Product Safety Commission) to prohibit the sale of products for seemingly good reasons may establish a precedent which could lead to major changes we never expected. (Bicycles, for example, are a very hazardous consumer product—perhaps they should not be sold!) Clearly, such government actions could seriously reduce consumers' present "right" to freedom of choice—including "bad" choices.[28]

Therefore, consumer/citizens should be careful to distinguish between proposed changes designed simply to modify our system and those designed to change it—perhaps drastically. In either case, the consumer/citizen should have the opportunity to make the decision (through elected representatives). This decision should not be left in the hands of a few well-placed managers or government planners.

Marketing people may be even more necessary in the future

Regardless of the changes which might be voted by consumer/citizens, some kind of a marketing system will be needed in the future. Further, if satisfying more subtle needs—such as the "good life"—becomes our goal, it could be even more important to have market-oriented firms. It may be necessary, for example, not only to define individual's needs, but also society's needs—perhaps for a "better neighborhood" or "more enriching social experiences," and so on. As one goes beyond tangible physical goods into more sophisticated need-satisfying blends of goods and services, the trial-and-error approach of the typical production-oriented manager becomes even less acceptable.

CONCLUSION

Macro-marketing does *not* cost too much. Business has been assigned the role—by consumers—of satisfying their needs. Customers find it satisfactory—and even desirable—to permit businesses to cater to them and even to stimulate wants. As long as consumers are satisfied, macro-marketing will not cost too much—and business firms will be permitted to continue as profit-making entities.

It must always be remembered that business exists at the consumers' discretion. It is only by satisfying the consumer that a particular business firm—and our economic system—can justify its existence and hope to keep operating.

In carrying out this role granted by consumers, the activities of business firms are not always as effective as they might be. Many business managers do not understand the marketing concept—or the role that marketing plays in our way of life. They seem to feel that business has a God-given right to operate as it chooses. And they proceed in their typical production-oriented ways. Further, many managers have had little or no training in business management—and are not as competent as they should be. As a result, micro-marketing does cost too much. The situation is being improved, however, as training for business expands and as more competent people are attracted to marketing and business generally. Clearly, *you* have a role to play in improving marketing activities in the future.

Marketing has new challenges to face in the future. *All* consumers may have to settle for a lower standard of living. Resource shortages, rising energy costs, and slowing population growth may all combine to reduce income growth. This may force consumers to shift their consumption patterns—and politicians to change some of the rules governing business. Even our present market-directed system may be threatened.

To keep our system working effectively, individual business firms should work toward more efficient and socially responsible implementation of the marketing concept. At the same time, individual consumers have the responsibility to consume goods and services in an intelligent and socially responsible way. Further, they have the responsibility to vote and ensure that they get the kind of macro-marketing system they want. What kind do you want? What can and should you do to ensure that fellow consumer/citizens will vote for your system? Is your system likely to satisfy you, personally, as well as another macro-marketing system? You do not have to answer these questions right now—but your answers will affect the future you will live in and how satisfied you will be.

QUESTIONS AND PROBLEMS

1. Explain why marketing must be evaluated at two levels. Also, explain what criteria you feel should be used for evaluating each level of marketing, and defend your answer. Explain why your criteria are "better" than alternative criteria.

2. Discuss the merits of various economic system objectives. Is the objective of the American economic system sensible? Do you feel more consumer satisfaction might be achieved by permitting some sociologists or some public officials to determine how the needs of the lower-income or less-educated members of the society should be satisfied? If you approve of this latter suggestion, what educational or income level should be required before an individual is granted free choice by the social planners?

3. Should the goal of our economy be maximum efficiency? If your answer is yes, efficiency in what? If not, what should the goal be?

4. Cite an example of a critic using his own value system when evaluating marketing.

5. Discuss the conflict of interests among production, finance, accounting, and marketing executives. How does this conflict contribute to the operation of an individual business? Of the economic system? Why does this conflict exist?

6. Why does the text indicate that the adoption of the marketing concept will encourage more efficient operation of an individual business? Be specific about the impact of the marketing concept on the various departments of a firm.

7. It appears that competition sometimes leads to inefficiency in the operation of the economic system in the short run. Many people argue for monopoly in order to eliminate this inefficiency. Discuss this solution to the problem of inefficiency.

8. How would officially granted monopolies affect the operation of our economic system? Specifically, consider the effect on allocation of resources, the level of income and employment, and the distribution of income. Is the effect any different than if a monopoly were obtained through winning out in a competitive market?

9. Is there any possibility of a pure-competition economy evolving naturally? Could legislation force a pure-competition economy?

10. Comment on the following statement: "Ultimately, the high cost of marketing is due only to consumers."

11. Should the consumer be king or queen? How should we decide this issue?

12. Should marketing managers, or business managers in general, be expected to refrain from producing profitable products which some target customers want but which may not be in their long-run interest? Contrariwise,

should firms be expected to produce "good" products which offer a lower rate of profitability than usual? What if only a break-even level were obtainable? What if the products were likely to be unprofitable, but the company was also producing other products which were profitable so that on balance it would still make some profit? What criteria are you using for each of your answers?

13. Should a marketing manager or a business refuse to produce an "energy-gobbling" appliance which some consumers are demanding? Similarly, should it install an expensive safety device which does not appear to be desired by potential customers and inevitably will increase costs? Are the same principles involved in both of these questions? Explain.

14. Discuss how much slower economic growth or even no economic growth would affect your college community, and in particular its marketing institutions.

SUGGESTED CASES

NOTES

1. This section is based on Jack L. Engledow, "Was Consumer Satisfaction a Pig in a Poke?" *MSU Business Topics,* April 1977, pp. 88–90.

2. James U. McNeal, "Consumer Satisfaction: The Measure of Marketing Effectiveness," *MSU Business Topics,* Summer 1969, p. 33.

3. For an extensive discussion of the problems and mechanics of measuring the efficiency of marketing, see Stanley C. Hollander, "Measuring the Cost and Value of Marketing," *Business Topics,* Summer 1961, pp. 17–26; and Reavis Cox, *Distribution in a High-Level Economy* (Englewood Cliffs, N.J.: Prentice-Hall, Inc.; 1965).

4. "New Harris Consumer Study Causes Few Shocks in Adland," *Advertising Age,* May 30, 1977, p. 2; and Hiram C. Barksdale and William D. Perreault, Jr., "Can Consumers Be Satisfied?" *MSU Business Topics,* Spring 1980, pp. 19–30.

5. Jon Han, "How the BBB Works on the Consumer's Behalf," *Chicago Daily News,* May 8, 1976, p. 26.

6. Alan R. Andreasen and Arthur Best, "Consumers Complain— Does Business Respond?" *Harvard Business Review,* July–August 1977, pp. 100–101.

7. B. Charles Ames, "Trappings vs. Substance in Industrial Marketing," *Harvard Business Review,* July–August 1970, pp. 93–102; and Merchant's Service, National Cash Register Co., *Establishing a Retail Store,* p. 3.

8. This is improving but only 20 percent had in 1968. See "Government Crackdown on Unsafe Goods," *Detroit Free Press,* October 7, 1968, p. 9–B.

9. "AMA Code of Ethics Voted by Directors" (American Marketing Association), *Marketing News,* Mid-July 1970, p. 3.

10. F. M. Nicosia, *Consumer Decision Processes* (Englewood Cliffs, N.J.: Prentice-Hall, Inc., 1966), p. 39.

11. E. H. Chamberlin, "Product Heterogeneity and Public Policy," *American Economic Review,* May 1950, p. 86.

12. For more on this point see Robert L. Steiner, "Does Advertising Lower Consumer Prices?" *Journal of Marketing,* October 1973, pp. 19–26; and Robert L. Steiner, "Marketing Productivity in Consumer Goods Industries—A Vertical Perspective," *Journal of Marketing,* January 1978, pp. 60–70.

13. George J. Stigler, "The Economics of Information," *Journal of Political Economy,* June 1961, p. 213.

14. Arnold J. Toynbee, *America and the World Revolution* (New York: Oxford University Press, 1966), pp. 144–45; see also John Kenneth Galbraith, *Economics and the Public Purpose* (Boston: Houghton-Mifflin Co., 1973), pp. 144–45.

15. Russel J. Tomsen, "Take It Away," *Newsweek,* October 7, 1974, p. 21.

16. See Robert F. Hartley, *Marketing Mistakes* (Columbus, Ohio: Grid, Inc., 1976).

17. Engledow, "Was Consumer Satisfaction a Pig in a Poke?," p. 92.

18. "Intellectuals Should Re-Examine the Marketplace; It Supports Them, Helps Keep Them Free; Prof. Stigler," *Advertising Age,* January 28, 1963; see also E. T. Grether, "Galbraith versus the Market: A Review Article," *Journal of Marketing,* January 1968, pp. 9–14; and E. T. Grether, "Marketing and Public Policy: A Contemporary View, *Journal of Marketing,* July 1974, pp. 2–7.

19. Frederick Webster, *Social Aspects of Marketing* (Englewood Cliffs, N.J.: Prentice-Hall, Inc., 1974), p. 32.

20. See Richard P. Lundy, "How Many Service Stations Are 'Too Many'?" in Reavis Cox and Wroe Alderson, eds., *Theory in Marketing* (Homewood, Ill.: Richard D. Irwin, Inc., 1950), pp. 321–33.

21. Paul M. Mazur, "Does Distribution Cost Enough?" *Fortune,* November 1947.

22. John E. Smallwood, "The Product Life Cycle: A Key to Strategic Marketing Planning," *MSU Business Topics,* Winter 1973, pp. 29–35.

23. Irving Kristol, "The Corporation and the Dinosaur," *The Wall Street Journal,* February 14, 1974.

24. For more on this topic, see Etienne Cracco and Jacques Rostenne, "The Socio-Ecological Product," *MSU Business Topics,* Summer 1971, pp. 27–34.

25. R. E. Wilkes and J. B. Wilcox, "Recent FTC Actions: Implications for the Advertising Strategist," *Journal of Marketing,* January 1974, pp. 55–61.

26. R. Bauer and S. Greyser, "The Dialogue that Never Happens," *Harvard Business Review,* November–December 1967, pp. 2–12 and 186–90; and T. Levitt, "Why Business Always Loses," *Harvard Business Review,* March–April 1968, pp. 81–89.

27. James T. Roth and Lissa Benson, "Intelligent Consumption: An Attractive Alternative to the Marketing Concept," *MSU Business Topics,* Winter 1974, pp. 30–34; and Robert E. Wilkes, "Fraudulent Behavior by Consumers," *Journal of Marketing,* October 1978, pp. 67–75; and "How Shoplifting is Draining the Economy," *Business Week,* October 15, 1979, pp. 119–123.

28. "Dictating PRODUCT Safety," *Business Week,* May 18, 1974, pp. 56–62; Y. Hugh Furuhashi and E. Jerome McCarthy, *Social Issues of Marketing in the American Economy* (Columbus, Ohio: Grid, Inc., 1971); James Owens, "Business Ethics; Age-Old Ideal, Now Real," *Business Horizons,* February 1978, pp. 26–30; Steven F. Goodman, "Quality of Life: The Role of Business," *Business Horizons,* June 1978, pp. 36–37; William F. Dwyer, "Smoking: Free Choice," *Business Horizons,* June 1978, pp. 52–56; Stanley J. Shapiro, "Marketing in a Conserver Society," *Business Horizons,* April 1978, pp. 3–13; and Johan Arndt, "How Broad Should the Marketing Concept Be?" *Journal of Marketing,* January 1978, pp. 101–03.

Career planning in marketing

When you finish this appendix, you should:

1. Know that there is a job or a career for you in marketing.
2. Know that marketing jobs can pay well.
3. Understand the difference between "people-oriented" and "thing-oriented" jobs.
4. Know about the many different kinds of marketing jobs you can choose from.

One of the hardest jobs facing most college students is the choice of a career. Of course, we cannot make this decision for you. You are the best judge of your own objectives, interests, and abilities. Only you can decide what career *you* should pursue. However, you probably owe it to yourself to at least consider the possibility of a career in marketing.

THERE'S A PLACE IN MARKETING FOR YOU

We're happy to tell you that there are many opportunities in marketing. Regardless of one's abilities or training, there is a place in marketing for everyone—from a supermarket bagger to a Vice President of Marketing in a large consumer goods company such as Procter & Gamble or General Foods. The opportunities range widely—so it will be helpful to be a little more specific. In the following pages, we will discuss (1) the financial returns in marketing jobs, (2) setting your own goals and evaluating your interests and abilities, and (3) the kinds of jobs available in marketing.

MARKETING JOBS CAN PAY WELL

The supermarket bagger may earn only the minimum wage, but there are many more challenging jobs for those with marketing training.

Fortunately, marketing jobs open to college level students do pay well! At the time this text went to press, marketing undergraduates were being offered

687

starting salaries ranging from $13,000 to $16,000 a year. Of course, these figures are only averages. Starting salaries can vary considerably, depending on your background, experience, and location.

As shown in Table C–1, starting salaries in sales-marketing compare favorably with many other fields—and are only slightly lower than those for fields such as engineering, for which college graduates are currently in very high demand. How far and fast your income rises above the starting level depends on many factors—including your willingness to work, how well you get along with people, and your individual abilities. But most of all it depends on getting results,—individually and through other people. And this is where many marketing jobs offer the newcomer great opportunities. It is possible to show initiative, ability, and judgment in marketing jobs. And some young people move up very rapidly in marketing. Some even end up at the top in large companies—or as owners of their own businesses.

Table C–1
Average starting salaries of 1980 college graduates (with bachelor's degrees) in selected fields

Field	Average starting salary (per month)
Engineering	$1,678
Chemistry	1,427
Sales-marketing	1,328
Accounting	1,310
Economics-finance	1,206
Business administration	1,175
Liberal arts	1,108

Source: *The Endicott Report—1980* (Evanston, Ill., Northwestern University, The Placement Center), p. 4.

Marketing can be the route to the top

Marketing is where the action is! In the final analysis, the success or failure of a firm depends on the effectiveness of its marketing program. This doesn't mean the other functional areas aren't important. It merely reflects the fact that a firm will have little need for accountants, finance people, production managers, and so on if it cannot successfully market its products.

Because marketing is so vital to the survival of a firm, many companies look for people with training and experience in marketing when filling key executive positions. A recent survey of the nation's largest corporations showed that the greatest proportion of chief executive officers had backgrounds in marketing and distribution (see Figure C–1).

DEVELOP YOUR OWN PERSONAL STRATEGIC PLAN

Now that you know that there are many opportunities in marketing, your problem is matching the opportunities which are available to your own personal objectives and strengths. Basically the problem is a marketing problem: developing a strategic plan to "sell" a product—yourself—to potential employers. Just as in planning strategies for products, developing your own strategy takes careful thought. Figure C–2 shows how you can organize your own strategic planning. This figure shows that you should evaluate yourself first—a personal analysis—

Figure C–1
Main career emphasis of corporate chief executive officers*

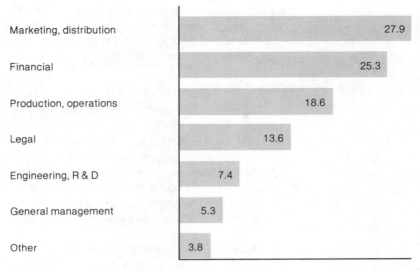

Marketing, distribution — 27.9
Financial — 25.3
Production, operations — 18.6
Legal — 13.6
Engineering, R & D — 7.4
General management — 5.3
Other — 3.8

Percent

* Based on a survey of the chief executive officers of the nation's 500 largest industrial corporations and 300 nonindustrial corporations (including commercial banks, life insurance firms, retailers, transportation companies, utilities, and diversified financial enterprises).
Source: Adapted from Charles G. Burck, "A Group Profile of the Fortune 500 Chief Executive," *Fortune,* May 1976, p. 172.

Figure C–2
Develop your own personal strategic plan

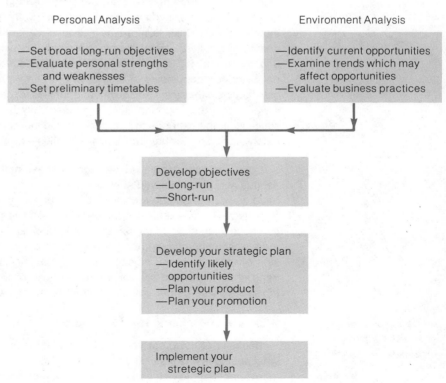

Personal Analysis

—Set broad long-run objectives
—Evaluate personal strengths and weaknesses
—Set preliminary timetables

Environment Analysis

—Identify current opportunities
—Examine trends which may affect opportunities
—Evaluate business practices

Develop objectives
—Long-run
—Short-run

Develop your strategic plan
—Identify likely opportunities
—Plan your product
—Plan your promotion

Implement your stretegic plan

and then analyze the environment—for opportunities. This will help you sharpen your personal long-run and short-run objectives—which will lead to developing a strategy. And, finally, you will start implementing your own personal strategic plan. These ideas are explained more fully below.

CONDUCT YOUR OWN PERSONAL ANALYSIS

You are the "Product" which you are going to include in your own strategic plan. So first you have to decide what your long-run objectives are—what you want to do, how hard you want to work, and how quickly you want to reach your objective. Be honest with yourself—or you will face eventual frustration. It's helpful to evaluate your own personal strengths and weaknesses, and decide what factors may become the key to your success. Finally, as part of your personal analysis, set some preliminary time tables—to guide your strategic planning and implementation efforts. Let's spell this out in detail.

Set broad long-run objectives

What do you want—a job or a career?

Strategic planning requires much "trial-and-error" decision making, but at the very beginning you should make some tentative decisions about your own objectives—what you are seeking out of a job, and out of life. At the very least, you should decide whether you are just looking for a "job" or whether you want to build a "career." And beyond this, do you want the position to be personally satisfying or is the financial return enough? And just how much financial return do you need—or are you willing to work for? Some people work only to support themselves and their leisure-time activities. Others work to support themselves and their families. These people seek only financial rewards from their job—and try to find job opportunities that provide adequate financial returns while not being too demanding of time or effort. Other people, however, look first for satisfaction in their job—and seek opportunities for career advancement. Financial rewards may be important too, but these may be used only as measures of success. In the extreme, the career-oriented individual may be willing to sacrifice much—including leisure and social activities—to achieve success in a career.

Once you have tentatively decided on these matters, then you can get more serious about whether you should seek a job—or a career—in marketing. If you have decided to pursue a career, you should set your broad long-run objectives to achieve it. For example, one long-run objective might simply be to pursue a career in marketing management (or marketing research). This might require more academic training than you had been planning for—as well as a different kind of training. If your objective is to get a "job" that pays well, on the other hand, then this would call for a different kind of training and different kinds of job experiences before completing your academic work.

Evaluate personal strengths and weaknesses

What kind of a job is right for you?

Because of the great variety of marketing jobs, it's hard to generalize about what aptitudes one should have, ideally, to pursue a career in marketing. Different jobs attract people with various interests and abilities. Here, we will provide some guidelines about what kinds of interests and abilities marketers should have. (Note: If you are completely "lost" about your own interests and abilities, you probably should see your campus career counselor and take some vocational aptitude and interest tests. These tests will enable you to compare yourself with people who are now working in various career positions. They will *not* tell you what you should do, but they can help—especially in eliminating things you are less interested in and/or able to do.)

Are you "people-oriented" or "thing-oriented"?

One of the first things you should try to decide for yourself is whether you are basically "people-oriented" or "thing-oriented." This is a very important decision. A "people-oriented" person probably would not be very happy in a bookkeeping job, for example, while a "thing-oriented" person might be quite miserable in a personal selling job which involves a lot of customer contact.

Marketing has both "people-oriented" and "thing-oriented" jobs. People-oriented jobs are primarily in the sales area, where company representatives must make contact with potential customers. This may be direct personal selling or customer service activities, for example at complaint desks or repair departments. Thing-oriented jobs focus more on creative activities and analyzing data—as in advertising and marketing research—or on operating warehouses, transportation agencies, or the "back-end" of retailing institutions.

People-oriented jobs tend to pay more, in part because such jobs are more likely to affect sales—the life blood of any business. Thing-oriented jobs, on the other hand, are often seen as "cost-generaters" rather than "sales-generaters." Taking a big view of the whole company's operations, the thing-oriented jobs are certainly necessary, but without sales no one is needed to do them.

Thing-oriented jobs are usually done at the company's offices. Further, especially in lower-level jobs, the amount of work that needs to be done—and even the nature of the work—may be spelled out quite clearly. The time it takes to design questionnaires and tabulate results, for example, can be estimated with reasonable accuracy. Similarly, running a warehouse, totaling inventories, packaging outgoing shipments, and so on are more like production operations. It is fairly easy to measure an employee's effectiveness and productivity in a thing-oriented job. At the least, time put in is a measure of the employee's contribution.

A sales representative, on the other hand, might spend all weekend thinking and planning how to make a half-hour sales presentation on Monday. For what should the sales rep be compensated—the half hour presentation, all of the planning and thinking that went into it, or the results? Typically, sales reps are rewarded according to their sales results—and this helps account for the sometimes extremely high salaries paid to effective order-getters. At the same time, some people-oriented jobs can be routinized and are lower paid. (For example, salesclerks in some retail stores are paid at or near the minimum wage.)

Managers needed for both kinds of jobs

We have oversimplified deliberately to emphasize the differences among types of jobs. Actually, of course, there are many variations between the two extremes. Some sales representatives must do a great deal of analytical work before they make a presentation. Similarly, some marketing reseachers must be extremely people-sensitive to get potential customers to reveal their true feelings. But the division is still useful—because it focuses on the primary emphasis in different kinds of jobs.

Managers are needed for the people in these two kinds of jobs. Managing others generally requires a blend of both people and analytical skills—but the people-skills may be the more important of the two. Therefore, we often see people-oriented persons being promoted as managers of either kind of job.

What will differentiate your "Product"?

After deciding whether you are generally "people-oriented" or "thing-oriented," you are ready for the next step—to try to identify your specific strengths (to be built upon) and weaknesses (to be avoided or remedied). It is important to become as specific as possible, so you can develop a better strategic plan. For example, if you decide you are more people-oriented, are you more skilled in verbal *or* in written communication? Or if you are more thing-oriented, what specific analytical or technical skills do you have? Are you "good" at working with numbers, solving complex problems, or coming to the root of a problem? Other possible strengths include past experience (career-related or otherwise), academic performance, an out-going personality, enthusiasm, drive, motivation, and so on.

It is important to see that your strategic plan should build on your strengths—after all, an employer will be hiring you to do something. And you probably should "promote" yourself as someone who is able to do something *well*. In other words, you should have some competitive differential advantage over other prospective employees—and this will be built on the unique things about *you* and what you can do.

While trying to identify strengths, you also must realize that you may have some important weaknesses—depending upon your objectives. If you are seeking a career which requires technical skills, for example, then you will have to obtain these skills. Or if you are seeking a career which requires much self-motivation and drive, then you should seek to develop these characteristics in yourself—or change your objectives.

Set preliminary timetables

At this point in your strategic planning process, you ought to set some preliminary timetables—to organize your thinking, and the rest of your planning. These can be tentative timetables, but you need to make some decisions at this point—to be sure you see where you are going. You might simply focus on getting your "first job," or you might decide to work on two strategic plans: (1) a short-run plan to get your first job and (2) a longer-run plan—perhaps a five-year plan—to show how you're going to accomplish your long-run objectives. People who are basically job-oriented may "get away with" only a short-run plan—just drifting from one opportunity to another as their own objectives and opportunities change. Those interested in "careers," however, need a longer-run plan. Otherwise, they may find themselves pursuing attractive first job opportunities which satisfy short-run objectives—but leave them quickly frustrated when they realize that they are not going to achieve their long-run objectives without additional training or other experiences.

ENVIRONMENT ANALYSIS

Strategic planning is a matching process—and for your own strategic planning this means matching yourself to career opportunities. So now let's look at opportunities available in the marketing area. (The same approach would apply, of course, in the whole business area.) Some of the possibilities and salary ranges are shown in Figure C–3.

An environment analysis looks at the kinds of business opportunities which are available, and current business practices and attitudes in areas which you might feel are opportunities for you.

Identifying current opportunities in marketing

Because of the wide range of opportunities in marketing, it will be helpful to try to narrow the possibilities for you. After deciding on your own objectives, and strengths and weaknesses, think about where in the marketing system you might like to work. Would you like to work for manufacturers, or wholesalers, or retailers? Or doesn't it really matter? And do you want to be involved with consumer goods or industrial goods? By analyzing your feelings about these possibilities, you can begin to zero in on the kind of job and the functional area which might interest you most.

One simple way to get a better idea of the kinds of jobs available in marketing is to review the chapters of this text—this time with an eye for job opportunities rather than new concepts. The following paragraphs contain capsule descriptions of job areas that are often of interest to marketing graduates—with references to specific chapters in the text. Some, as noted below, offer good starting opportunities, while others do not. While reading these paragraphs, keep your own objectives, interests, and strengths in mind.

Figure C–3
Some career paths and salary ranges

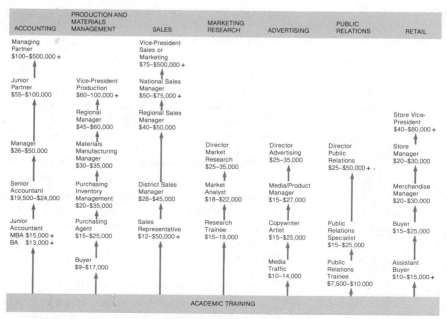

Source: Adapted from Lila B. Stair, *Careers in Business: Selecting and Planning Your Career Path* (Homewood, Ill., Richard D. Irwin, Inc., 1980) and other sources.

Marketing manager (Chapter 2)

This is usually not an entry level job, although aggressive students may move quickly into this role in smaller companies.

Marketing research opportunities (Chapter 5)

There are entry level opportunities at all levels in the channel (in large firms where formal marketing research is done) and in advertising agencies and marketing research firms. Quantitative and behavioral science skills are extremely important in marketing research, so many firms prefer to hire statistics or psychology graduates rather than business graduates. Nevertheless, there are many opportunities in marketing research for marketing graduates. A recent graduate might begin in a training program conducting interviews or coding questionnaires before being promoted to assistant project manager, and subsequent management positions.

Consumer researcher (Chapters 5, 6, and 7)

Opportunities as consumer analysts and market analysts are commonly found in large companies, marketing research organizations, and advertising agencies. Beginners start in "thing-oriented" jobs until their judgment and people-oriented skills have been tested. Because knowledge of statistics and/or behavioral sciences is very important, marketing graduates will find themselves competing with majors in fields such as psychology, sociology, statistics, and computer science.

Purchasing agent/buyer (Chapter 8)

Opportunities are commonly found in large companies, with beginners starting as trainees or assistant buyers under the supervision of experienced buyers.

Market analyst (Chapters 4 and 9)

See consumer researcher (Chapters 5, 6 and 7).

Product planner (Chapter 11)

This probably would not be an entry level position. Instead, people with experience on the technical side of the business and/or sales might be moved into new product development as they demonstrate judgment and analytical skills.

Product/brand manager (Chapters 10 and 11)

Many multiproduct firms have brand or product managers handling individual products—in effect, managing each product as a separate business. Some firms hire marketing graduates as assistant brand or product managers, although typically only MBAs would be considered. Most firms would prefer that recent college graduates spend some time in the field doing sales work before moving into brand or product management positions.

Packaging specialists (Chapter 10)

Packaging manufacturers tend to hire and train interested people from various backgrounds—because there is little formal academic training in packaging. There are many sales opportunities in this field—and the manufacturers can train interested people to be specialists fairly quickly in this growing area.

Distribution channel management (Chapter 12)

This work is typically handled or directed by sales managers, and therefore would not be an entry level position.

Retailing opportunities (Chapter 13)

Most entry level marketing positions in retailing involve some kind of sales activity. Retailing positions tend to offer lower-than-average starting salaries—but often provide opportunities for very rapid advancement. Most retailers require new employees to have some selling experience before managing others or buying. A typical marketing graduate can expect to do some sales work and manage one or several departments before advancing to a store management position—or to a staff position which might involve buying, advertising, marketing research, and so on.

Wholesaling opportunities (Chapter 14)

Entry level marketing opportunities probably would involve sales work, perhaps working with the wholesalers' retailers or other customers—either selling or supporting experienced salespeople. The buying side of wholesaling would be available after some sales experience had been gained. Some very large wholesalers, however, do have specialized buyers. See Purchasing Agent/Buyer (Chapter 8).

Physical distribution opportunities (Chapter 15)

There are many sales opportunities with physical distribution specialists—but there are also many "thing-oriented" jobs involving traffic management, warehousing, and materials handling. Here, training in accounting, finance, and quantitative methods could be quite useful. These kinds of jobs are available at all levels in the channels of distribution—remember that about half of the cost of marketing is caused by physical distribution activities.

Sales promotion opportunities (Chapter 16)

There will not be too many entry level positions in this area. Creativity and judgment are required—and it is difficult for an inexperienced person to demonstrate these skills. A beginner would probably move from sales or advertising jobs into sales promotion.

Personal sales opportunities (Chapter 17)

The greatest number of job opportunities and especially entry level jobs involve personal selling. This might be order getting, order taking, or missionary selling. Many students are reluctant to get into personal selling—but this field offers benefits that are hard to match in any other field. These include the opportunity to earn extremely high salaries and commissions—quickly—a chance to develop one's self-confidence and resourcefulness, an opportunity to work with minimal supervision—almost to the point of being one's own boss—and a chance to acquire product and customer knowledge that many firms consider a necessary prerequisite for a successful career in product/brand management, sales management, and marketing management. Note, however, that many salespersons spend their entire careers in selling, preferring the freedom and earning potential that go with the job over the headaches and sometimes lower salaries of management positions.

Sales management (Chapter 17)

This is a management position which usually is preceded by a variety of sales jobs.

Advertising opportunities (Chapter 18)

Job opportunities are varied in this area—and highly competitive. And because the ability to communicate and knowledge of the behavioral sciences are important, marketing graduates will often find themselves competing with majors from fields such as English, journalism, psychology, and sociology. There are "thing-oriented" jobs such as copywriting, media buying, art, and so on. And there are "people-oriented" positions involving sales—which probably would be of more interest to marketing graduates. This is a glamorous, but small and extremely competitive industry where young people can rise very rapidly—but can also be as easily displaced by new "bright young people."

Pricing opportunities (Chapters 19–20)

Pricing is generally handled by experienced executives, so there are no entry level opportunities here. In fact, in some companies pricing is not even handled by the sales or marketing people, as explained in the text.

Credit management opportunities

Specialists in credit have a continuing need for employees who are interested in evaluating customers' credit worthiness and ensuring that money gets collected. Both people skills and analytical skills can be useful here. The entry positions would normally involve a training program and then working under the supervision of others, until one's judgment and skills are tested.

International marketing opportunities (Chapter 23)

Many marketing students are intrigued with the adventure and foreign travel that are inherent in international marketing careers. However, very few firms hire recent college graduates for positions in international marketing—except some MBA graduates from schools that specialize in international trade. Graduates aspiring to a career in international marketing usually must be prepared to spend time mastering the firm's domestic marketing operations before being sent abroad.

Marketing cost and revenue analysis opportunities (Chapter 22)

Only progressive large firms use these kinds of techniques—usually as analytical tools in sales or marketing management. Some larger firms will have staff departments to do these kinds of analyses, but more typically they are simply tools applied by more analytical researchers and managers in their respective jobs. An MBA degree probably would be needed to go directly into a staff position requiring this sort of work.

Customer relations/consumer affairs opportunities (Chapter 18 and 24)

Some firms are becoming more concerned about their relations with customers and the general public. Employees for this kind of work, however, will have held various positions with the firm before filling customer relations positions.

Study trends which may affect your opportunities

A strategic planner should always be evaluating the future—because it is easier to go along with trends than to buck them. This means you should watch for political, technical, or economic changes which might open—or close—career opportunities. If you can spot a trend early, you may be able to prepare yourself to take advantage of it as part of your long-run strategy planning. Other trends might mean you should avoid certain career options. For example, rapid technological changes in computers and communications are likely to lead to major changes in retailing and advertising—as well as in personal selling. Cable television, telephone selling, and direct-mail selling may reduce the need for routine order-takers—while increasing the need for higher level order-getters. More targeted and more imaginative sales presentations—to be delivered by mail—and through the telephone or television screen may be needed. The retailers who survive may need to have a better understanding of their target markets and be supported by wholesalers and manufacturers who can plan more targeted promotions which make economic sense. This will require a better understanding of the production and physical distribution side of business—as well as of the financial sector. This means better training in accounting, finance, inventory control, and so on. So plan your strategy with trends in mind.

Evaluate business practices

Finally, you should know how businesses really operate—and the kind of training required for various jobs. We've already seen that there are many opportunities in marketing—but not all jobs are open to everyone, and not all jobs are entry jobs. Positions such as marketing manager, brand manager, and sales manager are higher rungs on the marketing career ladder. They become available only when you have a few years of experience and have shown leadership and judgment. Some positions require more education than others. So take a hard look at your long-run objectives and then look at what a business expects for the kinds of opportunities you might like. Will a two year degree get you where you want to go? Or will you need a four year degree, or even a graduate degree? Is a degree really necessary or would it only be "helpful"—perhaps offsetting lack of experience or speed your progress toward your objective?

Women may want to look at whether there are many women in the kinds of positions or kinds of firms they are considering. Some firms and industries are more "progressive" than others and a realistic strategic planner should try to find attractive opportunities which match with what you can offer. If there are no women in the positions or firms you are considering, you have to decide whether you want to be one of the first to "pioneer" in this area, or whether you might prefer to pursue opportunities with easier entry.

Fortunately, marketing positions are generally concerned with "getting results," and who is doing it is less important than that it gets done. Nevertheless, it is desirable for anyone planning a career to be realistic about the business practices in likely opportunities. Remember, it is usually better to go *with* trends than to buck them.

DEVELOP OBJECTIVES

Once you have done a personal analysis and environment analysis—identifying your personal interests, strengths and weaknesses, and opportunities in the environment—you must define your objectives more specifically—both long-run and short-run.

Develop long-run objectives

Your long-run objectives should clearly state what you want to be and what you will do for potential employers. You might want to be as specific as indicating a specific career area you will pursue over the next five to ten years. For example, your long-run objective might be to provide a set of marketing research and management goals to the food manufacturing industry—with the objective of becoming director of marketing research in a small food manufacturing company.

Your long-run objectives should be realistic and attainable. They should be objectives you have thought about and feel you have the necessary skills (or the capabilities to develop those skills) as well as the motivation to reach the objectives.

Develop short-run objectives

To achieve your long-run objective(s), you will also have to develop one or more short-run objectives. These would spell out the five year objectives that are related in some way toward reaching your long-run objective(s). For example, you might begin to develop a variety of marketing research skills *and* management skills—because both would be needed to reach the longer run objective. Or you might obtain an entry level position in marketing research in a large food manufacturer—to gain experience and background. An even shorter-run objective might be to take the academic courses which would be necessary to get that desired entry level job. In this example, you would probably need a minimum of an undergraduate degree in marketing—with an emphasis on marketing research. (Note that given the longer-run objective of managerial responsibility, it probably would be desirable to have a business degree rather than a statistics or psychology degree.)

DEVELOPING YOUR STRATEGIC PLAN

Now that you have developed your objectives, you can move on to developing your own personal strategic plan. This means zeroing in on likely opportunities and developing a specific strategy for these opportunities. Let's talk about that now.

Identify likely opportunities

An important step in strategy planning is to identify potentially attractive opportunities. Depending on where you are in your academic training, this can vary all the way from preliminary exploration to making detailed lists of companies that offer the kinds of jobs that interest you. If you are just getting started, you might talk to your school's career counselors and placement officers about the kinds of jobs being offered to your school's graduates. Your marketing instructors can help you be more realistic about ways you can match your training, abilities, and interests to job opportunities. Also, reading business publications such as *Business Week, Fortune, The Wall Street Journal,* the *Journal of Marketing* and *Advertising Age* can help. Don't overlook the business sections of your local newspapers to keep in touch with marketing developments in your area—and take advantage of any opportunity to talk directly with marketers—ask them what they are doing and what satisfactions they obtain from their job. Also, if your college has a marketing club, join it and participate actively in the club's programs. It will help you meet marketers and students with serious interest in the field. Some may have had very interesting job experiences and can provide you with leads on part-time jobs or exciting career opportunities.

If you are far along in your present academic training, you probably should list companies that you know something about or that you would be willing to investigate—trying to match your skills and interests with possible opportunities. You should narrow your list to a few companies you might like to work for. Then you should do some research on these companies. You should know how they are organized, their product lines, and in general their overall strategies. Try to get clear job descriptions for the kinds of positions you are seeking. Match these job descriptions against your understanding of these jobs and your objectives. Jobs with similar titles may offer very different opportunities. By researching job positions and companies in depth, you should begin to have a feel for where you would be comfortable as an employee. This will help you to narrow your "target market" of possible employers to perhaps five firms. For example, you may decide that your "target market" for an entry position is defined by a large corporation which has: (1) in-depth training programs, (2) a wide product line, and (3) a wide variety of marketing jobs which will enable you to get a wider range of experiences and responsibilities within the same company.

Planning your "Product"

Just like any strategic planner, you must decide what "Product" features are necessary to appeal to your target market. Identify what "credentials" are mandatory and what are optional. For example, is your present academic program enough or will you need more training? Also identify what technical skills—such as computer programming or accounting—are needed. Further, are there any business experiences or extra-curricular activities which will help make your "Product" more attractive to employers? This might involve active participation in college organizations—or work experience—either on the job or in internships.

Planning your Promotion

Once you have identified potential target markets and developed a Product you hope will be attractive to them, you have to tell these potential customers about your Product. You can either write directly to prospective employers—sending a carefully developed résumé which reflects your strategic planning—or visiting them directly (with your résumé). Many colleges run well-organized interviewing services—and their advice should be sought early in your strategic planning effort.

IMPLEMENTING YOUR STRATEGIC PLAN

When you have completed your personal strategic plan, you must implement it—starting with working to accomplish your short-run objectives. If as part of your plan you have decided that you will need specific outside experience—then you should arrange to get it. This may mean taking a "low-paying" job—or even volunteering to work in political organizations or volunteer organizations where you can get that kind of experience. If you have decided that you need skills that can be learned in academic courses, then you should plan to take these courses. Similarly, if you don't have a good understanding of your opportunities, then you need to begin to learn as much about alternative jobs as you can—by talking to professors, taking advanced courses, talking to business people, and so on. And, of course, trends and opportunities can change—so you should continue to read business publications, talk with professionals in your areas of likely interest, and be sure that the planning you have done still makes sense.

Strategic planning must adapt to the environment—and if the environment changes or your personal objectives change, then you will have to develop a new strategic plan. This is an ongoing process, and you may never be completely satisfied with your strategic planning. But even trying will make you look much more impressive when you begin your job interviews. Remember, while all employers would like to hire a "Superman" or a "Wonder Woman," they also are impressed with candidates who know what they want to do and are looking for a place where they can fit in—and make a contribution. So planning a personal strategy and seeking to implement it will almost guarantee that you will do a better job in career planning—and certainly it will help insure that you reach your own objectives—whatever they are.

Whether or not you decide to pursue a marketing career, the author wishes you the best of luck in your search for a challenging and rewarding career—wherever your interests and abilities may take you.

CASES

Guide to the use of these cases

Cases can be used in many ways. And the same case may be fruitfully considered several times for different purposes.

"Suggested cases" are listed at the end of most chapters, but these cases could also be used later in the text. The main criterion for the order of these cases is the amount of technical vocabulary or text principles which are needed to read the case meaningfully. The first cases are "easiest" in this regard. This shows why an early case could easily be used two or three times—for different purposes. Some early cases might require some consideration of Price, for example, and might be used twice, say in regard to product planning and, later pricing. But later cases which focus more on Price might be treated more effectively *after* the Price chapters have been covered.

1. Quenton, Incorporated

It is now 1973, and Mr. Donald Elsworth, newly elected president of Quenton, Inc., is faced with some serious problems. Quenton, Inc., is a 105-year-old California-based food processor. Its multiproduct lines are widely accepted under the "Quenton" brand. The company and subsidiaries prepare, can, package, and sell canned and frozen foods. Beginning with beef, the company expanded to include pineapple from Hawaii as well as other fruits, vegetables, pickles and condiments, Alaskan salmon, and can manufacturing. Operating more than 27 processing plants in the United States, Quenton became one of the largest U.S. food processors—with annual sales (in 1972) of $348,-065,000.

Until 1971, Quenton was a subsidiary of a major midwestern meat-packing company, and many of the present managers came up through the meat-packing industry. Quenton's last president recently said: "Almeat's (the meat-packing firm) influence is still with us. Quenton has always been run like a meat-packer. As long as new products show a potential for an increase in the company's sales volume, they are produced. Traditionally there has been little, if any, attention paid to margins. We are well aware that profits will come through good products."

Warren Austin, a 25-year Quenton employee and now production manager, is in full agreement with the multiproduct-line policy. Mr. Austin said: "Volume comes from satisfying needs. We at Quenton will can, pack, or freeze any meat, vegetable, or fruit we think the consumer might want." He also admitted that much of the expansion in product lines was encouraged by economics. The typical plants in the industry are not fully used. By adding new products to use this excess capacity, costs are spread over greater volume. So the production department is always looking for new ways to make more effective use of its present facilities.

The wide expansion of product lines coupled with Quenton's line-forcing policy has resulted in 85 percent of Quenton's sales coming from supermarket chain stores—such as Safeway, Kroger, and A&P. Smaller stores are generally not willing to accept the Quenton policy—which requires that any store wanting to carry its brand name must be willing to carry the whole line of 68 varieties of fruits, vegetables, and meats. Mr. Austin explains, "We know that only large stores can afford to invest the amount of money in inventory that it would take to be adequately supplied with our prod-

ucts. But, the large stores are the volume! We give consumers the choice of any Quenton product they want, and the result is maximum sales." Many small retailers have complained about Quenton's policy, but they have been considered to be too small in potential sales volume per store to be of any significance.

In 1973, a stockholders' revolt over low profits (in 1972, they were only $5,769) resulted in Quenton's president and two of its five directors being removed. Donald Elsworth, a lawyer who had been a staff assistant to the chairman of the board, was elected president. One of the first things he decided to focus on was the variable and low level of profits earned in the past several years. A comparison of Quenton's results with those of the California Packing Corporation (Calpack) and some other large competitors supported Mr. Elsworth's concern. In the past ten years, Calpack had an average profit return on shareholder's investment of 10.8 percent, H. J. Heinz averaged 9 percent, Hunt Food 6 percent, and Quenton 3.8 percent. Further, Quenton's sales volume, $348,065,000 in 1972, had not increased much from the 1956 level of $325 million—while operating costs have soared upward. Profits for the firm were about $8 million in 1956. The closest they have come since then is about $6 million—in 1964.

In his last report to the Quenton board of directors, the outgoing president blamed his failure on an inefficient marketing department. He wrote, "Our marketing department has deteriorated. I can't exactly put my finger on it, but the overall quality of marketing people has dropped and morale is bad. The team just didn't perform." When Mr. Elsworth confronted Jack Grey—the vice president of marketing—with the previous statement, his reply was, "It's not our fault. I think the company made a key mistake after World War II. It expanded horizontally—by increasing its number of product offerings—while competitors like Calpack were expanding vertically, growing their own raw materials and making all of their packing materials. They can control quality and make profits in manufacturing which can be used in marketing. I lost some of my best people from frustration. We just aren't competitive enough to reach the market to the extent we should with a comparable product and price."

In further conversation with Grey, Mr. Elsworth learned more about the nature of Quenton's market. Although all the firms in the food-processing industry advertise widely to the consumer market, there has been no real increase in the size of the market for processed foods. Further, consumers aren't very selective. If they can't find the brand of food they are looking for, they'll pick up another brand rather than go without a basic part of their diet. No company in the industry has much effect on the price at which its products are sold. Chain store buyers are used to paying about the same price per case for any competitor's product—and won't exceed it. They will, however, charge any price they wish on a given brand sold at retail (i.e., a 48-can case of sweet peas might be purchased from any supplier for $6.83, no matter whose product it is. Generally, the shelf price for each is no more than a few pennies different, but chain stores occasionally attract customers by placing a well-known brand on "sale.")

At this point Mr. Elsworth is wondering why Quenton is not as profitable as it once was. Also, he is puzzled as to why the competition is putting products on the market with low potential sales volume. For example, one major competitor recently introduced a small line of dietary fruits and vegetables—with a potential sales volume so small that almost every nationally known food processor had previously avoided such specialization.

Discuss Quenton's policies and what it might do to improve its situation.

2. Tom's Cleaning Company

Tom Wills is a 26-year-old ex-Navy frogman and a lifelong resident of Traverse City, Michigan—a beautiful summer resort area along the eastern shore of Lake Michigan. The permanent population is about 20,000—and this more than trebles in the summer months.

Tom spent seven years in the Navy after high school graduation, returning home in June 1977. Tom decided to go into business for himself, because he couldn't find a good job in the Traverse City area. He set up Tom's Cleaning Company. Tom felt that his savings would allow him to start the business without borrowing any money. His estimates of required expenditures were: $3,900 for a used panel truck, $475 for a steam-cleaning machine adaptable to carpets and furniture, $330 for a heavy-duty commercial vacuum cleaner, $50 for special brushes and attachments, $75 for the initial supply of cleaning fluids and compounds, and $200 for insurance and other incidental expenses. This total of $5,030 still left Tom with about $2,800 in savings to cover living expenses while getting started.

One of the reasons Tom chose this line of work is his previous work experience. From the time he was 16, Tom had worked part time for Joel Bidwell. Mr. Bidwell operated the only other successful carpet-cleaning company in Traverse City. (One other company was in Traverse City, but rumors suggest it is near bankruptcy.)

Mr. Bidwell prides himself on quality work and has gained a loyal clientele. Specializing in residential carpet cleaning, Bidwell has been able to build a strong customer franchise. For 35 years, Bidwell's major source of new business has been retailer recommendations and satisfied customers who tell friends about the quality service received from Mr. Bidwell. He is so highly thought of that the leading carpet and furniture stores in Traverse City always recommend Bidwell's for preventive maintenance in quality carpet and furniture care. Often Bidwell is trusted with the keys to Traverse City's finest homes for months at a time—when owners are out of town and want his services. Bidwell's customers are so loyal, in fact, that a Vita-Clean national household carpet-cleaning franchise found it next to impossible to compete with him. Even price cutting was not an effective weapon against Mr. Bidwell.

Tom Wills felt that he knew the business as well as Mr. Bidwell—having worked for him many years. Tom was anxious to reach his $20,000-per-year sales goal because he thought this would provide him with a comfortable living in Traverse City. While aware of opportunities for carpet cleaning in businesses, office buildings, motels, and so on, Tom felt that the sales volume available there was only about $8,000 because most businesses had their own cleaning staffs. As he saw it, his only opportunity was direct competition with Bidwell.

To get started, he allocated $600 to advertise his business in the local newspaper. With this money he was able to purchase two half-page ads and have enough left over to buy daily three-line ads in the classified section, listed under Miscellaneous Residential Services, for 52 weeks. All that was left was to paint a sign on his truck and wait for business to "catch on."

Tom had a few customers and was able to gross about $100 a week. He had, of course, expected much more. These customers were usually Bidwell regulars who, for one reason or another (usually stains, spills, or house guests), weren't able to wait the two weeks required until Bidwell could work them in. While these people did admit that Tom's work was of the same quality as Mr. Bidwell's, they preferred Bidwell's "quality-care" image. Sometimes, Tom did get more work than he could handle. This happened during April and May—when resort owners were preparing for summer openings and owners of summer homes were ready to "open the cottage." The same rush occurred in September and October—as resorts and homes were being closed for the winter. During these months, Tom was able to gross about $100–$120 a day—working ten hours.

Toward the end of his first year in business, Tom Wills began to have thoughts about quitting. While he hated to think of having to leave Traverse City, he couldn't see any way of making a living in the carpet- and furniture-cleaning business in Traverse. Mr. Bidwell had the whole residential market sewed up—except in the rush seasons and for people who needed fast cleaning.

Why wasn't Tom able to reach his goal of $20,000? Is there any way Tom can stay in business?

---

3. Kemek Manufacturing Company

Kemek Manufacturing Co. is a large California manufacturer of basic chemicals and polymer resins.

John Gorman, a bright young engineer, has been working for Kemek as a research engineer in the polymer resins laboratory. His job is to do research on established resins—to find new, more profitable applications for resin products.

During the last five years, John has been under heavy pressure from top management to come up with an idea that would open up new markets for the company's foamed polystyrene.

Two years ago, John developed the "spiral-dome concept," a method of using the foamed polystyrene to make dome-shaped roofs and other structures. He described the procedure for making domes as follows:

The construction of a spiral dome involves the use of a specially designed machine which bends, places, and bonds pieces of plastic foam together into a predetermined dome shape. In forming a dome, the machine head is mounted on a boom, which swings around a pivot like the hands of a clock, laying and bonding layer upon layer of foam board in a rising spherical form.

According to John, polystyrene foamed boards have several advantages:

1. Foam board is stiff—but capable of controlled deformation—and can be bonded to itself by heat alone.
2. Foam board is extremely lightweight and easy to handle. It has good structural rigidity.
3. Foam board has excellent and permanent insulating characteristics. (In fact, the major use for foamed board is as an insulator.)
4. Foam board provides an excellent base on which to apply a variety of surface finishes.

With his fine speaking and reasoning abilities, John had little trouble convincing top management of the soundness of the idea.

According to a preliminary study by the marketing department, the following were areas of construction that could be served by the domes:

1. Bulk storage.
2. Cold storage.
3. Educational construction.
4. Industrial tanks (covers for).
5. Light commercial construction.
6. Planetariums.
7. Recreational construction (such as a golf-course starter house).

The study focused on uses for existing dome structures. Most of the existing domes are made of concrete or some cement base material. It was estimated that large savings would result from using foam boards—due to the reduction of construction time.

Because of the new technology involved, the company decided to do its own contracting (at least for the first four to five years after starting the sales program). It felt this was necessary to make sure that no mistakes were made by inexperienced contractor crews. For example, if not applied properly, the plastic may burn.

After building a few domes to demonstrate the concept, the company contacted some leading architects across the country. Reactions were as follows:

It is very interesting, but you know that the Fire Marshal of Detriot will never give his OK.

Your tests show that foamed domes can be protected against fires, but there are no *good* tests for unconventional building materials as far as I am concerned.

I like the idea, but foam board does not have the impact resistance of cement.

We design a lot of recreational facilities and kids will find a way of sawing holes into the foam.

Building codes around L.A. are written for wood and cement structures. Maybe when the codes change.

After this unexpected reaction, management did not know what to do. John still thinks the company should go ahead. He feels that a few reports of well-constructed domes in leading newspapers would go a long way toward selling the idea.

What should Kemek do? Why did it get into the present situation?

---

4. Redi, Incorporated

Mr. Bob Wilson is the president and only stockholder of Redi, Incorporated, a small, successful firm in the restaurant and recreation business in the small town of Carroltown—the site of the state university (population 7,000 plus 20,000 students). Mr. Wilson attended the university in the 1930s—and paid most of his college expenses by selling refreshments at all of the school's athletic events. As he expanded his business, he hired local high school students to help him. The business became so profitable that Mr. Wilson decided to stay in Carroltown after graduation—renting a small building near the campus and opening a restaurant.

Over the years, his restaurant business was fairly successful. Mr. Wilson earned a $36,000 profit on sales of $1,462,500 in 1975. The restaurant now consists of an attractive 40-table dining room, a large drive-in facility, and free delivery of orders to any point on the campus. The only thing that hasn't changed much is Mr. Wilson's customers. He estimates that his restaurant business is still over 90 percent students—and that over three fourths of his sales are made between 6 p.m. and 1 a.m. There are several other restaurants with comparable facilities near to the campus, but none of these is as popular with the university students as his "Papa Bob's."

As a result of the restaurant's success with the student market, Mr. Wilson has aimed his whole promotion effort in that direction—by advertising only through the campus newspaper and over the campus and local rock music radio stations. In an attempt to increase his daytime business, from time to time Mr. Wilson has used such devices as coupon mealbooks priced at 85 percent of face value. And he features daily "lunch special" plates. Nevertheless, he admits that he has been unable to compete with the university cafeterias for daytime business.

In 1972, when Mr. Wilson was seeking a new investment opportunity, he contacted a national manufacturer of bowling equipment and supplies about the feasibility of opening a bowling lanes operation. Carroltown didn't have such a facility at the time, and Mr. Wilson felt that both the local and university communities would provide a good market. He already owned a large tract of land which would be suitable for construction of the bowling lanes. The land was next to the restaurant—and he felt that this would result in each business stimulating the other.

The decision was made to go ahead with the venture, and to date the results have been nothing short of outstanding. Several local and university groups have formed bowling leagues. The university's men's and women's physical education departments schedule several bowling classes at Mr. Wilson's bowling lanes each term. And the casual bowling in the late afternoons and evenings is such that at least 12 of the 16 lanes are almost always in use. Some local radio advertising is done for the bowling lanes, but Mr. Wilson doesn't feel that much is necessary. The success of the bowling lanes has encouraged the developer of a small shopping center in the residential part of town to make plans to include a similar facility in his new development. But Mr. Wilson believes that competition won't hurt his business, because he has more to offer in his recreation center—a restaurant and bowling.

Pleased with the profitability of his latest investment, Mr. Wilson decided to expand his recreational center even further. He noted that both students and local citizens patronized his bowling lanes and concluded that the addition of an attractive, modern billiard parlor would also have a common appeal. There were already two poolrooms in Carroltown. One was modern—about two miles from campus. The other one was considered to be a "hangout" and was avoided by townspeople and students. Mr. Wilson decided that distance and atmosphere were the factors which resulted in both operations being only marginally successful. Further, he felt that by offering a billiard parlor operation, he would be able to supply yet another recreational demand of his market. He obtained a loan from a local bank and began to build a third building at the back of his land. The billiard parlor was outfitted with 12 tables, a snack bar, wall-to-wall carpeting, and a soft-music background system.

Today, eight months later, Mr. Wilson is extremely disappointed with the billiard parlor operation. After the first two or three weeks, business steadily dropped off until now usually only one or two tables are in use—even during the evening hours when business at the bowling lanes is at its peak. Promotion for the billiard parlor has been combined with promotions for the other facilities—which are still doing very well.

In an effort to discover what went wrong, Mr. Wilson interviewed several of his restaurant and bowling customers. Some typical responses were:

—a coed: "I had enough trouble learning how to bowl—but at least it's sociable. Pool looks hard and everyone is so serious."

—a fraternity man: "My idea of a good date is dinner at Papa Bob's, then the movies or an evening of bowling. You just can't make a good impression by taking a girl to play pool."

—a Carroltown citizen: "I've never allowed my children to enter the local pool halls. What's more, as a kid I wasn't allowed either, and so I've never learned the game. It's too late to teach an old dog new tricks!"

Mr. Wilson is thinking about selling the billiard equipment and installing some pinball machines—because he has heard they can be very profitable.

Evaluate Mr. Wilson's overall position and suggest what should be done.

---

5. Midwest Steel Company

Midwest Steel Company is one of the two major producers of wide-flange beams in the Chicago area. The other major producer in the area is the U.S. Steel Corporation (USS)—which is several times larger than Midwest, as far as production capacity on this particular product is concerned. Bethlehem Steel Co. and USS have eastern plants which produce this product. Also, there are some small competitors in the Chicago area. And foreign competition is sometimes a factor. Generally, however, U.S. Steel and Midwest Steel are the major competitors in wide-flange beams in the Chicago area—because typically the mill price charged by all producers is the same and the customer must pay freight from the mill. Therefore, the large eastern mills' delivered prices would not be competitive in the Chicago area.

Wide-flange beams are one of the principal steel products used in construction. They are the modern version of what are commonly known as "I-beams." USS rolls a full range of wide flanges from 6 to 36 inches. Midwest entered the field about 15 years ago—when it converted an existing mill to produce this product. This mill is limited to flanges up to 24 inches, however. At the time of the conversion, it was esti-

mated that customer usage of sizes over 24 inches was likely to be small. In the past few years, however, there has been a definite trend toward the larger and heavier sections.

The beams produced by the various competitors are almost identical—since customers buy according to standard dimensional and physical-property specifications. In the smaller size range, there are a number of competitors, but above 14 inches only USS and Midwest compete in the Chicago area. Above 24 inches, USS has had no competition.

All the steel companies sell these beams through their own sales forces. The customer for these beams is called a "structural fabricator." This fabricator typically buys unshaped beams and other steel products from the mills and shapes them according to the specifications of his customer. The fabricator's customer is the contractor or owner of a particular building or structure which is being built.

The structural fabricator usually sells his product and services on a competitive-bid basis. The bidding is done on the basis of plans and specifications which are prepared by an architectural or structural engineering firm—and forwarded to him by the contractor wanting the bid. Although several hundred structural fabricators compete in the region, relatively few account for the majority of wide-flange tonnage. Since the price is the same from all producers, they typically buy beams on the basis of availability (i.e., availability to meet production schedules) and performance (reliability in meeting the promised delivery schedule).

Several years ago, Midwest production schedulers saw that they were going to have an excess of hot-rolled plate capacity in the near future. At the same time, a new production technique was developed which would enable a steel company to weld three plates together into a section with the same dimensional and physical properties and almost the same cross section as a rolled wide-flange beam. This technical development appeared to offer two advantages to Midwest: (1) it would enable Midwest to use some of the excess plate capacity, and (2) larger sizes of wide-flange beams could be offered. Cost analysts showed that by using a fully depreciated plate mill and the new welding process it would be possible to produce and sell larger wide-flange beams at competitive prices, i.e., at the same price charged by USS.

Midwest's managers were excited about the possibilities—because customers usually appreciate having a second source of supply. Also, the new approach would allow the production of up to a 60-inch depth of section and an almost 30-inch width of flange. With a little imagination, these larger sizes could offer a significant breakthrough for the construction industry.

Midwest decided to go ahead with the new project. As the production capacity was being converted, the salespeople were kept well informed of the progress. They, in turn, promoted this new capability—emphasizing that soon they would be able to offer a full range of beam products. Several general information letters were sent to the trade, but no advertising was used. Moreover, the market development section of the sales department was very busy explaining the new possibilities of the process—particularly to fabricators at engineering trade associations and shows.

When the new line was finally ready to go, the reaction was disappointing. In general, the customers were wary of the new product. The structural fabricators felt they could not use it without the approval of their customers—because it would involve deviating from the specified rolled sections. And, as long as they could still get the rolled section, why make the extra effort for something unfamiliar—especially with no price advantage. The salespeople were also bothered with a very common question: "How can you take plate which you sell for about $121 per ton and make a product which you can sell for $122?" This question came up frequently and tended to divert the whole discussion to the cost of production—rather than to the way the new product might be used.

Evaluate Midwest's situation. What should it do to gain greater acceptance for its new product?

6. The Capri

The Capri is a fairly large restaurant—covering about 20,000 square feet of floor space—located in the center of a small shopping center which was completed early in 1971. In addition to this restaurant, other businesses in the shopping center include a bakery, a beauty shop, a liquor store, and a meat market. There is parking space for several cars in front of each of the stores.

The shopping center is located in a residential section of a growing suburb in the East—along a heavily traveled major traffic artery. The nearby population is middle-income families, and although the ethnic background of the residents is fairly heterogeneous, a large proportion are Italians.

The Capri—which sells mostly full-course dinners (no bar)—is operated by Lu DeLuca, a neat-appearing man who was born in the community in 1920, of Italian

parentage. He graduated from a local high school and a nearby university and has been living in this town with his wife and two children for many years. He has been in the restaurant business (self-employed) since his graduation from college in 1945. His most recent venture—before opening this restaurant—was a large restaurant which he operated successfully with his brother from 1961 to 1967. In 1967, he sold out because of illness. Following his recovery, he was anxious for something to do and opened the present restaurant in April 1971.

Lu felt that his plans for the business and his opening were well thought out. He had even designed his very attractive sign three years before. When he was ready to go into this business, he looked at several possible locations before finally deciding on the present one. He said: "I looked everywhere, and this is one of the areas I inspected. I particularly noticed the heavy traffic when I first looked at it. This is the crossroads from north to south for practically every main artery statewide. So obviously the potential is here."

Having decided upon the location, Lu attacked the problem of the new building with enthusiasm. He tiled the floor; put in walls of surfwood; installed new plumbing and electrical fixtures and an extra washroom; and purchased the necessary restaurant equipment—all brand new. All this cost $32,000—which came from his own cash savings. He then spent an additional $600 for glassware, $1,500 for his initial food stock, and $675 to advertise his opening in the local newspaper. The local newspaper covered the whole metro area, so the $675 purchased only three quarter-page ads. These expenditures also came from his own personal savings. Next, he hired five waitresses, at $50 a week and one chef at $150 a week. Then, with $6,000 cash reserve for the business, he was ready to open. Reflecting his "sound business sense," Lu realized he would need a substantial cash reserve to fall back on until the business got on its own feet. He expected this to take about one year. He did not have any expectations about "getting rich overnight."

The business opened in April and by August had a weekly gross revenue of only $1,200. Lu was a little discouraged with this, but he was still able to meet all his operating expenses without investing any "new money" in the business. However, he was concerned that he might have to do so if business didn't pick up in the next couple of months. It had not by September, and Lu did have to invest an additional $1,200 in the business "for survival purposes."

Business had not improved in November and Lu was still insisting that it would take at least a year to build up a business of this type. In view of the failure to "catch on rapidly," Lu stepped up his advertising to see if this would help the business any. In the last few weeks, he had spent $250 of his own cash for radio advertising—ten late evening spots on a news program at a station which aims at "middle-income America." Moreover, he was planning to spend even more during the next several weeks for some newspaper ads.

By February 1972, business had picked up very slightly—about a $50 increase in the average weekly gross.

By April 1972, the situation had begun to improve and by June his weekly gross was up to between $1,700 and $1,800. By March in the following year, the weekly gross had risen to about $2,100. Lu increased the working hours of his staff six to seven hours a week—and added another cook to handle the increasing number of customers. Lu was more optimistic for the future because he was finally doing a little better than "breaking even." His full-time involvement seemed to be paying off. He had not put any new money into the business since the summer of 1972 and expected business to continue to rise. He had not yet taken any salary for himself, even though he had built up a small "surplus." Instead, he planned to put in an air-conditioning system at a cost of $5,000—and was also planning to use what salary he would have taken for himself to hire two new waitresses to handle his growing volume of business. And he saw that if business increased much more he would have to add another cook.

In explaining the successful survival and growth of his business, Lu said: "I had a lot of cash on hand, a well-planned program, and the patience to wait it out."

Evaluate Lu's marketing strategy. How might he have improved his chances for success and achieved more rapid growth?

---

7. Sleep-Inn Motel

After several years as a partner responsible for sales in a medium-sized manufacturing concern, in 1975 Phil Barnes sold his interest at a nice profit. Then, looking for an interesting opportunity that would be less demanding, he spent considerable time studying alternatives. He decided to purchase the Sleep-Inn—a recently completed 60-room motel at the edge of a small town in a relatively exclusive but rapidly expanding resort area. He saw a strong market potential for public accommodations. The location was also within one-half mile of an interstate highway. Fifteen miles away in the center of the tourist area were several nationally franchised full-service resort motels suitable for longer vacations.

He was able to hire the necessary staff—which initially consisted of four maids and a handyman—to care for general maintenance. Mr. Barnes looked after registration and office duties—assisted by his wife. Since he had traveled a lot himself and had stayed at many different hotels and motels, he had some definite ideas about what vacationers wanted in accommodations. He felt that a relatively plain but modern room with a comfortable bed, standard bath facilities, and air conditioning would appeal to most people.

He did not consider a swimming pool or any other nonrevenue-producing additions to be worthwhile—and considered a restaurant to be a greater management problem than the benefits it would offer. However, after many customers commented, he arranged to serve a continental breakfast of coffee and rolls from a service counter in a room next to the registration desk.

During the first year after opening, occupancy began to stabilize around 50–60 percent of capacity. According to figures which Mr. Barnes obtained from *Trends in the Hotel-Motel Business,* published by the accounting firm of Harris, Kerr, Forster & Company, his occupancy rate ranked much below the average of 78 percent for his classification—motels without restaurants.

Comparison of these results after two years of operation began to disturb Mr. Barnes. He decided to evaluate his operation and look for a way of increasing both occupancy rate and profitability. He did not want to give up his independence—and was trying not to compete directly with the resort areas offering much more complete services. Mr. Barnes stressed a price appeal in his signs and brochures. He was quite proud of the fact that he had been able to avoid all the "unnecessary expenses" of the resorts and was able to offer lodging at a very modest price—much below that of even the lowest-priced resort. The customers who stayed at his motel said they found it quite acceptable, but he was troubled by what seemed to be a large number of cars driving into his parking lot, looking around, but not coming in to register.

Mr. Barnes was particularly interested in the results of a recent study by the regional tourist bureau. This study revealed the following information about area vacationers:

1. 68 percent of the visitors to the area are young couples and older couples without children.
2. 40 percent of the visitors plan their vacations and reserve rooms more than 60 days in advance.
3. 66 percent of the visitors stay more than three days in the area and at the same location.
4. 78 percent of the visitors indicated that recreational facilities were important in their choice of accommodations.
5. 13 percent of the visitors had family incomes of less than $7,500 per year.
6. 38 percent of the visitors indicated that it was their first visit to the area.

Evaluate Mr. Barnes' strategy. What should he do to improve the profitability of the motel?

8. Arctic Palace

Lyle Riley is the manager of the Arctic Palace—an ice-skating rink with a conventional hockey rink surface (85 feet x 200 feet). He has a successful hockey program and is almost breaking even—which is about all that he can expect if he emphasizes hockey. To try to improve his financial condition, Lyle is trying to develop a public skating program. If he had such a program, instead of limiting the use of the ice to 12–24 people per hour, it would be possible to have as many as 700 people in a public session at one time. While the receipts from hockey might be $90 an hour (plus concessions), the receipts from a two-hour public skating session charging $1.50 per person could generate as much as $1,050 for a two-hour period (plus much higher concession revenue). Clearly, the potential revenue from large public skating sessions could add significantly to total receipts and make the Arctic Palace a profitable operation.

Lyle has put several public skating sessions into his ice schedule, but so far they have not attracted as many people as he hoped. In fact, on the average, they don't generate any more revenue than if the times were sold for hockey use. Even worse, more staff people are needed to handle a public skating session—guards, a ticket seller, skate rental, and more concession help.

The Sunday-afternoon public skating sessions have been the most successful—with an average of 300 people attending during the winter season. Typically, this is a "kid-sitting" session with more than half of the patrons being young children who have been dropped off by their parents for several hours. There are some family groups. In general, the kids and the families do seem to have a good time, and a fairly loyal group comes back Sunday after Sunday during the winter season. In spring and fall, however, attendance drops about in half, depending on how nice the weather is.

It is the Friday- and Saturday-evening public sessions which are a big disappointment to Lyle. The sessions run from 8:00 until 10:00—a time when he had hoped to attract couples. At $1.50 per person, plus 75 cents for skate rental if necessary, this could be a more economical date than going to the movies. In fact, Lyle has seen quite a few young couples—and some keep coming back. But he also sees a surprising number of 8 to 12-year-olds who have been dropped off by their parents. In other words, there is some similarity to the Sunday-afternoon kid-sitting session. The younger kids tend to race around the rink, playing tag. This affects the whole atmosphere and makes it less appealing for dating couples.

Lyle feels that is should be possible to develop a teenage and young-adult market based on the format used by roller-skating rinks. Their public skating sessions feature a variety of "couples-only" and "group games" as well as individuals skating to danceable music. This is not the format offered at the usual public ice skating session, however. The idea of making them social activities has not been common, although there are reports in the industry that a few operators have had success with the roller-skating program.

Lyle installed some soft lights to try to change the evening atmosphere. The music was designed to encourage couples to skate together. For a few sessions, Lyle even tried to have some "couples-only" skates, but this was strongly resisted by the young boys who felt that they had paid their money and there was no reason why they should be "kicked off the ice." Lyle also tried to attract more young couples by bringing in a local disc jockey to broadcast from the Arctic Palace and advertise the public sessions. But all this has had little effect on attendance—which varies from 50 to 100 per two-hour session.

Lyle seriously considered the possibility of limiting the evening sessions to people over 13—to try to change the environment. But when he counted the patrons, he realized that this would be risky. More than half of his evening patrons on an average night are 12 or under. This means that he would have to make a serious commitment to building the teenage and young-adult market, but so far his efforts have not been very successful. He has already invested over $2,000 in lighting changes, and over $6,000 promoting the sessions over the youth-oriented radio station, with almost no results.

Some days, Lyle feels it is hopeless. Maybe he should just resign himself to the public skating sessions being a "mixed-bag." Or maybe he should just sell the time to hockey groups.

What should Lyle Riley do about the evening public skating sessions?

---

9. Annie's Floral

Annie's Floral is a florist shop owned and operated by Harold and Anne Clark (a husband-and-wife team). Offering hundreds of varieties and arrangements of flowers, Annie's also carries small gift items to complement a floral arrangement. Mr. Clark serves as manager and sales clerk, while Mrs. Clark uses her artistic talents to select and arrange flowers. Since opening in 1974, sales have been good. Mr. Clark, however, is concerned about the failure of a recent addition to the gift line.

The Clarks bought the present operation in 1974 from Jack Boyd—who had been in the location for 20 years. Called Boyd's Florists, the shop was then grossing about $100,000 a year. Harold and Anne were confident that their previous 12 years' experience owning a smaller floral shop in a tiny (population 6,500) resort town less than 20 miles south would help them become a success in their new location.

Harold Clark feels their new store is in an excellent location. Located in a residential area of a northeast Indiana community of 130,000 population, the new Annie's Floral is somewhat isolated from other neighborhood stores. It is eight blocks to the nearest store—a drugstore—and three and one-half miles to the closest shopping center. But it is near the intersection of the major north-south and east-west streets.

Mr. Clark understood his primary customers' characteristics. This helped him to direct his efforts more efficiently. As a result, sales increased steadily from $150,000 at the end of 1974 to $300,000 in 1980. Most of the regular customers were women—from medium- to high-income families living in the local middle-class residential areas. Also, Mr. Clark was pleased to see that some of his old customers from the resort town come to Annie's—probably because a strong customer acceptance had been built on friendly service and quality floral arrangements. Those customers who stopped in less frequently were assumed to be similar to the "regulars."

The largest part of the shop's business consists of weddings, funerals, parties, dances, and other big, one-time events which need flowers. However, about 25 percent of the purchases are by casual buyers who like to browse and chat with the Clarks. Approximately 60 percent of the sales are telephone orders, while the remaining 40 percent are made in the shop. Almost all of the telephone orders are for special, one-time events, while the walk-in traffic is divided equally between special events and spur-of-the-moment purchases. Almost no one buys flowers on a daily or regular basis. There is some FTD (Florist Telegraph Delivery) business, but Mr. Clark considers this to be an added service. It is only about 5 percent of his volume.

Mr. Clark feels that flowers are fairly homogeneous, unbranded products. Therefore, he feels that he must charge competitive prices to meet those of his 14 competitors throughout the community.

The shop was remodeled in 1976—and selling space was doubled. To fill in the increased display area, it was decided to add several complementary gift items—such as a famous brand of candies, high-quality flowerpots and vases, a quality line of leather vests for men and woman, pen-and-pencil sets, and candles. All the new lines—except the vests—have taken hold and have increased in sales each month since the items were added. Sales of vests have been very disappointing. In fact, they haven't paid their way on the basis of display area allotted (about 1/50 of the total display area).

When the busiest store traffic occurs (during a three- to four-day period before traditional flower-giving days), additional help is used. When available, Mary and Will Clark—the high school-aged children of the owners—fill these jobs. (It was the children who suggested that the market for leather vests was growing in their high school during the last school year.) At other times, only one of the owners and a full-time sales clerk handle store traffic.

Samples of everything the shop has for sale are on display. The main activity of the sales clerk is to show customers various selections which could be used for a particular occasion—and then ring up the sale. Other than store display, advertising consists only of what is printed on the delivery truck, an ad in the Yellow Pages of the local telephone directory, and an occasional ad (five or six times per year) in the daily newspaper. None of the advertising mentions anything but flowers—because the Clarks wish to maintain their identity as florists.

Mr. Clark is wondering if more display area, a lower price, or extra promotion by the sales clerks might move more vests. Further, he is thinking of disposing of them, but isn't sure what should replace them if he did.

Evaluate the present operation and why leather vests don't sell. What strategy should the shop follow?

---

10. Byron Pharmaceutical Company

The Byron Pharmaceutical Company is a well-known manufacturer of high-quality cosmetics and ointments. A little over a year ago, Mr. Alcott, the president of Byron, was scanning the income statements for the last three quarters and did not like what he saw. At the next board meeting he stated that Byron should be showing a larger profit. It was generally agreed that the reason for the profit decline was that the firm had not added any new products to its line during the last two years.

Management was directed to investigate this problem—and remedy it if possible.

Mr. Alcott immediately asked for a report from the product planning group and found that it had been working on a new formula for a toothpaste that might be put into production immediately if a new product were needed. Mr. Emerson, the head of the research department, assured Mr. Alcott that the new ingredients in this toothpaste had remarkable qualities. Clinical tests had consistently shown that the new, as yet unnamed, dentifrice cleaned teeth better than the many toothpastes furiously battling for market share. Based on these tests, Mr. Alcott concluded that perhaps this product was what was needed and ordered work to proceed quickly to bring it to the market.

The marketing research department was asked to

come up with a pleasing name and a tube and carton design. The results were reported back within two months. The product was to be called "Pearly" and the package would emphasize eye-catching colors.

The marketing department decided to offer Pearly along with its other "prestige" products in the drugstores which were carrying the rest of Byron's better-quality, higher-priced products. Byron's success had been built on moving quality products through these outlets, and management felt that quality-oriented customers would be willing to pay a bit more for a better toothpaste. Byron was already well established with the wholesalers selling to these retailers and had little difficulty obtaining distribution for Pearly.

It is now six months after the introduction of Pearly, and the sales results have not been good. The regular wholesalers and retailers carried the product, but relatively little was purchased by final customers. And now many retailers are asking that Byron accept returns of Pearly. They feel it is obvious that it is not going to catch on with consumers—despite the extremely large (matching that of competitors) amounts of advertising which have supported Pearly.

Mr. Alcott has asked the marketing research department to analyze the situation and explain the disappointing results thus far. An outside survey agency interviewed several hundred consumers and has tabulated its results. These are pretty well summarized in the following quotes:

> The stuff I'm using now tastes good. Pearly tastes terrible!
>
> I never saw that brand at the supermarket I shop at.
>
> I like what I'm using . . . why change?
>
> I'm not going to pay that much for any toothpaste . . . it couldn't be *that* much better!

What recommendation would you make to Mr. Alcott? Why?

---

11. Bing Corporation

Bing Corporation is one of the larger chemical companies in the United States—making a wide line of organic and inorganic chemicals, plastics, bio-products, and metals. Technical research has played a vital role in the company's growth.

Recently, Bing's research laboratories developed a new product in the antifreeze line—Pro Tek 20. Much research was devoted to the technical phase, involving various experiments concerned with the quality of the new product.

The antifreeze commonly used now is ethylene glycol. If it leaks into the crankcase oil, it forms a thick, pasty sludge that can produce bearing damage, cylinder scoring, or a dozen other costly and time-consuming troubles for both the operator and the owner of heavy-duty equipment.

Bing Corporation believed that Pro Tek 20 would be very valuable to the owners of heavy-duty diesel and gasoline trucks—as well as other heavy-equipment owners. Chemically, Pro Tek 20 uses methoxy propanol—instead of the conventional glycol and alcohol products. It cannot prevent leakage, but if it does get into the crankcase, it will not cause any problems.

At first, Bing thought it had two attractive markets for this product: (1) the manufacturers of heavy-duty equipment, and (2) the users of heavy-duty equipment. Bing sales reps have made numerous calls and so far neither type of customer has been very interested. The manufacturers are reluctant to show interest in the product until it has been proven in actual use. The buyers for construction companies and other firms using heavy-duty equipment have also been hesitant. Some felt the price was far too high for the advantages offered. Others didn't understand what was wrong with the present antifreeze—and dismissed the idea of paying extra for "just another" antifreeze.

The price of Pro Tek 20 is $14.98 per gallon—which is more than twice the price of regular antifreeze. The higher price is the result of higher costs in producing the product and an increment for making a better type of antifreeze.

Explain what has happened so far. What would you do if you were responsible for this product?

12. Ski Haus Sports Shop

Tom and Ida Cory graduated from a state university in California in 1977. Then, with some family help, they were planning to open a small ski equipment shop in Aspen, Colorado. They were sure that by offering friendly, personal service they would have something unique and be able to compete with the many other ski shops in town. They were well aware that there are already many competitors, because many "ski bums" choose the Aspen area as a place to live—and then try to find a way to earn a living there. By keeping the shop small, however, the Corys hoped to be able to manage most of the activities themselves—thereby keeping costs down and also being sure the service is good.

Now they are trying to decide which line or lines of skis they should carry. Almost all the major manufacturers' skis are offered in the competing shops, so Tom and Ida are seriously considering specializing in the Hoffwurtz brand—which is not now carried by any local shops. In fact, the Hoffwurtz sales rep has assured them that if they are willing to carry the line exclusively, then Hoffwurtz will not sell its skis to any other retailers in Aspen. This idea appeals to Tom and Ida because it would give them something unique—a full line of German-made skis which have just been introduced into the American market with supporting full-page ads in skiing magazines. The skis have an injected foam core that is anchored to the glass layers above and below by a patented process which causes the glass fibers to penetrate the foam. This process is used in a full line of skis, so the Corys would have a unique story to sell for skis which could satisfy everyone's needs. Further, the suggested retail prices and markups were similar to other manufacturers, so the Ski Haus could emphasize the unique features of the Hoffwurtz skis while feeling confident that their prices were competitive.

Besides the exclusive fiber-penetrative construction offered by Hoffwurtz—for strength and durability—the German company had developed a special recreational ski for women—with the help of Olympic triple-medal-winner Heidi Schmidt. The Corys felt that this might be a special selling point for the Hoffwurtz line. Many women need and want recreational skis (skis that are easier to use) and a ski designed specifically for them might be appealing and very profitable.

The only thing that worries the Corys about committing so completely to the Hoffwurtz line is that there are many other manufacturers—both domestic and foreign—which offer full lines and claim to offer unique features. In fact, most ski manufacturers regularly come out with new models and features and the Corys realize that most consumers are confused about the relative merits of all of the offerings. In the past, Tom, himself, has been reluctant to buy "off-brand" skis—preferring instead to stay with major names such as Hart, Head, K2, and Rossignol. So he is wondering whether a complete commitment to the Hoffwurtz line is wise. On the other hand, the Corys want to offer something unique. They don't want to open just another ski shop carrying lines which are available "everywhere." The Hoffwurtz line isn't their only possibility, of course. There are other off-brands which are not yet carried in Aspen. But the Corys like the idea that Hoffwurtz is planning to give national promotional support to the skis during the introductory campaign in the U.S. markets. They feel that this might make a big difference in how rapidly the new skis are accepted. And if they provide friendly sales assistance and quick binding-mounting service, perhaps their chances for success will improve. Another reason for committing to the Hoffwurtz line is that they like the sales rep, Kurt Basse, and they feel he would be a big help in their initial stocking and set-up efforts. They talked briefly with some other firms' salespeople at the major trade shows, but had not gotten along nearly so well with any of them. In fact, most of the sales reps didn't seem too interested in helping a newcomer—preferring instead to talk with and entertain buyers from established stores. The major ski shows are over, so any more contacts with manufacturers will require the Corys to take the initiative. But from their past experience, this does not sound too appealing. Therefore, they seem to be drifting fast toward having the Ski Haus specialize in selling the Hoffwurtz line.

Evaluate the Corys' thinking. What would you suggest they do?

13. Andrews Photo, Inc.

Andrews Photo, Inc., is located in a residential area along a major street about two miles from the downtown of a metropolitan area of 450,000. It is also near a big university. It sells high-quality still and movie cameras, accessories, and projection equipment—including 8mm and 16mm movie projectors, 35mm slide projectors, opaque and overhead projectors, and a large assortment of projection screens. Most of the sales of this specialized equipment are made to area school boards for classroom use, to industry for use in research and sales, and to the university for use in research and instruction.

Andrews Photo offers a wide selection of film and a specialized film-processing service. Instead of processing film on a mass production basis, Andrews gives each roll of film individual attention—to bring out the particular features requested by the customer. This service is used extensively by local industries who need high-quality pictures of lab or manufacturing processes for analytical and sales work.

To encourage the school and industrial trade, Andrews Photo offers a graphics consultation service. If a customer wants to build a display—whether large or small—professional advice is readily available. Along with this free service, Andrews carries a full line of graphic arts supplies.

Andrews Photo employs four full-time store clerks and two outside sales reps. These sales reps make calls on industry, attend trade shows, make presentations for schools, and help both present and potential customers in their use and choice of visual aids.

The people who make most of the over-the-counter purchases are (1) serious amateur photographers and (2) some professional photographers who buy in small quantities. Price discounts of up to 25 percent of the suggested retail price are given to customers who buy more than $500 worth of goods per year. Most regular customers qualify for the discount.

In the last few years, many more "amateurs" have been taking 35mm slide pictures. Because of this, Kevin Arnold, the manager of Andrews Photo, felt that there ought to be a good demand for some way of viewing them. Therefore, he planned a special pre-Christmas sale of inexpensive slide projectors, viewers, and home-sized projection screens. Hoping that most of these would be purchased as Christmas gifts, Arnold selected some products which offered good value and discounted the price to competitive levels—for example, projectors at $99.50, viewers at $9.95, and screens at $29.95. To promote the sale, large signs were posted in the store windows—and ads were run in a Christmas-gift-suggestion edition of the local newspaper. This edition appeared each Wednesday during the four weeks before Christmas. At these prices and with this promotion, Arnold hoped to sell at least 150 projectors, 150 screens, and 200 viewers. When the Christmas returns were in, total sales were 22 projectors, 15 screens, and 48 viewers. He was most disappointed with these results—especially because trade estimates suggested that sales of projection equipment in this price and quality range were up 300 percent over last year.

Evaluate what happened. What should Mr. Arnold do in the future?

14. Deller Company

Jim Deller graduated in business from a large midwestern university in 1977. After a year as a car salesman, he decided to go into business for himself. In an effort to locate new opportunitites, Jim placed several ads in his local newspaper—in Toledo, Ohio—explaining that he was interested in becoming a sales representative in the local area. He was quite pleased to receive a number of responses. Eventually, he became the sales representative in the Toledo area for three local manufacturers: the Caldwell Drill and Press Co., which manufactured portable drills; the T. R. Rolf Co., a manufacturer of portable sanding machines; and the Bettman Lathe Co., which manufactured small lathes. All of these companies were relatively small and were represented in other areas by other sales representatives like Jim Deller.

Deller's main job was to call on industrial customers. Once he made a sale, he would send the order to the respective manufacturer, who would in turn ship the goods directly to the particular customer. The manufacturer would bill the customer, and Deller would receive a commission varying from 5 percent to 10 percent of the dollar value of the sale. Deller was expected to pay his own expenses.

Deller called on anyone in the Toledo area who might use the products he was handling. At first, his job was relatively easy, and sales came quickly because there was little sales competition. There are many national companies making similar products, but at that time they were not well represented in the Toledo area,

In 1979, Deller sold $150,000 worth of drills, earning a 10 percent commission; $100,000 worth of sanding machines, also earning a 10 percent commission; and $75,000 worth of small lathes, earning a 5 percent commission. He was encouraged with his progress and was looking forward to expanding sales in the future. He was especially optimistic because he had achieved these sales volumes without overtaxing himself. In fact, he felt he was operating at about 70 percent of his capacity.

Early in 1980, however, a local manufacturer with a very good reputation—the Bonner Electrical Equipment Company—started making a line of portable drills. It had a good reputation locally, and by April 1980 Bonner had captured approximately one half on Caldwell's Toledo drill market by charging a substantially lower price. Bonner was using its own sales force locally, and it was likely that it would continue to do so.

The Caldwell Company assured Deller that Bonner couldn't afford to continue to sell at such a low price and that shortly Caldwell's price would be competitive with Bonner's. Jim Deller was not nearly as optimistic about the short-run prospects, however. He began looking for other products he could handle in the Toledo area. A manufacturer of hand trucks had recently approached him, but he wasn't too enthusiastic about this offer because the commission was only 2 percent on potential annual sales of $150,000.

Now Jim Deller is faced with another decision. The Phillips Paint Company in Cleveland, Ohio, has made what looks like an attractive offer. They heard what a fine job he was doing in the Toledo area and felt that he could help them solve their present problem. Phillips is having trouble with its whole marketing effort and would like Jim Deller to take over.

The Phillips Paint Company has been selling primarily to industrial customers in the Cleveland area and is faced with many competitors selling essentially the same product and charging the same low prices. Phillips Paint is a small manufacturer. Last year's sales were $140,000. They would like to increase this sales volume and could handle at least double this sales volume with ease. They have offered Deller a 12 percent commission on sales if he will take charge of their pricing, advertising, and sales efforts in the Cleveland area. Jim was flattered by their offer, but he is a little worried because there would be a great deal more traveling than he is doing at present. For one thing, he would have to spend a couple of days each week in the Cleveland area, which is 110 miles away. Further, he realizes that he is being asked to do more than just sell. But he did have some marketing courses in college and thinks the new opportunity might be challenging.

What should Jim Deller do? Why?

15. Watson Sales Company

Bill Watson—now 55 years old—has been a salesman for over 30 years. He started selling in a department store, but gave it up after ten years to work in a lumberyard because the future looked much better in the building materials industry. After drifting from one job to another, he finally settled down and worked his way up to manager of a large wholesale building materials distribution warehouse in Kansas City, Kansas. In 1958, he decided to go into business for himself, selling carload lots of lumber to large retail yards in the Western Missouri and eastern Kansas area.

He made arrangements to work with five large lumber mills on the West Coast. They would notify him when a carload of lumber was available to be shipped, specifying the grade, condition, and number of each size board in the shipment. Bill wasn't the only person selling for these mills, but he was the only one in his area. He was not obligated to take any particular number of carloads per month—but once he told the mill he wanted a particular shipment, title passed to him and he had to sell it to someone. Bill's main function was to buy the lumber from the mill as it was being shipped, find a buyer, and have the railroad divert the car to the buyer.

Bill has been in this business for 20 years, so he knows all of the lumberyard buyers in his area very well—and is on good working terms with them. Most of his business is done over the telephone from his small office, but he tries to see each of the buyers about once a month. He has been marking up the lumber between 4 and 6 percent—the standard mark-up, depending on the grade—and has been able to make a good living for himself and his family.

In the last few years, however, interest rates have been rising for home loans and the building boom slowed down. Bill's profits did, too, but he decided to stick it out—figuring that people still needed housing, and business would pick up again.

Six months ago, an aggressive salesman—much younger than Bill—set up in the same business, covering about the same area but representing different mills. This new salesman charged about the same prices as Bill, but would undersell him once or twice a week in order to get the sale. Many lumber buyers—knowing that they were dealing with a homogeneous product—seemed to be willing to buy from the lowest-cost source. This has hurt Bill financially and personally—because even some of his "old friends" are willing to buy from the new man if the price is lower. The near-term outlook seems dark, since Bill doubts if there is enough business to support two firms like his, especially if the markup gets shaved any more.

One week ago, Bill was contacted by Mr. Talbott, representing the Talbott and White particleboard manufacturing plant. Mr. Talbott knew that Bill was well acquainted with the local building supply dealers and wanted to know if he would like to be the sole distributor for Talbott and White in that area—selling carload

lots, just as he did lumber. Mr. Talbott gave Bill several brochures on particleboard, a product introduced about 20 years ago, describing how it can be used as a cheaper and better subflooring than the standard lumber usually used. The particleboard is also made with a wood veneer so that it can be used as paneling in homes and offices. He told Bill that the lumberyards could specify the types and grades of particleboard they wanted. Therefore, they could get exactly what they needed, unlike lumber where they choose from carloads that are already made up. Bill knew that a carload of particleboard cost about 30 percent more than a carload of lumber and that sales would be less frequent. In fact, he knew that this product has not been as well accepted in his area as many others, because no one has done much promotion in his area. But the 20 percent average markup looks very tempting—and the particleboard market is expanding.

Bill has three choices:

1. Take Mr. Talbott's offer and sell both products.
2. Take the offer and drop lumber sales.
3. Stay strictly with lumber and forget the offer.

Mr. Talbott is expecting an answer within another week, so Bill has to decide soon.

Evaluate what Bill Watson has been doing. What should he do now? Why?

---

16. The Donell Company

The Donell Company is a full-line department store chain operating in and around Seattle, Washington. The company began in the 1920s in the downtown business district of Seattle, and has now expanded until it operates not only the downtown store but also branches in eight major shopping centers around Seattle.

One of the more successful departments in the Donell stores is the cosmetic and drug sundries department. This department sells a wide variety of products—ranging from face powder to vitamins. But it has not been in the prescription business, and does not have a registered pharmacist in the department. Its focus in the drug area has been on "proprietary" items—rather than on the ethical drugs which are normally sold only under the supervision of a registered pharmacist.

The Donell Company is now considering the proposal of the Bentley Drug Company—which is trying

to introduce a wholesale prescription service into Donell cosmetic and drug sundries departments. Bentley is a well-established drug wholesaler which now wants to expand its business by serving retailers such as the Donell Company.

Basically, the Bentley Drug Company's proposal is as follows:

1. Donell's customers would leave their prescriptions in the drug sundries department one day and then pick up their medicines the following day.
2. A representative of the Bentley Drug Company would pick up the prescriptions every evening at closing time and return the filled prescriptions before each store opened the following day. The Donell Company would not have to hire a pharmacist or carry any drug inventory.
3. Donell's could offer a savings of from 30 to 35 percent to their customers. This savings would be

due to the economies of the operation, including the absence of a pharmacist and the elimination of local inventories.

4. The Donell Company would earn a 40 percent commission on the selling price of each prescription sale.

5. Donell's name could be identified with the service and be printed on all bags, bottles, and other materials associated with the prescription drug business. In other words, the Bentley Drug Company would serve as a wholesaler in the operation, and would not be identified to Donell's customers.

The representative of the Bentley Drug Company pointed out that retail drug sales were expanding and were expected to continue to expand. Further, they noted that prescription drug prices were rising, so the Donell Company would have an opportunity to participate in an expanding business. Further, by offering

cost savings to its customers, Donell's could provide another service for them and also build return business and stimulate traffic. Also, since Donell's wouldn't have to hire additional personnel or carry inventory, the 40 percent margin for the Donell Company would be almost all net profit.

The Bentley Drug Company is anxious to begin offering this service to the Seattle area and has asked Donell's to make a decision very soon. If the Donell Company agrees to work with Bentley, the Bentley executives have agreed not to offer the service to any other Seattle stores. On the other hand, if Donell decides not to offer the service, Bentley does plan to approach other Seattle retailers.

Evaluate the Bentley proposal. What should the Donell Company do?

---

17. Spears National Bank

Roger Spears was recently appointed director of marketing by his father, Andrew Spears, president of the Spears National Bank. Roger is a recent graduate of a marketing program at the nearby state college. He has worked in the bank during summer vacations—but this is his first full-time job.

The Spears National Bank is a profitable, family-run business located in Denton—the county seat. The town itself has only about 7,000 population, but it serves farmers as far away as 20 miles. About ten miles south is a metropolitan area of 350,000. Banking competition is quite strong in the metropolitan area. But in Denton, there is only one other bank—of about the same size. The Spears National Bank has been quite profitable, last year earning about $300,000—or 1 percent of assets—a profit margin that would look very attractive to big-city bankers.

Spears National Bank has prospered over the years by emphasizing a friendly, small-town atmosphere. The employees are all local residents and are trained to be friendly with all customers—greeting them on a first-name basis. Even Roger's father tries to know all the customers personally and often comes out of his office to talk with them. The bank has followed a conservative policy—for example, insisting on 25 percent down payments on homes and relatively short maturities on loans. The interest rates charged are competitive or slightly higher than in the nearby city, but they are

similar to those charged by the other bank in town. In fact, the two local banks seem to be following more or less the same approach. Since they both have fairly convenient downtown locations, Roger feels that the two banks will continue to share the business equally unless some change is made.

Roger has developed an idea which he feels might attract a greater share of the local business. At a recent luncheon meeting with his father, he presented his idea and was disappointed that it was not enthusiastically received. Nevertheless, he has continued to push the idea.

Basically, Roger's idea involves trying to differentiate the bank by using a visual appeal. In particular, his proposal is to try to get all of the people in town to "Think Pink." Roger wants to paint the inside and outside of the bank pink and have all the bank's advertising and printed materials refer to the "Think Pink" campaign. The bank would give away pink shopping bags, offer pink deposit slips, mail out pink interest checks, advertise on pink billboards, and have pink stationery for the bank's correspondence. Roger realizes that his proposal is "far-out" for a conservative bank. But that is exactly why he thinks it will work. He wants people to be startled into thinking about the Spears National Bank, instead of just assuming that both banks are similar. He feels that after the initial surprise, the local citizens will think even more positively about the Spears National Bank. Its reputation is very good now, but he would like it to be recognized as "different." Roger feels that this would help attract a larger share of new residents and businesses. Further, he hopes that his "Think Pink" campaign would cause people to talk about the Spears National Bank—and given that word-of-mouth comments are likely to be positive, the bank might win a bigger share of the present business.

Roger's father is less excited about his son's proposal. He feels the bank has done very well under his direction, and he is concerned about changing a "good thing." He worries that some of the older farmers who are loyal customers might question the integrity of the bank—or even wonder if it had gone "big city." Further, he feels that Roger is talking about an important change which would be hard to undo once the decision had been made. His initial suggestion to Roger was to come up with some other way of differentiating the bank without running the risk of offending present customers. At the same time, he liked the idea of making the bank appear quite different from its competitor. People are continuing to move into Denton and he would like to get an increasing share of this business. But he was having difficulty accepting "Think Pink."

Evaluate Roger's proposal. Should it be accepted?

---

18. Billing Sports Company

Two years ago, Tom Billings bought the inventory, supplies, equipment, and business of Western Sport Sales—which was located in one of the suburbs of Spokane, Washington. The business was in an older building along a major highway leading out of town, but it was several miles from any body of water. The previous owner had achieved sales volumes of about $200,000 a year—just breaking even. For this reason—plus the desire to retire in southern California—the owner had been willing to sell to Tom for roughly the value of the inventory. Western Sport Sales had been selling two well-known brands of small pleasure boats, a leading outboard motor, two brands of snowmobiles, and a line of trailer and pickup-truck campers. The total inventory was valued at about $78,000 and Tom used all of his own savings and borrowed some from two friends to buy the inventory. At the same time, he took over the lease on the building—so he was able to begin operations immediately.

Tom had never operated a business of his own before, but he was sure that he would be able to do well. He had worked in a variety of jobs as an auto repair man, service man, and generally a jack-of-all-trades in the maintenance departments of several local businesses.

Soon after opening his business, Tom hired a friend who had had a similar background. Together, they handled all selling and set-up work on new sales, and performed maintenance work as necessary. Sometimes they were extremely busy—at the peaks of each sport season. Then, both sales and maintenance kept them going up to 16 hours a day. At these times it was difficult to have both new and repaired equipment available as soon as desired by customers. At other times, however, Tom and his friend, Bud, had almost nothing to do.

Tom usually charged the prices suggested by the various manufacturers, except at the end of a weather season when he was willing to make deals to minimize his inventory. Tom was a little annoyed that some of his competitors sold mainly on a price basis, offering 10 to 20 percent off the manufacturer's suggested list prices. Tom did not feel he wanted to get into that kind of business, however, because he wanted to build a loyal following based on friendship and personal service. He didn't feel he really had to cut price, because all of the lines he carried were "exclusive" for him in the area. No stores within a ten-mile radius carried any of his brands.

To try to build a favorable image for his company, Tom occasionally placed advertisements in local papers and purchased some radio spots. The basic theme of this advertising was that the Billing Sports Company was a good place to buy the equipment needed for that season of the year. Sometimes he mentioned the brand names he carried, but generally he was trying to build his own image. He decided in favor of this approach because, although he had exclusives on the brands he carried, there generally were 10 to 15 different manufacturers' goods being sold in each product category at any one time—and most of the products were quite similar. Tom felt that this similarity among competing products almost forced him to try to differentiate himself on the basis of his own store's services.

The first year's operation was not profitable. In fact,

after paying minimal salaries to Bud and himself, the business just about broke even. And this was without making any provision for return on his investment. In hopes of improving his profitability, Tom jumped at a chance to add a line of lawn tractors and attachments as he was starting into his second year of business. This line was offered by a well-known equipment manufacturer who was expanding into Tom's market. The equipment was similar to that offered by other lawn equipment manufacturers, but had a number of unique features and specialized attachments. The manufacturer's willingness to do some local advertising on his own and to provide some point-of-purchase displays appealed to Tom. And he also liked the idea that customers probably would be wanting this equipment sometime earlier than they would become interested in boats and other summer items. So, he would be able to handle this business without interfering with his other peak selling seasons.

Now it is two years after Tom started the Billing Sports Company and he is still only breaking even.

Sales have increased a little, but he has had to hire some part-time help. The lawn-equipment line did help to expand sales as he had expected, but unfortunately it did not appear to increase profits. The part-time helpers were needed to service this business—in part because the manufacturer's advertising had generated a lot of sales inquiries. Relatively few of these resulted in sales, however, and so it is possible that Tom may have even lost money handling the new line. He hesitates to give up this line, however, because he has no other attractive choices right now and he doesn't want to give up that sales volume. Further, the manufacturer's sales rep has been most encouraging—assuring Tom that things will get better and that they will be glad to continue their promotion support for Tom's business during the coming year.

Evaluate Tom's overall strategy. What should he do in the future, especially regarding the lawn-tractor line?

19. Debmar Corporation

The Debmar Corporation produces wire rope and cable ranging from one-half inch to four inches in diameter. The Chicago-based company sells throughout the United States. Principal users of the products are manufacturing firms using cranes and various other overhead lifts in their operations. Ski resorts, for example, are customers because cables are used in the various lifts. The main customers, however, are still cement plants, railroad and boat yards, heavy-equipment manufacturers, mining operations, construction companies, and steel manufacturers.

Debmar employs its own sales specialists to call on the purchasing agents of potential users. All the sales reps are engineers who go through an extensive training program covering the different applications, strengths, and other technical details concerning rope and cable. Then they are assigned a region or district— the size depending on the number of customers.

Phil Larimer went to work for Debmar in 1952, immediately after receiving a civil engineering degree from the University of Minnesota. After going through the training program, he was assigned, along with one other representative, to the Ohio, Indiana, and Michigan region. His job was to service and give technical help to present customers of rope and cable. He was expected to call on new customers when inquiries

came in. But his primary duties were to: (1) supply the technical assistance needed to use rope or cable in the most efficient and safe manner, (2) handle complaints, and (3) provide evaluation reports to customers' management regarding their use of cabling.

Phil Larimer became one of Debmar's most successful representatives. His exceptional ability to handle customer complaints and provide technical assistance was noted by many of the firm's customers. He also brought in a great deal of new business— mostly from the automobile manufacturers and ski resorts in Michigan.

Larimer's success established Michigan as Debmar's largest-volume state. As a result, Michigan became a separate district, and Phil Larimer was assigned as the representative for the district in 1959.

Although the company's sales in Michigan have not continued to grow in the past few years, the replacement market has been steady and profitable. This fact is mainly due to the ability and reputation of Phil Larimer. As one of the purchasing agents for a large automobile manufacturer mentioned, "When Phil Larimer makes a recommendation regarding use of our equipment and cabling, even if it is a competitor's cable we are using, we are sure it is for the best for our company. Last week, for example, a cable of one of his competitors broke and we were going to give him a contract. He told us it was not a defective cable that caused the break, but rather the way we were using it. He told us how it should be used and what we needed to do to correct our operation. We took his advice and gave him the contract as well!"

Four years ago, Debmar introduced an expensive wire sling device for holding cable groupings together. The sling makes operations around the cable much safer—and its use could reduce hospital and lost-time costs due to accidents. The profit margin for the sling is high, and Debmar urged all its representatives to push the sling.

The only sales rep to sell the sling with any success

was Phil Larimer. Eighty percent of his customers are currently using the wire sling. In other areas, sling sales are disappointing.

As a result of his success, Debmar is now considering forming a separate department for sling sales and putting Phil Larimer in charge. His duties would include traveling to the various sales districts and training other representatives in how to sell the sling. The Michigan district would be handled by a new person.

The question Debmar's management faces now is: should they gamble on losing profitable customers in Michigan in hopes that sling sales will increase?

What would you advise? Why?

20. Bayer Furniture Company

Mrs. Carol Raines has been operating the Bayer Furniture Co. for ten years and has slowly built the sales to $575,000 a year. Her store is located in the downtown shopping area of a city of 150,000 population. This is basically a factory town, and she has deliberately selected "blue-collar" workers as her target market. She carries some higher-priced furniture lines, but puts great emphasis on budget combinations and easy credit terms.

Mrs. Raines is most concerned because she feels she has reached the limit of her sales potential—because sales have not been increasing during the last two years. Her newspaper advertising seems to attract her target customers, but many of these people come in, shop around, and then leave. Some of them come back, but most do not. She feels her product selections are very suitable for her target market and is concerned that her salespeople do not close more sales with

potential customers. She has discussed this matter several times with her salespeople. They respond that they feel they ought to treat all customers alike, the way they personally would want to be treated—that is, they feel their role is just to answer questions when asked, not to make suggestions or help customers arrive at their selections. They feel that this would be too "hard sell."

Mrs. Raines argues that this behavior is interpreted as indifference by the customers who are attracted to the store by her advertising. She feels that customers must be treated on an individual basis—and that some customers need more encouragement and suggestion than others. Moreover, she feels that some customers will actually appreciate more help and suggestion than the salespeople themselves might. To support her views, she showed her salespeople the data from a study about furniture store customers (Ta-

Table 1

In shopping for furniture I found (find) that:	Demographic groups				Marital status	
	Group A	Group B	Group C	Group D	Newly-weds	Married 3–10 yrs.
I looked at furniture in many stores before I made a purchase	78%	57%	52%	50%	66%	71%
I went (am going) to only one store and bought (buy) what I found (find) there	2	9	10	11	9	12
To make my purchase I went (am going) back to one of the stores I shopped in previously	48	45	39	34	51	49
I looked (am looking) at furniture in no more than three stores and made (will make) my purchase in one of these	20	25	24.	45	37	30
No answer	10	18	27	27	6	4

Table 2
The sample design

Demographic status

Upper class (group A); 13% of sample
  This group consisted of managers, proprietors, or executives of large businesses. Professionals, including doctors, lawyers, engineers, college professors and school administrators, research personnel. Sales personnel, including managers, executives, and upper-income sales people above level of clerks.
  Family income over $20,000.
Middle class (group B); 37% of sample
  Group B consists of white-collar workers including clerical, secretarial, sales clerks, bookkeepers, etc.
  It also includes school teachers, social workers, semiprofessionals, proprietors or managers of small businesses; industrial foremen and other supervisory personnel.
  Family income between $10,000 and $20,000.
Lower middle class (group C); 36% of sample
  Skilled workers and semiskilled technicians were in this category along with custodians, elevator operators, telephone linemen, factory operatives, construction workers, and some domestic and personal service employees.
  Family income between $10,000 and $20,000.
  No one in this group had above a high school education.
Lower class (group D); 14% of sample
  Nonskilled employees, day laborers. It also includes some factory operatives, domestic and service people.
  Family income under $10,000.
  None had completed high school; some had only grade school education.

bles 1 and 2). She tried to explain to them about the differences in demographic groups and pointed out that her store was definitely trying to aim at specific groups. She argued that they (the salespeople) should cater to the needs and attitudes of their customers and think less about how they would like to be treated themselves.

Evaluate Mrs. Raines' thinking and suggest implications for her promotion.

21. Owens Dance Studio

Anne Owens has been operating the Owens Dance Studio for five years—in a suburban community of about 50,000. Slowly, she has built a clientele—mostly young girls whose mothers want them to have some ballet experience.

The studio is conveniently located downtown—within walking distance of two grade schools (grades 1–5) and one middle school (grades 6–8). Some of Anne's customers come from these schools, but even more come from more remote schools. Most are driven and picked up by their mothers.

There are a few competitors offering classes in their "rec rooms" to neighborhood children, but none of them has facilities or quality of instruction comparable to Anne's. The school district offers some classes at lower prices on Saturday and during the summer, but these have not been seen as real competition by Anne.

Most of Anne's students come only one hour a week, and slowly make enough progress so that Anne can hold spring recitals which show off the girls' accomplishments to their parents and friends. Even first-year students are able to make a reasonable showing—and "success" in the spring recital tends to encourage mothers to re-enroll their daughters in the fall classes. Anne has not had much luck developing an interest in summer classes—and last year she stopped trying. She decided that her students associated ballet with the nine-month school year. So Anne took off for a three-month summer vacation. Fortunately, there had been enough business in the previous nine months so she could afford to do this.

Now it is February 1974, and Anne is very much concerned about her financial prospects for the future. The "energy crisis" caused the local school system to change the opening and closing hours of school to save energy—moving the opening from 8:00 to 8:40 a.m. and the closing from 3:00 to 3:40 p.m. This has drastically cut into Anne's after-school business. Further, she just heard that the school plans to continue with the late schedule for the coming year.

The reason for changing the school schedule was to start later so the students would be getting up later and going to school later—thereby saving energy during the dark morning hours. There is some doubt whether this really did accomplish its purpose, but the school system has decided that the new schedule will be continued indefinitely.

At first Anne did not see the implications for her business when the change was announced for January 1974. But it quickly became clear that her 3:30–4:20 class was at the wrong time when no one signed up for the class during the first week of January. Not only did she lose many of the girls who were formerly enrolled in her 3:30 class, but enrollment in the later classes dropped almost in half. Some of the 3:30 girls did move to the 4:30 and 5:30 classes, but probably only about 20 percent of them. It is hard to get exact figures on enrollment because there's usually at least a 20 percent turnover from fall to winter to spring terms. Anne has become used to a continual flow of new girls. Few girls stay more than a couple of years—because the program is not designed to build serious ballet students, but rather to cater to the "recreational" ballet student. But, it is quite clear to Anne that the change in school schedule has drastically cut her business—and she is trying to decide what to do for the spring term and beyond.

Given that most parents seem to need about one-half hour to get their children from school to the studio, she could move the starting time of the first class to about 4:15 (from 4:30) to try to use a little more after school time. But this would still mean that she could only offer two "prime-time" classes after school (instead of the three which she offered before) because classes starting after 6:00 p.m. would be viewed as being "too late." Alternately, she could forget about trying to change the after-school schedule and try to fill later times with older, more serious students. Anne has the credentials and training for offering more advanced courses, but thus far there has not been much demand for them. The local school district does offer

some adult education classes at lower prices—and this may take care of the older market.

Another possibility that Anne is considering is to persuade the local school system to allow "early release" of interested students—with a view to filling the 3:30–4:20 or a 3:10–4:00 slot. Anne has heard that some children are now being released an hour early for advanced training in ice skating. But the number of students involved is quite small, and she fears that such an arrangement for ballet is not likely because her students aren't "advanced."

Now that the total amount of time available between the end of school and dinner time is almost an hour shorter, some parents may feel that there just isn't enough time for extra recreation activities. This may help account for the substantial drop in business after school. Anne's Saturday business has not been affected by the change in school schedule, but very few of the week-day students have moved to Saturday, either. This concerns her for the long run, because total revenue has dropped about one quarter—bringing her studio below the breakeven point. Clearly, the studio needs more students to break even, because it cannot cut costs very easily. Rent, light, taxes, insurance, and other fixed costs can't be changed. Further, her two part-time assistants are paid a fixed amount for the five after-school periods and Saturday. Saturday classes are full, so something must be done after school if the business is to survive. Before and after the school schedule change, the following numbers of students were enrolled in the various classes at approximately $3 per class:

Class	Fall 1973	Winter 1974
3:30–4:20	20	0
4:30–5:20	20	9
5:30–6:20	18	9
6:30–7:20	10	6

What has happened to the Owens Dance Studio? What would you recommend Anne Owens do?

22. A–A Fabricators, Inc.

A–A Fabricators, Inc.—located in Minneapolis, Minnesota—is a custom producer of industrial wire products. The company has a great deal of experience bending wire into many shapes—and also has the facil-

ities to chrome- or gold-plate finished products. The company was started ten years ago, and has slowly built its sales volume to $1 million a year. Just one year ago, Frank Josephs was appointed sales manager of the consumer products division. It was his responsibility to develop this division as a producer and marketer of the company's own branded products—as distinguished from custom orders which the industrial division produces for others.

Mr. Josephs has been working on a number of different product ideas for almost a year now, and has developed several unique designs for letter holders, flowerpot holders, key and pencil holders, and other novelties. His most promising product is a letter holder in the shape of a dog. It is very similar to one which the industrial division produced for a number of years for another company. In fact, it was experience with the seemingly amazing sales volume of this product which interested the company in the consumer market—and led to the development of the consumer products division.

Mr. Josephs has sold hundreds of units of his various products to local chain stores and wholesalers on a trial basis, but each time the price has been negotiated and no firm policy has been set. Now he is faced with the decision of what price to set on the dog-shaped letter holder which he plans to push aggressively wherever he can. Actually, he hasn't decided on exactly which channels of distribution he will use—but the trials in the local area have been encouraging, and, as noted above, the experience in the industrial division suggests that there is a large market for the product.

The manufacturing cost on this product is approximately 10 cents if it is painted black, and 20 cents if it is chromed or gold-plated. Similar products have been selling at retail in the 75 cents to $2.50 range. The sales and administrative overhead to be charged to the division would amount to $35,000 a year. This would include Mr. Joseph's salary and some office expenses. It is expected that a number of other products will be developed in the near future, but for the coming year it is hoped that this letter holder will account for about half the consumer products division's sales volume.

Evaluate Mr. Josephs' marketing strategy. What price should he set?

---

23. Ace Photofinishing Company

Organized in 1948, the Ace Photofinishing Company soon became one of the four major Colorado-based photofinishers—each with annual sales of about $2.5 million.

Ace was started by three people who had a lot of experience in the photofinishing industry—working in Kodak's photofinishing division in Rochester, New York. Ace started in a small rented warehouse in Boulder, Colorado. Today it has seven company-owned plants in five cities in Colorado and western Kansas. The two color-processing plants are located in Boulder and Hays, Kansas. Black-and-white-processing plants are located in Boulder and Hays, as well as Pueblo, Denver, and Colorado Springs, Colorado.

Ace does all of its own processing of black-and-white films, slides, prints, and movies. While they do own color-processing capability, Ace has found it more economical to have most color film processed by the regional Kodak processing plant. The color film processed by Ace is of the "off-brand" variety—or is special work done for professional photographers. Despite this limitation in color finishing, the company has always given its customers fast, quality service. All pictures—including those processed by Kodak—can be returned within three days of receipt by Ace.

Ace started as a wholesale photofinisher—and later developed its own processing plants in a drive for greater profit. Its customers are drugstores, camera stores, department stores, photographic studios, and any other retail outlets where photofinishing is offered to consumers. These retailers insert film rolls, cartridges, negatives, and so on, into separate bags—marking on the outside the kind of work to be done. The customer is handed a receipt, but seldom sees the bag into which the film has been placed. The bag has the retailer's name on it—not Ace's.

Each processing plant is fronted by a small retail outlet for drop-in customers who live near the plant. This is a minor part of Ace's business.

The company is also engaged in direct-mail photofinishing within the state of Colorado. Each processing plant in Colorado is capable of receiving direct-mail orders from consumers. All film received is handled in the same way as the other retail business.

A breakdown of the dollar volume by type of business is shown in Table 1.

All processing is priced at the level established by local competition. Ace sets a retail list price, and each retailer then is offered a trade discount based on the volume of business generated for Ace. The pricing schedule used by each of the major competitors in

Type of business	Percent of dollar volume
Sales to retail outlets	80
Direct-mail sales	17
Retail walk-in sales	3
	100

the Colorado-Kansas market is shown in Table 2. All direct-mail processing for final consumers is priced at the 33⅓ percent discount off retail price—but this is done under a disguised name so that retailer customers are not antagonized. Retail walk-in accounts are charged the full list price for all services performed.

Table 2

Monthly dollar volume (12-month average)	Discount (2/10 net 30)
$ 0–$ 100	33⅓%
$ 101–$ 500	40
$ 501–$1,000	45
$1,001–above	50

Retail stores offering photofinishing are served by Ace's own sales force. Each processing plant has at least three people servicing accounts. Their duties include daily visits to all accounts to pick up and deliver all photofinishing work. These sales reps also make daily trips to the nearby Greyhound bus terminal to pick up and drop off color film to be processed by Kodak.

Since the consumer does not come in contact with Ace, the firm has not found it necessary to advertise its retail business. To reach retailers, Ace is listed in the Yellow Pages of all telephone books in cities and towns served by its seven plants. There has been no attempt to make the consumer aware of Ace's service—since all consumers are served through retail stores.

The direct-mail portion of Ace's business is generated by regular advertisements in the Sunday pictorial sections of newspapers servicing Pueblo, Denver, Col-orado Springs, and Boulder. These advertisements usually stress the low-price service, two-week turn-around, and fine quality. Ace does not use its own name for these markets. Mailers are provided for the consumer to send in to the plant. Some people in the company felt this part of the business might have great potential if pursued more aggressively.

Recently, Ace's president, Mr. Randall, has become worried over the loss of several retail accounts in the $500–$1,000 discount range. He has been with the company since its beginning—and has always stressed quality and rapid delivery of the finished product. Demanding that all plants produce the finest quality, Mr. Randall personally conducts periodic quality tests of each plant through its direct-mail service. Plant managers are called on the carpet for any slips in quality.

To find out what is causing the loss in retail accounts, Mr. Randall is reviewing sales rep's reports and talking to various employees. In their weekly reports, Ace's sales reps have reported a possible trend toward higher trade discounts being offered to retailer customers. Fast-Film—a competitor of equal size that offers the same services as Ace—is offering an additional 5 percent discount in each sales volume category. This really makes a difference at some stores—because these retailers feel that all the major processors can do an equally good job. Further, they note, consumers apparently feel that the quality is acceptable, because there have been no complaints so far.

Ace has faced price cutting before—but never by an equally well-established company. Mr. Randall cannot understand why these retailer customers would leave Ace, because Ace is offering higher quality and the price difference is not that large. He is considering a direct-mail and newspaper campaign to consumers to persuade them to demand Ace's quality service from their favorite retailer. Mr. Randall feels that consumers demanding quality will force retailers to stay with—or return to—Ace. He says: "If we can't get the business by convincing the retailer of our fine quality, we'll get it by convincing the consumer."

Evaluate Ace's strategies and Mr. Randall's present thinking. What would you do?

---

24. The Schmidt Manufacturing Company

The Schmidt Manufacturing Co.—of Los Angeles, California—is a leading manufacturer in the wire machinery industry. It has patents covering over 200 ma-chine variations, but it is rare for Schmidt's customers to buy more than 30 different types in a year. Its machines are sold to wire and small-tubing manufacturers—when they are increasing production capacity or replacing outdated equipment.

Established in 1865, the company has enjoyed a steady growth to its present position with annual sales of $27 million.

About ten firms compete in the wire machinery market. Each is about the same size and manufactures basically similar machinery. Each of the competitors has tended to specialize in its own geographic area. Five of the competitors are in the East, three in the Midwest, and two—including Schmidt—on the West Coast. All of the competitors offer similar prices and sell F.O.B. their factories. Demand has been fairly strong in recent years. As a result, all of the competitors have been satisfied to sell in their geographic areas and avoid price cutting. In fact, price cutting is not a popular idea, because about 20 years ago one firm tried to win additional business and found that others immediately met the price cut but industry sales (in units) did not increase at all. Within a few years prices had returned to their earlier level, and since then competition has tended to focus on promotion.

Schmidt's promotion has depended largely on company sales reps who cover the West Coast. They usually are supported by sales engineers when the company is close to making a sale. Some advertising is done in trade journals. And direct mailings are used occasionally, but the main promotion emphasis is on personal selling. Personal contact outside the West Coast market, however, is through manufacturers' agents.

Errol Lang, president of Schmidt Manufacturing Co., is not satisfied with the present situation. Industry sales have begun to level off and so have Schmidt's sales—although the firm has continued to hold its share of the market. Lang would like to find a way to compete more effectively in the other regions, because he sees that there is great potential outside of the West Coast, if he can only find a better way of reaching it.

Schmidt has been acknowledged by competitors and buyers as one of the top-quality producers in the industry. Its machines have generally been somewhat superior to others in terms of reliability, durability, and productive capacity. The difference, however, has not been great enough to justify a higher price—because the others are able to do the necessary job. In short, if a buyer had a choice between Schmidt's and another's machines at the same price, Schmidt would probably get the business. But it seems clear that Schmidt's price must be at least competitive.

The average wire machine sold by Schmidt (or any of its competitors) sells for about $115,000, F.O.B. shipping point. Shipping costs within any of three major regions averages about $1,500—but another $1,000 must be added on shipments from the West Coast to the Midwest (either way) and another $1,000 from the Midwest to the East.

Mr. Lang is thinking about expanding his market by being willing to absorb the extra freight costs which would be incurred if a midwestern or eastern customer were to buy from his West Coast location. In other words, he would absorb the additional $1,000–$2,000 in transportation costs. By so doing, he would not be cutting price in those markets, but rather reducing his net return. He feels that his competitors would not see this as price competition and therefore would not resort to cutting prices themselves. Further, he thinks such a move would be legal—because all the customers in each major region would be offered the same price.

The sales manager, Robert Dixon, felt that the proposed freight absorption plan might actually stimulate price competition in the midwestern and eastern markets and perhaps on the West Coast. He proposed instead, that Schmidt hire some sales reps to work the midwestern and eastern markets—rather than relying on the manufacturers' agents. He felt that an additional three sales reps would not increase costs too much—and could greatly increase the sales from these markets over that brought in by the agents. With this plan, there would be no need to absorb the freight and risk disrupting the status quo with respect to competitive methods. He felt this was especially important, because competition in the Midwest and East was somewhat "hotter" than on the West Coast due to the number of competitors in these regions. The situation had been rather quiet in the West—because only two firms were sharing this market.

Mr. Lang agrees that Mr. Dixon has a point, but in view of the leveling off of industry sales, he feels that the competitive situation might change drastically in the near future and that he would rather be a leader in anything that is likely to happen rather than a follower. He is impressed with Mr. Dixon's comments about the greater competitiveness in the other markets, however, and therefore is unsure about what should be done—if anything.

Evaluate Schmidt's strategy planning in the light of its market situation, and explain what it should do now.

25. Valley View Company

The Valley View Company is a well-established manufacturer in the highly seasonal vegetable canning industry. It packs and sells canned beans, peas, carrots, corn, peas and carrots mixed, and kidney beans. Sales are made mainly through food brokers to merchant wholesalers, supermarket chains (such as Kroger, Safeway, A&P, and Jewel), cooperatives, and other outlets—mostly in the Chicago area. Of secondary importance, by volume, are sales in the immediate local market to institutions, grocery stores, and supermarkets—and sales of dented canned goods at low prices to walk-in customers.

Valley View is the second-largest vegetable canner in the Devil's River Valley area of Wisconsin—with sales in excess of $10 million annually (exact sales data is not published by the closely held corporation). Plants are located in Riverside, Portertown, and Williamston, Wisconsin, and in Clearview, Minnesota—with main offices in Riverside. The Valley View brand is used only on canned goods sold in the immediate local market. In most other cases, the goods are sold and shipped under the retailer's label, or the broker's/wholesaler's label.

Operating since 1905, Valley View has an excellent reputation for the consistent quality of its product offerings. And it is always willing to offer competitive prices. Strong channel rapport was built by Valley View's former chairman of the board and chief executive officer, E. J. McWirter. Mr. McWirter—who owns controlling interest in the firm—had "worked" the Chicago area as an aggressive company salesman in the firm's earlier years—before he took over from his father as president in 1931. He was an ambitious and hardworking executive, active in community affairs, and the firm prospered under his direction. He became well known within the canned food processing industry for technical/product innovations. During World War II, he was appointed to a position in Washington, D.C.—on the board which helped set wartime food rationing policies.

During the off-canning season, Mr. McWirter traveled widely. In the course of his travels, he arranged several important business deals. His 1968 and 1970 trips resulted in the following two events: (1) inexpensive pineapple was imported from Formosa and marketed in the central United States through Valley View—primarily to expand the product line; and (2) a technically advanced continuous process cooker (65 feet high) was imported from England and installed at the Riverside plant in February/March 1975. It was the first of its kind in the United States and cut process time sharply.

Mr. McWirter retired in 1975 and named his son-in-law, the 35-year-old Mr. King, as his successor. Mr. King is intelligent and hard-working. He had been concerned primarily with the company's financial matters, and only recently with marketing problems. During his seven-year tenure as financial director, the firm had received its highest credit rating ever—and was able to borrow working capital ($3 million to meet seasonal seed, fertilizer, can stockage, and wage requirements) at the lowest rate ever received by the company.

The fact that the firm isn't unionized allows some competitive advantage. However, minimum wage law changes have increased costs. And these and other rising costs have caused profit margins to narrow. The narrowed profit margins led to the recent closing of the Williamston plant and then the Portertown plant—as they became comparatively less efficient to operate. The remaining two plants were considerably expanded in capacity (especially warehouse facilities), so that they could operate more profitably due to maximum use of existing processing equipment.

Shortly after Mr. McWirter's retirement, Mr. King reviewed the company's current situation with his executives. He pointed out narrowing profit margins, debts contracted for new plant and equipment, and an increasingly competitive environment. Even considering the temporary labor-saving competitive advantage of the new cooker system, there seemed to be no way to improve the "status quo" unless the firm could sell direct—as they do in the local market—absorbing the food brokers' 5 percent commission on sales. This was the plan of action decided upon, and Mr. Freds was directed to test the new method for six months.

Mr. Freds is the only full-time salesman for the firm. Other top executives do some selling—but not much. Being a relative of Mr. McWirter's, Freds is also a member of the board of directors. He is well qualified in technical matters—he has a college degree in food chemistry. Although Mr. Freds formerly did call on some important customers with the brokers' sales reps, he is not well known in the industry or even by Valley View's usual customers.

Five months later, after Mr. Freds has made several selling trips and hundreds of telephone calls, he is unwilling to continue sales efforts on his own. He insists that a sales staff be formed if the present operation is to continue. Orders are down in comparison both to expectations and to the previous year's operating results. And sales of the new pineapple products are very disappointing. Even in regular channels, Mr. Freds sensed a reluctance to buy—though basic consumer demand had not changed. Further, some potential customers have demanded quantity guarantees considerably larger than the firm can supply. Expanding supply would be difficult in the short run—because the firm typically must contract with farmers for production acreage, to assure supplies of the type and quality they normally offer.

Mr. McWirter, still the controlling stockholder, has scheduled a meeting in two weeks to discuss the status of Valley View's current operations.

Evaluate Mr. King's strategy planning. What should he tell Mr. McWirter? What should be done next?

26. Demmer Mfg. Company

Bill Carson is currently employed as a sales representative for a plastics goods manufacturer. He calls mostly on large industrial accounts—such as refrigerator manufacturers—who might need large quantities of custom-made products. He is on a straight salary of $20,000 per year, plus expenses and a company car. He expects some salary increases, but does not see much long-run opportunity with this company. As a result, he is seriously considering changing jobs and investing $20,000 in the Demmer Mfg. Co.—an established midwestern thermoplastic molder and manufacturer. Carl Weiss, the present owner, is nearing retirement age and has not developed anyone to run the business. He has agreed to sell the business to Robert Watson, a lawyer-entrepreneur, who has invited Bill Carson to invest and become the sales manager. Mr. Watson has agreed to give Carson his current salary plus expenses, plus a bonus of 1 percent of profits. However, Bill must invest to become part of the new company. He will obtain a 5 percent interest in the business for his $20,000 investment.

The Demmer Mfg. Co. is well established—and last year had sales of $1.5 million, but no profits. In terms of sales, cost of materials was 46 percent; direct labor, 13 percent; indirect factory labor, 15 percent; factory overhead, 13 percent; and sales overhead and general expenses, 13 percent. The company has not been making any profit for several years—but has been continually adding new machines to replace those made obsolete by technological developments. The machinery is well maintained and modern, but most of it is similar to that owned by its many competitors. Most of the machines in the industry are standard. Special products are then made by using specially made dies with these machines.

Sales have been split about two-thirds custom-molded products (that is, made to order for other pro-

ducers or merchandising concerns) and the balance proprietary items (such as housewares and game items, like poker chips and cribbage sets). The housewares are copies of articles developed by others—and indicate neither originality nor style. Carl Weiss is in charge of the proprietary items distributed through any available wholesale channels. The custom-molded products are sold through three full-time sales engineers who receive a 5 percent commission on sales up to $10,000 and then 3 percent above that level, as well as by three manufacturers' reps getting the same commissions.

Financially, the company seems to be in fairly good condition—at least as far as book value is concerned. The $20,000 investment would buy approximately $30,000 in assets.

Mr. Watson feels that—with new management—the company has a real opportunity for profit. He expects to make some economies in the production process and hold custom-molding sales to approximately the present $1 million level. The other major expectation is that he will be able to develop the proprietary line from a sales volume of about $500,000 to $2 million a year. Bill Carson is expected to be a real asset here because of his sales experience. This will bring the firm up to about capacity level—but of course it will mean adding additional employees. The major advantage of expanding sales would be spreading overhead. Some of the products proposed by the lawyer for the expansion of the proprietary line are listed below.

New products for consideration:
Women's tool kit—molded housewares.
Six-bottle soft drink case.
Laminating printed film on housewares—molded.

Short legs for furniture—molded, $0.5 million minimum market.

Home storage box for milk bottles, $0.5 million minimum market.

Step-on garbage can without liner.

Importing and distributing foreign housewares.

Black-nylon-handled table utensils.

Extruded and embossed or formed wall coverings.

Extruded and formed wall decorations—nursery-rhyme figures, etc.

Formed butyrate outside house shutters.

Formed inside shutters in lieu of venetian blinds.

School and toy blackboards.

Translucent bird houses.

Formed holder for vacuum cleaner attachments.

Formed household door liners.

Formed "train terrain" table topography for model trains.

Formed skylights.

There is heavy competition is these markets from many other companies like Demmer. Further, most retailers expect a wide margin, sometimes 40 to 50 percent. Even so, manufacturing costs are low enough so some money can be spent for promotion, while still keeping the price competitive. Apparently many customers are willing to pay for the novelty of new products—if they see them in their stores.

How would you advise Bill Carson? Explain your reasoning.

27. Lewis Tool Company

Lewis Tool Co. is a manufacturer of industrial cutting tools. These tools include such items as lathe blades, drill press bits, and various other cutting edges used in the operation of large metal cutting, boring, or stamping machines. The president of the company, Chuck Taylor, takes great pride in the fact that his company—whose $1,759,000 sales in 1979 is small by industry standards—is recognized as a producer of the highest-quality line of cutting tools to be found.

Competition in the cutting-tool industry is intense. Lewis Tool faces competition not only from the original manufacturers of the machines, but also from many other relatively powerful companies offering cutting tools as one of many diverse product lines. This situation has had the effect, over the years, of standardizing the price, specifications, and in turn, the quality, of the competing products of all manufacturers.

About a year ago, Mr. Taylor was tiring of the tremendous financial pressure of competing with companies enjoying economies of scale. At the same time, he noted that more and more potential cutting-tool customers were turning to small custom tool-and-die shops because of specialized needs that could not be met by the mass production firms. Mr. Taylor considered a basic change in strategy. Although he was unwilling to become strictly a custom producer, Mr. Taylor felt that the recent trend toward buying customized cutting edges might be a good indication of the development of new markets which would be too small for the large, multiproduct-line companies to serve profitably. He thought that the new markets might be large enough for a flexible company of Lewis Tool's size to make a good profit.

An outside company, Ampex Research Associates, was hired to study the feasibility of serving this potential new market. The initial results were encouraging. It was estimated that Lewis Tool could increase sales by 50 percent and double profits by servicing the emerging market.

The next step taken by Lewis Tool was to develop a team of technical specialists to maintain continuous contact with potential cutting-tool customers. They were supposed to identify any present or future needs which might exist in enough cases to make it possible to profitably produce a specialized product. The technical specialists were not to take orders or "sell" Lewis Tool to the potential customers. Mr. Taylor felt that only through this policy could these representatives easily gain access to the right persons.

The initial feedback from the technical specialists was most encouraging. The company, therefore, decided to continually adapt its high-quality products to the ever-changing, specialized needs of users of cutting tools and edges.

The potential customers of Lewis Tool's specialized tools are widely scattered. The average sale per customer is not expected to exceed $250 at a time, but the sale will be repeated several times within a year.

Because of the widely dispersed market and low sales volume per customer, Mr. Taylor doesn't feel that selling the products direct—as is done by small custom shops—is practical. At the present time, the Lewis Tool Company distributes 90 percent of its regular output through a large industrial supply wholesaler which serves the entire area east of the Mississippi River. This wholesaler, although very large and well known, is having trouble moving cutting tools. It is losing sales of cutting tools in some cities to newer wholesalers specializing in the cutting-tool industry. The new wholesalers are able to give more technical help to potential customers, and therefore better service. The Lewis Tool wholesaler's chief executive is convinced that the newer, less-experienced concerns will either realize that a substantial profit margin can't be maintained along with their aggressive tactics, or they will eventually go broke trying to "overspecialize."

From Mr. Taylor's standpoint, the present wholesaler has an established reputation and has served Lewis Tool well in the past. The traditional wholesaler has been of great help to Lewis Tool in holding down the firm's inventory costs—by increasing the amount of inventory maintained in the 34 branch wholesale locations operated by the wholesaler. Although he has received several complaints about the lack of technical assistance given by the wholesaler's sales reps, Mr. Taylor feels that the present wholesaler is providing the best service it can. He explains the complaints as "the usual trouble you get into from just doing business."

Mr. Taylor feels that there are more urgent problems than a few complaints—profits are declining. Sales of the new cutting-tool line are not nearly as high as forecasted—even though all indications are that the company's new products should serve the intended market perfectly. The high costs involved in the high-quality product line and the technical specialist research team—together with lower-than-expected sales—have significantly reduced the firm's profits. Mr. Taylor is wondering whether it is wise to continue to try to cater to the needs of specific target markets when the results are this discouraging. He also is considering increasing advertising expenditures in the hope that customers will "pull" the new products through the channel.

Evaluate Lewis Tool's strategy. What should Mr. Taylor do now?

28. Cando, Inc.

Jerry Bullard and Joel Flynn are partners in several small businesses—operated under the name of Cando, Inc. They are now seriously considering whether they should take on the local franchise for "Save-A-Life" products. Jerry saw an advertisement in *The Wall Street Journal* and called for more information about the product and the franchise possibility. Now he and Joel are considering whether they should take on the local franchise and hire two more people to do the direct selling which is required. Joel is sure that he could hire and supervise the right kind of sales people without taxing his available time. In fact, the partners are looking for something more for Joel to do because his current responsibilities to the partnership do not fully use his time. So supervision and personnel aren't the problem. What is bothering the partners is whether this particular franchise is the right thing for them to do. Even more, Joel is worried that there is an ethical problem. Is it "right" to send sales people with a "good story" to call on "vulnerable" people?

The main Save-A-Life product involves a small radio transmitter which a person can carry around the house and a larger receiving unit which can be placed anywhere in the house. Just a push of a button on the transmitter will cause the receiver to dial up to four telephone numbers and play a prerecorded message. Depending on the situation, these calls could be to the police, fire department, or an emergency service, the person's doctor, and/or relatives. An obvious market is older people who live alone and are worried about what happens to them if they get sick, have an accident, or are bothered by intruders. Further, women of all ages might be interested in the product if they are concerned about their personal safety. It seems likely that there would be more potential customers in urban areas where there is great concern about crime.

The national distributor of the franchise has found that it is possible to get leads for prospective customers by running advertisements in local newspapers—with pictures stressing emergency situations. Then, personal sales follow-up is necessary. Sometimes several calls are needed. The system sells for $600. Jerry and Joel would have to pay $300 for each system—leaving $300 to cover the cost of sales, advertising, and general overhead. The national organization indicates that some franchise holders pay direct salespeople a commission of $100–$150 per unit sold. In addition, paying about $25 per installation seems to be adequate for proper installation by "handymen" who are willing to make the necessary connections to the telephone system. The national organization is willing and able to train technical people and salespeople in all the necessary functions as part of the original franchise fee. To get started, a franchise fee of $7,000 is required to cover the purchase of 15 systems, all necessary sales and promotion aids, and the right to unlimited home-office training of sales and technical personnel.

Jerry and Joel operate in a metropolitan area of about 450,000 people with a higher-than-average percentage of upper-income people. So they feel the economic potential may be adequate—although it is quite clear that an aggressive sales effort is required. The national distributor's sales rep feels that Jerry and Joel's salespeople (they are thinking of hiring two) ought to be able to sell at least 20 units each per month after a two-month break-in period—but, of course, no guarantee can be made.

Clearly, aggressive salespeople will be necessary. That is why the relatively "generous" return to the salespeople is suggested by the national distributor. But Joel wonders if it is really fair to appeal to sickly old people—or those who are worried about their safety. Further, is it right to take such a big markup? Joel realizes that without the $300 markup, there may not be any profit in it for the partners—but he still has nagging doubts about the whole idea.

Evaluate the Save-A-Life possibility for Jerry and Joel. Is this a good economic opportunity? Would it be "socially responsible" for them to take on this line?

---

29. Rundle Manufacturing Company

Rundle Manufacturing Company is a supplier of malleable iron castings for several automobile and aircraft manufacturers—and a variety of other users of castings. Last year's sales of castings amounted to over $50 million.

In addition to the foundry operations which produce the iron castings, Rundle also produces roughly 50 percent of all the original equipment bumper jacks installed in new automobiles each year. This is a very price-competitive business, but Rundle has been able to obtain this large share of the market by relying on close personal contact between the company's sales executives and its customers—supported by very close cooperation between the company's engineering department and its customers' buyers. This has been extremely important because the wide variety of models and model changes frequently requires alterations in the specifications of the bumper jacks. All of Rundle's bumper jacks are sold directly to the automobile manufacturers. No attempt has been made to sell bumper jacks to final consumers through hardware and automotive channels—although they are available through the manufacturers' automobile dealers.

Mr. Karns, Rundle's production manager, would now like to begin producing hydraulic jacks for sale through automotive-parts wholesalers to garages, body shops, and (in the case of one specialized design with some extra accessories) to fire and police departments—to aid in rescuing accident victims in cases where risks of fire prevent the use of cutting torches. Mr. Karns saw a variety of hydraulic jacks at a recent automotive show, and saw immediately that his plant could produce these products. This especially interested him because of the possibility of using excess capacity. Further, he feels that "jacks are jacks," and that the company would merely be broadening its product line by introducing hydraulic jacks. As he became more enthusiastic about the idea, he found that his engineering department already had a design which appeared to be technically superior to the products now offered on the market. Further, he says that the company would be able to produce a product which is better-made than the competition (i.e., smoother castings, etc.) although he agrees that customers probably wouldn't notice the differences. The production department's costs for producing products comparable to those currently offered by competitors would be about one half the current retail prices.

Mr. Phil Wolf, the sales manager, has just received a memo from William Harrison, the president of the company, explaining about the production department's enthusiasm for broadening its jack line into hydraulic jacks. He seems enthusiastic about the idea, too, noting that it may be a way to make fuller use of the company's resources and increase its sales. Recognizing this enthusiasm, Phil Wolf wants to develop a well-thought-out explanation of why he can't get very excited about the proposal. He knows he is already overworked and could not possibly promote this new line himself—and he is the only salesman the company has. But more basically, he feels that the proposed hydraulic-jack line is not very closely related to the company's present emphasis. He has already indicated his lack of enthusiasm to Mr. Karns, but this has made little difference in Karns' thinking. Now, it is clear that Phil will have to convince the president or he will soon be responsible for selling hydraulic jacks.

What would you advise Phil to say and do?

30. Canadian Food Limited*

Stan Roberts has been the marketing director of Canadian Foods Limited for the last two years—since he arrived from international headquarters in New York. Canadian Foods—headquartered in Toronto—is a subsidiary of a large U.S.-based consumer packaged-food company with worldwide sales of more than $2 billion in 1976. Its Canadian sales were just under $250 million—with the Quebec and Ontario markets accounting for 65 percent of the company's Canadian sales.

The company's product line includes such items as cake mixes, puddings, pie fillings, pancakes, and prepared foods. The company has successfully introduced at least six new products every year for the last five years. Its most recent new product was a line of frozen dinners successfully launched last year. Products from Canadian Foods are known for their high quality and enjoy considerable brand appeal throughout Canada—including the Province of Quebec.

Sales of the company's products have risen every year since Mr. Roberts has taken over as marketing director. In fact, the company's market share has increased steadily in each of the product categories in which it competes. The Quebec market has closely followed the national trend except that, in the past two years, sales growth in that market began to lag (Exhibit 1).

According to Mr. Roberts, a big advantage of Canadian Foods over its competitors is the ability to coordinate all phases of the food business from Toronto. For this reason, Mr. Roberts meets at least once a month with his product managers—to discuss developments in local markets that might affect marketing plans. While each manager is free to make suggestions—and even to suggest major departures from current marketing practices—Mr. Roberts has the final say.

One of the product managers, Claude Aylmer, expressed great concern at the last monthly meeting about the weak performance of the company's products in the Quebec market. While a broad range of possible reasons—ranging from inflation to politics—were reviewed to try to explain the situation, Mr. Aylmer maintained it was due to a basic lack of understanding of that market. Not enough managerial time and money had been spent studying the Quebec market. As a result, Aylmer felt that the current marketing approach to that market needed to be reevaluated. An inappropriate marketing plan may well be responsible for the sales slowdown. After all, "80 percent of the market is French-speaking. It's in the best interest of the company to treat that market as being separate and distinct from the rest of Canada."

Mr. Aylmer supported his position by showing that per capita consumption in Quebec of many product categories in which the firm competes is above the national average (Exhibit 2). Research projects conducted by Canadian Foods also supports the "separate and distinct" argument. The firm has found—over the years—many French-English differences in brand attitudes, lifestyles, usage rates, and so on.

Mr. Aylmer argued that the company should develop a unique Quebec marketing plan for some or all of its brands. He specifically suggested that the French-language advertising plan for a particular brand be developed independently of the plan for English Canada. Currently, the agency assigned to the brand adapts its English-language plan to meet the perceived

---

* This case was adapted from one written by Professor Robert Tamilia, University of Windsor, Canada.

Exhibit 1
Sales, Quebec and Canada (1973 = 100)

A. Quebec

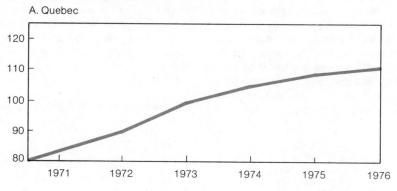

B. Canada

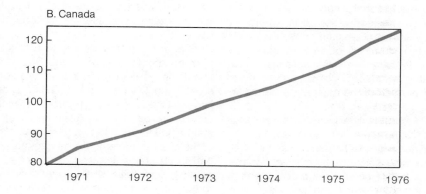

Exhibit 2
Per capita consumption index, Province of Quebec (Canada = 100)

Cake mixes	103	Pie fillings	115
Pancakes	91	Frozen dinners	84
Puddings	111	Prepared packaged	
Salad dressings	87	foods	89
Molasses	129	Cookies	119
Soft drinks	122		

needs of the French market. Mr. Roberts pointed out that the existing advertising approach assured Canadian Foods of a uniform brand image across Canada. However, the discussion that followed suggested that a different brand image might be needed in the French market if the company wanted to stop the brand's decline in sales.

The food distribution system in Quebec was then discussed. The major chains have their lowest market share of the food business in that province. Independents are strongest there. Specifically, the "mom-and-pop" food stores fast disappearing outside Quebec remain alive and well in the province. Traditionally, these stores have stocked a higher proportion (than supermarkets) of their shelf space with national brands—a point of some interest to Canadian Foods.

Finally, various issues related to discount policies, pricing structure, sales promotion, and cooperative advertising were discussed. All of this suggested that things were different in Quebec—and that future marketing plans for the firm's brands should reflect these differences to a greater extent than they do now.

After the meeting, Mr. Roberts stayed in his office to think about what had been said. Although he agreed with the basic idea that the Quebec market was in many ways different, he was unsure as to how far his company should go in recognizing this fact. He knew that regional differences in food tastes and brand purchases existed not only in Quebec, but in other parts of Canada as well. People were people, on the other hand, with far more similarities between them than differences.

Mr. Roberts was afraid that giving special status to one region might conflict with top management's goal of achieving standardization whenever possible. He was also worried about the long-term effect of such a policy change on costs, organizational structure, and on brand image. Still, enough product managers had expressed their concern over the years about the Quebec market to make him wonder if he shouldn't order a reevaluation of the company's current approach.

What would you tell Mr. Roberts? What are the future implications of your recommendations?

31. Modern Homes, Inc.*

Michael Good—marketing manager of Modern Homes, Inc.—is finding it difficult to get his fellow executives interested in exporting. He has been impressed by reports of the buying power of the newly wealthy Middle East nations. His own company's receipt of an export inquiry from a customer in Saudi Arabia has further confirmed his feeling.

Modern Homes, Inc. is a New England producer of wooden factory-built homes. The company was formed in the 1960s, when industrial house production methods began to be accepted. One of the major attractions of such housing is the 20–30 percent price advantage that it offers over contractor-built homes. Modern Homes produces modular homes in two or three sections, which are shipped to the site, placed on a foundation, assembled, and finished.[1] From its beginning, Modern Homes, Inc. has actively competed with other producers of factory-built homes in the East. The plant capacity is about 600 units a year. While sales have been improving over the last few years, the current year's sales are estimated to be about 400 units. The underutilized capacity is a big concern to the company's management—and one for which they have no easy solution. Domestic sales were hard to expand since a troubled economy held back many prospective home purchasers. Expansion of sales westward is not considered practical since transportation costs would make Modern's homes more expensive than those of Western competitors. Good's feeling, however, is that export sales might help solve the capacity problem—and provide longer-term growth prospects. There is no illusion on his part that exporting is easy. He had some experience with exporting to Iran in the past, and understands some of the problems.

It was in this climate that management began to more seriously consider export marketing. While there was agreement within the company that the Middle East presented good opportunities, there was uncertainty about the type of home that Modern Homes might export. While modular homes are reasonably priced in the U.S. market, a major problem with exporting is transportation costs. Modular homes are essentially big empty boxes. Since shipping costs are based on volume, shipping such homes is very costly. For example, the cost of shipping four homes to Iran was $80,000—with the homes themselves only valued in total at $100,000. Exporting panelized homes might be more sensible since the shipping costs of such homes were roughly one quarter those for modular homes. This results from the possibility of knocking down the walls of the home and folding everything into a smaller "box."

Attention also had to be paid, however, to the different assembly skills each type of home required in the export market. A panelized home could take about three to four weeks to erect, whereas a modular home could be completed in four to five days. Given the relative wealth of some Middle East consumers, a modular home might be worth its high transportation charges. Good had been told that Modern's houses would sell in the range of $80,000 to $100,000 in Saudi Arabia. A typical modular home with a delivered cost of $45,000 would offer quite a profit margin to a would-be Saudi middleman.

---

* This case was based on one written by Prof. Philip Rosson who, at the time of its preparation, was associated with the Centre for International Business Studies at Dalhousie University, Canada.

[1] In contrast, *panelized* construction is a knocked-down form of building, where completely finished panels are placed in position on the site; *precut* construction implies that all components are precut and then assembled on the site.

While there was agreement on the potential of export markets, contrasting points of view were expressed by individual executives. The general manager recognized the potential of the Middle East, but was uncertain about how to proceed, what the operation would cost, and how exports could best be handled. On this latter point, there were three main alternatives:

1. Modern Homes to export directly and to handle the overseas sales operation themselves.
2. Modern Homes to appoint overseas sales agents.
3. Modern Homes to seek out other interested parties and to "go in on their coattails."

Michael Good and the sales manager, Bill Comeau, felt that an overseas trip should be made to investigate the markets in depth. As Comeau said, "No one in the company knows what is wanted in the various export markets." Comeau felt that once a market had been selected by the company, Modern would probably need to develop a strong relationship with a local company. Overall, he felt that while there were good long-term prospects in the Middle East, the company shouldn't rush into exporting. A great deal of money has been made and *lost* by exporters in this area. Good agreed but was turned down when he asked the controller whether he would approve $50,000 to investigate and develop Middle East markets. The controller argued that the company knew that a market existed. What was required was to put together the right package, i.e., a product that shipped easily. He pointed to the requests for sales literature as strong enough indication that Modern Homes had a "hot" product.

In December 1980, the Modern Homes management was planning through 1983. Part of the company plan could involve export marketing if some agreement could be reached on the matter. The only additional information on hand (Exhibit 1) had been obtained at an Industry, Trade, and Commerce seminar held just a few days earlier.

Exhibit 1
Notes from an industry, trade, and commerce seminar on manufactured homes industry—December 1978

1. The Oil Crisis and aftermath has changed picture for Middle East as export markets for many goods, including manufactured homes.

Market ratings:		
	Saudi Arabia	+3
	Iran	+3
Markets range in rating from +5	Iraq	+2
to −5, based on a number of crite-	Kuwait/Trucia	
ria, with plus ratings showing areas	States	+2
of best potential.	Syria	+1

   Israel and Lebanon ratings have deteriorated such that both are rated negatively. However, the long-term prospects for both countries are good. Currently, there is an embargo on imports of house components in Israel, and income levels are being squeezed. In Lebanon, it was the opinion of ITC officials that it would be at least one year after peace before rebuilding would start.

2. Attitudes toward wood as a building material have improved, mainly because it is available and can be brought into the market quickly.

3. Two types of Canadian involvement have prevailed, mainly in Iran and Saudi Arabia:

   a. Demonstration homes—2–3 units for individual buyers—testing consumer acceptability.
   b. Contractual erections of 100–300 units on planned development sites.

4. Sales have almost exclusively been on the panellized variety. Modular homes have been erected for camp use, but most modular designs are either too small, or if they are large enough transportation costs make them costly.

5. Four Canadian companies are active in the area. Competition is stiff involving U.S., U.K., Romanian and Scandinavian companies.

6. Price is not the only important factor, perhaps more critical are quality, reliability and delivery.

7. ITC review of most would-be exporters reveals:

   a. Little experience.
   b. Little assessment of company capabilities or goals.
   c. Little knowledge of what is involved.

   ITC suggests companies *first* review what units they want to sell, when they want to sell them, and what level of involvement they desire, and then to review markets with the objective of making a compatible fit.

What action should Modern Homes now take regarding the Middle East market?

32. The Adanac Manufacturing Company*

William Johnson is president of the Adanac Manufacturing Company—located in Milwaukee, Wisconsin. The firm manufactures high-quality, hot-air oil furnaces. Prior to 1956, Mr. Johnson worked for a large furnace manufacturer in Chicago—first as production manager, and later as general manager of the firm. With $200,000 his aunt left him in her estate, Mr. Johnson established the Adanac Manufacturing Company in 1956.

In 1977, the Adanac Manufacturing Company had gross sales of $8 million (all in the United States).

* This case was adapted from one written by Dr. Herman Overgaard, Wilfried Laurier University, Canada.

At this time, the firm was operating at 65 percent of capacity and was barely profitable—in part because it had to compete with many other furnace manufacturers, some of whom were much larger and well established.

On Saturday, June 24, 1978, Adanac's vice president of marketing, Grant Oxley, was married in Chicago. At a party for the couple, Mr. Oxley met Ian Smyth, a U.S. embassy aide stationed in London.

Upon learning of the kind of products Adanac manufactured, Mr. Smyth suggested that Mr. Oxley give serious consideration to exporting some of his firm's production to Britain. That country, Mr. Smyth believed, was badly in need of better heating equipment. Mr. Oxley promised to take the matter up with his company's president. Upon further inquiry, Mr. Oxley discovered that, since the United Kingdom had joined the European Economic Community, the duty on oil furnaces imported from abroad (including the United States) was 18 percent. He also learned that the term used in the United Kingdom for furnaces in the home was *central heating units* or *domestic boilers*.

By consulting various publications during his honeymoon in England, Mr. Oxley found some data about the furnace industry in Britain. In 1974 there were nine manufacturers of central heating units in the United Kingdom—using various types of fuel. Of the over 20 million dwellings in the United Kingdom, 78 percent of the households occupied the entire house, 21 percent of the households occupied apartments and flats, and the remaining 1 percent occupied mobile homes.

Mr. Oxley also discovered from the 1973 General Household Survey that 34.9 percent of the households in the United Kingdom had central heating units installed. Also in 1974, 91 percent of all new dwellings in England and Wales were constructed with central heating units. Permanent new dwellings completed in the United Kingdom in 1974 numbered 278,363. Mr. Oxley also learned that about 8.5 million homes had been built in the United Kingdom since 1945. Some 24,923 central heating units were imported in 1974 at a total value of 1,864,529 pounds sterling.

What should Mr. Oxley do next? Explain what you would suggest if the company decided to compete in the U.K. market.

---

33. Metro Nurses Association

The Metro Nurses Association is a nonprofit organization which has been operating—with varying degrees of success—for 20 years. Some of its funding comes from the local "community chest"—to provide emergency nursing services for those who can't afford to pay. The balance of the revenues—about 80 percent of the $1 million annual budget—comes from charges made directly to the client or to third-party payers—including insurance companies and the federal government—for Medicare and Medicaid services.

Jane Burns has been director of the association for two years now—and has developed a well-functioning organization—able to meet the requests for service which come to it from some local doctors and from the discharge officers at local hospitals. Some business also comes to the association by self-referral—the client finding the name of the association in the Yellow Pages of the local telephone directory.

The last two years have been a rebuilding time—because the previous director had had personnel problems. This led to a weakening of the association's image with the local referring agencies. Now, the image is more positive. But Jane is not completely satisfied with the situation. By definition, the Metro Nurses Association is a nonprofit organization—but it still has to cover all its costs in order to meet the payroll, rent payments, telephone expenses, and so on—including her own salary. She can see that while the association is growing slightly and now breaking even, it doesn't have much of a cushion to fall back on if (1) people stop needing as many nursing services, (2) the government changes its rules about paying for the association's kind of nursing services—either cutting back on what would be paid or reducing the amount that would be paid—or (3) if new competitors enter the market. In fact, the latter possibility is of great concern to her. Some for-profit organizations are developing around the country—to provide home health care services—including nursing services of the kind offered by Metro Nurses Association. Reports from the industry indicate that these for-profit organizations are efficiently run—offering good service at competitive—and sometimes even lower—prices than some nonprofit organizations. And seemingly they are doing this at a profit—which suggests that it would be possible for them to lower their prices if the nonprofit organizations tried to compete on price.

Jane is trying to decide whether she should ask

her board of directors to let her begin to expand the association's activities by moving into the home health care market.

Now, the association is primarily concerned with providing professional nursing care in the home. But her nurses are much too expensive for routine health-care activities—such as helping fix meals, bathing and dressing patients, and so on. A registered nurse is not needed for these jobs. All that is required is an ability to get along with all kinds of people—and a willingness to do this kind of work. Generally, any mature person can be fairly quickly trained to do the job—following the instructions and under the general supervision of a physician, a nurse, or family members. There seems to be a growing demand for home health-care services as more women have joined the work force and can't take over home health care when the need arises—either due to emergencies or long-term disabilities. And with older people living longer, there are more single-survivor family situations where there is no one nearby to take care of their needs. Often, however, there are family members—or third-party payers such as the government or insurers—who would be willing to pay for such services. Now, Jane sometimes assigns nurses to this work—because the association is not in a position to send home health-care aides. Sometimes she recommends other agencies, or suggests one or another of three people who have been doing this work on their own—part-time. But with growing demand—she is wondering if the association should get into this business—hiring aides as needed.

Jane is concerned that a new, competitive, full-service home health-care organization—which would provide both nursing services *and* less-skilled home health-care services—might be very appealing to the local hospitals and other referers. So she can see the possibility of losing nursing service business if the Metro Nurses Association does not begin to offer a more complete service. This would cause real problems for the association—because there are overhead costs which are more or less fixed. A loss in revenue of as little as 10 or 20 percent could require laying off some nurses—or perhaps laying off some secretaries, giving up part of the office, and so on.

Another reason for seriously considering expanding beyond nursing services—using paraprofessionals and relatively unskilled personnel—is to offer a better service to present customers *and* make more effective use of the organization structure which has been developed over the last two years. Jane estimates that the administrative and office capabilities could handle 50 to 100 percent more clients without straining the system. It would be necessary to add some clerical help—if the expansion were quite large—as well as expanding the hours when the switchboard was open. But these increases in overhead would be minor compared to the present proportions of total revenues which go to covering overhead. In other words, additional clients could increase revenue and assure the survival of the association—providing a cushion to cover the normal fluctuations in demand—and providing some security for the administrative personnel. Further, she feels that if the association were successful in expanding its services—and therefore could generate some surplus—it would be in a position to extend services to those who are not now able to pay. One of the least attractive parts of her job is cutting off service to clients whose third-party benefits have run out—or for whatever reason can no longer afford to pay the association. Jane is uncomfortable about having to cut off service, but must schedule her nurses to provide revenue-producing services if she's going to be able to meet the payroll every two weeks. By expanding to provide more services, she might be able to keep serving more of these nonpaying clients. This possibility excites her because her nurse's training has instilled a deep desire to serve people—whether they can pay or not. This continual need to cut off service—because people can't pay—has been at the root of many disagreements—and even arguments—between the nurses serving the clients and Jane, as director and representative of the board of directors.

Expanding into home health-care services will not be easy, however. It may even require convincing the nurses' union that the nurses should be available on a 24-hour schedule—rather than the eight-to-five schedule six days a week, which is typical now. It would also require some decisions about relative pay levels for nurses, paraprofessionals, and home health-care aides. It would also require setting prices for these different services and telling the present customers and referers about the expanding service.

These problems aren't bothering Jane, however, because she thinks she could handle them. She is sure that the services are in demand and could be supplied at competitive prices.

Her primary concern is whether this is the right thing for a nurses' association to do. The name of her group is the Metro Nurses Association and its whole history has been oriented to supplying nurses' services. Nurses are dedicated professionals who bring high standards to any job they undertake. The question is whether the Metro Nurses Association should offer less "professional" services. Inevitably, some of the home health-care aides will not be as dedicated as the nurses might like them to be. And this might reflect unfavorably on the nurse image. At the same time, however, Jane is concerned about the future of the Metro Nurses Association and her own future.

What should Jane Burns do? Why?

34. West City's Committee on Fitness*

The members of the Mayor's Committee on Fitness listened attentively while Professor Henry Morgan, chairman of its research subcommittee, presented the findings of a research study the committee had authorized. The committee had been formed 12 months earlier when the mayor of West City had invited each of a number of clubs and organizations concerned with fitness and health—the YMCA, the medical association, the parks and recreation commission, sports clubs, and so forth—to appoint a representative to the committee. In his invitation, the mayor suggested the following objectives for the Committee on Fitness to consider:

1. To indicate to the people of West City the opportunities existing within the community for living more fully through personal involvement.
2. To suggest ways in which every member of the community can be encouraged to take part in his or her own way in fun-associated activity on a regular basis.
3. To involve the citizens of West City in physical activity—particularly of a vigorous nature, over an extended period of time.

Committee representatives subsequently discussed the reason for the formation of the committee. They generally agreed that there was a genuine need to develop programs designed to meet the objectives given in the mayor's invitation. The sedentary lifestyles of the people, developed over the last century as industrialization and urbanization increased, had led to some serious problems. A large proportion of the community's health costs, existing inefficiencies in labor productivity and even low enjoyment or satisfaction with life itself could be attributed to inappropriate lifestyles. Lack of physical activity and fitness, poor eating habits, and excessive use of alcohol, tobacco, and drugs could all be viewed as contributing factors. The level of physical fitness was considered especially important since it was known that people with high physical activity levels also ate better and made far less use of alcohol, tobacco, and drugs.

The members of the committee agreed that the objectives of the committee should go well beyond the first and second points mentioned by the mayor. It would not be enough "to indicate" or "to suggest." Rather, the committee should strive to bring about increased participation of the citizens of West City in physical activities of a "vigorous nature" over an "extended period of time." Since there was no well-known method of creating the major shift in lifestyles and behavior that achievement of their objective would require, the committee decided to seek the cooperation of several experts in physiology, human kinetics, recreation, and applied behavioral science on the staff of the local university. Accordingly, a research subcommittee was formed with the assistance of various faculty members. Professor Henry Morgan was chosen as that subcommittee's chairman.

After meeting several times, the research committee approved the following statement of its objectives:

> To describe the current physical activities, fitness capabilities, and predispositions toward physical activity of West City residents in a manner which will:
>
> a. Provide measures for use in future evaluations of the impact and effectiveness of programs implemented by the mayor's committee.
>
> b. Help to identify target markets and objectives suitable for program development.
>
> c. Provide information which is useful in designing and implementing programs.

Given these objectives, the research committee then designed a research project to measure three main classes of variables: (1) attitudes related to fitness; (2) rates of participation in physical activities; and (3) attitudes toward fitness and health. Using volunteer university and high school students as interviewers, 354 interviews were conducted in West City homes. A significant response bias was experienced

---

* This case was adapted from one prepared by Dr. John Liefeld, who at the time of its preparation was associated with the Department of Consumer Studies at the University of Guelph, Canada.

Exhibit 1
Attitude responses—physical activity

Statement	Disagree	Disagree somewhat	Agree somewhat	Agree
1. In our modern society there is no need for strenuous physical activity	69.4%	11.6%	9.3%	9.6%
2. I would participate more in physical activities if my doctor advised me to be more active	15.3	4.3	18.8	61.6
3. My athletic skills and capabilities are below average	34.7	21.9	22.2	21.3
4. I don't know enough about the role of exercise in health and fitness	43.3	16.5	21.1	19.1
5. I enjoy being a spectator of sports and physical activities more than being a participant	33.6	15.4	21.7	29.3
6. The companionship and socializing I get when participating in physical activities are more important to me than the health benefits of physical activities	35.0	23.9	27.1	14.0
7. I would participate more in physical activities and sports but I am embarrassed about my lack of physical skills	55.1	17.3	14.8	12.8
8. The health benefits of physical activities and sports are more important to me than the companionship and socializing I get from such activities	14.0	22.3	25.5	38.1
9. Medical science can keep us healthy and fit; exercise is not necessary	84.4	6.8	5.1	3.7
10. I prefer active recreations such as skating, swimming, or other physical activities to passive recreations such as reading, watching TV, or doing crafts	14.8	22.5	19.7	43.0
11. I would participate more in physical activities but my job is too tiring	43.6	14.0	23.5	18.9
12. I like my body the way it is	34.8	27.9	16.8	20.5
13. I want to know more about exercise, health, and fitness	11.4	11.4	31.1	46.0
14. In the summer it is too hot for me to participate in physical activities	66.0	16.7	9.6	7.6
15. I am personally committed to participation in active physical activities	45.5	13.9	15.9	24.7
16. I would participate more in physical activities and sports but there are not enough facilities in West City (i.e., fields, gyms, pools, courts, etc.)	57.9	16.6	13.8	11.7
17. In our modern society there is a real need for strenuous physical activity	15.1	14.2	21.7	49.0
18. It is important to me to be physically fit in order to manage my daily life and make my work and leisure more meaningful	5.9	10.5	20.4	63.2
19. I am too busy to participate in physical activities	45.0	17.6	27.8	9.6
20. I would participate in more physical activities if more of my friends would also participate	37.6	13.1	29.3	19.0
21. When I start some form of physical activity I always continue it	28.2	26.7	21.3	23.9
22. In the past year, I would have participated more in physical activities and sports but the programs cost too much money	54.7	12.9	18.6	13.8
23. A nutritious diet by itself will guarantee health and fitness	63.7	19.0	12.5	4.8
24. I would participate more in physical activities and sports but I don't have the time	34.0	14.7	32.9	18.4
25. Other people think I am fit	21.5	21.8	33.5	23.2

Exhibit 2
Physical activities during the past year

	Number of respondents		*Number of respondents*
Walking to, or at, work	236	Gardening	213
Walking for recreation	180	Snow shovelling	186
Jogging	64	Social dancing	129
Competitive running	7	Dancing classes	11
Calisthenic exercises	79	Yoga	22
Recreational bicycling	97	Horseback riding	9
Bicycling to work	32	Boxing, judo, karate	7
Bicycle racing	3	Tennis	41
Recreational swimming	171	Table tennis	30
Competitive swimming	3	Badminton	27
Platform diving	5	Handball or squash	8
Skin diving	4	Volleyball	21
Scuba diving	1	Curling	20
Recreational sailing	15	Bowling	50
Sailboat racing	3	Golfing	44
Recreational skating	45	Touch football	17
Figure skating	2	Soccer	9
Competitive skating	2	Hardball	7
Downhill skiing	23	Softball	20
Cross-country skiing	29	Ice hockey	16
Snow shoeing	6	Floor hockey	10
Repairs around the house	209	Basketball	20

in this interviewing as students reported that people who were overweight or negative in their attitudes toward physical activities were less likely to agree to be interviewed.

Striking findings were revealed when two activity indices were calculated. In the week prior to the study, 55 percent of the sample had an activity index number of 2.3 or less. To achieve an index number of 2.3, the individual need only move his or her body for 14 hours out of a 168 hour week. In other words, two hours or less per day of movement was the norm for 55 percent of the sample. Even given a sample which was biased toward those who are more fit—very little physical activity took place in the week prior to the study!

In terms of the index for the previous year's activity, similar results were reported. Seventy one percent of the sample had an index score of 200 or less. To achieve this index number, the individual need only move his or her body for one and a quarter hours a day every day of the year. This means that they spent less than 5.2 percent of the year in any kind of movement. That a very large majority of the residents of West City are extremely sedentary was an inevitable conclusion.

The responses of the subjects to the survey's probing as to attitudes are summarized in Exhibit 1. The physical activities of respondents during the previous year are presented in Exhibit 2 and the reasons given for so participating are shown in Exhibit 3.

Exhibit 3
Reasons for participating in physical activity (multiple responses possible)

		Percent of subjects
1.	It makes me feel good	85.6
2.	To maintain health and fitness	80.7
3.	To help control weight	63.7
4.	For social contacts	56.9
5.	For excitement	42.4
6.	Advised to do so by doctor	16.1
7.	To get recognition and admiration from friends	12.5

After Professor Morgan's presentation, the committee discussed the implications of the research findings for the programs which the mayor's committee might introduce. Some members of the committee advocated programs which would increase the number of organized fitness-related activities people could select. Others argued for an educational program to make people more knowledgeable about the relationship between fitness and health. A third group maintained that fitness motivation was the central problem. They insisted that programs designed either to educate or to offer more activities were doomed to failure until people could be motivated to change their way of life.

Given the data presented, what are the problems confronting the committee? What, if anything, can marketing contribute to their solution?

GLOSSARY

accessory equipment—short-lived capital items.

accumulation process—collecting products from many small producers.

administered channel systems—channel systems in which the various channel members informally agree to cooperate with each other.

administered prices—consciously set prices.

adoption curve—shows when different groups accept ideas.

adoption process—the steps which individuals go through on the way to accepting or rejecting a new idea.

advertising—any paid form of nonpersonal presentation of ideas, goods, or services by an identified sponsor.

advertising agencies—specialists in planning and handling mass selling details for advertisers.

advertising allowances—price reductions to firms further along in the channel to encourage them to advertise or otherwise promote the firm's products locally.

advertising managers—manage their company's mass selling effort.

agent middlemen—wholesalers who do not own the goods they sell.

agri-business—the move toward bigger and more businesslike farms.

AIDA model—costs of four promotion jobs: (1) to get Attention, (2) to hold Interest, (3) to arouse Desire, and (4) to obtain Action.

allocation process—breaking bulk—breaking carload or truckload shipments into smaller quantities as goods get closer to the final market.

allowance—(accounting term) occurs when a customer is not satisfied with a purchase for some reason and the company gives a price reduction on the original invoice (bill) but the customer keeps the goods or services.

allowances—given to final consumers, customers, or channel members for doing "something" or accepting less of "something."

assorting process—putting together a variety of products to give a target market what it wants.

attitudes—are reasonably permanent points of view about an object or class of objects.

auction companies—agent middlemen who provide a place where buyers and sellers can come together and complete a transaction.

automatic vending—selling and delivering products through vending machines.

average cost—obtained by dividing total cost by the related quantity (i.e., the total quantity which causes the total cost).

average-cost pricing—adding a "reasonable" markup to the average cost of a product.

average fixed cost—obtained by dividing total fixed cost by the related quantity.

average variable cost—obtained by dividing total variable cost by the related quantity.

bait pricing—setting very low prices to attract customers—but not to sell products.

balance sheet—statement of financial condition—an accounting statement which shows the assets, liabilities, and net worth of a company.

basic list prices—prices that final customers or users are normally asked to pay for products.

basic sales tasks—order getting, order taking, and supporting.

battle of the brands—the competition between dealer brands and manufacturer brands.

bid pricing—offering a specific price for each possible job.

black-box approach—using a "canned" or prepared sales presentation—building on the black box (stimulus-response) model.

bonded warehouses—public warehouses which specialize in storing imported goods or other goods (such as liquors or cigarettes) on which a tax must be paid before the goods are released for sale.

box store—a small-supermarket-sized retail store which carries a reduced assortment of staples—selling them out of their own boxes—at much lower prices.

brand familiarity—how well customers recognize and accept a company's brand.

brand insistence—customers insist upon a firm's branded product and would be willing to search for it.

brand managers—manage specific products.

brand name—a word, letter, or a group of words or letters.

brand preference—target customers will generally choose the brand over other brands—perhaps because of habit or past experience.

brand recognition—customers have heard of and remember the brand.

branding—the use of a name, term, symbol, or design—or a combination of these—to identify a product.

break-even analysis—analyzes whether the firm would be able to break even—i.e., cover all its costs—with a particular price.

break-even point (BEP)—the quantity where the firm's total costs will just equal its total revenue (i.e., total sales).

breakthrough opportunities—opportunities which enable innovators to develop hard-to-copy marketing mixes which will be very profitable for a long time.

brokerage allowance—a discount to buyers for performing the broker functions.

brokers—agent middlemen who bring buyers and sellers together.

buying function—looking for and evaluating goods and services.

capital items—durable goods which are charged off over many years, i.e., depreciated.

cash-and-carry wholesalers—merchant wholesalers who operate like service wholesalers—except that the customer must pay cash.

cash discounts—reductions in the price to encourage buyers to pay their bills quickly.

catalog showroom retailers—retailers who sell several lines out of a catalog and display showroom—with backup inventories.

central markets—convenient places where buyers and sellers can meet face-to-face to exchange goods and services.

chain store—one of several stores owned and managed by the same corporation.

channel captain—a manager who helps direct the activities of a whole channel and tries to avoid or solve channel conflicts.

channel of distribution—any series of firms from producer to final user or consumer.

class rates—transporting rates charged for general manufactured products that are shipped in amounts too small to justify much negotiation by shippers.

clustering techniques—research techniques which try to find similar patterns within sets of data.

cold-storage warehouses—public warehouses that are designed for storing perishable or easily spoiled products.

combination export manager—a blend of a manufacturers' agent and a selling agent—handling the entire export function for several manufacturers of similar but noncompeting lines.

combined target market approach—combining two or more homogeneous sub-markets into one larger target market as a basis for one strategy.

combiners—try to increase the size of their target markets by combining two or more sub-markets.

commission merchants—agent middlemen who handle goods shipped to them by sellers, complete the sale, and send the money—minus their commission—to each seller.

commodity rates—transporting rates for specific commodities between specific points or over specific routes.

commodity warehouses—public warehouses that are designed for storing perishable or easily spoiled products.

common carriers—transporters who must maintain regular schedules and accept goods from any shipper.

communication process—shows how a source tries to reach a receiver with a message.

community shopping centers—planned shopping centers which offer some shopping stores as well as the convenience stores found in neighborhood shopping centers—serving 40,000 to 150,000 people within a radius of three to four miles.

comparative advertising—makes specific brand comparisons—using actual product names.

competitive advertising—tries to develop selective demand.

competitive environment—the number and types of competitors the marketing manager must face—and how they might behave.

component parts and materials—expense items which have had more processing than raw materials.

confidence interval—the range on either side of an estimate which is likely to contain the "true value" with some percent of certainty (which depends on the size of the sample).

conscious level (of need awareness)—consumers are aware of their needs and are willing to talk to others about them.

consumer cooperatives—groups of consumers who buy together.

consumer goods—products meant for the final consumer.

consumer surplus—the difference to consumers between the value of a purchase and the price they pay.

consumerism—a social movement seeking to increase the rights and powers of consumers and buyers.

contract carriers—transporters who can work for anyone for an agreed sum and for any length of time.

contract farming—the farmer gets supplies and perhaps working capital from local middlemen or manufacturers who agree to buy the farmer's output—sometimes at guaranteed prices.

contract manufacturing—turning over the production to others, while retaining the marketing process.

contractual channel systems—channel systems in which the various channel members agree by contract to cooperate with each other.

contribution-margin approach (cost analysis)—all functional costs are not allocated in all situations.

control—the feedback process that helps the manager learn (1) how ongoing plans are working and (2) how to plan for the future.

convenience (food) stores—a variation of the conventional limited-line food stores which offer convenience—not assortment—and often charge prices 10–20 percent higher than those charged at nearby supermarkets.

convenience goods—products the customer needs but isn't willing to spend much time or effort shopping for.

convenience store—a convenient place to shop—either centrally located "downtown" or "in the neighborhood."

cooperative advertising—middlemen and producers sharing in the cost of ads.

cooperative chains—retailer-sponsored groups—formed by independent retailers—to run their own buying organization and conduct joint promotion efforts.

copy thrust—what is to be communicated by the written copy and illustrations.

corrective advertising—ads to correct deceptive advertising.

cost of goods sold—the total value (at cost) of all the goods sold during the period of an operating statement.

CPM—critical path method—a flowcharting technique.

cues—products, signs, ads, and other stimuli in the environment.

cultural and social environment—affects how and why people live and behave as they do.

culture—the whole set of beliefs, attitudes, and ways of doing things of a reasonably homogeneous set of people.

cumulative quantity discounts—apply to purchases over a given period—such as a year—and normally increase as the amount purchased increases.

customer service level—a measure of how rapidly and dependably a firm can deliver what customers want.

dealer brands—brands created by middlemen—sometimes called "private brands."

decoding—the receiver translating the message.

demand-backward pricing—starts with an acceptable final consumer price and works backward to what a producer can charge.

demand curve—a "picture" of the relationship between price and quantity in a market—assuming that all other things stay the same.

department stores—large retail stores—organized into separate departments.

derived demand—the demand for industrial goods is derived from the demand for final consumer goods.

description buying—buying from a written (or verbal) description of the product.

determining dimensions—the dimensions which actually affect the purchase of a specific product type or specific brand in a product-market.

direct-mail advertising—selling directly to the customer via his mailbox.

direct type advertising—aims for immediate buying action.

discount houses—retailers who offer "hard goods" (cameras, TVs, appliances) at substantial price cuts—to customers who go to the discounter's low-rent store, pay cash, and take care of any service or repair problems.

discounts—reductions from list price that are given by a seller to a buyer who either gives up some marketing function or provides the function for himself.

discrepancy of assortment—the difference between the lines the typical producer makes and the assortment wanted by final consumers or users.

discrepancy of quantity—the difference between the quantity of goods it is economical for a producer to make and the quantity normally wanted by final users or consumers.

discretionary income—what is left of disposable income after paying for necessities.

disposable income—what is left of income after taxes.

dissonance—a form of tension growing out of uncertainty about the rightness of a decision.

distinctiveness stage—the stage in the fashion cycle when some consumers seek—and are willing to pay for—products different from those satisfying the majority.

distribution center—a warehouse designed to speed the flow of goods and avoid unnecessary storing.

diversification—a firm moving into totally different lines of business.

diversion in transit—redirection of rail carloads already in transit.

door-to-door selling—going directly to the consumer's home.

drive—a strong stimulus which causes a tension that the individual tries to reduce by finding ways of satisfying this drive.

drop-shippers—merchant wholesalers who own the goods they sell—but do not actually handle, stock, or deliver them.

dual distribution—a manufacturer using several competing channels to reach the same target market—perhaps using several middlemen and selling directly himself.

dyad—the relationship between the customer and the salesperson.

early adopters—adopters who are relatively high in social status and usually high in opinion leadership—see **adoption curve.**

early majority—adopters who are above average in social status—see **adoption curve.**

economic and technological environment—affects the way firms—and the whole economy—use resources.

economic emulation stage—the stage in the fashion cycle when many consumers want the currently popular fashion—but at a lower price.

economic men—people who logically compare choices in terms of cost and value received—to maximize their satisfaction from spending their time, energy, and money.

economic needs—concerned with making the best use of a customer's limited resources—as the customer sees it.

economic system—the way an economy is organized to use scarce productive resources to produce goods and services and distribute them for consumption—now and in the future—among various people and groups in the society.

economies of scale—as a company produces larger numbers of a particular product, the cost for each of these products goes down.

elastic demand—the quantity demanded would increase enough to increase total revenue if price were decreased (and vice versa if price were increased).

elastic supply—the quantity supplied does stretch more if the price is raised.

emergency goods—products which are purchased only when the need is great.

emulation stage—the stage in the fashion cycle when many more consumers want to buy what is satisfying the original users.

encoding—the source deciding what it wants to say and translating it into words that will have the same meaning to the receiver.

Engel's laws—generalizations about consumer spending patterns.

equilibrium point—where the quantity and the price that sellers are willing to offer are equal to the quantity and price that buyers are willing to accept.

equilibrium price—the going market price.

exception rates—special low transporting rates set to meet competition.

exclusive distribution—selling through only one middleman in a particular geographic area.

expense items—short-lived goods and services which are charged off as they are used—usually in the year of purchase.

expenses—costs subtracted from the gross margin to get the net profit on an operating statement.

experience curve pricing—average-cost pricing using an estimate of future average costs.

experimental method—uses experiments to test hypotheses.

export or import agents—manufacturers' agents in international marketing.

export or import brokers—brokers in international marketing.

export or import commission houses—brokers in international marketing.

exporting—selling some of what the firm is producing to foreign markets.

extensive problem solving—when a need is completely new to a person—and much effort is taken to understand the need and how to satisfy it.

factor—a variable which shows the relation of some variable to the item being forecasted.

factor method—tries to forecast sales by finding a relation between the company's sales and some other factor (or factors).

factors—wholesalers of credit who buy their client's accounts receivable.

fad—a particular fashion that seems fashionable only to certain groups who are enthusiastic about it—but so fickle that it is short-lived as a fashion.

family brand—a brand name for several products.

farm products—products grown by farmers.

fashion—the currently accepted or popular style in a given field.

fashion cycle—pattern of consumer acceptance of fashions which usually goes through three stages: the distinctiveness, emulation, and economic emulation stages—which roughly parallel the product life cycle stages.

fast freight service—special, faster trains for freight (needing speed).

Federal Trade Commission (FTC)—the federal government agency which polices anti-monopoly laws.

fertility rate—number of children born per woman.

field warehouser—a firm which segregates some of a company's finished goods on its own property and issues warehouse receipts which can be used to borrow money.

fighting brand—an individual brand which is used to meet competition.

financing function—provides the necessary cash and credit to manufacture, transport, store, sell, and buy products.

fishy-back service—similar to rail piggy-back—using ships and trucks.

fixed-cost—contribution per unit—the assumed selling price per unit minus the variable cost per unit.

flexible-price policy—offering the same product and quantities to different customers at different prices.

floor planning—financing of display stocks for auto and appliance retailers.

F.O.B.—"free on board" some vehicle at some place.

focus group interview—interviewing a group of people rather than one at a time.

food brokers—manufacturers' agents who specialize in grocery distribution.

form utility—utility provided when a manufacturer makes something out of other materials.

franchise operations—like voluntary chains—with the franchiser developing a good marketing strategy and the franchise holders carrying out the strategy in their own units.

freight-absorption pricing—absorbing freight cost so that a firm's delivered price meets the nearest competitor's.

freight forwarders—combine the small shipments of many shippers into more economical shipping quantities.

full-cost approach (cost analysis)—all functional costs are allocated to products, customers, or other categories.

full-line pricing—setting prices for a whole line of products.

functional accounts—show the purpose for which the expenditures are made.

general-line (or single-line) wholesalers—full-service merchant wholesalers who carry a narrower line of merchandise than general merchandise wholesalers.

general merchandise warehouses—public warehouses which store almost every kind of manufactured goods.

general merchandise wholesalers—merchant wholesalers who carry a wide variety of nonperishable staple items such as hardware, electrical supplies, plumbing supplies, furniture, drugs, cosmetics, and automobile equipment.

general stores—retailers who sell anything the local consumers will buy in enough volume to justify carrying it.

generic market—a market in which sellers offer substitute products which are quite different physically or conceptually.

generic products—products which have no brand other than the identification of their contents.

grading and standardization functions—sorting products according to size and quality.

gross margin (gross profit)—the money left to cover the cost of selling the products and managing the business—and hopefully, leaving a profit—after subtracting these expenses on an operating statement.

gross national product (GNP)—the total market value of goods and services produced by an economy in a year.

gross sales—the total amount a company charges to all customers during some time period.

heterogeneous shopping goods—shopping goods that the customer sees as different—and wants to inspect for quality and suitability.

homogeneous shopping goods—shopping goods that the customer sees as basically the same—and wants at the lowest price.

horizontal integration—acquiring firms at the same level of activity.

hypodermic needle model—a theory of mass communication which assumes that the mass media has direct, immediate, and powerful effects on people.

hypotheses—educated guesses about the relationships between things or what will happen in the future.

iceberg principle—much good information is hidden in summary data.

ideal market exposure—makes a product widely enough available to satisfy target customers' needs—but not exceed them.

imitative combiner—tries to offer a better marketing mix for the innovator's target market.

imitative segmenter—tries to offer a better marketing mix to a market segment that has already been identified by an innovator—and perhaps even by other imitators.

impulse goods—goods which are bought quickly—as unplanned purchases—because of a strongly felt need.

indirect advertising—points out product advantages—to affect future buying decisions.

industrial goods—products meant for use in producing other products.

inelastic demand—the quantity demanded would increase if the price were decreased, but the quantity demanded would not increase enough to avoid a decrease in total revenue.

inelastic supply—the quantity supplied does not stretch much (if at all) if the price is raised.

inner-directed—people who have their own value systems and direct their own activities.

innovative combiner—tries to find a new combination of sub-markets for which he could offer a differentiated marketing mix.

innovative segmenter—looks for sub-markets with relatively "unsatisfied" needs and tries to develop a uniquely satisfying marketing mix for one (or more) of them.

innovators—the first to adopt, young, and high in social and economic status—see **adoption curve.**

inspection buying—looking at every item.

installations—important long-lived capital items.

institutional advertising—tries to develop goodwill for a company or even an industry—instead of a specific product.

intensive distribution—selling a product through all suitable wholesalers or retailers who will stock and/or sell the product.

intermediate customers—any buyers between producers of basic raw materials and final consumers.

interurbia—a strip of several urban-suburban areas.

introductory price dealing—temporary price cuts—to speed new products into a market.

job description—shows what a person is expected to do.

joint venturing—a domestic firm entering into a partnership with a foreign firm.

jury of executive opinion—combines the opinions of experienced executives as a method of forecasting.

laggards or nonadopters—low in social status and income—see **adoption curve.**

late majority—adopters who are below average in social status and income—see **adoption curve.**

law of diminishing demand—if the price of a product is raised, a smaller quantity will be demanded—and if the price of a product is lowered, a greater quantity will be demanded.

leader pricing—setting some very low prices—real bargains—to get customers into retail stores.

leading series—a time series which changes in the same direction but ahead of the series to be forecasted.

licensing—selling the right to use some process, trademark, patent, or other right—for a fee or royalty.

lifestyle analysis—analysis of many dimensions—including consumers' demographics, Activities, Interests, and Opinions.

limited-function wholesalers—merchant wholesalers who provide only some wholesaling functions.

limited problem solving—involves some effort to understand a person's need and how best to satisfy it.

lower-lower class—includes unskilled laborers and people in nonrespectable occupations.

lower-middle class—the white-collar workers—small-business people, office workers, teachers, technicians, and most sales people.

lower-upper class—socially prominent new rich.

macro-marketing—a social process which directs an economy's flow of goods and services from producers to consumers in a way which effectively matches supply and demand and accomplishes the objectives of society.

mail-order retailing—using mail-order catalogs to let customers "see" the offerings and delivering the purchases by mail or truck.

mail-order wholesalers—merchant wholesalers who sell out of a catalog which may be distributed widely to smaller industrial customers or retailers.

management contracting—the seller provides only management skills—the production facilities are owned by others.

manufacturer brands—brands which are created by manufacturers—sometimes called "national brands."

manufacturers' agent—an agent middleman who sells similar products for several noncompeting manufacturers—for a commission on what is actually sold.

manufacturers' sales branches—separate wholesaling businesses which manufacturers set up away from their factories.

manufacturing—actually producing goods and services.

marginal analysis—focuses on the last unit which would be sold and equates marginal revenue and marginal cost to find the most profitable price and quantity.

marginal cost—the change in total cost that results from producing an extra unit.

marginal profit—the extra profit on the last unit.

marginal revenue—the change in total revenue which results from the sale of one additional unit of product.

markdown—a retail price reduction which is required because the customers will not buy some item at the originally marked-up price.

markdown ratio—a tool used by many retailers to measure the efficiency of various departments and their whole business.

market—a group of buyers and sellers (usually producers and consumers) bargaining over the terms of exchange for goods and/or services.

market development—a firm trying to increase sales by selling its present products in new markets.

market-directed economic system—economic system in which the individual decisions of the many producers and consumers make the macro-level decisions for the whole economy.

market growth—the stage in the product life cycle when industry sales are growing fast—but profits rise and then start falling.

market information function—the collection, analysis, and distribution of information needed to plan, carry out, and control marketing activities.

market introduction—the stage in the product life cycle when a new idea is being introduced to a market.

market maturity—the stage in the product life cycle when industry sales level off—and competition gets tougher.

market penetration—a firm trying to increase sales of its present products in its present markets.

market potential—what a whole market segment might buy—rather than a sales forecast.

market segmentation—the process of identifying more homogeneous sub-markets or segments within a market—for the purpose of selecting target markets and developing appropriate marketing mixes.

marketing audit—a systematic, critical, and unbiased review and appraisal of the basic objectives and policies of the marketing function—and of the organization, methods, procedures, and people employed to implement the policies.

marketing company era—a time when the whole company effort is guided by the marketing concept.

marketing concept—a firm aims all its efforts at satisfying its customers—at a profit.

marketing department era—a time when all marketing activities are brought under the control of one department.

marketing information system (MIS)—an organized way of continually gathering and analyzing data to get information that will help managers make decisions.

marketing manager's job—consists of the basic management tasks: planning, implementing, and control—and planning consists of two parts: (1) finding attractive opportunities and (2) developing marketing strategies.

marketing mix—the controllable variables which the company puts together to satisfy its target market.

marketing orientation—trying to carry out the marketing concept.

marketing program—blends all a firm's strategic plans into one "big" plan.

marketing research—gathers and analyzes data to help marketing managers make decisions.

marketing strategy—a target market and related marketing mix.

markup—the dollar amount added to the cost of goods to get the selling price.

markup (percent)—percentage of selling price which is added to the cost to get the selling price.

mass marketing—the typical production-oriented approach which aims at "everyone."

mass merchandisers—large, self-service retail stores with many departments—which emphasize "soft goods" (housewares, clothing, and fabrics) but still follow the discount house's emphasis on lower margins to get faster turnover.

mass merchandising concept—retailers should offer low prices to get faster turnover and greater sales volumes—by appealing to larger markets.

mass selling—communicating with large numbers of customers at the same time.

merchant wholesalers—wholesalers who own (take title to) the goods they sell—and provide some—or all—of the wholesaling functions.

message channel—the carrier of the message.

micro-macro dilemma—what is "good" for some producers and consumers may not be "good" for society as a whole.

micro-marketing—the performance of activities which seek to accomplish an organization's objectives by anticipating customer or client needs and directing a flow of need-satisfying goods and services from producer to customer or client.

middleman—someone who specializes in trade rather than production.

missionary salespeople—work for manufacturers—calling on their middlemen and their customers.

modified rebuy—an in-between process where some review of the buying situation is done—though not as much as in new-task buying or as little as in straight rebuys.

monopolistic competition—a market situation which develops when: (1) a market has different (heterogeneous) products—in the eyes of some customers—and (2) sellers feel they have some competition in this market.

multinational corporations—have a direct investment in several countries and run their businesses depending on the choices available anywhere in the world.

multiple buying influence—the buyer shares the purchasing decision with several people—perhaps even top management.

multiple target market approach—segmenting the market and selecting two or more homogeneous sub-markets, each of which will be treated as a separate target market requiring a different marketing mix.

multi-step flow model—a theory of mass communication which assumes that there are a variety of ways that messages can flow from the mass media (or other sources) to people in the mass audience.

nationalism—an emphasis on a country's interests before everything else.

natural accounts—the categories to which various costs are charged in the normal accounting cycle.

natural products—products which occur in nature.

need-satisfaction approach—a sales presentation which involves developing a good understanding of the prospective customer's needs before trying to close the sale.

needs—basic forces which motivate an individual to do something.

negotiated contract buying—agreeing to a contract that allows for changing the purchase arrangements.

neighborhood shopping centers—planned shopping centers which serve 7,500 to 40,000 people living within six to ten minutes' driving distance.

net—payment for the face value of the invoice is due immediately.

net profit—what the company has earned from its operations during a particular period. It is the amount left after the cost of goods sold and the expenses have been subtracted from net sales.

net sales—the actual sales dollars the company will receive.

new product—one that is new in any way for the company concerned.

new-task buying—the buying process which occurs when a firm has a new need and the buyer wants a great deal of information.

new unsought goods—products offering really new ideas that potential customers don't know about yet.

noise—any factor which reduces the effectiveness of the communication process.

noncumulative quantity discounts—quantity discounts which apply only to individual orders.

nonprice competition—aggressive action on one or more of the Ps other than Price.

nonrecognition (brand)—a brand is not recognized by final consumers at all—even though middlemen may use the brand name for identification and inventory control.

observation method—a research method which involves observing potential customers' behavior.

odd-even pricing—setting prices which end in certain numbers.

oligopoly—a market situation which develops when a market has: (1) essentially homogeneous products, (2) relatively few sellers, and (3) fairly inelastic industry demand curves.

one-price policy—offering the same price to all customers who purchase goods under essentially the same conditions and in the same quantities.

1/10 net 30—a 1 percent discount off the face value of the invoice is allowed if the invoice is paid within ten days. Otherwise, the full face value is due within 30 days.

operating ratios—the ratio of items on the operating statement to net sales.

operating statement—a summary of the financial results of the operations of a company over a specified period of time.

opinion leaders—people who influence others.

order getters—salespeople who are concerned with getting new business.

order getting—aggressively seeking out possible buyers with a well-organized sales presentation designed to sell a product, service, or idea.

order takers—salespeople concerned with selling the regular or typical customers.

order taking—routine completion of sales made regularly to the target customers.

other-directed—people whose characters are formed mainly by those around them.

packaging—protecting and promoting the product.

penetration pricing policy—trying to sell the whole market at one low price.

performance analysis—looks for exceptions or variations from planned performance.

performance index—a number—such as a baseball batting average—which shows the relation of one value to another.

personal needs—concerned with the need of an individual to achieve personal satisfaction—unrelated to what others think or do.

personal selling—direct face-to-face communication between sellers and potential customers.

PERT—program evaluation and review technique—a flowcharting technique.

phony list prices—prices that customers can be shown to suggest that the price they are to pay has been discounted from "list."

physical distribution (PD)—transporting and storing of physical goods within individual firms and along channel systems.

physical distribution (PD) concept—all the transporting and storing activities of a business and a channel system should be thought of as part of one system—which should seek to minimize the cost of distribution for a given level of customer service.

physical distribution manager—manager concerned not only with physical product flow—but also the location of place facilities through which the flows move.

physiological needs—concerned with food, drink, rest, sex, and other biological needs.

piggy-back service—loads truck trailers on rail cars to provide both speed and flexibility.

pioneering advertising—product advertising which tries to develop primary demand.

place—concerned with building channels of distribution.

place utility—utility provided by having the product available *where* the customer wants it.

planned economic system—economic system in which government planners decide what and how much is to be produced and distributed by whom, when, and to whom.

planned shopping centers—a group of stores planned as a unit—to satisfy some market needs.

pool car service—allows several shippers to pool their like goods as a full car on a railroad.

portfolio management—a management approach which treats alternative products, divisions, or strategic business units (SBUs) as though they were stock investments—to be bought and sold using financial criteria.

possession utility—utility obtained by completing a transaction and gaining possession so that one has the right to use a product.

preconscious level (of need awareness)—customers may be aware of their needs, but would rather not discuss them with others.

prestige pricing—setting a rather high price to suggest high quality or high status.

price—what is charged for "something."

price discrimination—selling the same goods to different buyers at different prices—which injures competition.

price leader—seller who sets price for all to follow and (without any collusion) other members of the industry follow.

price lining—setting a few price levels for a product class and then marking all items at these prices.

primary data—information which is gathered specifically to solve a current problem.

primary demand—demand for a product idea—not just a company's own brand.

private carriers—company-owned transportation facilities.

private warehouses—storing facilities owned by companies for their own use.

producers' cooperatives—operate almost as full-service wholesalers—with the "profits" going to the cooperative's customer-members—in the form of "patronage dividends."

product assortment—the set of all product lines and items that a firm sells.

product development—a firm offering new or improved products for present markets.

product item—a particular product within a product line.

product liability—the legal obligation of sellers to pay damages to individuals who are injured by defective or unsafely designed products.

product life cycle—the stages a new product goes through from beginning to end—divided into four stages: market introduction, market growth, market maturity, and sales decline.

product line—a set of products that are closely related.

product manager—manages specific products.

product-market—a market in which sellers offer substitute products which are similar—either physically or conceptually.

product positioning—shows where proposed and/or present brands are located in a market—as seen by customers.

production era—a time when a company focuses on production.

production orientation—making products which are easy to produce—and then trying to sell them.

profit maximization objective—the firm seeks to get as much profit as it can.

promotion—communicating information between seller and buyer—to influence attitudes and behavior.

prospecting—following down all the "leads" in the target market.

psychographics—analysis of many dimensions—including consumers' demographics, Activities, Interests, and Opinions.

psychological pricing—setting prices which have special appeal to target customers.

public relations—communication with noncustomers—including labor, consumerists, stockholders, and the government.

public warehouses—independent storing facilities.

publicity—any unpaid form of nonpersonal presentation of ideas, goods, or services.

pulling—getting consumers to ask middlemen for the product.

purchase discount—a reduction of the original invoice amount for some business reason.

purchasing agents—buying specialists for manufacturers.

pure competition—a market situation which develops when a market has: (1) homogeneous (similar) products, (2) many buyers and sellers who have full knowledge of the market, and (3) ease of entry for buyers and sellers.

Push Money (or Prize Money) allowances—allowances given to retailers by manufacturers or wholesalers to pass on to the retailers' sales clerks—for aggressively selling particular items.

pushing—using normal promotion effort-personal selling and advertising—to help sell the whole marketing mix to possible channel members.

qualifying dimensions—the dimensions which are relevant to a product-market.

quantity discounts—discounts offered to encourage customers to buy in larger amounts.

quotas—set the specific quantities of goods which can move in or out of a country.

rack jobbers—merchant wholesalers who specialize in nonfood items which are sold through grocery stores and supermarkets—often displaying them on their own wire racks.

random sample—a sample which insures that all members of the population have a chance of being included in the sample.

raw materials—unprocessed goods—such as logs, iron ore, sand, and freshly caught fish—that are handled as little as is needed to move them to the next step in the production process.

receiver—a potential customer.

reciprocity—trading sales for sales—i.e., "if you buy from me, I'll buy from you."

reference group—the people to whom the individual looks when forming attitudes about a particular topic.

regional shopping centers—the largest planned shopping centers—emphasizing shopping stores and shopping goods.

regrouping activities—adjusting the quantities and/or assortments of goods handled at each level in a channel of distribution.

regularly unsought goods—products—like gravestones, life insurance, and encyclopedias—that may stay unsought but not unbought forever.

reinforcement (of learning)—occurs when the response is followed by satisfaction—i.e., reducing the drive tension.

rejection (brand)—potential customers won't buy a brand—unless its current image is changed.

relevant market—the market which is suitable for the firm's purpose.

reliability—concerned with the representativeness of research data.

reminder advertising—tries to keep the product's name before the public.

resident buyers—independent buying agents who work in central markets for several retailer or wholesaler customers in outlying markets.

response—an effort to satisfy a drive.

response function—shows (mathematically and/or graphically) how the firm's target market is expected to react to changes in marketing variables.

retailing—activities involved in the sale of goods and/or services to final consumers.

return—a customer sends back purchased products.

return on assets (ROA)—the ratio of net profit (after taxes) to the assets used to make the net profit— times 100 to get rid of decimals.

return on investment (ROI)—the ratio of net profit (after taxes) to the investment used to make the net profit—multiplied by 100 to get rid of decimals.

risk-taking function—marketing function concerned with bearing the uncertainties that are a part of the marketing process.

Robinson-Patman Act (of 1936)—makes illegal any price discrimination which injures competition.

routinized response behavior—buying process which involves mechanically selecting a particular way of satisfying a need whenever it occurs.

rule for maximizing profit—the firm should produce that output where marginal cost is just less than or equal to marginal revenue.

safety needs—concerned with protection and physical well-being.

sales analysis—detailed breakdown of a company's sales records.

sales decline stage (in the product life cycle)— when new products replace the old.

sales era—a time when a company emphasizes selling—because of increased competition.

sales finance companies—finance inventories.

sales forecast—an estimate of how much an industry or firm hopes to sell to a market segment.

sales managers—manage personal selling.

sales-oriented objective—the firm seeks to get some level of sales or share of market—without referring to profit.

sales presentation—a salesperson's effort to make a sale.

sales promotion—promotion activities which complement personal selling and mass selling.

sales promotion managers—manage their company's sales promotion effort.

sampling buying—looking at only part of a potential purchase.

scientific method—a research approach consisting of four stages: (1) observation, (2) developing hypotheses, (3) predicting the future, and (4) testing the hypotheses.

scrambled merchandising—retailers carrying any product lines which they feel they can sell profitably.

seasonal discounts—discounts offered to encourage buyers to stock earlier than present demand requires.

secondary data—information which is already published or collected.

segmenters—aim at one homogeneous sub-market (at a time) and try to develop a marketing mix that will satisfy that smaller market very well.

segmenting—an aggregating process.

selective demand—demand for a company's own brand rather than a product category.

selective distribution—selling through only those middlemen who will give the product special attention.

selective exposure—our eyes and mind seek out and notice only information that interests us.

selective perception—we screen out or modify ideas, messages, and information that conflict with previously learned attitudes and beliefs.

selective retention—we remember only what we want to remember.

selling agents—agent middlemen who take over the whole marketing job of manufacturers—not just the selling function.

selling formula approach—a sales presentation which uses a prepared outline—building on the black box (stimulus-response) model—taking the customers through some logical steps to a final close.

selling function—promoting the product.

senior citizens—people over 65.

service wholesalers—merchant wholesalers who provide all the wholesaling functions.

services—expense items which support the operations of a firm.

shopping goods—those products that customers feel are worth the time and effort to compare with competing products.

shopping stores—stores which attract customers from greater distances because of the width and depth of their assortments.

single-line (or general-line) wholesalers—full-service merchant wholesalers who carry a narrower line of merchandise than general merchandise wholesalers.

single-line or limited-line stores—stores which specialize in certain lines rather than the broad assortment carried by general stores.

single target market approach—segmenting the market and selecting one of the homogeneous sub-markets as the target market.

skimming pricing policy—trying to get the "cream" of a market (the top of a demand curve) at a high price before aiming at the more price-sensitive segments of that market.

social needs—concerned with love, friendship, status, and esteem—all things that involve a person's interaction with others.

sorting-out process—grading or sorting products.

source—the sender of a message.

specialty goods—consumer goods that the customer really wants—and is willing to make a special effort to buy.

specialty shop—a type of limited-line store—usually small, with a distinct "personality."

specialty stores—stores for which customers have developed a strong attraction because of service, selection, or reputation.

specialty wholesalers—merchant wholesalers who carry a very narrow range of products.

Standard Metropolitan Statistical Area (SMSA)—an integrated economic and social unit having a fairly large population nucleus.

standardization (and grading) functions—sorting products according to size and quality.

staples—consumer convenience goods which are bought often and routinely—without much thought.

status quo objectives—"don't-rock-the-pricing-boat" objectives—e.g., "meeting competition" or "avoiding competition" or "stabilizing prices."

stimulus-response model—people respond in some predictable way to a stimulus.

stockturn rate—a measure of the number of times the average inventory is sold during a year.

storing—the marketing function of holding goods.

storing function—holding goods.

straight rebuy—a routine repurchase which may have been made many times before.

strategic business unit (SBU)—an organizational unit within a larger company which focuses its efforts on some product-markets and is treated as a separate profit center.

strategic plan—a strategy and the time-related details for carrying out the strategy.

strategic planning—the managerial process of developing and maintaining a match between the resources of an organization and its market opportunities.

style—a characteristic or distinctive mode or method of expression, presentation, or conception.

substitute method—a sales forecasting method involving careful analysis of sales of products which a new one may displace.

substitutes—goods or services that offer a choice to the buyer.

supermarket—a large retail store specializing in groceries—with self-service and wide assortments.

super-stores—very large retail stores that try to meet all the customer's routine needs—at a low price.

supplies (industrial goods)—expense items that do not become a part of the final product.

supply curve (for a market)—shows the quantity of goods that will be supplied at various possible prices by all suppliers together.

supporting salespeople—help the order-oriented salespeople—but don't try to get orders themselves.

survey method—a research method which asks people questions.

tactics—short-run plans to help implement strategic plans.

target market—a fairly homogeneous (similar) group of customers to whom a company wishes to appeal.

target marketing—focusing on some specific target customers.

target return objective—a pricing objective which sets a specific profit-related goal.

target return pricing—adding a "target return" to the cost of a product.

tariffs—taxes on imported goods.

task method (budgeting)—basing the budget on the job to be done.

technical specialists—salespeople who provide technical assistance to order-oriented salespeople.

technological base—the technical skills and equipment which affect the way the resources of an economy are converted to output.

threshold expenditure level—the minimum expenditure level needed just to be in a market.

time-series—historical records of the fluctuations in economic variables.

time utility—utility provided by having the product available *when* the customer wants it.

ton-mile—the movement of a ton of goods one mile.

total cost—the sum of total fixed and total variable costs.

total-cost approach (to selecting a PD system)—evaluates all costs of various possible PD systems.

total fixed cost—the sum of those costs that are fixed in total—no matter how much is produced.

total variable cost—the sum of those changing expenses that are closely related to output.

trade (functional) discount—a list price reduction given to channel members for a job they are going to do.

trade-in allowance—a price reduction given for used goods when similar new goods are bought.

trademark—the words, symbols, or marks that the law says are trademarks.

trading stamps—free stamps (like "Green Stamps") given by some retailers with every purchase.

traditional channel system—a channel system in which the various channel members make little or no effort to cooperate with each other.

transit privilege—allows for processing of goods being transported by railroad.

transloading privilege—allows for combining several smaller (rail) shipments into a carload for part of the distance.

transporting function—the movement of goods from one place to another.

trend extension—a forecasting method which extends past sales experience into the future.

truck wholesalers—limited function merchant wholesalers who specialize in delivering goods which they stock in their own trucks.

two-step flow model—a theory of mass communication which assumes that mass media messages flow mainly to opinion leaders who react to these messages and then relay them to the people with whom they interact.

unchanging list prices—published prices that remain the same for long periods of time—perhaps years—but the actual price is adjusted upward or downward by add-ons or discounts.

unconscious level (of need awareness)—customers are not even aware of what forces are driving them.

unfair trade practice acts—laws which put a floor under prices, especially at the wholesale and retail levels.

uniform delivered pricing—making an average freight charge to all buyers.

unit pricing—placing the price per ounce (or some other standard measure) on or near the product.

universal functions (of marketing)—buying, selling, transporting, storing, standardization and grading, financing, risk taking, and market information.

universal product code—identifies each product with marks that can be "read" by electronic scanners and related to prices by computers.

unsought goods—consumer goods that potential customers do not yet want or know they can buy.

upper class—wealthy old families (upper-upper class) and the socially prominent new rich (lower-upper class).

upper-lower class—factory production-line workers, skilled workers, service workers—the "blue-collar" workers—and local politicians and union leaders who would lose their power if they moved out of this class.

upper-middle class—successful business people, professionals, and top salespeople.

upper-upper class—wealthy old families.

utility—the power to satisfy human needs.

validity—concerned with whether research actually measures what it intends to.

vertical integration—ownership of the natural product source by the user (or acquiring firms at two or more successive stages of production or distribution).

voluntary chains—wholesaler-sponsored groups which work with "independent" retailers.

wants—"needs" which are learned during an individual's life.

warranty—explains what the seller guarantees about its product.

wheel of retailing theory—new types of retailers enter the market as low-status, low-margin, low-price operators and then—if they are successful—evolve into more conventional retailers offering more services—with resulting higher operating costs and higher prices. They are then threatened by new low-status, low-margin, low-price retailers—and the wheel turns again.

Wheeler-Lea Amendment—bans "unfair or deceptive acts in commerce."

wholesaler—a firm whose main activity is providing wholesaling functions.

wholesaling—concerned with the activities of those persons or establishments (wholesalers) which sell to retailers and other wholesalers, and/or to industrial, institutional, and commercial users—but who do not sell in large amounts to final consumers.

wholly owned subsidiary—a separate firm—owned by a parent company.

zone pricing—making an average freight charge to all buyers within specific geographic areas.

AUTHOR INDEX

SUBJECT INDEX

This book has been set CAP VideoComp, in 9 and 8 point Spectra, leaded 3 points. Part numbers and titles are 64 and 24 point Souvenir Demi-Bold. Chapter numbers and titles are 72 and 20 point Souvenir Demi-Bold. The size of the type page is 37 by 50 picas.